1

(Continued on back endsheets)

WITHDRAWN

Twentieth-Century Italian Poets
Second Series

Dictionary of Literary Biography® • Volume One Hundred Twenty-Eight

Twentieth-Century Italian Poets
Second Series

Edited by

Giovanna Wedel De Stasio
Glauco Cambon
and
Antonio Illiano

A Bruccoli Clark Layman Book
Gale Research Inc.
Detroit, London

Advisory Board for
DICTIONARY OF LITERARY BIOGRAPHY

John Baker
William Cagle
Jane Christensen
Patrick O'Connor
Peter S. Prescott

Matthew J. Bruccoli and Richard Layman, Editorial Directors
C. E. Frazer Clark, Jr., Managing Editor
Karen L. Rood, Senior Editor

Printed in the United States of America

Published simultaneously in the United Kingdom
by Gale Research International Limited
(An affiliated company of Gale Research Inc.)

The paper used in this publication meets the minimum requirements
of American National Standard for Information Sciences–Permanence
Paper for Printed Library Materials, ANSI Z39.48-1984. ∞ ™

This publication is a creative work fully protected by all applicable copyright laws, as well as by misappropriation, trade secret,
unfair competition, and other applicable laws. The authors and
editors of this work have added value to the underlying factual
material herein through one or more of the following: unique
and original selection, coordination, expression, arrangement,
and classification of the information.

All rights to this publication will be vigorously defended.

Copyright © 1993 by Gale Research Inc.
835 Penobscot Building
Detroit, MI 48226

All rights reserved including the right of reproduction in
whole or in part in any form

Library of Congress Catalog Card Number 93-12732
ISBN 0-8103-5387-3

The trademark ITP is used under license.

10 9 8 7 6 5 4 3 2 1

Contents

Contents

Plan of the Series

. . . Almost the most prodigious asset of a country, and perhaps its most precious possession, is its native literary product — when that product is fine and noble and enduring.

Mark Twain*

The advisory board, the editors, and the publisher of the *Dictionary of Literary Biography* are joined in endorsing Mark Twain's declaration. The literature of a nation provides an inexhaustible resource of permanent worth. We intend to make literature and its creators better understood and more accessible to students and the reading public, while satisfying the standards of teachers and scholars.

To meet these requirements, *literary biography* has been construed in terms of the author's achievement. The most important thing about a writer is his writing. Accordingly, the entries in *DLB* are career biographies, tracing the development of the author's canon and the evolution of his reputation.

The purpose of *DLB* is not only to provide reliable information in a convenient format but also to place the figures in the larger perspective of literary history and to offer appraisals of their accomplishments by qualified scholars.

The publication plan for *DLB* resulted from two years of preparation. The project was proposed to Bruccoli Clark by Frederick C. Ruffner, president of the Gale Research Company, in November 1975. After specimen entries were prepared and typeset, an advisory board was formed to refine the entry format and develop the series rationale. In meetings held during 1976, the publisher, series editors, and advisory board approved the scheme for a comprehensive biographical dictionary of persons who contributed to North American literature. Editorial work on the first volume began in January 1977, and it was published in 1978. In order to make *DLB* more than a reference tool and to compile volumes that individually have claim to status

as literary history, it was decided to organize volumes by topic, period, or genre. Each of these free-standing volumes provides a biographical-bibliographical guide and overview for a particular area of literature. We are convinced that this organization — as opposed to a single alphabet method — constitutes a valuable innovation in the presentation of reference material. The volume plan necessarily requires many decisions for the placement and treatment of authors who might properly be included in two or three volumes. In some instances a major figure will be included in separate volumes, but with different entries emphasizing the aspect of his career appropriate to each volume. Ernest Hemingway, for example, is represented in *American Writers in Paris, 1920-1939* by an entry focusing on his expatriate apprenticeship; he is also in *American Novelists, 1910-1945* with an entry surveying his entire career. Each volume includes a cumulative index of the subject authors and articles. Comprehensive indexes to the entire series are planned.

With volume ten in 1982 it was decided to enlarge the scope of *DLB*. By the end of 1986 twenty-one volumes treating British literature had been published, and volumes for Commonwealth and Modern European literature were in progress. The series has been further augmented by the *DLB Yearbooks* (since 1981) which update published entries and add new entries to keep the *DLB* current with contemporary activity. There have also been *DLB Documentary Series* volumes which provide biographical and critical source materials for figures whose work is judged to have particular interest for students. One of these companion volumes is entirely devoted to Tennessee Williams.

We define literature as the *intellectual commerce of a nation:* not merely as belles lettres but as that ample and complex process by which ideas are generated, shaped, and transmitted. *DLB* entries are not limited to "creative writers" but extend to other figures who in their time and in their way influenced the mind of a people. Thus the series encompasses historians, journalists, publishers, and screenwriters. By this means readers of *DLB* may be aided to perceive literature not as cult scripture in

---

*From an unpublished section of Mark Twain's autobiography, copyright by the Mark Twain Company

the keeping of intellectual high priests but firmly positioned at the center of a nation's life.

DLB includes the major writers appropriate to each volume and those standing in the ranks immediately behind them. Scholarly and critical counsel has been sought in deciding which minor figures to include and how full their entries should be. Wherever possible, useful references are made to figures who do not warrant separate entries.

Each *DLB* volume has a volume editor responsible for planning the volume, selecting the figures for inclusion, and assigning the entries. Volume editors are also responsible for preparing, where appropriate, appendices surveying the major periodicals and literary and intellectual movements for their volumes, as well as lists of further readings. Work on the series as a whole is coordinated at the Bruccoli Clark Layman editorial center in Columbia, South Carolina, where the editorial staff is responsible for accuracy of the published volumes.

One feature that distinguishes *DLB* is the illustration policy – its concern with the iconography of literature. Just as an author is influenced by his surroundings, so is the reader's understanding of the author enhanced by a knowledge of his environment. Therefore *DLB* volumes include not only drawings, paintings, and photographs of authors, often depicting them at various stages in their careers, but also illustrations of their families and places where they lived. Title pages are regularly reproduced in facsimile along with dust jackets for modern authors. The dust jackets are a special feature of *DLB* because they often document better than anything else the way in which an author's work was perceived in its own time. Specimens of the writers' manuscripts are included when feasible.

Samuel Johnson rightly decreed that "The chief glory of every people arises from its authors." The purpose of the *Dictionary of Literary Biography* is to compile literary history in the surest way available to us – by accurate and comprehensive treatment of the lives and work of those who contributed to it.

The *DLB* Advisory Board

Introduction

Dictionary of Literary Biography 114 presented entries on a group of Italian poets belonging to the time frame that extends from the beginning of the twentieth century to the end of World War II. This second series, *DLB 128,* covers poets who wrote mostly in the second half of the century.

Italian poetry after 1945 reflected the profound changes undergone by Italian culture, including those caused by attempts at reconstruction after the end of the destructive conflict that brought down the Fascist regime. All the major Italian journals — starting with the *Politecnico* (1945–1947), edited by Elio Vittorini — expressed the necessity felt by Italian intellectuals for a new type of culture, capable of transforming human existence. Interest in communicating and in dealing with current problems of an ethical and sociopolitical nature overcame the earlier literary tendency toward fragmentary and hermetic monologues. Thus all apolitical and escapist poetry was severely criticized because it suggested a lack of moral and historical responsibility or, worse, a complacent attitude toward Fascism. Yet new poetry often showed an excess of good intentions and was marred by a propensity for populism.

In 1952 Luciano Anceschi grouped six poets in his anthology *Linea lombarda* (Lombard Line). In his view these poets — including Vittorio Sereni and Luciano Erba — aimed for a *poesia in re,* that is, a poetry committed to depicting the realistic aspects of everyday life (as was typical of the poetic tradition of the Lombardy region). The poets represented in *Linea lombarda* had the same crepuscular intonation present in the works of Eugenio Montale, but they opposed the obscurity of Montale and of hermeticism in general. They rejected all modes of abstractness and abstraction, and yet they did not adhere completely to the precepts of the new realism so distinctive of Italian culture in the postwar years.

In his essay "Le generazioni della poesia italiana del Novecento" (The Generations of Twentieth-Century Italian Poetry), published in the journal *Paragone,* in 1953 the critic Oreste Macrì examines twentieth-century Italian poetry by adopting a system of septennial generations. He concluded that the so-called fourth generation of poets, born between 1922 and 1930, was virtually nonexistent.

The following year Erba and Piero Chiara polemically responded to Macrì's article by publishing *Quarta generazione* (Fourth Generation), an anthology that includes work by thirty-three poets, including Elio Filippo Accrocca, Bartolo Cattafi, Margherita Guidacci, Pier Paolo Pasolini, Rocco Scotellaro, Maria Luisa Spaziani, and Andrea Zanzotto. In the introduction Erba explains that many critics do not highly regard the fourth generation because its poetry did not correspond to their postwar literary expectations. The fourth generation was formed by a heterogeneous group of writers who later went in different directions. Yet in the 1950s their low-key expressive mode showed a common repudiation of the poetic magniloquence that preceded the war and of the new rhetoric that followed it. Their reaction against declamatory modes and sensationalism, already begun by the *crepuscolari,* the poets of the "twilight" school, also revealed a tendency toward ironic humor, evasion, lack of commitment, and rejection of history.

Many poets maintained an ambiguous relationship with their recent literary tradition, as they were partly influenced by the style of the hermetic poets while recovering the appeal of the prosaic style with the composition of longer narrative poems. This constant relationship with tradition is exemplified by books in the poetry series "Il Canzoniere," which was edited by Accrocca and Cesare Vivaldi in the 1950s and which published poets who were open to experimentation but whose language was still rooted in the recent past. This new trend, as Macrì notes in his *Caratteri e figure della poesia italiana contemporanea* (Features and Figures of Contemporary Italian Poetry, 1956), deserved attention because it avoided the shifts and breaks of useless polemics and gave a thoughtful and authentic conclusion to an exemplary tradition while expressing, with honesty and authenticity, the feelings and expectations of a generation. At that same time Enrico Falqui offered a wide but careful selection of new poetry in *La giovane poesia* (Young Poetry, 1956). This anthology did not approach poetry from sectional viewpoints and thus avoided the sociopolitical conditioning of the postwar atmosphere. According to Falqui, poets could be divided at the most into two groups: the "Post-Hermetics," which included some poets of religious inspiration, and the "Neo-Realists," which encompassed the socially committed as well as the religious poets. But the complex evolution of postwar Italian poetry has been a central concern of other critics as well. See for instance Alberto Frattini's "Ragguaglio sulla critica della giovane poesia del dopoguerra" (A Review of Criticism of the New Postwar Poetry), in his *Poesia nuova in Italia tra ermetismo e neoavanguardia* (New Poetry in Italy between Hermeticism and Neo-avant-garde, 1967), and "Dopo l'ermetismo" (After Hermeticism), in his *Dai crepuscolari ai novissimi* (From the Twilight Poets to the Newest Ones, 1969).

Between the end of the 1950s and the beginning of the 1960s Italy entered a phase of economic prosperity and neocapitalism. Yet, despite its technological development, many of its social problems — such as illiteracy, poverty, unemployment of the lower classes, and overly rapid economic and industrial development in the south — were not solved. These imbalances added to the popularity of Marxist ideology. Regarding ideology and poetry, the journal *Officina* (1955–1959) was important. Founded and edited by three poets, Pier Paolo Pasolini, Roberto Roversi, and Francesco Leonetti, it was based on some of Italian Communist party leader Antonio Gramsci's ideas; it included debates on critical and literary issues, thus sustaining the renewal of the popularity of poetry. Pasolini theorized three different orientations for neo-experimentalism: toward social commitment, represented by the new realism; toward a religious, if not professional, inspiration, as shown by the posthermeticists; and toward the pure experimentation of the neo-avant-garde. *Officina* and neo-experimentalism contested the past and present and fostered a new literary climate, which was also promoted by such international movements as pop art and the Beat Generation.

Neo-avant-garde Italian culture found its forum for literary discussion and development in the Milanese journal *Verri,* founded in 1956 and directed by Anceschi. This journal, independent from any established ideology, attracted contributions by various authors. In 1961 a group of five poets collaborating with this journal — Elio Pagliarani, Alfredo Giuliani, Edoardo Sanguineti, Nanni Balestrini, and Antonio Porta — published an anthology titled *I Novissimi.* In this important collection of their poems, they tried to expose through their experimental writing the new social and cultural reality of Italy. They also attempted to express the alienation of the artist in a modern industrialized society. In the introduction Giuliani explains

that the *novissimi* intend to depict and criticize the modern condition in all its schizophrenic forms and tendencies. Their provocative attack against traditional lyricism, syntactic coherence, and neorealistic social reform, and also their lack of a clear sociopolitical program (in spite of their Marxist orientation), caused them to fall into a new type of sterile rhetoric. Unlike the futurists in the first half of the century, who opposed and intended to modernize traditional language in the light of new technological developments, the *novissimi* reacted against what they perceived as humankind's entrapment within a technological and industrial civilization. By imitating the alienating and neurotic condition of the contemporary age, the *novissimi* adopted one of the Aristotelian forces of poetry, mimesis, but they utilized it to contest a deceived and deceiving society. Their writing was influential also because it rejected syllabic versification and utilized techniques of provocation with a style that mixed the trivial with the sublime, nonsense with farce and visionism, irony and sarcasm with elegy, automatic writing with collage and juxtaposition, the materials of technology and consumerism with the feeling of individual and collective exasperation, parody with erudition, and existential anxiety with common rage at the mediocrity of the sociopolitical system.

In 1963 a group of writers and critics later called "Gruppo '63" gathered at a convention in Palermo to discuss the problematic interrelations between art and technology. A drastic divergence of opinions emerged from this meeting and from the ones they held in 1964 and 1965. As a whole the Gruppo '63, which included promoters of the *Verri* and the *novissimi,* believed in the modernization of language and in the adoption of technological means of communication to disclose the contradictions latent within mass culture. The volume *Gruppo '63* (1964), a series of debates and essays edited by Giuliani and Balestrini, set out the motivations and accomplishments of the neo-avant-garde movement and set the stage for a new climate of wide-ranging creativity and multifaceted eclecticism.

Radical experiments were performed to legitimize the writer's survival in a technological society that seemed to prefer iconographic and audiocommunicative media over verbal ones. Attempts were made to produce poetry with a computer, the Tape Mark I. Other experiments included "symbiotic poetry," which consists of the interaction of phonetic, graphic, and visual elements, and *poesia ginnica* (athletic poetry), which blends words and body movements. Still other experiments centered on phonetic and theatrical effects.

Visual writing, which simultaneously communicates a message at both the verbal and visual level, attracted a large group of followers and reached a high degree of development. Within the realm of Italian visual poetry, however, it is necessary to make a distinction between *poesia visuale* and *poesia visiva,* both of which are translated into English with the term *visual poetry.* In the introduction to his well-known anthology of concrete poetry, *Imaged Words and Worded Images* (1970), Richard Kostelanetz differentiates between "imaged words," which consist of "a word or phrase endowed with a visual form, so that the language is enhanced through pictorial means," and "worded images," which are "pictures made or embellished through linguistic means." In the latter case the shape of the image becomes a frame that contains words. Both types of poetry fit within the Italian category of *poesia visuale,* which relies on linguistic structures endowed with a visual form, while *poesia visiva,* a phenomenon more distinctly indigenous to Italy, combines words with nonverbal material and thus requires a decoding process that is disengaged from any ordinary temporal sequence. The visual poets tend to dismember sentences and words, establishing a relationship between the white spaces and the fragments. For instance, in Balestrini's creations called *cronogrammi* (chronograms) the writing includes overlapping or intersecting elements. Adriano Spatola's poems in *Zeroglifico* (1966; translated as *Zeroglyphics,* 1977) are made with the collage technique, which consists of dismembering sentences and words and then creating collages with the fragments. As Spatola states in his *Verso la poesia totale* (Toward a Total Poetry, 1969), the collage poem invents a personalized reading code without denying communication, which takes place somewhere beyond a verbal reality and a linguistic system.

As the postindustrial civilization offered more and more complex computerized systems of communication, traditional poetic notions and techniques appeared more and more inadequate. Consequently writers felt the urge to invent arbitrary new means of communication. The "Gruppo '70," founded by Lamberto Pignotti (who had been part of the Gruppo '63), attempted a cultural revolution against stereotyped mass communication through experiments in *poesia visiva.* The poets of the Gruppo '70 planned to influence the cultural and ideological development of society by operating within the existing communication channels. Pignotti, for instance, advocated publicizing poetry by printing it on boxes of matches or using neon signs.

The year 1968 is regarded by most critics as the one that saw a generalized rejection of institutionalized literature, poetry in particular, because literature appeared to be inadequate to communicate something significant in modern mass culture. An interdisciplinary concept of art, aiming at a fusion of different expressive means, was sustained. Quite a few journals flourished during the 1970s and encouraged new poetic forms that stressed either the signifying word or the signified thing. The politically oriented *Quindici* was founded in 1967 in Rome by Giuliani; *Tam Tam* was started in 1971 near Parma and directed by Spatola and Giulia Niccolai; Franco Cavallo's *Altri termini* was born in 1972 near Naples; and Mariella Bettarini's *Salvo Imprevisti* was founded in Florence in 1973. There were many others.

The variety of poetic tendencies and ideologies after 1968 is exemplified by the different and opposing criteria used to edit poetry anthologies in the 1970s and 1980s. In the introduction to *Il pubblico della poesia* (The Public of Poetry, 1975), edited with Franco Cordelli, Alfonso Berardinelli claims that, since common perspectives are lacking among the poets born after 1936 and writing in the years between 1968 and 1975, it is impossible to divide them into clearly identifiable groups. However, these poets do share, from the sociopsychological point of view, the common feeling of moving adrift in the poetic world.

In the 1970s and 1980s many volumes that explore recent poetry developments in Italy were published. Among them is the series "Quinta Generazione/Antologie," from the Forum/Quinta Generazione publishing house in Forlì. This series includes anthologies that collect work by poets from different Italian regions. Each poet is introduced by a brief critical description. Frattini edited *Poesia e regione in Italia* (Poetry and Region in Italy, 1983), which focuses mainly on poets from Tuscany, Abruzzi, Latium, Marches, and Lucania (now Basilicata), and published the essay "Poesia e regione in Italia nel secondo Novecento" (Poetry and Region in Italy in the Second Half of the Twentieth-Century) in the journal *Cultura e Scuola* (April–June 1987). Another important essay is Giovanni Raboni's "Poeti del secondo Novecento" (Poets of the Second Half of the Twentieth Century), included in Natalino Sapegno's enlarged and updated edition of *Storia della Letteratura Italiana: Il Novecento* (History of Italian Literature: The Twentieth Century), published in 1987. Raboni analyzes various generations of twentieth-century Italian poets and examines particular historical moments that had an impact on them: from the generation of 1945 to the generation of 1956 (the year of the repressed revolution in Budapest), to the generation of 1968 and the work of the new vernacular poets.

"Is Poetry Still Possible?" was the question asked (and the title of the speech given) by Montale in Stockholm when, on 12 December 1975, he received the Nobel Prize for literature. Undoubtedly poetry has survived the threats posed by mass media and technology. The continuous and sometimes sudden metamorphoses of modern times corresponded to the transformation of its means of expression. If one considers the most recent experimental poetry, which followed neo-avant-garde poetry, one will notice that technical innovations are accompanied by a rediscovery of the private, intimistic, and spiritual aspects of life. In the essay "Poesia" (Poetry) in the *Enciclopedia del Novecento* (Encyclopedia of the Twentieth Century, 1980), critic D'Arco Silvio Avalle identifies two main currents of poetry: one moves fundamentally away from the importance of form and technique, while the other is aimed at sustaining creativity with electronic means and transcending the traditional idea of a "geometrically defined" art form, emphasizing instead the idea of a process or system. On the basis of this interpretation, one may hypothesize the future direction of Italian poetry: it will continue to exist and prosper, even though poetics and styles will continue to change. As long as there is humankind, there will be poetry.

The second half of the century is teeming with poets, often working with very dissimilar ideological and artistic goals. Due to the wide variety of poetic trends and writers, we do not claim that *DLB 128* is exhaustive. In performing the difficult task of selection, our first concern was to integrate the lines of continuity and development with the voices of innovation. We have also endeavored to recognize those poets who appear to be isolated but whose work has contributed to the evolution of their art, along with the work of those who can be viewed as more decisively influential. There remain, nonetheless, emerging poets whose production so far, while clearly promising, has yet to reach its full maturity or its most representative stage of growth. Future *DLB* volumes may offer the opportunity to extend the series by highlighting other outstanding poets of the last three decades of the twentieth century.

– *Giovanna Wedel De Stasio and Antonio Illiano*

ACKNOWLEDGMENTS

This book was produced by Bruccoli Clark Layman, Inc. Karen L. Rood is senior editor for the *Dictionary of Literary Biography* series. Jack Turner was the in-house editor.

Photography editors are Edward Scott and Timothy C. Lundy. Layout and graphics supervisor is Penney L. Haughton. Copyediting supervisor is Bill Adams. Typesetting supervisor is Kathleen M. Flanagan. Samuel Bruce is editorial associate. Systems manager is George F. Dodge. The production staff includes Rowena Betts, Steve Borsanyi, Barbara Brannon, Patricia Coate, Rebecca Crawford, Margaret McGinty Cureton, Denise Edwards, Sarah A. Estes, Joyce Fowler, Robert Fowler, Brenda A. Gillie, Bonita Graham, Jolyon M. Helterman, Ellen McCracken, Kathy Lawler Merlette, John Myrick, Pamela D. Norton, Thomas J. Pickett, Patricia Salisbury, Maxine K. Smalls, Deborah P. Stokes, and Wilma Weant.

Walter W. Ross and Suzanne Burry did library research. They were assisted by the following librarians at the Thomas Cooper Library of the University of South Carolina: Linda Holderfield and the interlibrary-loan staff; reference librarians Gwen Baxter, Daniel Boice, Faye Chadwell, Cathy Eckman, Rhonda Felder, Gary Geer, Qun "Gerry" Jiao, Jackie Kinder, Laurie Preston, Jean Rhyne, Carol Tobin, Carolyn Tyler, Virginia Weathers, Elizabeth Whiznant, and Connie Widney; circulation-department head Thomas Marcil; and acquisitions-searching supervisor David Haggard.

The editors are grateful for the generous assistance of Prof. Corrado Federici and Prof. Alberto Frattini in the preparation of this volume.

Twentieth-Century Italian Poets
Second Series

Dictionary of Literary Biography

Elio Filippo Accrocca
(17 April 1923 -)

Achille Serrao

BOOKS: *Portonaccio* (Milan: Scheiwiller/All'Insegna del Pesce d'Oro, 1949);

Caserma, 1950 (Rome: Canzoniere, 1951);

Reliquia umana (Milan: Scheiwiller/All'Insegna del Pesce d'Oro, 1955);

Ritorno a Portonaccio (Milan & Verona: Mondadori, 1959);

Ritratti su misura di scrittori italiani (Venice: Sodalizio del Libro, 1960);

Innestogrammi-Corrispondenze (Padua: Rebellato, 1966);

Del guardare in faccia (Trieste: ALUT, 1968);

Paradigma [ten poems with French translation by Arthur Praillet] (Luxembourg: Origine, 1972);

Europa inquieta (Rome: CIAS/Tormargana, 1972);

Vagabondaggi per l'Europa (Rome: CIAS, 1972);

Roma così (Rome: De Luca, 1973);

Due parole dall'al di qua (Manduria: Laicata, 1973);

Siamo, non siamo (Milan: Rusconi, 1974);

Versi mignotti (Rome: Blocchetto, 1975);

Bicchiere di carta (Rome: Quaderni di Piazza Navona, 1977);

La funzione del poeta oggi (Palermo: Centro Pitré, 1977);

Il discorrere delle cose (Rome, 1978);

Il superfluo (Milan: Mondadori, 1980);

Scultogrammi (Rome, 1981);

I binari di Apollinaire (Rome: Quaderni di Piazza Navona, 1982);

Pesominimo (Abano Terme: Piovan, 1983);

Treangoli (Urbino: Spinello, 1983);

Videogrammi della prolunga (Rome: Lucarini, 1984);

Bagage (Rome: Ventaglio, 1984);

Esercizi radicali (Foggia: Bastogi, 1984);

Transeuropa, with Dutch translation by N. Morina Oostveen (Luxembourg: Euroeditor, 1984);

Copia difforme (Pisa: Giardini, 1986);

Contromano (Livorno: Nuova Fortezza, 1987);

Forse arrivi forse partenze (Parabita: Laboratorio, 1988);

Poesie: La distanza degli anni 1949-1987 (Rome: Newton Compton, 1988).

OTHER: *Antologia poetica della Resistenza italiana,* edited by Accrocca and Valerio Volpini (Florence: Landi, 1955);

Roma allo specchio nella narrativa da De Amicis a Moravia, edited by Accrocca and Livio Jannattoni (Rome: Istituto di Studi Romani, 1958);

Ungaretti: Poesie, edited, with an introduction, by Accrocca (Milan: Nuova Accademia, 1964);

Roma, paesaggio e poesia, edited by Accrocca (Rome: Canesi, 1965);

Lirici pugliesi del Novecento, edited by Accrocca and Ferruccio Ulivi (Bari: Adriatica, 1967);

Rèpaci 70 e la cultura italiana, edited by Accrocca (Rome: Costanzi, 1968);

Prosatori e narratori pugliesi del Novecento, edited by Accrocca and Ulivi (Bari: Adriatica, 1969);

Cronaca e poesia, edited by Accrocca and Luciano Luisi (Rome: Servostampa, 1976);

L'inquietudine, edited by Accrocca (Rome: System Graphic, 1980).

The well-known Italian poet and editor Elio Filippo Accrocca was born on 17 April 1923 to Livio and Caterina Pistilli Accrocca in the city of Cori, in the province of Latina — the family's place of origin. Several years later Livio Accrocca, a railway worker, moved the family from Cori to Rome so that he could find work. They settled in the popular district of San Lorenzo, one of the most important railway and commercial centers of the Lazio region. On 19 July 1943 San Lorenzo was the scene of a violent bombing attack, which destroyed the

Elio Filippo Accrocca circa 1984

Accroccas' home. Two years after the catastrophe Elio Filippo Accrocca wrote these lines:

Ho dormito l'ultima notte
nella casa di mio padre
al quartiere proletario.

La guerra, aborto d'uomini
dementi, è passata sulla
mia casa di San Lorenzo.

(I have slept for the last
time in my father's house
in the proletarian district.

War, the abortion of demented
men, has passed over
my home in San Lorenzo.)

This untitled poem is included in the opening section of *Portonaccio* (Portonaccio Street, 1949), Accrocca's first book.

In 1947 Accrocca obtained his degree in modern and contemporary literature at the University of Rome with a thesis on the Italian poetry of the resistance period. His thesis director was Giuseppe Ungaretti, who wrote an introductory note to *Portonaccio* in which he characterizes the voice of the poet from Cori as one "di estrema tenerezza davanti alla terribilità degli eventi, voce di una tenerezza quasi silenziosa per la sua intensità di commozione davanti a inermi povere cose, a poveri esseri travolti" (of extreme tenderness in the face of the horrifying events of the day, a voice of almost silent tenderness, as though overcome by the intensity of its response to the sight of defenseless things and helpless, crushed human beings).

Portonaccio includes poems written in the 1942–1947 period and reflects the war experience from the viewpoint of the victims. Every element is situated in the cultural context of prewar and postwar Italy. Accrocca found a spiritual guide in the legendary poet Salvatore Quasimodo, whose father was also a railway man. Accrocca, like Quasimodo, set out to remake humanity by helping people recover from the devastation and despair of the war and by building a bridge between the living and the dead. Accrocca also hoped to rebuild humanity in an ethical sense, so people could live without accepting evil as an inescapable necessity.

The cultural climate of Accrocca's literary debut was marked by the critical and ideological postulates of what is commonly referred to as *neorealismo* (neorealism). Neorealism grew out of the philosophical and aesthetic concepts that were formulated in England and in the United States during the first decades of the twentieth century to counteract the philosophy of idealism. These notions managed to infiltrate Italian literature in the 1930s. Neorealism in literature is characterized by the prevalence of the author's interest in concrete problems, pursued at the expense of style and form. Apparently neorealism in Italian poetry came into existence in 1936 with the publication of Cesare Pavese's *Lavorare stanca* (Hard Labor); there is a dramatic difference between Pavese's text and the prevailing hermetic poetry. Neorealist poetry was debated in several prestigious postwar journals, such as *La Strada, Momenti,* and *Il Contemporaneo*. A list of neorealist poets would include Franco Matacotta (pseudonym of Francesco Monterosso), Rocco Scotellaro, and Accrocca.

Accrocca's early poetry deals with themes suggested by society and biography; that is, his poetry is a record of the deaths, violence, destruction, sorrows, and pitiful circumstances to which he was witness. These themes coincide with the general conditions narrated in neorealist novels. Nevertheless, the rhetorical devices adopted by Accrocca, as well as his formal poetic structures, are clearly derivative of Ungarettian and neohermetic models. Accrocca's poems feature a meticulous "formalization," which acts as an effective vehicle for articulating twentieth-century experiences. A close reading of *Portonaccio* reveals a stylistic signature already beginning to take shape, an aspiration to achieve a personal tone that draws evocative power from a solid moral sense, and an ethics of combativeness sustained by the formal instruments appropriate to poetic discourse. These rhetorical features act as a literary mediation: the book is a stylistic and linguistic unit that includes typical neorealist subject matter and yet is not reduced to a mere *cronaca* (chronicle) of events — which most theorists of the period felt was sufficient and necessary for the socially involved *dire* (speech act) of the neorealist.

Ungaretti's preface to *Portonaccio* contributed to the error of reading the poems exclusively as elegiac compositions, because he spoke of Accrocca's tender voice in the face of terrifying events. However, in spite of the occasional use of mannered metaphors — particularly in the earliest poems — as Raffaele Pellecchia correctly noted in 1980, the poems of Accrocca's first publication indicate "Una coerenza interna e una reciprocità fra piano espressivo e livello concettuale, fra il polo dell'io e quello del reale, in un organismo sintattico compatto e unitario, senza cedimenti a sbavature sentimentali e ad estetismi di sorta" (an internal coherence and correspondence between the level of expression and the level of conceptual content, between the poetic subject and the empirical world, contained in a compact and unified text free of lapses into maudlin sentimentality and aesthetism of any kind).

In the early and mid 1950s Accrocca's literary career was marked by the appearance of two new collections of his poems: *Caserma, 1950* (Barracks, 1950), published in 1951, and *Reliquia umana* (Human Relics, 1955). The dialogue between Accrocca and the visual arts was continuous, as confirmed by his many monographs on the subject of art and by his many important writings of a technical, expressive nature. Painting and the graphic arts exerted considerable influence on his poetry. Alongside the thematic and formal aspects, allusions to the visual arts constitute a connecting thread that runs through Accrocca's entire output in poetry and prose. His need to establish an intimate and fruitful link between poetry and painting (augmented by the fact that Accrocca taught the history of art at the Academy of Foggia starting in 1960) is at the center of his creative and critical thought. This same desire represents a preview of the multimedia or interdisciplinary nature of art production "discovered" several decades later.

With *Caserma, 1950,* which comprises poems written between 1945 and 1951, Accrocca's stylistic evolution became more sharply focused. In the development of his social themes, humanity occupies a central position. Poetry's function is not only that of consoling humanity but also that of offering it an instrument with which to carry on its struggle. Imitative of Quasimodo's notion of *rifare* (remaking) humankind, *Caserma, 1950* assumes qualities that are at times epic and at other times apocalyptic. On the stylistic level, the book shows Accrocca's gradual abandonment of the lessons learned from the Ungarettian school of poetry. The lexicon and syntax, instead, are endowed with the expressive rhythms of colloquial speech inserted into expansive verses that derive their vigor from the poet's attempt to achieve a correspondence of word and sentence, of sound and meaning, without indulging in linguistic escapism. According to Accrocca the word is designed to lash and warn; it must, therefore, be a *piombo* (plumb) in relation to reality or, in other words, "un filo diretto e verticale . . . sul centro delle cose" (a direct, vertical line . . . to the center of things). Poetry must have sufficient weight and urgency to render with convincing realism the trauma of contemporary events. The "grafting" of past to present continues in *Caserma, 1950,* while the need intensifies for humanity to resume, in hope, its journey (interrupted by political events) toward the rediscovery of lost identity and toward material and moral recovery. As Accrocca writes in "Poem VIII,"

Quando scavata avremo la miniera
delle menzogne a ritrovare l'uomo
nel sacco verde di questa prigione,
quando legato avremo il nostro nome
a quello dei compagni, quando il suono
delle parole avrà il significato
reale delle cose, quando libera
uscita corrisponderà al segreto
umano desiderio, finalmente
il volto avremo degli uomini liberi.

(When we've dug deep in the mine
of lies to rediscover man
in the green sack of this prison,

when we've linked our names
to those of our comrades, when the sound
of words have the real meaning
of things, when man's secret desire
is to avoid combat, only then
shall we have the faces of free men.)

On 10 June 1953 Accrocca married elementary-school teacher Adriana Tambone, who devotedly supported him in his literary endeavors until her death in 1985. In 1955 *Reliquia umana* and *Antologia poetica della Resistenza italiana* (Poetry Anthology of the Italian Resistance) were published. The second volume was edited by Accrocca and Valerio Volpini. Both volumes appear to be products of the same critical views. *Reliquia umana* seems to be a conclusion or a synopsis of Accrocca's account of the history of humankind (history seen as a *ponte* [bridge] between the living and the dead, as well as an *innesto* [graft] of past onto present), started in *Portonaccio* and continued in *Caserma, 1950*. It is a synthesis dictated by a lucid critical conscience. Pellecchia has observed, with justification, that in Accrocca's work "il fare e la coscienza del fare, del cosa e come fare . . . coincidono: in lui il processo creativo procede sempre sotto la vigile luce della coscienza critica" (the doing and the awareness of doing, the knowing what to do and how to do it . . . coincide: in his work, the creative process always proceeds under the watchful eye of a critical conscience).

Therefore, while *Portonaccio* represents the fearful and painful awareness of ruin and death, and *Caserma, 1950* shows optimism as to the future salvation of humanity, in *Reliquia umana* the angle of vision is narrowed and concentrated. Accrocca compares his personal culture and history with the times in which he lives and to which his autobiography is "grafted" (as seen in "Poem III"):

L'origine mi resta dentro il sangue:
unica eredità da tramandare.
La custodisco come una reliquia.

(The origins are in my blood:
the only heirloom to hand down.
I treasure them like a relic.)

The comparison is made possible by the active participation of a memory that is not the recollection of a lost, mythical past but a historical, anthropomorphic entity, a repository of blood and values to be handed down to future generations. As a consequence of this view, according to critic Lorenzo Gigli, the poet's personal tale — which runs from a childhood lived in the stables of Cori and

the barns of Agro, through an adolescence spent in the houses of suburban Rome, up to the present moment of *consegna* (delivery) of sentiments and passions to the succeeding generation — "assurge a simbolo di catarsi comune, traduce nei propri trasalimenti l'angoscia e l'aspettazione di tutti" (becomes symbolic of a common catharsis and expresses, in its own vicissitudes, the anguish and anxiety of all people).

Reliquia umana concludes this phase of Accrocca's literary activity, which is generally defined as neorealistic, although not without reservation. *Ritorno a Portonaccio* (Return to Portonaccio Street, 1959) is a compendium of his three previous volumes, with the addition of some poems written between 1954 and 1958. These later poems open new vistas in terms of metrical/lexical form and thematic content, including the seemingly cheerful *disimpegno* (uninvolvement) of "Altri versi" (Other Poems), dedicated to the birth of Accrocca's only child, Stefano, on 6 July 1955. In these new poems Accrocca's unfailing attention to formal details is predominant — an attention that is sharpest when he composes in sonnet form, as in "I sonetti del carattere" (Sonnets on Human Character). In the broad sweep of lines modeled on Dantean and Leopardian moralizing verse, Accrocca displays dexterity for metrical construction (including the use of enjambment) and for clever implementation of rhetorical devices familiar to him. His skill, however, never results in the production of compromised or superficial utterances. His commitment to the concreteness of his social themes remains intact.

In a review of *Innestogrammi-Corrispondenze* ("Graftograms"-Correspondences, 1966) Giancarlo Vigorelli called it "un libro-germe, un libro-innesto di tutta una nuova misura di poesia" (a book that is the seed or grafting of a whole new style of poetry) (*Tempo*, 29 June 1966). A key word in Accrocca's vocabulary, *innesto,* reappears performing a function quite different from the one it had previously. What does one "graft," at the level of substance, in modern poetry? Vigorelli claimed that Accrocca "si è buttato già nel solco del domani, del Duemila, appunto perché del futuro ha preveduto e li innesta nel sangue, nel canto, i cambiamenti di *sostanza,* non di *forma*" (has thrown himself into the furrow of tomorrow, the year 2000, precisely because in the future he has foreseen changes of *substance,* not of *form,* which he grafts, in a sense, to his blood and his song). The most immediate changes Accrocca anticipates pertain to an extremely diversified and highly stratified Italian society of the late 1960s and early 1970s, to the new contradictions created by that society, to the wave of demonstrations and protests sweeping the nation, and to the behavioral models, the pseudo values of a capitalist consumer society. As a consequence of such anticipated social upheaval, problems that have long plagued European civilizations enter Accrocca's poetry: for example, society is threatened with spiritual annihilation brought about by excessive affluence; but he is able to maintain a hope for renewal.

Such a jagged reality calls for a poetry with increased penetrating power, one that expands the front of intellectual inquiry. As Accrocca says in his introductory note to the book, poetry should utilize the extraliterary material provided by the mass media and the fields of politics, economics, and sociology. Poets must be aware of forms of linguistic corruption and scientific falsification. Poetry represents an *innestografia* (graphic grafting) of the arts. The title of the book also contains the word *corrispondenze,* which is intended to be interpreted as a word of bivalent meaning, implying relationship as well as similarity between different contexts in which the poetic inquiry is conducted – namely the Italian or European culture as each relates to the personal experiences of Accrocca.

He exploits various visual techniques in the book, including italics, the arrangement of words in one or two columns (to be read either horizontally or vertically), the creation of spatial echoes by repetition, and the deployment of newspaper headlines or advertisements as slogans. The possibility of a multidimensional reading and the multiple meanings generated by such a reading make the text resemble a series of communicating vessels set up in different directions; through them flow the phenomenological and cultural elements of many disciplines, which obey a kind of psychological law of balance, just as water seeks its own level in accordance with physical laws. At the base of Accrocca's procedures is a commitment to the search for an understanding of the relationships or correspondences among the elements he explores.

The following passage, from the third section, "Osservazioni e analisi" (Observations and Analyses), illustrates his techniques:

Cover for one of Accrocca's 1984 books, poems that mix reality and fantasy with autobiographical reflections

Apriti, guarda oltre	*non ti stancare, ombra*
oltre di te, ombra . . .	*ombra amica del tempo*
Che so di me	*radice della mia radice*
di quanto d'aria attornia	*piuma della mia àncora*
questo corpo e quest'anima indifesa	*veritiera testimone della luce*
mobile l'uno e l'altra	*sublime satellite*

ad inattesi traguardi fissa	*una volta non ti notavo neppure*
e quasi se ne invoglia procedendo nel tempo	*e ti calpestavo spavaldo spezzandoti impietoso sui muri*
e s'appresta a superare i malintesi orgasmi	
scogli non ebbe mai così l'onda	*cosa inutile ti credevo*
né foglia apprese mai	*alla tua fedeltà mai ho badato*
inquietudine di tanto vento.	*peso degli anni insignificante.*
(Open up, look beyond	*don't tire yourself out, shadow*
beyond yourself, shadow What do I know of me of the air that encircles this body and this helpless soul	*shadow friend of time root of my root feather of my anchor true witness to the light*
the one mobile and the other focused on unexpected goals	*sublime satellite at one time I never noticed you and I crushed you defiantly*

which it almost
wants proceeding
through time
and it prepares to
overcome the mis-
understood de-
lights
the surf has never
seen such break-
ers
no leaf ever learned
restlessness from
such a wind.

*pitilessly smashing you on the
walls*

useless thing I thought of you

*to your loyalty I never paid
attention
the insignificant weight of
years.)*

When *Innestogrammi-Corrispondenze* was first published, some critics spoke of Accrocca's conversion from a lyrical poet to a socially involved "technological poet." This view was noted, for example, by Bruno Romani in 1977. Other critics have emphasized elements of *neosperimentalismo* (neoexperimentalism) that the collection supposedly contains. *Innestogrammi-Corrispondenze* does, indeed, have a generic "technological" quality, by virtue of the *innestografici* techniques implemented on the linguistic and semantic level (coincident with the new and multiplying sociological problems Accrocca points to). Nevertheless, the concept of conversion is unacceptable because Accrocca never was a "lyrical" poet in the strictest sense, and because the collection includes compositions in which there is no reference at all to technological man. Instead there are references to humanity that are characteristic of Accrocca's early work *Portonaccio,* according to which humanity occupies a central position in the poetic process. Humanity lives in symbiotic relationship with the literary text, which gives representation to the human condition. This symbiosis is especially evident in poetry, which is, according to Accrocca, a vehicle whose autonomy from conditioning factors and from enslavement of any sort must be safeguarded at all costs. These considerations permit one to appreciate the factors that differentiate Accrocca's position from that of the avant garde, for whom nothing is certain outside of literature. Even if *Innestogrammi-Corrispondenze* has an experimental surface, in the broadest sense, it is not possible to define the text in terms of the stylistic traits or the ideological tenets of the avant garde.

Other aspects of Accrocca's work include occasional stream-of-consciousness or internal-monologue techniques. These moments appear in Roman type; however, they are in a sense drawn into the *area di riflessione* (zone of reflection), printed in ital-

ics, by a dynamic process that confers a rational characteristic to the manifestations of the unconscious mind and, at the same time, a spontaneous characteristic to the logical statements – one of many possible uses of different type. Generally speaking, the print type meets Accrocca's need to give poetry a multidimensional quality and as wide a spectrum of communication, or communicative power, as possible. The results achieved are made possible by his impressive command of the *apprendimento del reale* (acquisition of reality) – a procedure that does not preclude borrowing from the visual arts, about which Accrocca became increasingly more knowledgeable, the proof being his appointment to the position of instructor of art history at the Academy of Fine Arts in Foggia. He continued to work in that capacity until 1977 and was director of the academy for brief periods. This was followed by his appointment to the post of inspector of academies for a five-year term, from 1978 to 1982.

The special attention accorded the volume *Innestogrammi-Corrispondenze* is justified on the basis of its importance within the framework of Accrocca's entire output. The book constitutes a technical and aesthetic turning point since it affects subsequent publications, especially *Europa inquieta* (Restless Europe, 1972), which comprises many of his poems composed between 1959 and 1971. Also in 1972 the same publisher released Accrocca's *Vagabondaggi per l'Europa* (Wanderings Through Europe). The second volume complements the first: the mixture of prose and poems in the second book is a record of "vagabondaggi sulle ruote lente di un viaggiatore disinteressato . . . un ritratto minimo dell'Europa . . . attraverso la particolare angolazione di una libera fantasia" (wanderings on the slow-moving wheels of a disinterested traveler . . . a miniportrait of Europe . . . from the special viewpoint of an uninhibited imagination), as the introduction states. The two books also complement each other in that both are marked by the same intense *sguardo* (gaze) that scrutinizes places, names, and monuments – so much so that Europe as a cultural entity is present to the sensations and modes of analysis of the poetic subject. Europe is a cultural entity in an anthropological sense rather than a strictly literary one.

Unquestionably, then, this phase of Accrocca's work opens with the theme of the journey, developed not as a travelogue or curiosity but as a "gnoseological" odyssey: a journey toward knowledge of self as well as of others. Places, names, and monuments offer the stimuli required to reconstruct what critic Walter Pedullà defines as an "autobiografia per interposta persona o paese o sentimento" (autobiography through the mediation of people, places, and feelings), in his review of *Europa inquieta* (*Avanti,* 1 June 1973). The journey to knowledge implies a continuous reflection on the things that present themselves to the perception of the poetic narrator, and, at the same time, it leads to "un esame di coscienza sul 'mosaico' di noi stessi, sulle nostre avarie, esperienze, intemperanze" (an examination of conscience performed on the 'mosaic' of our identities, on our failings, experiences, excesses), as Accrocca notes in the preface to *Europa inquieta.* In the final analysis, the journey is propelled by the poet's need to establish harmony between himself and others, as well as the need to find affinities and *corrispondenze.* If one considers Accrocca's foresightedness in the light of recent events in Europe and the world, one can better appreciate the importance of *Europa inquieta* in the larger context of European poetry. The journey takes the reader through a tragic Europe cloaked in solitude and fear; Accrocca makes his most dramatic stops at the sight of repression in Greece, violence in Ireland, and the ruins caused by an earthquake at Skopje, Yugoslavia. These traumatic events of modern history cannot be glossed over with indifference.

Accrocca's quest is a restless one, mirrored in the nervous graphic form and pagination of his text, including the *innestografia* of disparate elements, already experimented with in his 1966 volume — a technique that receives even broader application. Italics and capital letters reappear, allowing for conventional or "parallel" reading. Accrocca also adds his own drawings and illustrations, the implementation of still another tool in the production of a poetic discourse that exploits several interconnected "voices."

Accrocca's *Roma così* (This Is Rome, 1973) collects poems dating from the 1968–1971 period and composed virtually at the same time as *Europa inquieta,* with only a few exceptions. Whereas *Europa inquieta* expresses the need to know reality in the "correspondences" within the vast European context, *Roma così* brings that need to the more immediate surroundings of the poet's experience. This shift had already occurred to a certain extent in *Reliquia umana,* in which the poetic subject reflects on his life and on his condition as survivor, after the more general account of war and death in *Portonaccio* and *Caserma, 1950. Roma così* suggests a comparable psychological difference in relation to *Europa inquieta*: it represents a reduced area of analysis or a narrower

field of reflection. However, despite the fact that the eye of the poet focuses on a specifically urban landscape, the Roman one, the city is a symbol of an entire civilization ruined by the times, an enigma that cannot be grasped fully, as he intimates in "Questa città" (This City): "per capire i primi elementi di questa città devi crescere / come una pianta nei rioni dove s'impara a vivere / e non ti basta l'arco di una vita" (to understand the prime elements of this city you must grow / like a plant in the districts where you learn to live / and the span of a lifetime is not enough time). Rome is the place where Accrocca spent most of his life, but it is also the new Tower of Babel — a modern setting marked by a different and anonymous language that perplexes and exasperates, as seen in "Piazza del popolo" (People's Square):

Ai piedi dell'obelisco di Piazza del Popolo
sosta sui calli della pietra egizia e ascolta
confondersi nella cascata d'acqua il rumore diurno
e traduci nella tua lingua le parole del gergo
le frenate degli autobus
il fischio dei vigili
la sirena dei pompieri
la messa in moto delle macchine.

(At the foot of the obelisk in People's Square
pause in the avenues of Egyptian stone and hear
the daily din become one with the cascading water
and translate into your language the jargon of
the braking sounds of buses
the whistles of traffic cops
the siren of firemen
the start-up of automobiles.)

Some of the poems in *Roma così* reappear in *Siamo, non siamo* (We Are, We Are Not, 1974). *Due parole dall'al di qua* (A Few Words from the Here and Now), published in 1973, is somewhat disappointing. Even a cursory examination reveals Accrocca's more-limited use of the range of literary devices he had developed to this point. For instance, the alignment of the verses is more restricted; the ideographics and "graftograms" are almost completely absent; infrequent are the exchanges of reality and fiction, and of reflections on the present and recollections of the past, as suggested by the alternation of roman and italic type; and capital letters appear only rarely. Above all, the creation of composite words, so prominent a practice in preceding volumes, is almost completely abandoned. The word alone acquires a different dimension, a more "physical" or "material" consistency, in a sense. Even though there persists a pagination reminiscent of the "graphic grafts" of previous works, the words seem to be the object of the discourse; they become points of concentration. In essence they distract the author from exploiting the resources of his previous techniques.

In some cases it appears that Accrocca is attempting to personify or animate the word by attributing to it affective qualities, as in, for example, the following lines from "Perché" (Why):

> La parola allora è tornata su se stessa
> un po' confusa, è diventata rossa,
> poi lievemente ha infilato la porta
> rimettendosi la museruola sull'ultima lettera.
>
> (The word changed back into itself
> a bit confused, it turned red,
> then it slipped quietly through the door
> replacing the muzzle on its last letter).

Even the lexicon reveals the high frequency of the term *parola* and of terms that are of the same semantic field, such as *verbo* (verb), *paradigma* (paradigm), *sillaba* (syllable), *lingua* (language), *nome* (noun), and *voce* (headword). Along these lines, the primary theme of *Due parole dall'al di qua* is the *scrivere versi* (writing of verses). Connected to this theme is the motif of the autonomy of the writing process, particularly the writing of poetry — autonomy from standardization, fashion, servitude, and the bumptiousness of the well read.

Accrocca's ethical position implies separateness, solitude, and an unassailable moral rigor that tends to generate judgments and condemnations expressed in a tone that is not sermonizing. More often than not he resorts to irony, which is otherwise almost entirely alien to his canon. Equally rare in Accrocca's work is the use of rhyme. In this volume, however, metrical schemes recur frequently, in the form of conventional meter, internal rhyme, and assonance.

Due parole dall'al di qua had just been published when a tragic event marked Accrocca's life: on 6 September his only child, Stefano, was killed in a traffic accident shortly after his eighteenth birthday. The event deeply affected Accrocca's life and poetry, to the point where he questioned the value and purpose of his craft. After the death of his son Accrocca's despair grew; sorrow became his constant companion and blocked his creative output because he could not find the words needed for him to carry on writing, especially in the *inquieto* (restless) manner that had become his trademark. Despite the acute pain, or perhaps because of it, he composed the most beautiful and moving pages of *Siamo, non siamo* between October and December 1973. In the next year these pages were published in the fifth section, "Domande" (Questions). The experience is similar to that of Ungaretti, who composed his *Il Dolore* (Grief, 1947) in memory of his own son's death. Accrocca's *Siamo, non siamo* features a rich and thoughtful introduction by Giorgio Petrocchi. The book was awarded the 1974 Premio Tagliacozzo. It is divided into five sections; of these, "Italiaminima" ("Minimalitaly") and "Domande" had not been previously published. The remaining three sections comprise poems from the collections *Roma così, Due parole dall'al di qua,* and *Innestogrammi-Corrispondenze,* selected to be representative work.

"Italiaminima" includes verses written from 1962 to 1973, poems that belong to different creative periods. However, these works, not arranged in chronological order, constitute a unified project that has little or nothing to do with the journey, contrary to what many readers suggest. "Italiaminima" moves instead in a completely different direction; it appears to take up the problems treated in *Due parole dall'al di qua,* especially in the most recent compositions. The central theme of *Due parole dall'al di qua* resurfaces: the craft of the poet and the relationship between his personal life and the written page. This theme, in turn, recalls the symbiosis between literature and humanity. The title "Italiaminima" suggests that reality appears in fragments of *minimal* events, according to Accrocca. In another sense the effects produced by the poet's voice may be considered minimal.

In the poem "Ritratto" (Portrait) one reads the following lines:

> Una stagione
> è un tratto d'alfabeto, nient'altro,
> semicerchio di una piazza,
> la sosta in un bar . . .
> l'attesa di un evento che si alterna
> tra corsa e corsa . . .
> la sillaba che non può andare a capo.
>
> (A season
> is a portion of the alphabet, nothing more,
> semicircle of a piazza,
> the pause in a café . . .
> the anticipation of an event between
> one run and another . . .
> the syllable that can't start a paragraph.)

The reader is already in the presence of piercing personal sorrow and can sense, from the verses, the tragic and incomprehensible loss the poet is about to experience. Then come the poems of "Domande" addressed to Stefano. As the title suggests, direct and indirect questions are formulated in the context of Accrocca's frantic and often bitter need to understand, as in the poem "Non ti accadrà più nulla" (Nothing Else Can Happen to You):

> S'aggrovigliano in me rabbia e follia:
> vivo nell'indecifrabile
> che si avvolge di tenebre.
>
> Moltiplico e divido all'infinito
> il numero degli anni
> per decifrare tutti i tuoi respiri.
>
> Quando s'incepperà il mio cuore
> qualcuno scoprirà che nascondevo il tuo nel mio
> e invano m'illudevo di difenderlo.
>
> (Anger and madness enmesh in me:
> I dwell in the indecipherable
> that wraps itself in shadows.
>
> Endlessly I multiply and divide
> the number of years
> to glean your every breath.
>
> When my heart succumbs to clotting
> they will find that I concealed your heart in mine,
> and in vain I tried to protect it.)

Given the enormous weight of the pain endured, one might have expected the poems of "Domande" to be incapable of transcending raw emotion, but, on the contrary, Accrocca expands his search for adequate expressiveness to convey his more profoundly felt sorrow. He manages to give voice to absence and consistency to memory, precisely through the vehicle of his formal structures, as in "Il resto" (The Remainder):

> Non posso offrirti altro che parole,
> unico filo per tenerti vivo
> almeno nel delirio della notte.
>
> (I can offer you nothing but words,
> the only thread that keeps you alive
> at least through the delirium of night.)

The poetry also concerns itself with the sorrow of Accrocca's wife, Adriana, to whom the section is dedicated; her sorrow is the subject of some of the poems, including "Non ti accadrà più nulla":

> Crescevi grammo a grammo
> vigilato dall'occhio di tua madre
> . . . .
> Se potessi vedere
> com'è ridotta tua madre,
> a quale pianto s'abbandona, lei . . .

> (You grew one ounce at a time
> under your mother's watchful eye
> . . . .
> If you could only see
> the state she is in,
> the tears she sheds for you . . .).

Similarly in *Il superfluo* (Surplus, 1980) Accrocca succeeds in transforming the emotions of a tragic event into sublime poetry. The theme of death, which, in explicit or implicit form, runs through much of Accrocca's work, in "Domande" and *Il superfluo* becomes predominant. It absorbs all the other motifs in the poems, with the possible exception of some compositions of *Il superfluo,* such as "Parla sol il Tamigi" (Only the Thames Speaks) and "Il segno" (The Sign); these appear to belong to a more reflective phase of Accrocca's work in view of the fact that they deal with the philosophical themes of being, infinity, time, and space. However, it could be argued that these moments of reflection are also occasioned by the poet's personal tragedy. The prevailing stylistic form of the volume is, once more, the rhetorical question, and the epigraph repeats the dedication "ad Adriana, per Stefano" (to Adriana, for Stefano) but adds the phrase "nostro battito" (our heartbeat). The poem "A consumare gomitoli" (Using Up the Skeins) includes these lines:

> A ricrearlo con la fantasia
> — dandogli ancora vita —
> non siamo rimasti che noi due:
> una parvenza
> che tu continui a nutrire.
>
> . . . io posso darti soltanto una mano,
> o tu a me
> se mi siedi accanto
> quando lavori a maglia,
> in silenzio continui a consumare gomitoli
> gomitoli gomitoli di lana.
>
> (To recreate him with our imagination
> — restore him to life —
> there are only two of us left:
> it's an illusion
> you continue to nourish.
>
> . . . I can offer you only my hand,
> and you offer yours to me
> if you sit beside me
> while you knit,
> in silence and use up skeins
> skeins skeins of yarn.)

Claudio Toscani, in his 1976 interview with Accrocca, pointed out that the technical/linguistic dynamics of Accrocca's poems dealing with emotional themes were noticeably impoverished since the stylistic repertoire of *Innestogrammi-Corrispondenze* had been virtually abandoned. Accrocca then defended the creative freedom of the artist and the need for an experimental form in the face of modern technological reality. He also argued that a less *impegnata* (involved) page, at the level of expression, was fully justified where the themes selected made it seem appropriate. However, also in the name of poetic license, Accrocca insisted that even emotional themes could be treated in the context of his *innestografia*. He concluded, "la pagina dovrebbe essere *globale* perché noi siamo continuamente *sperimentati* dalla vita, dalla realtà interna ed esterna" (the page should be *all-inclusive* because we ourselves are the *subjects of experimentation* for life and the reality within and outside us).

By the time *Il superfluo* appeared, Accrocca had already published the poetry collections *Versi mignotti* (Wanton Verses) in 1975 and *Bicchiere di carta* (Paper Glass) in 1977. *Versi mignotti* has an unusual physical appearance. The top edge of the pages, rather than the side, has a thumb index, and the volume includes an appendix comprising photocopies of restaurant receipts that waiters prepare in hopes of receiving a gratuity. The unusual format, in part justified on the basis of a need to find new outlets for poetry, and the adjective *mignotti,* a term taken from the Roman dialect, would seem to give the volume a spontaneous and humorous quality that avoids the artifice of literary device to offer speech that flows automatically from the poet's imagination. However, the caustic, satirical vein that courses through the text (and which, in many ways, connects directly with the dominant ironic mode of *Due parole dall'al di qua*) finds in the epigram a suitable expressive instrument that can be appreciated on the basis of artistic criteria, as in "Foro" (Hole):

Non arrogarti diritti che non hai, amico
impietoso, disperso, la cresta dell'onda
ti condurrà (scommetti?) dove affonda
la vanità: nel foro di sambuco.

(My lost, heartless friend, do not claim all
the rights you don't have; the waves of the sea
will transport you [bet?] to where vanity
sinks like a stone: through the hole in the vessel.)

The volume also features drawings by several artists, including Accrocca himself, thereby renewing the author's experimentation with combining poetry and graphic design. In *Il bicchiere di carta,* as in

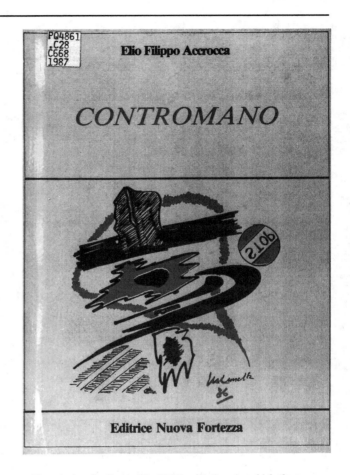

Dust jacket for Accrocca's 1987 collection, in which the poems reflect his depression following his wife's death in 1985

the poems "Parla solo il Tamigi" and "Il segno," the theme of death is integrated with the themes of existence, infinity, time, and space. The results are of questionable quality.

Near the end of 1960 Accrocca had become coeditor of the *Quaderni di Piazza Navona,* along with Raffaello Brignetti and Franco Fano. The periodical *Piazza Navona,* combined with a books-of-poetry series, revived the original objective of the *Quaderni del Canzoniere,* which was to promote collaboration among poets and artists. Although it took its name from a Roman square, *Piazza Navona* was more than a local journal. Indeed, Accrocca wrote in the May 1979 issue, "Una *Piazza Navona* come la intendiamo noi esiste nelle metropoli del nostro e di altri continenti. . . . 'Piazza' come centro di ritrovo, di scontro di idee con tutte le altre capitali d'Europa e del mondo" (*Piazza Navona,* the way we imagine it, exists in cities of our continent or any other. . . . 'Piazza' is meant in the sense of a meeting place where the ideas of all the capitals of Europe and the world can come together). Thus the original aim was expanded by the anticipated confluence of contributions from a wider geographic and cultural community. Once again one can detect in this project Accrocca's constant need to identify *corrispondenze* (in the sense of relationships and similarities) among different cultural and poetic contexts. A logical continuation of the work of *Piazza Navona* was *Carte d'Europa,* founded in 1983 by Accrocca. He brought to the new periodical his determination to make poetry an instrument with which to understand the *neuroconsumistica* (neurotic-consumer) face of the continent, as well as a means of surmounting geopolitical barriers, as voiced in *Europa inquieta.*

The poems in *Pesominimo* (Minimal Weight, 1983) take up again the themes and the "graphic grafting" techniques that characterize Accrocca's work prior to the appearance of *Il superfluo.* In *Pesominimo* Accrocca creates fresh forms of the "lexical grafting" he practiced previously and introduces two new concepts. The first is the notion of *peso* (weight). The term relates to the theory of the word's *materialità* (materiality) as well as to the aphoristic statement "la parola deve essere a piombo" (the word must be plumb), in *Caserma, 1950.* In *Pesominimo* Accrocca is alluding to the minimal weight of the word. However, he also suggests that, despite its scant substantiality, the word can undergo structural modifications through the author's manipulation of lexical, graphic, phonetic, and symbolic elements, as well as through his method of attaching one word to another. The second notion seems to pertain more explicitly to the *innestografia* of earlier texts, and it is an ideogramatic *radice* (root), a minimal unit that acts as the basis of the grafting technique. As Accrocca explains in the poem "Il segno dell'uomo" (The Signs of Humankind):

L'IDEOGRAMMA ha più età delle parole:
impronta, segno dell'uomo, forma che unifica
significati.

(The IDEOGRAM is older than words:
a mark, a symbol of humanity, a form that
unifies meanings.)

Pesominimo is divided into three sections. The first, "Pesominimo," features names such as P. M. Pasinetti, Giacomo Noventa, Bartolo Cattafi, and Leonardo Sinisgalli. The poems addressed to these important figures of contemporary Italian poetry suggest an air of consensus, which entails agreement on the nature of the poetic act and includes the taking of an ethical stand against the false

prophets of literature. Such a view is expressed in the poem "Al disperato orgoglio" (To Desperate Pride), dedicated to Noventa:

Ogni generazione ha bisogno
di un poeta come te
che sappia in sé riunire
lucidità e passione
intelligenza e ragione
equilibrio e ironia . . .

(Every generation needs
a poet like you
who can combine
lucidity and passion
intelligence and reason
balance and irony . . .).

The same is true for "A un filo di energia" (To a Power Line), addressed to Cattafi:

Dall'osso delle cose
hai raggiunto persino
il sottozero dell'anima.
L'immagine del vero
senza frange di polpa
è una tua scheggia informale
viaggiatore tra enigmi.

(From the bone of things
you managed to reach
the sub-zero soul.
The image of truth
without a trace of the pulp
is one of your formless splinters,
you who travel among enigmas.)

The second section of the book, "Carte d'Europa" (Maps of Europe) includes what Accrocca refers to as "pagine di viaggio: Est/Ovest. Zone geografiche dove mi spingono motivi di lavoro e sempre alla ricerca di 'rapporti,' mai di contrasti, sebbene le cronache volgano al peggio, come affermava [Eugenio] Montale, o mostrino più violenza che inquietudine" (pages on travel: East/West. Geographic locations to which my work leads me, always in search of 'relationships,' never of contrasts, even though, as Montale used to say, the news gets worse with each passing day, or displays more violence than restlessness). The cultural and anthropological referents of Accrocca's latest wanderings appear in Dublin, Moscow, Bergen, and Amsterdam, in their history, art, and politics. Nevertheless, Accrocca also continues to write his autobiography through the mediation of people and places.

The third section of the book is entitled "La prolunga" (Extension). In the opening poem, "Vai alla matrice" (Go to the Matrix), the concept of *radicale* (square roots) is presented in the following terms:

Regola radicale l'esercizio,
testo premonitore: innesto, impronta,
radice del possibile dialogo
        tra oggetti e forme.

(The exercise is the rule of square roots,
premonitory text: graft, trace,
root of the possible dialogue
        between objects and forms.)

The notion of *radicale* serves as the foundation of ideograms that come to Accrocca from Chinese culture. The acquisition of such a mode of writing resulted in his *Esercizi radicali* (Exercises in Square Roots, 1984), which contains mostly poetry based on "carte radicali/filologiche" (philological root maps), as Accrocca defines it; included are Chinese ideograms as well as graphic/digital designs intended to represent the "orme del possibile" (traces of the possible) beyond silence or to be an auxiliary to the word, which in itself is often insufficient for a speech act. In the introductory note to *Esercizi radicali* Accrocca clarifies some of the psychological and autobiographical motivations behind his use of the ideogram: the first impetus came from his studies of the Chinese language and of the works of Ezra Pound, James Joyce, and Guillaume Apollinaire at the University of Rome.

Esercizi radicali, in the context of Accrocca's experimentation, represents the point of maximum energy, where his exploration of the ideogrammatic form is augmented by the introduction of the *scultogramma* (lexical sculpture). Accrocca's tendency to innovate and experiment is never gratuitous. His metapoetry always takes into account a wide spectrum of things that are the substance of the existential passages of his texts. The most conspicuous feature of *Esercizi radicali* is the use of the *scultogramma*. Accrocca had been interested in the sculpturesque possibility of poetry for some time and had published a limited-edition catalogue of five poems and five etchings of Alba Gonzales titled *Scultogrammi* (1981). Earlier, in 1964, some of his sonnets, composed in accordance with this technique, had appeared in the journals *Alfabeto* and *Paese sera*. The following commentary was provided by Accrocca in the 15 February 1964 issue of *Alfabeto*: "Viaggiando, passavo davanti a Carrara, al marmo dell'Apuane. . . . È cosi che presi alcune pagine di Joyce e a furia di dar martellate estrassi sonetti. Identico esperimento ho fatto con il 'marmo' di [Alberto] Moravia, Gadda, Landolfi e altri" (In my

travels, I passed through Carrara and the marble quarries of Apuane. . . . Thus inspired, I set myself to work on some pages of Joyce; by sculpturing furiously, I extracted sonnets. I tried to duplicate my results with the 'marble' of Moravia, Gadda, Landolfi and others).

This technique derives from a creative method that is the exact opposite of the most commonly used device in Accrocca's poetry. Earlier he had proceeded on the basis of *accumulo* (accumulation) of linguistic units, manipulating and composing a broad range of lexical, metric, literary, and extraliterary products. In such a process Accrocca managed to fit pieces of language together to generate texts of rare beauty. By means of his "lexical sculptures" Accrocca offers the reader exercises in "decimazione verbale" (verbal decimation). In other words, he reduces a page from Gadda, Moravia, or others until he is left with a sonnet. It is an operation of "estrazione metrica dal marmo" (extraction of meter from marble), according to Accrocca's own definition.

In 1984 Accrocca also published *Videogrammi della prolunga* (Videograms of Extension), which was awarded the Premio Internazionale Taormina the following year, and *Bagage* (Baggage). The word *prolunga* refers to compositions in which memory extends the poet's *video-captante* (video-recording) abilities to allow a fuller contact with reality and a continuous juxtaposition of present and past. *Videogrammi della prolunga* includes a lengthy monologue or confession in which the poetic subject reviews his life – its successes, failures, events, and familiar faces – and dwells on literary and artistic recollections of Rome and Europe, as well as on individuals who acted as his guides: such as Vittorio Sereni and Niccolò Gallo, along with other protagonists of the arts, "presenze ormai invisibili di solidarietà silenziosa, di inquietudine partecipata e comune" (by now invisible representatives of a silent solidarity and of a collective disquiet), according to critic Giuseppe Pontiggia in his review of the book (*Epoca,* 7 December 1984). The personalities to which he is referring include Paul Valéry, Dino Campana, Carlo Emilio Gadda, Franz Kafka, Jorge Luis Borges, Tommaso Landolfi, Marc Chagall, Gino Bonichi, and Montale. The problematic, "gnoseological" odyssey through Europe, noted in earlier works, seems reduced to a crossing from one side of Rome's Via del Babbuino to the other. But this is merely an apparent effect. It is not a reduction, because the crossing of Via del Babbuino implies the full circle of Accrocca's existence, including the war experience, the residual affections, the cultural background, the "videograms" and "lexical grafts" of the later stages of his career, as well as the impressions formed in the course of his travels through Europe.

Mixing reality and fantasy, the present and the past, he engages in a dialogue with "lo sdraiato di pietra" (the reclining stone figure), the statue of a baboon, with "le mani mozzate / e la capoccia è rifatta che sembra di gesso" (its hands lopped off / and its head restored so it looks like plaster). Accrocca's long, uninterrupted confession in the presence of this "blocco di pietra dolente e fraterna" (block of suffering, brotherly stone) – which, as Andrea Zanzotto argues, "riassume in sé gli sporchi enigmi del nostro tempo paludoso eppure precipite" (symbolizes all of the dirty enigmas of our murky yet precipitous times) – expands like concentric circles. Each of the circles represents a thematic line. The primary motif is that of the city of Rome seen in a love/hate relationship, as the following lines suggest:

> Ma è la tua
> sanguisuga degli anni,
> la vorace città dove maturi
> di giorno in giorno
> all'ombra che raccoglie i tuoi ricordi,
> la più segreta delle capitali
> che non ha misteri per te
> e la puoi giudicare a viso aperto.
>
> (But it is the
> bloodsucker of your years,
> the voracious city where you grow
> day after day
> in the shadows that hold your memories,
> the most secretive of cities
> which has no mysteries for you
> and which you can judge openly.)

Along the pedestrian crossings of that capital city, Accrocca passes his life and it passes him. In the process he manages to glimpse only the *orme* (traces) it leaves behind as it completes its circle; the baboon is tarnished and mutilated more by the past and present than by an uncertain future. The *orme* are like the ideogramic *radici,* thereby suggesting the coherence of Accrocca's discourse on thematic and linguistic structural levels. He continues to perform his lexical grafting in this volume by taking material provided by various movements, including what Accrocca calls "innestografia psicologica" (psychological, graphic grafting), which might, for example, extract materials from a Joycean stream-of-con-

sciousness. His aim continues to be that of expanding the communicative power of poetry.

Another theme in Accrocca's work from the time of *Europa inquieta,* and which *Videogrammi della prolunga* combines with the motif of the city, is that of travel through Europe. The references to the Continent continue in *Bagage,* which comprises the poems of "Carte d'Europa," from *Pesominimo,* in addition to other documents, poetic "maps" of places not previously explored, such as Paris, Norway, Romania, Bulgaria, and Malta. Among the enigmas of the universe, the poet is a Ulysses on a raft that is more Joycean than Homeric. His "baggage" is the word or, perhaps, the voice that speaks of events, geography, sociology, syntax, and linguistic matters. That voice (the voice of poetry) holds the key to resolving conflicts, violence, terrorism, and crisis, as he intimates in "Col 'Testamento' di Arghezi" (With Arghezi's 'Testament'):

> spingo lo sguardo
>   all'archeologia dell'universo
> conosciute le spine anch'io
> faccio i conti con l'inchiostro del mattino
> e preferisco scegliere
>   le minuscole nell'alfabeto
> e raccolgo la parola in un vaso di terra
> e veglio sul mistero del linguaggio.
>
> (I strain to gaze
>   into the archeology of the universe
> I too have faced difficulties
> I come to terms with the morning ink
> and prefer to choose
>   the lower-case letters in the alphabet
> and I place the word in a flower pot
> and watch over the mystery of language.)

Much of the coordination of Accrocca's texts centers on the concept of the journey as travel through internal and external spatial dimensions; these two dimensions become one. The external exploratory journey through Europe, delineated in *Europa inquieta, Bagage,* and *Forse arrivi forse partenze* (Perhaps Arrivals Perhaps Departures, 1988) intersects and fuses with the seemingly internal travels presented in *Portonaccio*; *Caserma, 1950*; *Reliquia umana*; and in the more recent *Videogrammi della prolunga, Copia difforme* (Imperfect Copy, 1986), and *Contromano* (On the Wrong Side of the Road, 1987). External and internal categories are blurred in Accrocca's odyssey of the spirit. The formal structure of the text, based on lexical grafting, ideograms, "videograms," and lexical sculptures, is the glue that holds together the various elements of this journey to knowledge. In the final analysis,

Accrocca embarks on a journey into the word — one of the most innovative, complex, and anguished journeys of modern Italian poetry.

In 1985 Accrocca's wife died; from this point forward, Accrocca's work is characterized by moments of gloomy meditation. The journey becomes completely interiorized as he draws almost exclusively from his reservoir of memories. This stance is apparent in *Copia difforme,* in *Contromano,* and especially in the previously unpublished section of his *Poesie: La distanza degli anni 1949–1987* (Poetry: The Distance of the Years 1949–1987), published in 1988.

In the introduction, Accrocca writes: "Attraversato dalla vita e senza alcune rose dei venti, non inseguo che 'orme' ai limiti del campo che resta" (Passed through by life and without a wind rose, I'm only pursuing 'traces' at the edge of the field that remains). The circle of his fateful journey is nearly complete; all that remains are the residual memories — *orme* at the edge of the field. Nevertheless, life continues all around him; it is condensed in the alter ego with whom he converses: the stone baboon, that talisman and obsession, that block of suffering, fraternal stone.

It can be argued, however, that *Forse arrivi forse partenze* illustrates more clearly the transformation of the poet's journey from travel through real space to an interior journey to the deepest parts of memory, which motivates not only the odyssey but also the poetic discourse. The word of that discourse, then, satisfies in the poet the need to know himself as well as the world around him.

Interviews:

Claudio Toscani, "Incontro con Elio Filippo Accrocca," *Ragguaglio Librario,* 11 (November 1976): 367–369;

Emanuele Mandarà, "Da Portonaccio al Babbuino," *Sicilia,* 11 October 1985, p. 3.

References:

Enrico Falqui, "Elio Filippo Accrocca," in his *La giovane poesia* (Rome: Colombo, 1957);

Alberto Frattini, "Elio Filippo Accrocca," in his *Poesia nuova in Italia tra Ermetismo e Neoavanguardia* (Milan: IPL, 1967);

Lorenzo Gigli, "Stagioni di poesia," *Gazzetta del Popolo,* 15 October 1955, p. 3;

Mario Guidotti, "La riscoperta dell'Europa," *Gazzettino,* 7 November 1972, p. 3;

Raffaele Pellecchia, "Elio Filippo Accrocca," *Otto/Novecento,* 1 (January–February 1980): 199–225;

Ugo Reale, "I videogrammi di E. F. Accrocca," *Avanti!,* 28 July 1984, p. 5;

Claudio Rendina, "Accrocca: Un poeta romano ed europeo," *Regione Oggi,* 10 (October 1988): 27;

Bruno Romani, "I due 'registri' di Accrocca," *Albero,* 58, no. 1 (1977): 113–122;

Giacinto Spagnoletti, "Accrocca: Richiami e graffiti della coscienza," in his *Letteratura italiana del nostro secolo* (Milan: Mondadori, 1985), pp. 933–934;

Claudio Toscani, "'Siamo non siamo' di Accrocca," *Rapporti,* 5–6 (January 1975): 510;

Andrea Zanzotto, "Accrocca e il Babbuino, golem ispiratore," *Corriere della Sera,* 19 March 1989, p. 3.

Nanni Balestrini

(2 July 1935 –   )

Ernesto Livorni
Yale University

BOOKS: *Il sasso appeso* (Milan: All'Insegna del Pesce d'Oro, 1961);

Come si agisce (Milan: Feltrinelli, 1963);

Altri procedimenti (Milan: All'Insegna del Pesce d'Oro, 1965);

Tristano (Milan: Feltrinelli, 1966);

Ma noi facciamone un'altra (Milan: Feltrinelli, 1968);

Vogliamo tutto (Milan: Feltrinelli, 1971);

Prendiamoci tutto (Milan: Feltrinelli, 1972);

Le cinque giornate, by Balestrini and Dario Argento (Milan: Bompiani, 1974);

Ballate distese (Turin: Geiger, 1975);

La violenza illustrata (Turin: Einaudi, 1976);

Poesie pratiche, 1954–1969 (Turin: Einaudi, 1976);

Le ballate della signorina Richmond (Rome: Cooperativa Scrittori, 1977);

Blackout (Milan: Feltrinelli, 1980);

Ipocalisse: 49 sonetti, Provenza 1980–1983 (Milan: Scheiwiller, 1986);

Gli invisibili (Milan: Bompiani, 1987); translated by Liz Heron as *The Unseen* (London & New York: Verso, 1989);

Il ritorno della signorina Richmond (Oderzo: Becco Giallo, 1987);

La signorina Richmond se ne va (Milan: Corpo 10, 1988);

Osservazioni sul volo degli uccelli: Poesie 1954–1956 (Milan: All'Insegna del Pesce d'Oro, 1988);

L'orda d'oro 1968–1977, by Balestrini and Primo Moroni (Milan: Sugarco, 1988);

L'editore (Milan: Bompiani, 1989).

PLAY PRODUCTIONS: *Novae de Infinito Laudes,* text by Balestrini, music by Hans Werner Henze, 1962;

Mutazioni, subject for ballet by Balestrini, music by Vittorio Fellegara, Milan, Scala Theatre, 1963;

Milleuna, Milan, Out-Off Theatre, 1979;

Banana Morbid, Milan, Porta Romana Theatre, 1981.

RADIO: *Deposizione,* RAI, 1973;

Parma 1922, RAI, 1973.

OTHER: *Gruppo '63: La nuova letteratura, 34 scrittori,* edited by Balestrini and Alfredo Giuliani (Milan: Feltrinelli, 1964);

Gruppo '63: Il romanzo sperimentale, edited by Balestrini (Milan: Feltrinelli, 1966);

L'Opera di Pechino, edited by Balestrini (Milan: Feltrinelli, 1971);

Vittoria Bradshaw, ed. and trans., *From Pure Silence to Impure Dialogue: A Survey of Post-War Italian Poetry 1945–1965,* includes poems by Balestrini (New York: Las Américas, 1971), pp. 660–676;

Jack London, *Martin Eden,* preface by Balestrini (Milan: Sonzogno, 1974), pp. VII–XXIII;

Claude Simon, *Trittico,* translated by Balestrini (Turin: Einaudi, 1975) ;

"Linguaggio e opposizione," in *Critica e teoria,* edited by Renato Barilli and Angelo Guglielmi (Milan: Feltrinelli, 1976), pp. 77–79;

Alfonso Natella, *Come pesci nell'acqua inquinata,* preface by Balestrini (Milan: Librirossi, 1978), pp. 5–15;

"Indications du jeu," in *24 h? Satie* (Milan: Teatro di Porta Romana, 1980);

Banana Morbid in *Valeria Magli: Banana Lumière* (Milan: Cooperativa Intrapresa, 1981);

Lawrence R. Smith, ed. and trans., *The New Italian Poetry: 1945 to the Present. A Bilingual Anthology,* includes poems by Balestrini (Berkeley & Los Angeles: University of California Press, 1981), pp. 393–425;

Jean François Lyotard, *Il muro del Pacifico,* translated by Balestrini (Milan: Multipla, 1986);

Leon Battista Alberti, *Momo o del Principe,* edited by R. Consolo, preface by Balestrini (Genoa: Costa & Nolan, 1987), pp. v–x.

Cronogramma, *one of Nanni Balestrini's "visual poems" in poster form*

Nanni Balestrini's poetry is invariably linked with the activities and premises of the "Gruppo '63," the neo-avant-garde circle of poets, writers, and literary critics who added an important chapter to the history of the twentieth-century Italian lyric. Acting on the conviction that language exists in an alienated and reified condition, and wishing to revive the concept of language and literariness within a social structure felt to be alienating and oppressive, Balestrini intends to broaden the discussion on language by advancing the view that it is no longer a mere instrument of artistic expression but its own object. In his technical experimentations, from verses built up through the device of collage, to mechanical poems generated by the artificial intelligence of a computer, Balestrini pays special attention to the disengagement of normal syntactical links as well as to the effects of spoken language. Activity in this area has come to represent an important phase in the evolution of the neo-avant-garde and of the poetry produced in Italy from 1960 to the present.

Nanni Balestrini was born in Milan on 2 July 1935. Although his mother was of German descent, his own intellectual heritage places him squarely within the tradition of the so-called *Linea lombarda* (Lombard Line) – a term coined by critic and poet Luciano Anceschi; however, such a poetic tendency

has been mitigated to an extent by a dadaist vein, which has remained one of the peculiar aspects of Balestrini's art. While at the University of Milan he enrolled in the school of engineering, but his changing academic interests brought him to enter the faculties of economics and political science at the Università Cattolica, also in Milan. During this period he read the dadaists, as well as Guillaume Apollinaire, Bertolt Brecht, Ezra Pound, Carl Emilio Gadda, and, of course, the authors in the *linea lombarda,* particularly Luciano Erba; Balestrini was also actively interested in contemporary music and art. Shortly after Gillo Dorfles published some of Balestrini's poems in the journal *MAC* in 1945, Balestrini became a member of the group of poets who began to converge around Anceschi; by 1957 Balestrini had also published poems in *Il Verri,* the journal Anceschi had founded in the autumn of 1956. From 1957 on Balestrini served as a member of the journal's editorial board. The journal later played a significant role in the popularization and promotion of the movement that, a few years later, came to be called Gruppo '63. Balestrini continued to publish his poems in the magazine as well as to contribute translations of other poets, among whom was Jean Arp, a poet responsive to the allure of dadaist forms of poetry. In an explanatory note in *Il Verri* (April 1961) Balestrini voiced his attraction to dadaist experiments, which he preferred to those of other avant-garde movements. According to critic Alfredo Giuliani, "è significativo che alla delibazione delle situazioni oniriche del surrealismo Balestrini opponesse 'i puri regni di parole' dei poeti dadaisti" (it is significant that Balestrini rejects the predilection of the surrealists for oneiric situations, preferring the 'pure realms of words' of the dadaists).

Readers have an early probative demonstration of such a preference in Balestrini's poem "De cultu virginis" (On the Cult of the Virgin), in *Come si agisce* (How to Act, 1963):

Spesso preghiamo che Dio ci dia una mano
(un cilindro di carta d' amaretto, dateci fuoco in cima,
attenti! la cenere sale, su quasi fino al soffitto!)
e i bambini imparano che

sbocciano immobili giorni in cui non ricevono doni,
a non calpestare i fiori, strappare ali a gialle farfalle
o fidarsi di uomini che in tasca nascondono molte
    chiavi
e mutano in una fonte. Un uccello

bianco ogni tanto lacera aquiloni nel sole. TEOREMA:
Francesco Petrarca era forse infelice di non avere il caffè?

(We often pray for God to give us a hand
[a cylinder made from a cookie wrapper, you light the
    top,
watch out! the ashes climb, almost to the ceiling!] and
    the
 children learn that

motionless days blossom when they don't get gifts, not
    to
trample on flowers, tear the wings off yellow butterflies
    or
trust men who hide many keys in their pockets and
    change into
a fountain. A white

bird occasionally tears up kites in the sun. THEOREM:
    Could
it be that Francesco Petrarca was unhappy because he
    didn't
have coffee?)

— translation by Lawrence R. Smith

The entire composition appears to flirt with a certain symbolist lyricism without ever collapsing entirely into it. This persistent balancing act illustrates Balestrini's expressive power, especially at the level of poetic form; that is, formal composition is of paramount concern for Balestrini.

In his first book, *Il sasso appeso* (The Dangling Stone, 1961), his intention is transparent: to use a language that is not subjective and not, therefore, laden with personal metaphors that convey a specific meaning; instead, his language exploits the collective cultural baggage that, shattered into a series of common and familiar syntagmas, "comunica effettivamente al lettore una serie infinita di significati potenziali" (communicates effectively to the reader an endless sequence of potential meanings), according to Giuliani. Consider, for example, these lines from the opening (untitled) poem:

Gonfio di miele il fazzoletto sul sedile posteriore vuoto
e dopo un'ora ne avevamo abbastanza e continua (non
    ne usciremo)
fumando e raccontando *quand'ero tossicomane* può con-
    tinuare
con queste mani sempre pulite seppellivo disseppellivo i vivi . . .

E continua fino alla fine del continente (e un poco
    oltre),
aperti gli occhi dentro l'acqua, attenti all'elica e al
    crampo,
se non ce la fai non importa tanto meglio non ti bagni non
    sanguini

(Swollen with honey the handkerchief on the empty
    back seat
and after an hour we had had enough and continue [we
    won't get out]
smoking and telling of *when I was an addict* it can con-
    tinue
*with these hands always clean while I used to bury and exhume the
    living . . .*

And it continues until the end of the continent [and a bit
    beyond]
eyes open inside the water, watch out for the propeller
    and the cramp,
if you can't make it it doesn't matter better still you won't
    get wet you don't bleed)[.]

Such a stylistic approach was undoubtedly reinforced by Balestrini's study of Pound, T. S. Eliot, and Eugenio Montale. However, in Balestrini, this interest assumes fresh nuances. The following epigraph, written by French critic Roland Barthes and used by Balestrini to open his collection *Altri procedimenti* (Other Procedures, 1965), captures this sense of nuance: "faire du langage un *sujet,* et cela à travers le langage même, constitue encore un tabou très fort (dont l'écrivain serait le sorcier): la société semble limiter également la parole sur le sexe et la parole sur la parole" (to make language the *subject* of language still represents defying a formidable taboo [of which the writer himself is the sorcerer]: society seems to restrict the word pertaining to sex in the same way it restricts the word pertaining to the word).

The 1960s were years of intense curiosity about information theory, especially the notions of Norbert Weiner and Max Bense; these ideas were analyzed by Umberto Eco, a writer who was close to the neo-avant-garde group and who, in his *Opera aperta* (1962; translated as *The Open Work,* 1989), expressed a compatible theoretical position. In his poetry Balestrini profoundly rethinks the order-versus-disorder dialectic as a direct result of the contemporary research conducted on information. According to Weiner and Bense information is directly proportional to the degree of order; therefore, the degree of disorder, or entropy, is located at the opposite pole of information. However, it would be wrong to say that information corresponds to meaning; in fact, if order ensures the comprehensibility of a message, it also renders it banal, while disorder permits the attainment of authentic communication, at least in Balestrini's view.

Balestrini was already on the way to assimilating such a concept in 1963, when he became part of the editorial staff of the publishing company Feltrinelli, and when he collaborated with Vittorio Fellegara in the creation of the ballet *Mutazioni* (Mutations). Balestrini became increasingly involved with delving into the abyss that separates signifier and signified and by shattering the presuppositions that sustain the notion of order in communication.

It was also in 1963 that Balestrini organized the first meetings and conferences of the Gruppo '63. The label *novissimi* (brand new), applied by Edoardo Sanguineti to the group, demonstrates clearly the continuity and, at the same time, the discontinuity that existed between the neo-avant-garde writers and the *lirici nuovi* (new poets) so dear to Anceschi. Balestrini was the youngest of the five principal figures and had a precise ideological position. Of his sparse critical writings the short article "Linguaggio e opposizione" (Language and Opposition), written in 1963, is perhaps the most noteworthy. In it Balestrini argues that language is at an impasse since "il bisogno di servirsi con immediatezza delle parole porta infatti a un'approssimazione per difetto o per eccesso rispetto al contenuto originario della comunicazione" (the need to use words with immediacy leads in fact to the approximation due to deficiency or excess with respect to the original content of the communication).

He stresses the difference between spoken and written language, arguing that the latter "offre la possibilità di una stesura dilazionata" (offers the possibility of periodic revision), whereas in the former "cio che è detto è invece detto per sempre" (what is said, instead, is said once and for all).

Balestrini consequently proposes a fresh approach: "una poesia più vicina all'articolarsi dell'emozione e del pensiero in linguaggio" (a poetry that is closer to the process whereby emotion and thought acquire linguistic form); in such poetry "sarà una possibilità di *opporsi* efficacemente alla continua sedimentazione, che ha come complice l'inerzia del linguaggio" (it may be possible to resist effectively continuous sedimentation, to which the inertia of language contributes).

Come si agisce was awarded the 1963 Ferro di Cavallo Prize for the most experimental book of the year. In it Balestrini pushes to the limit the problem of the uneasy relationship between signifier and signified. He does not want to remain inside the linguistic system in his attempt to realize communication. Convinced that traditional communication leads eventually to a reduction of language to the status of merchandise (given its property as a commodity to be exchanged only on the condition that a specific market etiquette be respected), Balestrini chooses exile from the linguistic system; he repudiates grammatical codification and proposes noncommunication as a radical alternative. In order to expose the reification of language, he places his faith in the demystification of the order of language and appeals to its potential for disorder. The title of the volume itself is symptomatic of this conviction: it constitutes a behavioral prescription and appears to indicate the correct road to action. The peremptoriness of the title, as well as those of sections of the book, such as "Corpi in moto e corpi in equilibrio" (Bodies in Motion and Bodies in Equilibrium) – which demonstrates the points in common between *Come si agisce* and the linguistic experimentation of *Il sasso appeso* – underscores the volume's dynamic character. As a result of this characteristic, the text assumes the form of an *opera aperta,* which can be extended to infinity; at the same time, its individual components can be intersubstituted. The opening poem is titled "Avremmo potuto farne a meno" (We Could Have Done Without It):

Avremmo potuto farne a meno, gli alberi fanno troppo
rumore, ma cosa ci stanno a fare

i cavalli, ciascuno per suo conto
avremmo finito per perderci,
fare ritorno, fare

tutto quello che vuoi, certe
volte gli alberi riescono
a crescere in direzione del cielo

aspirando l'esplosione nell'istante
inatteso, aspettando che finisca
di piovere, ispirati dall'istinto

(We could have done without it, the trees make too
    much noise,
but what are they doing there

the horses, everyone on his own
we could have ended up getting lost,
returning, making

everything you want, at certain times
the trees manage to grow in the
direction of the sky

inhaling the explosion in the unexpected
instant, expecting it to stop
raining, inspired by instinct)[.]

The poem exploits to full advantage various verbal nuances, including certain semantically daring juxtapositions, such as "nell'istante / inatteso, aspettando che finisca" (in the unexpected / instant, expecting it to stop). This approach, which rejects any sort of selection criteria, has as its objective the negation of every shred of communication.

Balestrini extended his experimentation to the narrative genre with the publication of his novel *Tristano* (1966), which was written after Balestrini moved to Rome in 1964. In those years, he also worked on the publication of a journal called *Quindici;* its first issue appeared in 1967. This monthly magazine was edited by a group of intellectuals who did not remain together very long; in 1969, in fact, publication was suspended due to irreconcilable differences in the political choices made by the members of the editorial board. Nevertheless, these problems did not at first impede the journal in its (albeit short-lived) role as a rich, stimulating vehicle, not only for the literary and art criticism but also for dossiers on the political events that occurred in that period: the student protests, the labor struggle of Fiat employees, the so-called *Maggio Francese* (French May) and the *Primavera di Praga* (Prague Spring). The magazine officially signaled the start of Balestrini's involvement in matters more explicitly political. After *Quindici* ceased, he founded another magazine, *Compagni,* and he had a hand in the establishment of the left-wing, extraparliamentary political group known as *Potere Operaio* (Workers' Power).

During the late 1960s his poetry output was not abundant, but it did reflect his newfound political interests. Evidence of these are in his collection *Ma noi facciamone un'altra* (But Let's Make Another,

1968). This new stance did not mean that the research into language had become secondary for Balestrini; on the contrary, in this volume the tension between signifier and signified is dramatic and affects all levels of the enunciation. The sentence as syntactical unit is ignored. The first poem of the collection, "Non smettere" (Don't Stop), contains the word *che* (that), which is symptomatic of the semantic destabilization running through the entire volume, an integral part of Balestrini's discourse. The *che* could be a relative pronoun or a declarative conjunction. The reader does not know, because the hierarchy of syntactical units has been subverted. A sentence may be started and not completed, or vice versa; even the word at the end of a line may be truncated without regard for the rules of syllabication.

Many poems make clear Balestrini's intentions. "Disegno dello" (Design of the) states that "il problema è dare un significato alle parole" (the problem is ascribing a signified to the words). In "Che accadono continuamente" (Which Occur Continuously), the verses, structured simply on the stubborn repetition of a single consonant, reach the point of paroxysm. The sentence fragments available in this poem and in other poems, such as "I funerali di Togliatti" (Togliatti's Funeral), "Invece della rivoluzione" (Instead of the Revolution), and "Istruzioni" (Instructions), could be taken to indicate a fresh concern for the content of words — a concern stimulated by the political events of the time. However, for Balestrini the real revolution is the one waged by the new avant-garde against language. Further proof of this can be found in *Vogliamo tutto* (We Want It All, 1971), his novel which is, in many ways, a sequel to *Tristano.*

Following the tragic death of Giangiacomo Feltrinelli in March 1972 and the subsequent dissolution of *Potere Operaio,* Balestrini left Feltrinelli publishers to join the staff of the Marsilio publishing firm. At that time he also collaborated on screenplays, among which was *Le cinque giornate* (The Five Days, 1974), and worked on the production of radio plays. In 1974 he began to write a series of poems dedicated to a Signorina Richmond; these led to the collection known as *Ballate distese* (Extended Ballads, 1975). The same series was eventually republished in *Le ballate della signorina Richmond* (The Ballads of Miss Richmond, 1977).

In the meantime Balestrini's third novel, *La violenza illustrata* (Illustrated Violence, 1976), appeared in print, as did an anthology of his poetry, *Poesie pratiche* (Practical Poems, 1976). Balestrini participated in a project called *Autonomia* (Autonomy)

by collaborating in the newspaper *Rosso* and, later, by founding Arena, a center for publishing that facilitated the distribution of the material of smaller editorial firms; the center shut down a short time later, despite the success it enjoyed. By this time the first issue of the magazine *Alfabeto* was ready for release when, on 7 April 1979, a warrant was issued for the arrest of Balestrini and the other intellectual leaders of *Autonomia* – including Tony Negri – for being members of an armed subversive group. Among other crimes, they were charged with nineteen counts of murder, including one for the murder of Aldo Moro. Despite the fact that the so-called Trial of April 7 (held in 1984) absolved Balestrini of any wrongdoing, he continued to live in exile in Paris, where he had taken refuge on the day after the warrant was issued. There he worked as a consultant for the prestigious publisher Gallimard and wrote *Blackout* (1980), which was dedicated to his harassed companions. In the book, Balestrini uses an often-virulent satire to criticize Italian intellectuals who did not have the courage to rebel against the political repression of the period. The reader encounters the influence of Pound; the transcription of personal letters (in one particular case, the warrant for Balestrini's arrest); the psalmodic refrain of verses such as "perseguitate con la verità i vostri perseguitori" (persecute with the truth your persecutors); and strains of emotionalism seemingly modeled on the invective against Florence and the "serva Italia, di dolor ostello" (servant Italy, abode of sorrow), hurled by Dante from his place of exile (in *Purgatorio VI*). From the French region so important to the poetics of Dante, namely the Provence of the troubadours, Balestrini drew the inspiration to write *Ipocalisse* (Hypocalypse, 1986), a collection of forty-nine sonnets. (Balestrini had left Paris to live in the Provence region).

In autumn 1983 he founded the journal *Change International,* and in 1984 he organized the international poetry festival at Cogolin, near Saint-Tropez; he also continued to work on the adventures of Signorina Richmond, completing the second and third volumes of the series: *La signorina Richmond se ne va* (Miss Richmond Leaves, 1988) and *Il ritorno della signorina Richmond* (The Return of Miss Richmond, 1987), the third volume being published a year before the second.

The 1980s also marked Balestrini's return to the narrative genre, with the completion of his novel *Gli invisibili* (1987; translated as *The Unseen,* 1989), in which he again gives wide scope to the use of montage. Through the memories of the protagonist (a young man from the Milan hinterland involved in the *Autonomia* movement) he reviews the events of the second half of the 1970s. Since 1988 Balestrini has been living and writing in Berlin.

References:

Fausto Curi, "La 'distruzione del modello lineare' e la letteratura d'avanguardia" and "Poetica del nuovo terrore," in his *Metodo storia strutture* (Turin: Paravia, 1971), pp. 181–191, 207–217;

Roberto Esposito, "Produzione poetica e forme di reintroduzione," in his *Ideologie della neoavanguardia* (Naples: Liguori, 1976), pp. 127–193;

Gian Claudio Ferretti, "Il Gruppo '63 e l'area dello sperimentalismo," in his *La letteratura del rifiuto* (Milan: Mursia, 1968), pp. 274–299;

Alfredo Giuliani, "Poesie pratiche di Balestrini," in his *Le droghe di Marsiglia* (Milan: Adelphi, 1977), pp. 392–395;

Angelo Guglielmi, "Le tecniche di Balestrini," in his *Vero e falso* (Milan: Feltrinelli, 1968), pp. 138–142;

Niva Lorenzini, *Il laboratorio della poesia* (Rome: Bulzoni, 1978), pp. 45–80;

Walter Pedullà, "Balestrini ne fa un' altra," in his *La rivoluzione della letteratura* (Rome: Bulzoni, 1970), pp.123–129;

Pedullà, "A cavallo della contestazione," in his *La letteratura del benessere* (Rome: Bulzoni, 1973), pp. 514–526; republished in his *Il morbo di Basedow* (Cosenza, Italy: Lerici, 1975), pp. 115–140;

Pedullà, "La teoria della ricerca del significato," in his *L'estrema funzione* (Venice: Marsilio, 1975), pp. 93–183;

Pedullà, "La violenza ha l'orgasmo con Balestrini," in his *Miti, finzioni e buone maniere di fine millennio* (Milan: Rusconi, 1983), pp. 305–308;

Edoardo Sanguineti, "Come agisce Balestrini," in his *Ideologia e linguaggio* (Milan: Feltrinelli, 1970), pp. 84–90.

Luigi Ballerini

(20 April 1940 –   )

Thomas Harrison
University of Pennsylvania

BOOKS: *eccetera. E* (Parma: Guanda, 1972);
La piramide capovolta (Venice: Marsilio, 1975);
Logical Space, by Ballerini and James Reineking (New York & Milan: Out of London, 1975);
The Book of the Last of the Mohegans (Reggio Emilia: Maramotti, 1975);
Spelt from Sibyl's Leaves: Exploration in Italian Art (Milan: Electa, 1982);
La parte allegra del pesce, bilingual edition, translated by Thomas J. Harrison (Modena: Torchi del Bernini, 1983);
Selvaggina, bilingual edition, translated by Harrison (Milan: Scheiwiller, 1987);
Che figurato muore, bilingual edition, translated by Harrison (Milan: All'Insegna del Pesce d'Oro, 1988);
Italy Observed in Photography and Literature, by Ballerini and Charles Traub (New York: Rizzoli, 1988);
La torre dei filosofi, by Ballerini and Remo Bodei (Ravenna: Essegi, 1989);
Che oror l'orient (Bergamo: Lubrina, 1991);
The Coaxings of Our End, translated by Janet Izzo and Stephen Sartarelli (Ravenna: Essegi, 1991);
Una più del diavolo (Turin: Marco Noire, 1992).

OTHER: William Carlos Williams, *Kora all'inferno,* translated, with an introduction, by Ballerini (Parma: Guanda, 1971);
Scrittura visuale in Italia, 1912–1972, bilingual edition, edited by Ballerini (Turin: Galleria Civica d'Arte Moderna, 1973); also published as *Italian Visual Poetry, 1912–1972* (New York: Finch College, 1973);
Chelsea, 37 (December 1978), anthology of contemporary Italian poetry, edited by Ballerini;
Ruth Feldman and Brian Swann, eds. and trans., *Italian Poetry Today: Currents and Trends,* includes poems by Ballerini (St. Paul: New Rivers, 1979), pp. 20–22;

La rosa disabitata, edited by Ballerini and Richard Milazzo (Milan: Feltrinelli, 1981);
Thomas J. Harrison, ed. and trans., *The Favorite Malice: Ontology and Reference in Contemporary Italian Poetry,* bilingual edition, includes poems and prose by Ballerini (New York, Norristown, Pa. & Milan: Out of London, 1983), pp. 193–219;
Gertrude Stein, *La foresta di Arden,* translated, with an introduction, by Ballerini (Milan: Mondadori/Lo Specchio, 1992);
Shearsmen of Sorts: Italian Poetry, 1975–1993, edited by Ballerini and Paolo Barlera, includes poems and prose by Ballerini (New York: Forum Italicum, 1992);
I Novissimi, edited by Ballerini and Paul Vangelisti (Los Angeles: Sun & Moon, 1993).

Luigi Ballerini's poetry belongs to the ontological or grammatological style characteristic of a select group of poets, including Nanni Cagnone, Raffaele Perrotta, and Andrea Zanzotto, writing in the decades following the 1960s movement called the *novissimi* (newest poets). With Ballerini this style has usually taken the form of a poetry of enigma, composed of unlikely lexical choices arranged in difficult and often extragrammatical syntagmas. Implicit in these operations is a polemic against both the confessional lyric and mimetic aesthetics at large. Ballerini's theoretical roots lie in the alternative-language poetics of the twentieth-century avant-garde. These sources can be gauged by a rapid glance at the critical work that has most occupied Ballerini. He has written on Gertrude Stein and William Carlos Williams; Guido Cavalcanti and the *dolce stil novo* (sweet new style); and futurism and visual poetry – in *La piramide capovolta* (The Upside-Down Pyramid) and *Logical Space,* both published in 1975. His collection of poetry written be-

Luigi Ballerini, Alfredo Giuliani, and Reiner Schürmann of the New School for Social Research at a 1979 symposium called "The Favorite Malice," held at New York University. The proceedings were published in 1983 (photograph by Elsa Ruiz).

tween 1975 and 1988 takes its title from a phrase of Cavalcanti's — "Che figurato muore" (That Once Portrayed Must Die) — underscoring a problematic that informs every aspect of Ballerini's work: how to present a phenomenon that is killed by being named. The project is literally impossible and leads to paradoxical formulations such as the one serving as the epigraph to one of the sections of *Che figurato muore* (1988) — the first six lines of medieval poet Guillaume d'Acquitaine's "Farai un vers de dreyt nien" (I Will Write a Poem about Exactly Nothing). The stylistic audaciousness of Ballerini's poetry is an attempt to elude the mimetic fallacy governing the act of writing; he attempts to speak, instead, in a radically different way, sometimes outside of all but the sparest conventions of sense.

An only child, Ballerini was born to Umbertina Santi and Raffaele Ballerini in the outskirts of Milan on 20 April 1940. His father, called to arms,

died in combat against the Germans in Cephalonia, Greece, leaving Luigi to be brought up by his twenty-four-year-old mother and religiously strict maternal grandmother. In a poor suburban neighborhood at the outer edge of Porta Ticinese, whose inhabitants were mostly factory hands, Ballerini began working full-time at the age of fifteen, pursuing his studies on the side. Recalling the general squalor of the postwar years, Ballerini still remembers his childhood with fondness. An errand boy and later a shipping agent, he left Milan for a year in England in 1959, supporting himself with temporary jobs from dishwasher to research assistant. Upon his return to Italy he received another opportunity to leave, for a year of study at Wesleyan University in 1961. In the United States he met Julia Cullinan, whom he married in 1963. Returning to Italy, Ballerini left the Università Cattolica and transferred to the Università di Bologna. There he worked as an editor at the Rizzoli firm and received his *dottorato in lettere* with a thesis on Charles Olson in 1965. From 1965 to 1969 Ballerini worked mainly as a literary reviewer of American books for the periodicals *Avanti!, Unità,* and *Rinascita* and as an English teacher in high schools in the vicinity of Rome. In 1969 he returned to the United States, this time to become an assistant professor of Italian at the University of California at Los Angeles. A year later his only child, Edoardo, was born.

Ballerini told interviewer Ugo Rubeo that his second trip to the States was not intended to be any more permanent than the first one: "All'inizio, come molti della mia generazione, mi son detto: andiamo in America per un paio d'anni; si fa un'experienza americana e poi si torna a casa. Io ormai sono qui dal 1969 . . . " (At first, like many people of my generation, I said to myself: let's go to America for a couple of years; we'll see the States and come back home. I've been here since 1969 . . .). Two years of teaching at UCLA led to a job at the City College of New York, in the city Ballerini was most interested in experiencing firsthand. New York proved attractive, the contrastiveness, discontinuity, and entrepreneurial ethic appearing to him to be more culturally productive than any situation in Italy. Ballerini stayed, joining the comparative literature department of the Graduate Center of the City University of New York in 1973 and relocating to New York University in 1975. In 1982 Ballerini divorced his wife and three years later began a relationship with Paola Mieli, a Lacanian psychoanalyst from Milan who resides in Greenwich Village.

Professionally speaking, Ballerini's profile has been closely tied to New York University, and in particular to his administrative duties as the director of Italian studies. The move from professor to director heightened an interest already visible in Ballerini from the time he worked with Rizzoli: direct involvement with the cultural apparatus sustaining the arts, including journalism, institutional fund-raising, museum exhibits, and literary conferences. Ballerini wrote poetry while he dealt with this larger project of cultural and academic organization, manifested both by the nature of his research and the development of the New York University Program in Italian Studies. In this respect Ballerini is not a professional writer so much as a professional who writes. Beginning with his first collection in 1972, *eccetera. E* (etcetera. And), Ballerini's poetry has always appeared in small quantities alongside his other activities as a coordinator and point man for artistic and intellectual exchange between Italy and the United States.

In the early 1970s Ballerini's primary interest lay in the twentieth-century concept of visual writing. He toured Italy to collect texts and exhibited his findings both at the Galleria Civica d'Arte Moderna in Turin and the Finch College Museum in New York in 1973. The same concern for the intersections of writing and the visual arts resulted in many experiments in analogical aesthetics. *Logical Space* is entirely dedicated to the affinities between writing and the visual arts, and five editions of Ballerini's poems are elegant, expensive volumes accompanied by artwork.

Since 1971 Ballerini has translated some eleven books from English into Italian, and his second book including poetry is entirely in English (*The Book of the Last of the Mohegans,* 1975). Most subsequent collections of his have appeared with facing English translations. The Out of London Press, which Ballerini operated from 1975 to 1986, published more than twenty books of poetry and art criticism, some in bilingual editions. In 1979 he edited an anthology of contemporary Italian poetry for the journal *Chelsea* and two years later, with Richard Milazzo, an anthology of contemporary American poetry, *La rosa disabitata* (The Uninhabited Rose, 1981). What seems to have motivated Ballerini's work is the relationships and affinities of different artistic codes. This abiding interest in the languages, genres, and syntagmas of contemporary art has allowed his poetry to follow, and in some cases to push further, some of the more radical experiments of recent aesthetics.

In October 1991, one year after becoming a consultant for the Milano Poesia project and inviting American poets to Italy, Ballerini organized a festival of contemporary Italian poetry at New York University. More than a dozen poets and critics were flown from Italy to New York, along with several American counterparts, to participate in the conference, making it the largest gathering of its kind ever to be hosted on the continent. A companion book for the festival, a selection from two decades of Italian poetry, was published in 1992 as *Shearsmen of Sorts.* The gathering coincided with Ballerini's ending his tenure at New York University and relocating to the University of California at Los Angeles. Currently Ballerini is chairman of the Italian department there and senior editor of the Marsilio publishing house in New York and is coeditor, with Paul Vangelisti, of Blue Guitar books by the Sun and Moon Press.

Ballerini's first volume of poems, *eccetera. E,* exhibits a fragmentary collage technique, as seen in "Autopsia":

la somma possibile del moto e la sostanza l'apparenza e
    il modo
dell'apparenza et ke kontene
                        il numero nove uguale due
per la somma possibile del moto e tre per la sostanza
l'apparenza il modo dell'apparenza
                                    cui risponde
l'essere il non essere il diverso
dall'affermare il reale e il suo contrario
                                    cui risponde
l'amore negli organi del corpo

(the possible sum of motion and the substance the ap-
    pearance and the way
of the appearance and which contains
                        the number nine equals two
times the possible sum of motion and three times the
    substance
the appearance the way of the appearance
                        to which there corresponds
being nonbeing the different
from affirming the real and its opposite
                        to which there corresponds
love in the organs of the body)[.]

Much of the vocabulary of this selection returns in other poems, and its predominant imagery remains with Ballerini throughout his career, especially the emphasis on the organic, the theological, and the ontological.

As Ballerini's writing progressed, his poetic theorization became more and more central. The protagonists of his later poems are not people, things, and situations so much as acts of meaning. For example, Ballerini had originally intended to give the title *Onomaremalogos* (Name-Verb-Speech) to *Che figurato muore,* as though to signal that the true interest of the collection was not the object so much as the methodology of poetic creation. Theoretical speculation and linguistic invention are inseparable in Ballerini's writing, often bolstered by his philosophical readings. Two of the epigraphs in *Che figurato muore* are from Friedrich Nietzsche, and one of the sections of the volume is called "Le scarpe di [Martin] Heidegger" (Heidegger's Shoes).

Ballerini's poetic career began with a poetics of accumulation, conjunction, and montage, but by the late 1970s he was referring to his poetry as ablative. The act of taking away, rather than putting together, became the key to his shorter and increasingly enigmatic verses. While those of *eccetera. E* are titled and run between twenty-five and sixty lines, the poems of ten years later are untitled and consist of only four to eight.

The influence on Ballerini of the grammatological experiments of Gertrude Stein can be strongly felt, especially in the distortion of parts of speech and the nominalization of adjectives and adverbs. Ballerini's poems from the late 1970s and 1980s are articulated not as actual, functional statements but rather as hypothetical conjectures. One often sees a series of words without objective referents. The result of such nominal packing is an inevitable pressure on adverbs, adjectives, prepositions, and words ordinarily subordinated to others, as in phrases such as "l'appena del quasi" (the barely of almost). The poems of *Che figurato muore* include suspended clauses; ungrounded deictic words; and illogical, truncated sequences ("così stoviglia, liqueria, nuoto . . . e dopo fanale che allatta" [thus crockery, licorice, swim . . . and then a lamppost that suckles]). These indeterminate textual connections accompany a crisis of reference in which names are deliberately incongruous and parodic, as in this poem: "il rullo degli *stayers* / che si gonfia e marcisce, che si tinge / di lana refrattaria, di pelle d'oca" (the roller of *stayers* / that swells and rots, that is dyed / as fireproof wool, as goose-pimples). Many of Ballerini's phrases are naked paradoxes or idioms made strangely literal. "L'intensità," Ballerini writes in *eccetera. E,* "è più vera / del vero e del non vero" (intensity is truer / than the true and the untrue). In his later poems the intensity is consistently wrought by a process of abstraction, even on the basis of concrete images:

etimo è sfingefenice, sdoppia in uno
lo zucchero nervoso del raduno, la falce
di lievito e di sabbia, lo sterro dell'invito:
forse brughiera, forse tango,
ma nel ventaglio liquido di uccide

(etymon is phoenix-sphinx, uncouples in one
the assembly's nervous sugar, the scythe
of yeast and sand, the spoil of invitation:
heath, perhaps, or tango,
yet in the liquid fan of kills)[.]

The transition from Ballerini's first to his second phase of writing (from *eccetera. E* to *Che figurato muore*) was accomplished in *The Book of the Last of the Mohegans.* A jocular diary of performance, this amalgam of photography, poetry, and prose celebrates a scepter that fails to materialize. Present in the form of its absence, it acts as the target for a series of questions that, directed to the poetic image, are ultimately engulfed in silence. Silence comes to appear as the condition to which poetry most truly aspires, a theme later developed into an explicit invocation of death in *Che figurato muore:* "Oggetto ultimo e inimitabile dell'imitazione poetica è la morte" (Death is the ultimate and inimitable object of poetic imitation). The paradox of *eccetera. E,* in which every conclusion solicits a new discussion, appears in *Che figurato muore* as the negation of the referent in the very attempt to give it linguistic form, as Ballerini says in a note to the volume: "più si aggiunge, per precisare, più si allontana l'oggetto da precisare; più lo si cesella e più esso diventa segreto e impenetrabile, più partecipa dell'ombra" (piling up appositions for the sake of clarity may distance the object altogether; the more ornate you make it, the more secret and impenetrable it becomes, the more it recedes into its own shadow). Poetry thus becomes the voice of an "insopprimibile voglia di fare i conti con le infinitamente fuggevoli modalità dell'ombra" (irrepressible wish to come to terms with the infinitely fleeing degrees of shade).

The poems of *Che figurato muore* took thirteen years to write, in a distillation and chiseling of terse, tight forms. Closely knit, the eight sections of the book (including two essays on the nature of the art) trace a subtle progression from the oracular couplets at the beginning to the gradual insurgence of a more emotive language and personal voice at the end. Readers may finally understand that the Cavalcantian title of the collection alludes as much to love as to poetry and, more pointedly, to the relation between them.

The final sections of *Che figurato muore* signal Ballerini's move toward poetry in his native Milanese dialect, some of which have been published as *Che oror l'orient* (The Oriental Horror, 1991). For Ballerini this recuperation of a personal and suppressed dialect is partially based on a sense that its referentiality is psychologically more plausible than official Italian. "Se io andassi in analisi," Ballerini has said in conversation, "chiederei che questa analisi si facesse in milanese. Cioè, se è vero che lo stile nasce dai traumi, come vorrebbe [Roland] Barthes, allora io per rintracciare la fonte del mio stile devo farlo in milanese" (If I were to undergo analysis, I would want it to be conducted in Milanese. In other words, if it is true that style originates from traumas, as Barthes claims, then I must trace the source of my style in Milanese). Even so, this return to dialect does not entail a merely sentimental revisitation or autobiographical narration. The first poems in *Che oror l'orient* are short and elegiac, bearing witness to an impoverished "I" attempting to reconstitute its biographical foundations. As the volume progresses, dialect comes to appear as the arena of a poetic reworking, brought into play as an allegorical, "other" discourse. The temptation to speak directly is consistently transformed into a festive dance of words, as in the following poem:

te fo studià de pret, de sorvegliant, te porti
a vedè i sciori che mangen el gelato, te insebissi
come on piccett che'l tripilla, che per scondes el taca
a ziffolà l'aida, te fo rid de offellee, te confondi
cont on piatt de magioster, con i cavai selvadegh
de la strusa. Ah, ves bon de nodà fin a la sponda
negra de sto bigliard, spettà che vegna dì per lêg
el fond de la tazzinna, per voltass come'l vent a
    tormentà
la foeuia, la foeuia e la gainna, la legor e'l vitell, i sgiaff
a duu a duu fin che diventen disper

(I'll make you study like a priest, like a guardian, I'll
    take you
to see the rich eating ice cream, I'll display you
like a carousing robin that tries to hide itself by
whistling the aida, I'll provoke a sardonic smile in you,
    I'll confuse you
with a plate of strawberries, with wild horses
of fusing. Oh, how nice to be able to swim to the black
shore of this billiards, to wait until daybreak to read
the bottom of the cup, to turn like the wind tormenting
    the leaf,
the leaf and the hen, the hare and the calf, the slaps
that are coupled until they become odd)[.]

Another poem turns idioms of the mother tongue into strange linguistic monuments:

l'è com vun che'l spetta
de dagh ona scorlida,
magar de taccà balin,
l'è come refudà de dis'ciollass

(it's like sticking around
to shake off the drops
maybe to bend someone's ear
it's like refusing to wise up).

Che oror l'orient won the 1992 Feronia Award for poetry.

Ballerini's most recent poetry is characterized by two works still in progress: "Il Cavalcanti milanese" and "Il terzo gode" (The Third Party Wins). The first collection is an extended translation of Cavalcanti's poetry into Milanese, a dialect that links the verses to historical experiences. "Il terzo gode" is divided into three parts. The first, *Una più del diavolo* (One up on the Devil), was published as a book in 1992. The second, "Corse in pista e su strada" (Races on Tracks and Roads), appeared in the journal *Ritmica* that same year. The third, still in progress, bears the title of the collection.

In his latest phase Ballerini submits the materials of his personal experience to an intellectual transformation in which what is finally at stake is neither the referent of the words nor the words themselves but the shifty relation between them. He seeks a fusion – or a confusion – of linguistic registers, one in which they meet not to fix meanings but to amplify the process through which meanings are possible.

Interview:

Ugo Rubeo, in his *Mal d'America: Da mito a realtà* (Rome: Riuniti, 1987), pp. 75–86.

References:

Stefano Agosti, "The New Italian Poetry," in *The Favorite Malice,* edited and translated by Thomas J. Harrison (New York, Norristown, N.J. & Milan: Out of London, 1983), pp. 297–319;

Alfredo Giuliani, Foreword to Ballerini's *Che figurato muore* (Milan: All'Insegna del Pesce d'Oro, 1988), pp. 12–23;

Robert P. Harrison, "The Italian Silence," *Critical Inquiry,* 13 (1986): 81–99;

Thomas J. Harrison, Introduction to *The Favorite Malice,* pp. 19–55;

Franco Loi, "Il milanese scritto a New York: Giusta distanza per la poesia," *Sole – 24 Ore,* 12 January 1992;

Mario Lunetta, "Irregolari e sperimentali," *Paese Sera,* 15 October 1971;

Giulia Niccolai, "Pronto chi parla? E' l'ermo colle," *L'Europeo,* 2 August 1979;

Beniamino Placido, "A parer mio," *Repubblica,* 15 September 1986;

Placido, "Coraggio riscopriamo l'America," *Repubblica,* 27 February 1987;

Antonio Porta, "Poesia come salvezza," *Panorama* (26 June 1988);

Adriano Spatola, "etcetera. E," *Tam Tam,* 3–4 (1973): 94–95;

Tibor Wlassics, "Profili di poesia contemporanea: Luigi Ballerini," *Verri,* 4 (1973): 214–223.

Giorgio Bàrberi Squarotti

(14 September 1929 -   )

Gaetana Marrone
Princeton University

BOOKS: *Astrazione e realtà* (Milan: Rusconi & Paolazzi, 1960);

La voce roca (Milan: All'Insegna del Pesce d'Oro/Scheiwiller, 1960);

Poesia e narrativa del secondo Novecento (Milan: Mursia, 1961; enlarged, 1978);

Metodo, stile, storia (Milan: Fabbri, 1962);

Nel tempo delle metamorfosi (Florence: Linari, 1962);

Teoria e prove dello stile del Manzoni (Milan: Silva, 1965);

La declamazione onesta (Milan: Rizzoli, 1965);

La narrativa italiana del dopoguerra (Bologna: Cappelli, 1965);

La forma tragica del "Principe" e altri saggi sul Machiavelli (Florence: Olschki, 1966);

Simboli e strutture della poesia del Pascoli (Messina & Florence: D'Anna, 1966);

La cultura e la poesia italiana del dopoguerra (Bologna: Cappelli, 1966);

Manzoni, by Bàrberi Squarotti and Giuliano Martignetti (Padua: R.A.D.A.R., 1968);

Finzione e dolore (Pisa: Quindici, 1970);

Il gesto improbabile: Tre saggi su Gabriele D'Annunzio (Palermo: Flaccovio, 1971);

Camillo Sbarbaro (Milan: Mursia, 1971);

Il codice di Babele (Milan: Rizzoli, 1972);

Laberinto d'amore (1966–1971) (Naples: Centro Editoriale, 1972);

L'artificio dell'eternità (Verona: Fiorini, 1972);

Natura e storia nella letteratura italiana fra Otto e Novecento (Turin: Giappichelli, 1973);

Gli inferi e il labirinto: Da Pascoli a Montale (Bologna: Cappelli, 1974);

Il tragico nel mondo borghese (Turin: Giappichelli, 1974);

Poesia e ideologia borghese (Naples: Liguori, 1976);

Il velo (Milan: Bicordo, 1976);

Notizie dalla vita (Livorno: Bastogi, 1977);

Fine dell'idillio: Da Dante a Marino (Genoa: Melangolo, 1978);

Le sorti del tragico (Ravenna: Longo, 1978);

Il romanzo contro la storia: Studi sui "Promessi sposi" (Milan: Vita & Pensiero, 1980);

Ritratto di intellettuale (Manduria: Lacaita, 1980);

Il marinaio del Mar Nero e altre poesie (Padua: Rebellato, 1980);

La donna delle Langhe e altri fantasmi (Turin: L'Arzanà, 1981);

Dall'anima al sottosuolo: Problemi della letteratura dell'Ottocento da Leopardi a Lucini (Ravenna: Longo, 1982);

Giovanni Verga: Le finzioni dietro il Verismo (Palermo: Flaccovio, 1982);

Invito alla lettura di Gabriele D'Annunzio (Milan: Mursia, 1982);

Canto V dell'Inferno (Naples: Loffredo, 1982);

Da Gerico (Naples: Guida, 1983);

Il potere della parola: Studi sul "Decameron" (Naples: Federico & Ardia, 1983);

Gli Eredi di Verga (Randazzo: Comune di Randazzo, 1984);

Dal tramonto dell'ermetismo alla neoavanguardia (Brescia: Scuola, 1984);

Metamorfosi della novella (Foggia: Bastogi, 1985);

La poesia del Novecento (Caltanissetta: Sciascia, 1985);

Dalla bocca della balena (Turin: Genesi, 1986);

L'onore in corte: Dal Castiglione al Tasso (Milan: Angeli, 1986);

Machiavelli; o, La scelta della letteratura (Rome: Bulzoni, 1987);

La forma e la vita: Il romanzo del Novecento (Milan: Mursia, 1987);

Il sogno della letteratura (Milan: Angeli, 1988);

In un altro regno (Turin: Genesi, 1990).

OTHER: *La poesia italiana contemporanea dal Carducci ai giorni nostri,* edited by Bàrberi Squarotti and Stefano Jacomuzzi (Messina & Florence: D'Anna, 1963);

Pagine di teatro, edited by Bàrberi Squarotti (Turin: Società Editrice Internazionale, 1965);

Giuseppe Bonaviri, *Follia,* edited by Bàrberi Squarotti (Catania: Società di Storia Patria per la Sicilia Orientale, 1976);

Guido Gozzano, *Poesie,* edited by Bàrberi Squarotti (Milan: Rizzoli, 1977);

La poesia in Toscana dagli anni Quaranta agli anni Settanta, edited by Franco Manescalchi and Lucia Marcuzzi, includes essays and notes by Bàrberi Squarotti (Messina: D'Anna, 1981);

Vittorio Alfieri, *Del principe e delle lettere,* edited by Bàrberi Squarotti (Milan: Serra & Riva, 1983);

Dante, *Opere minori,* 2 volumes, edited by Bàrberi Squarotti and others (Turin: UTET, 1983, 1986);

La letteratura in scena: Il teatro del Novecento, edited by Bàrberi Squarotti (Turin: Tirrenia, 1985);

I bersagli della satira, edited by Bàrberi Squarotti (Turin: Tirrenia, 1987);

Prospettive sul Furioso, edited by Bàrberi Squarotti (Turin: Tirrenia, 1988);

Testi ed esegesi pascoliana, edited by Bàrberi Squarotti (Bologna: CLUEB, 1988);

Lo specchio che deforma: Le immagini della parodia, edited by Bàrberi Squarotti (Turin: Tirrenia, 1988);

Storia della civiltà letteraria italiana, edited by Bàrberi Squarotti (Turin: UTET, 1990).

Giorgio Bàrberi Squarotti's poetry expresses the dynamics of the Italian cultural scene of the last thirty years. As a literary critic and poet, he has enjoyed serious attention since 1960, when *Astrazione e realtà* (Abstraction and Reality), his first theoretical book, and *La voce roca* (The Raucous Voice), a collection of early poems, were published. Poetry is for Bàrberi Squarotti the "Other" opposed to social and phenomenological reality; it is an instrument for proclaiming personal liberty and knowledge in the horrid world of history. In *Poesia italiana del Novecento* (1986) Elio Gioanola has appropriately called the poetry of Bàrberi Squarotti "una tipica poesia 'indiretta,' che cerca i suoi referenti non nella realtà esterna e psicologica ma nello specchio della letteratura e della coscienza come deposito di simboli" (a typical "indirect" poetry, which finds its correspondences not with external or psychological reality but in the mirror of literature and conscience as a depository of symbols).

Bàrberi Squarotti's poetry ought to be measured against the literary parameters of the 1960s. His formation is that of the young generation of Italian poets concerned with departing from the confining boundaries of the hermetic tradition and with creating new linguistic codes. He evades the popular polemics of Marxist-idealist historicism and

chooses the stylistic innovations advanced by the European and American avant-garde: he actualizes a rational mode of experimentation, avoids autobiographical *occasioni* (occasions), and sublimates any emphasis on the *parola* (word) itself. His style conveys an exegetical search by means of recurring, abstract figurative patterns, which, in their oneiric structure, allow him to contemplate the conspicuous darkness of an age increasingly divested of human characteristics. As he writes in the poem "Per anni non fu che un'agonia" (For Years It Was Nothing but Agony), in *Ritratto di intellettuale* (Portrait of an Intellectual, 1980), life is "lotta o, meglio, una gara non voluta, una corsa obbligata / avanti agli occhi dei carnefici" (a struggle or, rather, an unwanted match, a set course / before the executioners' eyes). Memories and analogies mentally transpose an unseizable reality; an allegorical framework comprises existence as poetic *écriture* (writing,) the only true form of being. Bàrberi Squarotti's poetics is based on experimentation without indulging in mechanical exercises — "una ipotesi linguistica onesta" (an honest linguistic hypothesis), as Lorenzo Sbragi defined it in 1965.

Bàrberi Squarotti was born in 1929 in Turin, where he spent his childhood and most of his adult life. In 1953 at the age of twenty-four he received his doctorate in Italian literature after defending his dissertation on the style of Giordano Bruno. His director was Giovanni Getto, whom he subsequently succeeded at the University of Turin. Bàrberi Squarotti's first professional position was at the publishing house UTET, where in 1958 he became the chief editor of the celebrated *Dizionario della lingua italiana* by Salvatore Battaglia. In 1967 he returned to the university to teach modern and contemporary Italian literature.

An essayist of exceptional discernment and sensibility who has emphasized the study of modern authors, he has offered pivotal contributions to the readings of the works of such diverse artists as Dante, Giovanni Boccaccio, Alessandro Manzoni, Gabriele D'Annunzio, Camillo Sbarbaro, Giovanni Pascoli, and Dino Campana. His critical interpretations have shown a distinct independence from current ideological trends and have focused on the interpretation of the texts themselves. A regular contributor to numerous periodicals and newspapers, including *Giornale storico della letteratura italiana, Letteratura, Aut-aut, Paragone, Archivio glottologico, La gazzetta del popolo,* and *Paese sera,* he is also the coeditor of the book series titled "Civiltà letteraria del Novecento" (Twentieth-Century Literary Civilization) published by Mursia.

One of the poems of *La declamazione onesta* (The Honest Declamation, 1965), "In questo tempo" (In Our Times), provides a good introduction to Bàrberi Squarotti's poetics, as he confronts global concerns about life and art by devising a poetic space within which truth is exalted. Bàrberi Squarotti challenges "ambigua lingua" (ambiguous language) and false conscience:

E un tempo di palinodie e delazioni,
le parole d'ordine sono uguali e contrarie
come il crepuscolo dell'alba e quello della sera,
la verità e la menzogna sono nella luce e nelle tenebre,
nel prato verde e nello stagno delle bisce,
la lucertola fra le pietre, il fiore degli ireos,
la foglia d'erba, l'atropo nella luna,
la via cieca su cui regali dormono le volpi,
possono essere la viltà o il gesto che decide,
gli dèi del gelo o l'urto delle mutazioni.

(It is an age of palinodes and secret accusations,
passwords are alike and opposite
like the dusk at dawn and in the evening,
truth and lie are both in the light and in darkness,
in the green meadow and in the pond of snakes,
the lizard in between the stones, the flower of the
    irises,
the blade of grass, the Atropos in the moon,
the blind path where the foxes regally sleep,
it could be cowardice or the decisive action,
the gods of the ice or the impact of mutations.)

The psycholinguistic structures of this poem are violent and lead to an apocalyptic vision of nothingness. A hammering declamatory syntax scans the imaginary steps of "questa attesa ingannata dagli errori / degli astrolabi, dalle false carte delle eclissi, / dalle bestie impazzite dello zodiaco" (this wait deceived by the errors / of the astrolabes, by the false charts of the eclipses, / by the maddening animals of the zodiac).

Bàrberi Squarotti's early poems portray the existence of a defenseless man who grieves over his desolate loneliness. Paradigmatic of this mode of being are the themes of *errore* (error) and *inganno* (deceit), often represented by a rich heraldic bestiary: lion, hawk, dog, and unicorn; and by symbols of terror and threat: lightning, floods, and storms.

The "declamazione onesta" — as Silvio Ramat incisively points out — alludes to the rejection of evasive formalism and stresses the complexity of the poetic experience. The result is a self-questioning exploration of humankind's dramatic situation by means of a highly metaphorical language. In the last poem of the collection, "L'ottimo artista" (The Greatest Artist), the reader experiences irony: poetry accepts the necessity of hiding behind a mask

in order to disclose its prophetic vision, while the artist has chosen "il dominio dell'apparenza, l'ironia, / la doppia maschera, che muta colore secondo che la guardi" (the dominion of appearance, irony, the double mask, which mutes color according to the way you look at it).

In 1972 *Laberinto d'amore* (Labyrinth of Love) was printed in a private edition. The poems, written between 1966 and 1971, were all reprinted in *Notizie dalla vita* (News from Life, 1977), which also includes lyrics reflecting imaginary experiences with the oppression of governments: those of Vietnam, Chile, Greece, and Italy, as affected by obscure conspiracies. More openly political in inspiration than any of Bàrberi Squarotti's preceding works, *Laberinto d'amore* concentrates on a personal search for *salvezza* (salvation) in a world of inexhaustible allegories. Love may help people go through the labyrinth but cannot rescue them from the horrors of history. The moving force behind the thematic center of the *laberinto,* love can lead to transgression, blood, and violence. The status of a soul going through *percorsi d'amore* (love journeys) is symptomatic of the destiny of humankind, lost in an intricate world of fabulously peculiar emblems. The poems show the infernal labyrinthine *iter* of the outraged modern conscience witnessing the violation of the "Gran Teatro del Mondo" (The Great Theater of the World).

The year 1980 saw the appearance of two major collections by Bàrberi Squarotti, *Ritratto di intellettuale* and *Il marinaio del Mar Nero e altre poesie* (The Sailor of the Black Sea and Other Poetry). The "intellectual" of the first book refers both to the recurring *figura* of a self-centered poet, who proposes *écriture* as the absolute expression of reality, and to the *intellettuale organico* (organic intellectual) of poem "XXV," committed to resisting any form of institutional seduction:

. . . Disse: allora
facciamo la rivoluzione (a voce alta, nel vuoto cieco e
muto, nell'assenza, nel dominio di ciò che non c'è né
    esiste,
dove non c'è nessuno, e neppure ombre che alzino il
    pugno,
né lamenti né bandiere e neppure i discorsi alla folla di
fumo e aria e nulla o le canzoni d'
amore).

(. . . He said: then
let's have a revolution [aloud, to the blind and silent
empty space, to the absence, to the dominion of what is
    not nor exists,
where there is no one, and not even shadows that may
    raise their fists,

nor cries or flags and not even the speeches to the
    crowd of
smoke and air and nothingness nor the songs of
love].)

In "Di quelli che non se la cavano" (Those Who Do Not Survive), the protagonist is being persecuted in an imaginary "spazio pieno di grida e di furore" (space full of cries and furor): he rescues himself by mumbling "qualche verso, mescolando / Dante e i poeti marinisti e il Libro della / Sapienza" (a few verses, mixing / Dante and the marinist poets and the / Bible). The *intellettuale-poeta* sees the vastness of the opposition between life and *écriture*.

Il marinaio del Mar Nero e altre poesie ostensibly reinforces the programmatic acceptance of the poetic language as the only reality within the unreality of the world. The *écriture* becomes an ontological principle. Spatial and temporal images emerge with which Bàrberi Squarotti seeks to establish the poet's situation as unique. For example, in "Capodanno" (New Year's Day) "il vento nella notte" (the wind in the night) has the function of creating an absolute void; in "Il custode di Monchiero" (The Custodian of Monchiero) the speaker's hallucinatory perceptions denounce the destructive descent into "il cieco abisso" (the blind abyss), which is "la sorgente della morte" (the source of death) and "il principio di ogni nulla" (the beginning of every nothingness). Signs, ambiguous images, and confused names express an obsessive, unconscious life force; naked girls – recurrent images in Bàrberi Squarotti's poetic universe – are the authentic phantoms of nothingness, which connotes the failure of life and the negation of reality.

One of the topoi of Bàrberi Squarotti's recent poetry is the recovery of the past as a retrospective revelation of the present. The theme of the journey usually provides the framework for an elaboration of experience into abstract patterns of meaning. The narratives reflect a disfigured universe in which life and death coexist in altered states of existence, as manifest in his *Dalla bocca della balena* (From the Mouth of the Whale, 1986), which introduces twenty-two new poems preceded by selections from each previous collection. While in his early work the poetic voice assumes the passive traumatic role of a witness in front of the horrors of the reality, in *Dalla bocca della balena* it is divided into several characters, all participating in an "elogio della teatralità" (praise of theatricality) as defined by Giacinto Spagnoletti in his introduction to the volume.

Giorgio Bàrberi Squarotti's poetry does not draw on private history alone. The past to which the poems allude is also the collective past of literary and cultural tradition, including language itself, the common linguistic codes from which he forms his *écriture*. Poetry must find its space between tradition and innovation. Reality and history are essentially sites of violence; poetry is the place where violence is exorcized. Allegories of evil become the truth about sociohistorical abuse. Bàrberi Squarotti succeeds in being an alternative voice in an ideologically normative climate and achieves a perilous balance between the negativity of his message and the positivity of poetry as "Other."

References:

Elio Gioanola, "Giorgio Bàrberi Squarotti," in his *Poesia italiana del Novecento: Testi e commenti* (Milan: Librex, 1986), pp. 917–933;

Maria Grazia Lenisa, *Poetica di salvezza in Bàrberi Squarotti* (Foggia: Bastogi, 1985);

Mario Lunetta, "La metafora narrante: Giorgio Bàrberi Squarotti," in his *Poesia italiana oggi* (Rome: Newton Compton, 1981), pp. 231–234;

Giuliano Manacorda, *Storia della letteratura italiana contemporanea (1940–1965)* (Rome: Riuniti, 1974), pp. 397–398;

Silvio Ramat, "La declamazione onesta," in his *L'intelligenza dei contemporanei* (Padua: Rebellato, 1968), pp. 241–242;

Lorenzo Sbragi, "La poesia di Bàrberi Squarotti," *Nostro Tempo,* 14 (October–December 1965): 14–17;

Giacinto Spagnoletti, Introduction to Bàrberi Squarotti's *Dalla bocca della balena* (Turin: Genesi, 1986), pp. 7–14;

Claudio Toscani, "Giorgio Bàrberi Squarotti tra 'babele' e 'labirinto,'" *Ausonia,* 30, nos. 3–4 (1975): 86–88;

Giuseppe Zagarrio, "Il *Nulla/Morte* di Bàrberi Squarotti," in his *Febbre, furore e fiele: Repertorio della poesia italiana contemporanea 1979–1980* (Milan: Mursia, 1983), pp. 577–584;

Zagarrio, "L'onirico e il labirintico: La sintassi autogenerativa di Giorgio Bàrberi Squarotti," in his *Febbre, furore e fiele,* pp. 114–120;

Zagarrio, "Poesia e Vita," *Ponte,* 22 (April 1966): 516–525.

Giorgio Bassani

(4 March 1916 –   )

Corrado Federici
Brock University

BOOKS: *Una città di pianura,* as Giacomo Marchi
(Milan: Arte Grafica Lucini, 1940);
Storie di poveri amanti e altri versi (Rome: Astrolabio,
1945; enlarged, 1946);
Te lucis ante (Rome: Ubaldini, 1947);
Un'altra libertà (Milan: Mondadori, 1952);
Una lapide in via Mazzini (Rome: Estratto da Botteghe
Oscure, 1952);
La passeggiata prima di cena (Florence: Sansoni, 1953);
Gli ultimi anni di Clelia Trotti (Pisa: Nistri-Lischi,
1955);
Cinque storie ferraresi (Turin: Einaudi, 1956); repub-
lished as *Dentro le mura* (Milan: Mondadori,
1973); translated by William Weaver as *Five
Stories of Ferrara* (New York: Harcourt Brace
Jovanovich, 1971);
Gli occhiali d'oro (Turin: Einaudi, 1958); translated
by Isabel Quigly as *The Gold-Rimmed Spectacles*
(London: Faber & Faber, 1960; New York:
Atheneum, 1960);
Le storie ferraresi (Turin: Einaudi, 1960); translated
by Quigly as *A Prospect of Ferrara* (London:
Faber & Faber, 1962);
Una notte del '43 (Turin: Einaudi, 1960);
Il giardino dei Finzi-Contini (Turin: Einaudi, 1962);
translated by Quigly as *The Garden of the Finzi-
Continis* (New York: Atheneum, 1965; Lon-
don: Faber & Faber, 1965);
L'alba ai vetri: Poesie 1942–'50 (Turin: Einaudi,
1963);
Dietro la porta (Turin: Einaudi, 1964); translated by
Weaver as *Behind the Door* (New York: Har-
court Brace Jovanovich, 1972);
Due novelle (Venice: Sodalizio del Libro, 1965);
Venice des saisons, by Bassani and Mario Soldati
(Lausanne, Switzerland: Clairfontaine, 1965);
Le parole preparate, e altri scritti di letteratura (Turin:
Einaudi, 1966);
L'airone (Milan: Mondadori, 1968); translated by
Weaver as *The Heron* (New York: Harcourt
Brace Jovanovich, 1970; London: Panther,
1970);

Giorgio Bassani circa 1969

L'odore del fieno (Milan: Mondadori, 1972); trans-
lated by Weaver as *The Smell of Hay* (New
York: Harcourt Brace Jovanovich, 1975; Lon-
don: Weidenfeld & Nicolson, 1975);
Epitaffio (Milan: Mondadori, 1974);
Il romanzo di Ferrara (Milan: Mondadori, 1974);
In gran segreto (Milan: Mondadori, 1978);
In rima e senza (Milan: Mondadori, 1982);
Di là dal cuore (Milan: Mondadori, 1984).
Edition: *Rolls Royce and Other Poems,* bilingual edi-
tion, translated by Francesca Valente, Irving

Layton, Portia Prebys, and Greg Gatenby (Toronto: Aya, 1982).

Giorgio Bassani's reputation rests almost exclusively on the quality of his novels, even though he has been publishing poetry since 1947. This circumstance makes it difficult to contextualize Bassani's verse as does the tendency of critics to interpret that poetry from the perspective of its structural and thematic relationships with his prose. Also complicating the matter is the fact that Bassani's poetry does not often appear in anthologies of modern Italian poetry. Bassani's poems are interesting and coherent but generally fall short of breaking new ground or of producing a quintessential paradigm of the poetic modes that dominate the modern era. In other words his volumes written in the 1940s and 1950s reflect, parallel, and, to a degree, reinforce aspects of hermeticism and neorealism without achieving the status of definitive statements of either school. On the other hand Bassani's poems of the 1960s and 1970s do not significantly reflect or engage in the experimentalism or violent iconoclasm of the neo-avant-garde poets. There are critics who see in Bassani's verses echoes of works by the most classical of Italian poets; and there are those who situate his work in an intermediate position between crepuscularism and hermeticism — as well as those who either qualify or reject such a view. In the final analysis Bassani's poetry constitutes a unified vision that has a specific and consistent idealist basis. While it does reveal traces of crepuscularism, hermeticism, and neorealism, it is an autonomous, individualized entity that reveals subtle intricacies.

Giorgio Bassani was born in Bologna on 4 March 1916 to Dora and Enrico Bassani, a well-to-do Jewish couple from Ferrara. (Enrico was a surgeon.) Giorgio enrolled at the University of Bologna in 1934. Having as instructors Roberto Longhi and Carlo Calcaterra — disciples of Benedetto Croce and Giovanni Gentile — he came into contact with determining influences in the formation of his idealist aesthetic. He graduated in 1939. Another important biographical element is Bassani's reaction to Fascism. Initially his response to Benito Mussolini's policies was intellectual and did not translate into active opposition. The enactment of racial laws in 1938 did not at first affect Bassani personally; nor were they initially comprehended in the fullness of their tragic implications. To the contemplative Bassani the laws seemed the predictable policies of a dictatorship. A year later, however, his political activism began with his involvement in the Partito d'Azione (Action Party). Also at about this time his literary career began, with the story titled *Una città di pianura* (A City of the Lowlands, 1940), published under the pseudonym Giacomo Marchi, and with the composition of his first poems. In 1943 he married Valeria Sinigallia (they now have two children: Enrico and Paola). Also during 1943 Bassani's participation in the resistance movement landed him in jail, where he remained until the collapse of the Fascist government later the same year. That year saw Bassani move to Florence from where he combatted the nascent Salò regime. In the meantime his relatives from Ferrara had ended up in the death camp at Buchenwald. Bassani witnessed the tensions and horrors of the Allied invasion and the ensuing civil war — historical events that impressed the writer so profoundly that they emerge prominently in most of his works.

In 1945 Bassani published his first volume of poems, *Storie dei poveri amanti e altri versi* (Histories of Poor Lovers and Other Poems). At the time, he was teaching literature at the Naples Naval Institute and also working as a librarian. Recalling the circumstances under which he wrote, Bassani says, in a postscript to his 1963 book, *L'alba ai vetri* (Dawn at the Windows): "Nella primavera del '42, il primo impulso a scrivere versi mi venne, più che dalla vita e dalla realtà, dall'arte e dalla cultura" (In the spring of '42, the first impulse to write verses came, not so much from life and reality, as from art and culture). He identifies his primary influences as painters, sixteenth-century Ferrarese and Bolognese artists whose vibrant color schemes captured the essential texture and mood of the Emilian countryside that was such an important part of Bassani's adolescence. Alluding to this area, he writes in the same postscript: "mi si mostrava attraverso i colori, intrisi d'una luce come velata, di quelle antiche pitture" (it appeared before me, in the hues of those venerable canvasses, suffused with a light that seemed filtered). Bassani defines an equally significant feature of *Storie* — the evocation of a sun-drenched youth, crystallized in the brilliance of its symbolic aspects but undermined by a subtle yet stinging nostalgic distance: "Uscivo dalla giovinezza, lo sentivo bene, ma senza rimpianti . . . con una sorta di benigna condiscendenza. . . . Per la prima volta mi sentivo spettatore indulgente di me stesso" (I was emerging from my youth; I could sense it well, but without regret . . . with a sort of kind indulgence. . . . For the first time I felt I was a compassionate observer of my own self).

The limning of familiar scenes, both urban and rustic, is perhaps the most conspicuous thematic resource of *Storie*. Etched with traditional versification and rhyme schemes, the city of Ferrara — a recognizable topos in Bassani's narrative as well — appears magically depicted in rich hues, with red turrets and blue, ephemeral towers. The Emilian landscape is equally imbued with an emotional tonality, with its luminous farms, green fields of sunlight, and tepid rain. In such serenely impressionistic vistas there is no hint of the political maelstrom that overwhelmed Bassani's people at the time. He admits as much in the postscript to *L'alba*: "La primavera del '42! Stalingrad, El Alamein, e il futuro incerto, oscuro . . . . Eppure, nonostante tutto, la vita non mi è mai apparsa così bella, così bella e struggente come allora" (The spring of '42! Stalingrad, El Alamein, and an uncertain, obscure future . . . . Still, despite everything, life never seemed as beautiful, as beautiful and emotional as then). In idyllic symbiosis with their environment are the people of the area: tranquil, humble, radiant figures reminiscent of Giotto's protagonists. In "Sera a Porta Reno" (Evening at Porta Reno) readers find reference to "gentili / zingari" (gentle / wanderers), their "volti accesi / di indomabili speranze" (faces glowing / with irrepressible hopes). Their apolitical lives are characterized by unpretentious "miti tovaglie" (simple tablecloths) and "povere panche" (coarse benches). To an extent, the naturalistic light that bathes the characters acquires a spiritual valency that emphasizes their gentle goodness. The light also connotes grace or beatitude, showered upon them from above but also exuded, in Neoplatonic fashion, from within themselves. The overall effect is not dissimilar to that achieved by Bassani's contemporary Umberto Saba.

While Bassani's predilection is for late afternoons, early morning or twilight also commands his attention — hence the associations with crepuscularism. For example in "Verso Ferrara" (Toward Ferrara) one reads: "Questa è l'ora che vanno per calde erbe infinite / nel mio paese gli ultimi treni" (This is the hour when through the warm endless grasses / of my town pass the last trains). Although labeled by some critics as crepuscular, moments such as these lack the lacrimose or convalescent connotativeness of the poems of, say, Sergio Corazzini. Instead the prevailing tone is consolatory, as is also the case in "Monselice": "la luna m'amava, / quand'ero ragazzo, in segreto" (the moon loved me / when I was a child, secretly). However, a sense of tragic distance intrudes into the mediations. Many occasions remind one of typical Quasimodian structures, in that Bassani the

adult, riding on the same train on which he rode as a youth, reflects on his impressions of that remote past while he superimposes the bitterness of his present awareness. As he says of his past in the postscript to *L'alba*, "si svolgeva davanti ai miei occhi incantevole ma distante, distante per sempre" (It unfolded before my eyes enchanting but distant, forever distant).

The stylistic device exploited by Bassani to underscore his sense of the irretrievability of the past is that of isolating gestures of departure or separation, such as the "ultimi risa, baci, addii" (last laughter, kisses, good-byes) in "Cena di Pasqua" (Easter Dinner). He transforms the referential train of his commuting into a metaphor of separation and loss, the "ultimi treni, con fischi lenti" (last trains with muffled whistles) in "Verso Ferrara." This funereal ethos extends through much of Bassani's subsequent lyrics.

On another level he employs the sleep motif. That is, alongside the images of glowing hills and brick turrets are intratexts suggestive of a blanket of sleep that descends from above, to shroud these scenes at day's end: in "Verso Ferrara" one reads that the trains "affondavano indolenti / nel sonno" (would sink listlessly / into sleep); in "Marina d'ottobre" (October Seascape) he suggests, "andremo per la bruma lieve soli / nel sonno che dalle verdi e segrete / risacche fuma" (we shall go amid / the light fog alone in sleep which / issues smokelike from the green and secret undercurrents). These same shadows are strongly suggestive of impending doom — both for the vision represented and for the memory of it lingering in the mind of the poet, as the following verse from "Lasciando Marina di Cervia" (Leaving Marina di Cervia) attests: "a sera scende l'oblio" (with night descends oblivion). The sleep/death analogy is reinforced in expressions such as "amari papaveri" (bitter poppies), from "Dopo la fiera di San Giorgio" (After Saint George's Fair). This is only one of an entire bouquet of death symbols that recur in *Storie*.

Montalian influences are apparent. Such a pessimistic view of human isolation within walls of incommunicability (treated by many modernist artists) is reiterated in utterances such as "sei sola, dentro le tue mura di spazio" (you are alone, within your walls of space), from "Saluto a Roma" (Farewell to Rome). The oxymoron of "walls of space" introduces the metaphor that recurs throughout Bassani's work: that of the wall as enclosure, barrier, and protective seal that isolates, insulates, delineates, and ultimately suffocates. In this vein the city walls of Ferrara function both as a naturalistic detail, in some poems of *Storie,* and as interiorized landscape. As occurs in the strongly metaphoric or analogic text of the hermetics, natural elements such as wind, rain, light, or darkness assume an elusive polyvalence and portentous signification by which the onset of some nonspecific cataclysm is connoted. On occasions such as these, Bassani's *Storie* anticipates, to an extent, the mystical force of Eugenio Montale's *La bufera e altro* (1956; translated as *The Storm and Other Poems,* 1978), as well as paralleling some of the poems of his *Le occasioni* (1939; translated as *The Occasions,* 1987) – especially when Bassani writes of the "vento crudele" (cruel wind), "le muraglie gelate" (frozen walls), or "la bufera di buie / lacrime" (storm of dark / tears).

Awareness of the threat of annihilation also affects Bassani's interpretation of the past. A profound sense of permanent loss becomes forcefully explicit when he meditates on the "labbra inaridite" (withered lips), "l'amaro sepolto riso" (the bitter buried smile), or "il nostro cuore sepolto" (our buried heart). In *Storie* the burial theme (destined to become a vital motif in subsequent works) aligns itself with an Ungarettian image of the heart as intimate cemetery, a Quasimodian metaphor of memory as a wind that pursues the poet, and a brusque Montalian mood of quiet despair wherein the past can be visualized only in a fragmentary manner and cannot be reconstituted meaningfully.

The same entombment motif is contiguous to another central theme: the ostracism of the Jewish people: "la nostra vita fu tra le ombre / le foglie e il fango del viale / indecifrabile, esile" (our life was among the shadows / the leaves and mud of the avenue / indecipherable and vile), he writes in "Mascherata" (Masquerade). At times the speaker includes himself in an encasement along with the subjects of his meditations; they are people who nervously anticipate an indistinct yet gruesome future, as in "I giocatori" (The Card Players): "lungo le muraglie gelate / sentiremo la luna passare . . . scrutare / le impassibili facciate" (along the frozen walls / we will hear the moon pass . . . scrutinize / the impassible façades).

Into this context Bassani inserts his narrator – the autobiographical, reflective persona who articulates his role as that of survivor and custodian of memory; the poet redefines his duty as that of preserving experience, thereby retaining his personal humanity. Implied, too, is the need of humanity in general to remember the past as humankind plunges toward oblivion; in "Lasciando Marina di Cervia" Bassani writes: "si va nelle notti d'estate lungo i sentieri / verso lontane lampade sepolte" (we move

along roads in the summer nights / toward distant buried lamps). The poet envisions his task as that of giving testimony. Consequently *Storie* includes symbols of death but also of undying faith in the survival of individual essence: candles, wreaths, plaques, lanterns, and headstones. The poet/survivor evokes the dead by representing their eyes, faces, and voices, which haunt him to the point where he prophesies an eventual reunion with them, as in "Lasciando Marina di Cervia": "forse torneremo . . . d'intorno a questa / tavola, sotto la lampada, commensali distratti" (Perhaps we will reunite around this / table, below the lamp, distracted table companions).

Following his break with the Partito d'Azione, Bassani published *Te lucis ante* (Before Thee Light, 1947), which he calls his most important book. On a formal level one notices few stylistic changes, with the possible exception of greater variety in the rhyme schemes. The language is elegantly conversational, blending features of prose and poetry, as Montale points out: "In lui il prosatore si avverte anche nel tessuto del verso che rifugge da ogni astrazione sonora e che si vale di un linguaggio che è realistico, ma non contraddice mai alle possibilità tonali della lirica" (In his work the novelist comes through even in the structure of the verses that avoid every form of sonorous abstraction and utilize a language that is realistic, but never negates the tonal possibilities of the lyric) (quoted by Giorgio Varanini in *Bassani,* 1970).

In *Te lucis ante* familiar references to the city of Ferrara, fusing the referential and the symbolic, reappear with the latter beginning to outweigh the former. The same afternoon light that gives the poems of *Storie* a Renaissance glow recurs, but it seems charged with spirituality. It corresponds to the light of divinity or the light of existence itself in poems such as "Pur se m'eri vicina" (Even If You Were Near Me): "io benedico tenera / luce che mi ridesta" (I bless the tender / light that reawakens me).

The presence of the light motif even in the title of the book reveals Bassani's intention to make this element the structural keystone of the entire volume. The phrase "te lucis ante" is the hymn chanted by the souls in Dante's *Purgatorio* (VIII). The spiritual connotations of Bassani's text increase by virtue of this Dantean allusion. Dante's tormented but optimistic expiators, who move the pilgrim/witness with their plaintive song, reappear in Bassani's poems. He frequently refers to their cries: "ogni grido è sopra il mare" (each cry is above the sea); "dirotte / voci d'amore, bocche trafelate" (broken voices of love, breathless mouths). These se-

Bassani at the Premio Viareggio awards reception in 1962

quences combine with references to eyes or faces that emit a consoling yet feeble light: "al fosco riso, agli sguardi, / sempre al bel riso atroce, / ti riconosco, oh tardi" (by the dark laughter, by the gaze, always by your lovely atrocious laughter / I recognize you, belatedly). Bassani also makes the light/memory analogy explicit in this way: "Un ultimo segnale, / forse l'estremo avviso, / mi folgorò, per nere / scale, impresso in un viso" (A final signal / perhaps the last admonition struck me along / dark stairways impressed upon a face). With a technique similar to that employed by Montale, especially in his *Satura* (1962), Bassani engages in an agonizing dialectic with voices, faces, and gestures that haunt him. Recalling some of Giovanni Pascoli's personae, the dead people whisper to the survivor in "Un ultimo segnale" (A Last Signal): "Questa lingua che adoperi, / così oscura è per me! / Mai l'intesi; fuorchè / per averne paura" (This language of yours / is so obscure for me! / I've never understood it; / except to fear it).

The relationship between the poetic voice and the interlocutor is usually ambiguous and prompts the image of mutual imprisonment. The metonymic voices are seen to be relegated to a dark purgatorial abode, while the poet himself senses that he resides in an existential concentration camp, writing letters of consolation to his "freer" relatives. In an untitled poem, he writes: "E riapprodi, ogni notte, / al mio carcere" (Each night you reappear / in my cell). The antithetical juxtaposition of freedom and enclosure reflects the strange interchangeability of existence and nonexistence in Bassani's vision. In another untitled composition, one reads: "Chissà . . . se questo / nostro vivere è un sogno" (Who knows . . . if this living of ours is a dream). His rapport with his ghosts, then, becomes one of anticipation, resistance, and communion. Obsessive, persistent images spontaneously emerge from the sepulchral darkness: "Dormo: o sei Tu che pungi / il mio sonno quieto" (Am I asleep: or is it You piercing / my tranquil slumber). That annoying intrusion can also be a deafening scream: "tuo il grido che di lungi / cerca me, il mio segreto" (yours is the scream that from afar / seeks me, my secret). The speaker, therefore, oscillates between a desire to avoid disconcerting memories and the acknowledgment that these same memories are an intimate, reliable source of spiritual nourishment.

The theme of persecution — broadly hinted at in *Storie* and destined to emerge as an ideological cornerstone of Bassani's narrative — is installed in *Te lucis* as a prime component of the purgatory metaphor that anchors the collection. The "febbre d'ingiurie, lacrime / cocenti" (fevers of insults, tears / burning) are those of prisoners held in death camps; as happens to the character Geo Josz of *Una lapide in via Mazzini* (A Headstone on Mazzini Street, 1952), the narrator is aware of his own privileged destiny with respect to that of his martyred community: "stato sarei del gregge / dei morti a capo chino" (I would have been part of the flock / of those who died with heads bowed). Also emulating the heroes of Bassani's novels, the poetic narrator intuits his own stinging isolation by virtue of his escape from the extermination: "chi escluso, con la gola / arida li vedrà / spegnersi senza piangere?" (who excluded, with parched / throat will watch them / perish without shedding a tear?).

Bassani's third poetry volume, *Un'altra libertà* (Another Freedom, 1952), came at a time when his commitment to poetry was about to be suspended temporarily in favor of short stories and novels. He was also an editor for the journal *Paragone*. *Un'altra libertà* exhibits few formal or thematic variants, since virtually all of the poems are short one- or two-stanza compositions with traditional rhyme. The only stylistic innovation is the tendency to use the rhetorical question as a vehicle for the expression of anguished bewilderment before an enigmatic reality. At times the speaker directs his queries to the interlocutor of previous poems, as he does in "Vide cor meum" (Behold My Heart): "chi chiama? . . . chi cerca? . . . tu chiami? tu cerchi?" (who's calling? . . . who's searching? . . . are you calling? are you searching?). Or he puts the question to the reader, as in "Dove sei?" (Where Are You?): "solo ai morti le viole ridon spente e lontane?" (do the extinguished and distant violets laugh only for the dead?). Bassani may even apostrophize death itself: "Non è tuo questo lume, morte, intriso e tremante?" (Isn't this your light, death, drenched and tremulous?). The use of the term *lume* (light) illustrates Bassani's abiding interest in chiaroscuro for the purpose of describing the interpenetration of life and death or of survival and extinction. As usual the light is initially naturalistic, but it immediately takes on a spiritual valence in phrases such as the "luce estrema dell'angelus" (last light of the Angelus), wherein waning daylight is connected with therapeutic prayer and faith. Similarly daybreak constitutes a moment of epiphany. In the poem "L'alba ai vetri" (Dawn at the Windows) daylight nudges against window panes, but the equation dawn equals life soon emerges: "Eri tu che passavi, vita, mia / tu che sopravvenivi" (It was you who was passing by, my life / you who was overtaking me).

The light of grace or immortality represents the standard Bassanian counterpoint to the shadow of death. In *Un'altra libertà* he strives to rescue spirits from the abyss of nonexistence by drawing them into the light of recognition. If it is not darkness that enshrouds these specters, it is a stunning sense of remoteness experienced by the speaker: "distante / isola del passato, che a morire ci invita" (distant / island of the past, which invites us to die). Communication from figures confined within a Dantean limbo may also be associated with a melody from the speaker's memory: "riudiva / la sua musica fedele e lontana" (I could hear / once more its faithful and distant music). Suggestive also of the Ungarettian heart-as-cemetery metaphor is the fact that Bassani occasionally specifies that images of the past reside in time and have no existence in and of themselves. In "A mio padre" (To My Father) he wonders what would happen "Se qui nel petto . . . s'entro me stesso seppellirti osai" (If here in my breast . . . if within myself I dared bury you). The analogy of burial/preservation is even more explicit in other lines: at one point the speaker calls his heart a "seppellita fonte" (buried spring). The allusion is to the secret tears shed by the contemplative poetic narrator who resuscitates, partly in Proustian fashion, the essence of his past, all the while being aware, with Montalian perspicacity, of the illusory nature of that recollection: "Tutto tornava. Eppure vano, oh fu" (All was being restored. And yet how vain, alas, it was).

By virtue of the tear imagery, Bassani's poetry distances itself somewhat from the unemotionalism of Montale and Giuseppe Ungaretti, while it moves measurably closer to the crepuscular lament, the fundamental distinction being that the crepuscular poet expressed emotion over his own moribund state, whereas Bassani's sorrow derives from an acute response to severed ties with members of his cultural community. Hence it derives, too, from the immutable isolation of the departed and the survivor.

With some editing, Bassani's first three collections of poetry were published together in 1963 as *L'alba ai vetri*. During the 1952–1963 period Bassani wrote short stories and novels that garnered for him national and international recognition, and beginning in 1958 he worked as an editor for the Feltrinelli publishing house. In 1962 he was awarded the prestigious Premio Viareggio for his novel *Il giardino dei Finzi-Contini* (1962; translated as *The Garden of the Finzi-Continis*, 1965). In *Le parole preparate* (The Prepared Words, 1966) he states: "Come scrittore a quell'epoca mi trovavo ancora involto nella presunzione giovanile, di origine forse ermetica, dell'ineffabilità. . . . Scrivere significava fornire dei lampi, dei segni fulminei, magari anche imprecisi" (As a writer at that time I still found myself operating under the juvenile presumption, perhaps of hermetic origin, of the ineffable. . . . Writing meant providing flashes, spontaneous signs, even if rather imprecise ones). The 1950s for Bassani was also a decade of intense collaboration in periodicals, such as the *Fiera Letteraria, Mondo, Nuovi Argomenti,* and the *Corriere della Sera*, and from 1957 to 1967 he taught the history of theater at the National Academy of Dramatic Arts in Rome.

Bassani reemerged as a poet in 1974 with his volume of poems *Epitaffio* (Epitaph), in which he breaks new stylistic ground while remaining true to his most cherished thematics. Among those themes taken up from the poems of *L'alba* is the evocation of Ferrara, with its luminous palaces, winding roads, and tranquil landscapes; it is revived in the matrix of memory with an emotionalism tinged with melancholy, originating in the realization that these scenes are indeed immaterial: "la luce del sole colpiva il roseo / impervio fianco sud-ovest di palazzo Sacchetti" (the sun's rays struck the pink / impervious southwest flank of the Sacchetti palace). Allusions to other typically Bassanian topics also appear throughout *Epitaffio*. These constitute reexperienced events, tied intimately to names such as Castello Este, Corso Giovecca, and the church of San Carlo; the mimetic and the poetic intermingle. In this context one notes an evolved poetics with respect to earlier texts: Bassani reveals an expanded sensitivity to the content of his writing as well as to critical response to it. One particular statement, in the poem "La porta rosa" (The Pink Door) confirms just such a development: "mi rimproveri di non occuparmi nei miei libri / che di Ferrara e del territorio immediatamente limitrofo" (You criticize me for not dealing in my books / with anything other than Ferrara and its immediate surroundings).

On a formal level certain features are also reintroduced; such is the case with the use of an interlocutor — an ambivalent, multiple persona. It may be a former love or a composite, symbolic female personage. While comparable in certain respects to Montale's Clizia, Mosca, and Esterina, Bassani's addressees do not appear to be endowed with salvific properties. Instead they are largely extensions of the poet's inner self. In conversing with such enti-

ties, he succeeds in resurrecting aspects of his former life.

In *L'alba* the subject matter, though provocatively lyrical, is narrow in scope. In *Epitaffio* one encounters a more impressive range of poetic stimuli. For example, there are numerous allusions to Bassani's novels and to critical reviews of his work. Some titles of poems are self-explanatory, such as "Conversazione letteraria" (Literary Conversation) and "A un critico" (To a Critic). Bassani indicates he is acutely aware of the content of his literature, and he speculates on the nature and value of poetry, as in "A un altro critico" (To Another Critic): "comunicare tramite l'arte del resto fu ognora / la mia suprema ambizione" (to communicate through art after all has always / been my greatest ambition). There are also letters to the contemporary poet Franco Fortini, with whom Bassani commiserates. All such situations are handled with a characteristic ease of language and with ample sensitivity.

Furthermore, in *L'alba* the geographic boundaries are those of a specifically circumscribed area; in *Epitaffio* the poetic mind crosses oceans and continents, endeavoring to articulate the concerns of a growing intellect. Recognizable are his references to North America, where he traveled extensively between 1972 and 1974: "E l'America ad averti / fatto male" (It was America that harmed you), he advises a colleague in "A un professore di filosofia" (To a Professor of Philosophy). While the allusions to the United States are plentiful, there is also an array of other settings, from southern France to Bucharest and Cairo.

Still another aspect of this extended poetics is the cultural axis. In *L'alba* the objects of poetic discourse are historical facts pertaining to Bassani's life in the 1930s. *Epitaffio,* instead, is a decidedly contemporary piece, because alongside autobiographical memorabilia is a rich assembly of modern cultural objects and terms. These include Emily Dickinson, blue jeans, Rolls Royces, and the Nobel Prize, as well as the Giulio Andreotti government.

In taking inventory of the innovations, one should not overlook Bassani's continued propensity for carefully crafted descriptions of people and locations — a direct manifestation of his narrative skills. *Epitaffio* contains incisive portraits as in "Arrivo mia madre non sta bene" (I Arrive My Mother Does Not Feel Well): "fragili zigomi / le stesse sottili stanche un po' viola / labbra nevrotiche le medesime / cartilagini gialline . . . la identica paziente sommessa / ironia ebraica" (fragile cheekbones / the same fine tired somewhat purple / neurotic lips the same / yellowish cartilage . . . the same subdued /

Jewish irony). Complementing such precise portraiture are the many finely detailed scenes — whether a city street or merely a sink, as in this quote from "Lettera" (Letter): "lavandino . . . abitato puntualmente dalla solita metallica / quant' oltre mai incarognita / povera mosca" (a sink . . . punctually inhabited by the usual metallic / and greatly broken down / wretched fly).

By virtue of a radically altered lexical and syntactic scheme, *Epitaffio* falls in line with the linguistic experimentalism of most modernist poetry. Bassani's personal form of experimentation with free verse is actually a fusion of classical restraint with a modernist thirst for freedom from the strictures of convention. The verse, however, falls within the parameters of a pattern: the words are arranged like those of inscriptions on tombstones; the poems are variable but always identifiable as epitaphs of some kind. Bassani's intention, in adopting this form, would appear to be that of transforming each poetic utterance into a sort of eulogy. *Epitaffio,* then, ties in emotionally with *L'alba*: in both volumes, he commemorates and ritualistically ensures the survival of the past. *Epitaffio* shows a high level of consciousness or intentionality in the poetic narrator. In previous works he is often closeted in a hermetic dialogue with the ghosts of his adolescence. Here the format advises the reader of the memorial/celebratory purpose of the poems. In this way the structure is the unifying principle, which extends over all of the compositions a common elegiac overtone regardless of the specific content.

Another effect of the epitaph form is that of illustrating Bassani's understanding of a significant function of art. Influenced by Crocean idealism and its tendency to privilege the eternalizing capacity of poetry, Bassani sets out to capture and preserve for posterity the spirit of generations that have vanished. Unlike the hermetic, walled up in a personal, inaccessible world of private symbols, Bassani calls for a deliberate, communicative posture. Art crystallizes the spirit of individuals or communities and conveys that life form to the reader/spectator, who, in interpreting the art form, re-creates its substance.

A profound sense of exclusion is sometimes expressed in terms of aborted communication. In "Da quando" (Since), letters sent to the speaker lie unanswered at his feet: "zitte / come me ormai / la mia / vita" (silent / like me my life / now). Alternatively a wall (a prototypical Bassanian symbol) is an analogue for psychological distance, as in "A un'amica" (To a Friend): "Mi dicevi . . . che faccio sempre sentire agli altri / me di qua gli altri di là" (You'd always tell me I make people feel / I am on one side, they on the other). The speaker also senses his separateness from his own child, in "I due sangui" (The Two Bloods): "dice che è la sua vita e che la vita / nasce e muore con me" (she says that it is her life and that life / begins and ends in me).

A motif that runs through *Epitaffio* but is only hinted at in *L'alba* is that of aging; it alternates, and at times merges, with the more prominent Bassanian theme of death. In earlier works, Bassani focused on the disappearance of his youth and family — including those in the Jewish community annihilated in the Holocaust. In *Epitaffio* there is a greater concentration on the destruction of the self. Certain phrases articulate his desire to disappear completely from the stage of life; in "A letto" (In Bed) he calls this desire "l'ansia di essere anch'io / niente" (the urge to be nothing / like the rest). Or, striking a visibly modernist pose in "Lettera," he sees himself as already dead: "mentre così ragionavo fra me e me rimirando me stesso morto" (I reasoned thus with myself observing / my dead self). In "Arriva mia madre non sta bene" he mentions "la dolcezza anche del vecchio che accoglie il quasi / vecchio altrettanto / o magari di chi defunto da assai più lungo / tempo l'appena" (the sweetness also of the old man who greets / the one who is nearly as old / or rather of the one who's been dead for some / time as he greets a man who recently has died).

In the contemplation of human mortality in general Bassani asserts the function of art as generational or epochal tombstone. To a degree, his vision of life and art reflects that of Ugo Foscolo. However, Bassani's worldview is bereft of glorious exploits to be preserved metonymically on sepulchral monuments. Nor does Bassani's poetics stress the consolatory function of art, since the role of the reader becomes that of cocreator, not only of meaning (as modern aesthetic theory asserts) but of the very subject matter described. How art acts to rescue the quotidian from obliteration is stated in "Bocca Trabaria" (Trabaria Pass): "Fra pochi giorni anche quassù . . . non ci si ricorderà più di te / se non per commemorare invidiandola / l'eleganza silente / del tuo trapasso" (In a few days even up here . . . no one will remember much of you / except to commemorate with envy / the silent eloquence / of your passing).

Lanterns, candles, and light, already utilized in *L'alba* as ritualistic objects endowed with a mystical efficacy, once more play a prominent role. They not only stand as metaphors of survival but of memories. The vivifying functionality of items such as votive candles and headstones is seen in lines such as these: "tre snelle candide / lapidi sobriamente /

Frontispiece and title page for a bilingual selection of Bassani's poetry

iscritte" (three thin white / stones succinctly / inscribed), in "Storia di famiglia" (Family History). Those stones show the names of Bassani's father, mother, and sister; the markers represent unpretentious yet effective fragments of lives that once were profoundly real in and of themselves; now they are real in another way.

By shaping each poem as an epitaph and by selecting the volume title he did, Bassani integrates his own identity with that of the souls he eulogizes; in a sense he writes his own epitaph. In a final, desperate act of faith, he speculates on his death. In "Rolls Royce" he imagines that, upon dying, he will be transported back to his youth: "Subito dopo aver chiuso gli occhi per sempre / eccomi ancora una volta chissà come a riattraversare Ferrara in macchina" (Just after I close my eyes forever / here I am once more who knows how riding through Ferrara in an automobile). He would be twelve years old again; he would race through the countryside, but something would be terribly different: the Rolls would fly "per strade ampie deserte / prive affatto di tetti ai lati e affatto / sconosciute" (over the wide deserted streets / entirely devoid of rooftops on either side and altogether / unrecognizable).

In 1978 Bassani published his poetry volume titled *In gran segreto* (With Great Secrecy). The book does not present real thematic or stylistic surprises, although one does find a more intense focus on the poet's personal destiny, as well as a correspondingly more oppressive sense of impending doom. Content with the authenticity and efficacy of the epitaph model, Bassani continues to employ the form. Also familiar is the propensity for epigrammatic or aphoristic statements. Conspicuous, too, in *In gran segreto* is the retention of the broader topological framework of *Epitaffio*. No longer restricted to the Emilian topography, Bassani reaches for a wider experiential horizon, locating his favorite motifs in Vienna, Detroit, and San Francisco. The American settings reflect Bassani's stay as a visiting professor at the University of California, Berkeley, in 1976. His existential drama unfolds, then, in such unlikely venues as Central Park, Telegraph Avenue, and the Shattock Hotel. In keeping with the cosmopolitan air of his recent volumes, memorabilia of contemporary culture – from Michelangelo Antonioni to George Gershwin and condominiums – dot the lyrical landscape. Also making *In gran segreto* seem an ideological/structural continuation of *Epitaffio* is the spectrum of topics. Poems are devoted to rebuttals to critical evaluations of Bassani's work; these reactions may introduce a humorous note; usually the tone is ironic or sarcastic. In the same spirit he is capable of making observations on the current state of Italian letters, defining it in "I congiurati" (The Conspirators) as "ufficioso / nazional-cattolico-postermetico / organingramma letterario" (an officious / national-Catholic-posthermetic literary organization chart).

Operative still is Bassani's descriptive expertise. Incisive portraits recur, as in these concise strokes from "Piazza Indipendenza" (Independence Square): "grandi baudelairiani / negri d'entrambi i / sessi / alcuni abbigliati all'occidentale i più no / simili a magre piante verdibrune ovvero a molli / sgargianti fiori" (large Baudelairean / negroes of both / sexes / some dressed in Western clothes most not / similar to thin dark-green plants or soft brightly colored flowers). Flanking such portraits are, once again, richly textured vistas such as the "solida e bella vecchia villa cubica fine secolo con le rade / persiane chiuse serrate e con da tergo emergente un folto / di verzura" (solid and beautiful turn-of-the-century cubic villa with a few closed locked shutters and in the back an emergent thicket / of greenery).

Out of this matrix of predictable topoi emerges the dominant thematic axis of Bassani's art: life during the *ventennio nero* (the black twenty-year period) of Fascism, particularly from a Jewish perspective. While they are not expressly chronicled, the agonies withstood are represented as forms of universal suffering. Mere mention of words such as *Fascist* or *Nazi* suffices, in this context, to stimulate a shudder in the poetic narrator, as in "15 giugno 1975," where he mentions "toccò a mio padre a partire circa il '30 fino ad almeno / il '38 e le leggi della Razza" (my father forced to leave from around 1930 to about / 1938 and the racial laws). There is in *In gran segreto* some of Bassani's understandable ambivalence toward his homeland and countrymen. He sees himself as nestled "nelle braccia del ceto moderato italiano eternamente / traditore incolpevole da sempre / fascista e innocente" (in the arms of the Italian middle class eternally / blameless traitors and always / innocent Fascists).

Bassani remains largely faithful to his *ars poetica* — his firm belief in the function of art and the moral responsibility of the artist. He announces such a principle in "Allo stesso" (To the Same Person): "[volevo] dar voce all'inesprimibile far sì / che l'inesistenza o / quasi finalmente / esistesse" ([I

wanted] to give voice to the inexpressible make / nonexistence or / almost finally / come to life). With this statement he elaborates on his conviction that history is the persistence of the human spirit, which art succeeds in encapsulating for transmission through generations. The notion sets Bassani apart from the hermetics, who broadly negate the reality of history. In a way Bassani's view resembles Alessandro Manzoni's reconstitution, via the historical novel, of the lives or essence of ordinary individuals situated on the fringe of formal history. Bassani breathes life into his personages by invoking them with words; eulogizing them in "Allo stesso," he says, "[preferisco] i colori vaghi al puro e squillante le sorti / di cui la Storia con la esse grande non si occuperà / non si curerà" ([I prefer] muted colors to pure and loud ones the destinies / with which History with a capital H will not bother). In a powerfully evocative image of a Hades-like domain, he visualizes such simple souls huddled together, for warmth and mutual comfort, as they await being brought into the light of remembrance and resurrection: "In quale segreto e / sotterraneo in quale mai tenebrissimo insospettabile scantinato / convenuti . . . vi incontrate / vi date la mano" (In what secret and underground in what darkest unthinkable pit / united . . . you meet / you hold hands).

The poet's absolute moral duty is that of responding to this urgent yet private appeal to vivify the lifeless. In this sense Bassani's poetry fulfills a social responsibility, though not in the manner of the neorealists. In fact neorealists such as Pier Paolo Pasolini resented what they saw as Bassani's withdrawal from social and political involvement. However, Bassani prefers to interpret his role as that of restoring life and dignity to the anonymous who existed in concrete historical contexts and who were victimized by political circumstance. Rather than focus his literary gaze on contemporary socio-economic problems, Bassani chooses to shed light on the reality of historical barbarism and perhaps, in this way, to realize a more valid or at least more universal objective. In "Allo stesso" he admits that his role is not the result of any deliberate ideological decision but, instead, is an unavoidable component of his sensibility: "io . . . ho sempre nel cuore i poveri / morti" (I . . . always have in my heart the poor / deceased). For the poet to be able to fulfill his responsibility, according to Bassani, he must concentrate on the afterlife, as does Dante. Consequently the subject matter of his poems must be stark. His lifelong task is to radiate the spiritual light of *Te lucis ante* into dark chasms.

Having before him the constant presence of death, rendered usually as absence of light or warmth, Bassani is led to meditate, in an increasingly intense way, on his own approaching demise. Typical of his later utterances is the oxymoronic image of the old child in "Allo stesso": "[volevo] che tu pure magari povero / vecchio semicanuto / bambino . . . in qualche modo per sempre ci / fossi" ([I wanted] that you too rather poor / almost white-haired child . . . somehow could always / be there). But, more often than not, Bassani reiterates his own precarious state through the repetition of key terms, as in "Da Alceo" (From Alcaeus): "Non so che cosa cerca in me che cosa diavolo / a me vecchio domanda alla mia vecchia / vita" (I don't know what he wants with me what the devil / he's asking of an old man like me of my old / life). In "Ciampino" (Ciampino Airport) Bassani betrays a general uneasiness: "il vecchio / mio occhio l'azzurra insaziata mia folle / iride" (my old / eye my blue dissatisfied crazy / iris).

Related to this strong sense of personal mortality are many poems in *In gran segreto* that disclose Bassani's sensitivity to the evanescence of life. Reminiscent of Salvatore Quasimodo's 1930 poem "Ed è subito sera" (And Suddenly It Is Evening) are the following lines from "In Maremma": "col suo fieno / uno andrebbe più forte del / treno / del baleno / e addirittura della / morte" (with his hay / one would go faster than / the train / the lightening / and even than / death). By means of a hypothetical dialogue in the poem appropriately called "Padre e figlio" (Father and Son), Bassani equates human destiny with the fate of a dragonfly: "Sta dicendo dimmi com'è / che la libellula non ce la fa / a vivere più d'un giorno / solo / capisci bene un'unica / giornata e / basta?" (He is saying tell me how is it / that the dragonfly can't manage / to live more than a day / only / one day do you understand / and that's it?). The child's questioning is the poet's own disbelief before the brevity of existence. The absence of all interior punctuation, here as well as throughout the volume, syntactically heightens Bassani's sense of abject awe as he witnesses the unstoppable transience of life's daily phenomena.

Finally, as the self-appointed life giver to those who have fallen off the precipice of existence into the chasm of nonexistence, he must come to grips with his own inconsolable isolation. The memories he transports within him constitute his "gran segreto"; this stance is similar to the opinion expressed in some of Montale's poems where allusions are made to the burden of knowledge or insight that makes the poet a solitary figure. In the case of

Bassani it is not the sublime isolation of the symbolist or neoromantic, nor the self-pitying retreat of the crepuscular poets, nor the solipsistic aloofness of the hermetics. Bassani's segregation is born of a profound meditation on life's painful mysteries. For this reason he occasionally has interlocutors allude to his predicament, as when he writes in "Dove vivi" (Where You Live), "Nessuno pensando a te saprebbe darti oggi il più / piccolo posto un po' tuo . . . proprio tu che fino / all'altro ieri soltanto / non ne hai abitato in fondo che / uno" (No one thinking of you would be able today to give you / the smallest place of your own . . . you who until / the day before yesterday / had not really occupied but / one).

Complementing the perspective of others is Bassani's own stated sense of alienation, as seen in "Muore un'epoca" (An Epoch Dies): "Muore un'epoca l'altra è già qua / affatto nuova e / innocente / ma anche questa lo so non la / potrò vivere che girato / perennemente all'indietro a guardare / verso quella testè / finita" (One era dies and the other is already here / not at all new or / virginal / but even this one I know I will not be able to live in / except facing / perpetually backward looking to the one that just ended). In the end such awareness of his own isolation (an entombment of sorts) within the walls of his memory and beliefs causes him to feel that he is actually closer to the dead, about whom he writes, than to the living. From the former he derives his true sense of historical and existential identity: "mi fa oggi ancora sì trasalire / però di / vita" (even today it [contact with the dead] makes me shudder / but with / life). His meditations resolve themselves into a desire to vanish from the physical world in order to join the personae he celebrates, thereby going from a tormented form of existence to a more serene and lasting one. This movement symbolically occurs in "Padre e figlio": "desiderio di andarci / subito anch'io proprio laggiù dove vanno / a terminare dove si / perdono [le vie]" (a desire to go there / myself right now down there where / they [the roads] end where they / disappear).

In 1982 Bassani collected all his published poems and added several others in the epitaph style to produce *In rima e senza* (Rhymed and Unrhymed). The compositions of *L'alba* constitute the rhymed segment of the volume, while *Epitaffio, In gran segreto,* and the new poems written between 1978 and 1982 comprise the unrhymed segment. It is therefore possible to comprehend at a glance Bassani's evolution in stylistic terms as well as his persistent return to a limited yet profitably mined group of themes. The opus represents a significant contribution to modern Italian poetry, even though no single piece of writing can be said to be the major achievement of a given poetic style. Nevertheless, while they echo at times faintly and at other times loudly the experimentalism of the crepuscular, hermetic, and posthermetic poets, the poems of *In rima* remain rooted in a specific aesthetic and cogently address the human condition in general, rather than issues that pertain to any given epoch.

Interviews:

"Risposte a nove domande sul romanzo," *Nuovi Argomenti,* 38–39 (1959): 1–5;

Dominique Fernandez, "Entretien: Cassola e Bassani," *Express,* 23 August 1962, pp. 22–23;

Claudio Varese, "Tre domande a Bassani sul film di Vancini," *Punto,* 8 October 1962, p. 9;

Lorenzo Mondo, "Bassani difende con coraggio la screditata verità del pudore," *Gazzetta del Popolo,* 5 December 1962, p. 3;

"In difesa di Ferrara," *Avanti!,* 30 December 1962, p. 8;

Donatella Bisutti, "Bassani," *Grazia,* 28 February 1968, pp. 37–41;

Grazia Livi, "Bassani, come nasce un romanzo," *Epoca,* 27 October 1968, pp. 120–124;

Manlio Cancogni, "Perchè ho scritto *L'airone*: Conversazione con Giorgio Bassani," *Fiera Letteraria,* 14 November 1968, pp. 10–12;

Ferdinando Camon, "Giorgio Bassani," in his *La moglie del tiranno* (Rome: Lerici, 1969), pp. 85–91;

Camon, "Intervista con Bassani," in his *Il mestiere di scrittore* (Milan: Garzanti, 1973), pp. 54–71;

Stelio Cro, "Intervista con Bassani," *Canadian Journal of Italian Studies,* 1 (Fall 1977): 37–45;

Davide De Camilli, "Intervista a Giorgio Bassani," *Italianistica,* 9 (September–December 1980): 505–508;

Anna Dolfi, "'Meritare' il tempo: Intervista a Giorgio Bassani," in her *Le forme del sentimento: Prosa e poesia in Giorgio Bassani* (Padua: Liviana, 1981), pp. 79–81.

References:

Stelio Cro, "Art and Death in Bassani's Poetry," *Canadian Journal of Italian Studies,* 1 (Winter 1978): 153–160;

Massimo Grillandi, *Invito alla lettura di Bassani* (Milan: Mursia, 1972);

Pier Paolo Pasolini, *Passione e ideologia* (Milan: Garzanti, 1960), pp. 415–419;

Bortolo Pento, "Tempi di un itinerario lirico," in his *Letture di poesia contemporanea* (Milan: Marzorati, 1965), pp. 14–17;

Douglas Radcliff-Umstead, *The Exile into Eternity* (Rutherford, N.J.: Fairleigh Dickinson University Press, 1987);

Giorgio Varanini, *Bassani* (Florence: Nuova Italia, 1970).

Dario Bellezza

(5 September 1944 –   )

Corrado Federici
Brock University

BOOKS: *L'innocenza* (Bari: De Donato, 1970);
Invettive e licenze (Milan: Garzanti, 1971);
Lettere da Sodoma (Milan: Garzanti, 1972);
Il carnefice (Milan: Garzanti, 1973);
Morte segreta (Milan: Garzanti, 1976);
Angelo (Milan: Garzanti, 1979);
Morte di Pasolini (Milan: Mondadori, 1981);
Libro d'amore (Milan: Guanda, 1982);
Storia di Nino (Milan: Mondadori, 1982);
Io (Milan: Mondadori, 1983);
Turbamento (Milan: Mondadori, 1984);
Colosseo: Apologia di teatro (Catania: Pellicanolibri, 1985);
Piccolo canzoniere per E. M. (Rome: Giano, 1986);
L'amore felice (Milan: Rusconi, 1986);
Serpenta (Milan: Mondadori, 1987);
Libro di poesia (Milan: Garzanti, 1990).

OTHER: Ruth Feldman and Brian Swann, eds. and trans., *Italian Poetry Today: Currents and Trends,* includes poems by Bellezza (Saint Paul: New Rivers, 1979), pp. 23–25;
Giuliano Dego and Lucio Zaniboni, eds., *La svolta narrativa della poesia italiana,* includes poems by Bellezza (Lecco: Agielle, 1984), pp. 21–25.

Dario Bellezza circa 1980 (photograph by Gabriella Maleti)

Dario Bellezza's literary career has included both narrative and poetry. He has also been a translator and a controversial figure both for the subject matter treated in his writing and for his public views. He continues to collaborate on the journals *Paragone, Nuovi Argomenti, Bimestre, Carte Segrete,* and *Paese Sera* and to contribute to other periodicals and newspapers. His first poems appeared in *Nuovi Argomenti,* although his first book published was the novel *L'innocenza* (Innocence, 1970), which established his autobiographical slant, noticeable in all subsequent works, as well as the tendency, noted by critic Giuliano Manacorda, "ribadire una tematica dalla quale egli sembra sin troppo condizionato" (to reiterate a thematics to which he seems excessively predisposed). Despite the qualified critical response to what may seem to be a narrow set of themes, Bellezza was hailed by Pier Paolo Pasolini as the best of the new poets of the 1970s.

It is difficult to situate precisely Bellezza's poetry within the context of the modern Italian lyric, largely because of the rather chaotic, Babel-like climate that typifies the post-neo-avant-garde era. Amid strains of *riflusso* (reflux), neo-hermeticism, neo-crepuscularism, and neo-experimentalism, the voice of Bellezza might seem to be lost amid the many consonant or dissonant voices of the 1970s and 1980s. Upon closer examination, though, one finds that Bellezza's place is among those writers who firmly restore the meaningful signification of words and make the subjective *I* once more the focus of the artist's creative attention. His place is also among poets such as Pasolini and Sandro Penna who deal with the question of homosexuality, seeing in that condition a metaphor for all the alienated, disenfranchised pariahs of modern society. In addition Bellezza echoes the criticisms leveled against a corrupt modern world by writers such as Giovanni Giudici, Giovanni Raboni, and Mario Lunetta.

Bellezza was born in Rome on 5 September 1944 and still resides there. His father was born in Rome and his mother in Taranto. Bellezza was a friend of Pasolini and Elsa Morante, to whom he has dedicated some of his works. Bellezza's first book of poems, *Invettive e licenze* (Invectives and Liberties), was published in 1971. From the formal perspective, the text is characterized by longish verses strung together in frenetic sequences that are generally unrestrained by punctuation or rhyme. Manacorda recognizes in this form the influence of Pasolini's *Le ceneri di Gramsci* (Gramsci's Ashes, 1957). The poetry also fits into the context of post-neo-avant-garde poetics that reassert the semantic weight of the word as well as the urgency of communicating a comprehensible message. In this case the meaning transmitted is that of a tormented soul trapped in an unlivable moral/emotional condition to which there is but one analgesic therapy: death. Using dialogue, monologue, and soliloquy structures in a frenzied, almost hysterical style, Bellezza engages in an always intense, sometimes incoherent, and often brilliantly desultory debate with his soul or with the empirical reader – the speaker is analyzing, lamenting, imploring, castigating, or pleading for compassion for himself and others who share his fate.

One might use the term *confession* or *private letter* to describe the dominant format. Bellezza himself resorts to such expressions in moments of metaliterary frankness: "solo tu, tristezza mia, capirai / questa lettera privata e non spedita" (only you, my sorrow, will understand / this private letter never mailed). Using the vehicle of an intimate diary, he undertakes a ruthless, almost masochistic analysis of his contorted psyche; the autobiographical bias is clearly denoted by the frequent appearance of the pronoun *io* (I) and of the first-person-singular form

of the possessive adjective, as when he cites "il mio incerto passato" (my uncertain past), "la mia incerta biografia" (my uncertain biography), or "l'amara mia sconfitta" (my bitter defeat). In performing his verbalized examination of conscience, Bellezza (or the implicit poetic narrator) adopts a language that is at times literate and at times mundane or even vulgar. In one of his more erudite moods, the speaker describes himself sarcastically as "il pedante Amleto / della più consolatrice borghesia" (the pedant Hamlet / of the most consolatory bourgeoisie). Also indicative of his literateness are his allusions to the Orpheus and Narcissus myths, as well as to the philosophy of Thomas Hobbes, as the following reveals: "non ho combattuto il Leviatano / Stato che vuole tutto inghiottire" (I have not fought the Leviathan / State that wants to devour everything). Biblical allusions also form part of Bellezza's cultural profile; for instance, he thinks of himself as being "simile a Giacobbe che lotta / con l'angelo della più profonda notte" (similar to Jacob who battles / against the angel of the darkest night).

Countervailing the literary subtexts is the coarse lexicon of everyday existence. Reflecting the poetics of the later Eugenio Montale and of the lesser-known Raboni, Bellezza looks with hyperrealist or minimalist eyes at the objects of daily existence, and from them derives his existential crisis. These physical signifiers include "zuppa di latte" (milk soup), "una tazza / screpolata" (a chipped / cup), "un lettino di scapolo" (a bachelor's bed), and the "ronzìo delle zanzare" (buzzing of mosquitos). Among these untransformed or unsublimated items he manages to insert his most intimate impressions and his most chaotic sentiments.

The primary thematic axis of *Invettive e licenze* is the narrator's homosexuality, in all its attendant psychological and emotional complexities. The phrase that epitomizes the problem of his condition is "la vergogna del sesso sconclusionato" (the shame of ambiguous sexuality). In other words he articulates his homosexual impulses without erotizing or eulogizing, and, at the same time, he gives voice to his turbulent awareness of the abnormality of these same instincts. *Invettive e licenze* consequently constitutes a song of personal freedom from the constraints of a morally intolerant society; it is also a plea for acceptance and for a redefinition of normalcy. The tense interplay between these two equally compelling propensities produces one of the most anguished voices of contemporary Italian poetry. Indicative of Bellezza's desire to assert the shameless innocence of his condition are references to "la mobile calma dell'amplesso" (the mobile calmness of the embrace) and "i maschili corpi accesi di furore" (male bodies afire with passion). Coexistent with the intention to compose a hymn to amoral ecstasy is a competing sense of confusion as to the true emotional identity of the implicit poet: "io / che sono solo all'Anagrafe maschio" (I / who am male only on my birth certificate). While the collection contains surprisingly explicit terms referring to genitalia, the primary aesthetic concern remains that of confessing and elucidating the intellectual and emotional implications of his condition as a liberated but suffering individual living in an age of unparalleled freedom. Bellezza painfully reveals his awareness of just such a paradox in utterances such as "dove / s'aggirano i mostri della mia diversità" (where / the monsters of my distinctiveness roam) and "fu la gelosia la normalità / dei ragazzi a spingermi a rifiutare" (it was the jealousy the normalcy / of boys that impelled me to recoil).

Expressive of Bellezza's nervous cohabitation with his narcissistic nature is the sterility/fertility motif. While he derives consolation or pleasure from his homosexual relationships, he recognizes the impossibility of achieving complete biological fulfillment in the form of procreation; this knowledge renders his rapport with others sterile and barren. "Dov'è la sterilità che t'accompagna / e trattiene i sorrisi ai fecondatori / che non riescono a fecondarti / perchè sei sterile" (Where is the sterility that accompanies / you and holds back the smiles of the fecundators / who can't make you fertile / because you are sterile). From this perspective he transcends the parameters of his homosexuality by focusing on sentiments that pertain to relationships in general: regret over lost opportunities for spiritual growth; sadness over wasted friendships; jealousy; resentment or a profound sense of betrayal; self-pity; self-deprecation; depression; and even the inclination to consider suicide. In light of these features *Invettive e licenze* constitutes one of the most piercing expressions of spiritual affliction and personal isolation in the modern Italian lyric.

A parallel thematic axis of the volume is that of insomnia. Due to the preponderance of sorrow and anxiety, the poetic narrator feels frequently unable to sink into a therapeutic sleep: "mi sveglio e non dormo ahimè!" (I awaken and do not sleep, alas!). The insomnia motif, in turn, is linked inextricably with that of conscience or guilt: "l'insonnia viene...a chi disubbidisce" (insomnia comes . . . to the disobedient). This disobedience pertains not only to defiance of the natural order of things, but, in line with much neo-avant-garde literature in Italy, it also pertains to defiance before the author-

ity of orthodoxy and traditionalism. Symptomatic of his contradictory approach to self and world, Bellezza rebels yet must withstand the pangs of an active conscience. Certain utterances bespeak the guilt of partaking in "piaceri proibiti" (prohibited pleasures).

As a direct consequence of his perceived state of fallen grace or exclusion from the Eden of acceptance, he occasionally descends into a Rimbaudian hell of despair. He is escorted to his abode by the "angelo della perdizione" (angel of perdition). The personal hell in which he is condemned to expiate his sin (thereby setting up a contradiction vis-à-vis the bourgeois religious values he seemingly assails) is often identified explicitly, as in the invitation to follow him "nell'Inferno / casto dei miei piaceri proibiti" (into the chaste / Hell of my prohibited pleasures). The hell/purgatory motif is sustained by semantically related terms such as *damnation, punishment,* and *atonement.* In Baudelairian paradoxical fashion Bellezza also shows a propensity for interchanging the spheres of heaven and hell: "anche l'Inferno / è l'infinito. Il sesso lo squallore" (even Hell / is infinity. Sex squalor). However, he also designates that same sexuality in paradisiacal terms.

Resulting from such experiences of ceaseless carnal and psychological torment, made worse by an oppressive guilt and a sense of being punished for a sin involuntarily or innocently committed, the speaker in desperation searches for lost innocence or at least the preguilt stage of development; that same pristine condition is related by Pasolini to the primordial, prerational phase of human evolution. The image of the angel runs through Bellezza's writing. That desired condition of innocence is synonymous with the serenity that accompanies the realization of one's full humanity, irrespective of sexual orientation, and the freedom from societal, conditioned guilt responses: "l'innocenza di saperti diverso" (the innocence of knowing you are different). Utterances proclaiming the desire to find or recover that innocence, in turn, revolve around the twin motifs of prayer and martyrdom. Often he describes his plight as persecution – reminiscent of Pasolini's stance – as when Bellezza becomes aware of being "nella stanza / del martirio" (in the chamber / of martyrdom). By the same token, he reverts to dramatic religious symbolism when he points to the "croci che ti crucifiggono" (crosses that crucify you). Emulating the supplicant posture of Christ in Gethsemane, the persecuted speaker beseeches his creator to remove the chalice of torture. He also prays for peace of mind and relief from the remorse of imperfect friendships, as well as for an orthodox sexuality: "sognare / di rinascere io maschio e tu femmina" (to dream / of being reborn I as male and you as female). On the other hand, he also prays for the courage to remain as he is: "Pregavo di essere sempre / così, castrato amante di ragazzi" (I pray to be always / thus, castrated lover of youths).

The dominant motif of *Invettive e licenze,* however, is that of death. Bellezza repeatedly laments the progressive disintegration of his body and soul, brought on by pernicious guilt or a sense of moral decay – defined not by the standards of society, namely as deviancy, but as the unattainability of lasting and meaningful relationships. Images of putrefaction and decomposition recur in descriptions of himself and of those around him. Sensing his demise in progress, the speaker may challenge death to erase him entirely or he may integrate the desire for cessation of pain with the prayer motif. In the poem "Quale sesso ha la morte?" Bellezza writes, "Signore, fammi morire tutto, eternamente" (Lord, let me die completely, eternally). With every breath he feels the presence of death, within and without him, conditioning his every response to the exigencies of living. The specter even intrudes in his dreams, stamps its sinister omens on the landscape, and contaminates his sexual fantasies; he eventually asks, "quale sesso ha la morte?" (of what sex is death?).

Closely associated with the death motif in *Invettive e licenze* is that of madness, which winds its way through much of Bellezza's poetry and links him with the *maudit* (damned) poets such as Charles Baudelaire, Arthur Rimbaud, and Dino Campana. Virtually every aspect of the speaker's existence is marked by the stigma of folly: "Folle è ritrovarti" (Folly is finding you again). The summation of his experience may well be this remark: "mi preparo / all'insonne pazzia quotidiana" (I prepare myself / for the daily sleepless madness). A strong factor in the insanity is the perception of the irrationality of time. The narrator expresses dismay over the futility of resisting time's sweeping movement: "tutto il tempo invano passato" (all the time vainly passed). When it does not merely pass, it can be a vicious aggressor, as in the phrase "l'assalto del Tempo" (Time's assault).

A final aspect of Bellezza's poetics is the use of violent language to express the emotional carnage that is the ultimate subject matter of his verses. His is a "massacrato amore" (massacred love). But the idea that resonates in all of Bellezza's later works is that of assassination, in all its morphological derivatives, including "vita assassinata alla poesia" (life assassinated for poetry) and the "assassinato ingegno insaccato" (assassinated bagged mind). By means of such expressions he vehemently denounces life for having filled him with anguish. His soul is a "vittima e carnefice / del mio senso di colpa" (victim and executioner / of my sense of guilt). The term *carnefice* reemerges in the title of one of Bellezza's novels (1973). His use of violent language also serves to inveigh against contemporary society. For instance, he views the state as a modern Leviathan that devours all. Society is also chaotic: he cites the "disordine del mondo" (disorder of the world). At other times the world seems hopelessly imbecile, "incredulo e cretino" (incredulous and cretin). In addition to these generic protestations, Bellezza directs his invectives against specific targets, usually the bourgeoisie; he speaks of his "repulsione / ai giovani borghesi" (repulsion / toward middle-class youths). He also rejects his own environment: "il chiuso mio io / reticolato intorno alla festa morta adulta / e adulterata della crescita borghese" (my cloistered ego / strung like barbed wire around the dead adult / and adulterated feast of a bourgeois upbringing). Not only does Bellezza's poetic voice harangue against a spiritually ossified and intolerant society, but it rails against modern city existence amid "sigarette drogate" (drugged cigarettes), "pasticche avvelenate" (poisoned pills), and "le pasticche dell'oblio" (pills of oblivion).

Bellezza's second poetry collection, *Morte segreta* (Secret Death), published in 1976, does not present noteworthy innovations in form, thematics, or diction, except to introduce greater experimentation with shorter compositions. Again the confessional mode prevails: "scrivo un testamento o calendario, a seconda / dei temi giornalieri destinati dal Caso" (I'm writing a will or diary, according to / daily themes dictated by Chance). Once more, too, ordinary, prosaic moments of quotidian living activate the intellectual, obsessive self-analysis that has become a trademark of Bellezza. Whether eating in his kitchen, strolling through the streets of Rome, or leafing through the pages of a newspaper, he transforms ordinary events into vehicles for the dissection of his own feelings: "racconto una favola negativa a me / stesso" (I'm reciting a negative fairy tale / to myself).

In a sense what Bellezza composes in *Morte segreta* and subsequent works is a *canzoniere* (songbook). The compositions, however, are mostly laments of unsuccessful relationships rather than paeans to ideal forms of love: "coprendomi di ridicolo scrivo lettere / d'amore a traditi amori di un'epoca trascorsa" (covering myself in ridicule I write love / letters to betrayed loves of a bygone age). *Morte segreta* is as much a dirge over misplaced opportunities for ennobling encounters, beyond the experiential vectors of homosexuality, as it is a panegyric to individual freedom and sensibility. In the name of uncensored self-expression, Bellezza, as was the case in *Invettive e licenze,* undertakes a furious, rage-filled analysis of himself. The ego, with all its aspirations, glorious exuberance, and delusions, once more is at the center of the verses. Manacorda calls the focus a "continuo rovello sul proprio io" (continuous preoccupation with the ego). Bellezza exposes intimate pretense and falsification, referring to himself as "teatrale, senza ferite apparenti che non siano / d'amore" (theatrical, without obvious wounds that are not / those of love).

Exploring the twists and turns of his own conscience, Bellezza again focuses on his sense of abnormality and exclusion from the psychosocial norm. One technique he employs to advantage is that of recording the discriminatory remarks of his companions: "Non c'è spazio per te, qui, Dario caro" (There is no room for you, here, dear Dario). Complementing this modality is his direct admission of alienation: "Come d'esiliato vivere implacabile tutto / in me prende le mosse" (As in an implacable exiled existence everything / derives its motion from me). Feeling pursued, like a criminal, he pleads his own innocence in the poem "A. e D.": "Non succhio / il sangue dei bambini, non ti preoccupare, non / mangio gli avanzi dei festini del Dio / selvatico e sensuale" (I don't drink / the blood of infants, don't worry, I don't / eat the leftovers from the banquet table of the / savage and passionate God).

Within this normalcy/abnormality antithetical imagery, the poet weaves his usual themes, ranging from insomnia to madness: "chiamatemi così: pazzo, deserto testimone / di un deserto da percorrere" (call me that: crazy, deserted witness / to a desert I must cross). The insanity motif is, as in *Invettive e licenze,* intertwined with that of innocence: "muratemi / in una galera con la bibbia e i santi" (lock me up / in a jail cell with my Bible and my saints). Such a cell intersects semantically with the Baudelairean/Rimbaudian hell metaphor. And with this motif of everlasting earthly damnation is the Christian concept of sin and expiation, which the poet unsuccessfully strives to transcend.

Also reintroduced in *Morte segreta,* as the title connotes, are the collateral themes of death and suicide. As in *Invettive e licenze* Bellezza obstinately equates his plight to a living death or the situation of a criminal sentenced to be executed; his attitude fluctuates erratically between fear of dying and determination to survive. He is "innamorato di non morire mai" (enamored of the idea of never dying). Sometimes the line between life and death blurs: "morire non è tortura più grande / della debole sopravvivenza quotidiana" (dying is a torture not greater / than the feeble act of daily survival). Eventually suicide seems an attractive option. This theme may acquire the form of an irresistible urge to throw himself from a window or to plead for euthanasia: "fatemi fuori, / presto, prima che pensi" (put me out of my misery, / quickly, before I think).

Bellezza is also capable of extrapolating from his private destiny in order to denounce the mortality of humankind. Usually this occurs when he contemplates the devastation of time: "trionfatore sarà / solo il Tempo e il suo nero oltraggio, la Morte" (triumphant will be / only Time and its black ravage, Death). He presents himself as a spokesman for all of victimized humanity when he delineates the horror of life as "un infinito terrore di sentire il tempo / che passa senza illusione o condanna" (an infinite terror of feeling time / that passes without illusion or condemnation).

While the vast majority of the poems in *Morte segreta* tend to reiterate the concerns contained in *Invettive e licenze,* there are several places in which the poet either ventures into fresh territory or develops his usual thematics in unexpected ways. For example, the mania for self-analysis begins to be expressed in images of schizophrenia. In this respect Bellezza's work resembles that of modernist artists such as Luigi Pirandello who dramatize the contemporary disorder of estrangement from oneself. In the case of Bellezza the splitting of the personality generates an antithetical dynamic between the living self and the dead alter ego: "così diviso da me, osservo il mio cadavere, / ne contemplo le mille epoche sopravvissute / alle illusioni, alla felicità passeggera" (thus divided from myself, I watch my corpse, / I contemplate its one thousand ages that survived / illusions and fleeting joy). This schizoid personality trait effectively articulates the extreme, incompatible urges that animate the lyrics of *Morte segreta.* In other words, as in the poems of Baudelaire, the speaker's essential personality seems to be paralyzed between ascent toward ecstasy and descent toward damnation. Ultimately the two personalities correspond to hatred and love of life. Whereas in *Invettive e licenze* the dominant role is played by hatred, in *Morte segreta* there is a greater balance between the two affections. In fact the scale might even be tipped in favor of love: "in realtà amo / la vita, sono forte in essa" (in truth I love / life, I am strong in it).

Finally, the sector in which there is the greatest innovation is that of metaliterary or self-reflexive statements. There is a more pronounced inclination in *Morte segreta* to explain, rationalize, or defend the poetics. Bellezza is fully cognizant of the content of his verses. In "Scherzo per Catullo e Verlaine" he writes of his "sregolati versi / pieni di angoscia o martirio o lussuria" (undisciplined verses / full of anguish or martyrdom or lasciviousness). He is also aware of the iconoclastic or anarchic nature of his linguistic register, calling himself "il tiranno osceno autore di invettive amorose" (the obscene tyrant author of amorous invectives). Bellezza further admits that his compositions have a confessional quality, calling them at one point "Le solite parole della solitudine dette / un po' prima di andare a letto" (The usual words of solitude spoken / a bit before going to bed).

Additionally Bellezza appears to be extremely sensitive to critical response to his *Invettive e licenze*. Striking a sacrificial-lamb pose, he invites his critics to flail his writings: "la mia poesia / definitela con crudeltà e livore come lubrica, / oscena, interessata e manigolda consigliera / di sventure o furto di anime giovanili" (my poetry / define it with cruelty and rancor as lewd, / obscene, self-serving and as wicked vehicle / of misadventures or theft of young souls). He seems to resent accusations of contrived sincerity or histrionics, repudiating "la fretta dei critici immortali nel giudicare la mia / forsennata poesia sospesa fra elaborata perizia / e sincerità programmata" (the haste of those immortal critics who interpret my / lunatic poetry as suspended between elaborate craftsmanship / and programmed sincerity). In self-denial he can be quite convincing, as he declares his integrity and cites his aspiration to portray reality in unretouched detail: "diranno che sono volgare, ma è il rischio / di chi scrive per l'oggi mortale e non per / lo ieri eterno delle luci funerarie dei / tempi secolari" (they will say that I'm vulgar, but it's the risk / of one who writes for mortal today and not for / the eternal yesterday of the funereal light of / immortal time).

Although Bellezza's third book of poems, *Libro d'amore* (Book of Love) was published in 1982, its contents were composed between 1968 and 1981. The title immediately discloses his reluctance to depart from the *canzoniere* concept. Readers encounter many familiar topoi, mostly related to the Eros motif — "l'erotico abbandono" (erotic abandon) and "i luoghi della libidine" (the places of the libido), for example — as well as allusions to genitalia. These images are again subordinated to the nuances of sentimentalism. Complementing the stark, often jar-

ring references to physical contact or gratification are lines such as these: "un Tempo quando Eros / ci legava e io ti bevevo tutto" (a Time when Eros / bound us together and I imbibed you completely). Present, too, is the persistence of violent language to convey the voraciousness of the speaker's passion, as well as the devastating effect life in modern times has on the psyche. Also familiar is the self-portraiture: "questa mia ambulante carcassa" (this ambulatory carcass of mine). Homicide and suicide resurface in *Libro d'amore* as virtually two aspects of the same obsession: "L'omicidio è / suicidio-sfarzo di povero / matto dal volto ancora adolescente" (The homicide is / a suicide-show of the poor / insane figure whose face is still juvenile). The concept of the *carnefice* (executioner) is reinstated in *Libro d'amore*. Here, for instance, it identifies time: "il tempo era ancora / un carnefice che non dava paura" (time was still / an executioner who did not frighten us).

The novelty of *Libro d'amore* lies in its modulated tone. Less frequent and less melodramatic are the protestations against violence and hypocrisy in contemporary society, and virtually abandoned are the almost fanatical rantings about Bellezza's insanity, insomnia, and putrefaction. Instead the reader finds a more crepuscular tonality as the poet dwells on his pervasive sense of weariness and discouragement, as if the strain of drafting rage-filled invectives in the two previous works had drained him of his fire. He now prefers to ask that someone merely "guarire il mio cuore stanco" (heal my tired heart). As though battered by life, he is suddenly content to bemoan his "stracca carne di bestia avvilita e reclusa" (exhausted flesh of a dejected and reclusive animal). A factor in the formation of this humiliated state is the awareness of the transience of life: "il pianto di così / poca felicità" (the tears shed over such a small / amount of happiness). Even ecstasy is tragically ephemeral; hence it is a "passeggera eternità" (a fleeting eternity). Another component of the weariness theme in *Libro d'amore* is the cognizance of wasted experiences: "sterminate primavere di ebbrezza / quando la carne era senza freni" (exterminated springtimes of inebriation / when the flesh knew no restraints).

A striking innovation in *Libro d'amore* is the occasional shift in narrative perspective. Bellezza normally has his poetic gaze fixed on his personal sensations, but in *Libro d'amore* he succeeds in communicating a profound regard for his fellowman — presenting an aspect of his poetics that one might label altruistic. He recognizes the vulnerability of a friend: "sei solo nel temporale" (you are alone in the storm); or he acknowledges the courage needed to survive in a modern wasteland: "tuo coraggio / di ragazzo che lotta con le serpi del Potere" (your courage / of a child who battles the serpents of Power). Bellezza's greatest expression of compassion pertains to the funeral of a friend: "mancai alla tua morte con la mia" (I missed your death on account of my own); "le scie alate della tua morte oscura / si spandono per tutto il cielo" (the alate wake of your obscure death / stretches across the whole sky). Along these same lines Bellezza's concern, which pertains to people such as Pasolini, extends to all victims of social prejudice and, ultimately, to all of victimized humanity.

Bellezza's fourth volume of poetry, appropriately entitled *Io,* was published in 1983, its poems dating from the 1975–1982 period. On a formal basis it continues the trend established in *Libro d'amore* toward shorter poems of a few compact stanzas and more conspicuous punctuation. The overall effect is one of diminished frenzy and a more contemplative posture. The thematic axes remain largely unchanged, as he laments his loss of desire to pursue the dream of innocence. Resignation to existential tedium is evident: "Il trionfo vero / è quello della quotidianità" (The real triumph / is that of daily existence). Less obsessive, too, is the ambivalent attitude toward the omnipresent specter of death, as readers see in "La fine del mondo" (The End of the World): "forse è la morte mia / che mi spaventa e la unisco / a quella del Mondo" (perhaps it is my own death / that scares me and I fuse / it with that of the World). This statement clearly exemplifies the somewhat new approach exhibited by Bellezza in *Io* – namely that of subsuming his own mortality with that of humankind, thereby transcending his private, restricted viewpoint. In line with this reformed attitude, Bellezza displays a less sardonic or virulent disposition regarding his own youth. As expected, he mourns its disappearance, but he confronts that loss with mature stoicism: "la giovinezza non verrà" (youth won't return). Wisdom seems to have displaced outrage: "Inganna gioventù / chi crede giovane la sua essenza" (Youth deceives / him who believes that his essence is young).

Visible also in *Io* is that current of altruism noted in *Libro d'amore*. Empathy is expressed for someone such as Pasolini, eulogized in "In Memoriam": "nel tuo sangue versato come Cristo / si dispera di non farne più parte" (in your blood spilled like Christ's / we despair of still being part of it). Appreciation of the sacrifices of others, to the point of considering them as martyrs, is a conspicuous part of that outlook. This specific concern, in turn, expands into a broad sensitivity to human suffering in general. In this context Bellezza feels dismay over the dwindling of rationality in the computer age or regret that power and evolution seem to have conspired to annihilate morality; he imagines "la fuga dei fossili nell'evoluzione-spavento / ai miserabili ingordi del Potere" (the drain / of fossils in the evolution-dread / before the wretched appetite of Power).

Another dimension that begins to play a prominent role in *Io* is the religious one, a logical extension of meditations on mortality. Bellezza's thoughts oscillate between a desperate need for faith and an abject despondency over the absence of a divinity that adjudicates or intervenes in human misconduct. The first impulse comprises an intense quest for "la luce / la luce del Signore" (the light / the light of the Lord). At times he feels a desperate sense of abandonment, as he says: "sento come decrepitezza questo corpo volante / verso le foci buie del tempo più cristiano / che inchiodato da un Dio misterioso e crudele / passa oltre i folti cuori" (I feel as decrepitude this body flying / toward the dark mouth of time more Christian / than being nailed to a cross by a mysterious and cruel God / that passes through thick hearts). In one poem, "Io e Dio" (God and I), he constructs a dialogue between his supplicant ego and an indifferent, condescending God. While the poet pleads, "fammi sentire vivo e vero, / calpesta l'infamia del corpo / che mi pesa, non ne posso più" (make me feel alive and true / crush the infamy of the body / that weighs me down, I cannot stand it any more), his interlocutor remains impassive.

The most noteworthy developments in the volume are the memorial poems – striking eulogies to fallen comrades – and the tendency toward aphorism. For example, in "Nel presente" (In the Present), Bellezza writes, "Bisogna vivere nel presente, non nei ricordi: / i ricordi invecchiano" (One must live in the present, not in memories: / memories age us).

In 1985 *Colosseo: Apologia di teatro* (Colosseum: Apologia for the Theatre) was published. It consists of eleven poems written in 1968 and a short play. The poems of *Colosseo* were not included in the 1971 *Invettive e licenze* because, as Bellezza himself speculates in a note to the book, "forse sembravano troppo 'attuali' o 'audaci' per i tempi" (perhaps they seemed too "topical" or "audacious" for the times); they contained "erotismo affogato, la provocazione a tutti i costi, il 'maledettismo' ostentato" (drowned eroticism, provocation at all costs, and a display of "accursedness").

Indeed these traits could be described as characteristics of Bellezza's poetry to date. As he himself suggests, his lashing out verbally against a society that grudgingly tolerates him is more direct or overt in *Colosseo* than in other books. His hostility toward society can be quite explicit, as in these lines from the poem "Colosseo": "lascio indietro il piccolo-borghese mondo / che m'offende" (I leave behind the small, middle-class world / that offends me). The question of offensive toleration of the nonconformist is often openly confronted: "La democrazia borghese permette la mia esistenza / e di questa diversità neutralizzata fa l'alibi / della sua sopravvivenza" (The democratic bourgeoisie permits my existence / and makes this neutralized nonconformity the alibi / of its own survival). Within such a context are metaphors of exclusion and involuntary inclusion.

The novelty of *Colosseo,* however, is to be found in the use of Roman architectural ruins, such as the Colosseum, to provide a historical perspective to the lamentations. In other words the antagonism between Eros and Amor, between isolation and communication, or between conformity and ostracism, played out against the imposing ruins of antiquity, produces a poetic plea for understanding and acceptance that traverses the ages and suggests the regression in moral posture evident in the modern age, as seen in "Colosseo": "Qui / nel decrepito, fatiscente mondo, tutte le diversità / proprio perchè tali, politiche, razziali, sessuali, / sono epifenomeni di una stessa angoscia / che fa esistere: quella del neo-capitalismo, / della borghesia che ha paura dei mostri / che essa stessa produce" (Here / in the decrepit, collapsing world, all differences / by virtue of being what they are, political, racial, sexual, / are epiphenomena of the same anguish / that keeps us alive: that of neocapitalism, / of the bourgeoisie that fears the monsters / it itself creates). From the modern schizoid social fabric (aptly represented in the writings of neo-avant-garde poets such as Edoardo Sanguineti and Antonio Porta) emerges the image of the Roman world, stripped of its romanticized connotations. It is a world that, in the mind of the speaker, appears less liberal than the contemporary one in which he resides: "Lì, in un mondo diverso, forse più giusto, / meno alienato di questo, io non avrei diritto / neppure alla vita" (There, in a different world, perhaps a more just one, / one less alienated than this one, I would perhaps not even have the right / to be alive).

In the "Note to the Editor" one discovers Bellezza's useful attempt at classifying his poetry as postmodernist: "Ero già postmoderno dopo le ubriacature della Neoavanguardia letteraria; ero postmoderno nel gesto, nella 'vita' straparlando di morti e di rinascite. Ero postmoderno nel sesso visto come vuoto residuo di un'incarnazione passata; nel sapermi diverso – non diverso in tutte le contaminazioni dell'Eros e degli Stili" (I was postmodernist already, after the stupor of the literary neo-avant-garde; I was postmodernist in gesture, and in 'life' talking excessively about deaths and rebirths. I was postmodernist in sexuality seen as empty residue of a previous incarnation; in knowing that I was different – not different in all of the contaminated forms of Eros and Styles). Equally valuable is his acknowledgement that the primary influences on his early poetry were Pasolini, Rimbaud, Dylan Thomas, and Konstantínos Kaváfis (who wrote as Constantine Cavafy).

In 1986 Bellezza published *Piccolo canzoniere per E. M.* (Little Songbook for E. M.). The initials in the dedicatory title allude to Elsa Morante, a writer and friend much admired by Bellezza. In the thirteen compositions that make up this modest volume, the narrator treats the addressee much the way he treats his reader in previous works – as someone in whom he confides to express his well-rehearsed litany of self-pitying, self-deprecating exclamations, as well as his acrimonious vituperations directed at the wasteland society in which he dwells. Perhaps he expects to strike a sympathetic chord in Morante as reader when the speaker portrays himself as one possessing the voice of a "topo purgatoriale" (mouse of purgatory), or when he characterizes his existence as insanity: "chiuso e stretto nella mia follia" (enclosed and shut within my madness). He articulates his anxiety over the normalcy/abnormality dialectic at frequent intervals, and he communicates the frustrations of living in an age that inhibits his genuine development as a poet. He describes himself as "solo, abbarbicato ad una fortuna / che mi volle poeta inguaribile e bastardo" (alone, clinging to a destiny / that wanted me to be an incurable and bastard poet).

Piccolo canzoniere is noteworthy in that it presents a prevailing sense of anguish shared with a writer of appreciably compatible capacity for suffering. In "Dopo una rottura" (After a Breakup), for example, Bellezza asserts his and Morante's virtual interchangeability: "siamo due forme di uno stesso lavorio" (we are two forms of the same piece of work). Fundamental to this perceived bond between narrator and addressee is the sense of shared condemnation and a mutual anticipation of some sort of spiritual rebirth: "insieme votati alla distruzione /

per rinascere santi" (together committed to destruction / in order to be reborn as saints). In the postscript to *Piccolo canzoniere* Bellezza quotes Morante as saying, "si rimane dentro il carcere senza uscita, murati fra due orrori, la sopravvivenza e la morte, l'una e l'altra impossibile" (we find ourselves within a prison with no way out, walled in by two horrors, survival and death, one as impossible as the other). Bellezza makes this statement the focus of his own reflections, which either echo or interact with the implications of Morante's outlook, thereby generating the despondency that permeates *Piccolo canzoniere*. However, the despondency scarcely conceals the poet's burning admiration and affection for Morante.

Bellezza's *Serpenta* (Serpents), published in 1987, represents his most impressive product, since it treats familiar thematics with artistic restraint. Whereas anger, rage, and invective characterize earlier works, the dominant mood of *Serpenta* is one of painful acceptance; protests against the pain caused by mistreatment at the hands of an unforgiving society are couched in the code of resignation and understanding. The tendency to lash out still flares up from time to time, but it is considerably muted, as is the lexicon that in preceding works symbolized his anti-authoritarian revolt.

One sees the altered perspective in Bellezza's treatment of Eros. While he does not apotheosize his homosexuality, the narrator does present it as a casualty of the era in which it is practiced. He is still capable of admiring young men, as the suite titled "Lodi del corpo maschile" (Praise of the Male Body) indicates; nevertheless, they are now perceived to be beyond his attainment. They remain available to others, but the narrator broods (speaking of himself in the second person): "cerchi solitudine, e la trovi / nel silenzio assoluto della casa / inquieto di saperti solo e imperfetto" (you seek solitude, and you find it / in the absolute silence of the house / nervous in the knowledge you are alone and imperfect). So disorienting is his exclusion from meaningful existence that he confuses the pleasures of paradise with the pains of hell, saying that the "Paradiso confuso di ricordi / vissuti in mezzo al guado di Caronte" (confused Paradise of memories / lived at Charon's crossing).

Likewise recurring is the death imagery. Bellezza examines with sober dismay the wreckage of his existence: "mi sfiguro a pensare / i lieti conforti di una età diversa, / priva del vizio della morte" (I disfigure at the thought / of the pleasant comforts of another age, / free from the vice of death). With utter disillusionment he acknowledges

the nullification of all experience: "tutto è spento / dentro" (everything has been extinguished / inside).

Intimately connected with the death-of-the-self imagery is the impotence/sterility motif. The anguish at not being able to find spiritual fulfillment in human relationships is transposed as impotence: "volo / e sono desto, rasoterra rasento / il muro di cecità senza sesso / impotente" (I soar / and am awake, I touch the earth I nudge / the wall of blindness sexless / impotent). A sense of rejection, born of an inadequacy complex, permeates *Serpenta*. Typically he exclaims, "Il tuo corpo adorato più non tocco" (Your adored body no longer do I touch); and he feels pursued by "i fantasmi del sesso impotente" (the phantoms of impotent sexuality).

At the root of the problem lies Bellezza's usual perception of abnormality. In *Serpenta* not only is society responsible for fostering his sensitivity to his own distinctiveness but destiny itself is to blame: "è il massimo / d'avventura riservata dagli Dei vendicatori / a chi si oppone alla norma" (it is the ultimate / adventure reserved by the vindictive Gods / for those who oppose the norm). On a more immediate level the middle class is the rapacious culprit, as the speaker cites the "scempio delle borghesie / inani e gagliarde che vogliono il mio sangue" (slaughter of the inane / and hardy bourgeoisie that wants my blood). As the reader has come to expect, the dialectic rages between a profound sense of guilt for being aberrant and an urgent need to be abnormal.

In the context of the articulation of the sentiments of an outsider, or pariah, recognizable exclamations of weariness appear. Tedium and lethargy prevail over the invective and exuberance of Bellezza's earlier poetry. Typical of his new lament are these lines: "ora mi spengo / in questo assorto tramonto di speranze" (I now expire / in this submerged sunset of hopes). So much energy has been expended asserting the legitimacy and authenticity of his life-style that the speaker is virtually withered: "intossicato / non guardo più né quasi parlo" (poisoned / I no longer see and barely talk); he forlornly concedes, "io non vivo più né deliro" (I no longer live nor rave). Where there was rage, indignation, and defiance, there is absence of emotionalism: "Non credo più all'amore" (I don't believe in love any more). Such is the degree of disenchantment that, at one point, he is practically speechless: "il sole in alto già che non riscalda / il cuore gelido, mi attacco / al poco che resta oltre la cenere" (the sun straight overhead still does not warm / the frozen heart, I cling / to the bit that remains after the ashes). The sense of desperation is also underscored by the inability to find evidence of a providential being; the narrator longs for the light emitted by the "occhio di un Dio che è sparito" (the eyes of a God who has vanished).

The single most significant feature of *Serpenta* is not the thematics or idiom but the increasingly precise view of the contemporary world. Bellezza gives voice to the paranoia and dread that are synonymous with living in the nuclear age: "Non resta che rassegnarsi: la morte / atomica strimpella i suoi vagiti" (There is nothing left to do but resign ourselves: atomic / death utters its newborn cries). Elsewhere he isolates the pervasive fears that hang like dark clouds over technological civilization: "La mia religione dunque non fu / amore in questo dopomillennio di paure / scontate che di notte fanno capolino / nei sogni di un malato" (My religion therefore has not been / love in the postmillenium of automatic / fears that at night pop up / in the dreams of the ill). Nor do ecological disasters escape Bellezza's scrutiny, as he invokes nature under siege in "Verde" (Green): "O alberi / fortunati preziosi immortali / non vi uccida del tutto la furia bieca / dei vivi nati morti" (O lucky / precious immortal trees / do not let the blind fury of those living born dead / destroy you entirely).

The image of the serpent becomes the prototypical metaphor of insidiousness. Endowed with polyvalence, the word is suggestive of a viperous society; it alludes to those elements that treacherously thirst for the poet's abnormal blood; it is also suggestive of original sin – a metaphor that runs through all the poetry of Bellezza. On another level he apostrophizes the serpent as a kindred spirit: "e tu, Serpenta, immagine sfocata degli anni cattivi, / siamo due forme di uno stesso lavorio / eterno delle cose e degli astri e del Destino" (and you, Serpent, blurred image of the bad years, / we are two forms of the same eternal / mechanism of things and stars and Destiny). The only solution that presents itself is that of suicide, as the following invocation of American poet Hart Crane reveals: "così gridasti Hart, o caro Hart / poeta americano morto suicida / così gridasti al vento notturno / dal gran ponte precipitando" (thus you screamed Hart, oh dear Hart / American poet dead of suicide / thus you cried to the night wind / as you hurled yourself from the great bridge).

In the final analysis the poetry of Dario Bellezza provides an intriguing twist on the concept of the writer as exile. In several instances the verses suggest the image of the poetic subject as pariah – an individual perceived to be perverted. At times the subject himself is aware of having transgressed against the laws of nature. In the end, however, Bellezza deliberately chooses to isolate himself from an environment that he considers to be morally bankrupt and vile due to its hypocrisy and vindictiveness. Perhaps the greatest literary contribution made by Bellezza lies in the fact that he challenges the fundamental question of who is truly innocent and who is not, in the context of contemporary social structures.

Interview:

Silvia Battisti and Mariella Bettarini, *Chi è il poeta* (Milan: Gammalibri, 1980), pp. 226–231.

Bibliography:

Gianfranco Contini, *Schedario di scrittori italiani moderni e contemporanei* (Florence: Sansoni, 1978), pp. 10–11.

References:

Daniella Ambrosiano, "La *Morte segreta* di Dario Bellezza," *Carte Segrete,* 35 (1977): 186–190;

Maurizio Cucchi, "Cinque libri di poesia," *Nuovi Argomenti,* 51–52 (July–December 1976): 341–350;

Gualtiero De Santi, "Il 'calepin' del ragazzo di vita," *Italianistica,* 2 (May–August 1973): 421–424;

De Santi, "Monodia dai gironi dell'emarginazione," *Nuovi Argomenti,* 56 (October–December 1977): 176–184;

Mario Lunetta, "Invettive e licenze," *Rinascita,* 34 (20 August 1971): 26;

Giuliano Manacorda, *Letteratura italiana d'oggi 1965–1985* (Rome: Riuniti, 1987), pp. 246–248;

Marco Marchi, "Il mare della soggettività," *Paragone,* 27 (December 1976): 135–147;

Pier Paolo Pasolini, *Descrizioni di descrizioni* (Turin: Einaudi, 1979), pp. 110–114;

Giovanni Raboni, "Quattro libri di poesia," *Paragone,* 23 (April 1972): 245–249;

Giuseppe Zagarrio, *Febbre, furore e fiele* (Milan: Mursia, 1983), pp. 106–109.

Attilio Bertolucci

(18 November 1911 –   )

Mark Pietralunga
Florida State University

BOOKS: *Sirio* (Parma: Minardi, 1929);
Fuochi in novembre (Parma: Minardi, 1934);
La capanna indiana (Florence: Sansoni, 1951; revised and enlarged, 1955; further revised and enlarged edition, Milan: Garzanti, 1973);
Viaggio d'inverno (Milan: Garzanti, 1971);
Poesie e realtà '45–'75 (Rome: Savelli, 1977);
La camera da letto (Milan: Garzanti, 1984; enlarged, 1988);
Aritmie (Milan: Garzanti, 1991).

OTHER: Luciano Anceschi, ed., *Poeti antichi tradotti dai "Lirici nuovi,"* includes poems by Walter Savage Landor and Archibald MacLeish translated by Bertolucci (Milan: Balcone, 1945), pp. 198–210;
Honoré de Balzac, *La ragazza dagli occhi d'oro,* translated by Bertolucci (Parma: Guanda, 1946);
D. H. Lawrence, *Classici italiani,* translated, with a preface, by Bertolucci (Milan: Bompiani, 1948);
Thomas Love Peacock, *L'abbazia degli incubi,* translated by Bertolucci (Parma: Guanda, 1952);
Anna Banti, *Artemisia,* preface by Bertolucci (Milan: Mondadori, 1953);
Poesia straniera del Novecento, edited, with several translations, by Bertolucci (Milan: Garzanti, 1958);
Autobiographical statement, in *Ritratti su misura,* edited by Elio Filippo Accrocca (Venice: Sodalizio, 1960), pp. 70–71;
Gli umoristi moderni, edited by Bertolucci and Pietro Citati (Milan: Garzanti, 1961);
Carlo Golino, ed., *Contemporary Italian Poetry,* includes poems by Bertolucci (Berkeley & Los Angeles: University of California Press, 1962), pp. 98–101;
Ernest Hemingway, *Verdi colline d'Africa,* translated by Bertolucci and Aldo Rossi (Turin: Einaudi, 1968);
Thomas Hardy, *Poesie,* translated by Bertolucci, in *Romanzi* (Milan: Mondadori, 1973);

Attilio Bertolucci in 1934

Charles Baudelaire, *I fiori del male,* translated by Bertolucci (Milan: Garzanti, 1975);
Edgar Allan Poe, *Arthur Gordon Pym,* preface by Bertolucci (Rome: Riuniti, 1981);
Alessandro Gentili and Catherine O'Brien, eds., *The Green Flame,* includes poems by Bertolucci (Dublin: Irish Academic Press, 1987), pp. 136–142.

SELECTED PERIODICAL PUBLICATIONS –
UNCOLLECTED: William Wordsworth, "La valle di Airey-Force," "Per nocciole," "Preludio,"

and "L'escursione," translated by Bertolucci, *Poesia*, 9 (1948);
"Dalla poetica dell'extrasistole," part 1, *Paragone*, 2 (October 1951): 66–69; part 2, *Paragone*, 17 (August 1966): 23–26;
"I pescatori," *Botteghe Oscure*, 20 (1957): 437.

Attilio Bertolucci (father of the filmmakers Bernardo and Giuseppe Bertolucci) holds a place apart in the development of twentieth-century Italian poetry. Although he has remained isolated by nature and by choice from any literary movement, Attilio Bertolucci has been an important presence in Italy as a poet and promoter of cultural awareness. His poetry is also significant, as it represented for many years an alternative to the once prevalent hermetic tradition. Unlike the hermetic poets, Bertolucci is drawn to the concrete elements of reality and chooses to render them in a natural and ordinary manner. This direction has resulted in an unusual style of expression. By his own admission Bertolucci discovered at an early age a greater literary affinity with other European cultures than with his own. Primarily in recent Anglo-Saxon and French literary traditions he found voices most congenial to his particular interests. Yet Bertolucci's essential inspiration is the familiar world of his origins. Like many of the British writers of the nineteenth century whose works are rooted in a well-defined landscape, Bertolucci has his poetry focus on the surrounding countryside of his native region of Parma; his poetry is based on memory. His childhood represented a period of happiness, and in his poems he returns almost obsessively to those simple elements of his land that recall the joys of his youth. With Marcel Proust as his model, Bertolucci attempts to transfer the past into an eternal present in order to defeat time and death. An impressionistic approach to his subject matter enables Bertolucci to identify truth with poetic fantasy; he instills an underlying sense of anxiety into a seemingly idyllic setting. His autobiographical tendency has led him to adopt a style that intersperses prosaic elements with traditional poetic ones. According to Bertolucci meter no longer exists. What is important to him is a rhythm that is not limited to any fixed rules but rather directly reflects the moods of the heart. Consequently an inseparable bond exists between the stylistic evolution of Bertolucci's poetry and actual events in his life.

Bertolucci was born in the town of San Prospero, near Parma, on 18 November 1911. Both his parents were landowners who came, however, from two very different areas of the province of Parma. His father, Bernardo Bertolucci (whom Attilio was to name his son after), was from a village in the Apennines, while his mother, Maria Rossetti Bertolucci, came from a town in the fertile plains of the Po River valley. Attilio Bertolucci traces the origins and events of his family history in his long narrative poem *La camera da letto* (The Bedroom, 1984). A few months after Attilio's birth his parents moved with him to Antegnano, where he spent the first years of his life in a large villa in the rich countryside of Emilia, only a few miles from Parma. When he reached the age of six, he was placed in a boarding school in Parma for practical rather than disciplinary reasons. This experience was so traumatic for him that he began to write in order to keep himself company. It was, in fact, not long after his arrival at the boarding school when he first began to write verses.

Bertolucci's readings were equally precocious. Not yet a teenager, he had already discovered Charles Baudelaire's *Les Fleurs du mal* (The Flowers of Evil, 1857) and Walt Whitman's *Leaves of Grass* (1855). In 1925, at the age of fourteen, he purchased and read Eugenio Montale's *Ossi di seppia* (Cuttlefish Bones, 1925). During a trip to Venice that same year, he discovered the works of Proust. In his interview with Sara Cherin, Bertolucci revealed the pleasure of this important literary discovery. He mentioned that, upon the purchase of the first two volumes of Proust's *A la Recherche du temps perdu* (1913, 1919) in a bookstore in Venice, he was almost miraculously struck by certain signs. He began to read the work immediately and passionately, even though he was only in his first year of French. His parents were unable to draw him out of his room. Bertolucci was not the least bit interested in Venice and its monuments; his only desire was to be allowed to read his beloved Proust. Bertolucci told Cherin about his precocious readings: "Proprio queste mie letture precoci costituiscono poi uno dei motivi per cui ho sempre pensato che, per certi aspetti, io appartengo alla generazione precedente alla mia, come se fossi, in un certo senso, nato prima. I miei coetanei hanno cominciato a leggere i sacri testi moderni qualche anno dopo, certo con più giudizio, ma con meno candore e ardore" (Precisely these precocious readings give rise to one of the reasons for which I have always considered myself, in some ways, part of the generation that preceded my own; it was almost as if I were, in a certain sense, born earlier. My contemporaries began to read the sacred modern texts a few years later, certainly with greater judgment, but with less candor and passion).

While a high-school student in the 1920s, Bertolucci discovered another of his passions, the cinema. This interest was strengthened by his friendship with one of the eventual founders of the neorealist cinematic movement in Italy, Cesare Zavattini, who had briefly been one of Bertolucci's high-school instructors. Zavattini was also among those friends who encouraged him to publish in 1929, at the age of eighteen, his first collection of poetry, *Sirio* (Sirius). In this early production of twenty-seven poems, Bertolucci invents the personal poetic landscape that will characterize his verses. He limits his world to a circumscribed geographical area identifiable with the familiar countryside near his native Parma. Within this private universe the speaker lives entirely absorbed. A magical aura pervades the elegiac autobiography of *Sirio,* as Bertolucci's childlike imagination transports the natural and human setting into the realm of dreams. The poem "Inverno" (translated as "Winter" in *The Green Flame,* 1987) illustrates this youthful reverie:

Inverno, gracili sogni
sfioriscono sugli origlieri,
giardini lontani fra nebbie
nella pianura che sfuma
in mezzo alle luci dell'alba.
Voci come in un ricordo
d'infanzia, prigioniere del gelo,
s'allontanano verso la campagna;
ninfe dagli occhi dolci e chiari
fra gli alberi spogli, sotto il cielo grigio,
cacciatori che attra versano un ruscello,
mentre uno stormo d'uccelli s'alza a volo.

(Winter, delicate dreams
languish on the pillows,
distant gardens between mists
on the plain which vanishes
in the midst of dawn light.
Voices like in a childhood
memory, prisoners of the frost,
move away toward the country:
nymphs with clear and sweet eyes
among the naked trees, beneath the gray sky,
hunters who cross a stream,
while a flock of birds rise up in flight.)

His recourse to regional surroundings for the source of inspiration for his unpretentious, ironic verse recalls the colloquial poetry of French symbolist Jules Laforgue, to whom Bertolucci claimed a special affinity. With regard to Italian sources, he appears to have in mind Giovanni Pascoli and the crepuscular poets. Highly relevant in his verse are the examples of Giosuè Carducci's landscape poems and Riccardo Bacchelli's *Poemi lirici* (1914).

Bertolucci stated in an interview with high-school students (in *Sulla poesia,* 1981) that his poetry often originates from a vision of reality but should not be categorized as realistic. Instead his verses are metaphors. He reveals the modus operandi of *Sirio,* as well as much of his subsequent poetry, in the following statement: "Io mi sono avviato ad esprimere il massimo di realtà profonda muovendo dal minimo di realtà visibile quotidiana" (I set out to express the most of a profound reality moving from the least of a visible everyday reality). This observation explains Bertolucci's tendency to represent reality through isolated fragments that acquire an oneiric and surreal quality as they are filtered through a child's imagination, as in the poem "Frammento" (Fragment):

Buoi rossi e neri
pestano la bianca neve
nel cristallo opaco della notte.

Fremono i grandi abeti
nel lume fermo degli astri.

Angeli invisibili e gravi
guidano la colonna
con suoni di corni selvaggi.

(Black and red oxen
tread on white snow
in the opaque crystal of the night.

The large fir trees rustle
in the still light of the stars.

Angels invisible and solemn
lead the column
with sound of wild horns.)

Bertolucci's explication of this poem illustrates his vision of the world. He indicates that the opening image was inspired by the daily experience of life in the country, while the last one may have been suggested by the sculptures at the baptistry in Parma. He completes his explanation of the poem by declaring that the "suoni di corni selvaggi" are another imaginary element, which evokes the idea of barbaric invasions.

Upon the completion of high school in 1931 Bertolucci enrolled unwillingly in the School of Law at the University of Parma. The following year he was ill and bedridden for several months. Bertolucci recalls that period in his interview with Cherin: "a un certo momento mi presi una pleurite; chissà, fors'anche per convincere la ragazza che mi piaceva, ad amarmi; poi, per trovare una scusa a non dover dare esami di giurisprudenza, che era una cosa terribile" (at a certain moment I contracted pleurisy; who knows, maybe even to convince the girl I liked, to love me; also, to find an excuse to avoid taking my law exams, which were dreadful). In 1933 Bertolucci participated in a national poetry contest, held during the Fascist era, and was awarded second place. His poetry also began to appear in prominent reviews and to draw the attention of important literary figures such as Eugenio Montale and Enrico Falqui.

In 1934 his second volume of poetry, *Fuochi in novembre* (Fires in November), was published. It is anachronistic with respect to the literary climate of the times. *Fuochi in novembre* appeared when the pure, sublime poetry of the hermetic movement was predominant. Bertolucci's faith in the common objects of a familiar world and his use of ordinary language partly explain his distance from the hermetic poets. He preferred to adopt a language and style that were consistent with the simple, unobtrusive reality depicted in his poetry. He did not feel that it was necessary to seek recourse in an obscure language in order to free his poetry from any realistic constraints. In *Fuochi in novembre* Bertolucci returns to the calm, natural setting of rural Emilia and to the intimate relationship that exists between the poet and his surroundings. This intimacy personalizes ordinary objects and invests them with a sense of uniqueness. In the poem "Emilia" Bertolucci offers an affectionate metaphorical display of this personal view of his natural environment:

> Emilia, ormai scurisce il tuo frumento
> e il papavero esce a fare il bullo
> e le viti mettono teneri ricci
> e la sera i biancospini illuminano le stradette
> dove non passano che tante biciclette.
> Emilia, ormai le tue donne fioriscono le contrade
> di nuove toilettes, e le rose rosse nei giardini
> ascoltano quei pazzi usignoli querelarsi
> senza ragione, come i soprani nelle opere.

> (Emilia, by now your wheat darkens
> and the poppy appears acting like a bully
> and the vines grow tender curls
> and at night the hawthorns brighten the narrow roads
> where only many bicycles pass.
> Emilia, by now the women adorn the countryside
> with new toilettes, and the red roses in the garden
> listen to those crazy nightingales complain
> for no reason, like sopranos in the operas.)

What differentiates Bertolucci from his contemporaries is his colloquial and proselike style,

which is substantially different from the hermetic poets' emphasis on the word. The long narrative verses of "Emilia" are characteristic of his later poetry, but for many of the poems in *Fuochi in novembre* Bertolucci employs an epigrammatic form with a humorous tonality, which recalls the *poésie fantaisiste* of Paul-Jean Toulet. Like the French poet, Bertolucci uses fantasy to free himself from any exasperated feelings. Under the mask of humor and irony he moderates his voice and conceals any possible anxiety. In the poem "Insonnia" (Insomnia) he overcomes an uneasiness, and a feeling of calm soon reigns over the dreamlike world:

> Come cavallo
> che meridiana ombra impaura
> s'impunta il sonno,
> finché l'alba sbianca l'oriente.
> Allora, stanco, si rimette a trottare
> per borgate che si svegliano,
> davanti a osterie che riaprono
> da cui escono voci
> e fresco odore di grappa.

> (Like a horse
> frightened by a midday shadow
> sleep grows restive
> until dawn whitens the east.
> Then, tired, resumes its trot
> through villages that awaken,
> in front of taverns that reopen
> out of which come voices
> and a fresh smell of brandy.)

After four unsuccessful years as a law student at the University of Parma, Bertolucci transferred in 1935 to Bologna University and studied the arts. During his three years at Bologna, Bertolucci came in contact with people such as Giorgio Bassani and Francesco Arcangeli, all of whom were students of the famed art historian Roberto Longhi. In 1938 Bertolucci married an elementary-school teacher, Ninetta Giovanardi. After he graduated from the university, he began a career as an art-history instructor in Parma. In 1939 he founded "La fenice" (The Phoenix), a series on foreign poets, for Guanda publishers; he directed the series for several years. He also began to contribute to the local Parma newspaper and to journals such as *Letteratura, Circoli,* and *Corrente.* After the declaration of an armistice in Italy on 8 September 1943, Bertolucci took a leave of absence from teaching and sought refuge with his family at the abandoned seventeenth-century family residence in the Apennine village of Casarola. Cardiac arrhythmia had prevented him from active participation in the war.

From 1935 to 1945 he wrote very little. In his interview with Cherin he explained that he was much too unhappy with outside circumstances and much too happy with his private life to write poetry. He attempted to combat the unhappiness of that period in Italy and Europe by enclosing himself in private happiness: "Io e la mia compagna Ninetta, in maniera dolce e ossessiva, si stava sempre insieme, leggendo gli stessi libri, vedendo gli stessi film, ascoltando gli stessi dischi" (My companion Ninetta and I, in a sweet and obsessive way, were always together, reading the same books, seeing the same films, listening to the same records). In 1951 Bertolucci and his family moved to Rome, where he again taught art history and contributed to several reviews. That same year he published, after a long silence, his third volume of poetry, *La capanna indiana* (The Indian Hut). The book was awarded the 1951 Premio Viareggio. It contains selections from *Sirio* and *Fuochi in novembre;* in addition Bertolucci collected poems written from 1935 to 1950 and included them in the section titled "Lettera da casa" (Letter from Home). The long, three-part poem "La capanna indiana" and the brief poem "Frammento escluso" (Excluded Fragment) complete the volume.

In the collection "Lettera da casa" Bertolucci's world begins to show signs of change. A different reality emerges, which contrasts with the circumscribed reality of his earlier poems. The timeless, privileged dimension is invaded by outside forces. The reality of war, the deaths of loved ones, and the sight of his children growing up have affected the serenity of his personal environment. Bertolucci reacts to these changes by retreating further into his protective, conservative space in order to defend himself from the violence of these new experiences. In the affectionate, idyllic verses of "Lettera da casa" he attempts to ignore them and seeks desperately to maintain the calm of a fleeting world. He chooses to focus on a tender domestic setting; however, time has penetrated his intimacy. Consequently the brightness and happiness of that fairytale atmosphere darken under the shade of change and the passing of time. The poem "Idilli domestici" (translated as "Domestic Idylls" in *The Green Flame*) underscores these changes. Furthermore the elegiac tone, which often fades into childlike reverie in his earlier poems, lingers as an accompaniment to his pain:

> Sole o nebbia, non importa, la dolce sera
> vede fanciulli in mesti giochi gridare
> sul cielo occidentale, sia cenere o oro,
> tardi, tardi, sino alle luci che si accendono.
> ·

Bertolucci at the door of his family's seventeenth-century family estate in Casarola

> E questo argenteo silenzio il declinare
> dell'anno, la nostra vita
> variano appena le dolorose feste del cuore,
> le memorie che migrano come nuvole.
>
> (Sun or fog, it matters not, the sweet evening
> sees children in sad games shout
> on the western sky, be it ashes or gold,
> late, very late, until the lights are lit.
> ·
>
> This silvery silence marks the declining
> year, our life is scarcely changed
> by the painful celebration of the heart,
> the memories which migrate like clouds.)

In the 269 lines of "La capanna indiana" Bertolucci directs his attention to an enclosed and protective place. His reaction to any possible change affecting his idyllic world is to establish a circumscribed territory, which has the capacity of assuming a mythic dimension. The simple storage place for agricultural equipment becomes the emblematic center of the universe, a type of womb:

> Dietro la casa s'alza nella nebbia
> di novembre il suo culmine indeciso:
> una semplice costruzione rurale
> ai limiti dei campi, una graziosa
> parvenza sulla bruma che dirada,
> si direbbe una capanna indiana.

> (Behind the house it lifts in the fog
> of November its indecisive culmination:
> a simple rural construction
> at the edges of the fields, a graceful
> shadow in the mist that clears,
> one would say it is an Indian hut.)

In this poem Bertolucci performs the Proustian operation of inventing an intermittent state, which enables him to recapture time and exorcize any sign of change:

> Le stagioni vengono e vanno, maggio
> è tornato e non ce ne siamo accorti
> . . . .
> siamo caduti in una rete d'oro
> mista di raggi e foglie, la mattina
> indugia, il tempo non finisce mai.

> (The seasons come and go, May
> has returned and we did not realize it
> . . . .
> we have fallen into a net of gold
> mixed with rays and leaves, the morning
> lingers, time never ends.)

In Rome, Bertolucci had difficulty adapting to a new life and longed to return to Parma. He suffered dramatically from this separation. Nevertheless he recognized that the pain caused by this uprooting was necessary for his poetry. He refers to this experience in his autobiographical sketch in *Ritratti su misura* (Portraits Made to Order, 1960): "Certo lo sradicamento è terribile, anche se è vero che è necessario per la poesia. Se io me ne restavo sempre nella mia città, o provincia, meglio, v'era il pericolo che 'l'agnosticismo epicureo-municipalistico' rimproveratomi una volta, assai dolcemente da [Carlo Emilio] Gadda, sanasse, irrimediabilmente, la ferita" (Certainly the uprooting is terrible, even if it is true that it is necessary for poetry. If I always remained in my city or, better yet, province, there was the danger that the "municipalistic-epicurean agnosticism" I was accused of, so good-naturedly by Gadda, would heal the wound).

Bertolucci left the teaching profession in 1954 and became more involved in several other activi-

ties. He was a collaborator for the RAI (Italian Broadcasting Company), a contributor to newspapers, an editor of literary journals, and an editorial adviser to the Garzanti publishing company. During his early years in Rome he met Gadda and Pier Paolo Pasolini and introduced them to the Garzanti firm.

In 1955 a second, enlarged, edition of *La capanna indiana* was published. It included the eighteen new poems of "In un tempo incerto" (In an Uncertain Time). These verses mark a transition in Bertolucci's vision of the universe. Although he remains faithful to the same themes and to the myth of a private space, he recognizes the reality of the separation from his beloved territory; he attempts to come to terms with the trauma of leaving Parma and its surroundings for Rome. The nostalgia that was already a part of his poetry, even when he lived in contact with his land, is mixed with a sense of resignation. He intensifies the idyllic aspects in order to compensate for the pain and anxiety of the loss. In "Pensieri di casa" (Thoughts of Home) he attempts to recover his land through memory:

> Non posso più scrivere né vivere
> se quest'anno la neve che si scioglie
> non mi avrá testimone impaziente
> di sentire nell'aria prime viole.
> . . . .
> Forse a noi ultimi figli dell'età
> impressionista non è dato altro
> che copiare dal vero, mentre sgoccia
> la neve su dei passeri aggruppati.

> (I can no longer write nor live
> if this year the snow that melts
> will not have me as an impatient witness
> to feel the first violets in the air.
> . . . .
> Perhaps we the last children of the age
> of impressionism have no other choice
> but to copy from the real, while the snow
> drips on some sparrows flocked together.)

The last stanza is testimony to Bertolucci's adherence to a realistic tendency, which corresponds to the poetic trend of the 1950s. The many changes in his life appear to have encouraged him to speak about his intimate reality with everyone rather than with a select few. Consequently the elegiac tone of his previous poetry yields to a more epic expression.

The death of Bertolucci's father in 1954 was extremely traumatic for the poet. He began to experience severe anxiety and was eventually hospitalized for psychological problems in 1958. In that same year he had edited an anthology of twentieth-century foreign poetry, *Poesia straniera del Novecento,* which includes several of his translations of French and Anglo-American writers.

In 1971 Bertolucci published his fourth collection of poems, *Viaggio d'inverno* (Winter Voyage). The volume was awarded the Etna-Taormina and the Tarquinia-Cardarelli prizes later that year. *Viaggio d'inverno* comprises eighty-four poems composed between 1955 and 1971. Bertolucci divided the book into six sections, which have almost the same function as chapters.

The collection shows the painful stages of a crisis that began with his separation from his paradise. The opening poem, "I papaveri" (The Poppies), documents the effect of the penetration of time into his world. The aging speaker has lost the power to dictate the development of events in his circumscribed territory. His children have grown up and broken through the boundaries of the paternal "prison" he has constructed:

> A metà della vita ora vedevo
> figli cresciuti allontanarsi soli
> e perdersi oltre il carcere di voli
> che la rondine stringe nello spento
>
> bagliore d'una sera di tempesta . . .
>
> (Midway in life I now saw
> grown children depart alone
> and disappear beyond the prison like the flight
> of the swallow that hastens in the spent
>
> flash of a stormy night . . .)[.]

Even after the separation from his land he still believes that a brief return there may offer a remedy for his condition, which has deteriorated into an apparent illness. The monologue form of "Ritratto di un uomo malato" (Portrait of a Sick Man), from the section "Per una clinica demolita" (For a Demolished Clinic), underlines the process of self-examination that takes place throughout *Viaggio d'inverno.* In "Ritornare qui" (Returning Home) he recognizes that he is only a passing traveler:

> Ritornare qui è come risuscitare
> e sentirsi chiedere per quanto tempo
> oh non molto l'inverno arriva presto
> e siamo attrezzati tutt'al più per l'autunno.
>
> (Returning here is like being revived
> and being asked for how long
> oh not long winter arrives quickly
> and we are prepared at the most for autumn.)

In "Lasciami sanguinare" (Let Me Bleed) the metaphor of hemorrhaging underscores a sense of slow dissipation and consumption of the speaker's days, his affections, and his possessions:

> Lasciami sanguinare sulla strada
> sulla polvere sull'antipolvere sull'erba,
> il cuore palpitando nel suo ritmo feriale
> maschere verdi sulle case i rami
>
> di castagno, i freschi rami, due uccelli
> il maschio e la femmina volati via,
> la pupilla duole se tenta
> di seguirne la fuga l'amore
>
> per le solitudini aria acqua del Bràtica,
> non soccorrermi quando nel muovere
> il braccio riapro la ferita . . .
>
> (Let me bleed on the road
> on the dust on the gravel on the grass
> my heart beating at its working-day rhythm
> green masks on the houses the branches
>
> of the chestnut trees, the fresh branches, two birds
> a male and a female flown away
> the eye suffers if it attempts
> to follow their flight the love
>
> for solitude air water of the Bràtica,
> do not help me when in moving
> my arm I reopen the wound . . .)[.]

"Lasciami sanguinare" reveals a stylistic evolution in Bertolucci's poetry. The complex syntax and the lack of punctuation evoke sensations that correspond to an emotional crisis. Bertolucci's reaction to the negations in his life, imposed by time, is to adopt a strategy that enables him to suture, at least stylistically, his wounds. He accomplishes this with an original style, comparable to that of "action painting," which reflects his obsession with a privileged, idyllic world and the terror of losing it. Consequently the poetry of *Viaggio d'inverno* teems with sharp contrasts between lightness and darkness, solitude and sociability, time and eternity, stasis and movement, and life and death.

In 1984 Bertolucci published book 1 (chapters 1–29) of *La camera da letto.* It was awarded the Biella Prize that same year. In 1988 book 2 (chapters 30–41) was added. Bertolucci began to write *La camera da letto* in 1955, soon after the publication of the second edition of *La capanna indiana.* In a 1977 interview for the newspaper *Repubblica,* Bertolucci discussed his motivation to write a long narrative poem: "Avevo la sensazione di scrivere buone poesie ma al tempo stesso mi ero stancato. La poesia mi pareva girare a vuoto. [Edgar Allan] Poe, nella sua 'Philosophy of composition' [1846] dice che le poesie lunghe non si possono scrivere, altrimenti si cade nella prosa. Ecco: contro la tradizione ermetica e simbolista io ho pensato che bisogna proprio cadere nella prosa perché la poesia rinasca. Sono assai più d'accordo con [Gerard Manley] Hopkins, per il quale il linguaggio poetico è il linguaggio comune intensificato" (I had the feeling I was writing good poetry, but at a certain point I grew tired of it. The poetry seemed to be going around in circles. Poe, in his "Philosophy of Composition," says that long poems cannot be written, otherwise they fall into prose. That's it: against the hermetic and symbolist tradition I thought it was necessary to fall precisely into prose so that poetry may be reborn. I am much more in agreement with Hopkins, for whom poetic language is intensified ordinary language).

Bertolucci constructed *La camera da letto* in the form of a novel. He registers, with the precision of a chronicler, the events of his family from 1798 to 1951. The long poem begins with the story of the migration of his ancestors from Maremma to the region of the Apennines between Tuscany and Emilia, and it concludes with an autobiographical description of his departure from Parma for Rome. He directs attention to his maternal grandfather, Giovanni Rossetti, a rich landowner in the Po River valley; his strong-willed mother, Maria; his young sister Elsa, who died at the age of six; his brother, Ugo; his uncle and godfather, Don Attilio, the mysterious priest who gives him the much cherished edition of Torquato Tasso's *Gerusalemme liberata*; his wife, Ninetta; his two sons; and the many servants, relatives, and unnamed characters who pass in and out of Bertolucci's world over the many years.

Fundamental is the obsessive pleasure derived from the description of his natural surroundings and domestic environment. He is particularly sensitive to the daily events and concrete details of life in the country. With a childlike exuberance Bertolucci describes the trees, seasons, places, and activities of his world. Each chapter of *La camera da letto* starts anew to repeat the description of those same ordinary elements, as if he were attempting to relive his own sensations of the past along with those of the other characters. The repetition of the seasons and the other experiences that accompany them produces a cyclical quality and a means of exorcising historical time:

Giugno ha finito di scaricare i suoi fulmini
azzurri nelle brevi notti diurne dei temporali

senza che la grandine abbia prodotto danni a noi, è
tempo di mietere, ancora una volta tempo
di trebbiare con riti d'obbligo cui benigna si sottomette
Maria, annodatasi un fazzoletto rustico rosso e blu
sui capelli neri, indossato un abito di cretonne
a fiori: vestizione che le serve disapprovano . . .

(June stopped discharging its blue
thunderbolts in the brief diurnal nights of the storms
without the hail causing us any damages, it
is time to reap, yet again a time
to thresh with the rites of obligation to which Maria be-
    nignly
submits, having knotted a rustic blue and red handker-
    chief
around her black hair, having put on a flowery cotton
dress: a ceremony her servants disapprove of . . .)[.]

In a similar manner Bertolucci turns to the ordinary and seemingly insignificant aspects of reality to reconcile poetically the mystery of death. He relates to death with the same concreteness that he treats all the other elements of his universe. The pain generated by the loss of loved ones becomes the inspiration for peaceful memories that endure. The premature death of Bertolucci's sister Elsa evokes in her family members a desire to recuperate the particulars of the young girl and to relive those moments of the past with the same vivid and sweet sensations:

Non era proprio dolore, ma voglia
di parlarne, di ricordarne i capelli
o le guance, o le gambe: non ti lasciava
mai, s'intrometteva nei discorsi
all'improvviso, e si perdeva, poi
riprendeva, ed era proprio come
faceva lei correndo il sesto anno,
ultimo della sua vita . . .

(It was not exactly pain, but the desire
to talk about her, to remember her hair
or her cheeks, or her legs: she never left
you alone, she entered suddenly in
conversations, and she disappeared, then
returned, and she was exactly how
she ran at the age of six,
the last year of her life . . .)[.]

In a 16 February 1984 review published in the *Corriere della Sera,* critic Pietro Citati comments, "Lo stile della *Camera da letto* è il più molteplice della letteratura italiana" (The style of *La camera da letto* is the most varied of Italian literature). Citati refers to Bertolucci's masterful stylistic amalgam, which includes blank verse, classic hendecasyllables, septenarii, hexameters, and a diarylike prose. Bertolucci also employs the complex and extensive sentence structure that is typical of several poems in *Viaggio d'inverno.*

Bertolucci claims that there are no models for *La camera da letto* either in Italian or any other literatures. For Bertolucci this fact is most common and stems from a natural refusal to follow literary fashions or movements. Montale, in reviewing *Fuochi in novembre* in September 1934 for the journal *Pan,* first recognized and admired Bertolucci's originality in relation to literary trends. Nevertheless this nonconformist attitude resulted, initially, in Bertolucci's remaining in the shadows of his contemporaries, since critics were unable to categorize him. It is still impossible to classify his poetry. His decision to attempt a long narrative poem is an exceptional event for contemporary Italian poetry and clearly confirms his position of autonomy among poets in Italy today.

Interviews:

Anonymous, Interview with Bertolucci, *Repubblica,* 9–10 January 1977, p. 16;

Sara Cherin, *Attilio Bertolucci: I giorni di un poeta* (Milan: Salamandra, 1980), p. 106;

Giuliana Massini and Bruno Rivalta, eds., *Sulla poesia: Conversazioni nelle scuole* (Parma: Pratiche, 1981), pp. 9–29;

Marco Sorteni, "Nella camera da letto di un poeta," *Domenica del Corriere* (3 March 1984): 45–51;

Mirella Serri, "Bertolucci: Scrivo per restare quello di sempre," *Tuttolibri,* 16 (19 November 1988): 3.

References:

Alberto Bevilacqua, "Attilio Bertolucci," *Fiera Letteraria* (25 May 1958): 1;

Pietro Citati, "Viaggio d'inverno," in his *Il tè del cappellaio matto* (Milan: Mondadori, 1972), pp. 215–219;

Giuseppe De Robertis, "La capanna indiana," in his *Altro Novecento* (Florence: Le Monnier, 1962), pp. 418–483;

Ugo Dotti, "Per il ritratto di un poeta: Attilio Bertolucci," *Rassegna della Letteratura Italiana* (January–December 1979): 327–338;

Marco Forti, "Bertolucci: Elegia, memoria e esperimento," *Paragone,* no. 288 (February 1974): 90–99;

Franco Fortini, "Sandro Penna e Attilio Bertolucci," in his *I poeti del '900* (Rome & Bari: Laterza, 1977), pp. 93–97;

Renzo Frattarolo, "La capanna di Bertolucci," in his *Notizie per una letteratura* (Bergamo: San Marco, 1961), pp. 158–162;

Antonio Girardi, "Rilievi variantistici sul poema di Bertolucci," *Studi Novecenteschi,* 11 (December 1984): 295–319;

Antonio Iacopetta, *Attilio Bertolucci: Lo specchio e la perdita* (Rome: Bonacci, 1984);

Keala Jewell, "Epos and Fragment," in her *The Poiesis of History* (Ithaca: Cornell University Press, 1992), pp. 120–145;

Paolo Lagazzi, *Attilio Bertolucci* (Florence: Nuova Italia, 1982);

Mario Lavagetto, "Pratica pirica," *Nuovi Argomenti,* 23–24 (July–December 1971): 221–233;

Mario Luzi, "*La capanna indiana* di Bertolucci," *Paragone,* no. 20 (August 1951): 40–43;

Giuseppe Marchetti, "La pudica stagione: Per una lettura di *Fuochi in novembre* di Attilio Bertolucci," *Aurea Parma,* 62 (September 1982): 124–135;

Pier Vincenzo Mengaldo, "Attilio Bertolucci," in his *Poeti italiani del novecento* (Milan: Mondadori, 1978), pp. 567–572;

Pier Paolo Pasolini, "Bertolucci," in his *Passione e Ideologia (1948–1958)* (Milan: Garzanti, 1960), pp. 184–207;

Giovanni Raboni, "Dissanguamento e altre metafore nella poesia di Bertolucci," *Paragone,* no. 262 (December 1971): 119–124;

Vittorio Sereni, "Un poeta ha girato intorno al sole," *Milano-Sera,* 29–30 June 1951, p. 3;

Enzo Siciliano, "Ritmi feriali," in his *Autobiografia letteraria* (Milan: Garzanti, 1970), pp. 184–207.

Carlo Betocchi

(23 January 1899 – 25 May 1986)

Louis Kibler
Wayne State University

BOOKS: *Realtà vince il sogno* (Florence: Frontespizio, 1932);

Altre poesie (Florence: Vallecchi, 1939);

Notizie di prosa e poesia (Florence: Vallecchi, 1947);

Un ponte nella pianura (Milan: Schwarz, 1953);

Poesie, 1930–1954 (Florence: Vallecchi, 1955);

Mistici medievali, by Betocchi, Nicola Lisi, and Luigi Fallacara (Turin: Radio Italiana, 1956);

Il vetturale di Cosenza, ovvero viaggio meridionale (Lecce: Salentina di Pajano/Critone, 1959);

Cuore di primavera: Prose narrative e poesie (Padua: Rebellato, 1959);

L'estate di San Martino (Milan: Mondadori, 1961);

Sparsi pel monte (Cittadella Veneta: Rebellato, 1965);

Vino di Ciociaria (Rome: De Luca, 1965);

L'anno di Caporetto (Milan: Saggiatore, 1967);

Un passo, un altro passo (Milan: Mondadori, 1967);

2 poesie inedite di Carlo Betocchi; 13 disegni di Enzo Faraoni (Florence: Galleria Pananti, 1969);

Lo stravedere (Padua: Rebellato, 1970);

Prime e ultimissime 1930–1954, 1968–1973 (Milan: Mondadori, 1974);

Poesie scelte, edited by Carlo Bo (Milan: Mondadori/Gli Oscar, 1978);

Il segno e la morte (Florence: Galleria d'Arte Moderna "L'Indiano," 1980);

Poesie del sabato (Milan: Mondadori, 1980);

Il sale del canto (1934–1977) (Parma: Pilotta, 1980);

Del sempre (Padua: Pandolfo, 1982);

Memorie, racconti, poemetti in prosa (Florence: Pananti, 1983);

Tutte le poesie (Milan: Mondadori, 1984);

Confessioni minori (Florence: Sansoni, 1985);

Carlo Betocchi: Saggi (Florence: Lettere, 1990).

Edition in English: *Carlo Betocchi: Poems,* translated by I. L. Salomon (New York: Clarke & Way, 1964).

OTHER: André Lafon, *Mattutino,* translated by Betocchi (Milan: Grappolo, 1936);

Festa d'amore: Le più belle poesie d'amore di tutti i tempi e di tutti i paesi, edited by Betocchi (Florence: Vallecchi, 1952; revised, 1969);

Festa d'amore: Le più belle lettere d'amore di tutti i tempi e di tutti i paesi, edited by Betocchi (Florence: Vallecchi, 1954; revised, 1969);

Autobiographical statement, in *Ritratti su misura di scrittori italiani,* edited by Elio Filippo Accrocca (Venice: Sodalizio del Libro, 1960), pp. 71–73;

Carlo L. Golino, ed., *Contemporary Italian Poetry,* includes poems by Betocchi (Berkeley: University of California Press, 1962), pp. 88–91;

Contemporary Italian Verse, translated, with an introduction, by Ghan Singh (London: London Magazine, 1968), pp. 20–27;

Margherita Marchione, ed. and trans., *Twentieth-Century Italian Poetry: A Bilingual Anthology,* includes poems by Betocchi (Rutherford, N. J.: Fairleigh Dickinson University Press, 1974), pp. 42–49;

William Jay Smith and Dana Gioia, eds., *Poems from Italy,* includes poems by Betocchi (St. Paul: New Rivers, 1985), pp. 390–393.

A product of no literary school and without advanced academic training in literature, Carlo Betocchi constructed poetry founded on his reading of poets, his Christian faith, and his direct contact with the world of labor. His principal themes – God, nature, mother, family, his beloved Tuscany, and its inhabitants – may seem at first sight old fashioned and trite; Betocchi avoided banality, however, by filtering his perceptions through what critic Oreste Macrì has called a "grazia sensibile" (sensitive grace). Moreover these themes are reflected in Betocchi's poetic meditations and are the source of a continuing, albeit subdued, drama that unfolded and became more richly complex as his career grew. The result is a body of work that, though it has roots in the nineteenth century, is unmistakably modern.

Carlo Betocchi circa 1960

With Clemente Rèbora, Betocchi was one of the most highly regarded Christian poets in twentieth-century Italy. Yet his Catholicism is never dogmatic, never evangelical; instead it mirrors the conflict of a man who, without abandoning his faith, was imbued with so deep a love for earth that one suspects he adored the created more than the creator. His thirst for the concrete led him to inspect and admire all that surrounded him, to observe and to record, as in a diary, all that he met in his daily life. In his poetry the concreteness of nature is represented by the physical word, while ineffable mysteries reside in a metalanguage. Ultimately Betocchi's attitude toward the world around him was essentially spiritual, even mystic: the most intimate possession of the things of the world occurs through observation of and meditation on the objects, not through physical seizure — appreciation of the object for what it is, not for what one can make it become. In similar fashion, the most effective poetry is

not the shout but the whisper, a quiet and passive patience, the giving of oneself, not appropriation.

Although Carlo Betocchi was born in Turin on 23 January 1899, he is usually regarded (and he so regarded himself) as a Florentine. His family moved to Florence in 1906, and, except for periods when his work required him to live elsewhere, he spent most of his life there. His father, Alessandro, a railroad technician, died when Carlo was very young; his mother, Ernesta, a native Tuscan, reared him, his brother, and his sister under conditions of extreme poverty. Only the meager proceeds from the sale of a farm that the mother had inherited from a sister enabled the Betocchi children to receive a secondary-school education. Despite privations and the lack of a father, the Betocchi household was happy and harmonious; family life centered on Ernesta, whose pious and kind nature worked a profound influence on the young Carlo. In an autobiographical statement in Elio Filippo

Accrocca's *Ritratti su misura di scrittori italiani* (1960) Betocchi recalls his early years:

> La famiglia . . . viveva con parsimonia ma in una grande armonia: spirava da mia madre, in quella armonia, una religiosa intimità, profonda. . . . Studiammo bene, ma verso gli ultimi anni delle scuole secondarie, fra grandi strettezze e i miei rimedi, compreso il monte di pietà. Insisto sulla famiglia, perché credo che essa, penetrando tutti i miei sentimenti con il suo amore e con la sua unità, e infliggendomi i dolori delle sue disgrazie sia stato il miglior fondamento della mia capacità di comprendere e della mia capacità di abnegazione.

> (My family . . . lived frugally but in a great harmony inspired by my mother's deep religious feelings. . . . We studied hard, but toward the last years of secondary school we encountered difficult times with customary remedies, including the pawn shop. I emphasize my family, because I believe that, by instilling in me its love and unity and by inflicting on me the sorrows of its misfortunes, it was the basis of my capacity for understanding and for self-abnegation.)

While still a teenager Betocchi married Emilia de Palma on 27 November 1913; they later had two children.

Betocchi graduated in 1915 from the Istituto Tecnico Galilei with a diploma as a surveyor. In 1917 he was drafted into the army, served as an officer, and took part in the last battles of World War I. An account of his wartime experiences was published in 1931 in the journal *Frontespizio* (Frontispiece) and collected in his *Cuore di primavera* (Heart of Spring, 1959) and *L'anno di Caporetto* (The Year at Caporetto, 1967). Betocchi volunteered in December 1918 to go to Cyrenaica in Libya, where he remained until he left the army in April 1920. Upon his return to Italy he began his long career in the construction industry, traveling in France and in northern and central Italy to build or rebuild roads, bridges, dikes, and canals. It was heavy work, but the camaraderie among his fellow workers, the experience of working firsthand with earth and with concrete objects, and the rigors of weather and living conditions satisfied Betocchi's need for a simple, hardworking life. In his 1960 statement for Accrocca's book he described the value that his work held for him:

> Trent'anni della mia vita, da subito dopo la guerra, se ne sono andati vagando un po' per tutto, in Italia e fuori, con le imprese di costruzioni: stare con le imprese significava conoscere il lavoro nella sua concretezza, meritarsi davvero il pane. . . . Ho amato il mio lavoro. . . . Ho sanato gran parte della mia morbosità vicino alla semplice, inimitabile saggezza, al coraggio dei minatori . . .

> degli sterratori . . . : ho goduto le allegre giornate di aperta campagna con gli innocenti canneggiatori. Questo, con gli affetti familiari, fa parte della mia poesia: il lavoro è stato il mio bagno nell'innocenza, una difesa che s'è gagliardamente battuta con i miei vizi.

> (Thirty years of my life, from right after the war, were spent wandering almost everywhere, in Italy and abroad, following construction work: to be involved in construction meant knowing work in its concreteness, really earning your bread. . . . I loved my work. . . . I cured a large part of my morbidity in the presence of the simple, courageous, inimitable wisdom of . . . miners, of diggers . . . : I enjoyed happy days in the field with innocent surveyor's assistants. This, along with my feelings for my family, is part of my poetry: work was my bath of innocence, a defense that has valiantly done battle with my vices.)

Betocchi's interests were not limited, however, to the work that earned him a living. The young surveyor preferred reading the literature of the Italian Middle Ages and Renaissance, but he was also well acquainted with poets of later times and other places: Alessandro Manzoni and Giacomo Leopardi, François Villon and Arthur Rimbaud, John Keats and Percy Bysshe Shelley. Betocchi had begun writing in secondary school, and in 1923 one of his former schoolmates, Piero Bargellini, invited Betocchi to join him and Nicola Lisi in the founding of a small review, the *Calendario dei Pensieri e delle Pratiche Solari* (Almanac of Thoughts and Solar Practices), which sided informally with the proponents of the philosophy called *strapaese*. (During the early years of the 1920s, there were two major cultural currents in Italy, both of them a reaction against the middle-class liberalism of the nineteenth century. *Strapaese* proclaimed the traditional values and common sense of the people, and it advocated an unquestioning adherence to Catholicism and to the simple rural life. It was not, however, simply a new aspect of regionalism: the advocates of *strapaese* maintained that its values were universal and not limited to any single region nor even to Italy itself. Its opposite was *stracittà*. Whereas *strapaese* rejected modern industrial progress, contemporary art, and aestheticism, *stracittà* embraced all of these and exalted the ideas of risk and adventure.)

The *Calendario* ceased publication after a year, but it afforded Betocchi the opportunity to enter into an active literary career; his next journalistic endeavor broadened his experience and brought him prominence. In May 1929 Bargellini, Betocchi, and Lisi founded the *Frontespizio,* which, after modest beginnings as a bibliographic bulletin of the Libreria Fiorentina, became one of the leading Italian cultural and literary reviews until its demise in 1940. The *Frontespizio* did not have a specific program; its only tenet was its strong adherence to Catholicism, which was understood as a total experience that influenced every aspect of cultural and political life. Under such a broad banner it welcomed a variety of interests and literary styles, treated moral as well as artistic questions, and in general reflected better than any other journal the intense moral and cultural life of Florence during the 1930s, both its good aspects and its bad ones. The founding date of the review occurred in the year in which Benito Mussolini signed the concordat with the Catholic church, an event that would affect profoundly both Italy and the *Frontespizio*. In response to the ever closer relations between the church and fascism, the character of the journal changed; eventually, in 1938, Bargellini was replaced as editor, and the *Frontespizio* became little more than an organ of Fascist conformism. The review also evolved in other ways. From its beginning Bargellini and Giovanni Papini had represented literarily conservative interests; more-liberal tendencies, which came to be known as hermeticism, were espoused by Carlo Bo and later by his young followers, among whom were Macrì, Mario Luzi, and Alessandro Parronchi. Bo and his hermetic poets eventually left the *Frontespizio* in the late 1930s, as did Betocchi, who, while less radical than Bo and his group, was nonetheless closer to them poetically than he was to the conservative wing.

Betocchi matured artistically during his years with the *Frontespizio,* which published in 1932 his first collection of poems, *Realtà vince il sogno* (Reality Conquers the Dream). Of greater importance, however, was the experience that Betocchi gained in reading and criticizing the work of contributors, editing it, and writing essays and book reviews. Moreover the intense intellectual ferment that surrounded and characterized the journal permitted the young poet to know and to exchange ideas with some of the leading literary figures of the time. When Betocchi began his affiliation with the journal, it might be said that he did so as a Catholic who wrote verse; when he left it, he was a poet whose firm faith was tempered by a broadened outlook on life and art and by intellectual maturity.

In 1938 Betocchi received a chair in literature at Florence's Conservatorio Cherubini. His second book of verse, *Altre poesie* (Other Poems), was published the following year. He spent the early 1940s in Bologna, after which he returned to construction work in 1945. He was living in Rome when his *Notizie di prosa e poesia* (Notices of Prose and Poetry)

was published in 1947. Five years later he left his surveying job because of ill health. Returning to Florence, Betocchi resumed his teaching career, from which he retired in 1969. Earlier, in 1961, he had assumed the editorship of a review, *L'Approdo Letterario* (The Literary Landing), and held the post until the review ceased publication in 1977. Betocchi's book of collected poems, published under the title *Poesie, 1930–1954,* received the prestigious Viareggio Prize in 1955, the year of its publication. In later years Betocchi was awarded the Montefeltro and Dante Alighieri prizes (both in 1961), the Feltrinelli Prize (1967), and the Elba Prize (1968). Among the most admired poetic works of Betocchi are *L'estate di San Martino* (Indian Summer, 1961), *Un passo, un altro passo* (One Step, Then Another, 1967), *Prime e ultimissime 1930–1954, 1968–1973* (First and Latest, 1974), and *Poesie del sabato* (Sabbath Poems, 1980); his complete collected poetry, including dispersed and unpublished poems, appears in *Tutte le poesie* (All the Poetry, 1984).

The life of Betocchi, however, can be only partially represented by dates, activities, and lists of works. It is equally important to take into consideration the effect that he had on his colleagues and fellow poets. In *Maestri ed amici* (Masters and Friends, 1969) Leone Piccioni writes of his first meeting with Betocchi: "avevo l'impressione di un uomo duro, tagliato nel legno o nella roccia (com'è, del resto, il suo volto teso e scavato). . . . Ero molto intimidito: che impressione trovare . . . la sua schietta cordialità, la sua disponibilità di simpatia, come uno di famiglia, alla prima!" (I had the image of a hard man, carved from wood or stone [as is indeed his taut, meager face]. . . . I was very intimidated: what a surprise to meet right from the start with . . . his sincere cordiality, his ready understanding, as though I were a member of the family!)

Realtà vince il sogno had revealed to the Italian reading public a new and important poet; it had also indicated what kind of poet Betocchi was to be, for it includes many examples of the influence of his literary predecessors, of his themes, and of the qualities that would remain relatively constant throughout his work. More so than in his later works, Betocchi's debt to nineteenth-century writers is much in evidence. His poetic vocabulary is sprinkled with traditional forms that, among most of his contemporaries, were already regarded as archaic.

The religious themes recall the great Italian novelist and poet Manzoni, but Manzoni's sometimes doctrinaire fascination with and exaltation of a redeeming Christ are absent. Betocchi's God is not the Redeemer but the Creator, whose work is mirrored in both nature and in the soul of the poet. Manzoni's glorification of the mysteries of Catholicism gives way in Betocchi to a more personal and even mystical fusion of the poet's soul with the deity, as is evident in Betocchi's poem "Vetri" (Windowpanes):

> Sei vetri della finestra
> nell'angolo della stanza
> sono la strada maestra
> d'ogni nuvola che avanza.
>
> Io, dal mio angolo pigro
> tendo insidiosi agguati,
> dai poveri tetti emigro
> verso quei correnti prati.
>
> (Six windowpanes
> in the corner of the room
> are the highway
> for every cloud that passes.
>
> From my indolent corner
> I insidiously lie in wait;
> from the poor roofs I wander
> toward those flowing meadows.)

Echoes of Leopardi's poems are heard throughout *Realtà* in the themes of solitude and an animate nature as well as in the language. There are differences, of course: Betocchi's loneliness is only partial, for he is accompanied by his faith; his heaven and all of nature, unlike Leopardi's, exhibit God's compassion. Betocchi also resembles the nineteenth-century poet when he portrays the plain folk of the Tuscan countryside in such works as "Allegrezze dei poveri a Tegoleto" (The Joys of the Poor People of Tegoleto), "L'ultimo carro" (The Last Cart), "La sera di fiera" (The Night of the Fair), and "Piazza dei fanciulli la sera" (The Children's Square at Evening). In these simple poems Betocchi captures not only the activities but also the attitudes of peasants and simple folk – their love for the village, their joys, and their griefs.

Betocchi often mentioned the influence that Rimbaud and the early-twentieth-century poet Dino Campana exercised over his first (though not so much his later) poems, yet comparisons can be misleading: there is not in Betocchi any of the violence of these two rebels. His debt to them is limited to their capacity for imaginative, evocative, and visionary images, which appear in Betocchi's poems such as "Io un'alba guardai il cielo" (One Dawn I Looked at the Sky), "Quando al tempo, ecc." (When in the Days, etc.), and "Il dormente" (The Sleeper). A deeper affinity may be found between Betocchi and Paul Verlaine. Both frequently achieve their effects by a combination of metrical patterns and the sonorous qualities of the words they choose. In some of the best works of these two poets, there is a subdued melancholy, a mild impressionism that does not so much express a state of mind as it suggests such a state; both are masters at establishing an atmosphere. Of equal importance is the sense of simple joy that emanates from some of Verlaine's works and from many of Betocchi's, such as "Musici, giocolieri, bambini, gioia" (Musicians, Jugglers, Children, Happiness), "Alla danza, alla luce, ode" (To Dancing, to Light, Ode), and "Canto per l'alba imminente" (Song for the Approaching Dawn). The word *allegrezza* (joy) flows often from Betocchi's pen, and though there are moments of shade, light always seems to return to illuminate the poems of *Realtà*. Indeed if certain poets of early-twentieth-century Italy can be called crepuscular, one should then designate Betocchi as their opposite, for dawn (three of the thirty poems in *Realtà* have *alba* in their title) is the time of day cherished by him. His is not the flaming and dramatic sunset of romanticism nor yet the scorching, sterile, and arid midday of the poets Eugenio Montale and Leonardo Sinisgalli; Betocchi's songs are of muted melancholy, a guarded optimism, and a suggestion of impressionism. The Betocchi of this first collection is a late romantic in a minor key.

Although his versification is not radically different from that of his contemporaries, nor even from that of Giovanni Pascoli, there is nonetheless an originality in *Realtà* that is attributable not to a change in form but rather to the absence of any preconceived pattern. At first Betocchi's verses seem quite ordinary: he prefers the quatrain as a stanza, and the meters look as though they are regular. But scansion reveals that he does not adhere to a single metrical pattern. The choice is determined by the needs of the poem itself and not by a preconceived model. It is rare, however, to find stanzas in which long lines are mixed with short ones. Betocchi does not go to extremes; nevertheless, within the narrow range that he has chosen, there is a refreshing variety of tones and moods that the poetry, sculpted by the subtle and sensitive hands of an artist, is able to convey. His versifying techniques and the frequent prosaic cast of his verses give his poetry a disarming flavor of sincerity and even naiveté, yet study of the works reveals a poet of depth and substance.

With a few exceptions, all of Betocchi's verses published before 1961 are rhymed. Betocchi, perhaps more than any other Italian poet of the twentieth century, attributes to rhyme a function that borders on the sublime. In 1964 he wrote in "Diario della poesia e della rima" (Diary of Poetry and Rhyme), collected in *Tutte le poesie,* that "la rima è soprattutto un avamposto della poesia. . . . E' stata il primo grandissimo mezzo per connaturare alla poesia il dono d'una sublime oggettività. La rima è in questo senso tutt'altro che abbandono alla musicalità: è figura dell'oggettività che riflette le grandi e superbamente ordinate costruzioni metafisiche dell'intelletto d'amore" (rhyme is an outpost of poetry. . . . It was the first important means for integrating into poetry the gift of a sublime objectivity. In this sense rhyme is not mere musicality: it is an objective figure that reflects the grand and superbly ordered metaphysical constructions of the intellect of love).

Betocchi had a very fine ear for words; especially subtle is his handling of assonance, near rhyme, and the various sonorities that, interspersed with traditional rhyme, give his poetry a coloring that effectively blends the traditional with the new. Consider the exceptionally careful composition of the first two stanzas of "Quando al tempo, ecc.":

> Quando al tempo del malinconico
> autunno, lontana,
> spandeva un armonico
> canto la solitaria campana,
>
> volavano soffici e grigi
> i nordici uccelli,
> calando sui pigri
> stagni in sonnolenti anelli.
>
> (When in the days of melancholy
> autumn, from afar,
> the lonely bell
> gave forth a harmonious song,
>
> soft and gray
> the northern birds were flying,
> drifting down to lazy
> ponds in sleepy circles.)

Despite its outward simplicity, Betocchi's work evades facile summation. There are few ideas in his work; it is composed of sentiments and perceptions that, when paraphrased by the critics, often seem generalized and pedestrian. On the other hand, his work progresses by means of images and visions — seized during a particular moment — that then disappear or become transformed into other images. Contradictions and reversals are common, as in the first stanza of "Il dormente":

> Io mi destai con un profondo
> ricordo del mio sonno.
> Dalla mia veglia guardavo
> il mio corpo dormente;
> era giorno, era un chiaro
> giorno silente.
>
> (I awoke with a deep
> memory of my sleep.
> From my wakefulness I watched
> my sleeping body;
> it was day, a clear
> silent day.)

The phenomenon of being awake and sleeping at the same time recurs in Betocchi's poetry, indicative of a consciousness that is self-reflective, which, one might say, is the central perspective in both his earlier and his later poems. Betocchi is neither a philosopher nor a rationalist who analyzes and establishes a system in order to compare past and present with the hope of determining a future. On the contrary, he is a contemplator who, detached from the objects of his contemplation like a person awake gazing at himself sleeping, is capable of seeing only what is before him in the present and who fixes on it all his attention and savors its continuous evolution. There is substantial mysticism in Betocchi's attitude; his experience is almost — though never completely — a mystic transcendence. Rather it is the product of a fertile imagination that, while knowing no bounds, is constantly restrained by faith in God and love for the concrete world.

Betocchi's next collection of poetry, *Altre poesie,* is stylistically bolder than his first. Enjambments are frequent, and he makes wider use of a prose rhythm that, unfortunately, is often rendered awkward by the insistent presence of rhyme. However, certain poems are distinguished by their complex system of sonorities and their rich internal rhyme, as in the second stanza of "Pastorale":

> dove già inalba
> come scialba lanterna
> l'inverno, il pecoraro
> col flauto amaro sverna
> mandrie dal passo avaro.
>
> (where winter's
> wan lantern is
> already dawning, the shepherd
> with bitter flute
> winters his slow-footed flock.)

The poems continue many of the themes of *Realtà.* There are several Tuscan poems, among which the songs of women of the people — "Canto d'una vendemmiatrice" (Grapepicker's Song) and "Canto d'una rammendatrice" (Song of the Darner), for example – are especially well done. Religion is also present in *Altre poesie.* "La Pasqua dei poveri" (The Easter of the Poor) is almost Franciscan in its simple sincerity, and, like *Realtà,* this volume closes with a prayer. The harmony and unity of all, a major theme in Betocchi's work, is emphasized: in "Del riposo serale" (Evening Rest) he says: "Una e comune è la materia / delle cose" (The stuff of things / is one and the same).

The most striking feature of *Altre poesie,* however, is the personal tone. The pronoun *tu* (you), rare in his earlier poems, is common in these, for many of them are addressed directly to people: "All'amata" (To My Beloved), "Alla moglie" (To My Wife), and "Alla sorella" (To My Sister). The last is a masterpiece of tenderness and yet disturbing in its almost Leopardian contrast of an idyllic youth and an uncertain future.

Notizie di prosa e poesia, published after World War II, includes Betocchi's most uncharacteristic works. Poetically it is his most experimental effort, and as Pietro Civitareale has noted in his monograph *Carlo Betocchi* (1977), it is the Betocchian work that is closest to hermeticism. The metrically varied verses and the beauty of the rhymes show Betocchi's mastery of versification. He takes great liberties with syntax, which, combined with sparse punctuation and extraordinarily fluid transitions, imparts a stream-of-consciousness tone to many of the pieces. There recurs in these poems an image that, in various guises, is a significant feature of Betocchi's poetry: the image of a line, initially straight, which during its progress slowly curves away. It is emblematic of the poet's attitude, of his gaze, which is so often fixed on the heavens and which penetrates empty space until, either having approached its physical limit or else humble before God, departs from its straightness and bows into a gentle curve.

The most memorable works of *Notizie* are those in which the speaker reflects on the absurdity and destruction of the recent war, as in the poems "Ricostruzioni" (Reconstruction), "Rovine 1945" (Ruins 1945), and "Lungo la Casilina, 1945" (Along the Casilina Way, 1945). There are no polemics, however, no recriminations or outrage against the blindness of the Fascists, the cruelty of the Nazis, or the indiscriminate destruction by the Allies. Betocchi's works are apolitical, even ahistorical. The mild irony that the poet directs to the forthcoming republic in the poem "1946" is typical of his attitude toward politics and history: he regards them as passing trivialities that, when compared with nature, God, or the human heart, have little enduring importance. Throughout his works Betocchi dreams of and pursues liberty, but not a political liberty: it is a liberty of the spirit, the freedom to pursue a spiritual quest unencumbered by politics, society, or history.

Poesie, 1930–1954 mostly consists of poems from his three previously published volumes, although the number and arrangement of the poems are not identical to those of their first publications. He added a section titled "Tetti toscani" (Tuscan Roofs), the twenty-two poems of which constituted Betocchi's highest achievement to date. His return to Florence in 1952 seems to have rekindled his love for the solid virtues of the Tuscan countryside, and he raised his voice again to sing of the simple values of home, family, and God. Unlike lesser poets, Betocchi makes trite subjects such as mother, religion, and one's children seem new, either because of the sincerity of his feelings, his admiration for a woman who has resisted and endured, or his recognition of an imperfect god. Above all he has matured artistically in *Poesie,* his mastery of verse is almost complete, and there are Montalian overtones that give his poetry a force that was often lacking in his earlier works. At times, as in "La casa" (The House), Betocchi's art is found in complex rhyme schemes; elsewhere it appears in the rapid, insistent, proselike verses of "Dialoghi di amanti" (Dialogues of Lovers) or in his sure use of assonance and near rhyme throughout the new section. Betocchi retained the most successful elements of the experiments of *Notizie* and melded them into a poetry that is unique to him.

Joy unites "Tetti toscani." Sometimes it is a joy that cries out to all; at other times it is subdued, mitigated by reverence for creation and creator. Yet always it is a joy that issues from the heart of the poet, the elated joy that he feels when, upon his return, he gazes upon the beloved roofs of Florence. Or it might be the more intense, serene joy found in the opening stanza of "Tetti," where strong rhymes and dense, staccato rhythm crackle sharply, then, in Betocchian fashion, soften into a deep appreciation of his home and the heavens above it:

Tetti toscani secchi
fulvi di vecchi
tegoli,
. . . . .
Ma i tetti non han vizi,
a' bei solstizi
d'estate; e l'anima viaggia,
che dai tetti s'irraggia,

pei cieli asciutti,
chiari per tutti.

(Dry Tuscan roofs
tawny with old
tiles,
. . . .
But the roofs have no vices,
in the beautiful solstices
of summer; and the soul wanders,
radiating out from the roofs,
    through dry skies,
    clear for everyone.)

Betocchi's passion transforms objects, and, seconded by his technical skill, it results in masterpieces.

Betocchi's poetry reached its apogee with the publication in 1961 of *L'estate di San Martino,* a volume of poems written between 1943 and 1961. The work reveals a more observant and meditative Betocchi. Although all of Betocchi's work has the air of a daily journal of his observations and reflections (numerous critics have spoken of his *diarismo*), this tendency is especially marked in *L'estate.* Published in 1959 as a separate book, the fourth section, "Il vetturale di Cosenza, ovvero viaggio meridionale" (The Coachman of Cosenza, a Trip to the South), is the record of a trip taken to southern Italy, and the final section is titled "Diarietto invecchiando" (The Little Diary of a Man Growing Old), which could characterize most of Betocchi's subsequent poetry.

Although objects and places are still present, their symbolic aspects are more evident. The roofs, for example, are no longer emblematic of domesticity and the native town; they have acquired a transcendental component, have fused with other parts of nature and with spirituality. In "Dai tetti" the familiar roofs become a sea that speaks directly to the poet:

E' un mare fermo, rosso,
un mare cotto, in un'increspatura
di tegole. E' un mare di pensieri.
. . . .
. . . sento
che mi parla. . . .

(It is a still, red sea,
a baked sea, in a frill
of tiles. It is a sea of thoughts.
. . . .
. . . I feel
that it speaks to me. . . .)

The unbridled joy of Betocchi's earlier volumes has been replaced by an intensified introspection and a greater sense of wonder at the complexity of life and of the intricate and essential relations among him, others, nature, and God. There is a new tenderness and a compassion, even for animals, which, though not absent from earlier works, is more evident in *L'estate.* His friends enjoy a larger role in his poetry because of their presence and their deaths. The speaker seems haunted, even obsessed with the passing of time, aging, and the prospect of death. "Il tempo ci rapisce" (time steals us away), Betocchi writes in "Diarietto invecchiando"; and in "Canto dell'erba secca" (Song of Dry Grass), a prose piece that summarizes the tonal quality of *L'estate,* he states: "Si vede la terra, e la morte della terra; e la dolcezza siderale della morte della terra. Ma siamo ancora steli, anche se duri e irrigiditi. Tra stelo e stelo l'urto dà un piccolo suono chioccio, e il sibilo appena sensibile del venticello che li carezza, fraziona gli spazi fra le note, prende in considerazione e i quarti e i quinti e forse i decimi dei toni e semitoni. Ma il mio libro non registrerà che l'effetto sinfonico" (We see the earth, and the death of the earth; and the sidereal sweetness of the death of the earth. But we are still stalks, even though dried out and hard. And the rustling of the stalks gives off a husky sound, and the faintly audible sighing of the breeze caressing them fractures the spaces between the notes, breaks them into the fourths and the fifths and perhaps even the tenths of the tones and the semitones. But my book will register only the symphonic effect).

More so than in earlier collections, auditory images are prominent. In "Alla Chiesa di Frosinone" (In the Frosinone Church) the church clock chimes out each quarter hour, and the speaker says:

            . . . sembra
che siamo soli noi due, io e il tempo.
E sembra non ci sia carità; che il mondo
sia un'arida clessidra, e noi come sabbia
che, dentro, vi scivoliamo.

            (. . . it seems
that we two are alone, just me and time.
And it seems that there is no love; that the world
is a sterile hourglass, and we are like the sand,
inside, trickling down.)

Along with anguish, patience is one of the two dominating qualities of *L'estate* and the rest of Betocchi's work. In 1976 critic Silvio Ramat admitted that he was tempted to title the second stage of

Betocchi's work (his post-1961 publications) "Il dèmone e la pazienza" (The Demon and Patience). The first section of *L'estate,* dedicated to Bo, is called "Pazienza." "Bevvi pazienza" (I drank patience), the speaker declares in "Diarietto III," and the beneficial effects can be seen throughout the volume as an old man meditates, unhurriedly, at his own speed and in his own way, free of outside influences and literary fashions. At times Betocchi's patience takes on the characteristics of stoicism, as in "Diarietto II":

> Ma tutto sta nel precedere
> ciò che sarà, o nel lasciare
> che tutto ci preceda,
> senza mai trarre un lamento,
> nella fede duratura
> che verdeggia all'infinito.

> (Everything depends on what precedes
> what will be, or in letting
> everything precede us,
> without ever complaining,
> with the lasting faith
> that looms in infinity.)

At other times patience resembles spiritual passivity: instead of seeking God, the speaker often seems to be waiting for God to come to him, as he does in "Dai campi" (From the Fields). Although he is very conscious of his past and present sin, at times even obsessed by it, Betocchi does little in his poems to expiate or eradicate it. God in *L'estate* is more remote than in any of Betocchi's previous works. In reading *L'estate,* one has the impression that Betocchi's religion has lost most of its divine character and has been distilled into an intense sentiment of gratitude for existence itself. As for existence the speaker is incapable of explaining it, for his relation with it is neither intellectual nor rational. Rather he experiences toward it an instinctive attraction and an unquenchable love.

Although he confesses in "Il canto d'erba secca" that he feels besieged by death, the speaker's distress is neither total nor unrelenting. He finds comfort in prayer or in the memory of his mother. Although Betocchi may have felt physically old and often emotionally sad, his spirit nonetheless retained the lightness and hope of a youth, as when he writes in "Nel cortile di quand'ero ragazzo" (In the Courtyard When I Was a Boy), "Pesa il mio cuore: salta / la mia anima . . . " (My heart is heavy: my soul leaps up . . .); and in "Sosta laziale" (Stopover in Lazio): "Il cuore con un palpito più nero / dell'antracite ha la speranza azzurra" (My heart that beats blacker / than anthracite is filled with azure

hope). This contrast between the dark heaviness of the corporeal and his spiritual lightness is evocatively described in "Diarietto IX": "sento che in me ripullula un gorgoglio / come di fango fatto e di preghiera" (I feel within me a teeming gurgling / made of mud and prayer).

Contradictions abound in *L'estate;* Betocchi agonizes about his aging body and his youthful spirit, a past that seems empty and a future that is uncertain, and a god that is distant but omnipresent; yet these polarities are resolved, as they are throughout Betocchi's work, in a sentiment of harmony and unity in which diversity becomes one and unity diverse in a complex world of interacting feelings, beliefs, and visions.

Betocchi's next major collection of poems, *Un passo, un'altro passo,* continues, as is indicated by the title, the patient progress of *L'estate,* and, like its predecessor, it exhibits rhyme less frequently than his earlier works. Including poems written between 1950 and 1966 as well as many pieces published in *Sparsi pel monte* (Scattered about the Hillside, 1965), *Un passo* adds more physical aspect to the anguish of the speaker. The sections titled "Nel giardino di Susanna" (Susanna's Garden) and "Da più oscure latebre" (From Darker Hidden Places) chronicle the plight of an old man who has fallen in love. They present a touching and sensitive portrait of the pain that occurs when the emotions are young but the body is old. In the first of these sections Betocchi shows that he recognizes such love as foolish: "Non c'è cosa più sciocca / d'un vecchio innamorato" (There is nothing more foolish / than an old man in love). But he also observes that love "è delicato anche nei vecchi" (is delicate even among the old). The tension between spirit and body is almost Petrarchan, as when the speaker describes the inevitable losses wreaked upon him in the battle of love:

> Certo, questo corpo non perdona a nessuno;
> né lo spirito: in guerra aperta si battono;
> ed ora l'hanno vinta le passioni, ed ora
> le virtù. Ma, il più spesso, vittorie di Pirro.

> (Certainly, this body gives no quarter;
> nor does my spirit: they battle each other in all-out warfare;
> and sometimes passion wins, and sometimes
> virtue. But usually they are Pyrrhic victories.)

The poems of the latter half of the volume change brusquely in tone and subject: "Lettera d'autunno" (Autumn Letter) contains some of the most religious poems in all of Betocchi's work. His mother appears as a character in many of them, almost as though the thought of the saintly Ernesta can vanquish his passions and push aside earthly concerns.

Prime e ultimissime unites some of Betocchi's earliest poems with his more recent ones, the latter having been written between 1961 and 1973. Similar to *Prime e ultimissime, Poesie del sabato* comprises works dating from 1932 to 1979. Although many of the pieces from the final decade of Betocchi's poetic career present a reasoned consideration of everyday life in a prosaic and conversational tone, their overall tenor is more abstract than the works of *L'estate* and *Un passo:* Betocchi is preoccupied with the question of God. He attempts to reconcile the idea of a loving God with the suffering of the world; at times the speaker appears to be on the verge of renouncing God. Elsewhere he makes great efforts to convince himself of his faith and of God. If one can draw a conclusion (Betocchi has difficulty in doing so), it is that the existence of God, like the existence of everything, is an enigma. Ultimately, though fully cognizant of the absence of a definitive and concrete solution to this enigma, Betocchi falls back on his faith: he is unable not to believe in God. In the penultimate poem of *Prime e ultimissime* he writes:

Cosi mi ha fatto chi mi amò
fino a morire per me, libero
di non credergli, fino a dimenticarlo,
ma dimenticarlo era impossibile. . . .

(Thus he who loved me
enough to die for me gave me the freedom
not to believe in him, even to forget him,
but I could not forget him. . . .)

For Betocchi his faith is, like his view of existence, a *mistero necessario* (necessary mystery). Poetry was the mediator between him and God; it initially provided Betocchi a means for expressing gratitude and, later in his life, served as an instrument of reflection and of deliverance from the ordeal of living.

Interview:

Ferdinando Camon, *Il mestiere di poeta* (Milan: Lerici, 1965), pp. 67–75.

Letters:

Emerico Giachery, ed., *Incontro a Tursi: Lettere di Betocchi a Pierro, poesie, testi critici vari* (Rome & Bari: Laterza, 1973).

References:

Pietro Civitareale, *Carlo Betocchi* (Milan: Mursia, 1977);

Fiera Letteraria, special issue on Betocchi, 11 (17 June 1956);

Alberto Frattini, "Interpretazione di Betocchi," in his *Studi di poesia e di critica* (Milan: Marzorati, 1972), pp. 374–380;

Frattini, "Metamorfosi stilistica e coerenza d'anima nella poesia di Betocchi," *Humanitas,* 29 (December 1974): 919–922;

Massimo Grillandi, "Carlo Betocchi: Poesia e passione," *Letterature moderne,* 12 (March–June 1962): 191–198;

Oreste Macrì, "Della grazia sensibile," in his *Esemplari del sentimento poetico contemporaneo* (Florence: Vallecchi, 1941), pp. 53–76;

Cristiana Maggi Romano, "L'ultimissimo' Betocchi," *Paragone,* 26 (June 1975): 104–112;

Maria Serafina Mazza, *Not for Art's Sake: The Story of "Il Frontespizio"* (New York: King's Crown, 1948), pp. 73–81;

Pier Paolo Pasolini, *Descrizioni di descrizioni* (Turin: Einaudi, 1979), pp. 341–344;

Giorgio Petrocchi and Giannantonio Pompeo, *Letteratura, critica e società del Novecento* (Naples: Loffredo, 1974), pp. 655–662;

Leone Piccioni, *Maestri ed amici* (Milan: Rizzoli, 1969), pp. 20–21;

Gianni Pozzi, *Poesia italiana del Novecento da Gozzano agli ermetici* (Turin: Einaudi, 1967), pp. 343–354;

Giovanni Raboni, "Esempi non finiti della storia di una generazione," *Aut Aut,* 61–62 (January–March 1961): 73–92;

Silvio Ramat, *Storia della poesia italiana del Novecento* (Milan: Mursia, 1976), pp. 322–334, 648–655;

Luigina Stefani, ed., *Carlo Betocchi: Atti del convegno di studi* (Florence: Lettere, 1990);

Valerio Volpini, *Betocchi* (Florence: Nuova Italia, 1971);

Volpini, *Letteratura italiana: I Contemporanei,* 2 volumes (Milan: Marzorati, 1963), II: 1281–1295.

Mariella Bettarini

(31 January 1942 –   )

Elio Costa
York University

BOOKS: *Il pudore e l'effondersi* (Florence: Città di vita, 1966);

Il leccio (Florence: Centauri, 1968);

La rivoluzione copernicana (Rome: Trevi, 1970);

Terra di tutti e altre poesie (Caltanissetta & Rome: Sciascia, 1972);

Dal vero (Caltanissetta & Rome: Sciascia, 1974);

In bocca alla balena (Florence: Salvo Imprevisti, 1977);

Storie d'Ortensia (Rome: Donne, 1978);

Felice di essere: Scritti sulla condizione della donna e sulla sessualità (Rome: Gammalibri, 1978);

Diario fiorentino (Caltanissetta & Rome: Sciascia, 1979);

Ossessi oggetti/Spiritate materie (Siena: Barbablù, 1981);

Il viaggio/Il corpo (Turin: L'Arzanà, 1982);

La nostra gioventù (Caltanissetta: Sciascia, 1982);

Psicografia (Milan: Gammalibri, 1982);

Poesie vegetali (Siena: Barbablù, 1982);

Vegetali figure (Naples: Guida, 1983);

I Guerrieri di Riace di Mario Grasso (Caltanissetta: Sciascia, 1984);

Tre lustri ed oltre: Antologia poetica 1963–1981 (Caltanissetta & Rome: Sciascia, 1986);

Amorosa persona (Florence: Salvo Imprevisti/Gazebo, 1989).

OTHER: Simone Weil, *Lettera a un religioso,* translated by Bettarini (Turin: Borla, 1970);

"Donne e poesia," in *Poesia femminista italiana,* edited by Laura di Nola (Rome: Savelli, 1978), pp. 17–23;

"Trittico per Pasolini," *Almanacco dell Specchio,* 8 (1979): 359–368;

Chi è il poeta?, edited, with an introduction, by Bettarini and Silvia Batisti (Milan: Gammalibri, 1980);

"Il gregge," in *Etrusca-mente* (Florence: Gazebo, 1984), pp. 11–17.

Mariella Bettarini (photograph by Gabriella Maleti)

Mariella Bettarini's literary output is characterized from the beginning by a constant focus on the autobiographical. Far from entailing an escape into the sentimental or a withdrawal from the real, her writings display attention to, and at times a high degree of involvement in, the objective conditions around her and the often turbulent events that have transformed Italian society in the past twenty-five years. The personal and psychological dimension of her writings and her strong advocacy of feminist issues have contributed to the impression of Bettarini as aggressively confrontational. Some critics have interpreted her uncompromising outspokenness as naive moralistic posturing. Others have labeled her a radical feminist, a classification she rejects. Bettarini has, in fact, consistently and successfully resisted attempts to define her work according to ideologies and movements (political or otherwise). This refusal has, in turn, led to a sense of isolation, compounded by what is perceived as antagonism and resentment on her part by both the literary/publishing establishment and the avant-garde. Some have relegated her to an important but provincial role, thus damning her with faint praise for her intense activity with *Salvo Imprevisti,* the small, independent literary journal she has edited and published since 1973, along with a series of poetic and prose monographs called "Gazebo." This situation has made it difficult for Bettarini to receive an adequate critical assessment or for her work to be published in the first place. Her uncompromising independence, both artistic and ideological, which she sees as moral and civil commitment, is an uncomfortable anomaly in the Italian literary and publishing environment, where allegiances to power structures are necessary for survival and success. To some extent Bettarini embodies the paradoxes, doubts, and inconsistencies of many Italian artists and intellectuals of the postwar period. An example of such thinkers is Pier Paolo Pasolini, in whose writings and life the Christian and Marxist matrices coexisted without being reconciled, except as utopian aspirations. Pasolini is, with Carlo Emilio Gadda, one of the two avowed masters to whom she has devoted considerable critical attention.

Mariella Bettarini was born in Florence on 31 January 1942. Her father, Luciano, was originally from Prato; her mother, Elda Zupo Bettarini, and her family were from Lombardy. Luciano Bettarini was a musician who played for the symphony orchestra of RAI, the government-owned radio network. In Florence, Mariella completed the five years of elementary school. In 1952 the family, which included her younger brother, moved to Turin to follow the requirements of her father's job. A year and a half later he received a new assignment by RAI, this time in Rome, where Mariella continued to attend school. Adolescence and youth were painful, even dramatic years, characterized by physical illness and psychological problems. Their cause is attributed by Bettarini to a conflict with her father, whose authoritarian presence has loomed since then in her personal life and her writings. The event that heightened this trauma and the breakup of the family was her father's relationship with

another woman. It continues to be, after all these years, an open wound and a source of tension and conflict, even after the divorce of her parents and her father's remarriage. Bettarini's sickly, oppressive adolescence was relieved only by intensive reading and, starting at the age of eighteen, by the writing of her first poems. The poems only worsened the tension with her father: his fear of losing his primacy as the artist in the family manifested itself in various ways, especially when it became apparent that the daughter was to achieve some measure of critical attention for her literary efforts. Her teacher's diploma, obtained in Rome in 1964, was followed by her first few part-time teaching assignments, frequently interrupted by sickness. In 1965 Bettarini and her mother moved back to Florence, where they still live together and where she teaches in an elementary school.

The first collection of Bettarini's poems to be published was *Il pudore e l'effondersi* (Modesty and Self-effusion, 1966). The booklet, with its twenty-eight compositions, reveals a poetic voice whose main characteristic is a youthful reverence for nature. The passage of the seasons, the coming of evening, and natural spaces are transformed into private, psychological experiences. The apparently ecstatic contemplation, which at times borders on the mystical if not the religious, shows Bettarini's debt to writers such as Mario Luzi, the Florentine hermetic poet whom Bettarini considers an important fatherly figure in her apprenticeship. Another telling influence, readily admitted, is that of Giacomo Leopardi, whose echoes are especially perceivable in the short poem "Settembre":

> Già tutta sa di distacco
> l'incombente sera, nella quale
> incantarsi vedo fanciulli
> presso sentieri cancellati
> di segrete cose fantasticando
> che la lontananza mi rende magiche
>
> (Now the looming evening
> suggests parting, in it
> I see children spellbound
> near erased paths
> daydreaming of secret things
> that distance makes magic in me)[.]

Her second collection of poetry, *Il leccio* (The Holm Oak, 1968), presents a notable shift in tone, evident in the presence of a tension barely perceivable in the earlier poems but now no longer contained. *Il leccio* also draws on nature, but the serenity and contemplative calm of the first collection are at least partly gone. At bottom there is confidence in one's inner strength, but there also appear the first signs of a pent-up rage and anger, the source of which is not yet definable. The language acquires a more agitated rhythm and tone. In "Il tempo della disobbedienza" (The Time of Disobedience), which concludes the collection, there emerges a clear indication of things to come. A revolt against the past can no longer be repressed, and momentous changes are about to take place:

> è il tempo
> della disobbedienza al tempo – ti dici –
> ma il fuoco represso brucia
> più forte, e questo è vero
> anche di te presa
> isolatamente, soffocata d'aria,
> detentrice di potere impotente, anche se è
> nella linea delle cose
> il rifiuto a parole d'ordine rivolte a noi
> nati negli anni Quaranta e
> Cinquanta.

> (is the time
> of disobedience to time – you say to yourself –
> but the repressed fire burns
> more strongly, and this is also
> true of you taken
> in isolation, suffocating with air,
> holder of impotent power, even if it is
> in the order of things
> to refuse passwords handed on to us
> for us born in the Forties
> and Fifties.)

The problematic refusal and rejection of a given order continues to be a theme in Bettarini's next collection, *La rivoluzione copernicana* (The Copernican Revolution, 1970). Rage surfaces explicitly in poems such as "I giorni dell'ira" (The Days of Anger) and in the title poem, in which personal liberation is seen as the historical transition from a Ptolemaic to a Copernican view of the universe and in biblical terms as the veil of the temple being rent to reveal a fundamental truth. The personal hardships, family traumas, and daily grind of teaching, which make life a constant struggle, are more than compensated for by the optimism with which she professes her belief in some hard-won truth:

> Anche ora – che il diciassette di aprile
> sta per andare nel mucchio e che la mia situazione
> si direbbe di debolezza –
> sento che le articolazioni malate
> e il manto della tigre su un corpo di pecora
> preludono a una libertà più grande,
> magari quella della verità strappata a morsi.

> (Even now – that the seventeenth of April
> is about to end up on the heap and that my situation
> could be considered weak –
> I feel that the sickly articulations
> and the tigress's skin on a sheep's body
> are the prelude to a greater freedom,
> perhaps that of the truth bitten off piece by piece.)

For Bettarini 1968 was a watershed year to which she refers repeatedly in her writings. Artists and intellectuals throughout Europe were hard-pressed not only to express opinions but to take new positions in the face of events such as the war in Vietnam, student protests and riots, the invasion of Czechoslovakia, and in Italy the beginning of political violence, which in a few years seemed to bring the old order to the brink of collapse. To Bettarini the late 1960s were marked by a critical re-examination of her Catholic background and by a rapid ideological radicalization. The first step was her involvement with a Catholic social-reform group called the Isolotto, from the name of the working-class neighborhood in which it operated. Headquartered in the parish church of Saint Thomas, the Isolotto gained national notoriety for its opposition to the conservative, authoritarian leadership of Florit, the archbishop of Florence.

In 1970 and 1971 Bettarini worked with *Testimonianze,* a Catholic intellectual journal still published in Florence. She soon came to realize, however, that such movements as the Isolotto, although motivated by praiseworthy Christian sentiments and carried on by well-meaning people, were not the solution for her, since they were either too naive in their assumptions or perpetuated, in a different guise, the old authoritarian structures and mentalities of the past – a feeling expressed in part in her poem "L'Isolotto è un triangolo" (The Isolotto Is a Triangle), from *La rivoluzione copernicana.* Her participation in Catholic social activism was a prelude to her definitive break with the Catholic church. Bettarini calls this phase in her life a "bagno nella realtà" (bath in reality), a relatively brief period of intense politicization, marked by the reading of Marxist texts, the works of Antonio Gramsci, and those of Sigmund Freud. This reading was accompanied by an equally intense series of encounters, discussions, and projects with other young artists and intellectuals in search of new answers. She emerged from this phase of her life with a new awareness of the link between politics and culture, and of feminist issues that were then surfacing. Florence was at the time a city in which various groups and individuals – outside the powerful traditional literary establishment and the neo-avant-garde, which seemed to deny the value of any content in literature – attempted to elaborate a new sense of artistic and literary relevancy. The journals in which the new ideas were debated and circulated were usually in mimeographed form, which was both a statement against the industrialization of culture and a money-saving device. Bettarini took active part in several of these groups and projects in the late 1960s and early 1970s, including the journals *Quartiere* and *Quasi.*

In 1973, along with a small group of friends, she founded her own journal, *Salvo Imprevisti.* Most of these journals did not last very long. As commitments lagged and financial resources waned, the people who worked on them went on to other things. *Salvo Imprevisti* itself was not expected to last even by the people who started it, as the title (meaning Barring the Unforeseen) whimsically implies. It has survived mainly through the efforts of Bettarini and her friends. The philosophy of the journal was summed up by her in the first issue: "Realmente non esistono per un poeta, per un rivoluzionario (ma non dovrebbero essere la stessa cosa?) per un filosofo, per un ricercatore di verità e di consapevolezza storica, due verità, due strade, ma una soltanto, e la conquista della libertà di parola e della libertà individuale (poesia, cultura) dovrebbe risultare contemporanea conquista di una coscienza collettiva, preoccupata per il bene di tutti (politica)" (In reality there do not exist for a poet, for a revolutionary [but should they not be one and the same?] for a philosopher, for a seeker of truth and historical consciousness, two truths, two roads, but only one, and the conquest of freedom of speech and individual freedom [poetry, culture] should in the end be contemporaneous conquest of a collective conscience, concerned with the welfare of all [politics]).

This radical concept of poetry – which seemed at the time to be the only apt response to those who considered the traditional concept of art no longer relevant in a world where the distinction between thought and action was soon to disappear – was modified in a 1978 issue of the journal: Bettarini had to admit that poetry was not, and could not be, a "strumento diretto, immediato, espressione di ire proletarie, retorica populista. . . . So che poesia è libera coscienza critica della realtà . . . luogo aperto all'incontro e allo scontro dialettico" (direct, immediate instrument, expression of proletarian angers, populist rhetoric. . . . I know that poetry is the free critical conscience of reality . . . the place available to dialectical encounter and conflict). The journal has evolved over the years but has consistently tried to articulate, according to

Bettarini, a sense of the civic role of poetry and literature. Each of its issues (it is published every four months) explores a specific theme, topic, or author.

Salvo Imprevisti is in some measure the response to important events taking place in Italian society and in the world, an effort to enter the wide-ranging debate Bettarini considers vital, and her poetry is not immune to the same stimuli and shocks. Her heightened awareness of the importance of politics, and of the relationship between it and poetry, shows in her work, particularly in *Terra di tutti e altre poesie* (Everybody's Earth and Other Poems, 1972), with the references, for example, in "Dal massacro" (From the Massacre) to the increasing terrorist violence that lasted to the end of the decade. In a later poem, "Spedizione '71" (Expedition '71), from *In bocca alla balena* (In the Mouth of the Whale, 1977), Bettarini describes the impact of these events on her life and the way they forced themselves into the private domain of her creativity. These violent and tragic events signaled a new and increasingly problematical phase in her life, which she refers to as a journey outside herself:

a mente riposata il mare ("fors'anche lo
mare della storia"), questo viaggio all'estero
di una persona avvezza
a viaggi all'interno-dentro

(with mind at ease the sea ["perhaps even the
sea of history"], this trip abroad
of a person used
to voyages within-inside)[.]

The pent-up anger and violence, which had been directed inward, would now be channeled toward other targets. In much of Bettarini's work the need to speak in the first person translates into an impassioned and cathartic invective against another person, the father, who also becomes the embodiment of all that is repressive and tyrannical, as in the poem "Paternale" in *Dal vero* (From Reality, 1974). Yet, beyond the invective, the great merit of this poetry is Bettarini's ability to transcend the personal and to project the violence onto an epic plane. Her style of language owes much to the lesson of Gadda, whom Bettarini explicitly acknowledges in the epigraph to *Dal vero.* In "Paternale," as in other poems in the collection, words and phrases are charged with a force that cannot, it seems, be contained by traditional grammatical forms of punctuation. Yet, paradoxically, traditional words and expressions are also used to expose not just the father as a product of his culture but the father *as* the culture:

proprio allora nacque
la mia rivolta il mio riscatto principiò allora
a realizzarsi contra te padre del nostro pane
nostri sonni nostri vestiti nostri corpi
e di due donne l'un contra l'altra armate

(exactly then was born
my revolt my emancipation began then
to take shape against you father of our bread
our slumbers our clothes our bodies
and of two women one against the other armed)[.]

Pasolini is another strong presence in Bettarini's poetry. Her great admiration for his courageous, often polemical pronouncements on the issues of the day and his provocative presence in Italian life and letters can be glimpsed in her writings. There is also evidence of Pasolini's influence in certain linguistic choices, such as the Tuscan flavor of some verses, for which Pasolini's early Friulian dialect poetry can be cited as precedent. To this can be added the recollection of rural roots, the memory of grandparents and old aunts, a sense of the sacredness of nature, and what poet and critic Roberto Roversi has called the "tensione oracolare" (oracular tension) of some of Bettarini's poetry.

In an introductory note to the 1984 collection *Etrusca-mente* (a play on words meaning both "Etruscan-ly" and "Etruscan-mind"), in which she published the poem "Il gregge" (The Flock), she mused on the reasons for her fascination for Etruscan culture and art: "fascino e mistero cui non è certo estraneo l'appello della storia, tanto più se antica; la passione inesauribile per le radici, il legame carnale e mentale insieme alla terra (ventre-amore-morte, provenienza e ferale/ferace ritorno là da dove si è misteriosamente giunti)" (the fascination and mystery that cannot be separated from the appeal of history, especially if it is ancient; the inexhaustible passion for roots, the simultaneously carnal and mental link to the land [womb-love-death, as source and feral/fertile return there from where we have mysteriously arrived]). The shocking and violent death of Pasolini in 1975 left a deep impression on Bettarini. The January 1976 *Salvo Imprevisti* was dedicated to him. In addition Bettarini wrote several critical pieces, as well as the poem "Trittico per Pasolini" (Triptych for Pasolini, 1979), in which she pays tribute to the murdered man. In this long piece, which starts from her contemplation of Pasolini's dead body, Bettarini slowly moves from a sense of physical pain to outrage and invective at a hypocritical society that breathes a sigh of relief at Pasolini's death while it fakes sorrow. The poem, in which some of his works are alluded to, is struc-tured in the form of an intimate monologue in which poetry and prose seem at first to coexist, as Bettarini gradually conflates the image of the corpse and that of Italy, which is seen as lifeless and cold:

Eri uno dei nostri tiepidi padri vestito da ragazzo? A ripensarti direi di sì. Sono rimasti qua zii astenici – limoni acidi – e servitori della menzogna: le comparse che beffeggiavi – parenti borghesi (asfittici) – teste coronate – i digiuni d'idee. Hai fatto il vuoto intorno. Ora hai un corpo da più di mille chilometri – che si ghiaccia.

(Were you one of our mild fathers dressed as a boy? In remembering you I tend to think so. We are left with asthenic uncles – bitter lemons – and servants of deceit: the stand-ins you derided – bourgeois relatives (washed out) – crowned heads – the empty-headed. You have created a void all around. Now you have a body a thousand kilometers long – which is freezing.)

The next phase of Bettarini's poetry is marked by what she called, in the introduction to *Diario fiorentino* (Florentine Diary, 1979), a return to the psychobiographical roots of ten or more years earlier and to the poetry of *Il leccio*. This development is not an involution; the poetry of *Diario fiorentino,* written in the space of two weeks, displays the sureness and confidence of a mature poet. At work in these poems is the magnetic pull of the past and the attempt to find answers in the present to questions that had gone unanswered before. *Diario fiorentino* is also, therefore, an evocative psychoanalytical reenactment of relationships and betrayed friendships. *Il viaggio/Il corpo* (The Voyage/The Body, 1982) continues this difficult process of constructing some semblance of reality from echoes of past events and encounters and from the moments of a daily existence that seems to unfold as if in a daydream or nightmare. The language of these poems projects a disconnected, fragmentary reality, and any meaning it acquires does not derive from a logical or grammatical order but from the free association between the various parts, unimpeded by any punctuation or pause. In the title poem a sea journey, an obvious metaphor for life, takes place among a chaotic series of dangers, which the mind can only feebly notice but never control, and it ends in a shipwreck:

. . . il mare
            luogo di scoperte
e di funghi
            corpo mangiato dalle
cose
      colate a picco

                    segno di un breve
regno come
sfondare porte aperte
fare un buco nell'acqua
puntare sul pensiero.

            (. . . the sea
                    place of discoveries
and mushrooms
                    body eaten by
things
            gone to the bottom
                        sign of a brief
kingdom like
breaking down open doors
making a hole in the water
aiming at thought.)

The 1970s saw the full emergence of the feminist movement as a political and cultural force. Bettarini soon became a prominent, articulate, and passionate voice in feminist politics, and she took an active part in debates and discussions. *Felice di essere* (Happy to Be, 1978) is the sum of her statements on feminist issues up to that point, although she continues to speak and write about them. The book is a collection of her articles, book reviews, papers given at artists' gatherings, and letters written to periodicals and newspapers. The topics are divided into two main headings: "Per una cultura delle donne" (For a Women's Culture) and "Sessualità e politica" (Sexuality and Politics). The pieces contained in the first part are typical of Bettarini in the way they integrate the social and cultural with the personal and autobiographical, as seen in her opening statement: "La mia esperienza femminista . . . si può facilmente far risalire agli anni di una non ancora troppo lontana adolescenza e al confronto-conflitto col padre, simbolo (oltreché persona) deputato all'insorgere di qualunque autentico e non destinato a perdersi principio di critica e dunque di rivolta" (My feminist experience . . . can easily be traced back to the period of my not yet distant adolescence and to the encounter-conflict with the father, symbol [as well as real person] chosen as object of any authentic and lasting principle of criticism and revolt). Personal experience is brought to bear on the perception of history, as Bettarini anticipates some of the main ideas she would elaborate in the following years. The first of these ideas is that feminism is a revolt against an authority embedded in culture at all levels: the economic, psychological, and sexual, as well as the religious and political. The feminist experience is not so much a process of liberation from men as it is a struggle for equal dignity and parity with the archetypal father, "the source of power."

Bettarini has argued that it is not possible to discuss literature or poetry without first pointing out the links between them and political reality with its institutions, including language. In the essay "Donne, poesia, linguaggio, sessualità" (Women, Poetry, Language, Sexuality) she says it is language that forms the bridge between sexuality and politics or between the pleasure principle (subconscious sexuality) and the reality principle (conscious thought and politics). In arguing for a true feminist creativity, Bettarini postulates, therefore, not only the development of essentially new themes, with the implicit rejection of traditional female roles, but also a new language.

With *Chi è il poeta?* (Who Is the Poet?, 1980), which she coedited with Silvia Batisti — at that time a collaborator and member of the editorial board of *Salvo Imprevisti* — Bettarini tried, as the title implies, to "identify" the poet and his or her role at that specific moment in history. The book is made up of the answers to three questions submitted by Bettarini and Batisti to about forty poets. The list includes the most representative names in Italian poetry, thirty-three of whom replied.

In *Poesie vegetali* (Vegetable Poems, 1982) and *Ossessi oggetti/Spiritate materie* (Obsessed Objects/Spirited Matters, 1981) the objects of Bettarini's poetry are two exhibitions of photographs by her friend, fellow poet, and coworker on *Salvo Imprevisti,* Gabriella Maleti. In *Poesie vegetali,* made up of ten brief poems, Bettarini's interest in and study of plants and flowers, which emerge clearly in many of her poems, is joined by a more philosophical, theoretical link between the word and the image. What particularly fascinates her is that the photographic image, while static, becomes dynamic when the same object is photographed from different angles and distances. The observation of this "movement" in the still images, in Bettarini's poems, becomes at times a linguistic/visual interplay of imaginative associations. In *Ossessi oggetti/Spiritate materie* the fascination for Bettarini, as well as for the reader, is with images from the house of another artist friend and with the almost magical effect the photographed objects have on the observer. The mind is free to linger on the mystery evoked by, for example, an old bottle of perfume:

chi sa (chi mai
saprà) lo contenuto
del contenitore (KIMBER, London)

dark di profumo o veleno
                 e la sorella
che lo guarda ergersi
dolciastro avvelenato
                 sugo
di morte o d'arte
                 tinta
 per tele o telamoni.

(who knows [who will ever
know] the content
of the container [KIMBER, London]
dark with perfume or poison
                 and its sister
who sees it rise
bittersweet poisoned
                 juice
of death or art
                 dye
for canvas or telamones.)

In 1978 Bettarini had published a short prose work, *Storie d'Ortensia* (Ortensia's Stories), in which she drew heavily from the life of a great-aunt who in the 1920s and 1930s had been a strong anti-Fascist. Published by a small, feminist-oriented press, the booklet did not receive wide distribution. It was therefore extensively revised, with the dialect parts rewritten in more accessible form, and published with Bettarini's next narrative work, *Psicografia* (Psychography, 1982), a strictly personal, autobiographical account of the conflict and final breakup with her father. In the book the dividing line between literature and life is removed, as Bettarini makes extensive use of pages from her diary to chronicle events and their impact on the psyche, making *Psicografia* a dark, foreboding work. It is nevertheless an important, perhaps invaluable, key to the understanding of Bettarini the person.

In 1986 a significant portion of Bettarini's poetic output was collected and published with the title *Tre lustri ed oltre* (Fifteen Years and Beyond), dedicated to the memory of the publisher Salvatore Sciascia, who had also published some of her earlier works and who had died a short time before. The book marks an important stage in Bettarini's poetic career and was an opportunity for her to measure the artistic distance traveled. It was an opportunity, too, to make more easily accessible poems published years before, which had received limited distribution. Bettarini also used the occasion to revise and rewrite some of her poems. In her dedication Bettarini remembers Sciascia as an "editore amico indimenticabile, / in un tempo drammaticamente avaro / di amici, di editori, / tanto più di editori-amici" (unforgettable friendly publisher, / at a time dramatically lacking / in friends, in publishers, / even more so in publisher-friends). This dedication speaks eloquently of the difficulties Bettarini has had over the years in having her works published. A case in point is her latest prose work, *Amorosa persona* (Amorous Person, 1989). As she explains in the preface, the novel, if such a complex work can be called a novel, was completed six years earlier. In that long period, and even with the help of Luigi Baldacci, the noted critic whose 1984 letter to Bettarini serves as the introduction, no publisher accepted it for publication. Finally Bettarini had it printed in the Gazebo series, published by *Salvo Imprevisti*. With this last work, more ambitious in scope than any of her previous narratives, Bettarini once again makes no concessions to literary fashions or to commercial considerations, reasons given by the more honest editors for not publishing it. The book is a succession of diary entries, letters, poems, dreams, quotations, and recollections that serve to delineate events in the life of the protagonist, Romilda. Once again, as in virtually all of Bettarini's works, at the center of *Amorosa persona*, amid the crises and traumas and the hopelessness of love, is the stoic, unavoidable acceptance of life.

Interviews:

Alberto Frattini and Mario Gabriele Giordano, eds., "Inchiesta sulla poesia italiana in prospettiva Duemila," special issue of *Riscontri,* 9, nos. 1–2 (1987);

Angelo Gaccione, ed., *Le crisi della ragione e le ragioni della crisi: Gli anni '80 fra caduta della razionalità e incubo nucleare* (Milan: Nuove Scritture, 1987), pp. 47–49.

References:

Silvana Folliero, "Fatale gestazione delle cose nella poesia di Mariella Bettarini," *Idea,* 43 (December 1987): 30–34;

Maria Grazia Lenisa, "L'impegno di Antigone contro la disumanità dell'ordine," *Arenaria,* 8–9 (December 1987): 115–118;

Roberto Roversi, "La verità di Cassandra," *Almanacco dello Specchio,* 8 (1979): 352–357;

Giuseppe Zagarrio, *Febbre, furore e fiele* (Milan: Mursia, 1983), pp. 260–266;

Zagarrio, *Poesia fra editoria e anti* (Trapani: Celebes, 1971), pp. 123–129.

Piero Bigongiari

(15 October 1914 –)

Adapted from an original essay by
Giancarlo Quiriconi
University of Florence

BOOKS: *L'elaborazione della lirica leopardiana* (Florence: Le Monnier, 1937);
La figlia di Babilonia (Florence: Parenti, 1942);
Studi (Florence: Vallecchi, 1946);
Il senso della lirica italiana e altri studi (Florence: Sansoni, 1952);
Rogo (Milan: Meridiana, 1952);
Testimone in Grecia, by Bigongiari and G. B. Angioletti (Turin: ERI, 1954);
Il corvo bianco (Milan: Meridiana, 1955);
Testimone in Egitto, by Bigongiari and Angioletti (Florence: Fiorino, 1958);
Le mura di Pistoia (Milan: Mondadori, 1958);
Poesia italiana del Novecento (Milan: Fabbri, 1960; enlarged edition, Florence: Vallecchi, 1965; enlarged again, 2 volumes, Milan: Saggiatore, 1978, 1980);
Il caso e il caos (Lecce: Critone, 1961);
Leopardi (Florence: Vallecchi, 1962);
Torre di Arnolfo (Milan: Mondadori, 1964);
Stato di cose (Milan: Mondadori/Lo Specchio, 1968);
Poesia francese del Novecento (Florence: Vallecchi, 1968);
Capitoli di una storia della poesia italiana (Florence: Le Monnier, 1968);
Prosa per il Novecento (Florence: Nuova Italia, 1970);
Antimateria (Milan: Mondadori, 1971);
La poesia come funzione simbolica del linguaggio (Milan: Rizzoli, 1972);
Il Seicento fiorentino: Tra Galileo e il Recitar cantando (Milan: Rizzoli, 1975; revised edition, Florence: Sansoni, 1982);
Moses (Milan: Mondadori/Lo Specchio, 1979);
Dal barocco all'informale (Bologna: Cappelli, 1980);
Poesie, edited by Silvio Ramat (Milan: Mondadori, 1982);
Autoritratto poetico (Florence: Sansoni, 1985);
Visibile, invisibile (Florence: Sansoni, 1985);
L'evento immobile (Milan: Jaca, 1986);
Col dito in terra (Milan: Mondadori, 1986);
Diario americano (Treviso: Amadeus, 1987);
Nel delta del poema (Milan: Mondadori, 1989).

Piero Bigongiari circa 1960

OTHER: Autobiographical statement, in *Ritratti su misura,* edited by Elio Filippo Accrocca (Venice: Sodalizio del Libro, 1960), pp. 78–79;
Il vento d'ottobre: da Alcmane a Dylan Thomas, translated by Bigongiari (Milan: Mondadori, 1961);
Gli inni, edited by Bigongiari (Florence: Sedicesimo, 1986);
Alessandro Gentili and Catherine O'Brien, eds., *The Green Flame: Contemporary Italian Poetry,* includes poems by Bigongiari (Dublin: Irish Academic Press, 1987), pp. 164–172.

SELECTED PERIODICAL PUBLICATIONS –
UNCOLLECTED: "Autoritratto poetico," *Paragone,* 9 (June 1959): 43–50;

"La donna miriade (romanzo mancato)," *Forum Italicum*, 2–3 (June–September 1975): 264–278.

Piero Bigongiari's long career in Italian poetry and literary criticism has been characterized by a strong commitment to innovation. It has also been marked by continuous theoretical reflection and awareness of developments within literary culture. These factors have prompted the Tuscan writer to make of his own creative activity the testing ground for extensive intellectual experimentation. Through such a dense dialectic between the theoretical and the creative process, Bigongiari has sought to bring into the heart of his work some linguistic notions derived from poststructuralism – notions capable of producing a poetic spark. He has been especially influenced by concepts generated by the intersection of linguistics and psychoanalysis, as in the ideas of Jacques Lacan and Jacques Derrida. This same inclination has brought Bigongiari into contact with the ideas and direction of the new science, as expounded by Ernst Toller and Ilya Prigogine. As a result the semantic nuclei and, indeed, the entire linguistic universe created by Bigongiari's poetry are isomorphic. Like subatomic particles, minimal phonetic units, which are active in language while activating it, generate linguistic structures that are unstable because they are forever changing and evolving.

Born in Navacchio (just a few kilometers from Pisa on the Arno River) on 15 October 1914, Bigongiari belongs to that illustrious and almost legendary *terza generazione* (third generation) of hermeticists, which also includes Carlo Bo, Mario Luzi, Vittorio Sereni, and Oreste Macrì. Between the mid 1930s and the end of World War II, these men produced one of the most important poetic and cultural movements of twentieth-century Italy: new hermeticism. Not only did it initiate a break with the past, including recent literary history, it also proved to be an extraordinary force that had a profound impact on developments in succeeding decades.

The first years of Bigongiari's life were characterized by frequent changes of residence, taking place mostly along the Arno (Pescia, Pistoia, Florence, with a brief stay in Grosseto). This period is of interest not so much for those who are curious about the man's life but for the fact that it served as a spiritual substratum to which Bigongiari's poetry was to adhere, because it provided the images, symbols, places, and situations that are archetypes of an existential condition, as opposed to a purely personal one.

In 1932 Bigongiari enrolled to study the humanities at the University of Florence and graduated in 1936; his thesis was *L'elaborazione della lirica leopardiana* (The Genesis of [Giacomo] Leopardi's Poetry), published one year later. Bigongiari's interest in the poet of Recanati was not merely academic, since Leopardi's work affected deeply Bigongiari's own verse – so much so that this interest persisted for the duration of Bigongiari's career. In the meantime the city of Florence lodged itself in his imagination as the end of an ideal journey from the place of birth to a privileged destination. In parallel fashion his arrival there after an exhausting odyssey coincided with the discovery of his own identity. In a self-portrait in Silvio Ramat's *Invito alla lettura di Bigongiari* (Invitation to the Reading of Bigongiari, 1979) he wrote, "L'eterno Arno sulle cui rive l'autore tuttora vive a Firenze, quasi *speculum* archetipico della propria foce origine" (The eternal Arno, on whose shores the author currently resides, in Florence, is almost an archetypal *image* of his own origins).

His poetic odyssey could not be fully understood if one did not take into account the formative years spent between Pistoia and Florence. The climate then was determined, on the one hand, by the increasingly monolithic presence of Fascism and the imminent outbreak of war – which gave rise to enormous tensions. On the other hand, perhaps as a response to historical events, the atmosphere contained the seeds of a vibrant revitalization of culture. Florence was a city that expressed, to the highest degree possible, the fusion of such opposing thrusts, a fusion promoted by the imposing presence of Eugenio Montale. In such a climate of resistance to the ethical and cultural impositions of the Fascist regime and of heightened awareness with respect to innovative trends in European culture, the *terza generazione* took shape. As it grew, the group developed the need to go beyond the limits of a static condition from which the masters (Montale, Giuseppe Ungaretti, and Salvatore Quasimodo) seemed unable to break free. As Bigongiari says in *Autoritratto poetico* (Poetic Self-Portrait, 1985), "Fu l'epoca dei prigionieri in patria. E fu in questo straordinario ma drammatico silenzio che nacque la parola della terza generazione, quando aperta a una sorta di intenerimento interiore, quando orogliosamente chiusa a una civiltà esterna ch'essa rifiutava in blocco" (It was a time of prisoners in their own homeland. It was also in this extraordinary but dramatic silence that the word of the "third generation" was born, when the word opened itself up to a sort of intimacy, and at the same time closed itself off from an external civilization that it rejected wholesale).

"Letteratura come vita" (Literature as Life), the essay that Bo published in 1938 in the journal *Frontespizio,* constitutes more than a manifesto of objectives. It is a generation's index of self-awareness and indicates the moods and aspirations of a group of young men who determinedly stressed the need for a spiritual liberation, to be realized in art as well as in life. They urgently wanted to remove literature from the sterile academic environment into which it had been forced and to make it responsive to the most vital aspects of spirituality – in clear opposition to the numbing of social and cultural life at the hands of the Fascist government. In this sense the centrality of poetic discourse was restored because, in its infinite workings, poetry came to be seen as the only instrument that could enable the human spirit to realize its full potential.

A common point of departure and a common faith in the liberating potential of poetry did not cause a homogenizing of theoretical positions or of individual inclinations among the members of the third generation. Hermeticism was not a monolith but an ideal to which each writer made a personal contribution and which each author interpreted independently of his colleagues.

In the case of Bigongiari the same origins caused an increasingly marked tendency to stress the autonomy of the poetic text and the inexhaustible potential of its language. Poetry is the ideal place where the circuit is completed between silence and verbalization and from verbalization back to silence, in a kind of endless orphic spiral. Artistic creation is a continuous process that cannot be encased within a closed set of meanings. In its initial stages Bigongiari's poetry gives indications of procedural tendencies that have become theoretically justified and codified in the last few years.

Freedom from the constraints of the formative, minor phase of his career was achieved within the tentative goals of the nascent hermetic movement, including the aim to be a comprehensive movement and the search for a rhythm and meter that would be the direct expression of a continuous sense of becoming. The hermetics also proposed to articulate the sense of a voyage into the reality of humanity and the reality of the word – a quest for lyricism. But those ideas appear so clearly on the pages of Bigongiari's work and are so purified as to constitute a highly personal vision within the generation. In this sense *La figlia di Babilonia* (The Daugh-

ter of Babylon) is a unique book. It was published in 1942, when hermeticism had already achieved maturity; yet it expresses all of the turmoil of that brief but intense period of maturation. In the volume all biographical references are deleted or hidden beneath thick layers of metaphoric allusions that disguise physical landscapes. Bigongiari negates every reference to external reality in order to restore absolute autonomy to personal feelings, to a pure sense of expectancy, in addition to the presence of memory, which is totally disembodied.

La figlia di Babilonia gathers poems written as early as 1937. The inspirations are even older and parallel an attempted epistolary novel written from 1933 to 1939, partially published with the title "La donna miriade" (Multiple Woman) in *Forum Italicum* in 1975. Dabbling in the novel genre was typical of the emergent hermetic movement, as verified by the presence of narratives among the works of other poets of the third generation. The same tendency was also a response to the need to experience the process or duration of creative activity, as well as a reaction to the central importance accorded to the permanence of the written word.

In addition to certain other aspects of "La donna miriade" the concept of the novel is seen directly in *La figlia di Babilonia.* The narrative line is established by the titles of the three sections: "Ella andava verso la notte" (She Was Moving Toward the Night), "Era triste, forse piangeva" (She Was Sad, Perhaps Crying), and "Si è voltata, sono perduto" (She Has Turned Around, I Am Lost). Bigongiari creates a progression that is clearly suggestive of a sequence comprising a woman's movement toward liberation and absence, her surmounting of obstacles in order to become absolutely free, and the account of the impact that process has on the poetic subject. But human nature is multiple: the drama, therefore, cannot and must not be linear. On the contrary, it unfolds in a continuous interplay of absence and presence, void and fullness, ascent toward infinite space and descent into existential nothingness, past and future, and hope and despair.

Bigongiari manages to evoke a metaphoric balance in which the events of existence are continually subjected to a force that destroys yet transcends them while conferring on them, in paradoxical fashion, a sort of absolute status. In "Il silenzio del moto" (The Silence of Motion) he writes of his ambiguous memory, poised between the past and the future:

O memoria tu libera ricordi
l'avvenire vissuto nel mio cuore,

Portrait of Bigongiari, painted in 1945 by Mario Marcucci
(Collection of Piero Bigongiari)

il cielo perso negli spazi sordi
tu conduci il vespero in amore
sui tuoi passi; t'attendo: sulla bianca
spalletta, dentro gli occhi di chi è
riflessa in una stanca
pace di luna d'un giro d'eterna
primavera che langue come piuma.

(O memory you freely recall
the future lived in my heart,
the sky lost in the deaf spaces
you lead the evening to love
on your steps; I await you: on the white
roadside, inside the eyes of one who is
reflected in the weary
lunar peace of one turn of eternal
spring that languishes like a feather.)

The last section of *La figlia di Babilonia* emphasizes the notion of the loss of self due to the existential uncertainty of the other (the moment of weak-
ness represented by the woman's turning around),
as in the poem "Trama" (Plot):

Io lungamente attesi il mio morire
da uno sguardo più lungo, ma se niente
sopravanzava fuor che il tuo transire
sempre là dove inalterata i sogni

tradisci per non esser men vera,
nelle lacrime dove mi specchiai,
nella spera impazzita, nel segreto
della mia vita incalcolato, andrai

per sempre, o sognante, col tuo passo
o sia esso un po' di sole che ti giustifica.

(I have long awaited my dying
from a longer look, but if nothing
remained beyond your ceaseless
movement to where unaltered you betray

dreams in order not to be any less real,
into the tears that mirrored me,
into the crazed sphere, into the accidental
secret of my life, you will go

forever, dreamer, with your step
which may be a ray of sunshine that justifies you.)

By 1941 Bigongiari had fully settled in Florence. Following the attainment of his degree, he
chose not to enter the competition for teaching
posts at the Scuola Normale Superiore in Pisa or at
the University of Timisoara in Romania, preferring
to remain in the cultural milieu of Florence. He
eventually obtained a teaching position at the Liceo
Artistico in Florence.

But those were also the years that saw Italy
swept by the storm of Fascism. In that tragic circumstance, Bigongiari's poetic voice went silent, as
though muted by the gloomy presence of death and
the triumph of barbarism. In the postscript to *Torre
di Arnolfo* (Arnolfo's Tower, 1964), he recalls that silence: "Il mio lettore vedrà uno iato tra il primo e il
secondo volume . . . ma, a parte il fatto che
all'inspirazione, come dicevano i nostri padri, non si
comanda, il richiamo agli avvenimenti vissuti in
quegli anni potrà forse far capire che il vero
s'avverava allora, e non solo in Italia, e non solo per
l'autore di questo libro, attraverso un'azione non
più mediata dalla parola" (My reader will notice a
gap between the first and second volume . . . but,
apart from the fact that, as our forefathers used to
say, you cannot dictate inspiration, my recollection
of the events of those years may help to understand
that truth was in fact being affirmed at the time, not
only in Italy, and not only by the author of this
book; the truth was being asserted in actions that
were not necessarily accompanied by words).

The reemergence of Bigongiari's voice at the
end of the war occurred with a renewed emphasis
on material as well as existential concerns; this
focus would not have been imaginable for him previously. Of course, he was not alone in such an ap-

proach. One need only consider some of the post-war books by other Italian poets, including Franco Fortini, Luzi, Ungaretti, and Quasimodo. In *Rogo* (Pyre, 1952) Bigongiari articulates a flow of emotions no longer containable, which is immediately evident in the opening poem, "A labbra serrate" (With Pursed Lips), one of his most noteworthy compositions:

Inutile parlarvi, miei morti sconosciuti,
inutile cercarvi, voi uomini della terra,
per la troppa terra che nasconde il vostro cielo.
Solo vostro è il cielo per cui soffriamo tutta la terra.

(There's no point talking to you, my unknown dead;
it's pointless to look for you, people of the earth,
because too much earth covers your sky.
Yours only is the sky for which we suffer the whole world.)

Death acquires connotations different from those in *La figlia di Babilonia*. It is no longer the scene of absence nor the cathartic manifestation of the absolute. A powerful pathos emanates from what seems to be an impossible dialogue between the speaker and the choral mass of the dead who assert themselves firmly into the reader's imagination as victims of the war and of other violence. They also seem tinged with an existential and historical coloring:

Con un passo più lungo commettiamo la stanchezza, a
    che cosa?
la rosa in un vortice repentino scopre la primavera in
    un deserto
e le stagioni si salvano dai cannoni ma non dagli
    sguardi degli uomini
che forse esistono sulla terra per uno scompenso di
    menzogne
come il vento in un dislivello barometrico.

(With a longer stride we commit our weariness, to
    what?
the rose in a sudden vortex signals spring in the desert
and the seasons are saved from the cannons but not
    from the eyes of men
who exist on this earth perhaps through an imbalance
    of falsehoods
like the wind in a barometric asymmetry.)

Awareness of existential pain becomes acute and roots itself in a context that leaves no room for evasive maneuvers.

Caught between pain and its latency, between the available bits of information on existence and the lack of information about absence, and between natural and human history, the speaker's attention focuses directly on the problem of deciphering the contradictory and ambiguous signs that govern the world. The poetry of Bigongiari assumes this important role; it is no longer the exclusive site of absolute freedom but a place where language's full potential can uncover life's hidden meanings and contradictions. As he writes in "La tempesta" (The Tempest),

Forse è questa l'ora di non vedere
se tutto è chiaro, forse questa è l'ora
ch'è solo di sé paga, ed il tuo incanto
divaga nell'inverno della terra,
nell'inferno dei segni da capire.

(Perhaps this is the hour of not seeing
if everything is clear, perhaps this is the hour
that is satisfied only with itself, and your spell
is diffused throughout the winter of the earth,
throughout the hell of signs to be decoded.)

The poet's perspective, therefore, is to be located "dentro le cose" (inside of things), as he states in "Non so" (I Don't Know). A point is reached, though, where happiness erupts out of all the suffering endured, and clarity of vision out of the blindness. On this basis the informal tone of much of Bigongiari's later poetry becomes firmly established. This can be defined in terms of two sets of factors. One of these is the inherent materiality of language, as a result of which the word (in its semantic extension and phonetic composition) is treated as a physical entity that not only conveys direct meaning but also moves toward an ever-changing and always new signification — by virtue of its autonomy as well as its semantic derivatives. Bigongiari pays constant attention to the phono-symbolic value of each word, in addition to the word's capacity to create unusual metaphoric fields out of the centrifugal and centripetal forces active within and between linguistic units. The other set of factors comprises the growing emphasis on what may be called semantic materiality; that is to say, prime elements such as water, fire, air, and earth are tightly bound to existential, biographical, historical, and cultural events. Together they are a set of mythical and archetypal elements that inspire Bigongiari's verses.

In *Stato di cose* (The State of Things, 1968) he addresses just such informal materiality. He chose this particular title for a collection of several of his works including *La figlia di Babilonia*, *Rogo*, and *Il corvo bianco* (The White Crow, 1955). Bigongiari states in a note that the title *Stato di cose*, does not indicate a compact reality or a static entity. Instead it alludes to a state of continuous evolution and change, which characterizes the reality of matter and of poetry: "Credo a una verità come avverarsi del vero: cioè a una verità colta come stato improprio ... tra quello che era e quello che sarà. ... Credo cioè ancora a una poesia come movimento e di tramite che il titolo complessivo *Stato di cose* può forse apparentemente smentire; ma esso ... implica, in definitiva, l'idea di rapporto oggettivo nell'insieme di una situazione" (I believe in a truth that is the realization process of the true: that is, truth understood as an improper state ... between what was and what will be. ... Where he contradicts himself, man brings his humanity and creativity into the indefiniteness of existence ... I still believe, in other words, in poetry as a movement and a vehicle, which the title *Stato di cose* might contradict; however ... it definitely suggests the idea of an objective relationship within an overall situation). Bigongiari structures his poetry as the expression of movement that shifts at times syntagmatically, as it changes from one state to another along a temporal axis. At other times the slide is vertical, along a paradigmatic axis, as it changes from one field to another within a spatial dimension. He compares it to a "romanzo dove cause ed effetti collidono in una materia che è continuamente, e insieme, causale ed effettuale" (novel in which causes and effects collide in a material that is simultaneously cause and effect).

Il corvo bianco, *Le mura di Pistoia* (The Walls of Pistoia), and *Torre di Arnolfo,* all published from the mid 1950s to the mid 1960s, depict a bold odyssey into a chaotic world undertaken aboard an equally chaotic linguistic code. As a consequence readers encounter unresolved but vital contrasts, as in "Inno primo" (First Hymn), from *Il corvo bianco:*

> abbandònati a questo inconsistente
> pulviscolo di cose e di pensieri,
> abìtuati all'inferno dell'effimero:
> ieri è già eterno se altro tempo cade
> dal suo cielo e vi porta visi, cose
> fuggiasche nella loro lenta traccia:
> questa la loro libertà: seguire
> lievi il declino, drizzarsi dentro
> la loro gravità che le raccoglie
> e le figge quaggiù dentro la ghiaccia
> senza un grido.

> (Abandon yourself to this unsubstantial
> dust of things and thoughts,
> get accustomed to the hell of ephemerality:
> yesterday is already eternal if another time falls
> from its sky and brings you faces, things
> that will not last in their slow trace:
> this is their freedom: to follow

> gently the decline, to veer toward
> the gravity that envelops them
> and fixes them down here inside the ice
> without a scream being uttered.)

Inside this framework the poetry brings to light the events of Bigongiari's life and the situations that recur in his memory, not merely because they have personal significance but because events great and small, together with the sensations of a moment and occurrences that may seem insignificant at the time, all assume an almost prophetic role when brought into focus inside the mind. Inevitably they tend to become projections of the poetic subject into the reality of objects, sights, and sounds, such as the Arno, whose waters once flooded Bigongiari's home; a fire in a local liquor factory; the road on which his home in Pistoia stood when he was an adolescent; the railway lines; the shriek of circus tigers; the various colors reflected off Florentine palaces and pavements; and the flight of seagulls viewed from his terrace on the banks of the river. Memory performs an even more central role than before. It obscures the present by activating, in the flux of recollections, a series of anticipations. Memory participates in the development of the images it evokes since those images transform the reality they convey and are altered, in turn, by that reality, as seen in "Inno primo":

> . . . è un vuoto lo ieri, un vuoto quello
> che al tuo occhio s'illumina, ma, vedi,
> fiorisce, si diffonde, cretta i massi
> più densi, si dirama, esplode, è quello
> che diroccia il futuro e ti fa strada.

> (. . . yesterday is a void, a void that
> lights up before your eyes, but, you see,
> it flourishes, spreads, cracks the densest
> masses, splinters, explodes, it is what
> demolishes the future and opens the way for you.)

Bigongiari embraces in this later poetry all the aspects of experience, personal as well as historical. In doing so, he penetrates beyond the limits that restricted his early artistic growth. He opens himself up to a richer variety of references. He becomes an instrument, as it were, that enables distinctive forms to emerge from amorphous existence and vice versa. As a consequence *non sapere* (not knowing) and *indecisione* (indecision) ultimately appear as the only ways of gaining access to final truth, as he indicates in "Il fuoco di Sant'Ermete" (The Fire of Saint Ermete), from *Le mura di Pistoia*:

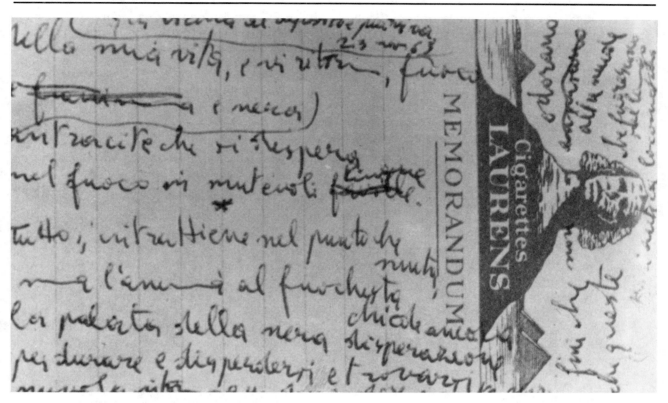

Notes by Bigongiari for his poem "La Scala della Vergine," which is collected in Torre di Arnolfo *(by permission of Piero Bigongiari)*

. . . io sono qui indeciso
se il fuoco l'ombra o l'ombra attizza il fuoco,
io sono qui lungo il mare indeciso
qual è il silenzio, quale la sua voce.

. . . .

dico l'attimo più doloroso della gioia al culmine,
dico che tutto già decide, il tronco
che si corruga, la maniglia appena
toccata, tutta l'ombra, tutto il fuoco
di un'inespressa verità indivisa.

(. . . I am undecided here as to whether
the fire stirs the shadow or the shadow stirs the fire,
I am here next to the sea undecided as to
what is the silence, what is its voice.

. . . .

I call the moment of utmost joy pain,
I say everything is already decided, the tree trunk
that corrugates, the handle barely
touched, all of the shade, all of the fire
of an inexpressed and undivided truth).

During 1953 and 1954 Bigongiari had taken some important trips that left an indelible mark on his work. As a representative of the Italian radio network R.A.I., he accompanied Giovanbattista Agnoletti to Greece and Egypt, as well as to the Sinai. In that area Bigongiari encountered a world that was new and, at the same time, as ancient as humanity itself; it presented fresh avenues of exploration for his poetry. To a certain extent, *Il corvo bianco* is based on the impact of such Eastern culture. The myths and history of ancient Greece and, above all, the narrative and meaning of the Scriptures penetrate Bigongiari's poetry; they act as an inexhaustible reservoir or resources for the creation of new myths out of the ancient ones. These resources constituted an extended area in which to interpret the signs of the world and humanity's history. The title and meaning of *Il corvo bianco* are directly related to the passage in Genesis that describes the end of the deluge. It is a biblical episode that Bigongiari's text reworks by fusing the image of the white dove and that of the black crow – birds released by Noah in order to determine the level of the receding waters.

However, in *Le mura di Pistoia* readers encounter the first deliberate attempt to link the biography of the poetic subject with the history of humanity and to identify the poetic subject with the figure of Moses. These procedures open a perspective that becomes more complete in Bigongiari's 1979 volume, *Moses*.

In 1964 *Torre di Arnolfo* encapsulated Bigongiari's quest. The first narrative sweep (the "novel") of his poetry culminates in that work. As is usually the case in Bigongiari's poetry, the completion of the cycle postulates a new beginning for more discourse. The "novel" implied in his work thus consists of a long poem with the function of exalting the infinite orchestration of opposites and performing an ongoing revision of its own objectives. If truth hides in the highest forms of fiction, happiness in sorrow, and essence in transitoriness, the whole of his work up to 1964 captures, as few other oeuvres do, the infinite gradations that mark the passage from one extreme condition to the other, as well as their oxymoronic convergence. Bigongiari's poetry, then is a place where these gradations manifest themselves; the poetic text is inseparable from them and exists by virtue of their presence, as in the title poem of *Torre di Arnolfo:*

E vero questo scendere del fiume
è vera l'acqua, la mota, la luce
immota sul perpetuo suo sottrarsi
come nell'illusione, orma, un pensiero.
Dove ti appoggi più non trovi uguale
alla carezza l'impeto, all'ardore
la fiamma: e nel crollare dei tizzoni
è larva che consegna a verità
l'antico sforzo ed il futuro . . .

(It is real the river's descent,
true are the waters, the sludge, the light
motionless on its perpetual slippage
as in an illusion, a trace, a thought.
Where you lean you no longer find
the touch the same to the caress, the flame
to the ardor: and in the collapse of embers
is the larva that consigns to truth
the ancient effort and the future . . .).

From the 1960s onward Bigongiari's life became increasingly marked by journeys that brought him to various places, especially and repeatedly to France and North America (mostly the United States, but also Canada). Nevertheless his center of operations remained Florence, at whose university he taught starting in 1965 as a professor of modern and contemporary Italian literature. The centrality of his home base and his sojourns in countries with geographies and cultures different from Italy became a sort of metaphor destined to acquire structural importance in his poetry. That discourse is marked increasingly by the linkage of stasis and motion, the center and the perimeter.

The narrative thrust of Bigongiari's poetry, from *Antimateria* (Antimatter, 1971) onward is based on such linkages. The effect is of the uncontrolled, mutable mobility of all the textual material (biographical, cultural, historical, and natural) drawn into the creative crucible. The mobility even extends to his critical theory, as theory and creativity become henceforth extremely interdependent intellectual activities.

At the base of *Antimateria,* as in his later volumes, lies the realization that each limit also implies the negation of limits and that the principle of contradiction is the only principle that can lead to the elimination of contradictions and, hence, to elusive truth. From *Antimateria, Moses,* and *Col dito in terra* (With a Finger in the Ground, 1986) to *Nel delta del poema* (Into the Delta of the Poem, 1989), Bigongiari's last volumes exploit a creative process that oscillates in circular fashion between coalescence and dispersal. The circularity leads from the entities of physical reality to the entities of the imagination and back again, in a continuous reciprocal activation. Thus the poetry becomes self-reflexive. In the act of capturing the world, the word constructs reality in the sense that verbalization allows the poetic subject to establish a link between himself and the empirical world. One can easily understand, then, the essential value assigned to the creative act, viewed as a process of actualization through the word and as a way of giving substance to the abstract reality beyond the sensible world. In such a context, poetic discourse can only move along a nonthematic line; it does so even more than in previous works by Bigongiari.

The inevitable contradictions and antitheses of life, as well as the existential flux in which Bigongiari's poetry is immersed, find a necessary complement and their essence in the linguistic structures. Even at this level the poetry does not renounce the law of the unavoidable clash of opposites. The word is paradise and creative power, but it is also hell in that it signals human impotence against the resistant mass of occult truth. As in the poetry of Stéphane Mallarmé, the word ends up repudiating its own impotence to formulate absolute statements. But, unlike the French symbolist, Bigongiari does not have faith in the blank page that succumbs under the persistence of fate. In "Ocelli II," from *Antimateria,* Bigongiari attacks the source of linguistic expression at the site where silence has been broken but thought has not yet been verbalized. There, at the point of origin, in the "filo di sangue puro la parola / non udita dilaga" (trickle of pure blood the unheard / word gushes forth).

In *Moses* readers are on the road to undeciphered language or to faint inscriptions in the rocks. In the title poem the narrator (Moses) says, "non so se sono io l'assetato / o il salvato dalle acque" (I don't know if I'm the one dying of thirst / or the one saved from the waters). In the same way, all the extraordinary experiences narrated in *Col dito in terra* and *Nel delta del poema* are consumed in the search for an unwritten sign or for what has already been erased: "Col dito in terra scavi l'amore rappreso, / scrivi del malinteso quanto non si può intendere, / allontani la morte dall'arreso, l'arreso dalla morte" (With a finger in the ground you dig up coagulated love, / you write incomprehensible things about the misunderstood, / you distance death from the surrendered, the surrendered from death).

Col dito in terra and *Nel delta del poema* are effectively one work. After the narrative dream of *Moses,* these two collections depict not so much the end but the inevitable and possible ramifications of *Moses*. In these two 1980s volumes the poetic act is positioned between the extremes of personal and collective history, and the presence of the law and transgression of the same for the sake of finding an absolute law. In such a perspective of openness to all possibilities, the fate of the word unfolds between what is said and what cannot be said, between what is written and what cannot be written. In the endless multiplication of life's symbols, the word, caught in the spiral of its multiple and always deferred meanings, seems to betray an essential defect — if one expects to find "laringe ultima che / vibrerà la parola decisiva" (the last larynx that will vibrate the definitive word).

Truth does not shine forth from a simple utterance, and it eludes the definition into which language forces it. Truth and falsehood, life and death — all come together in the enigma that envelops essence and emerges from the most unlikely instances of individual and collective existence. Caught between the sign and its many signifieds, between voice and silence, hymn and mutterings, the word subsumes within itself the mystery that surrounds it. Hence Bigongiari chooses the most difficult path, even if it is the one to which his entire poetic research led him inexorably. The path implies problematizing the autonomy of the poetic subject and of his song, as well as the ability of each to come to terms with life's inexplicable mysteries. In this sense, the poem breaks into countless fragments that merge at its delta, where every rivulet disperses it then unifies it with the sea of being. From this point of view, even Bigongiari's literary skill cannot prevent conveying the implicit deficiency of the word in realizing its function, which is to transcend the fixity of objects and to articulate the infinite interpersonal relationships connecting the subject and the world. Bigongiari is aware that the word distances him from his own material. Words ironically conceal the ultimate meaning of the enigma while pointing to it. The poem breaks up into brilliant shards. It is a hymn understood as a song that interrupts the emergence of an indistinct cry. The hymn sets everything in motion at the moment the poetic subject rejects the biographical and ideological unity of his being.

Col dito in terra and *Nel delta del poema,* with their endless patterns of dispersion and recombination, develop to full realization the countermelody established in Bigongiari's poetry from *Antimateria* onward. It is a countermelody in the sense that it resists the spiritual and historical disintegration of the Western world, in which life is precarious. The descent to the depths of the ineffable sign in search of a trace of the mysterious or the divine assumes the form of a dramatic appeal, an appeal capable of incorporating in itself all the events of existence — everything that, in one way or another (even by the force of poetry alone), eludes the relentless erosion of all things. In "Inno diciannovesimo" (Nineteenth Hymn), from *Col dito in terra,* Bigongiari writes:

> Avanza tra le tese, qui, del mare
> e le rocce rare dell'avventura
> qualche cosa che se vuol dirsi luce
> cerca gli anfratti più esalati, il morbido
> ondeggiare quasi, se avesse le ali
> – o le ha? – il vento fosse, il vento che
> mentre toglie la mente alle chimere
> scava le fosse e le riempie, trova
> l'occulto, il rarefatto, e lo raccoglie
> con mano leggera, – e legge foglie
> – quelle ancora che escono dall'antro
> di sibilla, da quel picciòlo stanco
> di trattenere tra il passato e
> il futuro inevaso il bel presente.

> (Something approaches here among the sea
> tides and the rare rocks of adventure,
> something that if it means light
> seeks out the airiest crevices, almost
> the gentlest undulation; if it had wings
> – or does it? – if it were wind, the wind
> that sweeps nightmares from the mind
> as it digs trenches only to refill them, finds
> the occult, the rarefied and gathers it up
> with a gentle hand, – and reads leaves
> – those that still issue from the sybil's
> cave, from that reed tired
> of holding the lovely present between the
> past and the unevaded future.)

The ultimate significance of the odyssey depicted in Bigongiari's poetry comprises the search for "l'occulto, il rarefatto." It is an odyssey that is movement and stasis together; it relates the efforts of the poetic subject to go outside himself in order to return promptly, but terrified and sobered by fresh insights. It also constitutes a journey into existence and being. What sustains the peregrination is Bigongiari's desperate faith in the word — that spark of creativity that can still be saved from compromise — and its ability to express meaning even in the most sterile of contexts, in an existential wasteland that is becoming increasingly alien to the human spirit. The odyssey expresses hope that the word's penetrating properties, like the hand of God, can point toward heaven or toward earth and identify the key that unlocks the mystery of life.

Interviews:

Despina Mladoveanu, "Conversatie cu Piero Bigongiari," *Romania Literara,* 2 (2 January 1969): 22;

Claudio Toscani, "Incontro in due tempi con Piero Bigongiari," *Ragguaglio Librario,* 40 (October-November 1973): 326–329, 362–365;

Silvio Ramat, "La vita," in his *Invito alla lettura di Bigongiari* (Milan: Mursia 1979), pp. 19–23.

Bibliography:

Maria Carla Papini, *Bibliografia di Piero Bigongiari* (Florence: Opus Libri, 1986).

References:

Luigi Baldacci, "*Antimateria:* Una svolta nella poesia di Bigongiari," *Epoca* (19 March 1972);

Carlo Bo, "Poesia come virtù: Bigongiari," in *Gli inni,* edited by Bigongiari (Florence: Sedicesimo, 1986), pp. 7–9;

Jean-Michel Gardair, "La poétique ininterrompue de Piero Bigongiari," *Critique,* no. 263 (April 1969): 304–311;

Ruggero Jacobbi, "Commento agli *Inni* di Bigongiari," in *Gli inni,* pp. 87–100;

Oreste Macrì, "La cultura poetica dell'ermetismo in Bigongiari," in his *Caratteri e figure della poesia italiana contemporanea* (Florence: Vallecchi, 1956), pp. 197–217;

Macrì, "L'enigma della poesia di Bigongiari," in his *Studi sull'ermetismo* (Lecce: Milella, 1988);

Macrì, "Fisica del simbolo in Piero Bigongiari," in his *Realtà del simbolo* (Florence: Vallecchi, 1968), pp. 195–214;

Roberto Mussapi, "Bigongiari e le dinamica del visivo," in his *Il centro e l'orizzonte* (Milan: Jaca, 1985), pp. 79–91;

Adelia Noferi, "Ipotesi sull'informale e la poesia della terza generazione," in her *Il gioco delle tracce* (Florence: Nuova Italia, 1979), pp. 329–363;

Noferi, "Piero Bigongiari: La critica come segno di contraddizione," in her *Le poetiche critiche novecentesche* (Florence: Le Monnier, 1970), pp. 149–223;

Maria Carla Papini, "Bigongiari tra ermetismo e no," in her *Il sorriso della Gioconda* (Rome: Bulzoni, 1989), pp. 173–229;

Papini, "Resistenza e tensione nel linguaggio di Piero Bigongiari," in her *Il linguaggio del moto* (Florence: Nuova Italia, 1981), pp. 103–143;

Giancarlo Quiriconi, "Norma e infrazione: Il vortice segnico di Bigongiari," *Michelangelo Oggi,* 71–72 (January–April 1989);

Quiriconi, "Piero Bigongiari," in his *I miraggi, le tracce* (Milan: Jaca, 1989), pp. 199–234;

Silvio Ramat, Introduction to Bigongiari's *Poesie,* edited by Ramat (Milan: Mondadori/Oscar, 1982), pp. ix–xxxvi;

Ramat, *Invito alla lettura di Bigongiari* (Milan: Mursia, 1979);

Luigi Tassoni, *L'occhio, la madre* (Catanzaro: Fucina Jonica, 1982);

Tassoni, "Il senso delle cose" and "Dal ciclo della memoria ai frammenti del poema," in his *Finzione e conoscenza* (Bergamo: Lubrina, 1989), pp. 117–119, 177–182.

Vittorio Bodini
(6 January 1914 – December 1970)

Joseph Perricone
Fordham University

BOOKS: *La luna dei Borboni* (Milan: Meridiana, 1952); enlarged as *La luna dei Borboni e altre poesie, 1945–1961* (Milan: Mondadori, 1962);

Dopo la luna (Rome & Caltanissetta: Sciascia, 1956);

Poesie (Milan: Mondadori, 1962); enlarged as *Poesie, 1939–1970,* edited by Oreste Macrì (Milan: Mondadori, 1972);

Studi sul barocco di Gòngora (Rome: Ateneo, 1964);

Metamor (Milan: All'Insegna del Pesce d'Oro, 1967);

Segni e simboli nella "Vida es sueño" (Bari: Adriatica, 1968);

Estudio estructural de la literatura clásica española, translated (into Spanish) by Angel Sánchez-Gijón (Barcelona: Martinez Roca, 1971);

31 disegni delle anime e 13 poesie inedite (Bari: Adriatica, 1973);

La lobbia di Masoliver e altri racconti, edited by Paolo Chiarini (Milan: All'Insegna del Pesce d'Oro, 1980);

Tutte le poesie, 1932–1970, edited by Macrì (Milan: Mondadori, 1983);

I fiori e le spade, edited by Fabio Grassi (Lecce: Milella, 1984).

Edition in English: *The Hands of the South: Poems by Vittorio Bodini,* translated by Ruth Feldman and Brian Swann (Washington, D.C.: Charioteer, 1980).

OTHER: "Antologia della poesia spagnola del '900," edited by Bodini, *Poesia,* 5 (July 1946);

Federico García Lorca, *Teatro,* translated with an introduction, by Bodini (Turin: Einaudi, 1952);

Galleria, special issue on Spanish literature, 1–2 (January–April 1955), edited by Bodini;

Miguel de Cervantes, *Don Chisciotte della Mancia,* translated, with an introduction, by Bodini (Turin: Einaudi, 1957);

Pedro Salinas, *Poesie,* translated, with an introduction, by Bodini (Milan: Lerici, 1958);

Vicente Aleixandre, *Picasso,* translated by Bodini (Milan: Scheiwiller, 1962);

Vittorio Bodini circa 1974

I poeti surrealisti spagnoli, translated by Bodini (Turin: Einaudi, 1963);

Rafael Alberti, *Poesie,* translated, with an introduction, by Bodini (Milan: Mondadori, 1964);

Francisco Quevedo, *Sonetti amorosi e morali,* translated, with an introduction, by Bodini (Turin: Einaudi, 1965);

Alberti, *Degli angeli,* translated, with an introduction, by Bodini (Turin: Einaudi, 1966);

Alberti, *Il poeta nella strada,* translated, with an introduction, by Bodini (Milan: Mondadori, 1969);

Juan Larrea, *Visione celeste,* translated, with an introduction, by Bodini (Turin: Einaudi, 1969);

José Moreno Villa, *Giacinta la rossa,* translated by Bodini (Turin: Einaudi, 1971);

Alberti, *Roma, pericolo per i viandanti,* translated by Bodini (Milan: Mondadori, 1972);

Cervantes, *Intermezzi,* translated by Bodini (Turin: Einaudi, 1972);

Renato Aymone, *Poesia e poetica del Sud,* includes prose and poetry by Bodini (Salerno: Edisud, 1980);

"Stazzema Series," translated by Ruth Feldman and Brian Swann, *American Poetry Review,* 9 (November–December 1980).

SELECTED PERIODICAL PUBLICATIONS –
UNCOLLECTED: "A F. T. Marinetti," *Vecchio e Nuovo,* 2 (17 April 1932);

"Aprile – ore 9 mattutine," *Voce del Salento,* 10 (1 May 1932);

"Cammino," *Vecchio e Nuovo,* 2 (11 December 1932);

"Aeroplano" and "Poesia," *Voce del Salento,* 10 (31 December 1932);

"Alberetto malato," *Voce del Salento,* 11 (15 January 1933);

"Proposito," "Giardini D'Azeglio," "Una foglia," "Solitudine a San Miniato," "Per una villa presso Settignano," and "Convergenze," *Letteratura,* 14 (April–June 1940);

"Sul poggio che cantava dei tuoi passi," *Vedetta Mediterranea* (31 March 1941);

"Tu non conosci il Sud," "Quando tornai," and "Appena la conchiglia," *Mercurio,* 29 (January 1947);

"Omaggio a Gòngora," *Letteratura,* 4 (January–April 1958);

"Morta in Puglia," *Cynthia,* 1–2 (January–April 1963);

"Due poesie per il surrealismo: Pseudosonetto, Night" and "Davanti a un mare," *Marcatrè,* 26–29 (December 1966);

"Valentina," "Canto al colombo Serapione," and "Madama di Trebe," *Paragone,* no. 232 (June 1969).

With a dynamic innovative spirit and an awareness, from a very young age, of European and world trends in art and thought, Vittorio Bodini typifies in his poetry the existential anguish of the people of the southern regions of Italy, their metaphysical dimension and their social characteristics. His intellectual vigor was a stimulus to the continued renewal of cultural life in his native region of Apulia and brought to the national literature a new voice that was an original blend of the baroque and the surreal, traditions that played relevant roles in the growth of his poetics. However, the quotidian reality of his region, the plight of the oppressed, and the problems of social injustice remained a constant throughout his poetic evolution, whether thematically present, as in his first two collections of poetry, or as a background allusion in his later poems.

Bodini was born in Bari, the capital of Apulia, on 6 January 1914 to an aristocratic family originally from Lecce. His was a timely birth because it coincided with a renaissance in the intellectual and social life of the region. (Donato Valli, in *La cultura letteraria del Salento* [1971], traces the sociopolitical and literary evolution in the Salento province and in the Apulia region in general.) This spiritual rebirth was fostered by several good journals that played a key role in providing an ideal forum to stimulate debate, which is indispensable to the evolution of a community. The discussion focusing on literary, artistic, and social themes was particularly animated in the Salento province of Apulia, centering on the cultural hub of that area, the baroque city of Lecce. Pietro Marti, Bodini's maternal grandfather and an influential figure in his life – particularly since Bodini's father had died while Bodini was still an infant – was an erudite scholar and historian in Lecce. A well-respected intellectual, he was also the editor of several prestigious journals at various times in his long life. Therefore, Bodini can be said to have been born in the heart of the heated debates that flourished among important journals published in Lecce during the first decades of the twentieth century.

Readers of the region preferred the works of Giosuè Carducci, the national bard of Italy at the turn of the century, who in 1906 was awarded the Nobel Prize and whose less attractive aspect was a penchant for declamatory nationalistic verse. For this reason several journals engaged in an effort to broaden the literary horizons of this retrograde readership. Publications such as the *Gazzetta delle Puglie, Gazzettino Letterario,* and *Studente Magliese* were among the most fashionable and were also very receptive to foreign authors and brought to the public knowledge of Charles Baudelaire, Emile Zola, Gérard de Nerval, Heinrich Heine, and others. Through such journals Bodini was able to develop his interests in a broader European literary tradition. Through his contact with this relatively small but lively and alert artistic ambience, Bodini was able to overcome both the general widespread mood of apathy and the inherent limitations of a culture that lagged behind mainstream national developments by several decades.

The dialogue between the supporters of Carducci and those who favored less anachronistic expressive modes was primarily hosted by the journal *Vecchio e Nuovo* during the first years of the 1930s. The young Bodini entered this arena and sided with the advocates of the new trends, which at this time essentially meant adherence to the recently relaunched futurist movement. In 1925 the futurists, disguised and profoundly modified, had made a comeback, in Filippo Tommaso Marinetti's anthology *I nuovi poeti futuristi* (The New Futurist Poets). The fact that the new futurists were influenced by recent political developments did not bother the Leccese group. For them as for Bodini the movement signified first of all an opening, a window through which to welcome something new. The advent of this second wave of futurism reinvigorated the debates centering on social and literary issues and polarized the population into two groups: those who defended the old ways and those who fought to make way for the new.

At this point of the literary-cultural debate in Lecce the eighteen-year-old Bodini made his publishing debut with a series of articles showing his staunch support of the faction favoring renewal and modernization. These early writings, in his grandfather's journal *Voce del Salento* and in *Vecchio e Nuovo,* also testify to Bodini's openness to transalpine literary influences, which included Leo Tolstoy and Franz Kafka among other authors that he was reading at that time. The position taken by Bodini in these polemical essays was consistently that of denouncing the supine acceptance of traditional values and defending a rational analysis of problems in the light of a broad perspective of points of view.

With Elemo d'Avila, a Roman activist for the futurist movement, Bodini launched the shocking "Manifesto ai Pugliesi della provincia" (Manifesto to the Apulians of the Province) in the journal *Vecchio e Nuovo* in 1932. Prompted by his spirit of rebellion, Bodini would also on occasion replace the *passatista* (traditionalist) poems submitted by old professors and postmasters with his own futurist poems just moments before his grandfather's journal went to print. These early compositions represent the first poetic efforts by Bodini. They were excluded from any edition of his works until his friend and editor Oreste Macrì included them in the appendix of *Tutte le poesie* (All the Poetry, 1983).

The youthful compositions reveal a poetic temperament, a manner of filtering reality, and the presence of certain themes that were to recur in Bodini's later poetry. They document certain images of southern ambience, elements of attraction, repulsion, affection, and disillusionment. This cluster of poems finds its thematic unity in the opposition between static, worn-out, languid objects – symbols of the old and the outmoded – and the dynamic, revolutionary, rebellious emblems of futurism. Spiritual strength and flaccid passivity, and youth and senility, are contrasted in a series of images suggested by the cultural landscape: quaint courtyards, church steeples, falling walls, and svelte country roads that lead toward the *ignoto* (unknown). Fire and light symbolize the new half of the binomial of oppositions; a purifying fire is pitched against a dormant, melancholy decor. In a 1932 poem dedicated to Marinetti, the founder of the futurist movement is apostrophized as a benign incendiary type who can spark the imagination of the provincial inhabitants. There is an element of Aldo Palazzeschi's *L'Incendiario* (1910) recognizable in Bodini's jocular tone: "Torrente instancabile di fede Futurista / che Incalzi incendiando ariacquamareterra / al tuo liquido soffio-fuoco crepitanti . . ." (Untiring torrent of Futurist faith / you who advances setting on fire airwatersealand / before your liquid breath-fire crackling . . .). In the 1932 poem "Aprile – ore 9 mattutine" (April – 9 O'Clock in the Morning) the sun is personified as an incendiary, angry person invading the passive landscape as it pushes forward its fiery glance. Both these early poems are collected in *Tutte le poesie.*

The train appears in these poems as a harbinger of the new and a symbol of freedom rather than revolution: a means of escaping from the humdrum reality obsequious to a dogmatic tradition. Flight from the potentially destructive tranquillity of the province is a much-dreamed-of alternative. Escape is also the aspiration projected with various other objects – plants, machines, asphalt roads, and electric lights – in this nucleus of poems. There is irony and sarcasm. Bodini caresses the objects and the places of his landscape with almost filial love, but at the same time he distances himself from them with scoffing superciliousness as one who wants to flee. The cars, airplanes, and locomotives, more than a celebration of technology, are symbols of escape and manifest the young Bodini's energetic characteristics. The languor that is present in some compositions is a projection of the perceived hopelessness of his plight, the consequence of his frustrated aspirations. The environment is consistently depicted in a state of decay with some elements that are generally attempting to flee, but they are often too delicate or weak to accomplish their goal.

The futurist experience was significant for young Bodini because, in addition to representing the baptismal moment of his poetic initiation, it provided him with the proper forum to begin to elaborate his aspiration for freedom and renewal and his sense of a civic mission for poetry. Those initial poems also reveal a constant of Bodini's inspiration: his deep-rooted inclination for a poetics of revolt, which later was revealed in his admiration of the surrealists and led to the evolution of his own personal blend of avant-garde poetry. Also reflected in these early poems is the vivacity with which Bodini assimilated the suggestions of other poets and poetics that he was discovering through his voracious if somewhat unfocused reading. There are echoes of Giuseppe Ungaretti in the poem "Cammino" (Road) and of Ardengo Soffici in the poem "Aeroplano"; a certain Parnassian decantation of experience in crystalline imagery is detectable in "Poesia" (in *Tutte le poesie*): "Lacrima repressa / racchiusa / entro i ricami / d'un vetro di Murano" (A tear suppressed / enclosed / within the lace / of a Murano glass").

This first phase of Bodini's evolution as an artist and intellectual, with a strong commitment and dedication to a cause, came to its conclusion by the end of the year 1932 because of circumstantial and political factors. The *Voce del Salento* ceased publication, as did *Vecchio e Nuovo,* as the Fascist regime imparted more forcefully its aversion to variety and difference of opinion. The next several years were relatively uneventful as Bodini completed his secondary education and then went to Rome to attend the university. However, the vacuous rigidity of academic life, the oppressive political ambience, and the atmosphere of unauthenticity that prevailed in the social milieu of the capital persuaded him to leave Rome after a year. One of his uncles intervened to help Bodini find work in Florence as a clerk at an automobile club. Thus in 1937 Bodini moved to Florence, where he supported himself through school until the completion of his university education three years later.

Bodini recounts the substantive aspects of that invaluable experience in an autobiographical prose piece in the appendix of Renato Aymone's *Poesia e poetica del Sud* (Poetry and Poetics of the South, 1980). Most important for the understanding of his poetic evolution is the story of his first meeting with a group of hermetic poets. He was admitted to this group after some of his poems were published in the journal *Letteratura,* which had accepted them upon consulting with Eugenio Montale, the dean of Italian poetry at that time. The hermetic group, whom Bodini then admired profoundly, preferred fleeting, esoteric verse, nearly inscrutable images, and an essential, compressed language. The group would gather informally at the Giubbe Rosse café, where they enacted their political protest by mournful silence:

> Andai alle Giubbe Rosse e vi trovai infatti fra i tavolini all'aperto, un Montale, a cui mi presentai, parco di gesti e di parole; pareva dirigere o muovere dei fili invisibili dentro di sé; era con [Mario] Luzi, di cui mi colpì il fuoco interiore che pareva avesse arrossato il suo viso asciutto. Saputo che ero di Lecce mi chiesero subito se conoscevo [Oreste] Macrì, se avevo sue notizie. Poi vennero altri alla spicciolata, sedendosi al nostro tavolino o ai tavoli accanto: [Carlo Emilio] Gadda, [Ottone] Rosai, [Carlo] Bo, [Tommaso] Landolfi, [Vasco] Pratolini, [Piero] Bigongiari, [Alessandro] Parronchi e quel silenzio che era caduto sul nostro tavolino e che mi imbarazzava un po' per il sospetto che fosse dovuto alla mia presenza, nonostante qualche occhiata amichevole che Luzi mi lanciava di tanto in tanto, era invece la regola del gruppo. Dopo uno scarno saluto sedevano, o in compagnia o anche a un tavolino da soli, e tacevano tutti (all'infuori di Rosai che lanciava ogni tanto delle imprecazioni) con bellissime fronti levate come in caccia di bianche figure dell'assenza.

> (I went to the Giubbe Rosse and indeed there at the tables outdoors I found Montale, to whom I introduced myself, sparing in gestures and words; he seemed to direct or to move some invisible threads within himself; he was with Luzi, whose dry red face seemed the consequence of an internal fire that made an impression on me. Having learned that I was from Lecce they asked me whether I knew Macrì, and if I had news of him. Then others arrived separately, sitting at our table or at others nearby: Gadda, Rosai, Bo, Landolfi, Pratolini, Bigongiari, Parronchi and that silence that fell on our table and that embarrassed me a little because I imagined that it was due to my presence, in spite of an occasional friendly glance that Luzi sent me from time to time, that silence was in fact a rule of the group. After a meager salutation, they would sit down either together or also alone at a table, and all remained silent [except for Rosai, who from time to time uttered imprecations] with their very beautiful foreheads raised as though chasing white images of absence.)

Unlike his futurist compositions, which Bodini later repudiated on the grounds that they pertained to the "prehistory" of his development, the poems written between 1939 and 1942 under the aegis of the hermetic style are remembered as a vital phase of his poetic beginnings. These poems were first published in *Letteratura* and *Vedetta Mediterranea,* the journal Bodini and Macrì edited together in Lecce between 1939 and 1942. Two examples from this small nucleus of eight poems are in the 1962 edition of *Poesie* (as well as later editions). He offered in the appendix a justification for their retention: "a memoria di un punto di partenza, e nello stesso tempo, d'un clima generale che non meritano d'essere rinnegati" (to remember a point of departure and at the same time a general climate, which do not deserve to be renounced). Those poems are cast in the suggestive imagery and language of the hermetic poets, whose concept of poetry was in some ways similar to that of the French symbolists. It focused on the evocative potential of the word, conceived as pure, that is to say disentangled from its prosaic, common, and concrete referential restrictions. Bodini's verses have as their overt subject an emblematic presence, probably an allusion to the Englishwoman Isobel, whom he met in those years in Florence and who had to return to England as a consequence of the outbreak of World War II. Her name is probably the three-syllable name that the 1940 poem "Giardini D'Azeglio" (D'Azeglio Gardens, in *Tutte le poesie*) refers to:

Un'altra volta
la presentii, sfiorando l'esistenza
d'una che un giro arguto di tre sillabe
distingue ancora, e un volto che balena
sempre più rado e breve, se l'evochino
le dita casuali del ricordo.

(Once more
I sensed her presence, brushing near the existence
of one whom the sharp turn of three syllables
still identifies, and a face that flashes
ever more rarely and briefly, when the casual fingers
of
memory should evoke it.)

While the persona lies abandoned in the anguish of existential solitude, the only solace may come from the platonic memory of a distant and unattainable perfection. Yearning is therefore the principal theme of these poems, as well as, implicitly, a human condition devoid of grace and fraught with suffering and abnegation. The woman is a salvific essence, perhaps capable of succoring the speaker. All the phonetic resources of the language are subtly but fully exploited by a poetics that aims to capture the undefinable, as in these verses from "Convergenze" (Convergences, in *Tutte le poesie*): "Vibrò nell'ala d'un colombo un verbo / di primavera . . ." (A word of spring vibrated / in the wing of a dove . . .).

By 1940 Bodini had completed his university studies in Florence with a dissertation on G. D. Romagnosi, a political thinker of the nineteenth century. In that same year, Bodini left Florence and after a brief stopover in Rome, where he met the rather reserved and laconic poet Alfonso Gatto, he proceeded to Lecce, where he was to remain until 1945. The years during the war were filled with intense political engagement and activism and saw Bodini gradually drift away from the strict observance of the hermetic style toward a more active involvement in grassroots political organizations. With Macrì he collaborated in the preparation of *Vedetta Mediterranea.* On its *terza pagina,* or cultural page, they regularly engaged in a subtle anti-Fascist campaign, which eventually may have caused the suppression of the journal.

As early as 1941 Bodini had joined the then-clandestine group called Giustizia e Libertà (Justice and Freedom), an anti-Fascist organization founded by Carlo Rosselli, and, with Vittore Fiore, Bodini played an important role in the Partito d'Azione (Action Party). He even took part in an expedition with a group of volunteers, affiliated with the Garibaldi brigades, who were to join the war of liberation. After 1945, however, the failure of this expedition, due to intrigues by opposing political factions, left such a bitter memory for Bodini that he recorded the experience in a poem that was never published in his lifetime because, in his opinion, it lacked any literary elaboration. "Colonna Pavone" (in *Tutte le poesie*) is nonetheless significant, as it records the disappointment of a defeat that left a deep mark on his conscience:

Qualcuno formava a Nocera
una brigata garibaldina.
[Pietro] Badoglio parlò con gli inglesi
per farla sciogliere:
promise in cambio i volontari del re.

(Someone was forming at Nocera
a Garibaldi brigade.
Badoglio spoke with the English
to have it disbanded:
he promised instead the king's volunteers.)

This important political parenthesis in Bodini's life lasted well into 1946. It coincided with a period of low poetic output due to his preoccupation with matters of historical consequence. Such a time, he must have felt, required his turning to prose because of its greater immediacy and directness. This period of political activism corresponds with what was perhaps the most disenchanting

Bodini in 1969 (drawing by Marcello Tommasi; from Omaggio a Bodini, *edited by Leonardo Mancino, 1972)*

period of his life. A detailed account of his intense participation in ideological battles during this period and throughout his lifetime, as well as the relevant articles, letters, and other testimonials, is in *I fiori e le spade* (The Flowers and the Swords, 1984).

In 1945 Bodini left Lecce to go to Rome, where he was called to serve in the leadership of the Partito Democrazia del Lavoro (Workers' Democratic Party). Full of enthusiasm, Bodini was also hopeful of reestablishing there his contacts with the literary intelligentsia and continuing his creative artistic activities. However, his socioethical aspira-

tions encountered further discouragement and defeat. It became ever more apparent to him that the new political forces shaping postwar Italian society were not going to implement those drastic reforms that Bodini thought could bring about the rebirth of his beloved southern provinces. His prose of this period, especially the creative, narrative prose, documents a shift from purely political to less immediate concerns. The exploration of a timeless southern folklore began to assume greater importance, a fact that attests to his ever-deepening awareness of the southern reality. His interest in poetry was renewed, and he resumed writing. His poems began to include an ever-greater presence of the southern elements: the flora and the fauna, and the characteristic objects of an age-old spiritual condition that are the major focuses of the collections *La luna dei Borboni* (The Moon of the Bourbons, 1952) and *Dopo la luna* (After the Moon, 1956).

His experience with Spanish culture and literature received renewed emphasis when he accepted in 1946 a scholarship from the Spanish government and took an appointment with the Italian Istituto de Cultura in Madrid. He was commissioned to write a series of articles on Spanish cultural life. Newspapers and journals also gave Bodini assignments of a similar nature. His stay in Spain, which originally was to last only a few months, was extended until 1949, with only a brief interruption in 1947. The Spanish sojourn opened a new and fruitful season for Bodini's poetry, giving him an opportunity to renew old literary interests in authors such as Federico García Lorca, whose works he had read in 1936 at the time of that poet's execution. In Lorca's writings Bodini discovered humble folk traditions, a timeless world, that in Bodini's conscience became associated with his native region. He also renewed his interest in other poets, including Rafael Alberti, Vicente Aleixandre, Antonio Machado, and others he was later to translate and anthologize, along with a critical study, in his *I poeti surrealisti spagnoli* (The Spanish Surrealist Poets), published in 1963. Through these poets he rediscovered the baroque Spanish literature of Luis de Góngora, Francisco Quevedo, Miguel de Cervantes, and Lope de Vega, authors whose works he later translated and discussed as the subject of critical studies. Spain was casting a new light on Salento, as Bodini began to discover affinities between Spanish culture and his own ancestral area. The result of Bodini's reflections on certain aspects of Spanish culture and on its contiguity with his native Salento is in part responsible for the poetry in *La luna dei Borboni* and *Dopo la luna.*

Salento and the whole southern region were a geographical entity and an area of Bodini's self. Realistic, concrete elements of the landscape were filtered by the poetic imagination according to the neobaroque and surrealist poetics so congenial to Bodini. Because of the thematic material and the treatment it receives, he has often been associated with other poets of the Italian South who constitute what has come to be called the "Linea Meridionale" (Southern Line) of twentieth-century Italian poetry.

In his first books of poetry Bodini seems possessed by an inner demonic force, and his poetry is fashioned from the depths, personal as well as ancestral, as the image of "fiumi paterni" (paternal rivers) suggests in the following lines from "O mio dio": "O mio dio a cui non credo, / ti leggo come una poesia profonda, / piena di occulti sensi e di fiumi paterni" ("O my god in whom I do not believe, / I read you as a profound poem, / full of recondite meanings and paternal rivers). Poetry is a process of discovery designed to bring to light the subterranean ancestral waters generative of the self.

The presence of mysterious sounds as emblems of the self within the folds of the soul is the theme of another poem from the same period. "Vorrei avere la gola d'una lucertola" (I Would Like to Have the Throat of a Lizard) has the central image of the chthonic lizard, the archetype of rebirth being an animal that lives close to the earth and obtains rejuvenation through the sloughing of its skin. The poem is a metaphor for the superhuman effort needed to liberate the soul from its suffocating demonic possessions. The speaker wishes to assimilate the divine property of the reptile, whose throat bulges like a big red balloon at the time of the seasonal change, contracting and expanding, while the mouth remains open as if a very loud scream were about to burst forth, while not a sound is produced, reminiscent of Ungaretti's similar image in *Vita d'un uomo* (Life of a Man, 1962): "La vita non mi è piu, / arrestata in fondo alla gola, / che una roccia di gridi" (Arrested deep in my throat, / my life is not more / than a boulder of screams).

Bodini's southern poetry is embroidered with the delicate filament of memory, a jutting out of the speaker's own life mixed with the familiar landscape. Fleeting moments of remembrance of a pristine and primordial time are sustained by a series of subtle associations established among the various elements: the azure sea, the pink sky, a smile, the dawn, a tree, and the noise of a cart. All these amount to the vanishing metaphor of childhood, of its purity.

Elsewhere in *La luna dei Borboni* and *Dopo la luna* the plexus of feelings toward the motherland is unraveled and becomes evident as an oscillation of love and hate, a centripetal and a centrifugal force, as in these lines from poem 8 in *La luna dei Borboni*: "Qui non vorrei morire dove vivere / mi tocca, mio paese, / cosi sgradito da doverti amare . . ." (I do not wish to die here / where it is my lot to live, my land, / so distasteful that I must love you . . .). The feeling of love is heightened by the repulsion felt as a consequence of the misery and the degradation of the countryside and the people. The landscape becomes the metaphor for a condition of abuses whose most obvious sign is the inertia embodied in the very flatness of the plain. The image of the "insensata pianura" (unfeeling plain) in the poem "Se un giorno uno sprone d'Apennino" (If One Day a Spur of the Apennine) reveals much of the bitter anger of the persona desperately wishing that everything could change, that the people could unite, and that the senselessness and absurdity could be wiped away by a simple kick from the Apennines delivered to the low-lying inert plains.

One of the earliest instances of the South as a central theme appears in the first section of *La luna dei Borboni*; the section is made up of a series of poems numbered one through twelve and provides a first portrait of the southern landscape, as much a physical entity as it is a metaphysical zone of the psyche. The first poem has the dramatic strength of an accusation: "Tu non conosci il Sud / le case di calce / da cui uscivamo al sole come numeri / dalla faccia d'un dado" (You do not know the South / the whitewashed houses / whence we came out to the sunlight like numbers / from the face of a die).

Some verses of *La luna dei Borboni* seem at times to be too abstruse, even cerebral in the unusual combination of their disparate elements. Nonetheless even the most daring of these can be justified because it is the flavor of a certain experience that Bodini wants to convey, never simply the inert physical detail alone: " – Che erba hai in mano? – Ho un mazzetto / di balconi e di capre / di calce azzurra . . ." (– What herbs have you in your hand? – I have a little bundle / of balconies and goats / of blue plaster . . .).

Dopo la luna continues essentially in the same style with perhaps a greater emphasis on socioeconomic themes. The poem "Morta in Puglia" (A Woman's Death in Apulia) provides one of the most poignant lyrical moments. The neorealist component of Bodini's poetics is more evident as the daily struggles, the humble conditions, and the suffering of the people are clearly at the thematic forefront: "Quando seppe l'aumento del prezzo dei pomodori / capì che il tempo dei palpiti era finito. / Imparò a brontolare / e a mettere le mani nella liscivia bollente" (When she learned of the increase in the cost of tomatoes / she understood that her carefree days were over. / She learned to complain / and to put her hands in boiling leach). The finale of the poem introduces a mythical paradise, an invention of folk traditions, in a delicate reverie in which through magic, the oppressive conditions are relieved: "Risorgi nell'Inutile, morta in Puglia: / nei coralli del mare o negli orti del vento / nella tua

terra d'ostriche e di lupi mannari" (Resurrect in the Realm of Non-necessity, dead woman in Apulia: / in the corals of the sea or the howls of the wind / in your land of oysters and of werewolves). These verses complete the portrait of a microcosm, typical of a specific social sector of the region. The label "magic realism" aptly describes these two booklets of poetry.

Aymone's suggestion that the theme of the South is exhausted in the poetry of *La luna dei Borboni* and *Dopo la luna* is accurate only to the extent that in later collections, including *Metamor* (1967), "Zeta," "Poesie ovali"(Oval Poetry), and "Collage" (the last three in *Tutte le poesie* only), the archaic, ancestral lore of the region is not as pervasively present, and much of the demonic charge inherent in the two earlier books has been exorcised. However, the South continues to be the focus of Bodini's poetic meditations as the socioethical conditions of that region are the principal concerns in the later production, where the denunciation of abuses and oppression is presented in an even wider, universal vision. *Metamor* expresses the frustration of Bodini's long-nurtured hope of bringing about social changes – an unrealized economic and egalitarian rebirth of the southern community. A tone of hopelessness and existential anguish pervades the poems. The title of this booklet is an original coinage and suggests a variety of possible meanings. Macrì is inclined to think of it as an amalgam of the words *meta* (half), *amor* (love), and *mor* (death) that refers to a spiritual state suggested by "half love" and "half death." Perhaps the title was formed with the Greek prefix *meta* (beyond) and a combination of *mor* and *amor,* thus giving the possible meanings of "beyond love" and "beyond death." These are plausible interpretations since they echo the essential theme and atmosphere of the poems, based on vanished hopes and defeated aspirations. An alienated and disheartened persona, surviving the aftermath of a great loss – perhaps the loss of love, harmony, and the expectations of youth – decants his bitterness in powerful images. The poems of *Metamor* can also be read as a significant document about the defeat of the ideals of social reforms that had inspired many advocates of the resistance in the immediate postwar period; the reforms were neglected and forgotten as time passed. Still more disheartening for Bodini must have been the reinstatement of political practices that ensured a continuation of social injustice and oppression for a certain sector of the population.

One stylistic element of these poems is rhetorical questioning. The effect of this strategy is to underline the sense of loss and desperation through the fact that the questions asked have obvious answers. The interrogative in these poems is somewhat reminiscent of Giacomo Leopardi's own use of that device to suggest, among other things, the loss of certainty and teleology in a meaningless universe, in which people are alone before an uncaring nature and distant celestial bodies. A variation of the age-old theme of the flight of time constitutes the inspirational nucleus of the poem "Conosco appena le mani" (I Barely Know My Hands). But, in addition to that theme, there is the perplexed and anguished self confronting loneliness and isolation:

Conosco appena le mani,
le scarpe che metto ai piedi.
Conosco il giorno e la notte
e i terrori del vento.
Ma gli anni? Dove sono gli anni,
e tutti i libri che ho letto?
. . . .
Ah, dove son le acute presenze del
passato, le sue calde forme,
la cera su cui incidevano
i miei sentimenti?
Dove si nasconde il senso
delle cose che ho vissuto,
e i brividi lucenti
e i cieli dell'avventura?

(I barely know my hands,
the shoes I am wearing.
I know the day and the night
and the terrors of the wind.
But the years? Where are the years,
and all the books that I read?
. . . .
Ah, where are the sharp witnesses
of the past, its warm shapes,
the wax on which my sentiments
used to leave a trace?
Where hides the sense
of the things I experienced,
and the brilliant shudders
and the skies of adventure?

The questioning strategy allows Bodini to describe a lost aspect of reality while at the same time lamenting its loss. The questions underlie the negative consequences of a consumerist society and the failure of postindustrial political ideology. The speaker cannot find any consolation, since even the avant-garde has become ineffective as a tool of social and political criticism:

Limpida gioia, di che mano sei morta
sotto i duri piumaggi di palmizi senza profeti?
. . . .
Come potremo ora vivere perdendo quota in noi
stessi?
O forse nei mattini senza specchi
ringrazieremo la morte dei suoi cortesi anticipi?

(Limpid happiness, by what hands did you die
under the harsh plumage of palm trees without prophets?
. . . .
How can we now live losing altitude in ourselves?
Or perhaps in the morning without mirrors
we will thank death for its courteous anticipations?)

Criticism of postindustrial social conditions in the 1960s is an essential thematic component of *Metamor* and of Bodini's subsequent collections. The facile, superficial amelioration of economic conditions, which benefitted merely a sector of the population while leaving others in the same old conditions of need, brought with it even more serious problems of a moral nature; personal alienation; migration, with the inherent disintegration of the family structure and the decline of the agricultural sector; the worsening of prejudices and racial conflicts as workers moved to the cities of the North to pursue the mirage of a better life; and the blights of the sexual revolution. These issues are addressed in Bodini's poems of this period. The economic boom is perceived as coiled, destructive, and serpentlike in "Nelle spire del boom" (In the Coils of the Boom), from *Metamor:* "Presi nelle spire del boom ne gustiamo anche noi / gli alti palazzi e le piante nane / piume serpenti chiomati sotterfugi intimi" (Caught in the coils of the boom we get a taste also / of the tall buildings and the dwarfed plants / plumage wigged serpents intimate subterfuges). "Nei viali ovali" (In the Oval Promenades) denounces the perils of internal migration but, more fundamentally, the injustice done to a population that has been shortchanged by the political system of the postwar period:

I bagnini
i muratori
i meridional i emigrati al Nord
propagano il testamento di un'aurora perduta
fra le rampe d'un coito che s'affaccia sul nulla.
Si punge elettrizzata la carne ai chiodi freschi
di uccelli come fari usciti in cerca di cibo.

(The lifeguards
the bricklayers
the southerners immigrated to the North
propagate the testament of a dawn that failed

among the ramps of a coitus that looks onto nothingness.
Electrified flesh is pricked by fresh nails
of birds like headlights gone out looking for food.)

A prolonged and painful illness (cancer),
which eventually culminated in the death of Bodini
at the age of fifty-six in 1970, did not stop him from
continuing his creative productivity while also ful-
filling his role of professor of Spanish literature,
first at the University of Bari and later at the University of Pescara. His death prevented him from
preparing for publication the poems he had been
composing. The task of preparing the complete
works of Bodini fell upon Macrì, his close friend
who was well acquainted with his recent developments and work in progress. The criteria used for
ordering the works, particularly those of the last
phase, are thoroughly elucidated in the preface to
the 1983 edition. One of Bodini's compositional
habits, that of using at a later date poems composed
as much as a decade earlier, by inserting them in a
thematically and stylistically appropriate section of
a new collection, is responsible for the chronological overlapping of the poems in "Zeta" (1962–1969)
with those of *Metamor* (1962–1966) and "Poesie
ovali" (1966–1970). "Collage" (1969–1970) is a
book in the nucleic stage only, made up of fragments of verses and syntagms that in some cases
were already used in earlier poems. Macrì included
these fragments for completeness.

The themes encountered in these last collections are essentially similar to those of the earlier
ones – the concerns always at the center of Bodini's
poetic search: the South; the degradation of human
values in a utilitarian, industrial society; the corruption of political mores; and the destruction of the
natural environment. The anguished persona characteristic of these poems suffers alienation and
hopelessness and is afflicted by an ever-deteriorat-
ing social environment. The verses of this period
are exemplary civic poetry in which the denunciation of an unsatisfactory social system is carried out
ingeniously, with an acutely perspicacious and innovative linguistic manipulation. "L'angelo dei baffi"
(The Angel with the Moustache), for example, is a
portrait of a new social type, a petulant, detestable,
insensitive being: "Coi suoi denti più falsamente
bianchi / ghigna squittisce litiga . . ." (With teeth
more falsely white / he frowns squeaks quar-
rels . . .). "Rapporto del consumo industriale" (Report on Industrial Consumerism) focuses on the
detrimental consequences of industrialization on the
agrarian South:

Dov'erano anfiteatri d'uve dizionari d'ombre
si alzano nidi di plastica di cemento di calcoli di gittata
e tra pungoli e gemiti di notti senza fiori
il numero nemico dell'uomo e della bellezza
coordina coiti prolifici che assicurano all'industria
un più grande mercato di consumatori.

(Where there were amphitheaters of grapes dictionaries of shadows
rise now plastic nests calculations of stretches of cement
and among stings and cries of nights without flowers
the number enemy of beauty
coordinates prolific coituses that ensure to industries
a larger consumer market.)

Bodini searches his own and the collective
consciousness for signs of the durable and enduring
values of the human race, but disillusionment and
hopelessness are recurrent. A pristine time of auro-
ral promise now lost forever is a frequently used
motif in the poems of this last phase, with images of
a utopian dawn that the persona yearns for and invokes, as in "Credevo che credesse" (I Thought He
Thought):

. . . Tornasse anche così
sulle piazze del vento quella lontana rosa
e di colpo fiorissero sui balconi
le immense ciglia. . . .

(. . . Would it return even so
on the wind's squares that distant rose
and suddenly would flourish on balconies
the immense eyelashes. . . .)

The unusual inventiveness of the imagery engages
the reader's attention while never rendering too
obscure the objective concrete data; the imagery
intensifies the apperception of reality and heightens
its impact.

Vittorio Bodini was primarily a poet, and to
the art of poetry he made a lifetime commitment.
However, his narrative fiction and journalistic reportage also show his expressive creativity, while
his works of literary criticism on Góngora,
Quevedo, Pedro Calderón de la Barca, and other
Spanish authors are exemplary essays on baroque
literature.

Bodini also had talent as an artist in pen and
ink; some of his sketches have appeared in the journal *Albero* with a commentary by Macrì. One trait,
however, dominated his multiform personality and
bound all the other characteristics into one: his profound dedication and unflinching courage in decry-
ing abuses and injustices wherever he found them.
This is Bodini's most singular quality, as Giuseppe

Sansone stresses in his *Le trame della poesia* (The Plots of Poetry, 1988). Bodini's most valuable aspect as a writer was his search for human dignity and spiritual freedom.

References:

Renato Aymone, *L'età delle rose: note e letture di poesia* (Naples: Scientifiche Italiane, 1982), pp. 145–207;

Luciano De Rosa, "Storia e cultura in vent'anni di poesia italiana (1940–1960)," *Albero,* nos. 41–44 (1966): 87–104;

Lucio Giannone, *Bodini prima della "luna"* (Lecce: Milella, 1982);

Giovanni Giudici, "Poesia," *Espresso* (23 July 1972): 21;

Oreste Macrì, "Due Salentini a Firenze," *Critica politica,* 7–8 (July–August 1981): 7;

Macrì, "Il Foscolo giocatore di Bodini," in his *Il Foscolo negli scritti del Novecento* (Ravenna: Longo, 1980), pp. 129–133;

Macrì, "Poesia grafica di Vittorio Bodini," *Albero,* no. 51 (1974): pp. 75–98;

Macrì, "Saluto a Vittorio Bodini," *Albero,* no. 46 (1971): 12–18;

Macrì, Ennio Bonea, and Donato Valli, eds., *Le terre di Carlo V: Studi su V. Bodini* (Galatina: Congedo, 1984);

Giuliano Manacorda, *Prometeo,* 1 (June 1981): 9–11;

Leonardo Mancino, ed., *Omaggio a Bodini,* (Manduria: Lacaita, 1972);

Mario Marti, "Ipotesi filologico-critica su Bodini e il suo Salento," *Critica Letteraria,* 33 (1982): 143–149;

Bortolo Pento, *Letture di poesia contemporanea* (Milan: Marzorati, 1965), pp. 22–26;

Joseph Perricone, "Objects and Landscape in *La luna dei Borbini,*" *Forum Italicum* (Fall 1984): 302–320;

Perricone, *Vittorio Bodini: Saggio critico* (Fasano: Schena, 1986);

Silvio Ramat, *L'ermetismo* (Florence: Nuova Italia, 1969), pp. 462–464;

Giuseppe Sansone, *Le trame della poesia* (Florence: Vallecchi, 1988), pp. 297–313;

Alba Tremonti, *Zucchero e assenzio in Vittorio Bodini* (Fossalta di Piave: Rebellato, 1981).

Giorgio Caproni

(7 January 1912 – 22 January 1990)

Emilio Speciale
University of Chicago

BOOKS: *Come un'allegoria* (Genoa: Degli Orfini, 1936);

Ballo a Fontanigorda e altre poesie (Genoa: Degli Orfini, 1938);

Finzioni (Rome: Tiberino, 1941);

Giorni aperti (Rome: Letture d'Oggi, 1942);

Cronistoria (Florence: Vallecchi, 1943);

Stanze della funicolare (Rome: De Luca, 1952);

Il gelo della mattina (Caltanissetta: Sciascia, 1954);

Il passaggio d'Enea (Florence: Vallecchi, 1956);

Il seme del piangere (Milan: Garzanti, 1959);

Congedo del viaggiatore cerimonioso & altre prosopopee (Milan: Garzanti, 1965);

Versi nella nebbia & dal monte (Trieste: ALUT, 1968);

Il "Terzo libro" e altre cose (Turin: Einaudi, 1968);

Versi fuori commercio (Luxembourg: Origine, 1970);

4 poesie inedite di Giorgio Caproni — 9 dipinti di Mario Marcucci (Florence: Pananti, 1975);

Il muro della terra (Milan: Garzanti, 1975);

Poesie (Milan: Garzanti, 1976; enlarged, 1989);

Erba francese (Luxembourg: Origine, 1979);

L'ultimo borgo, edited by Giovanni Raboni (Milan: Rizzoli, 1980);

Il franco cacciatore (Milan: Garzanti, 1982);

Genova di tutta la vita, edited by Giorgio Devoto and Adriano Guerrini (Genoa: San Marco dei Giustiniani, 1983);

Tutte le poesie (Milan: Garzanti, 1983);

Il labirinto (Milan: Rizzoli, 1984);

Il Conte di Kevenhüller (Milan: Garzanti, 1986);

Allegretto con brio (Lugano, Switzerland: Laghi di Plivtice, 1988);

Res amissa, edited by Giorgio Agamben (Milan: Garzanti, 1991).

OTHER: Ruth Feldman and Brian Swann, eds. and trans., *Italian Poetry Today: Currents and Trends,* includes poems by Caproni (Saint Paul: New Rivers, 1979), pp. 38–39.

TRANSLATIONS: Marcel Proust, *Il tempo ritrovato* (Turin: Einaudi, 1950);

Giorgio Caproni circa 1969

René Char, *Poesia e prosa* (Milan: Feltrinelli, 1962);

Charles Baudelaire, *I fiori del male* (Rome: Curgio, 1963);

Louis-Ferdinand Céline, *Morte a credito* (Milan: Garzanti, 1964);

Guy de Maupassant, *Bel-Ami* (Milan: Garzanti, 1965);

Blaise Cendrars, *La mano mozza* (Milan: Garzanti, 1967);

André Frénaud, *Il silenzio di Genova e altre poesie* (Turin: Einaudi, 1967);

Frénaud, *Non c'è paradiso* (Milan: Rizzoli, 1971);

Jean Genet, *Tutto il teatro* (Milan: Saggiatore, 1971);

Federico García Lorca, *Il maleficio della farfalla* (Turin: ERI, 1972);

Wilhelm Busch, *Max e Moritz ovvero Pippo e Peppo* (Milan: Rizzoli, 1974);

Genet, *Quattro romanzi* (Milan: Saggiatore, 1975);

Guillaume Apollinaire, *Poesie* (Milan: Rizzoli, 1980).

In the panorama of twentieth-century Italian poetry, the work of Giorgio Caproni represents a centrifugal force with respect to official trends. He was more responsive to the Italian literary tradition in its entirety than to a particular school of his time. Nevertheless, Caproni's poetry is embedded in contemporary experience; it is aimed at answering everyday existential and ethical questions as well as searching for poetical forms adequate to express such questions. He was a poet who looked beyond and over the various poetical trends and schools of his time; he leaned on the solid foundations of Italian literary tradition in order to restore it in a fragmentary mode for the modern reader's taste.

Born in Leghorn, Italy, on 7 January 1912 (and consequently belonging to the same generation as Attilio Bertolucci, Piero Bigongiari, Alfonso Gatto, Mario Luzi, and Vittorio Sereni – the so-called Third Generation), Caproni moved with his family to Genoa when he was ten years old. Genoa was to become in many of his poems the mythical city. To follow his chosen profession, that of an elementary-school teacher, he lived in different small towns until he moved to Rome in 1939. He fought in World War II on the western front and was actively involved in the resistance. At the end of the war he returned to Rome, where he lived until his death. His life included a beloved wife, a son, a daughter, and a secure job as teacher. Caproni's poetic production was constant, without big gaps, though there was a brief silence right after the end of the war.

In his first book, *Come un'allegoria* (Like an Allegory, 1936), which includes Caproni's poetry from 1932 to 1935, one notices a strong, mannered naturalism that will tend to disappear in the following collections. It is a continuous description of country scenery, especially in changing moments: dawn and sunset, the passage of the seasons, fires and wind, and so on. In these moments young boys and girls are privileged characters, in a tradition that goes from Giacomo Leopardi to Giovanni Pascoli to Umberto Saba to Sandro Penna. In Caproni's poems there is the entire life of a village seen through the eyes of youth in images of transition:

> ma se mi passa accanto
> un ragazzo, nel soffio
> della sua bocca sento
> quant'è labile il fiato
> del giorno.
> . . . .
>   Ma io sento ancora
> fresco sulla mia pelle il vento
> d'una fanciulla passatami a fianco
> di corsa.

> (but if a boy
> walks by me, in the breath
> of his mouth I feel
> how transient is the breath
> of the day.
> . . . .
>   But I still feel
> fresh on my skin the wind
> of a girl who passed by me
> running.)

Labile (transient) is one of the most used adjectives in these poems to describe the fragile world of the young poet. But *labili* (transciencies) are not the forms Caproni adopted in this first book: one immediately notices his literary skills in many lines. There are bold metaphors with strong alliteration, as in this line: "nell'ora in cui l'aria s'arancia" (in the hour in which the air oranges [turns orange]), and complicated alliterative play with sibilant and fricative letters, as in these lines: "e se si sono spente / le risse e le sassaiole / chiassose, nel vento è vivo" (and if ceased / the fights and the volley of stones / noisy, in the wind are alive). The title of this first collection comes from a line in Caproni's poem "Borgoratti":

> Come un'allegoria
> una fanciulla appare
> sulla porta dell'osteria.
> Alle sue spalle è un vociare
> confuso d'uomini – e l'aspro
> odore del vino.

> (Like an allegory
> a young girl appears
> at the tavern's door.
> Behind her [inside] is a vague shouting
> of men – and the pungent
> smell of wine.)

The young girl is like an allegory of life in front of a young boy who looks at her face; he is ready to enter the adult world, the blurred and smelly world of the tavern.

This small-town and naturalistic dimension persists as the background in Caproni's second collection, *Ballo a Fontanigorda*, (Dance in Fontanigorda, 1938), which includes poems written between 1935 and 1937. Here again are mutable landscapes as well as fleeting young figures and fresh sensations. A young bride is "cosa tanto precaria" (a very precarious thing), like Caproni's first girlfriend, Olga Franzoni, who died very young. Nevertheless, youth remains a vivacious experience, a dance. In this collection is the first appearance in Caproni's poetry of Rina, his wife, who lived in Fontanigorda. Moreover, the poet's first sexual feelings appear in connection with sea imagery. The emblem of Venus is in this vein, as is this quatrain of septenarii:

Questo odore marino
che mi rammenta tanto
i tuoi capelli, al primo
chiareggiato mattino.

(This smell of the sea
which reminds me so much of
your hair, in the first
morning light.)

The Italian literary tradition is always present, as in the phrasing of this stanza, very similar to Leopardi's style:

E quanto mai
dolce è per un istante
indugiare allora sul tempo
andato — sul giorno,
in così varie e tante
guerre, vinto oramai.

(And how sweet
it is for an instant
to linger then on the times
bygone — on the day,
in so different and many
wars, now overcome.)

Finzioni (Fictions, 1941) is part, together with the first two collections, of what Caproni called his "Primo Libro" (First Book). There is a thematic continuity among these early collections. But in *Finzioni* one notices how Caproni has acquired a secure technique and uses rhyme with ease. In this collection are short poems with lines of six or seven syllables — mostly love poems. The landscape is still one of the sea, on which the image of woman stands out, as in this poem:

Come dev'esser dolce
della tua carnagione
il fiore, alle prim'ore
d'alba colto in stagione
chiara, quando di nuove
cose commuove l'aria
pudicissimo odore,
e il petto tocca e tenta
lo svegliarsi del mare.

(How sweet must be
your complexion
the flower, in the first hours
of dawn picked in a clear
season, when new
things touch the air
with a very bashful scent,
and the breast touches and tempts
the awakening of the sea.)

The reader should also notice these lines: "Sei donna di marine, / donna che apre riviere" (You are a woman of seashores, / a woman who opens coasts). In these recurring landscapes and moments of joy and dance, Caproni lives his *romanza*, a love story in which moments of sadness for the absence of the beloved person predominate along with hopes for the future. In contrast with these feelings, there is also the awareness of time's inevitable passing. The collection concludes with two sonnets, a form often used by Caproni as his career progressed. The concluding poems in *Finzioni* summarize the main themes of his work: the collective feast, the noisy joy of youth, the happy face of the woman, the taverns, and the month of May — a month of passages that foreshadows "grandiose / notti più umane" (grandiose / nights more human).

Cronistoria (Chronicle, 1943) is divided into two sections — "E lo spazio era un fuoco" (And the Space Was a Fire) and "Sonetti dell'anniversario" (Sonnets for the Anniversary) — which are extremely dissimilar in form and content. In the first section, which includes mostly short poems, the woman's image is still in the foreground, a strong image of fire and burning, in which the color red prevails: "E lo spazio era un fuoco / dove ardevi per gioco / coi tuoi abiti . . ." (And the space was a fire / where you were burning for fun / with your clothes . . .). Blood, embers, face, and clothes are all symbolic elements that return obsessively in poems dedicated to the woman. Red is also the color associated with Caproni's youth, which he left behind when he moved away to discover cities such as Udine, Pisa, Rome, Tarquinia, and Assisi. In this book the language becomes closer to the essential and analogic language of the hermetic school:

I sassi
soli compagni, gridi,
lo sento, nel tuo silenzio
l'amor cieco – ai nidi
di vipere la tua paura
come un tempo riaffidi.

(The stones
as only companions, you yell,
I hear it, in your silence
the blind love – you again
entrust as in the past
your fear to nests of vipers.)

In section 2 Caproni chooses the sonnet, a closed form, but in his hands not rigidly perfect, to narrate in a dramatic and exclamatory tone the death of his girlfriend Olga. In a continuous dialogue with the lost young girl, the speaker evokes the happy time spent together with her, and the mourning in which he is now enveloped. The poem is a hymn to the precariousness of life and to the certainty of death:

Di te riavrò solo nell'aria
esulcerata un'ardente lettura
dai segni che v'hai inciso – una precaria
chiusa grafia, che nessuna figura
allenterà, se non morte plenaria.

(Of you I will have only in the distressed
air a burning reading
of the signs you engraved on it – a precarious
secret writing, which no figure
will loosen, if not a plenary death.)

Il passaggio d'Enea (The Passage of Aeneas, 1956) constitutes the high point of Caproni's first poetic phase. It features several *poemetti* (long poems divided into shorter ones), in which he reflects on the human condition after a devastating war (World War II). The collection opens with two sonnets, as a prelude, in which Caproni indicates a condition of inner death: "io ho fermo / il polso" (my pulse / has stopped). The first section, "Gli anni tedeschi" (The German Years), includes two *poemetti* – "I lamenti" and "Le biciclette" – and a closing sonnet. "I lamenti" has a vigorous civic tone and underlines the weakening of life's values during the war, the uselessness of the poetical word in the face of such a calamity. This is a poetry with exclamatory sentences (typically the lament's form) or interrogative ones, with no answers. "Le biciclette," dedicated to the

Caproni in 1964 (drawing by Franco Gentilini; Collection of the Caproni Family)

poet Libero Bigiaretti, consists of eight stanzas of sixteen lines (close to a combination of two ottava rimas) of rhyming hendecasyllables. Caproni reached a very sophisticated metric technique, which is repeated in the other *poemetti* of this collection but which he abandons in his later production. The bicycles in the poem bring the sound of youth, a time in which the speaker might have considered himself full of *ardore*. That "tempo ormai diviso" (time now divided) is characterized by a series of mistakes, a time that may be recovered by a different pedaling, one not done by the speaker: "E se il mio piede / melodico ormai tace, altro pedale / fugge sopra gli asfalti bianchi al bordo / d'altr'erba millenaria" (And if my melodic foot / is by now silent, another pedal / runs away on the white asphalts on the edge / of another millennial grass).

The next poem in *Il passaggio d'Enea* is *Stanze della funicolare* (Stanzas of the Funicular, separately published in 1952), which opens with an interlude introducing the populist hell of a small dairy, where a Proserpina figure/waitress serves a few patrons. The long poem describes a run on the funicular above Genoa, a vehicle that does not move the passenger from one place to a very different one. Indeed, the funicular elevates a passenger above the same landscape; only the perspective of the ascending person is changed. The poem is an unceasing trip toward death in twelve stanzas, which always conclude with a variant of the lines "non è l'ora / questa, nel buio, di chiedere l'alt" (this is not the time, / in the dark, to ask for a halt). From the funicular, often transformed into an ark in Caproni's imagination, one can see Genoa at the time of awakening, with the road sweepers, market people, the trolley, various girls, some sailors, and others. All are surrounded by the darkness and the first light of morning in a dense, pervasive fog, which symbolize the difficulty of knowing the world:

> Perché è nebbia, e la nebbia è nebbia, e il latte
> nei bicchieri è ancora nebbia, e nebbia ha
> nella cornea la donna che in ciabatte
> lava la soglia di quei magri bar
> dove in Erebo è il passo.

> (Because it is fog, and the fog is fog, and the milk
> in the glasses is still fog, and fog is what is
> in the cornea of the woman who in slippers
> washes the threshold of those lean cafés
> where the passage to the Erebus is.)

This is the human condition, a suspended trip in a landscape with only a few lights, enveloped in fog until:

> la funicolare
> già lontana ed insipida, scolora
> nella nebbia di latte ove si sfa
> l'ultima voglia di chiedere l'ora
> fra quel lenzuolo di chiedere l'alt.

> (the funicular
> already far away and tasteless, discolors
> in the fog of milk where the last desire
> to ask for the time decays
> between those sheets of asking for a halt.)

The next poem is "All alone" (the title is in English), and it has three parts: "Didascalia" (Subtitle), "Versi," and "Epilogo." The first one is an introduction and describes the poet's arrival in Genoa at night, in the dark, through "una porta stretta" (a narrow door). The second – six stanzas of sixteen lines – describes the return of "Uomini miti" (meek men) to their home, in realistic snapshots, from the opening of the main door in the morning to their awakening the next day, ready to leave again. These are men who, in their "minimi traffici" (small businesses), live their lives between faith and hope, two key words that recur several times in the *poemetto*.

In the "Epilogo" these meek men become the poet himself, who finds himself knocking at a door through which one enters and exits Genoa. He then remembers his last entrance in Genoa: the "Salita della Tosse" area, the girls, and the sea.

The *poemetto* that gives the title to the entire collection, "Il passaggio d'Enea," is also composed of three sections, with identical titles from the previous *poemetto*. This long poem, considered by critics to be Caproni's masterpiece, refers to a sculpture of Aeneas seen by the poet in a Genoa square. The sculpture represents Aeneas carrying his father on his shoulders and taking his son by hand. In "Didascalia" (three stanzas of short lines) the poet finds himself in a roadman's house, and, hearing noises through the shutters, he sees:

> lampi erranti
> d'ammotorati viandanti.
> Frusciavano in me l'idea
> che fosse il passaggio d'Enea.

> (wandering flashes
> of motorized wayfarers.
> They rustled in me the idea
> that this was Aeneas's passage.)

In "Versi" (five stanzas of sixteen lines) Caproni invokes again some images of Aeneas:

> Enea che in spalla
> un passato che crolla tenta invano
> di porre in salvo, e al rullo d'un tamburo
> ch'è uno schianto di mura, per la mano
> ha ancora così gracile un futuro
> da non reggersi ritto.

> (Aeneas who on his shoulders
> a collapsing past in vain tries
> to save, and at the roll of a drum
> which is a crash of walls, by hand
> has such a still frail future
> unable to stand up by itself.)

This is a very clear existential statement of a generation who came out of a destructive war, a generation without a past to lean on and with a very fragile future.

In "Epilogo" the speaker, now tired, approaches the sea in the evening:

> Avevo raggiunto la rena,
> ma senza avere più lena.
> Forse era il peso, nei panni,
> dell'acqua dei miei anni.

> (I had reached the sand,
> but I had no more energy.

Perhaps it was the weight, in my clothes,
of the water of my years.)

The appendix to the book contains several poems, almost all dedicated to Genoa, including the very long final poem "Litania."

Of the same period are many poems Caproni collected in *Il seme del piangere* (The Seed of Crying, 1959), but the style of these poems is quite different. Caproni goes back to the short lines of his first collections but shows his technical maturity, especially in presenting the canzonet form, in which popular tone, spoken language, and the prosaic mode prevail. Far from the poetry of *Il passaggio d'Enea*, the poems are more readable and singable, and there are easy rhymes. These are used to evoke, in the section "Versi livornesi" (Verses from Leghorn), Annina Picchi Caproni, mother of the poet and busy seamstress, and the town of Leghorn, the happy background of her days until she died in 1950. Line after line, the poem is the story of Annina's life, with Annina a symbol of youth who regenerates everything she touches and passes:

Livorno, quando lei passava,
d'aria e di barche odorava.
Che voglia di lavorare
nasceva, al suo ancheggiare!

(Leghorn, when she passed by,
smelled of air and boats.
What a desire to work
arose, at the sight of her swaying by!)

Caproni revisits many places, the simple feelings of Leghorn people, the bicycles, the seamstresses, and the cafés. In "Eppure" (And Yet) he describes his mother's wedding and, in the poem that gives the title to the collection, her loss:

La mamma-più-bella-del-mondo
non c'era più – era via.
Via la ragazza fina,
d'ingegno e di fantasia.

(The most-beautiful-mother-of-the-world
was no more – she went away.
Away the refined girl,
in her intellect and imagination.)

Metapoetic considerations surface in the section's opening poem, "Perch'io ..." (Because I ...) – which is an evident allusion to Guido Cavalcanti – and "Battendo a macchina" (Typing):

Caproni circa 1965

Mia mano, fatti piuma:
fatti vela; e leggera
muovendoti sulla tastiera,
sii cauta. E bada, prima
di fermare la rima,
che stai scrivendo d'una
che fu viva e fu vera.

(My hand, become a feather:
become a sail; and lightly
moving on the keyboard,
be prudent. And mind, before
fixing the rhyme,
that you are writing about
someone who was alive and real.)

These metapoetic considerations appear also in "La gente se l'additava" (People Pointed Her Out), "Per lei" (For Her), and other poems. Caproni essentially asks how to talk about such a delicate subject (a working-class mother, a young seamstress, true and beautiful in her son's memory) without slipping into "crepuscolarism." He solves this problem by complicating his poetry with the literary tradition, using well the popular and cantabile forms of the canzonet and the ballad. The "Versi livornesi" section concludes with this summarizing verse:

> Freschi come i bicchieri
> furono i suoi pensieri.
> Per lei torni in onore
> la rima in cuore e amore.

> (Fresh as glasses
> were her thoughts.
> For her, let there return with honor
> the rhyme in *cuore* [heart] and *amore* [love].

Il seme del piangere also includes a section of "Altri versi," with the same style and tone but different themes (youth, school days, May Day, and so forth).

The short collection *Congedo del viaggiatore cerimonioso & altre prosopopee* (The Departure of the Ceremonious Traveler & Other Prosopopoeias, 1965) opened a new phase of Caproni's poetry. Some characteristics are typical of all his poetry to follow. Caproni abandons the closed metrical forms and uses rhyme seldom and less rigidly. He adopts short lines and brief poems for a more epigrammatic style, in which an aphoristic tone, irony, and paradox prevail, together with more stress on the spoken language. In this collection prosopopoeia is the core of poetry: he introduces characters who speak about themselves. Prosopopeia presupposes the absence or death of the person who speaks, and in reality these voices of the poet are voices from another world. The voice of the poet, indeed, takes its leave from human conversation. He is ready to face the unknown, where "il buio è così buio / che non c'è oscurità" (the darkness is so dark / that there is no obscurity). He seems to have reached his destination:

> Congedo alla sapienza
> e congedo all'amore.
> Congedo anche alla religione.
> Ormai sono a destinazione.

> Ora che più forte sento
> stridere il freno, vi lascio
> davvero, amici. Addio.
> Di questo, sono certo: io
> son giunto alla disperazione
> calma, senza sgomento.

> Scendo. Buon proseguimento.

> (Farewell to wisdom
> and farewell to love.

Farewell also to religion.
Now I have arrived.

> Now that I can hear more acutely
> the brake screeching, I leave you
> indeed, my friends. Farewell.
> I am sure of this: I
> have arrived to a calm
> despair, without dismay.

> I am getting off. Enjoy the rest of your journey.)

In "Il fischio (parla il guardacaccia)" (The Whistle [a Gamekeeper Speaks]) Caproni presents another theme, the ambiguity of hunting: "Il guardacaccia, caccia / ed è cacciato" (The gamekeeper hunts / and is hunted). In "Lamento (o boria) del preticello deriso" (The Lament [or Haughtiness] of the Fooled Young Priest) Caproni introduces a religious theme through the blasphemous confession of the priest: "So anche che voi non credete / a Dio. Nemmeno io. / Per questo mi sono fatto prete" (I also know you do not believe / in God. Neither do I. / This the reason why I became a priest). The priest speaks of his conversion to the church, with the help of a prostitute. The language verges on obscenity, and the speaker inveighs against the corruption of the world, because he sees everything under the market economy's spell. In conclusion he prays not because God exists, but because God should exist.

Caproni's collection *Il muro della terra* (The Wall of the Earth, 1975), its title from Dante's *Inferno*, where *terra* indicates the city of Dis, was enthusiastically received by literary critics. The collection is divided into sections of different length (sometimes a single poem) but with unitary content. The condition of despair is accentuated. The speaker becomes certain of not being able to break "the wall" of the other and the world, and of being condemned to a solitary life "nel grigiore / che non ha nome" (in the grayness / which has no name). It becomes very difficult to find a way of saving who is lost or is in the process of losing himself:

> M'ero sperso. Annaspavo.
> Cercavo uno sfogo.
> Chiesi a uno. "Non sono,"
> mi rispose, "del luogo."

> (I was lost. I was groping.
> I was looking for some relief.
> I asked someone. "I am not,"
> he answered, "from this place.")

This search for a light in the darkness, which enwraps the speaker like an insuperable wall, constrains him to ask for a guide and consequently to pray to a supernatural being. Then he directly asks God to appear, to become light, but without success, because God has disappeared or killed himself: "(Non ha saputo resistere / al suo non esistere?)" ([He did not know how to resist / his nonexisting?]) Unable to bear the fact that his divine presence is not felt anymore on the corrupted earth, God has decided to eliminate himself. This disappearance of God produces dizziness and confusion in human beings. The speaker is not able to distinguish between the guide and the guided, as in this example, in which he asks his son to be his guide: "Portami con te lontano / . . . lontano . . . / nel tuo futuro. // Diventa mio padre, portami / per la mano" (Take me with you far away / . . . far away . . . / in your future. // Become my father, take me / by the hand), where one may notice the resumption of the myth of Aeneas.

There is also confusion between the I and the other (often God), as in this poem:

Cercai,
a urtoni, d'aprirmi un passo
tra la calca, ma lui
(od ero io?) lui
già s'era alzato: sparito,
senza che io lo avessi incrociato.

(I tried,
with pushes, to open for myself a passage
in the crowd, but he
[or was it I?] he
already had stood up: had disappeared,
without my having run into him.)

Then the speaker is not able to recognize the places where he was:

Tutti i luoghi che ho visto,
che ho visitato,
ora so – ne sono certo:
non ci sono mai stato.

(All the places I have seen,
I have visited,
now I know – I am sure:
I have never been there.)

All the elements that keep together the identity of a person have completely disappeared: family ties, spatial location, religion, and relationship with other persons. Everything and everybody has left, leaving the speaker to doubt the necessity of his existence, as in "Lasciando Loco" (Leaving Loco)

and "Parole (dopo l'esodo) dell'ultimo della Moglia" (Words [After the Exodus] of the Last Inhabitant of the Moglia). This poetry is highly epigrammatic and very close to paradox, by means of which Caproni wants to demonstrate the discouraging logic of the modern human condition. This poetry is also extremely learned (including many citations – some in English and French – and references to past poets, above all, Dante), but the language comes closer and closer to the spoken form, and syntax and metrics are simplified.

The poems of *Il franco cacciatore* (The Free Shooter, 1982) continue the aphoristic discourse of *Il muro della terra*, varying the same theme of the disappearance of the divine and of the solitude of humankind: "Vi sono casi in cui accettare la solitudine può significare attingere Dio. Ma v'è una stoica accettazione più nobile ancora: la solitudine senza Dio" (There are cases in which to accept solitude can mean reaching God. But there is a stoic resignation that is nobler: solitude without God). This condition does not precipitate Caproni into a state of melancholy or rage; on the contrary, it produces in him an "allegria indicibile" (unutterable joy), the happiness of being able to believe in God, knowing that God does not exist. The disappearance of the divine is caused by the desacralization of the human being. In this condition the human being has lost the knowledge of his "luoghi giurisdizionali" (jurisdictional places): "Errata / Non sai mai dove sei. // Corrige / Non sei mai dove sai" (Errata / You never know where you are. // Corrige / You never are where you know). Even the journey of life appears to be a journey without a departure or arrival: "Il mio viaggiare / è stato tutto un restare / qua, dove non fui mai" (My traveling / has all been a remaining / here, where I have never been). The only certainty of the journey is death, which Caproni contemplates from an even closer position: "Mi sono avvicinato troppo. / Fra poco precipiterò" (I have come too close. / Very soon I will fall); and "Sono già vicino al Forte. // Son già dentro la morte" (I am already near the Fort. // I am already inside death). Death is in any case a homicide/suicide, in which it is difficult to distinguish the hunted from the hunter. Caproni does not see any form of redemption against death, not even the consolatory redemption of the poet through his poetry:

Bravo. Sei stato lirico.
Lirico fino all'orgasmo.
Ora va' a letto. Dormi,
beato, nel tuo entusiasmo.

(Bravo. You have been lyric.
Lyric up to an orgasm.
Now go to bed. Sleep,
happy, in your enthusiasm.)

Caproni's poetic discourse has arrived at a total fragmentation and an obsessive repetition of the same themes. More and more often, his poems consist of only one word or one line. The syntax tends to be dislocated and minimal. In these poems nominal sentences, unfinished sentences, and isolated verbs prevail: the homicide/suicide of the word.

His comprehensive collection *Tutte le poesie* (All the Poems, 1983) is closed by two sections. The first includes some previously unpublished poems that, he says, "si sono scritte da sole" (wrote themselves on their own), and these poems wished to be published, almost without the consent of the author. They are "Versicoli del Controcaproni" (Little Verses of the Counter-Caproni) and are variants of the same themes seen earlier, as in "Proverbio dell'egoista" (Proverb of the Selfish Man): "Morto io, / morto Dio" (Once I am dead, / God is dead).

The last section, *Erba francese* (French Grass, separately published in 1979), is a sort of travel diary and an impressionistic description of the Parisian places visited by Caproni and his daughter, Silvana. These short poems are like postcards of memory: "Parigi impressionista. / Già persa di vista" (Impressionistic Paris. / Already lost sight of it). His complete works conclude with an added poem that has the function of a farewell to the world: "Chiusi la finestra. / Il cuore. / La porta. / A doppia mandata" (I locked the window. / The heart. / The door. / Double-locked).

But this was not so, because Caproni in 1986 published another book of poems. *Il Conte di Kevenhüller* (The Count of Kevenhüller) starts with a hunting notice posted by the count in 1792. The first part of the book tells of an opera at the beginning of which the director dies. Caproni was an amateur violinist, and music had an important role in his poetry. In this collection music is at the core of the project: the opera is divided into "Il Libretto" and "La Musica." It is the story of the hunting of a beast, which successively metamorphoses into God, the I, the name, and life in general. The rhythm of the poems becomes the rhythm of the hunt, and the reader follows this fugue, this impossible mission to catch evil. It is also a continuous naming of the beast:

La Bestia assassina.

La Bestia che nessuno mai vide.

La Bestia che sotterraneamente
— falsamente mastina —
ogni giorno ti elide.

La Bestia che ti vivifica e uccide
· ·
Io solo, con un nodo in gola,
sapevo. E' dietro la Parola.

(The murderous Beast.

The Beast nobody ever saw.

The Beast which from underground
— like a false mastiff —
annuls you everyday.

The Beast which livens and kills you
· ·
Only I, with a lump in my throat,
knew. It is behind the Word.)

The beast haunting Caproni is the emptiness of the name, the fading of the word, and the void which remains. Poetry thus becomes an increasing effort to avoid the disappearance of the word. In *Il Conte* Caproni again uses white spaces, nominal sentences, syntactical fragments, and a minimal presence of rhyme. In the second part, titled "Altre cadenze" (Other Cadences), he presents several poems reflecting his last years. Among them is the singular poem titled "(" — which consists of the following line: "La morte non finisce mai" (Death never ends); whereas on the next page, the poem graphically titled ")" does not have any text.

In 1991 Giorgio Agamben edited a new collection of poems on which Caproni was working before his death. The title of the collection, *Res amissa* (The Lost Thing) refers to "the Good" according to a note by Caproni: "il tema è la Bestia (il male) nelle sue varie forme e metamorfosi. Tutti riceviamo in dono qualcosa di prezioso, che poi perdiamo irrevocabilmente. (La Bestia è il Male. La *res amissa* [la cosa perduta] è il Bene)" (the theme is the Beast [the evil] in its different forms and metamorphoses. We all receive as a gift something precious, that we irrevocably lose. [The Beast is the Evil. *Res amissa* (the lost thing) is the Good]). In this collection Caproni continues his search for an after-the-death-of-God theology: "Mio Dio, anche se non esisti, / perché non ci assisti?" (My God, even if you do not exist, /

why do not assist us?). This theme appears to be linked to the necessary departure of the poet himself. Caproni reflects more in his last poems on death, even if in an ironic vein. His epigrammatic style and craftsmanlike use of rhyme continues to characterize his poems, as in "La fatalità della rima" (The Fatality of Rhyme):

La terra.
La guerra.

La sorte.
La morte.

(Earth.
War.

Faith.
Death.)

Giorgio Caproni was a first-class figure in the Italian poetry of the twentieth century. It is impossible to enclose his poetry in a formula. He always worked intensively on the planning of his books, each one of which has a unified theme. If one wishes to find a unifying motif for his poetry it may be his working and reworking of form itself, as any great poet has done. One may define Caproni as a mannerist poet: he obsessively repeated and used a few themes, and he worked in the presence of the entire Italian poetical tradition, which he appropriated with grace, as in his homage to Torquato Tasso (in *Tutte le poesie*):

Dedica,
per amor di rima:
a Torquato Tasso,
con cordiale stima.

(Dedication,
due to a love of rhyme:
for Torquato Tasso
with cordial esteem.)

But this search for new forms and the labor to attain perfection were strictly connected by Caproni with the depressing journey of life.

Biographies:

Luigi Surdich, *Giorgio Caproni: Un ritratto* (Genoa: Costa & Nolan, 1990);

Adele Dei, *Giorgio Caproni* (Milan: Mursia, 1992).

References:

Antonio Barbuto, *Giorgio Caproni: Il destino d'Enea* (Rome: Ateneo & Bizzarri, 1980);

Giorgio Devoto and Stefano Verdino, eds., *Genova a Giorgio Caproni* (Genoa: San Marco dei Giustiniani, 1982);

Antonio Girardi, "Metri di Giorgio Caproni," in his *Cinque storie stilistiche* (Genoa: Marietti, 1987), pp. 99–134;

Antonio Iacopetta, *Giorgio Caproni: Miti e poesia* (Rome: Bonacci, 1981).

Bartolo Cattafi

(6 July 1922 – 13 March 1979)

Giovanna Wedel De Stasio

BOOKS: *Nel centro della mano* (Milan: Meridiana, 1951);

Partenza da Greenwich (Milan: Meridiana, 1955);

Le mosche del meriggio (Milan: Mondadori, 1958);

Lo stretto di Messina e le Eolie, by Cattafi and Alfredo Camisa (Rome: Lea, 1961);

Qualcosa di preciso (Milan: All'Insegna del Pesce d'Oro, 1961);

L'osso, l'anima (Milan: Mondadori, 1964);

L'aria secca del fuoco, marzo 1971-gennaio 1972 (Milan: Mondadori, 1972);

Il buio (Milan: All'Insegna del Pesce d'Oro, 1973);

Lame (Verona: Sommaruga, 1973);

Quattro poesie e quattro acqueforti (Verona: Sommaruga, 1974);

Ostuni (Milan: Edizione 32, 1975);

La discesa al trono, 1971-1973 (Milan: Mondadori, 1975);

Ipotenusa (Senningerberg, Luxembourg: Origine, 1975);

Marzo e le sue idi, 1972-1973 (Milan: Mondadori, 1977);

Nel rettangolo dei teoremi (Rome: L'Arco / Milan: Scheiwiller, 1978);

18 dediche, '76-'77 (Milan: All'Insegna del Pesce d'Oro, 1978);

Se i cavalli . . . (Milan: Scheiwiller, 1978);

Poesie scelte (1946-1973), edited by Giovanni Raboni (Milan: Mondadori, 1978);

L'allodola ottobrina, 1976-1977 (Milan: Mondadori, 1979);

Oltre l'omega (Milan: All'Insegna del Pesce d'Oro, 1980);

Chiromanzia d'inverno (Milan: Mondadori, 1983);

Dieci poesie inedite (Pesaro: Pergola, 1983);

Segni (Milan: Scheiwiller, 1986);

Poesie, 1943-1979, edited by Vincenzo Leotta and Raboni (Milan: Mondadori, 1990).

Edition: *The Dry Air of the Fire: Selected Poems,* bilingual edition, edited and translated by Ruth Feldman and Brian Swann (Ann Arbor: Translation Press, 1981).

OTHER: Vittoria Bradshaw, ed. and trans., *From*
Pure Silence to Impure Dialogue: A Survey of Post-War Italian Poetry 1945-1965, includes poems by Cattafi (New York: Las Américas, 1971), pp. 172-187;

Lawrence R. Smith, ed. and trans., *The New Italian Poetry: 1945 to the Present. A Bilingual Anthology,* includes poems by Cattafi (Berkeley: University of California Press, 1981), pp. 253-269.

Bartolo Cattafi's poetry is a significant testimony to the return of a baroque style in twentieth-century literature. The important presence of Cattafi's work in the evolution of Italian poetry during the last two decades is also due to his gradual refusal of the hermetic tradition and to his new usage of poetic language. Like the English Metaphysicals, Cattafi tries to grasp the fragments of an unseizable reality by exploring verbal logic to the verge of absurdity. He bestows a metaphysical significance upon common physical objects; existential interrogations mold the ethical and aesthetic import of his poems. The metaphorical use of words creates the symbolic transposition of emotional phenomena into objects. By using literary emblems, Cattafi, like the Metaphysicals, conveys a concept figuratively, so that it can be perceived by the mind and by the senses simultaneously. He combines separate and distant experiences into what T. S. Eliot defines, in his essay "The Metaphysical Poets," as "a direct sensuous apprehension of thought, or a recreation of thought into feeling." Although Cattafi reveals an affinity of taste and intellectual attitude with writers of the baroque age in his choice of stylistic devices, he does not share their drama of transcendence and remains locked in a secular immanence. He is essentially a poet of the twentieth century, the century of free verse and widespread, if uneasy, freethinking. In his attempt to find a clue to the interpretation of a disorderly and unstable universe, Cattafi is deeply aware of the inadequacy of human reason to find the ultimate meaning of existence. Cattafi portrays the condition of modern man, whose knowledge of some structures of the universe determines a degradation of his own image, for he loses power to his

Cover for the volume of Cattafi's poems selected by poet Giovanni Raboni in 1978

own indispensable and ominously proliferating artifacts. In his perception of the human predicament, Cattafi has internalized the *horror vacui,* the frightful feeling of nothingness so aptly defined by Giuseppe Ungaretti in *Vita d'un uomo* (The Life of a Man, 1974), to the extent that it becomes an inner fear for the crumbling of self-identity.

Cattafi was born in the town of Barcellona, Sicily, near Messina, on 6 July 1922. His well-to-do family included rich landowners and professionals, who had a solid tradition of cultural and political commitment. One of his uncles was a prominent political figure and a journalist who contributed to the socialist newspaper *Avanti.* Two other uncles, both lawyers, belonged to Sturzo's Popular party. Bartolomeo Cattafi, Bartolo's father, was a physician; he died four months prior to his son's birth. To him the author dedicated the poem "A mio padre" in *18*

dediche, '76–'77 (Eighteen Dedications, 1978). After Cattafi's birth, his mother, the former Matilde Ortoleva, moved with him to Mollerino, in the district of Terme Vigliatore (near Messina), where the poet spent his childhood. When Cattafi reached the age of ten, they moved back to Barcellona, where he continued his education, stressing classical studies. In 1934 Cattafi underwent a period of military training for infantry officers, in Forlì. This experience, which lasted only a few weeks, was so traumatic that he was hospitalized in Bologna. With a sick leave he was allowed to return to Sicily, where he began to write his first verses in the spring of 1943. In a statement reported by Giacinto Spagnoletti in his 1969 poetry anthology, *Poesia italiana contemporanea: 1909–1959,* Cattafi describes the beginning of his poetic activity:

Cominciai a scrivere versi non so come, ero sempre in preda a non so quale ebbrezza, stordito da sensazioni troppo acute, troppo dolci. Le mille cose che quella snervante primavera mi proponeva erano magicamente gravide di significati, ricche di acutissime, deliziose radiazioni. Come in una seconda infanzia, cominciai a enumerare le cose amate, a compitare in versi un ingenuo inventario del mondo. Tutt'intorno lo schianto delle bombe e le raffiche degli Hurricane, degli Spitfire. . . . Me ne andavo nella colorita campagna nutrendomi di sapori, aromi, immagini; la morte non era elemento innaturale in quel quadro; era un pesco fiorito, un falco sulla gallina, una lucertola che guizza attraverso la viottola. Scrissi così i miei primi versi.

(I don't exactly know how I began to write poetry. I was always prey to a kind of intoxication, dazed by sensations that were too sharp and too sweet. The thousands of things presented to me by that enervating spring were magically pregnant with meanings, rich in sharp delicious radiations. As in a second childhood, I began to enumerate loved things, to compile in verses an ingenuous inventory of the world. All around, the crashing of bombs and the explosions of Hurricanes and Spitfires. . . . I used to go into the colorful countryside nourishing myself on tastes, fragrances, images; death was not an unnatural element in that picture; it was like a peach tree in bloom, a hawk on a hen, a lizard darting across the path. This is how I wrote my first verses.)

In 1944 Cattafi earned a law degree at the University of Messina, yet he never practiced law. At Easter time in 1947, Cattafi went to Milan, where he wished to work as a journalist. He was hired as an errand boy by a playwright, who also contributed articles to many newspapers. When his employer informed him that he could not afford to pay him, Cattafi was forced to go back to Sicily. In spite of his first unfavorable sojourn, he soon returned to Milan, where he remained until 1967, working in journalism and advertising. He alternated his stay with travels to Sicily, in Europe, and in French Africa. In an interview with Enzo Fabiani published in *Gente* (1972), Cattafi reveals some of the adventures that occurred during his travels; many of these biographical details are identifiable in his poems. He mentions that in Seville he was nearly killed by the blade of a Spaniard, jealous of his splendid and unfaithful fiancée; in Orano, in 1953, two policemen were assigned to him as escorts, to protect him against the harassing of smugglers; in Dublin, where he did not speak a word of English, he pretended to be blind and begged for alms; in Lowonsford, England, he was hired to pick strawberries, but half an hour later he was fired because he had fallen asleep in a field. Cattafi's unlimited desire to understand and learn about the surrounding world is reflected in his poetry through his constant attempt to unveil the meaning of things. Of his travels he says in the *Gente* interview: "Dei miei viaggi mi è rimasto il loro 'senso ultimo,' la perentorietà dei dati reperiti. . . . Per me viaggiare è stato ed è un modo d'arricchirmi, d'abbracciare più umanità (per me sempre fraterna). E quindi fatale che viaggiando scriva poesie, su cose passate sulla mia pelle, e dentro il mio sangue" (Of my travels I preserved their "ultimate meaning," the peremptory quality of the data I collected. Traveling for me was a way of enriching myself, of embracing more geography [which is always maternal for me], of embracing more humanity [always fraternal for me]. It is therefore inevitable that, as I travel, I write poems about things that passed over my skin and inside my blood).

In Milan, Cattafi was in touch with Luciano Erba, Nelo Risi, Giorgio Orelli, and other poets of the "Linea Lombarda." In the Piazza Meda, during the afternoon, he often joined them at the Blue Bar (later called City Bar) in the summer and at the Caffè San Paolo in the winter. Cattafi shared with these poets the keen and disillusioned awareness of the moral failure that followed the war. Like them, he was diametrically opposed to the hermetic movement, and at the same time he did not adhere to the cultural commitment of the neorealists, accused of writing a nonobjective poetry of ideas. Postwar poets felt the necessity to free the language from the koine established by the hermetics and by their followers; they refused the smoothness and affection of hermetic poetry — although inevitably inheriting some of the expressive instruments they were denying; this is a trend that Cattafi exhibits in his use of a harsh poetic language as he depicts the aridity and whiteness of the calcareous southern landscape.

What differentiates Cattafi from other contemporary poets is his figurative language, which is substantially different from that of Giuseppe Ungaretti and close to Eugenio Montale's late style, which in turn is analogous to Eliot's usage of his objective correlative. Ungaretti believes in the centralization on the subject who organizes objects in relation to his inner experiences. Ungaretti's poetic process, which consists of elevating the object to the lyrical and then to the metaphysical level, is the opposite of Cattafi's. The latter shifts the emphasis from the subject to the object, from the metaphysical to the physical, and he establishes a coincidence of the two polarities. Like Montale and Eliot, he invests the objects with the function of expressing the subject's emotions, and he even discovers allegorical meanings within the objects. Cattafi's emblematic objects bring to mind the sixteenth- and seventeenth-century books of emblems, which derived from the medieval scholastic representation of the world as a figurative mystical alphabet. In the medieval tradition concepts were symbolically condensed into emblems so that they could be perceived and understood by the mind and by the senses simultaneously.

Cattafi's poetic style changes from a colorful exuberance not unlike Giambattista Marino's seventeenth-century version of the baroque to a progressively barer and more abstract kind, which recalls the intellectual tensions of John Donne and Andrew Marvell. This development is based on the ever-closer confrontation with looming death. The title of Cattafi's first major collection, *Le mosche del meriggio* (The Flies of Noon, 1958), composed after the distressful experience of World War II, carries the emblematic meaning of a mournful condition; the flies stand for the frailty of humans (particularly in the war), as they can be incinerated in an instant of incandescence or drowned at the bottom of a glass. Animals, atmospheric conditions, and natural elements acquire the symbolic power of conveying the poet's mental and existential state. Cattafi never portrays death as a terrifying experience; he minimizes its frightening effect by placing it within the limits of an indefinite framework (for example, the fog) or by carrying it to the symbolic level. *Le mosche del meriggio* won the Cittadella Prize in 1958.

Fundamental in Cattafi's poetry is the motif of a metaphysical journey; the poet's exploration of the most minute aspects of the world carries the deeper meaning of an existential itinerary. "Poesia è dunque per me avventura, viaggio, scoperta, vitale reperimento degli idoli della tribù, tentata decifrazione del mondo" (Poetry is for me adventure, voyage, discovery, vital tracing of the tribal idols, an attempt to decipher the world) – says Cattafi in the statement included in Spagnoletti's anthology. The fly, the butterfly, and the wilting flower, for instance, are common seventeenth-century emblems used by Cattafi to denote the ephemeral duration of life. The material object becomes the sensory representation of an abstract concept.

In *Le mosche del meriggio* the protagonist is an experienced sailor, who does not yet know what course to follow. Throughout the book the expressed need for security, the search for a direction in life, and the recurrent presence of religious invocations are symptoms of the postwar spiritual malaise, typical of the "fourth generation," to which Cattafi belongs. This generation consists of a group of poets born in the mid and late 1920s, whose work would eventually develop in different directions. In the 1950s they shared a moral rather than a metaphysical restlessness and a concern with the material events of daily life. In *Le mosche del meriggio* Cattafi appears to be within the limits of a traditional orthodoxy; later he would try to disclose, by means of his reason only, the essence that makes things exist and function. The imagery of *Le mosche del meriggio* expresses the author's postwar spiritual discomfort, whereas in the following books the same images will become universal emblems of the frailty of human existence. In "L'agave" ("The Agave," as translated in *The Dry Air of the Fire*, 1981) the plant is an emblem of the poet, who rises into the sky to begin his cognitive voyage:

Abbandona la sabbia siciliana, la musica e il miele
degli Arabi e dei Greci,
rompi i dolci legami, questo torpido
latte delle radiche,
discendi in mare regina sonnolenta
verde bestia con braccia di dolore
come chi è pronto al varco

(Abandon the Sicilian sand, the music and the honey
of Arabs and Greeks,
break the sweet ties, this torpid
milk of roots,
descend into the sea drowsy queen
green beast with arms of sorrow
like one who is ready for crossing)[.]

Unlike Montale's agave of "Scirocco," Cattafi's tropical plant is able to escape from its existential state of constriction.

In 1961 the *novissimi* (newest poets), produced a polemical anthology in which they attempted to renovate the poetic language and break away from the hermetic movement. In *L'osso, l'anima* (The Bone, The Soul, 1964), which was awarded the Chianciano Prize in 1964, Cattafi appears to be receptive to the new avant-garde poetry through the unconventional use of syntax and punctuation and a more impersonal style. Yet he does not sever all ties with the hermetic poets. His connection to Montale is still visible in the title of the volume, in which the "bone," unlike Montale's cuttlefish bone, has more metaphysical than physical value. In *L'osso, l'anima* the traveler of *Le mosche del meriggio* continues his exploration of the world within the physical boundaries of his room. He wishes to reach the "bone" of things, their immutable essence, the pure image of truth, devoid of superfluity and imperfection. However, the limitations of man's measuring instruments and the occurrence of unforeseeable events constantly undermine the acquisition of absolute knowledge. Man's impotence and existential precariousness are represented by the emblem of rust, also present in Montale's poetry. The book ends with "I colori del sud" ("The Colors of the South," as translated in *The Dry Air of the Fire*) and its mythical presentation of southern Italy, which is also part of the poet's metaphorical journey. For instance, the dazzling whiteness of the landscape reflects an internal state of emptiness:

> L'osso l'avorio il gesso
> calceviva e latte
> di calce carbonato
> di piombo camelia
> giglio magnolia gelsomino
> sabbia polvere sale.

> (Bone ivory chalk
> quicklime and milk
> of plaster
> of lead camellia
> lily magnolia jasmine
> sand dust salt.)

The poet lists a series of nouns without semantic or syntactic connection, evoking the visual perception of the color white; the subject is lost among objects that he is unable to distinguish.

In 1966 Cattafi married, and in July 1967 he moved with his wife back to Sicily, where he continued to reside in Mollerino. His return to Sicily was prompted by his desire to live and work in the tranquillity of his native land. In his *Gente* interview he explains that he returned to a specific area in Sicily, where he was born and raised; as a mature man he felt he could work serenely only in that corner of his native region. At the same time, he reveals the existential restlessness that was inborn in his personality; he adds, "al poeta conviene vivere, secondo me, in un'oasi, tra le palme e con l'acqua che gli zampilla sotto i piedi, oppure in un altoforno. Ma non è detto che chi vive nell'oasi non si senta in un altoforno, e viceversa" (the poet should live in an oasis, among palm trees, with the water streaming under his feet, or in a blasting furnace. But he who lives in an oasis may feel as if he lived in a furnace and vice versa).

In the fall of 1967 Cattafi devoted himself to painting, abandoning his poetic activity for a few years. He recalls that one night, in March 1971, he had to rise suddenly from his bed in order to look for pen and paper. During a period of just nine months he composed over three hundred poems collected in *L'aria secca del fuoco, marzo 1971–gennaio 1972* (1972; title section of the translated collection *The Dry Air of the Fire*). The book was awarded the Vann'Antò and the Sebeto prizes in 1972. It is dedi-

cated to Cattafi's friend Dr. Ninì Casdia, who died before its publication. In his preface the poet remembers the impossibility of his attempts to restrain the impetus of his inspiration: "Dopo sette anni di silenzio, durante i quali non ero riuscito a mettere insieme due versi, scrissi in dieci mesi circa quattrocento poesie. Scrissi continuamente e un po' dovunque: qui in Contrada Mollerino e in Jugoslavia, in provincia di Varese e in Francia" (After seven years of silence, in which I had been unable to put two lines together, I wrote about four hundred poems within ten months. I wrote continuously, and a little everywhere: here in the area of Mollerino and in Yugoslavia, in the area of Varese and in France).

L'aria secca del fuoco is a chronicle of the author's experiences, memories of the years of the war, observations, and encounters which took place during his numerous travels abroad and his visits to Sicily. In addition to the autobiographical dimension, the geographical, historical, and cultural data contain symbolic meanings. The title of this collection is a verse drawn from the poem "A pieni polmoni" (With Full Lungs), and it may refer to the pungent smell of spent ammunition during the war:

> In mezzo alle folate del tiraggio
> zolfo a pieni polmoni, dentro,
> nelle spire rigogliose
> di fantasmi sgorgati dai vetri rotti,
> nell'aria secca del fuoco.

> (In the middle of the gusts of shots
> with lungs full of sulphur,
> inside, in the luxuriant coils
> of ghosts sprung from broken glass,
> in the dry air of the fire.)

This poem is included in the section dedicated to the ending years of the war. The title of the volume may also refer to the dry wind which blows from Africa to Sicily, as in "Ghibli," the poem whose title is the name of this African wind:

> Questo vento che spinge al mare
> lontano dalla riva
> che vorrebbe ammucchiarlo all'orizzonte
> nato in Africa nei deserti
> svelle urla asciuga
> soffia sul fuoco. . . .

> (This wind which thrusts the sea
> away from the shore
> which would like to heap it on the horizon
> born in Africa in the deserts
> it uproots howls dries
> blows on the fire. . . .)

The title of the book indicates the harshness of life in southern Italy, and it may suggest, on a more general level, the state of man's submission to the destructive forces of nature. The poems of this collection are short and sometimes satirical; they are written in a witty epigrammatic style and are intricately structured.

In Sicily, Cattafi continued to write poems at a steady pace. The exploration of the microcosm becomes more particularized in *Il buio* (The Dark, 1973), *La discesa al trono, 1971–1973* (The Descent to the Throne, 1975), and *Marzo e le sue idi, 1972–1973* (March and Its Ides, 1977). *La discesa al trono* received the Ceppo Prize in 1975, and *Marzo e le sue idi* won the Vallombrosa Prize in 1977. The poet's eye focuses on an endless number of small objects which are endowed with enormous weight. The attempt to decipher the universe is expressed through a strained baroque style; the noun, stripped bare of any coloring modifiers and qualifying elements, comes to coincide with the emblematic object itself. Man moves to the level of inferior animals and objects by descending into the dark in "Ingresso" ("Entrance," as translated in *The Dry Air of the Fire*), Eurydice's underworld, where not even the power of art can change the irreversible reality of death. Images of a metaphorical descent recur frequently in *La discesa al trono*. The dark of *Il buio* corresponds to the natural course toward death, which is in all things: yet life and death cannot be separated, just as truth and appearance, or internal and external reality (subject and object), cannot be distinguished from one another. Ultimately the poetic subject "Marzo e le sue idi" distrusts any manifestation of the perceptible world and wishes to fulfill his ill-starred destiny:

Di tutto diffido
del pugnale di bruto
della tenera carne di cesare
dello stesso destino. . . .

(I distrust everything
the dagger of brutus
the tender flesh of caesar
destiny itself. . . .)

The abolition of the capital letter, already present in *L'aria secca del fuoco,* becomes systematic with few exceptions, indicating the reduction of the subject to the level of objects.

From April 1978 until he died of cancer on 13 March 1979, Cattafi lived in northern Italy, alternating his residence between the house of his parents-in-law in Cimbro, near Varese, and a hospital in Milan. In Cimbro and in Milan he wrote the poems later collected in *Chiromanzia d'inverno* (Fortune Telling in Winter) and published, after his death, in 1983. *L'allodola ottobrina* (1979; "The October Lark," as translated in *The Dry Air of the Fire*), also published posthumously, contains the poems written in Sicily in 1976 and 1977. The volume was awarded the Roberto Gatti Prize in Bologna in 1979. As the title suggests, the temporal dimension of autumn is central in the book. This seasonal choice discloses Cattafi's obsessive preoccupation with death, which is accepted as part of the natural order of life. The poetic subject aspires to a complete self-annihilation, including the obliteration of all memories, an idea which marks Cattafi's final differentiation from Montale. As the lark takes flight into the air during the hunting season, the poet is ready to complete his existential journey. The continual metamorphosis of all things in the process of composition and decomposition is emblematically portrayed by the life of the hermit crab. The shells changed by the crab represent the various stops of man's existential journey, which goes beyond the limits of one individual life. In "Metamorfosi" (Metamorphosis) Cattafi conceives life in a Pirandellian fashion, as the painful immobilization of essence into form:

lieve essenza imprecisa
lieta polvere pronta
a un'umida vita
all'impasto al compatto
al disastro più vasto
d'una prossima forma.

(a light imprecise essence
joyful dust ready
for a damp life
for the mixture the solid
the greater disaster
of a new form.)

Every existing form is the product of a casual arrangement of particles, which constantly undergoes transformation. Instead of circumnavigating the world, Cattafi discovers he is dragged by the planet into its revolutions; he is part of a system where orientation cannot be found by means of human instruments. Toward the end of his life the experienced sailor does not believe in his perception of reality. This is apparent in *Chiromanzia d'inverno,* which was awarded the Sicilia Prize in 1983. Cattafi had only begun to arrange his last poems into an organic volume intended for posthumous publication. Although it is unfinished, *Chiromanzia d'inverno* represents the author's final poetic legacy and the ultimate expression of his human condition. As Cattafi declared in 1973 during an interview with Diego Sergio Anzà for the *Gazzetta del Sud:* "La poesia per me è un fatto esistenziale, che appartiene alla dimensione dell'uomo, un modo come un altro, non particolarmente privilegiato, di essere e sentirsi uomo" (Poetry for me is an existential reality, which belongs to the human dimension, it is one of many ways, and not a very privileged way, to be and to feel human).

In "La battaglia" (The Battle), one of the poems of *Chiromanzia d'inverno,* life is allegorically portrayed as an "empty" or nonexistent battle, in which man imagines that he fights every day, wearing himself out for the real exertion. In "Nel grigio" (In the Gray), included in the same collection, the gray, which is the ambiguous reality of existence, is interrupted by the sudden certainty of the colors of fire, symbolic of death and destruction:

> . . . nel grigio quel giallo sfolgorante
> o amaranto che sia o rosso-arancio
> lo slancio di quei gridi
>
> (. . . in the gray that dazzling yellow
> or amaranth or orange-red
> the power of those screams)[.]

In "Geografo" (Geographer), another poem in *Chiromanzia d'inverno,* Cattafi acknowledges the emblematic nature of his verses:

> tutto ho stravolto mutato adattato
> a un diverso disegno
> ho parlato di me
> ho confessato andando
> dal massiccio montuoso all'alga all'erba
> spinto dalla bisogna
> ad una verità vestita di menzogna.
>
> (I have twisted changed adapted everything
> to a different design
> I talked about me
> I confessed moving
> from massive mountains to seaweed and grass
> driven by the need
> of a truth covered with falsity.)

Another posthumously published volume by Cattafi, *Segni* (Signs, 1986) comprises 117 poems composed in 1972 and 1973 and thus chronologically antecedent to the poems included in *L'allodola ottobrina.* Cattafi had begun to collect poems for this volume in 1976, but he never completed the project. Numerous poems in *Segni* had appeared in newspapers, periodicals, in Cattafi's *Nel rettangolo dei teoremi* (In the Rectangle of Theorems, 1977), and in *Dieci poesie inedite* (Ten Unpublished Poems, 1983). In *Segni* the poet's vision of the world comes to coincide with his own writing. His white pages become the unlimited space where the objects of the universe are arranged in an orderly or disorderly fashion. The letters of the alphabet form emblematic shapes on the page: they are signs of a truth that cannot easily be deciphered. In "Manifesti" (Posters) a nonsensical whirlwind of words occupies the world, while the searcher for truth has only the void of blank paper:

> Si perdono parole
> agli angoli delle strade
> nel giro delle piazze
> cadono con lo stesso
> sconforto delle foglie. . . .
>
> (Words get lost
> at the corners of the streets
> around the squares
> they fall with the same
> distress of leaves. . . .)

In "Nero su bianco" (Black or White) the poetic persona expresses the painful impossibility of grasping reality through the abstraction of his art. This reality that may not even exist is emblematically portrayed by the emptiness of words:

> copro colmo comando
> parole
> l'assenza certifico
> attesto la finzione.
>
> (I cover fill command
> words
> I certify the absence
> I testify the deceit.)

With the objects of his analysis — in *Segni* metaphorically represented by his writing — Cattafi has fashioned an allegory of his existential history, which is the history of modern man. It is still too soon to describe with certainty Cattafi's impact and influence on contemporary poetry. Although his works have been widely reviewed since the 1950s, interest in his poetry has increased since his death. Critically it would be appropriate to study Cattafi's dependence on and rejection of hermeticism as an indication of the direction taken by postwar Italian poets. Cattafi's early writing is still tied to that of hermetic poets, particularly to the verse of Salvatore Quasimodo and the late works of Montale. Later he moves in the direction of a personal poetic avant-garde, which constantly reflects his existential experience; yet his style is always controlled by cultural instruments received from the past. Cattafi's poetry tends to an abstract expressionism for its continuous and coherent transition from the objects to the metaphor, from the sensory to the intellectual level. At the same time it maintains a historical value for its verification of a reality which is unstable and fragmentary but also concrete and defined by spatial and temporal boundaries. The word and the object permeate each other in a perennial and deluding cognitive tension.

Interviews:

Enzo Fabiani, "In Sicilia a caccia di sirene," *Gente,* 29 (1972);

Diego Sergio Anzà, "La mia sicilianità è biologico-culturale," *Gazzetta del Sud,* 30 January 1973.

References:

Giuseppe Amoroso, "Chiromanzia di Cattafi," *Rassegna di cultura e vita scolastica* (May–July 1983): 8;

Giorgio Bàrberi Squarotti, "La strada di Atene," *Aut-Aut* (January–March 1961): 119–142;

Glauco Cambon, "Le epifanie di Cattafi," *Fiera Letteraria,* 18 February 1962, p. 3;

Piero Chiara and Luciano Erba, *Quarta generazione* (Varese: Magenta, 1954);

Ada De Alessandri, *La spiritualità di Bartolo Cattafi* (Messina: All'Insegna del Pesce d'Oro, 1989);

Enzo Fabiani, "Bartolo Cattafi: La sua ultima poe-sia," *Gente,* 13 (1979): 127–128;

Marco Forti, "Per Bartolo Cattafi," in his *Le proposte della poesia* (Milan: Mursia, 1963), pp. 239–243;

Forti, "Il secco fuoco di Cattafi," *Albero,* 49 (1972): 296–299;

Alberto Frattini, "Poesia ghestaltica di Cattafi," in his *Poesia nuova in Italia tra Ermetismo e Avanguardia* (Milan: IPL, 1968), pp. 70–75;

Lunario Nuovo, special issue on Cattafi, 6–7, edited by Mario Grasso (December 1980);

Dante Maffia, "Su Bartolo Cattafi," in *Operai di sogni: La poesia del Novecento in Sicilia,* edited by Giovanni Raboni (Randazzo: Alfa Grafica Sgroi, 1985), pp. 99–115;

Giovanni Occhipinti, "La verità di Cattafi," in his *Uno splendido Medioevo: Poesia anni '60* (Poggibonsi: Lalli, 1978);

Folco Portinari, "La poesia della quarta generazione," in his *Problemi critici di ieri e di oggi* (Milan: Fabbri, 1959), pp. 201–208;

Giacinto Spagnoletti, "Bartolo Cattafi," in his *Novecento siciliano* (Catania: Tifeo, 1986), pp. 274–284;

Giovanna Wedel De Stasio, *La poesia neobarocca di Bartolo Cattafi* (Caltanissetta & Rome: Sciascia, 1985);

Giuseppe Zagarrio, *Sicilia e poesia contemporanea* (Palermo: Sciascia, 1964), pp. 126–138.

Annalisa Cima

(20 January 1941 –)

Claire De Cesare Huffman
Brooklyn College, City University of New York

BOOKS: *6 quadri, 3 disegni, 1 serigrafia, lavori in corso* (Milan: All'Insegna del Pesce d'Oro, 1968);

Con Marianne Moore (Milan: All'Insegna del Pesce d'Oro, 1968);

Eugenio Montale, via Bigli, Milano (Milan: All'Insegna del Pesce d'Oro, 1968);

Allegria di Ungaretti (Milan: All'Insegna del Pesce d'Oro, 1969);

Terzo modo (Milan: All'Insegna del Pesce d'Oro, 1969); revised by Mary de Rachewiltz and translated by Sizzo de Rachewiltz as *Third Way* (New York: New Directions, 1977);

La Genesi e altre poesie (Milan: All'Insegna del Pesce d'Oro, 1971);

Incontro Palazzeschi (Milan: All'Insegna del Pesce d'Oro, 1972);

Incontro Montale (Milan: All'Insegna del Pesce d'Oro, 1973);

Immobilità (Milan: All'Insegna del Pesce d'Oro, 1974);

Sesamon (Parma: Guanda, 1977);

Ipotesi d'amore (Milan: Garzanti, 1984);

Ezra Pound a Venezia da "Cici" alla Salute (Milan: All'Insegna del Pesce d'Oro, 1985);

Quattro tempi (Lugano, Switzerland: Fondazione Schlesinger, 1986);

Aegri somnia/Sogni di malato (Lugano, Switzerland: Cima, 1989).

OTHER: *G. F. Malipiero a Venezia,* edited by Cima (Milan: All'Insegna del Pesce d'Oro, 1968);

Ezio Gribaudo, *Logografi 70,* introduction by Cima (Milan: All'Insegna del Pesce d'Oro, 1970);

Vittorio Cavicchioni, preface by Cima (Rome: Magma, 1973);

Murilo Mendes, *Di domenica,* edited, with an introduction, by Cima (Milan: All'Insegna del Pesce d'Oro, 1974);

Jorge Guillén, *Da Gilli, Firenze,* edited, with an introduction, by Cima (Milan: All'Insegna del Pesce d'Oro, 1975);

Annalisa Cima circa 1984

Eugenio Montale, profilo di un autore, edited by Cima and Cesare Segre (Milan: Rizzoli, 1977);

Di Terzet, preface by Cima (Genoa: Grillo, 1979);

Allen Mandelbaum, *Leaves of Absence,* includes translations by Cima (Milan: All'Insegna del Pesce d'Oro, 1980);

Edoardo Gatti, *Egocosmo,* preface by Cima (Milan: All'Insegna del Pesce d'Oro, 1980);

Rivoluzione dei fiori, edited by Cima (Lugano, Switzerland: Pegaso, 1986);

Poesie inedite di Eugenio Montale, 6 volumes to date, edited by Cima (Lugano, Switzerland: Fondazione Schlesinger, 1986–).

Annalisa Cima has occupied a significant position in the Italian literary landscape since the publication of her *Terzo modo* (1969; translated as *Third Way,* 1977). Her early poetry received praise from reviewers and academic scholars in Italy, and, later, her *Quattro tempi* (Four Times, 1986) was officially celebrated by a reception at the Italian Istituto di Cultura in New York, at which she read some of her poems. Cima's is a poetry of revelations and of semantic and linguistic inventiveness. The difficulties encountered in her work are rewarded by meaning far beyond anything an initial reading would lead one to suspect. Cesare Segre wrote, in his preface to her *Immobilità* (Immobility, 1974), "Ognuna si presenta autonoma nella sua concentrazione gnomica, simile a un *tanka* o ad un *haikai.* . . . Poi ci si accorge che tutte le poesie si collegano, ritornando su pochi temi, richiamandosi con le stesse parole-chiave: esse formano un piccolo ciclo, spirale meditativa ed espressiva" (Each [poem] appears autonomous in its aphoristic density, like a *tanka* or a *haiku.* . . . Then one sees that the poems are all bound together, returning to a few chosen themes, reverberating with the same key words. They form a small meditative and expressive spiral).

Cima's work has affinities with the poetry of Eugenio Montale and Paul Celan, among others. She reads and admires the works of T. S. Eliot and Emily Dickinson. Cima has written monographs on other authors from various countries, including Marianne Moore, Giuseppe Ungaretti, Murilo Mendes, Jorge Guillén, and Ezra Pound. Her strongest link, however, is with Montale; the editing and publication of poems left unpublished at his death were entrusted to her. Cima also attests to the influence of poets who equally attracted Montale, such as Friedrich Hölderlin, Charles Baudelaire, and Ugo Foscolo.

Cima was born in Milan on 20 January 1941. From 1958 on, she studied painting and exhibited widely – for instance, at the Galleria del Cavallino, Venice, in 1965 and the National Gallery, London, in 1967. In subsequent years she participated also in the Rome Quadriennale and the Venice Biennale. Like Segre, Andrea Zanzotto (in a review of *Immobilità* in *Corriere della Sera,* 25 May 1975) has insisted on the relationship between Cima's work as an artist and her writing, especially her tendency toward "un certo orientalismo e al frammento" (a certain orientalism and fragmentism).

Cima has always been sensitive to the relations between visual and linguistic phenomena. Her books on contemporaries and other authors blend literature, photography, interviews, and sketches. *Allegria di Ungaretti* (Ungaretti's *Allegria* [Joy], 1969), for example, includes three unpublished poems and one prose poem by Ungaretti and photographs by Ugo Mulas; *Incontro Montale* (Montale Encounter, 1973) has a sketch by Marino Marini. Interviews with Cima produce little autobiographical detail; instead they yield information on her encounters with writers and painters such as Moore, Mendes, Ungaretti, Robert Lowell, and Aldo Palazzeschi.

After studies in Lausanne and Geneva, Cima received a degree in philosophy. She insists that the themes of her poems cannot be extracted from political and cultural events and that, from early on, they have been based on a few central personal experiences. There is much "absence" in Cima's poetry: an absent mother and an absent geographical center. Important formative influences include writers such as Stendhal and the respiratory illness tuberculosis. This disease and its effects troubled her from the age of fifteen on, and even today it may be the chief thematic center of her poetry. Illness is the transfiguring element that, like her writing and by means of it, removes her from normality. Cycles of illness, love, and travel are the foci of the temporal dimension of her poems, and temporal and thematic dimensions are inseparable in the consideration of her life and work.

Cima's lifelong love for music – from her early study of the piano and the works of Wolfgang Amadeus Mozart to her love of the music of Ludwig van Beethoven – also pervades her poetry. She has often talked about the arduousness of achieving deep musicality in her poems and of writing the proper incipit and finale. Cima's ultimate maestro in this respect is Montale; she attributes to him "l'insegnamento della musicalità" (the teaching of musicality).

Though Cima's life has been one of movement and travel, she says she feels at home everywhere and nowhere. The mention of Vienna evokes memories of her grandfather who was a Jew, an anti-Fascist, and a pacifist. Perhaps this family history has produced the condition of unease she admits to today. Cima is uncomfortable with abstractions, traditions, groups, literary lines of descent, and any approach to literature and life that could be symbolized by an anthology-style, arbitrary grouping. She admits that much of her work is in the form of dialogue and that dialogue is her chief means of contact with others.

At a 1988 reading of her poetry at the City University of New York, a vigorous discussion ensued about the apparent narcissism in her work. Cima spoke of her discomfort with discursive and narrative forms and of her need to avoid generalities by exhausting the particular events and occasions of her life. She claimed that her desire has been to reach the essence of the events of her life, especially her bouts of illness. She sees her effort to achieve minimalism as inseparable from the effort to create a free linguistic space and time.

Cima has agreed that her philosophical position is expressed in "Bewusstsein," in *Terzo modo*: the best approach to knowledge is to "conosci te stesso" (know thyself) and to "ritornare su se stessi e diventare ciò che vogliamo / guardare" (return to oneself and become what we want / to look at). *Terzo modo* includes, in the title poem, these often-cited lines:

> Il terzo modo
> per distinguere A con-
> siste nel rapporto tra
> A e se stessi. A
> si identifica, non si ha
> alternativa da
> qui il monoteismo.
>
> (The third way
> to distinguish A con-
> sists of the relation between
> A and oneself. A
> identifies itself; there is
> no other way, and so
> we have monotheism.)

In Cima's early poetry, the theme of *essere* (being) is given as a philosophical problem; in the later poetry there are no differences among *corpo*, *pensiero*, and *amore* (body, thought, and love). In *Immobilità* love is absent, and the suspicion grows that people are simply used, and used up, by nature. There are no answers to solitude, precisely because solitude itself may be an illusion, comprehensible only as a kind of transcendence of the self in the thing-which-is-thought. *Immobilità* develops the theme of poetry that, like the self in solitary medita-

tion, seeks to consume and transcend itself, as in "Unica strada" (The Only Path):

> Unica strada
> l'essenza del dolore
> il pensare
> che avvicina senza limiti
> al pensato.
>
> (The only path
> the essence of suffering
> the thought
> that brings closer boundless
> to the thing which is thought.)

If Cima stops short of the radical semantic dislocations of Celan, she uses, as early as 1974 in *Immobilità,* a poetic language dissociated from reference, as seen in "Non usiamo la parola" (Let Us Not Use the Word):

> Cerchiamo di vedere
> il noncolore
> di sentire
> la nonvoce
> afferrare
> l'inesistente.
>
> (We seek to see
> the noncolor
> to hear
> the nonvoice
> to seize
> what does not exist.)

Segre has pointed out how Cima's *Immobilità* is "ben aperta a vicende e occasioni: purché sublimate a un livello di allusività o assoggettate a trasposizione meditativa" (open to events and occasions: provided that they are either sublimated to a level of allusiveness or subjected to meditative transposition). And he insists that loss of reference is paradoxically the result of insistence on corporeal things. Moreover, verbs are turned into metaphors and past participles into substantives. Words are stripped of materiality and connotation. In *Immobilità* transcendence is sought, and language is sometimes conceived as a barrier to surpass. Whatever their apparent conceptual reference, Segre denies that the poems of *Immobilità* are ever really philosophical: they deny, individually and collectively, the usefulness of conceptualization and even of words, as in these lines:

> Attribuisci importanza
> alle parole
> e le parole
> sono perdita di pensiero.

(Give importance
to words
and words
are loss of thought.)

Sesamon (1977) has been defined as a *canzoniere* (songbook) and is largely composed of thoughts wrested from real events. The contrast is not so much between what is thought and what is expressed (or may be expressed, without being tainted) as it is between new oppositions: "rispecchiamento e rovesciamento, presente e passato, desiderio e compimento, inconscio [e] normalità, realtà e immagine, [e] passione e controllo" (reflection and upset, present and past, desire and fulfillment, unconsciousness [and] normality, reality and imagination, [and] passion and control), as Segre notes in his preface to the volume. Cima has underscored in interviews the importance of finding resolution in thoughts that come whole and inseparable from their form, without ever falling into the trap of transient contingency. Concerning *Sesamon,* critics have noted that Cima emerges victorious over isolation. The poetry does not surprise insofar as it finds in love the answer to withdrawal, but it does surprise by the rebellious anticonformism so often noted by critics. Yet the import of the volume is more one of style than of content: rhymes are, in a Montalian sense, *avare* (scarce); verbal tense yields to the repeated use of infinitives; the lexicon is rarefied; and many words are coined and made up of odd junctures, then broken by line endings and pauses. These and others of Cima's devices are analyzed by Segre in his introductory remarks to *Sesamon* and connected with the palpably erotic content of the poems.

Segre's criticism of *Sesamon* points out an ultimate paradox in Cima's work itself: whatever overt content it may have, however it may disclose meanings, it is poetry that has a stylistic mission: to arrive at "l'indifferenziato, l'indistinto, l'indeterminato, [e] l'incerto" (the undifferentiated, indistinct, indeterminate, and uncertain). Although Cima has commented in personal interviews on the brilliant analysis by Segre, she is reluctant to separate stylistic from conceptual development. For instance, the use of the prefix *dis* is to be taken in the sense of loss, of undoing (including its sexual counterparts), and of recovery through loss. But *dis* also has a temporal dimension, that of the loosening of the past as it gathers into a new future of dissolution that leads to resolution. The word *stigma* is another example of a focusing element in the poetry; it may

convey a religious sense, but it is not without reference to the imprint of the past. *Umori* are body fluids, life-giving, almost sacramental ones; and all of nature may participate in this sacrament. One of the truths of the poems, says Cima, is that life spreads by ivory rains of hail, by silver granules, and by points of light that shed light but never a single truth. Cima admits to a certain archaism in the use of such images, but hers is a search for a future language, too, which uses the linguistic past and poetic models such as Montale, Dickinson, and Petrarch to move to a new language and to new revelations. *Sesamon* confirms what *Immobilità* hints at: that history is to be set aside.

The major symbol of *Aegri somnia* (Painful Dreams, 1989) is the character Filottete, who, Dario del Corno says in his preface,

> è chiamato a sciogliere il nodo della storia, perché egli è fuori della storia. Il suo male l'ha isolato dai traumi transeunti del contingente: lo salva dal tempo, gli offre come compenso l'immobilità della sapienza. Allo strazio del male egli ha opposto la forza d'acciaio di un "pensiero da pensare" . . . e la forza, la festa interiore di questi versi è la consapevolezza che esiste "l'evento che giustifichi il vivere, il pensare" – l'amore.

> (is called to free the nexus of history, because he is outside of history. His illness has isolated him from the transient blows of contingency: it saves him from time and offers him, as compensation, the permanence of knowledge. Against the agony of illness, he has set up the steel-like strength of a "thinker of thoughts" . . . and the strength, the internal celebration of these lines, is the knowledge that "the event justifying living, thinking" exists – [it is] love.)

No study of Cima would be complete without an outline of the aims and achievements of the Fondazione Schlesinger, founded in December 1978 in Milan (with an American branch opening in 1982 in New York) by Cima and Segre with Montale serving as honorary chairman from 1978 to 1981. Guillén, Italo Calvino, and Roman Jakobson have served on the board, among other distinguished critics, writers, and academics. The foundation has as its primary goal the linking of American and Italian culture, both literary and scientific, and it strives to do so by copublishing works of Italian and American writers and by translating American writers into Italian and vice versa. Under Cima's guidance the foundation has published collections of the poetry of Giovanni Bottiroli (1975), Edoardo Gatti (1980), and Guido Zavanone (1983). In collaboration with New Directions Press and the Scheiwiller company, Cima is preparing editions of the poetry of Mario Luzi, Edoardo Sanguineti, Giovanni Giudici, and Zanzotto. With New Directions, the foundation has coedited and published *Poesia-Poetry,* a collection of works by ten Italian and ten American poets. There are also plans to publish more selected poetry and prose by Montale, as well as "Conversazioni con Montale" (edited by Cima and introduced by Segre). The foundation has published six annual volumes of Poesie inedite di Eugenio Montale (Unpublished Poetry of Eugenio Montale, 1986–) as part of a long-range plan to bring to the public the entire group of poems entrusted to Cima directly by Montale.

Interviews:

Manuela Camponovo, "Un lungo sodalizio all'ombra della poesia," *Giornale del Popolo,* 25 September 1986;

Florinda Balli, "Due anni nel Ticino la Fondazione Schlesinger," *Azione,* 2 October 1986;

"Annalisa Cima," *Corriere della Sera,* 10 October 1986;

Marzio G. Mian, "Io e Montale, così realizzerò il suo 'American Dream,'" *Progresso,* 30 November 1986.

References:

Manuela Camponovo, "Soffio vitale di un Cherubino," *Giornale del Popolo*, (16 November 1984);

Dario del Corno, Preface to Cima's *Aegri somnia/Sogni di malato* (Lugano, Switzerland: Cima, 1989);

Stelio Crise, "Fuori del noviziato," *Piccolo,* 5 November 1977;

Benito Iezzi, "Erza 'Cici,' ciacole e calli," *Mattino,* 15 March 1986;

Alberto Lattuada, "Anticonformismo, eros e ribellione," *Paese Sera,* 6 November 1977;

Grazia Palmisano, "L'angolo della poesia," *Piccolo,* 5 November 1984;

P. D. P., "Al di là del pensato," *Fiera Letteraria,* 10 November 1974;

Cesare Segre, Preface to Cima's *Immobilità* (Milan: All'Insegna del Pesce d'Oro, 1974).

Milo De Angelis

(6 June 1951 –   )

Lawrence Venuti
Temple University

BOOKS: *Somiglianze* (Milan: Guanda, 1976; revised edition, 1990);
La corsa dei mantelli (Milan: Guanda, 1979);
Poesia e destino (Bologna: Cappelli, 1982);
Millimetri (Turin: Einaudi, 1983);
Terra del viso (Milan: Mondadori, 1985);
Distante un padre (Milan: Mondadori, 1989);
Cartina muta (Reggio Emilia: Elytra, 1991).

OTHER: Giancarlo Pontiggia and Enzo Di Mauro, eds., *La parola innamorata: I poeti nuovi 1976–1978,* includes poetry and prose by De Angelis (Milan: Feltrinelli, 1978), pp. 73–82;
Maurice Blanchot, *L'attesa l'oblio,* translated by De Angelis (Milan: Guanda, 1978);
Ruth Feldman and Brian Swann, eds., *Italian Poetry Today: Currents and Trends,* includes three poems by De Angelis (Saint Paul: New Rivers, 1979), pp. 66–67;
Adriano Spatola and Paul Vangelisti, eds., *Italian Poetry, 1960–1980: From Neo to Post Avant-garde,* includes a poem by De Angelis (San Francisco: Red Hill, 1982), pp. 41–42;
Charles Baudelaire, *I paradisi artificiali,* translated by De Angelis (Milan: Guanda, 1983);
Claudius Claudianus, *Il rapimento di Proserpina,* translated and edited by De Angelis and Marta Bertamini (Milan: Marcos & Marcos, 1984);
Dana Gioia and Michael Palma, eds., *New Italian Poets,* includes fifteen poems by De Angelis (Brownsville, Oreg.: Story Line, 1991), pp. 296–335.

Milo De Angelis is a sophisticated experimentalist who has set out to reinvent poetry in postmodern terms. His poems since the beginning of the 1970s draw on classical literature, existential phenomenology, and psychoanalysis but transform them according to the new conceptions of subjectivity and language that underlie poststructuralism. An early interest in Maurice Blanchot's critical speculations about the creative process and the nature of language and textuality led De Angelis to the study of Martin Heidegger and Ludwig Binswanger and finally to a belief in the overriding importance of Friedrich Nietzsche and Jacques Lacan for contemporary poetry.

In De Angelis's writing, the Heideggerian attempt to overcome Western metaphysical tradition and discover an originary way of thinking about human existence is joined to several Nietzschean and Lacanian arguments, particularly the critique of morality and representation as potent inventions of "value" and "truth" and the exposure of subjectivity as a linguistic construction in which desire is repressed by the very means of its expression. This configuration of ideas establishes the fundamental paradox of De Angelis's poetic project. He strives to represent and free the anarchic origins of existence from the cultural and social determinations that order and normalize them through language. At the same time, however, he knows that the origins remain ineffable, outside the poem, because language imposes order and normalcy, negating what it names, restraining what exceeds it, bringing the illusory comforts of intelligibility, coherence, and transparency to calm the panic of the unknown.

For De Angelis the function of poetry is to stimulate thinking by pushing at the limits of language and transgressing cultural norms, but he is always aware that their destruction is simultaneously tragic and creative, the end of existence and the ceaseless proliferation of new beginnings. His poems stage what critic Giuseppe Conte has described as a common project for Italian poets in the 1970s: "liberazione che è scatenamento e silenzio, irresponsabilità e gioia, attingimento, attraverso la perdita, dell'infinita semplicità delle cose" (liberation that is unchaining and silence, irresponsibility and joy, attainment, through loss, of the infinite simplicity of things). Over the past twenty years De Angelis has been exploring these ideas in writing that is strangely disquieting in its stylistic disloca-

NEW ITALIAN POETS

edited by

DANA GIOIA & MICHAEL PALMA

Cover for a 1991 bilingual anthology that includes poems by Milo De Angelis and nine of his contemporaries

tions and profound in its evocation of a peculiarly postmodern sense of tragedy.

De Angelis was born in Milan on 6 June 1951. He spent his childhood in Montferrat, a village in the Piedmont area. The childhood experiences of this rural setting, the agrarian practices, the proximity of nature, and the provincial legends would later prove formative to his poetry, reinforcing a central thematic preoccupation with natural cycles as well as serving as the basis for autobiographical allusions. During his late teens De Angelis became deeply involved in sports, initially in soccer, later in track and field. These experiences also reemerge in his poetry, as a pattern of athletic images that resonate with his philosophical speculations. He studied at the University of Milan from 1970 to 1974 and then at the University of Montpellier in France from 1975 to 1976, focusing on contemporary Italian literature and classical philology. He subsequently tutored private students in the Greek and Latin languages and literatures. He has traveled throughout Italy and to many foreign countries, including Greece, Czechoslovakia, and the former Soviet Union. In 1989 he married the poet Giovanna Sicari, and they have a son, Daniele. Currently they live in Rome.

De Angelis began writing poetry in his mid teens, when he was also reading widely in literature, philosophy, and literary criticism. His precocious literary debut occurred in 1975, when some of his poems appeared in two anthologies important in the history of contemporary Italian poetry: the prestigious annual *Almanacco dello Specchio* (Almanac of the Mirror), edited by Marco Forti, which usually prints poems by a few interesting newcomers along with recent work by respected major writers; and *Il pubblico della poesia* (The Audience of Poetry), a selection of works by twenty-five poets, edited by Alfonso Berardinelli and Franco Cordelli in an effort to characterize the social and cultural situation of Italian poetry in the 1970s. De Angelis's impressive contributions were favorably noticed by the senior poet and critic Franco Fortini in a 1975 survey of current Italian writing (a survey occasioned by Eugenio Montale's winning the Nobel Prize). De Angelis has gone on to publish five collections of poems and several books of prose and translation (a narrative, a collection of critical and theoretical essays, and translations from French and Latin), which have affirmed his early promise.

He develops the formal experimentation characteristic of the so-called neo-avant-garde literary movement that surfaced in Italy during the late 1950s and early 1960s in magazines such as Luciano Anceschi's *Verri*, founded in 1956, and in polemical anthologies, including Alfredo Giuliani's *I Novissimi: Poesie per gli anni '60* (The Newest: Poetry for the 60s, 1961). Giuliani's preface outlines the new poetic project as a materialist, cultural politics: language is fractured in a "visione 'schizomorfa' " ("schizomorphic" vision) that simultaneously reflects and resists the mental dislocations and illusory representations of consumer capitalism. Giuliani asserts that for him, as for other poets in his anthology (Elio Pagliarani, Edoardo Sanguineti, Nanni Balestrini, and Antonio Porta), poetry is a subversion of the dominant ideology, what he calls "lo smascheramento, sfidando il silenzio che sempre consegue, insieme con le chiacchiere, al deperimento di un linguaggio, esasperando l'insensatezza, rifiutando l'oppressione dei significati imposti, raccontando con gusto e con amore pensieri e bubbole di questa età schizofrenica" (the unmasking, challenging the silence that always follows, along with the idle talk, the deterioration of language, exasperating the nonsense, refusing the oppression of imposed meanings, relating with taste and with love the thoughts and lies of this schizophrenic age). De Angelis shares the view that discontinuous form is the most suitable way to address philosophical problems raised by language, representation, and subjectivity. But he eschews explicit political engagement, with which the neo-avant-garde treated these problems, for a poetic discourse that is both deeply personal and densely philosophical. De Angelis's more speculative treatment is suggestive of Heidegger's thinking. As Fortini notes in his essay "The Wind of Revival," the poems in De Angelis's first collection, *Somiglianze* (Resemblances, 1976) – which Fortini had read in 1975 – show De Angelis "fascinated with the Heideggerian vortices of origin, absence, recurrence, and the danger of death."

The critique of representation in *Somiglianze* is not articulated in historical-materialist terms but based on Heidegger's concept of "being-toward-

death," which De Angelis submits to a Nietzschean revision. In *Sein und Zeit* (1927; translated as *Being and Time*, 1962), Heidegger argues that human existence is perpetually "falling," always already determined by relations with people and things, its identity being dispersed into the "they" – until the possibility of death appears. The anticipation of death, the possibility of being nothing, constitutes a "limit-situation" in which the subject is forced to recognize the inauthenticity of his determinate nature and gains "a freedom which has been released from the illusions of the 'they,' and which is factical, certain of itself, and anxious."

De Angelis's poem "L'idea centrale" (The Central Idea) exploits the potential for drama in this climactic moment of truth by sketching a hospital scene, yet De Angelis resists any suggestion that such being-toward-death is the prelude to authentic existence:

E ancora, davanti a tutti, si sceglieva
tra le azioni e il loro senso.
Ma per caso.
Esseri dispotici regalavano il centro
distrattamente, con una radiografia,
e in sogno padroni minacciosi
sibilanti:
"se ti togliamo ciò che non è tuo
non ti rimane niente."

(And still, in front of everybody, there was choosing
between the actions and their meaning.
But by chance.
Despotic beings made a gift of the center
absentmindedly, with an X ray,
and in a dream threatening bosses
whispering:
"if we take from you what isn't yours
you'll have nothing left.")

This poem depicts being-toward-death as a state of physical and psychological extremity wherein the apparent unity of experience is split by competing representations, and consciousness loses its self-possession and self-consistency. "Actions" are decentered from intentionality: "their meaning" is never uniquely appropriate to the subject but is an appropriation by the "they," figured here as the "bosses" who are "threatening" because they speak "in a dream," having even colonized the unconscious. The "central idea" is that subjectivity is ultimately "nothing," mere action on which meaning is imposed, an ensemble of biological processes whose meaninglessness "despotic beings" inadvertently reveal when they attempt to impose meaning through scientific representations such as X rays.

The formal peculiarities of the poem – the shifts from realistic detail to abstract reflection to quoted statement, the scanty amount of information, and the fragmented syntax – mimic the identity-shattering experience of being-toward-death by destabilizing the signifying process, abandoning any linearity of meaning, and unbalancing the reader's search for intelligibility. What does become clear, however, is that De Angelis's disturbingly enigmatic poem does not assume Heidegger's idea of authenticity as being that is unified and free. In form and theme "L'idea centrale" instead reflects Nietzsche's corrosive ideas in *Der Wille zur Macht* (1901; translated as *The Will to Power,* 1967), in which human agency is described as not a subject but an action, a creative positing.

The limit-situations in De Angelis's *Somiglianze* challenge consciousness, threaten or suspend its rational coherence, break down its self-identity, and give it access to what is other than itself. The situations that recur most often include not only a brush with death, whether through accident, illness, or a suicide attempt, but also psychological suffering, sexual desire, drug intoxication, biological processes, the immaturity of childhood, and the unreflective spontaneity of athletic performance. These are situations of transgression because they are prelinguistic or they fracture or abandon language, releasing subjectivity from its web of determinations, allowing it to deviate from the concepts of rationality and moral value that shape it, revealing not only their exclusion of deviation and difference but also their fragile basis in the interaction between language and consciousness. Hence subjectivity in De Angelis's poetry is volatile and in process, often presented in dramatic scenes with snippets of dialogue and a rapid succession of evocative images. Metonymy is the dominant mode of representing this experience, and the rush of metonymic representations can be movingly resonant, even as their speed and heterogeneity endanger communication. The discontinuous form of De Angelis's poetry serves to evoke a notion of consciousness not as the stable, coherent origin of meaning, knowledge, and action but as constituted by its contradictory conditions, by language, by familial relationships, and by the culture at large – needing the limit-situation to be reminded of these forgotten conditions and to imagine new possibilities.

The concept of subjectivity as a determinate process makes De Angelis deeply skeptical of established moral values, leading him to adopt a morality based on Nietzsche's concept of tragedy, If the world, as Nietzsche argues in *The Will to Power,* "is 'in flux,' as something in a state of becoming, as a

falsehood always changing but never getting near the truth," then an "active" morality is required, a willingness to accept deviation, a joyful affirmation of multiplicity and uncertainty, an experimental creation of new values, "as a counterweight to this extreme fatalism." Yet insofar as this creativity depends on the transgression of limits, the deviation from cultural norms, and the annihilation of individuality, its joy exists simultaneously with suffering. The impact of these ideas on De Angelis can be seen in his essay "Tragedia Novecentesca" (Twentieth-Century Tragedy) from his theoretical work *Poesia e destino* (Poetry and Fate, 1982): tragedy from Aeschylus to Paul Celan is defined as "l'impatto tra telos e contingenza" (the collision between telos and contingency), which excludes transcendence and exposes the limitations of human subjectivity but welcomes them as conditions of new possibility, refusing to resolve them in metaphysics or idealism. For De Angelis tragedy is "ciò che continua a finire" (what continues to end). The project of his poetry, then, is to proliferate and intensify contradictions by abnegating the self, affirming difference, and inventing, willing, and cultivating what Nietzsche calls the Dionysian art through which the voice of nature can be heard.

In many poems, De Angelis indicates the fundamentally affirmative significance of this concept of tragedy by linking the theme of transgression to the natural cycle of birth, death, and rebirth. Violence, a limit-situation in which human action drifts from identity and social meaning toward the realm of becoming, is said to have a *stagione* (season) in "I sicari" (The Assassins):

Dove il passo
per esserci chiede una scelta
introvabile, sacra attesa, stagione:
ai confini del viso
le ombre, in ascolto,
si fermano nella solennità
che divide il pugnale
dal gesto.

(Where the step
to be here demands an undiscoverable
choice, sacred wait, season:
at the edges of the face
the shadows, in listening,
stop in the solemnity
dividing dagger
from act.)

The Nietzschean separation of action from motive is not only linked to a return to the temporality of nature, but treated as a religious experience.

Millimetri (Millimeters, 1983) shows a marked increase in the rapid discontinuity of De Angelis's poetry as he explores the murky origins and vicissitudes of subjectivity against the natural cycle. His penchant for staging dramatic scenes gives way to highly elliptical patterns of imagery, as in "Ora c'è la disadorna" (Now She Is Unadorned):

Ora c'è la disadorna
e si compiono gli anni, a manciate,
con ingegno di forbici e
una boria che accosta
al gas la bocca
dura fino alla sua spina
dove crede
oppure i morti arrancano verso un campo
che ha la testa cava
e le miriadi
si gettano nel battesimo
per un soffio.

(Now she is unadorned
and the years come to pass, in handfuls,
with the wit of shears and
an arrogance that draws
to the gas the mouth
persistent down to the spine
where it believes
or else the dead trudge toward a field
that has a hollow head
and the myriads
hurl themselves into the baptism
for a breath.)

References to agriculture, suicide, and religious ritual are combined with surreal juxtapositions to suggest the key idea that nature is creative only insofar as it is violent and self-destructive. The rapidity and resonance of the images and the sudden shifts in the syntax give this and other poems from *Millimetri* an obscure but exhilarating power, eliciting the sort of experience Nietzsche found in Dionysian art. The paradox is that to be primordially is to be nothing, dissolved in the ceaseless flux of becoming; being depends on discourse, on naming: it is "baptism" that gives "a breath" to "the myriads."

De Angelis's combination of discontinuous form with origin-centered thinking displays his strong affinity with Celan's poetry. De Angelis follows Celan's transformation of the lyric by developing a poetics of the limit-situation, but one that derives from a modern movement in Italian poetry, the hermeticism that dominated the 1930s and 1940s. In the essay "Andare a capo (autobiografia)" (Starting a New Line of Verse [Autobiography]), from *Poesia e destino,* De Angelis describes his early interest in the formal innovations of hermeticism —

its oblique means of signification, particularly the ambiguities released by the "attenzione sottile per le pause e gli accostamenti" (subtle attention to pauses and juxtapositions) in the poems of Mario Luzi, Alfonso Gatto, and Piero Bigongiari. De Angelis's strategy, however, was to push the hermetic fragmentation of meaning to an extreme: "ho cercato qualcos'altro: un andare a capo ancora più lontano dal senso — dal senso inerente a due versi separati e da quello orchestrale che ne illumina la separazione — ho cercato cioè una rottura della frase che fosse obbligata ma non innalzabile dalla frase stessa né dalla totalità delle frasi" (I sought something else: a starting over even further removed from meaning — from the meaning inherent in two separated lines and from that orchestral meaning that illuminates their separation — I sought, in other words, a rupture of the sentence that might be constrained by, but not derivable from, the sentence itself or the totality of sentences).

De Angelis's aim is to write poems whose very process of signification enacts the origin-centered thinking that is their theme, the tragic collision between telos and contingency. The telos of poetic composition includes not only the rules of syntax, the sentence, but also the experience chosen for representation and the elaborate signifying structures or poetics typical of literary texts. De Angelis introduces the contingent with syntactical irregularities, abrupt caesuras and enjambments, and shifts in discourse, all of which are circumscribed by the telos already animating the composition. The effect of these procedures is to break down the process of signification in the text, making it a site of incipient meanings and structures. De Angelis's poetry often takes as a point of departure specific episodes in his own life, but he renders them impersonal, thickening the representation with an intricate network of images and allusions and resisting any facile reduction of the text to authorial biography.

His third collection of poetry, *Terra del viso* (Land of the Face, 1985), is a mature synthesis of his poetics. Some poems show a return to the suspenseful dramatic style of *Somiglianze;* others show the impact of the heterogeneous and fragmentary images that characterize *Millimetri*. De Angelis's speculations on subjectivity examine a wider range of human experiences and relationships, including infancy and childhood, and the autobiographical references are at times more explicit, as in "Colloquio col padre" (Conversation with Father). The result is a provocative, remarkable meditation on human temporality.

"Ti benderai?" (Will You Put on the Blind-fold?) is a dramatic monologue that sketches a limit-situation in childhood: two boys are jumping across the roofs of houses. The speaker is the more Dionysian of the two and urges the other to jump, to act without reflection, to become merely a biological process. The childlike tone, full of innocent excitement, heightens the alarming nature of the scene:

Ti benderai? Io sono salito con la sciarpa
sugli occhi, ho graffiato i mattoni. Il muro
ha molte crepe, ma non temere, non devi temere:
salirai tra i rampicanti, i fratelli rampicanti.

E altissimo, quassù. Ti benderai? Io sono salito
in pochi minuti, guarda, ho le unghie insanguinate
e ti aspetto vicino all'antenna, non temere.

(Will you put on the blindfold? I climbed with my
     scarf
over my eyes, I scratched the bricks. The wall
has many cracks, but don't be afraid, you mustn't be
     afraid:
you'll climb up the creepers, the creeping brothers.

It is very high up here. Put on the blindfold? I climbed
in a few minutes, look, my nails are bloody
and I will wait for you near the antenna, do not be
     afraid.)

"Nei polmoni" (In the Lungs) treats infancy in De Angelis's distinctive way, with glimpses of a hospital scene in which Nietzschean ideas mix with nature imagery:

La coperta, la sua forza, mentre crescevamo.
O gli occhi che ieri furono ciechi,
oggi tuoi, ieri l'inseparable. Le fiale,
il riso in bianco diventano l'unico
mondo senza simbolo. Materia che
fu soltanto materia, nulla che
fu soltanto materia. Vegliare, non vegliare, poesia,
cobalto, padre, nulla, pioppi.

(The blanket, its weight, when we were growing.
Or the eyes which yesterday were blind,
today yours, yesterday the indivisible. The vials,
the boiled rice become the only
world without symbol. Matter that
was only matter, nothing that
was only matter. Watch, don't watch, poetry,
cobalt, father, nothing, poplars.)

The question of temporality enters De Angelis's poems not only through recurrent images drawn from biology but also formally, through the very recurrence of the imagery. The reader is led to construct intertextual relationships, initially among De Angelis's texts but also between them and the other cultural materials they appropriate. As a result, reading his poems forces an awareness of how language and subjectivity are constituted in time, by their difference within the cultural tradition. The intertextuality of De Angelis's poems situates them and the reader in a cultural tradition and thereby projects a concept of temporality.

This recursiveness becomes more pronounced in De Angelis's fourth collection, *Distante un padre* (A Distant Father, 1989). The poems are dominated by memories of relationships to family and friends. The last section, dedicated to De Angelis's mother, includes several poems in the Piedmontese dialect of Montferrat. The extreme formal discontinuity makes the memories obscure, impersonalizing them to the point of inscrutability, but the poems remain forcefully resonant because of De Angelis's recurrent ideas and images, as he occasionally quotes and revises lines from his earlier poems, forcing the reader to confront the changing conditions of language and subjectivity. "Telegramma" is typically allusive: it echoes "Le sentinelle" (The Sentries) from *Somiglianze,* which mentions those who "si ritraggono dalla morte per scortarla" (withdraw from death to escort it) with "simboli di seconda mano" (secondhand symbols). "Telegramma" shows the poet isolated by his estranging use of language:

La finestra è rimasta come prima. Il freddo
ripete quell'essenza idiota di roccia
proprio mentre tremano le lettere di ogni parola.
Con un mezzo sorriso indichi
una via d'uscita, una scala qualunque.
Nemmeno adesso hai simboli per chi muore.
Ti parlavo del mare, ma il mare è pochi metri quadrati,
un trapano, appena fuori. Era anche, per noi,
l'intuito di una figlia che respira
nei primi attimi di una cosa. Carta per dire
brodo e riso, mesi per dire cuscino. Gli azzuri mi
     chiamano
congelato in una stella fissa.

(The window remained as before. The cold
repeats that idiotic essence of rock
just as the letters of every word tremble.
With a half smile you point
out an exit, some stairs.
Not even now have you symbols for the dead.
I spoke to you of the sea, but the sea is a few square
     meters,
a drill, scarcely out. It was also, for us,
the intuition of a daughter breathing
in the first moments of a thing. Paper to say
broth and rice, months to say pillow. The blue ones
     call me
frozen in a fixed star.)

For De Angelis, language has a dual aspect: on the one hand, it transforms what it describes, imposing a conceptual system like mathematics ("a few square meters"); on the other hand, it brings awareness of the transformation, of the difference that exceeds linguistic determination, likened here to a parting and death but also to "the first moments of a thing." De Angelis's poem is a "telegram" from the edge of language, received in staccato bursts of lines, where the opaque details seem by turns realistic, autobiographical, and figurative – multiplying meanings by interrupting signification.

The postmodern concerns of De Angelis's poetic project give it an international currency, but it is also bears a fundamental resemblance to those of other Italian poets who began to publish during the 1970s, such as Nanni Cagnone, Angelo Lumelli, and Giuseppe Conte. Thomas J. Harrison describes the basic outline of this project in *The Favorite Malice: Ontology and Reference in Contemporary Italian Poetry* (1983): "the poet sings Dionysos – not in the hope of recalling the gods," as Heidegger's pursuit of being encourages, "but to celebrate their absence," following Nietzsche and poststructuralist thinkers such as Gilles Deleuze who have commented on and developed Nietzsche's antimetaphysical philosophy. De Angelis differs from other 1970s experimentalists in Italy in that his philosophical explorations coincide with his rigorous development of an original poetics and a repertoire of images and scenes, partly literary and partly autobiographical. The discontinuous form of his poetry derives from both the neo-avant-garde and hermeticism, but he avoids the explicit political engagement of the first and the controlled ambiguity of the second by fostering an indeterminacy of meaning that recalls the origins of language, subjectivity, culture, and society. The undeniable power of De Angelis's writing has distinguished him as one of the most compelling post–World War II Italian poets.

References:

Giorgio Bàrberi-Squarotti, "Introduzione a *L'idea centrale* di Milo De Angelis," *Almanacco dello Specchio,* 4 (1975): 373–375;

Alfonso Berardinelli, "Effetti di deriva," in *Il pubblico della poesia,* edited by Berardinelli and Franco Cordelli (Cosenza: Lerici, 1975), pp. 7–29;

Giuseppe Conte, "Le istituzioni del desiderio," *Verri,* 2 (September 1976): 53–76;

Franco Fortini, "Come certe danze del Caucaso," *Panorama* (2 June 1985): 31;

Fortini, "The Wind of Revival," *Times Literary Supplement,* 31 October 1975, pp. 1308–1309;

Robert P. Harrison, "The Italian Silence," *Critical Inquiry,* 13 (Autumn 1986): 81–99;

Thomas J. Harrison, "Nietzsche, Heidegger, and the Language of Contemporary Italian Poetry," in *The Favorite Malice: Ontology and Reference in Contemporary Italian Poetry,* translated and edited by Harrison (New York, Norristown, Pa. & Milan: Out of London, 1983), pp. 17–55;

Roberto Mussapi, "Milo De Angelis," *Nuova Corrente,* 29 (1982): 411–418;

Giancarlo Pontiggia and Enzo Di Mauro, "La Statua Vuota," in *La parola innamorata,* edited by Pontiggia and Di Mauro (Milan: Feltrinelli, 1978), pp. 9–17;

Antonio Riccardi, "Nell'itinerario poetico di Milo De Angelis," *Poesia,* 3 (March 1989): 85–86;

Enzo Siciliano, "Al confine delle parole," *Espresso* (19 February 1989): 182–183.

Fabio Doplicher
(11 September 1938 –   )

Mario B. Mignone
State University of New York at Stony Brook

BOOKS: *Il girochiuso* (Rome: Trevi, 1970);
La stanza del ghiaccio (Rome: De Luca, 1971);
I giorni dell'esilio (Manduria: Lacaita, 1975);
La notte degli attori (Rome: Carte Segrete, 1980);
Poesia diffusa (Brescia: Shakespeare, 1982);
La rappresentazione (Rome: Stilb, 1984);
Curvano echi dentro l'universo (Foggia: Vinelli, 1985).
Edition in English: *Selected Poems,* translated by Gaetano A. Iannace (New York: Garland, 1992).

OTHER: Adriano Spatola and Paul Vangelisti, eds., *Italian Poetry 1960–1980, from New to Post Avant Garde,* includes poems by Doplicher (San Francisco & Los Angeles: Red Hill, 1982), pp. 44–46;
Poesia della metamorfosi, edited by Doplicher, Umberto Piersanti, and Dino Zacchilli (Rome: Stilb, 1984);
Il pensiero, il corpo: Antologia della poesia italiana contemporanea, edited by Doplicher and Piersanti (Rome: Stilb, 1986);
Il teatro dei poeti: Antologia catalogo, edited by Doplicher (Rome: CTM, 1987).

Fabio Doplicher is one of the most versatile literary artists in Italy today. He writes poems, film scripts, plays, and criticism; he edits literary journals and organizes major cultural symposia. His reputation rests chiefly, however, on his poems, which have earned him high acclaim. In 1985, in presenting him the Premio Montale for *La rappresentazione* (The Performance, 1984), the poet Mario Luzi said (as reported in *Avanti!,* 12 July 1985):

> *La rappresentazione* è un libro di ispirazione unitaria che supera la casualità di una "raccolta," e che è degno del premio per lo stile e per la particolare coloritura dell'immagine e della metafora, lo è altresì per il pensiero sotteso, l'ossatura filosofica e l'implicita indagine figurata sui valori e la crisi dei valori di questo particolare momento della nostra civiltà. Altrettanto rilevante è l'apertura teatrale e narrativa che offre insolite prospettive al linguaggio poetico e alle sue situazioni.

> (*The Representation* is a book of unitary inspiration that overcomes the casualness of a "collection," and it is worthy of the prize for its style, for the particular coloration of the images, metaphors, the underlying thought, the philosophical frame, and the sharp inquiry into values and the crisis of values of this particular moment of our civilization. Just as relevant is its theatrical and narrative style, which offers unusual perspectives on our poetical language and settings.)

Doplicher's style was achieved by rejecting experimentalism for its own sake and assessing and opening new frontiers and new possibilities of poetical expression and literary techniques. Doplicher's poetry, however, does broadly reflect the evolution of Italian poetry in the last twenty-five years, from the abandonment of the hermetic tradition to the use of poetic language by the neo-avant-garde. While representing the reality of physical objects, he endows figurative language with metaphysical significance to shape existential questions and characterize a disorderly and unstable universe. Since he is fully aware of the inadequacy of human reason to find the ultimate meaning of existence, he conveys his understanding of the multiplicity of experiences through rich metaphors perceived by the mind as simultaneous realities.

The landscape of Doplicher's world, imagistically viewed, is strongly colored by Trieste and Rome, the two cities in which he has spent the greatest part of his life. He was born on 11 September 1938 and reared in Trieste; he has lived in Rome since the age of sixteen, when his father died. The Trieste years are important, not only because they encompass the critical formative years of childhood and adolescence but because the city, with its peculiar geographical position and its cultural milieu, peripheral to Italy but on the main cultural pathways to and from central Europe, contributed to a certain idiosyncratic development of his poetry. Trieste sidled Doplicher from the cultural main-

Fabio Doplicher in Kiev, 1983

stream. He found his strongest link to Italy in the rich library created by his father, a cultivated businessman who read widely and translated literary works: using the pseudonym Antonio Doraldi, he was the first Italian to translate works by August Strindberg. One of Fabio's uncles, a well-known musician, knew many important artists in Trieste, among them the poet Umberto Saba. This marginal background may explain Doplicher's isolation when he moved to Rome. In the early 1960s, when the neo-avant-garde held sway in Italy, Doplicher was still rooted in Triestine middle-European culture and classical literature. Something else that may have contributed to his personal dilemma is the fact that, with a Jewish mother, he was brought up in two cultural and religious traditions (Christian and Jewish). His heritage exacerbated his identity crisis, a prominent theme in his work. His writing becomes dark and prophetic when he describes humankind's woes and outrages, but he allows some hope for ultimate survival. He sees life as fascinating in its phenomenal richness.

Doplicher's poetic voice stems from a vision that may or may not reflect a shared reality, so crude and powerful is the force of his images. He dramatically raises the curtain on an urban world of exploitation and violence but gives to it a metaphysical candor suffused with mythical quality. Scenes of damnation engulf the reader in a modern-day inferno, but the condemning speaker also finds images of shy tenderness and beauty. As for Giacomo Leopardi, so for Doplicher, truth is poetic reality, and beauty can spring forth in a turn of phrase, a heartfelt comment, or a gentle meditation on the human condition.

The unmasking of urban realities is artfully accomplished in post-Pirandellian terms, and the theatrical quality is a special characteristic of Doplicher's poetic voice. Seeking a rational understanding or at least an awareness of the multiple layers of reality, he places himself in opposition to twentieth-century irrationalism, which he condemns for its anomalies while acknowledging that it represents a massive, predominant component of Western culture and its artistic identity. Reason, however, is valued by Doplicher not for its power to enlighten but for its capacity to stimulate a kind of dialectical play between the mathematical, physical sciences – by which he is fascinated (his theoretical physicist brother, Sergio, is for him a source of information) – and human intuitiveness. But reliance on pure reason alone suggests to Doplicher images of a soulless void toward which people are drawn in a process of self-destruction.

His first collection of poems, *Il girochiuso* (The Enclosed Circle, 1970), already shows Doplicher to be a materialist, in the Lucretian sense, with an increasingly cosmic vision tempered by humanitarian socialism. A first reading produces the impression that Doplicher enters the world of poetry as a neorealist, with his use of low-key conversational style and his focus on postwar social reality. Soon, however, the objective reality represented acquires a surreal color and gives to his art an epic quality of extraordinary force: his panoramic vision and epic-allegorical style engage readers' senses and imagination. This collection, divided into two sections – the first made up of "short stories" in verses, the second composed of short poems – is rather an atypical work for its time.

The first part dramatizes depersonalization, a theme that pervades Doplicher's oeuvre. It evokes the outskirts of a metropolis (Rome), where lonely characters roam through city refuse or prowl through ashes and smoke near convoluted highways leading in and out of the city like symbols of salvation and perdition. Humankind's reduction to nothingness and the inane search for identity in a socially cruel world are given cogent representation in "Luciano Creta," which is about a hobo found dead and stripped of papers:

> Luciano Creta, cadavere, mediaetà mediopeso,
> si è perso tra l'ingresso ai furgoni
> fumosi del traffico industriale
> e il deposito degli uomini e delle donne
> poveri per la sepoltura;
> ogni ricerca vana, s'informa a termini di legge
>   e nessun certificato al riposo
>   accompagnava Luciano Creta,
>   strana creatura, come sabbia
>   nella regola del morire umano.
>
> (Luciano Creta, a cadaver, middle-aged and medium
>   built,
> got lost between the smoky
> vans of the industrial traffic
> and the burial grounds
> of poor men and women;
> every vain search, is carried out with legal terms
>   and no certificate accompanied
>   Luciano Creta to his last rest,
>   now, strange creature, similar to sand
>   in the law of human destiny.)

Doplicher's poetry itself becomes a quest for identity. In the landscape of the "enclosed circle" he views emigration, exploitation, and debilitating working conditions as continuous perils, serious impediments to pride and selfhood.

In the second part of the collection the social forces that shape the personae are often less circumscribed and objectified. The compositions are more lyrical; images of Trieste, the Carso, the sea, contemporary violence, wars in progress, prevarications, and physical and moral decay are intertwined with archetypal images of history and myth. Past and present representations of evil are often linked together by verses from the Old Testament, testifying to the truth of prophetic words and the enduring presence of a collective consciousness and memory. According to Doplicher fantasy cannot and should not attempt to disassociate itself from myth, but should, on the contrary, reintroduce it to establish the continuity of human experience. The sea, a symbol of vitality and death, underlines origins and experiences and gives the poetical landscape a strong metaphysical significance, as in "Un ricordo" (A Memory):

> il mare è un lungo tappeto ordito di scogli
> e i nodi mi legano come gesti rituali
> al senso perduto nel reclinar d'antenne.
>
> (the sea is a long carpet warped with rocks
> and the knots tie me like ritual gestures
> to the lost significance of the bent antennae.)

The sea, the only entity comparable to time, harbors the idea of continuity and multiple forms, promising infinite possibilities.

In his first work Doplicher's diction and technique derive vigor from compound words, hammering rhythms, and verses energetically linked. There is constant interplay between the phonic level and the iconic level. Literary words are set on a collision course with colloquial expressions, gracious poetic images clash with figures of decaying objects reflecting the technological age, and a series of neologisms creates eddies of analogies. In "I raccordi" (The Connections), for example, the entangled sentences and meanings disorient both characters and readers and make them yearn for some guiding thread, for a key to language and meaning. Loneliness, lack of communication, and isolation thrive in a foggy world. Indeed, the fog is a recurrent metaphor: it induces sleep, hides things, and limits vision, but it is also a sentinel that guards intimacy and protects dreams and chimeras. The image of God is blurred by the mist, as in "Diosangue" (Bloody God):

noi non ti vediamo sangue
· ·
il silenzio Diosangue è pace all'altopiano
dove t'hanno dimenticato i morti
operosi per sciogliere al calcare
il proprio cantuccio inebriato
nel ruvido vento di pruno.

(we do not see your blood
· ·
silence Bloody God is peace on the plateau
where you have been forgotten by the dead
trying to free themselves from their tombs
their own nook intoxicated
by the rough wind of the prune tree.)

Verbal experimentation is more prevalent in Doplicher's next work, *La stanza del ghiaccio* (The Room of Ice, 1971). The long and short verses are voiced in familiar colloquialisms, business jargon, refined poetic discourse, proverbs, and metaphors, creating a collage akin to those so prevalent in the poetry of the neo-avant-garde. His poems cease to be confession, vision, or song — the expression of self — to become instead provocative linguistic objects, destructive impersonal creations designed to lay bare the untrustworthy validity of expression itself. Alongside the clear intent to break with tradition, there is a robust indictment of both the bourgeoisie and Marxist ideology. Doplicher's collages, however, are not merely systems of nonsense but platforms and pleas to expand the poetic imagination, to excite startling creative possibilities in a new dimension and through new insights. The plurality of linguistic registers offers the possibility of reading on many levels and the portrayal of a complex reality that finds a more adequate treatment in his later works. The linguistic fractures do not annul the significative value of the word or that of the poetical voice; the book is, rather, an effort intellectually and emotionally to enliven meaning and poetical expressiveness. Thus Doplicher's most neo-avant-garde book is also an alternate project directed against the neo-avant-garde, who sought to abolish lexical meaning but flattened poetical expression and value. Doplicher is a consummate formalist, but formalism is secondary to his attitude and to the verbal living of the instant. His craft is not employed to lock the poet inside his own troubled ego, and the reader with him, but to release both beyond such egocentricity.

Doplicher's word or logos is manifest in the context of a world and society in perpetual change, which is one of the major themes of his *I giorni del-l'esilio* (The Days of Exile, 1975), considered by many critics his first work of maturity

and a high moment of postwar Italian poetry. In this new phase the anguish of historic memory clamors for attention. Doplicher wants poetry, or at least his poetry, to be a cognitive fact, to be representative of his historical moment. In the first poem, "Premessa: Figli della parola" (Premise: Children of the Word), providing an exposition of his poetics, he says that his verses, in form and substance alike, must be a cognitive process nourished by both thought and emotion and achieved through the reinstatement of the word as an instrument of work and life:

È tempo di significati. È tempo di immagini
· ·
Compito del poeta
che ricerchi una nuova realtà, ridiscutendo se stesso
come parte di una condizione di lavoro, è ricreare le
    parole
in un momento comune di sofferenza e di speranza.

(It is the time for meanings. It is the time for images
· ·
It is the task of the poet
to search for a new reality, examining himself
as though a condition for work, and to re-create words

in a moment of shared suffering and hope.)

Reality can be changed by the instruments of work, and in the poet's case his tools are words. The Orphic myth is recast to represent a new reality, a music with different rhythm and a diverse timbre. In contrast to the poets of the neo-avant-garde, who relied on the ability of the self-reproducing word, Doplicher's "word chain" is the result of a deliberate effort to interpret better the perceived reality. It is a poetic search for truth, an adventure, a voyage of discovery, a deciphering of the world in an era of transition.

In the mid 1970s Doplicher aimed at elaborating a vision of poetry that would constitute a discourse on ethics and incorporate his deepening classicism. It was a period during which he felt increasingly more exiled, and he returned in thought to his native Trieste. The "days of exile" concern his childhood, evoked metaphorically as through a filtered memory. They also hark back to a lost paradise, a mythical age of fables that stands in contrast to a desolate present where one finds himself swallowed by avalanches of refuse, anxious, and enslaved by consumerism and high technology. The outskirts of Rome (representing any large urban center) emerge again in all their dreariness. Doplicher's vision of life, already denunciatory, grows even more somber. Even the candor and the beauty of Venus have sardonically changed into a cheap, papier-mâché mannequin, a relic goddess of love in decomposition, as seen in "La nascita di Venere" (The Birth of Venus):

Ogni giorno diventi più ruggine, che tu abbia traspor-
    tato ghiaia
che tu abbia portato fuoco, o soltanto
il peso del tuo sangue.
La vita, questo orinatoio: una nicchia a testa,
occhi imbambolati.
Allora lasciami.

(Every day you become more decayed, for the gravel
    you might have carried
for the fire you might have brought, or only
for the weight of your blood.
Life, this urinal: a place for everyone,
eyes dulled.
Now leave me.)

Doplicher's poetic search is marked by restlessness and anxiety.

The search becomes inquisitorial in his next collection, *La notte degli attori* (The Actor's Night, 1980). The title indicates that poetry is allied to theater, the classical mode of self-examination; indeed the book, in five parts, is a poetic discussion about actors and performances. The speaker imagines that the five fingers of his hand (by extension the act of writing and subjectivity) rebel on the stage of an old theater and become five characters with traditional roles: the first actor, the beloved, the comic, the old man, and the singer. During one night they act out all of history and the problems of faith before becoming fingers again and thus closing the cycle. Theater, thought, and poetry are to be understood as complementary representational components of reality.

Doplicher later intensified his search into the representational possibilities of poetry. In the early 1980s, when the neo-avant-garde had almost vanished and most of its practitioners had become conventional in their art, had rejected any social commitment, and had abandoned their utopian dreams, he followed his own way. He felt the need to create a poetry of images, hospitable to the ever-changing manner in which people perceive the world. His poetry of metamorphosis signals a gap between imagination and perception and a loss of contact with tradition. There are reflections on the materiality of the written text, on a cosmic awareness of human nature, on the emergence of a new *I,* and on poetry as the art of thinking, the interpreter of all the other arts, and a search for rationality in an irrational world.

To foster this new mode of considering the nature and function of poetry, in 1981 Doplicher cre-

ated a journal, *Stilb: Spettacolo, Scrittura-Spazio,* which served to connect the various arts, to allow them to confront one another, and to amalgamate the various modes of expression. The journal was not a passive medium but a forum in which practice and theory questioned each other. Divided into three sections — "Spettacolo" (Spectacle), concerning theater, film, and music; "Scrittura" (Writing), presenting literary debates through critical and creative texts; and "Spazio" (Space), focusing on environment, architecture, and ecology — *Stilb* offered the hope of endowing modern humankind with new signs, with original modes of representation to express a world in constant flux. Its premises did not exclude the search for a new political ethic that would brook no compromise. Doplicher became a cultural "animator," a promoter of symposia and politicocultural encounters on poetry and theater. Like all great theorists, he fought in defense of poetry.

La rappresentazione, published in 1984 in the Stilb book series, has been considered by critics to be Doplicher's major literary accomplishment. Written, as usual, in a variety of meters and fraught with complicated images, the poems develop a personal dialogue that achieves, at times, great lyrical intensity. Doplicher focuses on the agitation and anguish of a world that sees its survival in doubt. Garbage pollutes nature, and the sea gull, symbolizing human destiny, abandons its old ways, flies up rivers, and becomes an urban dweller. In "Metamorfosi del gabbiano" (Metamorphosis of the Sea Gull) Doplicher writes:

vieni a visitare il suolo, asseconda
il peso del corpo, il formicolio nelle mani, le volute
di un fumo cinereo, sospeso, senza origine.
. . . .
ammalati come la città, un dio avventuroso
la percorre sui mucchietti luridi che il mattino succhia.
questa è la storia che vivrai, mosca cieca e metastasi,
come è cominciata e dove porti ignori, per questo è tua.

(come to visit the ground, add to
your body weight, the tingling in your hands, the
    whorls
of ashen smoke, hanging in midair, without a source.
. . . .
get sick like this city, an adventurous god
crosses it on foul small heaps that the morning sucks.
this is the story that you will live, blindman's buff and
    metastasis,
how it began and where it leads you do not know, therefore
    it is yours.)

Like the sea gull, humankind is living a new reality to which it must learn to adapt, by which it will also be shaped.

Doplicher becomes the historian of a changing reality. In a world of destruction and of annihilation, poetry has to regain its power. Europe is still shaken from the horrors of the Holocaust, and the fearful past is still present in everyone's consciousness. A new European conscience is sought, a new brotherhood is announced, and a new humanism is proposed. Doplicher questions the present and interprets the future by invoking the cultural past exemplified by the works of Petrarch, Miguel de Cervantes, Denis Diderot, Percy Bysshe Shelley, Arthur Schopenhauer, and Friedrich Hölderlin. Schopenhauer's vision of the world as will and representation becomes a suggestion that, after the fall of all utopias, only representation of shattered dreams can give meaning to experience. Representation, a relation of unity between past, present, and future, comes to signify not only humankind's permanent state of change and conflict but also the conflict of matter with matter; it embodies the phenomenal reality of being. The main interest of Doplicher in Schopenhauer's ideas is not his pessimism but the reduction of fragmented reality into a unity, a poetical, representational unity. It is an effort to find justification and certainty in a period of doubt and uncertainty, even when the reality portrayed is apocalyptic destruction. The poet's task is to record the transformations people experience, to describe the continuous shift in ways of perceiving reality, and to explain, rationally and imaginatively, how self-destruction may father a new beginning. The fall of utopias and the vacuum of values will not destroy faith in the value and importance of human presence, provided the poet, reconciling belief and reason, keeps faith with humanity.

There are no simple solutions to the existential dilemma. In his identity crisis, unable to find the mythical youth of Faust, European man looks for a mask that would fix his features in changing times. He becomes an actor playing all roles but displaying a single countenance ("La maschera di Faust" [Faust's Mask] is the title of the second section of *La rappresentazione*). Words, however, must acquire old meanings to assure the representative value of new times, and Doplicher's main actor becomes Hypokrites, a Greek actor and poet, a man who pretends in order to find truth, to discover, to love, to approach the mysteries of fate, and to become god-like in his consciousness: "scoprire, amare, fingere: è il patto. . . . / L'uomo quale eri sta fondomare tra pesci e coralli" (to discover, to love, to pretend: that is the pact. . . . / The man you once were is at the bottom of the sea among fishes and corals).

Doplicher defines even more clearly the sense of his mission in the third section of *La rappresentazione*, "Difesa della poesia" (Defense of Poetry), which includes "Mano d'acqua" (Hand of Water) and "Miniature di Belbello" (Miniatures of Belbello). Reality is made of all the realities of the past, just as the perfume of a rose contains the essence of all past seasons:

il bianco degli occhi
degli enciclopedisti e dei gesuiti
è mobile come bolle di vetro incandescente.
i nostri appuntamenti, regolari e tristi
per dignità si chiamano amore. le cucchiaiate
di foglie secche, nell'intruglio del pensiero.

(the white of the eyes
of encyclopedists and Jesuits
quivering like bubbles of incandescent glass.
our encounters, regular and sad
for dignity we call love. spoonful
of dried leaves, in the brew of thought.)

Images of encyclopedists and allusions to victims of the Inquisition return again and again in Doplicher's poems, like a refrain; they, too, saw another reality others could not see.

The collection concludes with a terrifying image of hopelessness and despair, but Doplicher insists that such an image heralds a new dawn and states that even when the voyage toward self-destruction has run its course, the last, lonely creature finally aware of the end of everything has still kept his hope, his illusions, and his faith:

Contro un cielo nero, il giovane, livido nudo solo e
   ultimo,
cerca un padre che stia sui monti
e urla "sono soltanto un uomo."

(Against the black sky, the young man, ashen naked
   alone and last,
asks for a father that is on the mountains
and cries out "I am only a man.")

Evoking Hölderlin and Lucretius, the poem aspires to a poetry of intuition, feelings, and reason to represent the changing moments of the human journey on earth, the infinite multiplicity of nature, and the various ways of perceiving such a reality. Such a poetics assigns to poets the task of seeing more clearly and of anticipating the road to what lies ahead by opening the veils of mystery and conferring new validity and worth on words.

Fabio Doplicher's poetry is cultured but always at the edge of the abyss. In his view, poetry is a search for humankind's place in existence with the purpose of discovering a pragmatic direction, the best possible road toward survival and the creation of valid goals.

Interviews:

Giuseppe Tedeschi, "Metamorfosi del poeta," *Tempo* (16 December 1983): 17;

Franco Zangrilli, "Incontro con Fabio Doplicher," *Italian Quarterly,* 25 (Winter 1984): 57–72.

References:

S. Busin, "Fabio Doplicher e l'arte," *Alla bottega,* 10 (May–June 1972): 46–50;

Giovanna Wedel De Stasio, "*La rappresentazione,*" *Quaderni d'Italianistica,* 7 (Spring 1986): 143–147;

Rodolfo Di Biasio, "Ragione come allegoria e liricità nella poesia di Fabio Doplicher," *Lunario Nuovo,* 9, no. 45: 3–20;

Luigi Fontanella, "Rivolta e proiezione: Saggio sulla poesia di Fabio Doplicher," *Misure Critiche,* 9–10 (October–December 1979/January–March 1980): 87–109;

Paolo Guzzi, "Fabio Doplicher tra teatro, televisione e poesia," *Ridotto,* 8 (April–May 1985): 21–67;

Guzzi, "Poesia e teatro della metamorfosi in Fabio Doplicher," *Battana,* 21 (March 1984): 19–38;

Gaetano A. Iannace, "Il mito e la fantasia poetante in Fabio Doplicher," *Uomini e Libri,* 120 (September–October 1988): 51–53;

Ruggiero Jacobbi, "La poesia di Doplicher: Diario di un esilio," *Uomini e Libri,* 58 (March–April 1976): 40–43;

Jacobbi, "Premessa a tre testi di Fabio Doplicher," *Ridotto,* 3 (January–February 1980): 9–10;

Franco Mancinelli, "Fabio Doplicher," in his *Poeti di frontiera* (Rome: Stilb, 1983);

Remo Pagnanelli, *Fabio Doplicher* (Latina: Di Mambro, 1985);

Umberto Piersanti, "L'inquieto universo di Fabio Doplicher," *Ponte,* 39 (31 January 1983): 86–94;

Silvio Ramat, "Le nuvole di Urbino," *Forum Italicum,* 12, no. 2 (1978): 258–261;

Giacinto Spagnoletti, "Un linguaggio spietato a ritmo incalzante," *Sipario,* 389 (October 1978): 37–39;

Franco Zangrilli, "La poesia filosofica di Fabio Doplicher," *Cristallo,* 27, no. 2 (1985): 67–70.

Luciano Erba

(18 September 1922 –   )

Maria Nina Lombardo
University of Chicago

BOOKS: *Linea K* (Modena: Guanda, 1951);

Il bel paese (Milan: Meridiana, 1955);

Ipogrammi & Metaippogrammi di Giovanola (Milan: All'Insegna del Pesce d'Oro, 1958);

Il prete di Ratanà (Milan: All'Insegna del Pesce d'Oro, 1959);

Il male minore (Milan: Mondadori, 1960);

Magia e invenzione: Note e ricerche su Cyrano de Bergerac e altri autori del primo Seicento francese (Milan: All'Insegna del Pesce d'Oro, 1967);

Huysmans e la liturgia, e alcune note di letteratura francese contemporanea (Bari: Adriatica, 1971);

Il prato più verde (Milan: Guanda, 1977);

Il nastro di Moebius (Milan: Mondadori, 1980);

Françoise (Brescia, 1982);

Il cerchio aperto (Milan: All'Insegna del Pesce d'Oro, 1983);

Il tranviere metafisico (Milan: Scheiwiller, 1987);

L'ippopotamo (Turin: Einaudi, 1989).

OTHER: *Quarta generazione: La giovane poesia, 1945–1954,* edited by Erba and Piero Chiara, includes poems by Erba (Varese: Magenta, 1954);

Cyrano de Bergerac, *L'altro mondo,* translated by Erba (Florence: Fussi, 1956);

"Lo svagato" and "Terra e Mare," *Poetry,* 94 (April–September 1959): 308–311;

Jacques de Sponde, *Sonetti,* translated by Erba (Milan: Nuova Accademia, 1960);

Blaise Cendrars, *Poesie,* translated by Erba (Milan: Nuova Accademia, 1961);

de Bergerac, *Lettres,* edited and translated by Erba (Milan: Scheiwiller, 1965);

Vittoria Bradshaw, ed. and trans., *From Pure Silence to Impure Dialogue: A Survey of Post-War Italian Poetry 1945–1965,* includes poems by Erba (New York: Las Américas, 1971), pp. 112–140;

Ruth Feldman and Brian Swann, eds. and trans., *Italian Poetry Today: Currents and Trends,* includes poems by Erba (Saint Paul: New Rivers, 1979), pp. 74–76;

Lawrence R. Smith, trans., *The New Italian Poetry: 1945 to the Present. A Bilingual Anthology,* includes poems by Erba (Berkeley & Los Angeles: University of California Press, 1981), pp. 220–231.

In 1952 Luciano Anceschi included poems by Luciano Erba in the volume *Linea lombarda* (Lombard Line) along with works by five other poets: Vittorio Sereni, Roberto Rebora, Giorgio Orelli, Nelo Risi, and Renzo Modesti. Anceschi's categorization indicates less the existence of an official school than a perception of a poetic mood shared by these poets of the lakes region of northern Italy. The poetry of the *linea lombarda* is antiliterary and posthermetic, and Erba's poetry in particular is marked by a realism hardly characteristic of the hermetic school. Similar to his contemporary Risi, Erba utilizes images to tell existential minitales, adding a touch of Guillaume Apollinaire in the process. The young Erba balanced his existential explorations with lightheartedness or, according to critic Glauco Cambon, with a characteristic "ritmo felice nel ritmo grave della vita urbana" (happy rhythm in the somber rhythm of urban life).

Luciano Erba was born on 18 September 1922 in Milan. Despite sojourns of varying duration in Switzerland during World War II, Paris from 1948 to the 1950s, and the United States from 1963 to 1966, Erba has retained residence in his native city, graduating in 1947 from the Università Cattolica del Sacro Cuore there. As a teacher of French language and literature, Erba moved quickly to the university level and presently chairs the Department of French Language and Literature at the University of Verona, where he has taught since 1982. Besides being a poet and the author of a volume of short stories (*Françoise,* 1982), Erba is also a scholar whose interests embrace the French literature of the seventeenth and nineteenth centuries. He has translated the works of some French, English, and American poets, and in 1965 he published a critical edition of Cyrano de Bergerac's *Lettres*. Erba has written for Italian and foreign literary magazines such as *Fiera Letteraria, Officina, Botteghe Oscure, Poetry,* and the *Western Review.* In 1961 he married Maria Giuseppina Sain, and they have three daughters. Erba won the Premio Carducci in 1977 and the Premio Viareggio in 1980.

Erba's first poetry collection was published in 1951 with the title *Linea K.* The poems included in this small volume are combined with others from the 1950s in *Il male minore* (The Lesser Evil, 1960). Seventeen years elapsed before the release of Erba's next poetic venture, during which time he devoted himself to translation and other academic pursuits.

Il prato più verde (The Greenest Lawn) was published in 1977. *Il nastro di Moebius* (The Möbius Strip, 1980) reunites poetry from both *Il male minore* and *Il prato più verde* and offers only three new sections. Erba has published three other volumes of poetry: *Il cerchio aperto* (The Open Circle, 1983); *Il tranviere metafisico* (Metaphysical Conductor, 1987); and *L'ippopotamo* (The Hippopotamus, 1989), which won the Montale-Guggenheim Award in June 1989.

Erba's poetry is almost exclusively free verse: brief lyrics without rhyme and – notable particularly in *Il prato più verde* – often without punctuation. Erba's style is characterized by an intuitive metric order; his favorite stylistic devices are confined to the most simple, including alliteration, repetition, and the irony for which he has been frequently noted. Recurring images in Erba's poetry include the dawn, the city, and, most important, people – children leaving the city dreaming of a Milan of blue valleys; women on their way to work at inns along the river; and the well-known "Grande Jeanne" with a great blue hat. Furthermore, in earlier works such as *Linea K* and *Il bel paese,* one notes a distinct nostalgia for places, often identifiable with Milan. Understandably, then, Erba's poetry can be described as highly autobiographical, an assortment of memory fragments sometimes with no obvious plan of organization.

In a 1960 article in *Menabò,* poet and critic Franco Fortini divides Italian poetry of the postwar period into three categories by which he is able to evaluate and classify the poetic response to sociological conditions of the era. These three categories are *transito* (passage), *contraddizione* (contradiction), and *avvento* (advent). Poets who belong to the category of *transito* manifest passivity and patience in the face of problems of the day, and their poetry is characterized by the description of everyday experiences. These poets view passion as a useless or vain evasion of the existential condition and tend to use an ironic tone to distance themselves from their surroundings. Quite different from the first group, the poets in the *contraddizione* category make heavy use of opposition in various ways, creating a rebellious divarication between signifier and signified and adopting disturbingly unaesthetic technological and administrative languages in an effort to express their existential exasperation through stylistic tension. The poets who belong to the category of *avvento* see humanity wedged between the postwar period and the cold war. Their poetry hovers in immobility as they look anxiously toward the future for a welcome change from the present dilemma.

Fortini would classify Erba as a poet of *transito* for his ironic tone and interest in the objects, people, and places around him. Confronted with a tumultuous and discouraging reality, he has elected to encircle himself in the description of a quaint and personal universe, reclining passively in ignorance, the lesser of evils – thus the title of the collection *Il male minore.*

Fortini and Angelo Jacomuzzi, among others, have emphasized the concrete elements central to Erba's poetry. Zinnias, heliotrope, and animal tracks in the snow are images that dominate Erba's early poetry. Yet these elements serve as mere starting points from which Erba transports his lyrics to a universal level, departing from the concrete or decorative and arriving at the abstract and existential. Erba the poet embraces the human race, populating the silence of confusion with lively images, as in the poem "Sentimento del tempo" (Feeling of the Time):

> Tu mi parli
> della traccia di lepre sulla neve
> di Mahori cantata dalla radio
> quando ti svegli
> che danzano a New York.
> Ti fidi.
> Così se piove sul tetto,
> Io non so fermarmi
> al segno dell'infinito
> in quest'ombra di cose:
> la mia pioggia
> ha il rumore degli anni.
>
> (You speak to me
> of hare tracks in the snow
> of Mahori sung on the radio
> when you awaken
> that they are dancing in New York.
> You trust.
> So if rain falls on the roof,
> I don't know how to stop

at the sign of the infinite
in this shadow of things:
my rain
makes the noise of the years.)

Here the speaker declares himself a spokesperson
for global discontent: his effort to arrive at the
infinite meaning of objects and events is prevented
by his own experience, as his rain "makes the noise
of the years."

The intentionally ill-defined addressee whom
he engages in his existential discourse is present in
many of the other poems of *Il male minore* but almost
disappears in the longer and more complex lyrics of
Il prato più verde. In these later lyrics the speaker confronts his condition in solitude, expressing the un-
welcomeness of an age that does not share his memories. There is also more evidence in the volume of
what some critics call the "fantastic" element in
Erba's poetry, as "Gli anni quaranta" (The Forties)
demonstrates. Nostalgic references are less frequent, and one notes a distinct openness to poetic
experimentation.

The poem titled "Moebius" is of particular interest since it forms a link with the later volume to
which it lends its name and because it is essential
for an understanding of Erba's poetics:

Impreparato
ma sì, alla vita
il binario da prendere era un altro
arrugginito, in curva
svaniva in una trincea di foglie fresche
in un ninfeo di scambi e di rocaille

oggi sono tornato
sono tornato troppo lontano

(Unprepared
but yes, for life
the track to take was another
rusty, in a curve
it was vanishing in a trench of fresh leaves
in a nymphaeum of exchanges and of rocaille

today I returned
I returned too far away)[.]

In a note to the poem Erba acquaints the reader
with August Ferdinand Möbius, the nineteenth-century German astronomer and mathematician best
known for the Möbius strip, a one-sided geometric
figure that can be followed infinitely without crossing an edge or reaching its end. Erba's 1980 volume, *Il nastro di Moebius*, contains a majority of
poems from earlier volumes and a small percentage
of new material. Möbius's geometric figure is thus
applied to the poet's condition as to the human
condition in general: an endless repetitive process,
beginning where it ends, only to begin incessantly
again. In the poem "Moebius" this condition is
lamented: the speaker wishes he had chosen a completely different Möbius strip, and, acutely aware of
his helplessness to control his own destiny, he returns to the crucial point at which his path in life
was determined, capturing desperation with the
lines "today I returned / I returned too far away."

Such despair is perhaps already perceivable in
the poems of *Il prato più verde*, in which readers see
evidence of a nostalgia for the hopelessly lost past —
a looking back that is melancholy rather than affectionate, the only type of nostalgia realistic for a historical epoch marked by disappointment and confusion. Although Erba's literary production is far
from abundant, his poetic dossier documents the literary reaction to one of the most existentially turbulent periods of Western culture.

References:

Giorgio Bàrberi Squarotti, "Da 'Linea K' al 'Bel
paese,'" *Fiera Letteraria*, 7 July 1956, p. 4;

Glauco Cambon, "'Il prato più verde' di Luciano
Erba," *Forum Italicum*, 13 (Fall 1979): 359–364;

Giorgio Caproni, "Ezra Pound e Luciano Erba,"
Fiera Letteraria, 8 November 1959, pp. 1–2;

Arnaldo Di Benedetto, "L'impossibile Esiodo,"
Letteratura Italiana Contemporanea, 2, no. 4
(1982): 79–94;

Angelo Jacomuzzi, "La poesia di Erba 'Super
flumina,'" *Forum Italicum*, 13 (Spring 1979):
30–47;

Giorgio Luzzi, *Poeti della Linea Lombarda (1952–
1985)* (Milan: Nuova Stampa, 1987);

Silvio Ramat, *Storia della poesia italiana del novecento*
(Milan: Mursia, 1976), pp. 579–598.

Franco Fortini
(10 September 1917 –)

Thomas E. Peterson
University of Georgia

BOOKS: *Foglio di via e altri versi* (Turin: Einaudi, 1946; revised and enlarged, 1967);

Agonia di Natale (Turin: Einaudi, 1948); republished as *Giovanni e le mani* (Turin: Einaudi, 1972);

Sei poesie per Ruth e una per me (Milan, 1953);

Una facile allegoria (Milan: Meridiana, 1954);

In una strada di Firenze (Milan: Meridiana, 1955);

Asia maggiore: Viaggio nella Cina (Turin: Einaudi, 1956);

I destini generali (Caltanissetta & Rome: Sciascia, 1956);

Dieci inverni, 1947–1957: Contributi ad un discorso socialista (Milan: Feltrinelli, 1957);

Sestina a Firenze (Milan: Meridiana, 1957);

Poesia ed errore, 1937–1957 (Milan: Feltrinelli, 1959);

Poesia delle rose (Bologna: Palmaverde, 1962);

Una volta per sempre (Milan: Mondadori, 1963; enlarged edition, Turin: Einaudi, 1978);

Sere in Valdossola (Milan: Mondadori, 1963);

Tre testi per film: All'armi siam fascisti (1961), Sciopero a Torino (1962), La statua di Stalin (1963) (Milan: Avanti!, 1963);

Verifica dei poteri (Milan: Saggiatore, 1965; enlarged, 1969);

L'ospite ingrato: Testi e note per versi ironici (Bari: Da Vinci, 1966; enlarged edition, Casale Monferrato: Marietti, 1985);

I cani del Sinai (Bari: De Donato, 1967);

Ventiquattro voci per un dizionario di lettere (Milan: Saggiatore, 1968);

Questo muro, 1962–1972 (Milan: Mondadori, 1973);

Poesie scelte (1938–1973), edited by Pier Vincenzo Mengaldo (Milan: Mondadori, 1974);

Saggi italiani (Bari: De Donato, 1974);

I poeti del Novecento (Bari & Rome: Laterza, 1977);

Questioni di frontiera: Scritti di politica e di letteratura (Turin: Einaudi, 1977);

Una obbedienza: 18 poesie, 1969–1979 (Genoa: Marco dei Giustiniani, 1980);

Il ladro di ciliege (Turin: Einaudi, 1982);

Memorie per dopo domani (Milan: Fini, 1983);

Paesaggio con serpente (Turin: Einaudi, 1984);

Insistenze: Cinquanta scritti 1976–1984 (Milan: Garzanti, 1985);

La poesia ad alta voce (Siena: Barbablù, 1986);

Note su Noventa (Venice: Atti del Convegno, 1986);

Dei confini della poesia (Brescia: Obliquo, 1986);

Nuovi saggi italiani (Milan: Garzanti, 1987);

Poesie rare e inedite (Milan: Scheiwiller, 1987);

La cena delle ceneri; & Racconto fiorentino (Milan: Lombardi, 1988);

La morte del cherubino (Siena: Barbablù, 1988);

Tradizione, traduzione, società (Rome: Riuniti, 1989);

Extrema ratio: Note per un buon uso delle rovine (Milan: Garzanti, 1990);

Versi scelti (1939–1989) (Turin: Einaudi, 1990);

Non solo oggi: Cinquantanove voci (Rome: Riuniti, 1991).

Edition in English: *Poems,* translated by Michael Hamburger (Todmorden, U.K.: Arc, 1978).

OTHER: Rainer Maria Rilke, *Poesie,* translated by Gaime Pintor, introduction by Fortini (Turin: Einaudi, 1955);

Il movimento surrealista, edited by Fortini and Lanfranco Binni (Milan: Garzanti, 1959);

Profezie e realtà del nostro secolo: Testi e documenti per la storia di domani, edited by Fortini (Bari: Laterza, 1965);

Gli argomenti umani: Antologia italiana per il biennio delle scuole medie superiori, edited by Fortini and Augusto Vegesto (Naples: Morano, 1969);

Vittoria Bradshaw, ed. and trans., *From Pure Silence to Impure Dialogue,* includes poems and prose by Fortini (New York: Las Américas, 1971), pp. 470–516;

Giorgio Soavi, *Un banco di nebbia,* introduction by Fortini (Milan: Rizzoli, 1974);

La poesia di Scotellaro, edited by Fortini (Rome & Matera: Basilicata, 1974);

"Le ultime parole davanti alla corte," in *Retorica e politica* (Padua: Liviana, 1977), pp. 317–323;

Lawrence R. Smith, ed. and trans., *The New Italian Poetry,* includes poems by Fortini (Berkeley:

Franco Fortini in 1964

University of California Press, 1981), pp. 44–63;

"Poesia degli anni cinquanta," in *Novecento,* edited by Gianni Grana (Milan: Marzorati, 1982), IX: 8039–8046;

Mario Luzi, includes an essay by Fortini (Rome: Dell'Ateneo, 1983);

Luis de Góngora, *Sonetti,* introduction by Fortini (Milan: Mondadori, 1985);

Ferruccio Benzoni, *Notizie dalla solitudine,* introduction by Fortini (Genoa: Marco dei Giustiniani, 1986).

TRANSLATIONS: Gustave Flaubert, *Un cuore semplice* (Milan: Lettere d'oggi, 1942);

C. F. Ramuz, *Statura umana* (Milan: Comunità, 1947);

Søren Kierkegaard, *Timore e tremore* (Milan: Comunità, 1948);

Paul Eluard, *Poesia ininterrotta* (Turin: Einaudi, 1948);

Antonin Döblin, *Addio al Reno* (Turin: Einaudi, 1949);

André Gide, *Viaggio al Congo e ritorno dal Ciad* (Turin: Einaudi, 1950);

Simone Weil, *L'ombra e la grazia* (Milan: Comunità, 1951);

Bertolt Brecht, *Madre coraggio* (Turin: Einaudi, 1951);

Brecht, *Santa Giovanna dei Macelli* (Turin: Einaudi, 1951);

Marcel Proust, *Albertine scomparsa* (Turin: Einaudi, 1951);

Proust, *Jean Santeuil* (Turin: Einaudi, 1952);

Weil, *La prima radice* (Milan: Comunità, 1954);

Eluard, *Poesie* (Turin: Einaudi, 1955);

Johann Wolfgang von Goethe, *Goetz von Berlichingen* (Turin: ERI, 1956);

Brecht, *Il romanzo da tre soldi* (Turin: Einaudi, 1958);

Brecht, *Poesie e canzoni* (Turin: Einaudi, 1959);

Raymond Queneau, *Zazie nel metró* (Turin: Einaudi, 1960);

Lucien Goldmann, *Pascal e Racine: Studi sulla visione tragica nei* Pensieri *di Pascal e nel teatro di Racine,* translated by Fortini and L. Amodio (Milan: Lerici, 1961);

H. M. Enzensberger, *Poesie per chi non legge poesia: Trenta poesie* (Turin: Feltrinelli, 1964);

Goethe, *Faust* (Milan: Mondadori, 1970);

Peter Huchel, *Strade strade* (Milan: Mondadori, 1970);

Il ladro di ciliegie e altre versioni di poesia (Turin: Einaudi, 1982).

SELECTED PERIODICAL PUBLICATIONS –
UNCOLLECTED: "Come leggere i classici," *Politecnico*, 31–32 (July–August 1946): 54–58;

"La leggenda di Recanati," *Politecnico*, 33–34 (September–December 1946): 34–38;

"Lukács in Italia," *Officina*, new series 2 (May–June 1959): 77–101;

"Più velenose di quanto pensiate," *Quaderni Piacentini*, 10 (October 1971): 221–227;

"Gli scrittori e Manzoni," *Italianistica*, 2 (September–December 1973): 34–35;

"Lettera sul realismo," *Nuovi Argomenti*, 51–52 (July–December 1976): 3–4;

"Dialetto ucciso e mai morto: *Filò* di Andrea Zanzotto," *Corriere della Sera*, 20 February 1977, p. 3;

"A Santa Croce," *Forum Italicum*, 12 (Winter 1978): 457–459;

"Notizie e dichiarazioni di scrittori (1911–1917)," *Rassegna della Letteratura Italiana*, 85 (September–December 1981): 438–441;

"Le lettere antagonistiche (1952–1953)," *Belfagor*, 34 (30 November 1982): 685–699;

"Da un diario inesistente (1967–1970)," *Linea d'Ombra*, 1 (May 1983): 59–65.

Born in Florence on 10 September 1917 to a Catholic mother and non-Orthodox Jewish father, Franco Lattes (later Fortini) experienced firsthand the important literary culture of that city during the Fascist period. He studied the figurative arts (writing a thesis on Rosso Fiorentino) and then the law. His family suffered economic hardships even before the institution of the race laws in 1938. In addition, the young poet endured a life-threatening illness and operation. In 1939 he was baptized in the Waldensian church, a decision which he connected to his "Calvinistic" formation and to his "aesthetic religion" of choice, that of Dante and Masaccio. To avoid discrimination he adopted the beginning of his mother's surname (Fortini del Giglio) and in 1945 moved to Milan, where he still lives.

During World War II Fortini served in the Italian military until 8 September 1943, when he fled to Switzerland. He joined the Italian Socialist party in 1944 and worked for two years on its newspaper, *Avanti!* He left the party in 1957. Over the years Fortini has contributed to many other political and cultural-literary journals, including *Politecnico, Comunità, Ragionamenti, Officina,* and *Quaderni Piacentini,* keeping vigil over virtually every significant development in Italy's postwar history. He also collaborated with Roland Barthes and Edgar Morin on the Parisian journal *Arguments.* He worked for years as an advertising copywriter for the Olivetti corporation, and he conducted a remarkable career as a translator of poetry, prose, and nonfiction. In recent years, until his retirement, he taught the history of criticism at the University of Siena.

Fortini matured within a literary climate dominated by hermeticism, an influence evident in his earliest poems, begun around 1938. Yet at the same time he was drawn to Giacomo Noventa, a poet and philosopher whose Florence-based journal, *La Riforma Letteraria,* was opposed to the entire literary, political, and philosophical establishment. Fortini met Noventa, a dialect poet from the Venetian mainland, through Alberto Carocci, a friend and former director of the magazine *Solaria.* Noventa's critique of Italian intellectual life provided Fortini with a persuasive countermodel to the literary trends of postsymbolism and hermeticism. His intellectual maturity is evident in a novella, *Sere in Valdossola* (Evenings in Valdossola, 1963), where, amid accurate renderings of the war, one finds philosophical reflections.

A similar pattern occurs in Fortini's poetry; despite stylistic similarities with the hermetics, Fortini seeks a new generality, which might respond both to problems of private religious aspiration and public commitment. In *Foglio di via* (Deportation Order, 1946) he writes, in the title poem:

Dunque nessun cammino per discendere
se non questo del nord, dove il sole non tocca
e sono d'acqua i rami degli alberi.

Dunque fra poco senza parole la bocca.
E questa sera saremo in fondo alla valle.

(So just this road to go down
from the north, where the sun does not reach
and branches are made of water.

So before long the mouth without words.
And tonight we reach the bottom of the valley.)

The valley where the soldier/speaker descends into camp is symbolically the Valley of Jehoshaphat and the Twenty-third Psalm. Such allegorical landscapes (usually in winter) recur in

Self-portrait by Fortini, circa 1960

Fortini's work and come to signify a moral imperative, a focus on the general destinies of humankind. In this sense, despite stylistic similarities with the hermetics, critics speak of Fortini as an ascetic and a moralist. His literary message was derived from a political context that, more than a renunciation of Fascism, was a rejection of the entire bourgeois status quo, Fascist or anti-Fascist. It was also derived from an ontological context — that of the religious existentialists: Søren Kierkegaard (whose work Fortini has translated), Nikolay Berdyayev, Karl Barth, and Karl Jaspers.

Fortini published important literary essays in *Politecnico,* where he worked as an editor from 1945 to 1947 with Elio Vittorini. He dissented from the widespread notion that anti-Fascist literature adequately expressed the Marxist position. In 1946 he interviewed Paul Eluard, the French surrealist whose poetics of "desecration" denied bourgeois

forms of expression that ignored class conditions. He would later translate and introduce Eluard's collected poetry (1955), providing a definitive critical evaluation of this poet for whom surrealism was not an escape from the world but a return to its biological laws. Traces of Eluard remain apparent in Fortini's writings on poetics and in the utopian dimension of his verse. The same prophetic and allegorical dimension was also affected by his translations of Bertolt Brecht's lyric poetry and Johann Wolfgang von Goethe's *Faust.* In general the task of the translator is coterminous with that of the literary critic; Fortini maintains high academic standards, notably in his history of Italian twentieth-century poetry (*I poeti del Novecento,* 1977), in his anthology of French surrealism (*Il movimento surrealista,* 1959), and in his two volumes of essays on literary topics, *Saggi italiani* (Italian Essays, 1974) and *Nuovi saggi italiani* (New Italian Essays, 1987).

From the start Fortini was a poet of rectitude. The so-called new lyricists were an indisputable fact of his formation, as is evident in the closed sense of space and time and the intense rhetorical silences of *Foglio di via.* Yet while Giuseppe Ungaretti's poetics of analogy and Eugenio Montale's recondite poetics of the emblematic object found continuations in Fortini's early work, the individualism is absent, as is the tendency to free verse. One finds instead a choral or collective voice supported by a reliance on logic, plain statement, and metric composition.

In the years following World War II, in which the hopes for a leftist hegemony were crushed, Fortini invested his hope – a recurrent word throughout his opus – in those oppressed people who would eventually be liberated, the future addressees in whose minds lay his only worthy pursuit of immortality. In general, after his initial hermetic tendency, with the noted "choral" correction, Fortini moved to a composite style: part high lyric, part popular vernacular. He continued to compose metrically and to write a difficult, at times obscure, poetry. Yet with the same passion he refused to isolate the metrical fact from the political context; this willful paradox came to define his position.

The young Fortini was drawn, above all, to the examples of Piero Jahier, Ungaretti, and Montale. Fortini subsequently revolted, notably in the poems of *Poesia ed errore* (Poetry and Errors, 1959), against the idyll and toward a tragic romanticism, rejecting illusionism for the sake of a deliberate, though mediated, message. His voice stressed the importance of community and dialogue in any definition of self; he sought to attack those intellectuals who ignored the sociohistorical plane of discourse and treated literary forms as atemporal entities. For example, though he admired the poetry of Montale, he sensed in him a retreat, at the advent of Fascism, into a sanctuary of sorts, an avoidance of fundamental social and political conflicts. By denying ideology as a proper ground for their work, such poets have abdicated, forcing the genuine resistance into a kind of internal exile and replacing it with their own myth. Fortini's preoccupation with "error" and for the "verb in the future tense" (both concepts also found in the work of the Catholic socialist Noventa) were also concerns about the soul, basic to an evolving system of values, the *religio* of the "classical," and the sense of implied ideological interconnection of literary and philosophical cultures. One role of art in Fortini's view was to plot the convergence of knowledge and understanding, the analytic and the synthetic. Another was to provide authentic spiritual and affective imprints of the fluctuations of consciousness. The project of the artist was less linear than circular in this respect, owing to the recursive nature of the phenomena treated, among them the *ars poetica,* which involved an effacement of his own person and a respect for the words themselves, their materiality.

One obvious feature of this poetics is its prose discursiveness and self-effacement. These features have been interpreted as Brechtian, but there is also a subtle romanticism and rueful Cavalcantian metatextuality to Fortini's work. *Poesia ed errore* also contains a stronger ironic, at times grotesque, component. If the tendency to polemic led him to identify enemies, friendship, too, attained a high value, while love was pushed into the territory of the unsayable, the valley of silence. The often simple poetic diction (*wall, rose, valley, cross, ivy*) reflects a Leopardian generality and a continued pursuit of György Lukács's idea of the typical. (Fortini had introduced Lukács and his ideas to Italy in the mid 1950s.)

Fortini had followed Eluard in locating the historical importance of poetic expression in the mythic and spiritual identity of a people. Attempts to codify such a thought created much concern among the Italian Left after World War II, feeding polemics over prospectivism and socialist realism.

The sense of being stateless is at the heart of a concept Fortini borrowed from Noventa: that of the "guest" who rejects any possible unity of Fascist and anti-Fascist thought, and the virtuosic tendency in literature. *L'ospite ingrato* (The Ungrateful Guest, 1966), a book of ironic poems, includes "Per Noventa" (For Noventa):

Più d'ogni tua parola a me maestro,
per disperato orgoglio a falsi òmeni,
vecchio, fingevi d'arrenderti. . . .

(You more than any of your words old man,
were my teacher, your desperate pride toward false
   men,
to whom you pretended to surrender. . . .)

The pointed epigrams and topical pieces in *L'ospite ingrato* perform an important function: they exempt the main body of Fortini's poetic work from overtly dealing with such immediate and polemical topics.

With *Una volta per sempre* (Once and For All, 1963) Fortini arrived at maturity and consistency.

Amid a mixture of topical, biblical, and literary references, he produced messages in which the immanent, transcendent, historical, and eschatological interpenetrate, as in "Prima lettera da Babilonia" (First Letter from Babylon):

> Non è vero che siamo in esilio.
> Non è vero che torneremo in patria,
> Non è vero che piangeremo di gioia
> dopo l'ultima svolta del cammino.
> Non è vero che saremo perdonati.

> (It is not true we are in exile.
> It is not true that we will return home,
> It is not true that we will cry for joy
> after the last turn in the road.
> It is not true we will be forgiven.)

The sparse punctuation and adjectivization and the focus on meter over rhythm and on objective relations over sentiments reflect the insistence on a verification of the relation between poetic form and content. The "prose" clarity in his poetry does not preclude the existence of multiple levels of meaning; on the contrary, such natural ambiguity (or obscurity) is rooted in a language/world reciprocity. Beginning with his longest poem, *Poesia delle rose* (Poem of Roses, 1962), the dichotomy of communication and expression was exacerbated, as he directed fierce irony toward literary formalism. Critic Alfonso Berardinelli calls the poem "una perfetta figura di antitesi inconciliata, un'immagine di negazione irrudicibile e di violenta proiezione utopica" (a perfect figure of unreconciled antithesis, an image of irreducible negation and of violent utopian projection).

The rose of *Poesia delle rose* is a symbol of the liberty/slavery polarity, enjoined as the subject of myth and encrypted in contemporary reality. The logical trajectories of the 144-line poem are oblique; readers need a utopian vantage point to decipher its contradictory sense and vague augury. The poem assumes the Italian landscape as a political medium containing a sublimated passion, in which no code or figurative ideal can take precedence nor any bourgeois integration take place. A kind of witches' Sabbath is enacted in a Roman park, during which a random energy permeates the scene, like a magnetic charge. This deliriousness extends to the versification, at once an ironic rebuff of the fashionable neo-avant-garde and an exasperation of the chains of signification at the center of which stands the rose – repeated sixteen times – in its consummate ambiguity.

Fortini remained firm in his anticapitalism throughout the years of the Vietnam War; despite inequities and intransigence in the Soviet bloc, his poetic production quietly insisted on a Communist position that is at once noetic and lyrical. This stance led to a kind of mythognomic poetry in which subjective intensity was related to the objectivity of history. *Questo muro* (This Wall, 1973) clarifies Fortini's communicative purpose: to form a dialogue with those with a historical consciousness. "Il seme" (The Seed) addresses the theme of descendence and succession:

> Mio padre s'inteneriva sulla propria morte
> udendo l'allegretto della Settima.
> . . . Ma nulla
> sa più di noi e discorre da sola
> coi suoi corni e le tombe la musica
> tra questi muri sudati.
> In luogo di lui ci sono io
> o mio figlio o nessuno.

> Tutti i fiori non sono che scene ironiche.
> Ormai la piaga non si chiuderà.
> Con tale vergogna scenderò
> i seminterrati delle cliniche
> e con rancore.

> (My father felt compassion over his own death
> hearing the joyful sound of the Seventh Symphony.
> . . . But he knows nothing
> of us anymore and the music
> between these sweat-stained walls
> plays on alone with its horns and trumpets.
> In his place am I
> or my child or no one.

> All flowers are but ironic scenes.
> By now the wound will not close.
> With such shame I shall descend
> the half-basements of clinics
> and with rancor.)

The "wall" of the book's title is polysemous: a cultural condition of impending gravity; a delimiter of consciousness; and a wall of resignation but not of defeat.

In "Le difficoltà del colorificio" (Difficulties at the Dye Works) Fortini contrasts the political reality of China and the West by means of the logical distinction between *enemies* and *adversaries*. Error is to be hated in either, but the enemy is hated in his person, while the errors of one's adversaries may potentially occur in oneself. Whereas in China more adversaries and fewer enemies would be desirable, in the West the opposite is needed, to break the hypocrisy and paralysis of the status quo. The four-part "Deducant te angeli" (Dedicated to the Angels) is a plaintive, at times macabre, narration of war-related events, which ends in a conditioned apologia of the "not useless servant" (from the "useless servant" of the Gospels) who has seen and endured terror, in Vietnam and Austria. The poem also introduces a theme that persists in Fortini's subsequent work — ecologicaldegradation:

> Non questi abeti non
> il ribrezzo della cascata ma
> questa la sequenza.
> . . . .
> Dov'era l'ospizio
> ora c'è ecco
> lacrimante uno stabilimento.
>
> (Not these fir trees not
> the shock of the waterfall but
> this sequence.
> . . . .
> Look now where
> the inn was a
> factory in tears.)

In *Paesaggio con serpente* (Landscape with Serpent, 1984), the epigraph from Virgil "*cantando rumpitur anguis*" (By song is the snake burst asunder) recapitulates the use of the image in the title. The enemy is the snake; the earthly paradise recapitulates Eden, as the snake's original victory prefigures its eventual defeat. The joyous and terrible coexist in the archetypal garden, which contains both the poisoning tree of knowledge and the liberating tree of crucifixion.

There is also an irrepressible autobiographical component in Fortini's late poetry; this aspect is especially evident in poems about or addressed to other poets, such as the sonnet in *Paesaggio con serpente* dedicated to Andrea Zanzotto. Here the biblical rose, like the allusion to Minos that precedes it, is but a splendid metaphor:

> Qui stiamo a udire la sentenza. E non
> ci sarà, lo sappiamo, una sentenza.
> A uno a uno siamo in noi giù volti.
>
> Quanto sei bella, rosa di Saron,
> Gerusalemme che ci avrai raccolti.
> Quanto lucente la tua inesistenza.
>
> (Here we stand to hear sentence.
> And we know there will be no sentence.
> We are led downward into ourselves, one by one.
> How beautiful you are, oh rose of Sharon,
> Jerusalem who will have gathered us up.
> Oh how brilliant your nonexistence.)

Time itself provides the limit to the logos, to the "sentence" or map of any ideological certitude. The ones led most immediately downward "into themselves" (the reference is to Dante's *Inferno,* canto 5) include Pier Paolo Pasolini, Fortini's longtime correspondent, who was murdered a month before Fortini wrote the poem. Jerusalem stands as a wall of endurance of poetry, poised against the descent into hell. As he writes in "Allora comincerò . . . " (Then I Shall Begin . . .),

> E ancora:
> il clamoroso parlare, la lingua sonora
> degli italiani non potrà aiutarmi.
> Da quanti anni sappiamo, no? che una rosa
> non è una rosa, che un'acqua non è un'acqua,
> che parola rimanda a parola e ogni cosa
> a un'altra cosa, egualmente estranee al vero?
>
> (And still:
> the clamorous speech, the sonorous language
> of the Italians will not be able to help me.
> Have we not known this for many years? that a rose
> is not a rose, that water is not water,
> that words suggest other words and every thing
> some other thing, equally estranged from the true?)

After *Paesaggio con serpente* Fortini published various other poems and two books of essays — *Extrema ratio* (1990), published after the collapse of the Soviet Union, and *Non solo oggi* (Not Just Today, 1991), a "dictionary" of collected short essays from a forty-year period. Once again one witnesses Fortini's consummate ability to document intellectual history from the standpoint of the oppressed, as he reinforces his belief in a literature of values that finds its unity in general destinies and "argomenti umani" (human tools).

Letter:

"Una lettera di Franco Fortini," in Pier Vincenzo Mengaldo's *La tradizione del Novecento* (Milan: Feltrinelli, 1975).

Interviews:

Ferdinando Camon, *Il mestiere di poeta* (Milan: Lerici, 1965);

Alfredo Barberis, *Voci che contano* (Milan: Formichiere, 1978), pp. 117–123;

Giulio Nascimbeni, " 'Il mondo si è stretto senza migliorare,' un nuovo libro di versi: Intervista con Fortini," *Corriere della Sera,* 31 March 1984.

Bibliography:

Carlo Fini, "Nota bio-bibliografica su Franco Fortini," in *Per Franco Fortini,* edited by Fini (Padua: Liviana, 1980), pp. 200-214.

References:

Alberto Asor Rosa, "Alla ricerca dell'artista borghese," in his *Intellettuali e classe operaia: Saggi sulle forme di uno storico conflitto e di una possibile alleanza* (Florence: Nuova Italia, 1973), pp. 231-271;

Alfonso Berardinelli, *Franco Fortini* (Florence: Nuova Italia, 1973);

Gian Paolo Biasin, "Un poeta 'cataro,'" *Italica,* 9 (June-September 1975): 436-443;

Giampaolo Borghello, "Fortini e Lukács" and "Fortini: Il senno di poi," in his *Linea rossa* (Venice: Marsilio, 1982), pp. 68-78; 245-303;

Vincenzo Carini and Costanzo Di Girolamo, "Franco Fortini," *Belfagor,* 32 (May 1977): 281-310;

Luciana Ceccarelli, "Il coraggio di esitare: La *Poesia delle rose* di Fortini," *Paragone,* no. 338 (June 1982): 54-77;

Remo Ceserani, "Sonati sono i corni di Fortini," *Belfagor,* 32 (31 July 1983): 467-472;

Gian Carlo Ferretti, "Franco Fortini e la critica del presente," *Rinascita,* 18 May 1985, p. 20;

Ferretti, *"Officina" — Cultura, letteratura e politica negli anni cinquanta* (Turin: Einaudi, 1975);

Carlo Fini, ed., *Per Franco Fortini* (Padua: Liviana, 1980);

David Forgàcs, "Franco Fortini," in *Writers and Society in Contemporary Italy,* edited by Michael Caesar and Peter Hainsworth (Leamington Spa, U.K.: Berg, 1984), pp. 89-116;

Giuliano Gramigna, "La poesia espugnata di là dalla 'grazia': 'Paesaggio con serpente,' il nuovo libro di Franco Fortini," *Corriere della Sera,* 14 June 1984, p. 3;

Immaginazione, special issue on Fortini (June-July 1985);

Romano Luperini, *La lotta mentale: Per un profilo di Franco Fortini* (Rome: Riuniti, 1986);

Claudio Magris, "Liberarsi dall'alibi della falsa innocenza: Pasolini e Fortini, due riflessioni sulla colpa," *Corriere della Sera,* 4 June 1985, p. 3;

Pier Vincenzo Mengaldo, "Fortini e i *Poeti del Novecento,*" *Nuovi Argomenti,* 3 (1977): 159-177;

Mengaldo, "Per la poesia di Fortini," in his *La tradizione del Novecento* (Milan: Feltrinelli, 1975);

Pier Paolo Pasolini, "I destini generali," in his *Passione e ideologia* (Milan: Garzanti, 1960), pp. 463-465;

Pasquale Sabbatino, *Gli inverni di Fortini* (Foggia: Bastogi, 1981).

Alberto Frattini

(29 March 1922 –   )

Pietro Pelosi
University of Salerno

BOOKS: *Il problema dell'esistenza in Leopardi* (Milan: Gastaldi, 1950);

Giorni e sogni (Rome: Pagine Nuove, 1950);

Leopardi e Rousseau (Rome: Pagine Nuove, 1951);

Poeti italiani del Novecento (Alcamo: Accademia, 1953);

Fioraia bambina (Rome: Canzoniere, 1953);

Speranza e destino (Rome: Canzoniere, 1954);

La poesia della redenzione nel Tommaseo (Alcamo: Accademia, 1955);

Il Canto XXXIII dell'Inferno (Alcamo: Accademia, 1955);

Studi sulla poesia italiana del dopoguerra (Alcamo: Accademia, 1955);

Studi leopardiani (Pisa: Nistri-Lischi, 1956);

Come acqua alpina (Alcamo: Accademia, 1956);

Critici contemporanei (Rome: Gismondi, 1957);

La poesia e il tempo (Rome: Hermes, 1957);

Critica e fortuna dei "Canti" di G. Leopardi (Brescia: Scuola, 1957);

Cultura e pensiero in Leopardi (Rome: Ausonia, 1958);

Latomie (Florence: Vallecchi, 1958);

Da Tommaseo a Ungaretti (Bologna: Cappelli, 1959);

Il Canto XXVIII del Paradiso (Turin: S.E.I., 1960);

Il Canto XXVII del Purgatorio (Florence: Le Monnier, 1963);

La giovane poesia italiana (Pisa: Nistri-Lischi, 1964);

Il neoclassicismo e Ugo Foscolo (Bologna: Cappelli, 1965);

Salute nel miraggio (Rome: Storia e Letteratura, 1965);

Poeti e critici italiani dell'Otto e del Novecento (Milan: Marzorati, 1966);

Poeti italiani tra il primo e secondo Novecento (Milan: IPL, 1967);

Poesia nuova in Italia: Tra ermetismo e neoavanguardia (Milan: IPL, 1968);

Giacomo Leopardi (Bologna: Cappelli, 1969; revised edition, Rome: Studium, 1986);

Dai crepuscolari ai Novissimi (Milan: Marzorati, 1969);

Tra il nulla e l'amore (Rome: Società Edizioni Nuove, 1969);

Scoperta di paesi (Milan: IPL, 1969);

Studi di poesia e di critica (Milan: Marzorati, 1972);

Critica, strutture, stile (Milan: IPL, 1977);

Caro atomo (Venice: Locusta, 1977);

Letteratura e scienza in Leopardi (Milan: Marzorati, 1978);

Il vento e le gemme (Rome: Piazza Navona, 1981);

La sfida nel labirinto (Padua: Rebellato, 1982);

Poesia e regione in Italia (Milan: IPL, 1983);

Introduzione a Giorgio Vigolo (Milan: Marzorati, 1984);

Il sogno della morte (Padua: Piovan, 1986);

Stupendo enigma (Milan: IPL, 1988);

Giacomo Leopardi: Una lettura infinita (Milan: IPL, 1989);

Leopardi e noi (Rome: Studium, 1990).

OTHER: *Canti di Giacomo Leopardi,* edited by Frattini (Brescia: Scuola, 1960);

Poeti italiani del XX secolo, edited by Frattini and Pasquale Tuscano (Brescia: Scuola, 1974);

Poesie e tragedie di Alessandro Manzoni, edited by Frattini (Brescia: Scuola, 1981);

Poeti a Roma: 1945–1980, edited by Frattini and Marcella Uffreduzzi (Rome: Bonacci, 1983);

Poeti della Toscana, edited by Frattini and Franco Manescalchi (Forlì: Forum/Quinta Generazione, 1985).

Alberto Frattini's poetry contains a vigorously realistic power of connotation. During his early career, certain critics attempted to define his poetry as neorealistic; however, Frattini's kind of realism includes clear references to metaphysical as well as phenomenological and existentialist elements that unite individuals in a common humanity. The critics who argue in favor of a realistic tendency in Frattini's work do so largely on the basis of his reluctance to indulge in the outrageous linguistic structures and the baroque imagery that typify much of contemporary Italian poetry. His language is the product of sentiment and thought; it ex-

Alberto Frattini

presses in delicate but sometimes harsh tones the sentiment that frames the chain of being, as well as the sense of anxiety in the course of daily existence.

The importance of Frattini's poetry lies precisely in the profoundly felt adherence of thought and sentiment to language; the result is limpid lyrics that exclude experimentalism in order to articulate his dignity and mission, even in verses that denounce the pain of living. Frattini's poetry is positive in that it never discards the seeds of hope; instead every verse tends to evoke harmony and inner peace. Occasionally the poetry can be lean and incisive, condensed into intensely private statements, sung, as it were, to the point of attaining the crystalline freshness of spring water. The words of Frattini capture the reader's attention by virtue of a purity of style that stands out against the backdrop of modern Italian poetry. His adherence to his concept of the reality of nature, life, and the universe, as well as his curiosity about the enigma of existence, produces an unmistakable message of caution and hope for humankind.

Alberto Frattini was born in Florence on 29 March 1922 into a family rich in affection and moral sense. His father was a member of the corps of engineers and had substantial character and lively intelligence. His mother was a cousin of Christian philosopher Ernesto Buonaiuti; from her Alberto inherited his sense of the beautiful. At the age of five or six he began to compose verses, but family discreetness would not permit him to be treated as a child prodigy; it was felt that such treatment might cause him to lose the spontaneous quality of his poetry. Instead he was allowed to follow his instincts, with humility and affection, under the watchful eye of his parents.

As a youth, Frattini was acquainted with the ideas of Buonaiuti, a much-discussed figure in his day and the proponent of a renewed Christianity based on its old roots. Frattini attended many of Buonaiuti's lectures, which dealt with the interrelationship of poetry, thought, and culture. Buonaiuti exerted a profound influence on the character of Frattini and followed Frattini's studies and poetry

Drawing of Frattini by P. Novona

readings from a distance. Buonaiuti encouraged Frattini's family to move to Rome, where they resided for more than a decade on the via degli Acquasparta, only a few yards from Piazza Navona. Frattini obtained his degree in modern languages in 1945 at the University of Rome with a thesis comparing the works and ideas of Giacomo Leopardi and Jean-Jacques Rousseau. In 1946 Frattini obtained a second degree, in philosophy, choosing to specialize in Leopardi and his pessimistic eudaemonism.

A short time after graduation Frattini met his future wife, Lea, on the university campus. She was extremely fond of ancient poetry and also enjoyed reading his compositions. She belonged to a Catholic cultural milieu and had written her doctoral thesis on Christian inscriptions. The love between them grew out of a deep friendship; they found in poetry and spirituality an indissoluble bond.

The constant points of reference on which the poetry and critical work of Frattini converge are po-etry, thought, and ethics. In 1950 he published his first collection of poems, *Giorni e sogni* (Days and Dreams), which met with instant favor among some noted critics. Giorgio Petrocchi, writing for *La Via* (21 October 1950), said, "La formazione critica e saggistica del Frattini non pesa sul suo dono di poeta, anzi serve a rendere maggiormente cosciente ed agguerrita in lui la ricerca dei mezzi espressivi, sì che il linguaggio della sua lirica (pur non tentando raccordi espressivi di grande audacia) è raffina-tissimo, ricco di sensibilità musicale, mobile e colmo di delicatezza" (Frattini's critical preparation does not impair his talent for poetry; in fact it serves to intensify or heighten his search for appropriate means of expression, so much so that the language of his poetry [although it never strives for daring linguistic structures] remains extremely refined, rich in musical nuance, versatile and very delicate).

Fioraia bambina (Flower-seller Child) was published in 1953. In these poems water, skies, and silences fuse with a sense of anxiety. Compared to Frattini's first volume, this publication is more restrained and personal; although it maintains those basic qualities of lyrical delicacy and intellectual complexity, the collection represents an important stylistic step forward for the young poet. *Speranza e destino* (Hope and Destiny, 1954) constitutes a significant milestone. The lean quality of his poetry had originally made critics think of the posthermetic lyric, and his secure hold on the reality of daily existence had prompted critics to speak of neorealism, but this unpretentious volume eliminates all ambiguity. Like all genuine art, Frattini's poetry is the product of its time while transcending it, because his vision of time is an ethical and universal one. Every composition of the collection is permeated with sentiments and themes born of individual experience, and they acquire concreteness in the realm that is part of every reader's sensibility: the search for the meaning of God, the universe, and the most profound human emotions.

Come acqua alpina (Like Alpine Water, 1956) retains the most recognizable features of Frattini's precision and focus (namely, a landscape that extends to the point of embracing the entire cosmos, while it remains densely interiorized), and the collection explores the domestic aspects of the city and the arcanely splendid vistas of nature, subtended by the need to see oneself in the mirror of the external world, a projection of the poet. In the alternation of the seasons, the night rainfalls, and the fresh alpine waters, Frattini sees an omen of something that transcends the ordinary and predictable aspects of nature. Nourished by an ethic that might make the reader think of a modern version of the medieval concept of "the great book of nature" given to man for him to interpret, Frattini's markedly anthropocentric stance fuses with expressions of a clearly modern sentiment (understood in the Leopardian sense); although it acknowledges those values proposed by hermeticism, Frattini's anthropocentrism transcends those same values in the awareness of an inner impulse that reveals the soul's inclination toward the external world and other human beings in an act of communion with all of creation.

In 1958 Frattini published *Latomie* (State Prisons), which conveys a profound pity coexistent with ethical commitment and a spontaneity that occasionally overreaches this same moral sense in order to assume the form of an intimate and hushed confession. Through the alternation of sorrow and exuberance, a deep faith that reveals the presence of God in daily events asserts itself in the volume. As occurs in the works of the great poets whose sensi-

bilities were forged in the highly charged atmosphere of the postwar period, in the poems of *Latomie* the reader discovers an increased interest on the part of the poet in humankind and history.

Salute nel miraggio (Health in the Mirage) was published in 1965, in the midst of the neo-avant-garde movement. Lanfranco Orsini's remarks (in *Baretti,* July–October 1966) are, in this context, especially apt:

> Questo libro ci mostra un poeta tanto discreto nei mezzi quanto più ricco di umanità e di registri, con una immagine tra le più persuasive e fedeli ad una concezione della poesia che ricerchi la propria ragione di essere non già in convulsioni verbali ma in una trama di sentimenti e d'affetti da trasformare in parole. E se, come è logico, la liricità non ha sempre quel grado di intensità e di purezza che raggiunge nelle migliori composizioni, tutta la silloge testimonia una presenza, nell'ambito della nostra attuale poesia, significativa e di per se stessa polemica.

> (This book gives us a poet as subtle in the selection of his means of expression as he is rich in humanity and range of linguistic registers; his is one of the most convincing examples of loyalty to the concept of poetry as a search for one's own raison d'être, not in verbal gymnastics but in the network of feelings and emotions that need to be verbalized. If, as seems logical, the lyricism does not always have the level of intensity and purity that it attains in Frattini's better compositions, the entire work attests the presence of an important, as well as controversial, figure in the area of contemporary Italian poetry.)

In *Tra il nulla e l'amore* (Between Love and Nothingness, 1969) Frattini rejects facile effects and demands the reader's attentive and intelligent response. More than ever the reader becomes aware of Frattini's fertile and close readings of the classics of Italian poetry and thought, as well as of the best voices of modern Italian and European poetry. These readings constitute his linguistic and cultural heritage. The dialectic of classic and modern resolves itself into a language that is artfully orchestrated, one that rejects all compromises with the neo-avant-garde movement. According to Pasquale Tuscano (*Quaderno di Arti e di Lettere,* April 1969), "sempre in una dimensione moderna, il Frattini trova la sua collocazione naturale nell'alveo della nostra tradizione classica" (always in the modern way, Frattini finds his natural home in the stream of our classical tradition). Consider the opening lines of "Notte di primavera" (Spring Night):

Volevo imparare i nomi
delle stelle, spalancare l'anima

all'intatta innocenza d'ogni fuoco.
Ma forse è tardi,
la notte e il silenzio
danno altro senso
ai segreti del mondo,
un pudore di passi perduti.

(I wanted to learn the names
of the stars, open wide the soul
to the complete innocence of each fire.
But perhaps it is too late,
the night and the silence
give another meaning
to the world's secrets,
a decency of lost traces.)

In *Caro atomo* (Dear Atom, 1977) Frattini's poems show compassion toward humankind and are uncompromising in the indictment of spiritual and moral degradation. His criticism of the myth of false science and false freedom assumes the form of parodic treatment of scientific language; it is not ridiculed but subjected to irony in Frattini's occasionally strident word combinations. Scientific terminology amalgamates with the poetic word in unusual and jarring juxtapositions, in a sort of automatic writing style that evokes the image of human folly: humankind enslaved by technological language is nothing more than submission to the machine. Illustrative of this notion is the poem "C'è una grande onda schiumante" (There Is a Great Foaming Wave). In its apparently festive arrangement of words, the lyric warns of an ever-present danger within contemporary society:

C'è una grande onda schiumante:
schizofrenica trionfante.
Nella ragna macchinomane
l'antiuomo già s'invesca.
Per resistere alla tresca
forse è urgente realizzare
la proposta del contino,
per produrre in serie rapida
donne "honeste" e galantuomini.
. . . .

Qui ci vuole il frodicida,
l'antiautoma, l'antibestia.

(There is a great foaming wave:
schizophrenic triumphant.
In the machinomaniacal web
antiman already is trapped.
To resist the seduction
it is perhaps urgent to act on
the young count's recommendation
to mass-produce rapidly
"honest" women and gentlemen.
. . . .

What is needed here is the fraudicide,
the anti-automaton, the antibeast.)

Along these same lines is the collection *Il vento e le gemme* (The Wind and the Gems, 1981). According to critic Raffaele Pellecchia, the collection "nasce da un'esigenza di approfondimento del rapporto dell'uomo con la realtà. Si tratta, occorre subito dirlo, di un rapporto problematico, che suscita dubbi e perplessità, momenti di scoramento ma anche istanti di felici intuizioni e di definitive acquisizioni che danno il senso di una direzione che, tra impervi sentieri e disselciati camminamenti, conduce al possesso della verità, sottratta sia al pericolo di un capriccioso relativismo, sia al settarismo di ideologie transeunti" (is born of a need to deepen man's relationship with reality. It must be stated from the outset that this is a problematic relationship, which gives rise to doubts, confusion and moments of despair but also to instants of joyous epiphany or definite insight that point in the direction of a path that, through rugged and inaccessible terrain, leads to a truth free from dangerously capricious relativism and transient ideological sectarianism). In the composition "Se la gemma" (If the Gem) Frattini voices hope:

Se la gemma rispetta la gemma
se le foglie non contestano il vento
il miracolo umano più grande
è la volontà d'armonia
che accetta il diverso infinito,
e senza fine riscatta il messaggio
degli uccelli e dei gigli di campo.

(If the gem respects the gem
if the leaves do not resist the wind
the noblest human miracle
is the desire for the harmony
that tolerates infinite diversity,
and without end preserves the message
of the birds and the lilies of the field.)

In *La sfida nel labirinto* (The Challenge Within the Labyrinth, 1982) this need for human values seems affirmed even by the title. Frattini shows a thirst for knowledge free of arrogance, as in "Anche se non puoi salpare" (Even Though You Cannot Set Sail):

anche se il pensiero
della fine di tutto
fa del nonsenso l'unico
senso possibile: mettiti
dalla parte della ragione
non superba, accetta l'assurdo
come il prezzo di tante meraviglie,

ascolta dalla segreta saggezza
d'ogni cellula in cui consisti
il sì alla vita, all'esistere,
questa strana sfida
alle ombre voraci del nulla.

(even if the thought
of the end of everything
makes nonsense the only
possible sense: place yourself
on the side of reason
that is not arrogant, accept the absurd
as the price for so many marvels,
hear from the secret wisdom
of every cell that is you
the affirmation of life, existence,
this strange defiance
of the voracious shadows of nothingness.)

Il sogno della morte (The Dream of Death, 1986) returns to human experience poised amid daily events, past history, and an inner temporal existence. Typical are poems such as "Rispettate almeno la morte" (At Least Respect Death) and "Catacombe" (Catacombs), where an earthquake and the martyrdom of "legioni inermi / che consacrarono col sangue / il no alla violenza dei despoti" (the helpless legions / who consecrated with their blood / the rejection of the violence of despots) become the vivid reminders of a mystery that transcends generations.

Frattini's collection titled *Stupendo enigma* (Magnificent Enigma) was published in 1988. Here the forms of daily life fade into more-metaphysical reflections, but these are not abstract meditations.

What could be sermonizing becomes instead heartfelt reflection in apparent detachment but actually in passionate participation in the destiny of humankind, as in "Chimera":

La violenza i massacri gli scempi
continuano sul vecchio globo:
odio e ferocia senza più misura,
la bontà, spersa scintilla di follia.

(The violence massacre destruction
continue on the venerable globe:
hatred and ferocity without limit,
goodness, stray spark of madness.)

Still, something that poetry and love can offer transcends the network of madness and penetrates human destinies, "riscattando la pena / la piena di ogni lordura" (relieving the pain / the flood of all sordidness). Frattini's message is clear and unambiguous; it rests on the solid foundation of hope.

References:

Carmine Di Biase, "Critica e arte in A. Frattini," *Otto/Novecento,* 5 (1978): 195–198;

Antonio Iacopetta, "Frattini: Verità e prodigio," *Humanitas,* 2 (April 1989): 294–299;

Ferruccio Mazzariol, "Recente e ultima poesia di Alberto Frattini," *Studium,* 70 (1974): 278–283;

Raffaele Pellecchia, "La difficile speranza nella poesia di Alberto Frattini," *Fuoco,* 2 (1982): 16–26;

Giorgio Petrocchi and Walter Mauro, "Interventi critici sulla poesia di Frattini," *Quinta Generazione,* 167–168 (May–June 1988): 24–27.

Melo Freni

(19 July 1934 -)

Giovanna Wedel De Stasio

BOOKS: *Odor di pane caldo* (Padua: Lucciola, 1962);
Sicilia, continente inquieto (Milazzo: Mediterranea-Spes, 1964);
Il senso delle cose (Palermo: Flaccovio, 1966);
Morire a Palermo (Rome & Caltanissetta: Sciascia, 1968);
Bidiemme (Palermo: Ausonia, 1968);
Lu focu e la nivi (Palermo: Isola d'Oro, 1969);
Viaggio in Grecia (Palermo: Flaccovio, 1969);
Sui mimi di Francesco Lanza (Catania: U.P.C., 1970);
Dolce terra promessa (Padua: Rebellato, 1974);
Le calde stagioni (Naples: Marotta, 1976);
La famiglia Ceravolo (Milan: Rusconi, 1980);
Amore e logos (Venice: Rebellato, 1983);
Le passioni di Petra (Florence: Vallecchi, 1985);
Marta d'Elicona (Rome: Riuniti, 1987);
Verso la vacanza (Marina di Patti: Pungitopo, 1990).

OTHER: "Lucio Piccolo e la Feldman," *Fiera Letteraria* (12 December 1971): 5;
"Ho 23 anni dice Buttitta (ma ne ha 73)," *Fiera Letteraria* (16 July 1972): 14;
"Quasimodo e la Sicilia," in *Salvatore Quasimodo: La poesia nel mito e oltre,* edited by Gilberto Finzi (Bari: Laterza, 1986), pp. 497–502.

Within the wide and multifaceted cultural activity of Melo Freni, his poetic work qualitatively holds an eminent position. Freni, who is also a journalist, novelist, theater director, and filmmaker, is primarily a Sicilian writer, revealing topical affinities with other Sicilian poets such as Salvatore Quasimodo, Lucio Piccolo, and Bartolo Cattafi. Yet Freni's verse tends to exceed the limits of a strictly regional collocation as some of his social, philosophical, and existential themes may generally be found in other posthermetic Italian poetry. In *Febbre, furore e fiele* (Fever, Furor and Gall, 1983) critic and poet Giuseppe Zagarrio defines the *sicilitudine,* or insular condition, of Sicilian poets, as the painful awareness of the contradictions of their social and cultural separation from the mainland. Often, as in Freni's case, these writers left their native island and settled on the Italian peninsula, thus undergoing significant adjustments. As they share a complex feeling of attraction and rejection toward the island of Sicily, these poets display a tendency to idealize its glorious past and, at the same time, to denounce harshly its present socioeconomic problems. Their sense of exclusion (feeling of inferiority) and pride for their uniqueness (feeling of superiority) often translate into intellectualistic, baroque, oxymoronic, and ambiguous writing. In regard to Freni's particular case, Zagarrio points out the structural and stylistic contradictions of his writing, where pathos, irony, free experimentation, classical precision, and Italian and Sicilian dialects coexist.

Carmelo (known as Melo) Freni was born on 19 July 1934 in the town of Barcellona, Sicily, also the birthplace of the poets Cattafi and Emilio Isgrò. Nunzio Freni, Melo's father, was a pastry cook, following a long family tradition. As Melo admits, his growing up between the smell of honey and the crackling of wood ovens added sweetness and strength to his poems. His mother, Blanda Rizzo D'Amico Freni, was a Sicilian woman of ancient French origins. Melo was raised after age five in the town of Castroreale, where his family moved in 1939. In Castroreale he completed his elementary and junior-high education. He then pursued classical studies in Messina, at the Istituto Salesiano San Luigi, a high school run by Salesian priests. He also began his university education in Messina, but after one year he transferred to the Università di Palermo, where in 1957 he received a law degree. In 1958 Freni moved to Rome to work as a journalist, an activity he had already begun a year before. There he contributed to the periodical *Fiera Letteraria* and worked for the RAI, the Italian radio and television network. In 1960 Freni returned to Sicily and continued his journalistic activity; he also practiced law for a couple of years. In 1961 he married Franca Giordano, an elementary-school teacher from the Sicilian town of Naso, an ancient Greek colony. Their daughter, Blanda, was born in 1973.

Melo Freni in 1987

In 1963, as a result of a nationwide competition, Freni was selected to enter full-time employment at the RAI. Therefore he abandoned the law profession, and between 1963 and August 1964 he worked for the RAI in Palermo and in Catania as a radio news correspondent. During this period Freni conducted a series of programs on the socioeconomic problems of the newly industrialized Sicily. These studies were later collected in the volume *Sicilia, continente inquieto* (Sicily, Restless Continent, 1964). For the serious social and cultural commitment to his journalistic activity, Freni was awarded the Sileno-Gela prize, an official acknowledgment annually bestowed on Sicilians who distinguish themselves. Freni's interest in the dramatic social and human condition of his fellow Sicilians is also a recurring theme in his verse.

Between 1964 and 1970 Freni, still a radio news correspondent, was based solely in Palermo. During this period he traveled extensively, often due to his work, in Europe, the Soviet Union, the United States, and Africa. Since 1970 he has been residing in Rome, where at the RAI he directs the cultural programs of the TGI (television channel 1). Since 1968 he has also directed various theatrical productions, such as plays, concerts, and operas, for several Italian theaters.

Freni's first poetry collection, *Odor di pane caldo* (Smell of Warm Bread, 1962), was inspired by his native island, which is presented through its natural landscape, odors, sounds, and folklore. The primitive beauty of the island is viewed with a sense of religious veneration, sincere affection, and nostalgia. An element of grief for the harshness, misery, and violent reality of Sicilian life is also present in the book, creating a dramatic contrast with the lightness of its natural images, as in "Il cielo ascolta" (The Sky Listens):

Grandine estiva
cade sulla terra
che fete di sudore,
com'assoluzione
su un'anima imbrattata.

(Summer hail
falls on the earth
fetid with sweat,
as absolution
on a soiled soul.)

Only religion, a sort of natural pantheism, may comfort the aggrieved soul of the poetic subject. In the poem "Odor di pane caldo" oil and bread, two Christian symbols of physical and spiritual sustenance, figuratively join humankind, nature, and all things on the island during a joyful ritual of fraternity.

Despite its flashes of freshness (as Cattafi notes in his preface to the book) and moments of intense lyricism, *Odor di pane caldo* appears to be excessively impressionistic and lacking structural cohesion. Much more articulate and intellectually engaging is Freni's second poetry collection, *Il senso delle cose* (The Meaning of Things), which was awarded the Riviera dei Marmi prize when published in 1966. The book shows Freni's interest in the socioeconomic issues related to the transformation of modern Sicily. Yet the book may also be read as the search of modern people for an ultimate meaning that may yield a purpose and a sense of stability in a world where everything is subject to continuous metamorphosis and death. Two colors, black and red, recur insistently throughout the pages to convey the violent quality of modern Sicily: hunger, crime, and political corruption afflict life on the island even as the old baronial and cliental social system continues to prevail. Red stands for the blood of the dead, the fiery wine, and the passion of women, whereas the earth, the roads, and the clothes worn for mourning are black. The meaning of things can be identified in the historical immobility of the island and in the senseless, chaotic succession of its daily events, but precise calculations of meaning reach no clear solution in the poem "I morti lasciamoli stare" (Let Us Leave the Dead Alone), and order and systematization appear to be an illusion in "Statistiche" (Statistics).

In "La macina" (The Millstone), dedicated to Freni's father, the rotating wheel of the mill is an iconic representation of the passing of time, whereas the grinding of wheat symbolizes the unending continuation of life and also its gradual consumption. The poetic subject views the millstone as his only stronghold in life; family continuity, as life repeats itself from generation to generation, seems to provide the only stability in the chaos of existence. This is clearly manifest in the epigrammatic closing of the poem: "Non farmi testamento. Ho preso, padre / ogni cosa da te per macinare" (Do not leave me a will. Father, I took / everything from you in order to grind).

The influence of Cattafi's poetry on Freni, which the critic Lucio Zinna mentions in a 26 June 1966 review (in *Trapani Nuova*) of *Il senso delle cose,* is particularly evident in "La macina," with its existential interrogations and emblematic imagery. Other poems of this collection show affinities with the poetry of Quasimodo and other southern writers, who tend to present the Italian south in a mythical light. An example is Freni's "Isola" (Island):

Nacque all'alba del mondo.
Le case
erano bianche, era silenzio.
Una sola pianura
biancastra
all'ombra dei calcari inumiditi
di sapore di mare
profumava.

(She [the island] was born at the dawn of the world.
The houses
were white, there was silence.
Only a plain
whitish
in the shade of damp limestones
smelled
of sea flavor.)

Morire a Palermo (To Die in Palermo, 1968) stems from Freni's experiences while residing in Palermo. The first section, "Morire a Palermo," is a collection of tragic events, reported with bitter irony and grief. The last two sections, "La terra senza nebbie" (The Fogless Land) and "Villeggiatura" (Vacation), are general reflections on human destiny. In the preface to the book, Freni recounts how, upon his arrival in Palermo in the spring of 1963, he was told that the episodes of violent crime were diminishing and coming to an end. Instead he says he witnessed even crueller cases of violence during the next five years. In the preface Freni also explains his intention to narrate his poems without falsifying the truth, yet adding to them a symbolic and more universal meaning. He says he wanted to remain a reporter.

The narrative intent in the poems transpires from their colloquial intonation, from the use of the vocative, and from the occasional invitations to listen. The use of direct speech is effective in conveying each story with vividness and immediacy. At the same time the verses are extremely polished: the reiteration of words and a songlike rhythm make for a fascinating combination of journalism and poetry. In a lyric that tells of the murder of a florist, the closing revelation is pronounced with the vehemence and immediacy of a line yelled to a crowd:

> Erano troppo rossi quei gerani
> li toccava il fioraio
> con mani non pulite
> – l'hanno ucciso il fioraio
> per vendetta.

> (Those geraniums were too red
> the florist was touching them
> with hands that were not clean
> – the florist was killed
> in a vendetta.)

The poems of *Morire a Palermo* are short, clever, and concise. In one poem the reiteration of the opening line amplifies the sense of drama and irreversibility of the situation:

> Mohamed è stato assassinato
> e cercava l'amore città desolata
> in te lo cercava. Navigante
> bramoso d'amore
> Mohamed è stato assassinato.

> (Mohamed has been assassinated
> and he was looking for love desolate city
> in you he was looking for it. Seaman
> eager for love
> Mohamed has been assassinated.)

The chiasmatic structure of the poem and the contrast of love and death point to the contradictions of the reality of Sicily or, on a larger scale, of human existence. The book opens with a warning that may also refer to life in Sicily or to human life in general: living necessarily involves a moral compromise, as seen in these lines:

> Condizione precisa: stare al giuoco
> o morire di rabbia, rinunciare.
> Così com'hanno fatto anche le rose
> nelle ville di mare
> dove l'agave ancora si difende

> puntigliosa, precisa alla minaccia
> e sfida la paura
> con gli artigli decisi il temporale.

> (Precise condition: to go along with the game
> or to die of anger, to give up.
> As the roses also have done
> in the villas on the sea
> where the agave still resists
> with punctiliousness, precision to the threat
> and it defies the fear
> the storm with determined claws.)

The flowers that survive by adapting to environmental difficulties emblematically suggest the hardships of life; the storm, as elsewhere in Freni's verse, is an image of impending death. The speaker confronts the choice between existential struggle and renouncement or suicide, as is also suggested in "Suicide," in *Il senso delle cose,* where killing oneself is equated with the avoidance of a fight.

In the last two sections of *Morire a Palermo* Freni evokes his island with nostalgia. Sicily paradoxically becomes the land he must leave in order to survive and also his only destination in life. It is a point of departure and arrival, the beginning and end of all things. The contradictions of human existence expressed through the contrasts of the island are present also in an interesting small publication, *Lu focu e la nivi* (The Fire and the Snow, 1969), a song poem in Sicilian dialect depicting an earthquake on the island.

Viaggio in Grecia (Voyage to Greece, 1969), as the critic Alberto Bevilacqua points out in the preface, is a metaphorical return to the womb. The Sicilian traveler in search of his roots enters the mythical places of an ancestral Greece. His blood and his heart are the same as those of people from Crete. Elements of nature become the symbolic details of an itinerary rich with Christian overtones. The classical material and the picturesque southern imagery are treated in an original and lyrical manner. Mythical Greece and modern Greece are juxtaposed; history and imagination cannot be clearly separated. At times aestheticism and impressionism are the results of an idealizing mode. In the following example a Greek woman appears in Freni's imagination in perfect symbiosis with nature:

> Vestita di nero
> bianchissima
> contrasto fra nuvole e fiori
> rubavi profumo alle rose
> freschezza alla brina
> di primo mattino.

(Dressed in black
very white
contrast between clouds and flowers
you were stealing fragrance from the roses
freshness from the frost
in the early morning.)

Freni continues to seek his cultural roots in *Dolce terra promessa* (Sweet Promised Land, 1974). Natural elements, events, and places observed in everyday life awaken the memories of the exiled traveler who cannot reach his promised land. In "Naufrago relitto" (Shipwrecked Relic) his navigational course brings to mind Cattafi's similar circumnavigation and interior exploration of the soul. Each person is a survivor in a wasteland, kept alive only by dreams and memories. In the foam, which is all that is left after each disappearance of the promised land, the speaker searches for an existential reason. T. S. Eliot's verses from "The Burial of the Dead," cited at the opening of *Dolce terra promessa,* emphasize the allegorical quality of the poems, which often depict the squalor of existence. Time is the force "that crumbles / except for memories, everything." People may resist the action of time by preserving the continuity of the species, thus passing memories from one generation to the next.

Through *Amore e logos* (Love and Logos, 1983) it is possible to reconstruct the complete history of the poetic subject, who moves back in time. The book, in five sections – "Amore e logos," "Dolce terra promessa," "Viaggio in Grecia," "Morire a Palermo," and "Il senso delle cose" – incorporates previous poems (revised and in a different order) together with new poems. *Amore e logos* was nominated for the Premio Viareggio in 1983 and was awarded the Premio Pisa in 1984. The title of the book focuses on the two tracks followed in a journey that takes the direction of a vertical descent: it is the speaker's real or imagined return to the south and also his tormented penetration into his historical past. He views himself as a timeless poet who enacts a psychoanalytic exploration of a universal conscience, as in "Diario milanese" (Milanese Diary):

psicanalizzare
scavare
scovare
per riportare la causa alla radice
come si dice dell'inconscio
vissuto e non capito.

(to psychoanalyze
to dig

to uncover
in order to bring the cause back to the root
as they say about the subconscious
experienced and not understood.)

The concept of an introspective study carried out by probing into Sicilian culture reappears in "A occhi spenti" (With Closed Eyes), a touching poem dedicated to the artist Carlo Levi, who, after eye surgery, painted and wrote in the dark during a period of convalescence:

Con le mani scavando nel buio
e l'unghie che pulsavano graffiando
il sangue dell'aorta
hai riscoperto il senso della vita. . . .

(With your hands digging in the dark
and your nails pulsating as they scratched
the blood of the aorta
you rediscovered the meaning of life. . . .)

Through his work the artist discovers "the meaning of life," just as the poet utilizes linguistic means in his existential analysis. Yet in the opening poem of the book, "Logos," the speaker declares the inadequacy and evasiveness of his instruments. The Logos, the reasoning and investigation, may assume more and more subtle meanings, opening new angles of interpretation. Therefore the understanding of history (personal and universal) is never clear. In "Il conto" (The Computation) an entire life is examined in one night, and the number of days of which one can comprehend the significance amounts to one year at the most.

The term *Logos* can also be taken in a philosophical sense as a search for truth, which in Freni's poetry is always the equivalent of a search for cultural roots. Love and Logos are, therefore, the parallel roads of a metaphorical itinerary. They also reflect the perfect balance between thought and emotion in Freni's poetry. The new compositions included in the volume are stylistically elaborate. Often the final two lines rhyme. In the first section, "Amore e logos," the painful feeling of passing time, which pervades the entire book, is introduced. Eternal time flows untouched by death in "Senza fine" (Unendingly): "tutto comincia senza fine / e senza fine muore" (all begins without end / and dies without end). In "L'inizio" (The Beginning) any event occurs without changing the course of time: "dopo che tutto accadde tutto accade / senza nulla cambiare" (after everything happened everything happens / without changing anything). In "Sicut erat" (It Was like That) the speaker states that history is memory because only through memory may one chronologically differentiate moments in history. Through memory the narrator analyzes, interprets, and reconstructs the puzzle of human history, as in "Segreto" (Secret). From the dark and toward the dark moves the intellectual journey of *Amore e logos,* ending in the ultimate shipwreck of its own contradictions. The speaker is lost in the chaos of existence, which he has tried to reorganize through words that cannot be clearly deciphered.

In *Amore e logos* Freni utilizes traditional literary material as codified by southern Italian poets, reinventing it in a new context. Sicily becomes the point of departure and the center of a social and cultural discourse that does not concern so much the problems of southern Italy as those of modern civilization. Freni's poetry deserves more critical attention in the future. Further study of his work, as of that of other recent Sicilian poets, will contribute to evaluating the extent to which southern Italian writers are still indebted to or reject hermeticism and posthermeticism in favor of new styles and themes. Freni seems to incorporate a tasteful combination of tradition and experimentation in his verse. He also utilizes poetic language to present current issues of cultural or historical relevance, never giving in to sterile abstractionism.

References:

Cosimo Cucinotta, "La poesia di Melo Freni," *Atti del Convegno su Melo Freni narratore e poeta* (Messina: University of Messina, 1987);

Alcide Paolini, "Poesia, memoria e ironia," *Corriere della Sera* (14 December 1983);

Giuseppe Zagarrio, "Antigruppo 73," *Ponte,* 29 (31 May 1973): 719–721;

Zagarrio, *Febbre, furore e fiele* (Milan: Mursia, 1983), pp. 273–302.

Giovanni Giudici
(26 June 1924 –   )

Rosetta Di Pace-Jordan
University of Oklahoma

BOOKS: *Fiorì d'improvviso* (Rome: Canzoniere, 1953);

La stazione di Pisa e altre poesie (Urbino: Istituto Statale d'Arte, 1955);

L'intelligenza col nemico (Milan: All'Insegna del Pesce d'Oro, 1957);

L'educazione cattolica (Milan: All'Insegna del Pesce d'Oro, 1963);

La vita in versi (Milan: Mondadori, 1965);

Autobiologia (Milan: Mondadori, 1969);

O Beatrice (Milan: Mondadori, 1972);

Poesie scelte, edited by Fernando Bandini (Milan: Mondadori, 1975);

La letteratura verso Hiroshima e altri scritti (Rome: Riuniti, 1976);

Il male dei creditori (Milan: Mondadori, 1977);

Il ristorante dei morti (Milan: Mondadori, 1981);

Design Process (Turin: Olivetti, 1983);

Lume dei tuoi misteri (Milan: Mondadori, 1984);

La dama non cercata (Milan: Mondadori, 1985);

Salutz (Turin: Einaudi, 1986);

Frau Doktor (Milan: Mondadori, 1989);

Prove del teatro (Turin: Einaudi, 1989);

Fortezza (Milan: Mondadori, 1990);

Il paradiso (Genoa: Costa & Nolan, 1991).

OTHER: "Se sia opportuno trasferirsi in campagna," *Menabò,* 4 (1961): 185–212;

Giancarlo Buzzi, *Isabella della Grazia,* introduction by Giudici (Milan: All'Insegna del Pesce d'Oro, 1967);

Vittoria Bradshaw, ed. and trans., *From Pure Silence to Impure Dialogue: A Survey of Post War Italian Poetry (1945–1965),* includes poems by Giudici (New York: Las Américas, 1971), pp. 517–550;

Gustave Flaubert, *Tre Racconti,* introduction by Giudici (Milan: Garzanti, 1974);

Umberto Saba, introduction by Giudici (Milan: Mondadori, 1976);

Lawrence Smith, ed. and trans., *The New Italian Poetry: 1945 to the Present,* includes poems by Giudici (Berkeley & Los Angeles: University of California Press, 1981), pp. 127–137.

TRANSLATIONS: Sara Lidman, *Cinque diamanti* (Milan: Rizzoli, 1966);

Edmund Wilson, *Saggi letterari, 1920–1950* (Milan: Garzanti, 1967);

Jurij Tynjanov, *Il problema del linguaggio poetico,* translated by Giudici and L. Kortikova (Milan: Saggiatore, 1968);

Omaggio a Praga (Milan: All'Insegna del Pesce d'Oro, 1968);

Poesia Sovietica degli anni sessanta, translated by Giudici, J. Spendel, and G. Venturi (Milan: Mondadori, 1970);

Addio, proibito piangere e altri versi tradotti (1955–1980) (Turin: Einaudi, 1982).

As a poet and left-wing intellectual living in the urban environment of Milan, Giovanni Giudici succeeds in giving his poetry power by refusing the privilege of distance and the posture of radical individualism that the Italian hermetic poets had claimed and retained up to the end of World War II. The open tone of Giudici's poetry and its lack of elitism were well suited to both the time in which it began to appear and to the role of witness that he had chosen. Deeply aware of the problematic currents in postwar Italian society, with its rising materialism and the failure of political action to fuse the self and history into a more integrated whole, he was a representative voice of the cultural climate from which his poetry arose. In the article "Che cosa possiamo imparare da [Arthur] Rimbaud" (What We Can Learn from Rimbaud), collected in *La letteratura verso Hiroshima* (Literature toward Hiroshima, 1976), Giudici says that the poet need not resign himself to the role of history's notary public, for he is part of history. In trying to understand immediate reality, he can take a stand, judge history, and restate it in its more humane aspects. Throughout the course of his career Giudici has remained faithful to this manner of inquiry.

Giovanni Giudici (photograph by Gabriella Maleti)

Giudici was born on 26 June 1924 in Le Grazie (near La Spezia), where he spent his childhood. At nine he was sent to Rome to attend a Catholic school. In Rome he also studied French literature with the well-known teacher P. A. Trompeo and wrote his thesis on Anatole France. Giudici has lived in Rome, Ivrea, Turin, and Milan, where he retired as a copywriter at Olivetti. He continues to live in Milan with his wife and two grown sons. Giudici has been politically active both as a socialist and as a communist. Also active as a cultural journalist, he is a contributor to *Espresso* and *Unità*. He seems to have made up his mind early in life about social and political realities, as shown in his early books. At no time did he feel that political action is irrelevant to life, nor did he feel that the social condition is not synonymous to the human condition. As he has given much of himself to political activity, he has also chosen his verse as a vehicle of such commitment. In Giudici's poetry the special nature of this commitment takes the form more of resistance than of violent protest. His posture of resistance is pitted against what he feels are the artificial and conditioning myths of a society that, caught in a postwar economic boom, has clearly adopted a materialist way of life. Throughout *La vita in versi* (Life in Verse, 1965) he takes an overtly autobiographical stance, as one can see in the poem "Dal cuore del miracolo" (From the Heart of the Miracle):

Parlo di me dal cuore del miracolo:
la mia colpa sociale è di non ridere,

di non commuovermi al momento giusto.
E intanto muoio, per aspettare a vivere.

(I speak of myself from the heart of the miracle:
my social fault is that of not laughing,
of not feeling touched at the right moment.
And meanwhile I die, waiting to live.)

He is unable to give assent to myths about life and happiness. He considers these myths as false and inadequate to establish an authentic contact with reality. At the same time he often tells of his feeling of guilt for being inextricably implicated in the reality he depicts.

Giudici examines what he considers the tragic situation of contemporary Western society from his own personal experience, by portraying life in its daily, most ordinary dimension; thus his poetry acquires documentary value. His Catholic upbringing, which he overtly rejects in *L'educazione cattolica* (A Catholic Education, 1963), serves him in good stead nonetheless. In his poetry he has created a personal casuistry, not lacking in Jesuitic virtuosity, which makes it possible for him to conduct his special inquiry into reality from his own point of view and to be a political poet in the best sense of the word, especially when talking about himself, blending private confession with public testimony. Giudici's poetic voice cannot be confused with that of any other contemporary Italian poet. His method consists of showing that the problematic condition of the self reflects the same condition in the culture as a whole. In an effort to respect the boundary lines he has set for historical and emotional reality, he adheres to his own biography, which constitutes the subject matter of most of his poetry. His approach is, therefore, personal and contextual; it is that of an existentialist. In the poem "L'intelligenza col nemico" (The Understanding with the Enemy), from *La vita in versi,* one sees that the social sphere is always dissolving into the private one, a perfect example of Giudici's poetic strategy:

> trattengo
> fra due maschere avverse un volto solo,
> indifferente a come mi sorprenda
> l'esito, in fuga o nell'azzurra tenda
> d'un vincitore provvisorio.
> C'è
> chi mi crede un mercante intento ai traffici:
> tu sai soltanto che ambiguo è il mio cuore,
> ma non mente. Resistere è difficile.

> (I keep
> between two opposite masks one face only,
> indifferent to how the outcome will overtake me,
> in flight or in the blue tent of a temporary winner.

There are
those who see in me a dealer busy trading:
only you know that ambiguous is my heart,
but it does not lie. To resist is difficult.)

Giudici does not write from a position of isolated social comfort but from his own uneasy, problematic situation.

Besides showing the manner in which Giudici establishes an immediate, concrete, irreducible contact with reality, the above poem also points to the polarity between fixity and freedom, between a sense of determinism and a desire for action that is central to Giudici's poetic world. This duality is never fully overcome. He cannot reject all forms of determinism, for he feels that the stance of the absolutely free self is so undermined by social and psychological forces that it renders the Sartrean concept of freedom a purely formal one. However, if Giudici can no longer offer to be a guide in the romantic sense, if he cannot show a superior order to impose on the chaos of contemporary existence, then, in not being able to move past uncertainty, he can at least show his predicament. In this weak position lies much of the strength of Giudici's poetry. After all, a measure of free will is still implied in his concept of resistance, which not only allows him to keep on registering his special form of social protest but also has enough of a teleological dimension to ensure that the defeat of the self need not ever be final. If the poem comes to no resolution in terms of experience alone, the force of the aphoristic closure shows the way in which Giudici grounds meaning in experience itself. Critics have justly pointed to the aphoristic nature of Giudici's poetry. There are indeed many memorable lines, enough to be collected in the seventeenth-century manner of, for example, François la Rochefoucauld. Giudici's tone and import are, however, unmistakably twentieth-century ones, as in "Alcuni" (Some People): "Essere umani può anche significare rassegnarsi / ma essere più umani è persistere a darsi" (To be human can also mean to resign oneself, / but to be more human is to continue to give of oneself), and in "Una casa in città" (A House in the City): "È impossibile salvarsi da soli" (It is impossible to save ourselves by ourselves alone).

The genetic development of these abstract thoughts can be traced back to the lived moment of experience within the poem. They do not come from a source outside the poems, nor are they artificially attached to them as closures. They represent no verbal puzzle, and while their strength rests on the verbs instead of the nouns, which once more shows Giudici's activist bent, they do not lash out with gnomic violence. Typical of Giudici's attitude, their message is open, allusive. They reveal that Giudici's inclination toward self-realization is still tied to a Christian ethos. The two aphorisms above can be seen as paradigmatic of his strong Augustinian orientation in his concept of relatedness, of human love, of *caritas*. The individual can never be self-sufficient; self-realization needs to be always reciprocal in some way. *Autobiologia* (Autobiology, 1969) needs to be read in this light, from the perspective that relatedness is basic to human life in its biological and historical dimensions. Giudici, in accordance with his natural inclination toward others, which, in turn, is consistent with his political ideology, has not taken the opposite antinomian position of those who, like Jean-Paul Sartre, view all human relationships as basically negative in nature and conflictual in pattern. Giudici does not share in this defensive attitude. In aesthetic terms this means a moving away from the cooler, more distanced position of the hermetics, and by extension from the whole symbolist-modernist movement. His looking at human experience for the origin and meaning of poetry also means a rejection of the "mysticism of the word." In the explosive post-1968 era of the Italian political and literary world, through the chaotic atmosphere of ideologies and poetics of the 1970s and 1980s, Giudici has continued to maintain his position by using the same existential themes.

Not interested in projecting himself as an individual personality in the romantic sense, Giudici is much more concerned with characterizing his psychological states and their problematic nature, more in the manner of Umberto Saba than of Gabriele D'Annunzio. Like Saba, Giudici does not sublimate his emotions into purely aesthetic forms, and like Saba he finds the perfect measure of his art on the mundane level of his autobiography. This stance prevents his scrutiny of reality from dissipating into an abstract analysis of perceptions and emotions. The key figures from his life, mostly the members of his immediate family, keep primary psychic elements active, vital, and consequential. A well-known line from Eugenio Montale's "Voce giunta con le folaghe" (Voice Coming with the Moorhens) — "memoria non è peccato finché giova" (memory is not a sin as long as it is of use) — can help explain the critical role that Giudici has assigned to memory as a basic process of consciousness. By not being entirely submissive to the promptings of memory, Giudici has again taken a different attitude from the whole symbolist-hermetic line. Yet, by giving memory such empirical urgency in creating a network of

figures and events that give texture and coherence to his experience, he shows that his ontology is not one of radical discontinuity.

Giudici's way of evoking events from his life is to dramatize them. He writes his autobiography by addressing a constant monologue to his cast of figures, highlighting the lived moment in the manner of drama. In this style critics such as Franco Fortini have seen a direct relationship to the *crepuscolare* poet Guido Gozzano, especially the Gozzano of *I colloqui* (The Colloquies, 1911). While it is true that the dramatic monologue as a formal structure is present in both poets, as is the tendency of both toward self-irony and self-parody, Giudici's posture toward other people as objects of his consciousness needs to be assessed in its proper light. His sense of compassion toward others (the word *pietà* is ubiquitous in his work) precludes much of the sexual farce readers find in Gozzano's work. Emotional expressionism is typical of both poets, as is their predilection to take the pulse of actuality in its most ordinary dimension, but Giudici's consciousness is more conflictual, problematic, and urgent. He asks many more searching, troubling questions. Charles Baudelaire more than Gozzano comes to mind, since Giudici's poetry seems to develop more openly and more fully when his attention is directed toward others — as in *Il male dei creditori* (The Creditors' Evil, 1977), when he writes in the poem "Sottomissione e riconoscimento" (Submission and Confession),

Cerco di ridurti
A mia immagine – ma fossi
Tu la pace che è il tuo corpo
Quando "fammi il mare" ti supplico
Sotto o sopra la pancia – non si sa bene chi dei due
È acqua o barca

Cerco di rivoltarti
Stringerti – ma cosa chiedo
Ai tuoi occhi
Un te stessa invisibile benché
Ti tocco pezzo a pezzo mi ripeto "sei qui"
Ti misuro nel chiuso delle mie mani

(I try to reduce you
to the image I have of you, but if it were
you the peace that is your body
when I implore you "make me the sea"
under or above the belly, not being clear which one of
    us
is the water or the sail.

I try to overturn you
squeeze you, but what do I ask
of your eyes an invisible you

although I touch you piece by piece I repeat to myself
  "you are here"
I measure you in the fold of my hands)[.]

Giudici's intuition about the nature of psychic reality never fails him. He knows that one cannot change nature through an act of the will. He is also aware that the point at which instincts and actions connect eludes consciousness. This knowledge does not allow him to overestimate freedom or to underestimate the determining forces impinging on the self. His poetry is born out of this awareness. Much of the authenticity of his voice and its constancy reside in his inability to quiet his conflicting desires.

The feminine character that stands at the center of Giudici's poetry and has become its icon is given a literary identity only. She is not directly representative of his mother or wife. Above all she is the unforgettable voice in "La Bovary c'est moi" (I Am the Bovary) in *Autobiologia* and in the whole section "Persona femminile" (Feminine Person) in *Il ristorante dei morti* (The Restaurant of the Dead, 1981). In "La Bovary c'est moi" she appears as if under limelight; all alone, she seems to be reciting her minidrama onstage, as in the following brief excerpt:

Potrei supporre di non sapere come sono
e che anche lui si domandi come è possibile che.
Ma temo sia più vero quello che so di sapere
e lui se non oggi domani riaprirà gli occhi.
Forse ci sta già pensando a come cavarsene fuori
più avanti dei miei timori.

Non devo illudermi perché dopo sarà peggio.
Meglio dirglielo subito che se ha un sospetto è vero.
Che faccia conto sia stato come uno sbaglio al telefono.
Insomma niente – e che se vuole può andarsene.

(I could assume not to know the way I am
and that he too is asking himself how that is possible.
But I am afraid that what I know of knowing is more
  true
and that if not today tomorrow he will open his eyes.
Maybe he is already thinking of how to get out of it
ahead of my fears.

I must not delude myself because after it will be worse.
Better tell him right away that if he suspects something
  he is right.
He can make believe that it has been like a mistake on
  the telephone.
In short nothing – and that if he wants to he can leave.)

Giudici's father is also a central character in his poetry, especially in *Il male dei creditori,* in which he is seen as a dislocated, burned-out, but elegant drifter whose son has assumed all the burden of the relationship. While the father is absolved in an almost mythical fashion, the son gathers in himself all the guilt. Giudici moves from a social consideration of evil (that of the creditors) to a consideration of the coexistence of good and evil in the self, turning the book in many instances into a cruel auto-da-fé. His tendency to be a willing penitent is never erased from his Catholic consciousness.

One of the characteristic forms of Giudici's poetry is formal, rhetorical prayer, often as a litany or a hymn, as in *O Beatrice* (1972). The poem "Madonnina" (Little Madonna), from *Lume dei tuoi misteri* (Light of Your Mysteries, 1984), is among the most beautiful and disquieting of all of Giudici's prayers:

Un bravo poeta e un brav'uomo non sarà detto
Di me - e non per colpa del poeta

Non fu pronunciato in vano che assassina
Era l'anima mia se non la mano

Portami alle tue braccia mia madonnina
Così lontana a Czestochowa e a Loreto

Al gelo della tua pancia il graffio del diavolo
Che mi brucia la guancia

(A good poet and a good man will not be said
Of me - and not because of the poet's fault

It was not said in vain that murderous
Was my soul if not my hand

Take me in your arms my little madonna
So far away at Czestochowa and at Loreto

To the cold of your womb the scratch of the devil
That burns my cheek)[.]

Religious feeling is pervaded by a sense of menace. The key imperative *portami* (take me) is pivotal in shifting the invocation to the sudden perspective of shocking imagery.

The supplicant in "Madonnina" prefigures the one in Giudici's *Salutz* (Salute, 1986), a book that can be read as an indulgence. In a note, Giudici says that he has written it to satisfy a personal, private need. Inspired by the *lettera epica* (epic letter) written in 1205 by the troubadour poet Raimbaut de Vaqueiras, *Salutz* is a *canzoniere* (songbook) dedicated to "Minne" (his love). But the book only superficially endorses the tradition of courtly love lyrics. The tone is that of the lament of the servant of love. Between independence and enslavement, the main character of this book, which is not overtly autobiographical, has chosen to be the willing victim of love. Unlike in his other books, where Giudici has always been able to get away from the dark side of things with a clever or clownish gesture, here he gives in to obsession. However, the poem "L'Etica di Bonhoeffer" (Bonhoeffer's Ethics) is representative of Giudici's general attitude toward life and art. By sustaining the two forms of involvement he has chosen, that of personal relationships and that of politics, he resists the feeling of nothingness that threatens contemporary consciousness. By not being able to see human value in an individual and social vacuum, he makes an explicit connection between ethics and aesthetics. By assigning such a vital role both to art and experience, he projects a Christian vision of communion, of *caritas:*

> O uomo reale
> O speranza certamente non riposta più in basso
> Del cuore di Gesù
>
> O uomo che osi sbagliare
> O tu del quale
> La forza è non giudicare
>
> Più pazienza ti chiedo
> Ti chiedo più religione
>
> (Oh real man
> Oh hope certainly not placed lower
> Than Jesus' heart
>
> Oh man you who dare to err
> Oh you whose
> Strength is not to judge
>
> More patience I ask of you
> I ask you for more religion)[.]

Interviews:

Silvia Batisti and Mariella Bettarini, "Giovanni Giudici," in *Chi è il poeta* (Milan: Gammalibri, 1980);

Ferdinando Camon, "Giovanni Giudici," in *Il mestiere di poeta* (Milan: Garzanti, 1982), pp. 151–167.

References:

Fernando Bandini, "Giovanni Giudici," in Giudici's *Poesie scelte,* edited by Bandini (Milan: Mondadori, 1975), pp. 9–21;

Giorgio Bàrberi Squarotti, *Poesia e narrativa del secondo Novecento* (Milan: Mursia, 1978), pp. 34, 50–52, 474–479;

Glauco Cambon, "La poesia di Giudici fra satira e elegia," *Forum Italicum,* 7 (March 1973): 3–8;

Marco Forti, "Inizio di Giovanni Giudici," "Fortini e Giudici dopo l'ideologia," and "Ancora per Giudici: Autobiologia," in his *Le proposte della poesia e nuove proposte* (Milan: Mursia, 1971), pp. 315–337;

Franco Fortini, "F. Leonetti, R. Roversi, G. Giudici, N. Risi," in his *I poeti del Novecento* (Rome & Bari: Laterza, 1977), pp. 189–196;

Marco Marchi, "Poeti della 'Quarta generazione': Spaziani, Orelli, Giudici e Cattafi," in his *Alcuni Poeti* (Florence: Valecchi, 1981), pp. 111–136;

Silvio Ramat, "Lo sguardo di Giudici da realismo a finzione," in his *Storia della poesia italiana del Novecento* (Milan: Mursia, 1976), pp. 670–673;

Enzo Siciliano, "Autobiologia," in his *Autobiografia letteraria* (Milan: Garzanti, 1970), pp. 375–377;

Cesare Viviani, Introduction to his *I percorsi della nuova poesia italiana* (Naples: Guida, 1980), pp. xv–xxiv;

Giuseppe Zagarrio, "Giudici fra il 'normale' e il 'matto'" and "L'occhio di Giudici," in his *Febbre, furore e fiele* (Milan: Mursia, 1983), pp. 65–74, 228–233.

Alfredo Giuliani
(23 November 1924 –   )

John Picchione
York University

BOOKS: *Il cuore zoppo; Con sette versioni da Dylan Thomas* (Varese: Magenta, 1955);

Margherite al sole (Bologna: S.I.A., 1956);

Pelle d'asino, by Giuliani and Elio Pagliarani (Milan: All'Insegna del Pesce d'Oro, 1964);

Povera Juliet, e altre poesie (Milan: Feltrinelli, 1965);

Immagini e maniere (Milan: Feltrinelli, 1965);

Moro river: Cimitero di guerra canadese (Ascoli Piceno: S.T.E., 1969);

Il tautofono (Milan: Feltrinelli, 1969);

Gerusalemme liberata (Turin: Einaudi, 1970);

Il giovane Max (Milan: Adelphi, 1972);

Chi l'avrebbe detto (Turin: Einaudi, 1973);

Nostro padre Ubu (Rome: Cooperativa Scrittori, 1977);

Le droghe di Marsiglia (Milan: Adelphi, 1977);

Autunno del Novecento: Cronache di letteratura (Milan: Feltrinelli, 1984);

Versi e nonversi (Milan: Feltrinelli, 1986);

Tre recite su commissione (Bergamo: Lubrina, 1990).

OTHER: *I Novissimi: Poesie per gli anni '60,* edited, with an introduction, by Giuliani, includes poems by Giuliani (Milan: Rusconi & Paolazzi, 1961; revised edition, Turin: Einaudi, 1965);

La scuola di Palermo, edited by Giuliani (Milan: Feltrinelli, 1963);

Gruppo 63: La nuova letteratura, edited by Giuliani and Nanni Balestrini (Milan: Feltrinelli, 1964);

Dylan Thomas, *Ritratto dell'autore da cucciolo,* preface by Giuliani (Turin: Einaudi, 1966);

Poeti di Tel Quel, edited by Giuliani and Jacqueline Risset (Turin: Einaudi, 1968);

Vittoria Bradshaw, ed. and trans., *From Pure Silence to Impure Dialogue: A Survey of Post-War Italian Poetry 1945–1965,* includes poems by Giuliani (New York: Las Américas, 1971), pp. 638–659;

Tristan Corbière, *Tutte le poesie,* preface by Giuliani (Rome: Newton Compton, 1973);

Antologia della poesia italiana: Dalle origini al Trecento, 2 volumes, edited by Giuliani (Milan: Feltrinelli, 1975, 1976);

Lawrence R. Smith, ed. and trans., *The New Italian Poetry 1945 to Present: A Bilingual Anthology,* includes poems by Giuliani (Berkeley: University of California Press, 1981), pp. 311–329.

TRANSLATIONS: T. S. Eliot, *Sulla poesia e sui poeti* (Milan: Bompiani, 1960);

William Empson, "Poesie," *Verri,* 3 (1960): 56–60;

James Joyce, "Musica da camera," in *James Joyce: Poesie,* edited by Giuliani, Edoardo Sanguineti, Antonio Rossi, and J. R. Wilcox (Milan: Mondadori, 1961);

Dylan Thomas, "Poesie," in *Dylan Thomas, Poesie,* edited by Ariodante Marianni (Turin: Einaudi, 1965);

Edwin Arlington Robinson, *Uomini e ombre* (Milan: Mondadori, 1965);

Henri Michaux, *Un certo Piuma,* translated, with a preface, by Giuliani (Milan: Bompiani, 1971);

Ben Jonson, *Volpone* (Rome: Officina, 1977).

Alfredo Giuliani's name is linked with *I Novissimi: Poesie per gli anni '60* (The New Ones: Poetry for the Year 1960), an anthology he edited in 1961, which instantly caused so much turmoil in the Italian intellectual establishment that it was to change drastically the course of contemporary Italian poetry. Undoubtedly Giuliani's introduction to the five poets whose works make up the anthology (Elio Pagliarani, Edoardo Sanguineti, Nanni Balestrini, Antonio Porta, and Giuliani himself) represents one of the most daring and innovative statements of poetics to come out of postwar Italy. Giuliani's own poetry, from its beginnings, has constantly been guided by the necessity to explore new poetic paths in the attempt to overcome the limits of the sentimental, autobiographical character of a great part of twentieth-century Italian poetry. Starting in the early 1950s, mainly through his association with Luciano Anceschi, whose critical search for new literary expressions had led him beyond the Italian poetic tradition, Giuliani came into contact not only with the language of poets such as Ezra Pound and T. S. Eliot but especially with the image-oriented poetry of Dylan Thomas, whose influence was to constitute the core of Giuliani's first poetic experience.

Born in Mombaroccio, near Pesaro, on 23 November 1924, Giuliani has spent most of his life in Rome, where he earned a degree in philosophy at the University of Rome in 1949. Two years after the publication in 1955 of his first collection of poetry, *Il cuore zoppo* (The Lame Heart), Giuliani became a member of the editorial staff of the *Verri,* a journal founded and directed by Anceschi, who can certainly be considered a father figure for the five young rebels known as the *novissimi.* Later, as a member of "Gruppo '63" (a group that was immediately labeled the neo-avant-garde), Giuliani actively participated in the various literary debates organized by the group and became the director of its monthly newspaper, *Quindici,* from its foundation in June 1967 until his resignation in January 1969. He quit as a sign of protest against the gradual reorientation of Gruppo '63 toward predominantly political action rather than literary, and his resignation gave rise to a crisis that caused the group's demise. In the years to follow, Giuliani as a militant critic contributed to the newspapers *Resto del Carlino, Mondo operaio,* and *Repubblica.* Especially in the 1960s he was intensely active as a translator, publishing in Italian some works by Eliot, Thomas, William Empson, and James Joyce. Giuliani also taught Italian literature at the University of Bologna for many years. At present he teaches at the University of Chieti.

In spite of the presence of the analogical language of hermetic tradition, *Il cuore zoppo* owes much of its innovative searching to the poetry of Thomas. The suddenly explosive images, the hallucinatory symbols, and the visual and constantly sensuous language of the Welsh poet are the most striking features of Giuliani's first collection. Thomas's ambiguous style of diction and his transfiguration of reality into fantastic, chromatic images are adapted by Giuliani with a vital tension that oscillates between the vigor of adolescence and the menacing anticipation of death, as in these lines:

Nel mio sangue risuscitano i boschi
La mora la fragola la spina
Per il dolce saccheggio dei ragazzi.
Linfa di mari corre per le dita
Rompe ai polsi la risacca, scivola

Cover for the 1986 book that includes nearly all of Alfredo Giuliani's poetry

Nel membruto regno delle ossa
La luna di scoglio.
(In my blood the woods resurge
The blackberry the strawberry the bramble
For the boy's sweet pillage.
A lymph of seas flows through my fingers
On my wrists the surf breaks,
In my bones' limbed kingdom
The reef moon glides.)
            – translation by Vittoria Bradshaw

In later years Thomas's lessons were to be combined not only with Giuliani's phenomenological orientation but also with his attention to the artistic experience of the first avant-gardes and to the coeval developments in the fields of figurative arts and music.

However, Giuliani's first and deepest impact on Italian letters began with the publication of *I Novissimi,* certainly one of the most revitalizing literary events of the last few decades. In his introduction Giuliani conceives of poetry as a provocative linguistic construction. Against any instrumental view of language, Giuliani insists that a poet's attention must be devoted to the medium itself. A poet must be preoccupied with words and not with ideologies or "pre-verità" (pregiven truth). Refusing any form of degradation of Logos to an instrument, and opposing the contemporary consumeristic and reifying exploitation of language, Giuliani advocates a mode of writing concerned with the "semantica concreta della poesia" (concrete semantics of poetry). Such a poetics generates corollaries: subject and object of its operation, poetry is not seen in an ancillary, servile subordination to reality, and not even as its metaphor. Rather, poetry is conceived of as another pole, as a different dimension of the linguistic world of everyday life. In essence Giuliani rejects any drab conception of realism; he is in favor of a pragmatic, gestural attitude. By abandoning the constrictions of representational aesthetics, he shifts toward a deliberately arbitrary and abnormal poetic structure. Poetry for Giuliani is not an epistemological medium but a form of contact. Poetry's content is what it does – how it acts upon the reader, the action it exerts: "Ciò che la poesia *fa* è precisamente il suo 'contenuto' " (What poetry *does* is precisely its "content"). With a revolutionary formal structure, poetry must constantly put the reader in a state of shock or disquietude. By shattering the dominant literary models, a poet's task is that of thwarting the reader's expectations while provoking an "accrescimento di vitalità" (increase of vitality).

The deep aversion to literature centered on concepts or ideologies aimed at transforming the world leads Giuliani to focus his attention on the linguistic modalities of reality. Poetry's function is to create a distance from the normality and automatism of everyday linguistic models by demolishing the syntax and by violently fragmenting semantic articulation. Such a deranging operation not only aims at the degradation of signified things but engenders in readers a state of estrangement that forces them to establish with the text a more dynamic and active rapport. By exploiting the arbitrariness and ambiguity of the sign, poetry draws attention to its own artifice, to the way meaning is produced rather than to the meaning of things. Advocating a form of poetry with an "open" structure, Giuliani gives an unprecedented prominence, at least within the Italian literary context, to the role of the reader. The reader's task is not so much to interpret the text, to identify preestablished meanings, but to collaborate in creating the text with the act of reading. In its asemantic and asyntactic structure, the poetic text becomes the locus of disorder and

ambiguity, a defying and anarchic linguistic construct that, on one hand, expresses the negation of current forms of communication and ideologies and, on the other, affirms the necessity of the utopian and the imaginary as denials of the reality principle. This calculated linguistic madness, this "visione schizomorfa" (schizomorphous vision), as Giuliani defines it, seems to perform a twofold function: it produces an autonomous formal structure and, at the same time, an ersatz schizophrenia that characterizes contemporary society. Following the philosophical orientation of phenomenology, in his poetics of the "riduzione dell'io" (reduction of the "I") – a phenomenological bracketing of existence and subjectivity, interpretable also as a denunciation of traditional, sentimental lyricism – Giuliani asserts the urgency of employing language as an autonomous, autotelic entity generating its own realities.

Giuliani's theoretical writings display a constant rejection of all poetics that naively claim the possibility of a naturalistic representation of reality. He insists on a new type of poetry, viewed as a "mimesi critica" (critical mimesis), as a formal construct that reflects and opposes reality at the same time. As Giuliani clarifies it in his collection of essays *Immagini e maniere* (Images and Manners, 1965), the poetic structure becomes "neo-contenuto" (neocontent). What matters is not what poetry says: it is the perturbative effects on the reader caused by the formal derangements that constitute new "messages," new ways of establishing contact. By demolishing normal linguistic structures, Giuliani not only attempts to challenge the reader's vision of the world but aims, too, at recovering life's possible authentic dimension. In other words, Giuliani's poetics also reveals strong existential motivations. The emphasis on the formal transgression conveys the existential necessity to go beyond vacuous, mystifying conceptions of reality. For Giuliani the phenomenological *epochè* – the suspension of all preconstituted ideologies (any belief placed in abeyance as a matter of method) – represents the only possibility of confronting historical and social alienation. With the aim of overcoming existential and linguistic alienation, Giuliani's "poesia novissima," with its revolutionary forms, offers the only possibility of authentic self-expression capable of opening up alternative ways to exist.

In his aspiration to reach a new form of poetry that would make "i pensieri visibili come cose, non quali argomenti" (thoughts visible as things, rather than concepts), Giuliani, in *Povera Juliet* (Poor Juliet, 1965), attempts to free the poetic imagination from established hierarchies. Images are not intended to embody preconceived or preordered thoughts but to stem from the process of writing, from the internal vitality of language itself. Through a constant textual fragmentation, which precludes with its mobile and fluid construction any cohesion or progression of a discourse, Giuliani embarks on a linguistic and existential journey, totally guided by the desire to explore the inner movements of language. However, paradoxically, he soon realizes that the proliferation of images without a beginning or end, the vertiginous verbal adventure, is a constant reminder of the impossibility of arresting the flux, of finding any reassuring linguistic crystallizations. Language's vitality coincides with its own annihilation. The continuous movement from one image to another cannot but effect the dissolution of any possible unity. Poems such as "La cara contraddizione" (The Dear Contradiction) present poetry torn between presence and absence, voice and silence, between the search for an authentic reality free from a priori schemes of perception and the insurmountable mediation of language. Closed within itself, in its tautological movements, language becomes intransitive, dangerously sliding toward nothingness. Vitalistic and nihilistic at the same time, this stage of Giuliani's poetry hopelessly attempts to reconcile word and silence, life and death. In search of transparent contact with the world, he also explores the dimension of animal instincts, of the regression to a precognitive state that could provide an access to direct, primordial awareness. Recurrent references to the natural state of animal realities, in poems such as "Penuria e fervore" (Penury and Fervor), "E dopo" (It Is After), and "Predilezioni" (Predilections), with its lycanthropic images, reveal the aspiration to recover a genuine vitality, a liberating and immediate experience of the world. Toward the end of "Predilezioni" he writes:

Prendi il nero del silenzio, tanto parlare
disinvoglia la nuca, in sé pupilla, palato
di cane, oppure pensa le notti che risbuca
nel gelo il firmamento dei gatti, amore.

(Take the black of silence, talking so much
makes the skin of your neck crawl, pupil in itself, dog's
palate, or think about nights when
the firmament of cats punctures the ice, love.)
— translation by Lawrence R. Smith

However, there is no escape from the prison of language and from the alienating condition of existence: in the miserable struggle "non c'è onore, né calma, né tregua" (there is neither honor, nor peace, nor truce).

Beginning with "Prosa" (Prose) and "I mimi mescolati" (The Mixed Mimes), Giuliani enters a new phase, experimenting with poetry constructed as collages of everyday dialogues. Held together only by the metrical and rhythmical order of the sequences, devoid of any logical semantic articulation, these poems do not simply mirror the reified condition of contemporary language. On the contrary, through the delirious montage of heterogeneous linguistic scraps, Giuliani on one hand tries to reduce language to a nonreferential, material entity, and, on the other, he shows the desire to reactivate its power to create new possible realities. These experiments with collage led to the production of texts identified by Giuliani as "poesia di teatro" (poetry of theater), carried on in *Chi l'avrebbe detto* (Who Would Have Said It, 1973), comprised of poems written between 1952 and 1966. In "Io ho una bella pera, e tu cos'hai?" (I Have a Beautiful Pear, and What Do You Have?) and "Povera Juliet," Giuliani wants to abolish the representational dimension of theater in order to reduce the linguistic sign to pure movement, action, and gestural invention — not the arbitrary entity that replaces or represents objective reality. The aesthetic matrix of this operation includes the theater of Antonin Artaud or the "Living Theatre," if not dadaistic experiments. However, Giuliani, in his obsessive search for the verbal sign in its pure state, is providing a poetic equivalent of avant-garde music as practiced, for instance, by John Cage in his experiments with noises, environmental sounds, and sounds of nature. Besides his relationship with avant-garde music, Giuliani came into close contact with a group of Roman artists, including Gastone Novelli, Toti Scialoja, and Achille Perilli, who were pursuing an abstract form of painting based on the medium itself, on the gestural treatment of pictorial signs adopted as pure signifiers. In a poem titled "Una conferenza di Jorge Luis Borges" (A Lecture by Jorge Luis Borges) Giuliani carries his attempt so far as to reduce the word to dismembered phonemes, absolute noise:

KRAKUAC.boc.bok.Kuakk.uuus. . .
  bok.KUAKUARS.u
KK.uuu(!!!. . . . . !!. . .) UUUuAuau
AuAUUu.boc.**Martín**   **Fierro**
  boc.bok.KUAKUAS.UKK.
paisaje / uuUuuuauauauauuuuUUUUU.KUASkkc.
pampa[.]

Poems such as "Invetticoglia" and "Yé-Yé coglino" (whose titles are untranslatable), which close the collection, seem to approximate pure invention. The almost total collapse of the referential function of language allows for verbal acrobatics guided solely by a linguistic excitement, with puns, double entendres, neologisms, etymological games, and phonic equivalences. This joyous carnival of words, nevertheless, is opposed by Giuliani's critical awareness: as poetry cannot become pure animal utterances, so it cannot escape the mystifying and culturally determined linguistic signs. In "Le radici dei segni" (The Roots of the Signs), which opens both *Povera Juliet* and *Chi l'avrebbe detto,* the line "le culture sono alfabeti" (cultures are alphabets) reveals the impossibility of going beyond the linguistic sign, the hiatus that unavoidably marks the distance from an unadulterated contact with reality.

Giuliani's *Il tautofono* (The Tautophone, 1969) comprises poems written between 1966 and 1969. Readers enter a linguistic realm in which the differentiating elements of language are absent. As Giuliani points out in a short preface to the volume, *tautofono* represents a poetic equivalent of the Rorschach test. The inkblots are replaced by dismembered sentences, amputated narrative sequences, which in their nonsensical flow indicate that there is no possibility of intrinsic meaning. Contrary to the Rorschach test, however, the projective technique does not allow for absolute free associations. The poet guides the interpretations of these meaningless sounds. In this epos of death and nothingness readers witness the total collapse of reality; human identity seems no longer possible. In a psychotic delirium, an "ominicànide" (an antihero who cannot be defined as a human) moves in a labyrinth of signs that speak only of the death of all meaning. The "being-toward-death" of the sign is essentially the void, the being-toward-death of existence itself. In Giuliani's hallucinations, the distinctive features of vegetal, animal, or human realities no longer exist. The "ominicànide," in its voyage through spaces populated by "cadaveri frizzanti" (fizzy corpses) and "orribili embrioni con la coda urlanti" (horrible embryos with the tail howling), encounters "erba pelosa" (hairy grass), "vegetazione nasale" (nasal vegetation), "un verme coi piedi gonfi" (a worm with swollen feet), and "vigneti di tartaruga" (tortoise vineyards). In a world degraded to a garbage dump full of excrement, a world in which only absurd animalistic rites and onanistic acts are performed, "la natura non c'è più" (nature no longer exists). The absence of nature declares the absence of authenticity, the impossibility for the poet to disclose any trace of real existence.

This surreal voyage uncovers the meaningless rituals of daily existence; poems such as "Avventure di quando vivevo proprio in quel tempo" (Adventures of When I Was Living Right at That Time) and "Fuga in famiglia" (Escape from Family) are particularly revealing. *Tautofono,* however, should not be read solely as an epos guided by an anarchic, destructive, neodadaistic antidiscourse. With his collages, his fantastic accumulations of heterogeneous materials, Giuliani is providing, at the same time, a mimicry of surrealistic procedures: images are constructed and then, with a sort of clownish gesture, are erased. Signs remain an illusion of meaning and inevitably cannot but reveal their ambiguous state, as in "Il canto animale" (Animal Song):

la nostra piccola atmosfera soffre di un accumulo di
  onde disritmiche e ci perturba
più del barrito degli elefanti e poi c'è la grande lezione
  silenziosa dei gatti dio
com'era bello con la ventosa della gola godere le strisce
  d'aria e sputare sul sole
quanto mi piace il muso ottuso dell'amore che respira
  muto tra la vegetazione nasale

(our small atmosphere suffers from a buildup of
  arhythmical waves and it bothers us
more than the trumpeting of elephants and then there's
  the great silent lesson of cats goodness
how beautiful it was with the suction cup throat to
  enjoy the layers of air and spit on the sun
how I do like love's blunt snout which breathes silently
  in the nasal vegetation)[.]
                                                – translation by Smith

Closed into its own verbal space, *Tautofono* once again reveals the dualistic movement of Giuliani's poetry: the orgiastic vigor of the linguistic sign and the solitary void of its narcissistic nature.

The collage technique is also employed in *Il giovane Max* (The Young Max), first published in 1972 and later reprinted in *Versi e nonversi* (Verses and Nonverses, 1986), which, except for a few poems from *Il cuore zoppo,* includes all Giuliani's published poetry. Grotesque and linguistically eccentric, *Il giovane Max* defies any traditional classification: it is neither a poem nor a novel. It is, perhaps, as Giuliani defines it in the first section, a collection of "Poesie senza versi" (Poems without verses), a pasting together of scraps of alienated, desemanticized language. *Il giovane Max* can certainly be read as a mock narrative, a derisive, burlesque imitation of narration itself. Again in this collection, faced with a standardized and automatized linguistic code, Giuliani does not find any road leading to a subjective and authentic use of language. Experimenting with an alienated, pathological language is the only possibility left open to literature. Farcical and carnivalesque, *Il giovane Max* subverts any literary norm and, in its perversion, refuses any reduction of literature to social or political discourse. With its constant semantic void and linguistic absurdities, it also reaffirms Giuliani's courageous defense of literature against all the pressures to transform it into a medium, into an instrument other than itself. For Giuliani, literature, in its self-reflexivity, must constantly turn inward. By distancing itself from reality, literature becomes autorepresentation, capable of inversions and subversions, thus providing an imaginative exploration in the realm of language. For Giuliani, literature can be nothing else.

References:

Corrado Costa, "Il test di licantropo, a proposito di 'Povera Juliet,' ovvero per una concezione dell'amore nella poesia contemporanea," *Marcatré*, 26–29 (1966): 240–244;

Fausto Curi, "Appunti per due Novissimi," in his *Ordine e disordine* (Milan: Feltrinelli, 1965), pp. 79–81, 116–120;

Curi, "La forma, l'informe, il deforme," in his *Perdita d'aureola* (Turin: Einaudi, 1977), pp. 233–247;

Roberto Esposito, "La vita impossibile della poesia: Alfredo Giuliani," in his *Le ideologie della neoavanguardia* (Naples: Liguori, 1976), pp. 69–125;

Giulio Ferroni, "La poesia di Alfredo Giuliani o l'impossibilità dell'avanguardia," *Rassegna della Letteratura Italiana*, 1 (1970): 90–111;

Angelo Guglielmi, "Tecnicamente dolce," in his *La letteratura del risparmio* (Milan: Bompiani, 1973), pp. 141–146;

Niva Lorenzini, "Le avventure verbali di un poeta itinerante," in her *Il laboratorio della poesia* (Rome: Bulzoni, 1978), pp. 113–138;

Walter Pedullà, "Alfredo Giuliani/la fame della metafisica," in his *La rivoluzione della letteratura* (Rome: Ennesse, 1970), pp. 155–163;

John Picchione, "La dialettica negativa del Gruppo 63," *Otto/Novecento*, 2 (1987): 151–161;

Gianni Scalia, "La nuova avanguardia (o della miseria della poesia)," in *Avanguardia e neoavanguardia*, edited by Andrea Barbato (Milan: Sugar, 1966), pp. 55–60;

Giuseppe Ungaretti, "Per Giuliani," *Verri*, 19 (1966): 64–66;

Lucio Vetri, "Saggio d'antologia: Alfredo Giuliani e la poesia come 'scioglimento della tensione vitale e dell'ironia," *Verri*, 9–10 (March–June 1986): 103–125.

Tonino Guerra

(16 March 1920 –   )

Hermann W. Haller
City University of New York

BOOKS: *I scarabócc* (Faenza: Lega, 1946);

La s-ciuptèda (Faenza: Lega, 1950);

La storia di Fortunato (Turin: Einaudi, 1952);

Lunario (Faenza: Benedetti, 1954);

Dopo i leoni (Turin: Einaudi, 1956);

L'assassino, by Guerra and Elio Petri (Milan: Zibetti, 1962);

Il deserto rosso, by Guerra and Michelangelo Antonioni, edited by Carlo di Carlo (Bologna: Cappelli, 1964);

L'equilibrio (Milan: Bompiani, 1967); translated by Eric Mosbacher as *Equilibrium* (London: Chatto & Windus, 1969; New York: Walker, 1970);

L'uomo parallelo (Milan: Bompiani, 1969);

Millemosche senza cavallo, by Guerra and Luigi Malerba (Milan: Bompiani, 1969);

Millemosche mercenario, by Guerra and Malerba (Milan: Bompiani, 1969);

Millemosche fuoco e fiamme, by Guerra and Malerba (Milan: Bompiani, 1970);

Millemosche innamorato, by Guerra and Malerba (Milan: Bompiani, 1971);

I bu: Poesie romagnole, translated into standard Italian by Roberto Roversi (Milan: Rizzoli, 1972);

Il cannocchiale e altri testi, by Guerra and Lucile Laks (Milan: Bompiani, 1972);

Millemosche e il leone, by Guerra and Malerba (Milan: Bompiani, 1973);

Amarcord, by Guerra and Federico Fellini (Milan: Rizzoli, 1973); translated by Nina Roots as *Amarcord: Portrait of a Town* (London: Abelard-Schuman, 1974; New York: Berkley, 1975);

Millemosche e la fine del mondo (Milan: Bompiani, 1973);

I cento uccelli (Milan: Bompiani, 1974);

Millemosche alla ventura, by Guerra and Malerba (Milan: Bompiani, 1974);

Il polverone: Storie per una notte quieta (Milan: Bompiani, 1978);

I guardatori della luna (Milan: Bompiani, 1981);

Il miele (Rimini: Maggioli, 1981);

L'aquilone: Una favola del nostro tempo, by Guerra and Antonioni (Rimini: Maggioli, 1982);

Il leone dalla barba bianca, by Guerra and Michail Romadin (Milan: Emme, 1983);

La pioggia tiepida (Milan: Rusconi, 1984);

La capanna (Rimini: Maggioli, 1985);

Il viaggio (Rimini: Maggioli, 1987);

Il libro delle chiese abbandonate (Rimini: Maggioli, 1988);

L'orto d'Eliseo (Rimini: Maggioli, 1989);

Il profilo del conte (Rimini: Maggioli, 1990).

Collection: *Storie dell'anno Mille,* by Guerra and Luigi Malerba (Milan: Bompiani, 1977) – comprises all the *Millemosche* volumes.

OTHER: Hermann W. Haller, ed., *The Hidden Italy: A Bilingual Edition of Italian Dialect Poetry,* includes poems by Guerra (Detroit: Wayne State University Press, 1986), pp. 277–289.

As is the case for the majority of Italian regions, Emilia-Romagna has a long-standing literary tradition in dialect, with such key writers as the Bolognese playwrights Giulio Cesare Cortese and Alfredo Testoni, and the Romagnol poet Aldo Spallicci. A younger generation of poets, represented by Raffaele Baldini, Nino Pedretti, and Tonino Guerra, has perpetuated and rejuvenated this rich tradition, which parallels the region's well-known literary production in standard Italian. By choosing to write in dialect, the authors opt for a language of social reality or for a medium of personal and intimate expression.

Antonio (later Tonino) Guerra was born in the small town of Sant'Arcangelo di Romagna, near Ravenna, on 16 March 1920. He went to school there and later taught classes there while studying education at the University of Urbino, from which he graduated with a *laurea* (degree) in 1946. Two years earlier he had experienced one of the most traumatic and devastating events in his life when he was arrested by the Fascists and deported to the

Tonino Guerra circa 1985

German concentration camp Troisdorf; there he composed his first poems in dialect, to comfort and entertain his fellow prisoners in their mother tongue, Romagnol. When Guerra returned from Germany, a small bundle of dialect poems, *I scarabócc* (The Scribbles, 1946), was ready to be published. The choice of dialect is hardly a coincidence; it is consonant with his rebellious opposition to the Fascist threats and policies of the time. More poems followed in *La s-ciuptèda* (The Gunshot) in 1950 and *Lunario* (Almanac) four years later. All these poems, together with several others, gained wide critical attention in the 1972 collection *I bu* (The Oxen), with an introduction by Gianfranco Contini and standard Italian versions by the poet Roberto Roversi.

Guerra's poetry of this first phase (which he admits he likes the best) portrays a landscape of decay and dying, a world inhabited by the old, the poor, and the mad. Subtle observation is blended with powerful imagination, yielding a poetry of tension and contrasts between the real and the imaginary, past and present, and nature and art. Nature is portrayed in eternal dualities of perfection and imperfection, and innocuousness and violent rebelliousness. The marginal, deprived, and aberrant characters in Guerra's poems provide an impassioned look at the human condition in a world that is peripheral only in appearance. Death is one of the key themes, especially prominent in "I bu," the title poem:

Andé a di acsè mi bu ch'i vaga véa,
che quèl chi à fat i à fatt,
che adèss u s'èra préima se tratour.

E' pianz e' cór ma tótt, ènca mu mé,
avdai ch'i à lavurè dal mièri d'ann
e adèss i à d'andè véa a tèsta basa
dri ma la córda lònga de' mazèll.

(Go tell my oxen to go away,
that their work is done,
that now one works faster with the tractor.

And then we all cry, and even I,
thinking of the labor they endured for thousands of
    years
now that they have to go away with their heads down
behind the long rope of the butcher.)

The speaker grieves over a way of life that has grown useless and is vanishing in the name of progress. Transition and the relentless passage of time in the cycle of life are constants in Guerra's poetry. They are frequently symbolized by *e' mi fióm* (the Marecchia River), which is also a source of life.

A sense of timeless awe is evoked by the contrast of decay and simple beauty, as epitomized by spiderwebs discovered on a wall in the poem "I pidriul ad saida" (Spiderwebs):

E un dè la mi muraia
l'era pina
ad pidriul ad saida
che fa i ragn.

(And one day my wall
was covered
with those silken webs
the spiders spin.)

Other poems evoke the sensation of trauma and imminent disaster. Yet beneath all the madness and misery lies a redeeming strength, a subtle yet persistent force of optimism, a profound love of life and a search for regeneration, as in "La mi dòna" (My Woman):

Ma la mi dòna u i va i mi módi ad fè
sa scòrr, sa móv un braz,
sa dég qualcósa fórt dréinta un cafè.

Ma la mi dòna u i pis a la su vólta,
s'andém a lètt sla vòia ad divértéis,
ch'a n a séa un fug ad paia a fé iniquèl.

(My woman likes the way I walk
the way I talk, or move my arm,
when I say something loud in the coffeehouse.

But my woman also likes
when we go to bed with lust to play,
if only it's not done in a flash.)

Simplicity is one of the key ingredients in all Guerra's poetry, whether in the description of manmade walls or in the accounts of nature – the river, owls, doves, snakes, and geese. This same simplicity (which critic Giuseppe Prezzolini praised in his homage in *Tonino Guerra,* 1985) yields a sense of raw beauty in the epigrammatic poem "Rico":

Una sacòuna nira,
al schèrpi's strazz
sal fasci mi calzéun
e un fiòur tal mèni,
Rico.

Un po' a la militèra
e un po' da sociéta;
e tal bascòzi i suldaréll chi spéc
chi sòuna par la strèda,
quand che va.

(A black coat,
rugged shoes
waist bands on the pants
a flower in his hand,
Rico.

A bit like a soldier
and a bit like a gentleman;
with small change in his pocket
that clinks through the street,
when he walks.)

As Contini accurately points out in his introduction to *I bu,* Guerra's language seems unedited and virgin. The sounds of this particular Romagnol dialect – with its abundant nasals and diphthongs – and the free rhymes make for a homogenous yet powerful poetic language in which the real, the fantastic, the subtle, and the brutal interplay in a delicate act of balance.

In about 1953, after having taught secondary school in Savignano sul Rubicone for several years, Guerra moved to Rome and started to work on screenplays for some of the foremost Italian film directors. He also wrote novels and tales for children. There is a steady and intrinsic relationship between Guerra the poet and Guerra the prose writer, as Italo Calvino noted in his homage in *Tonino Guerra:* "Tutto per Tonino Guerra si trasforma in racconto e in poesia. . . . C'è sempre un racconto in ogni sua poesia; c'è sempre una poesia in ogni suo racconto . . ." (For Tonino Guerra everything turns into a tale or a poem.

... There is always a story in each of his poems; there is always a poem in each of his stories ...).

Guerra has been very productive as a screenwriter, working with some twenty-six film directors. He has contributed his visions and insights to some sixty films, working mostly with Michelangelo Antonioni and Francesco Rosi. However, as Rebecca West accurately notes, this activity did not bring Guerra the wide recognition he earned with his poetry. As in his narrative prose, there is in Guerra's scripts the imprint of the poet, with his feelings for the land and people of Romagna and his considerations of cosmic problems. This interplay has been aptly described by Antonioni in *Tonino Guerra*: "La condanna (o il privilegio?) di Tonino Guerra è di essere costretto ad andare sempre in giro con Tonino Guerra. Mi domando come faccia il primo, l'uomo, a sopportare senza un attimo di tregua la visione del mondo del secondo, il poeta. Mi domando anche come sia possibile che la carica vitale dell'uno, sanguigna quasi selvatica, si traduca attraverso l'altro in qualcosa di così puramente letterario come le sue opere" (Tonino Guerra's punishment [or his privilege?] is to be forced to always go around with Tonino Guerra. I wonder how the first manages to tolerate incessantly the second, the poet. I also wonder how it is possible that the vital energy of the first, sanguine and almost savage, translates itself into something so purely literary as his works). All filmmakers eager to work with Guerra must have sensed the importance of his poetry. In 1973 he began his association with Federico Fellini. One scene in the script for *Amarcord* (I Remember) calls to mind one of Tonino's early poems (in *I bu*), "E' gatt sòura e' barcòcall" (The Cat on the Apricot Tree):

Léu l'éra un matt
che féva féinta d'ès un animèli
tra al rèmi de *barcòcall*.

E' su pór ba l'è e' più bon òm ch'u i fóss
....
U i géva: "Gino va là vén zò;
da rèta, dòunca, ma quèl ch'u t déi e' tu ba" –
Ma e' matt u s'ranicéva se barcòcall
e tótt la nota e' féva i vérs de' gatt.

(He was a madman
pretending to be an animal
on the branches of an *apricot tree*.

His poor dad was the best man in the world
....
He told him: "Gino come on get down;
listen to the words of your dad" –

But the madman crouched down between the branches and made the sounds of a cat all night long.)

Guerra's involvement with the movies took him to many foreign countries. He traveled to the United States on the occasion of the opening of *Amarcord*. He was particularly familiar with the republic of Georgia in the former Soviet Union. In 1977 Guerra married Eleonora Kreindlina in Moscow.

During the 1980s Guerra returned to his first literary passion, composing four long poems in dialect: *Il miele* (Honey, 1981), *La capanna* (The Cabin, 1985), *Il viaggio* (The Journey, 1987), and *Il libro delle chiese abbandonate* (The Book of Abandoned Churches, 1988). A few dialect poems, inserted among the short stories of *Il polverone* (The Cloud of Dust, 1978), had already reintroduced the public to his continuing dialect muse. The 1980s quartet of books initiates a more narrative phase of Guerra's poetry. Two of the four poems are dedicated to people who speak dialect, including his parents, grandparents, the people of Romagna (*Il miele*), and the citizens of Naples (*La capanna*); *Il viaggio* is a tribute to the Marecchia River and its surroundings; and *Il libro* is dedicated to farmers who have not abandoned their land.

Il miele is a long poetic tale in thirty-six cantos, composed in free verse and in stanzas of differing lengths. It evokes the last years of life of two brothers in what could be called a Romagnol ghost town, where only the old and crazy are left: the old androgynous Bina walking behind her goat, the shoemakers, the old farmer Pinela looking for wild honey, and Filomena's retarded son. It is about a twilight world, with abandoned houses, forgotten trees, dead leaves, rain, fog, hail, and a town filled with tragic, clownlike human beings. One of the brothers sits at the train station, where he worked as a telegraph operator but where no train has passed in the last forty years. Filomena's thirty goats stopped eating one morning and slowly died. In this world in transition death is mysterious, feared but also seen as a natural part of the life cycle, sweet like honey at the tip of a sword. Honey, the main substance in the book, is also a symbol of regeneration. Throughout the narrative one senses Guerra's power of imagination and intuition in exploring the secrets of the human heart and of nature. Abrupt violence is contrasted with subtle observations and a sense of humor; reality and fantasy are contrasted through the use of different colors, sounds, and movements. *Il miele* clearly connects with and develops the themes, motives, and images of Guerra's earlier poetry.

La capanna shows another lost world with its timeless objects and harmony with nature. The main setting, a huge mazelike cabin, has a precise history: it was built, near San Giovanni in Galilea close to the seashore, by the character Zangalà, who had survived sanitation work in the infectious marshlands south of Rome. The abandoned cabin becomes inhabited by Homer, a mysterious stranger who lives there alone in communion with nature. Homer's life takes on an unusual dimension when a woman, Isolina, visits him to help him in the house. With her rich husband away on a business trip, she wants to come back to the country to live out her need to work. She is a fountain of memories, telling the stories of Nazzarena, who immigrated to Brazil, and of Bigliola, who made love with Zaira in the cane fields. She initially resists Homer's sexual advances – though he is entranced by her "tètti ch'al ridéva" (laughing tits) – but she finally gives in, and Homer vanishes from the cabin and from the town, like "un mat" (a madman). In Guerra's own explanation, the complex poem is related to his marriage and his Russian wife's dedication to work.

Il viaggio is an ode in ten sequences to the Marecchia valley, including the river and medieval castles there. It is an account of the honeymoon journey of an old couple, Rico and Zaira – a barber from Petrella Giudi and his wife. Neither of them has ever seen the sea, only twenty miles away; they have only heard of its mysteries, of whales washed ashore. Their walk takes them down along the river to the sea during the fall season. It is a trip of life and memory, a search for truth, yet also a journey toward death. Zaira fantasizes having a death similar to that of a gypsy who died while asleep. Rico wants to die screaming violently at everything. The couple spends a night in an abandoned mill, and the white dust reminds Rico of a cloud of white butterflies that once invaded their town. Further down the river, a crusher used to dig out the bed of the river, causing it to flow faster, symbolizes a ruthless modern world with no respect for nature. A dilapidated, roofless church with obscene graffiti on its walls is the couple's next discovery. Zaira confesses her past adventure with a gypsy to a priest, who puts food in little holes in the ground outside the church to attract singing birds. A fountain in Pietracuta, where the women used to wash their clothes, is also the place where Rico and Zaira proposed to each other. Later they see a young couple making love, and Zaira remembers her sexual awakening in the oat fields, two days after her wedding. Finally Rico and Zaira arrive at an abandoned wedding tent with only some leftovers to feed on. They are worn out and thirsty. A carter takes them on the last leg of their journey to the sea, which is shrouded in fog. Rico and Zaira first lose and then embrace each other, with the water already up to their heads. As the critic Dante Isella notes in his postscript, the trip symbolizes a journey to Hades, from the lively river to the still, mysterious sea. As in the other two long poems, as well as in Guerra's earlier poetry, from a crumbling and decaying world rises the power of human love, caring, and strength.

In *Il libro delle chiese abbandonate,* abandoned churches, encountered in *Il viaggio,* become the constant theme throughout the twenty-four short sections. The reader is led through the valley of crumbling and forgotten churches and convents, some with trees and birds inside, others burned to the ground or with only some murals left on the walls. There are frequent historical and geographical references, including Badia, Pietra Rubbia, Sogliano, Montetiffi, Montebotolino, and other locations. Each church has a story, tied to precise events – the breakout of World War I, for example – and to certain worshippers and friars. There is the story of a shopkeeper who miraculously finds his breakfast in the church he uses to store water closets and that of a shepherd whose unhappy sheep walk into a church to disappear into a painting with Saint Anthony. The stories of miracles portray the superstitious souls of simple folks and give a sense of timelessness to Guerra's poetry: the past blends with the present and future.

As in earlier poems the theme of death is contrasted by the pervasive power of life, by a sense of hope amid the decay, with nature continuing to thrive in victory and with people worshiping fallen temples. In Guerra's poetry, rich with fantasy and subtle humor, religious feelings and references, in their simplicity, are reminiscent of Saint Francis's writings. As in earlier poems by Guerra *Il libro* allegorizes transition, with farmers abandoning their land, birds leaving their old habitats, churches left abandoned by people, and the speaker abandoning the big city, Rome, to return to his native land, at least in his mind.

L'orto d'Eliseo (Eliseo's Garden, 1989) and *Il profilo del conte* (The Count's Profile, 1990) continue the poetic cycle of memory evoked by the Marecchia valley. In the first, the world is restricted to the space of a garden, where a fierce war is fought between an old man and a mole, a struggle against unpredictable destruction and death. Hopeful of keeping the mole from returning to destroy the garden, the old man revels in past memories but finally is almost longing to yield to the blind, nocturnal animal. The second book is the story of the Marecchia valley's last count, who returns to the enchanting surroundings of his castle.

As well as being an accomplished writer, Guerra is also a pictorial artist. His paintings have been called figurative metaphors inspired by Russian and oriental works. A poster series published by Maggioli is a vivid testimony to Guerra's active participation in public life – his concerns for a harmonious environment and improving education. His figurative art makes Guerra what critic Cesare Zavattini calls (in *Tonino Guerra*) "uno e trino: letterato, cineasta, pittore, e sempre poeta" (one and trine: a man of letters, a filmmaker, a painter, yet always a poet), and it is the blending of storytelling, existentialist thinking, and pictorial vision that makes for the compassion, intensity, and strength in all Guerra's poetic work.

Tonino Guerra received official recognition when he won the Premio Argentario (for his novel *L'uomo parellelo* [Parallel Man, 1969]), followed by the Premio Friulano "Risit d'aur" (1984), the Premio Comisso (1986), and the Premio Pasolini (1988). Two documentaries about him were screened at the 1986 Venice Film Festival.

References:

Gianfranco Contini, "*Excursus* continuo su Tonino Guerra," introduction to Guerra's *I bu: Poesie romagnole* (Milan: Rizzoli, 1972), pp. 7–15;

Natalia Ginzburg, "Un poeta di paesi," *Stampa,* 29 October 1972;

Dante Isella, Postscript to Guerra's *Il viaggio* (Rimini: Maggioli, 1987), pp. 71–77;

Lingua, dialetto, poesia: Atti del Seminario popolare su Tonino Guerra e la poesia dialettale romagnola (Ravenna: Girasole, 1976);

Tonino Guerra (Rimini: Maggioli, 1985);

Rebecca West, "Tonino Guerra and the Space of the Screenwriter," *Annali d'Italianistica,* 6 (1988): 162–178.

Margherita Guidacci

(25 April 1921 – 19 June 1992)

Natalia Costa-Zalessow
San Francisco State University

BOOKS: *La sabbia e l'Angelo* (Florence: Vallecchi, 1946);

Morte del ricco (Florence: Vallecchi, 1954);

Giorno dei Santi (Milan: All'Insegna del Pesce d'Oro, 1957);

Paglia e polvere (Cittadella Veneta: Rebellato, 1961);

Un cammino incerto/Un chemin incertain, bilingual edition, translated by Arthur Praillet (Luxembourg: Cahiers d'Origine, 1970);

Neurosuite (Vicenza: Neri Pozza, 1970); ten poems translated by Marina La Palma as *Poems from Neurosuite* (Berkeley, Cal.: Kelsey St., 1975);

Terra senza orologi (Milan: Edizioni 32, 1973);

Quindici poesie e sette disegni, by Guidacci and Giuseppe Banchieri (Milan: Edizioni 32, 1973);

Studi su Eliot (Milan: Istituto Propaganda Libraria, 1975);

Taccuino slavo (Vicenza: Locusta, 1976);

Il vuoto e le forme (Quarto d'Altino: Rebellato, 1977);

Studi su poeti e narratori americani (Cagliari: EDES, 1978);

L'altare di Isenheim (Milan: Rusconi, 1980);

Brevi e lunghe poesie, edited by Brenno Bucciarelli (Vatican City: Libreria Editrice Vaticana, 1980);

L'orologio di Bologna (Florence: Città di Vita, 1981);

Inno alla gioia (Florence: Centro Internazionale del Libro, 1983);

La via crucis dell'umanità (Florence: Città di Vita, 1984);

Incontro con Margherita Guidacci: Antologia di poesia scelta dall'autrice (Scarperia: Cassa Rurale ed Artigiana del Mugello, 1986);

Liber fulguralis (Messina: Hobelix, 1986);

Poesie per poeti (Milan: Istituto Propaganda Libraria, 1987);

Una breve misura (Chieti: Vecchio Faggio, 1988);

Il buio e lo splendore (Milan: Garzanti, 1989); part 1 translated by Ruth Feldman as *A Book of Sibyls* (Boston: Rowan Tree, 1989).

Collection: *Poesie* (Milan: Rizzoli, 1965) – comprises *La sabbia e l'Angelo, Morte del ricco,* and *Giorno dei Santi.*

Edition in English: *Landscape With Ruins: Selected Poetry,* translated by Ruth Feldman (Detroit: Wayne State University Press, 1992).

OTHER: "Idea di una società cristiana," *Cronache Sociali* (November 1949);

Vello Salo, trans., *Poeti estoni,* edited by Guidacci (Rome: Abete, 1973; enlarged, 1975);

Marian Arkin and Barbara Shollar, eds., *Longman Anthology of World Literature by Women, 1875–1975,* includes two poems by Guidacci translated by Claire Siegel (New York & London: Longman, 1989), pp. 641–642.

TRANSLATIONS: John Donne, *Sermoni* (Florence: Libreria Editrice Fiorentina, 1946);

Max Beerbohm, *L'ipocrita beato* (Florence: Vallecchi, 1946);

Emily Dickinson, *Poesie* (Florence: Cya, 1947; bilingual edition, Milan: Rizzoli, 1979);

Sacre rappresentazioni inglesi (Florence: Libreria Editrice Fiorentina, 1950);

Emmanuel Mounier, *L'avventura cristiana* (Florence: Libreria Editrice Fiorentina, 1951);

George Gissing, *Sulla riva dello Jonio* (Bologna: Cappelli, 1957);

Tu Fu, *Desiderio di pace* (Milan: Scheiwiller, 1957);

Ezra Pound, *Patria mia* (Florence: Centro Internazionale del Libro, 1958);

Pound, *A lume spento,* translated by Guidacci, Salvatore Quasimodo, and Giuseppe Ungaretti (Milan: Scheiwiller, 1958);

Sophocles, *Le Trachinie* (Florence: Centro Internazionale del Libro, 1958);

Archibald MacLeish, *Quattro poesie* (Milan: Scheiwiller, 1958);

Antichi racconti cinesi (Bologna: Cappelli, 1959);

Jorge Guillén, *Federico in persona: Carteggio* (Milan: Scheiwiller, 1960);

Henry James, *Roderick Hudson* (Bologna: Cappelli, 1960);

Joseph Conrad, *Destino* (Milan: Bompiani, 1961);

Racconti popolari irlandesi (Bologna: Cappelli, 1961);

Dickinson, *Poesie e lettere* (Florence: Sansoni, 1961);

Mark Twain, *Vita sul Mississippi* (Rome: Opere Nuove, 1962);

T'ao Ch'ien (T'ao Yüan-ming), *Poema per la bellezza della sua donna* (Milan: Scheiwiller, 1962); republished as *Poema d'amore* (Milan: Scheiwiller, 1970);

Conrad, *Racconti ascoltati; Ultimi saggi* (Milan: Bompiani, 1963);

Edith Sitwell, *Autobiografia* (Milan: Rizzoli, 1968);

Mao Tse-tung, *Quattro poesie,* edited by Guidacci and Giovanni Giudici (Milan: Scheiwiller, 1971);

Christopher Smart, *Inno a David e altre poesie* (Turin: Einaudi, 1975);

John Paul II, *Pietra di luce* (Vatican City: Libreria Editrice Vaticana, 1979);

John Paul II, *Il sapore del pane: Poesie,* translated by Guidacci and Alekandra Kurczab (Vatican City: Libreria Editrice Vaticana, 1979);

Due antichi poeti cinesi (Milan: Scheiwiller, 1980);

Padraig J. Daly, *Dall'orlo marino del mondo* (Vatican City: Libreria Editrice Vaticana, 1981);

John Paul II, *Giobbe ed altri inediti: Un dramma e sei poesie,* translated by Guidacci and Kurczab (Vatican City: Libreria Editrice Vaticana, 1982);

Elizabeth Bishop, *L'arte di perdere,* bilingual edition (Milan: Rusconi, 1982);

Jessica Powers, *Luogo di splendore: Poesie* (Vatican City: Libreria Editrice Vaticana, 1982);

Sarah Orne Jewett, *Lady Ferry e altri racconti* (Milan: Donne, 1982);

Friedebert Tuglas, *Ultimo addio; Popi e Huhuu; Il cerchio d'oro: Un romanzo breve e due racconti,* translated by Guidacci, Vello Salo, and Lorenzo Pinna (Milan: Jaca, 1983);

Sitwell, *Una vita protetta* (Milan: SE, 1989).

Margherita Guidacci circa 1960

Margherita Guidacci was one of the first among the poets of postwar Italy to abandon the hermetic tradition and find her own path. She did not seek a magic sound in cryptic words but preferred to use words for their concrete value in order to express an idea in finely structured verses. Her inspiration was existentialist and deeply religious. Yet her poems are not prayers in the old tradition; they simply include profound sentiments that derive from a search for regeneration, for a resurrection from death. Guidacci saw life as a passage and death as a means toward resurrection. Therefore all desolation and pain lead to redemption. In her poetry, water is either the nourishing element of life or oblivion, the sea is a means of communicating with the cosmos and with eternity, and sand and dust, elements that change shape constantly like creativity, are symbolic of human life. The predominant theme of death was treated by Guidacci with many variations. At the beginning her intonation was impersonal, but progressively she became more personal and autobiographical, as reflected in the use of the first person, though she frequently switched to a collective concept. The result is a gripping poetry expressed in clear and simple images that capture the constant struggle to comprehend life and death. Guidacci's contribution to Italian poetry is fully recognized by literary critics. Her work is included in major Italian anthologies and reference works, and she received the following prizes: Le Grazie (1948), Carducci (1957), Cervia (1965), Ceppo (1971), Gabicce (1974), Lerici (1975), Scanno (1976), Biella (1978), Pontano (1980), Silvi (1981), Tagliacozzo (1983), and Basilicata (1988).

Guidacci was born in Florence on 25 April 1921 of a family originally from Scarperia, Tuscany, and received all her education in her native city. She graduated from the classical Lycée Michelangelo and obtained her degree in literature from the University of Florence in 1943 with a thesis on the poetry of Giuseppe Ungaretti, written under the guidance of Professor Giuseppe De Robertis. Subsequently she took up the study of English, which shaped her future, for she became a translator of works by English and American writers, as well as an instructor of Anglo-American literature and English.

In 1949 she married the writer and sociologist Luca Pinna and moved with him to Rome, where she lived until her death on 19 June 1992. She had three children: Lorenzo, Antonio, and Elisa.

Guidacci had started teaching in 1947, but her career was mainly carried out in Rome, where she received tenure in 1954 as a professor in the state lycée. Her scholarly work as a specialist in English literature was recognized in 1972 through the granting of a *libera docenza* (license to teach at a university). She then taught at the University of Macerata from 1973 to 1982 and subsequently at the Istituto Universitario di Magistero Maria Assunta in Rome.

Guidacci was an only child who had a solitary childhood, saddened by the illnesses and deaths of persons dear to her — events that influenced her as a poet. At an early age she experimented with writing but then interrupted all creative activities until she became a university student. Her first book of verse, *La sabbia e l'Angelo* (The Sand and the Angel, 1946), written in 1945 in only a few days, was, according to her, a result of the released psychological tension that had accumulated in her during the war years and which resulted in a song of communication with the dead. Her epigraphic intonation is frequently based on a single image.

La sabbia e l'Angelo is divided into three parts: "Meditazioni e sentenze" (Meditations and Maxims), "Epitaffi" (Epitaphs), and "La sabbia e l'Angelo." Guidacci works mainly with symbols centered on the impossibility of penetrating the mysteries of the world, as in the poem "Meditazioni XV":

Il mondo a te offerto per similitudine facilmente
    decifrare tu credi.
Tu dici: "Le sabbie del tempo" ed "il vento dell'anima"
    e "la pallida erba
Della memoria." Ma come in se stesse
Vivano queste cose, e sabbia ed erba e vento,
Forse solo gli amanti intendono ed i morti.

(The world, offered to you in simile, is easy, you be-
    lieve, to decipher.
You say: "The sands of time" and "the wind of the
    soul" and "the pale grass
Of memory." But how, in themselves, do they live,
These things, and sand and grass and wind,
Perhaps lovers alone, and the dead, understand.)
                                        – translation by Claire Siegel

Death, the main leitmotiv, is treated almost in a baroque way, for it is everywhere and perpetual. Every death contains all deaths, those of animals, individual human beings, or entire nations. Her thoughts on war casualties form the basis of this collection of poems.

In 1948 Guidacci received recognition through the granting of the Grazie Prize (which she shared with the poet Sandro Penna) for a group of unpublished poems. Of the two poems eventually published in Giacinto Spagnoletti's anthology *Poeti del Novecento* (Twentieth-Century Poets, 1952), "La conchiglia" (The Shell) is the more notable. Guidacci gives a variant to an old theme by having the shell speak directly to the casual passerby who picks it up and places it against his ear. The mysterious murmur is the shell's lament for the sea it lost when a storm beached the shell.

During the period from 1945 to 1951 Guidacci translated John Donne's *Sermons* (1946), Max Beerbohm's *The Happy Hypocrite* (1946), Emily Dickinson's poems (*Poesie,* 1947), some English mystery plays (*Sacre rappresentazioni inglesi,* 1950), and Emmanuel Mounier's *L'affrontement chrétien* (The Spoils of the Violent, 1951). The choice of these authors indicates her particular literary preferences and points to the influences on her poetry. She also wrote an article, "Idea di una società cristiana" (An Idea of a Christian Society), which appeared in *Cronache Sociali* (November 1949).

Morte del ricco (Death of the Rich Man, 1954), was written between 1951 and 1953. It was defined by Guidacci as an oratorio based on the parable of the rich man and Lazarus (Luke 16: 19–31), which is the subject of many European mystery plays from the thirteenth to the sixteenth century. The structure of the poem, with a prologue by Guidacci and an epilogue supposedly by Death, recalls the pattern of these Christian plays, but Guidacci's oratorio, nevertheless, is an original work. The tragic content reflects a concern for the perennial injustice that people inflict on others, an injustice that cannot be erased by death.

Giorno dei Santi (All Saints' Day, 1957) consists of two separate collections having a common denominator. The first, "Pensieri in riva al mare" (Thoughts on the Seashore), comprises sixteen poems in which the sea and the shores repeatedly appear. Guidacci elaborates on the perennial change that all things must undergo. Human struggles come and go, cities and entire civilizations disappear without a trace, and life pulsates but must end in death. These existential and religious themes are expressed through the symbolism of the sea that does not have a memory, for it erases every trace along its shores and on its waters.

The second part of *Giorno dei Santi,* from which the title of the collection is derived, is dedicated to the month of the dead. The first of November is All Saints' Day, dedicated to all Christian martyrs, and 2 November is All Souls' Day, traditionally when Catholics go visit cemeteries. Moreover, late fall, when the last leaves are falling and everything is turning gray, leads one's thoughts toward death:

Guidacci circa 1980

> E arduo
> Oggi pensare al Paradiso; tutto
> Ci riconduce e prostra sulla terra.
> Occorre troppa fede a superare
> L'alta barriera di tristezza. Facile
> Sarà invece domani, nella scia
> D'una stagione di disfacimento,
> Ricordare la fine d'ogni carne.
>
> (It is hard
> To think of Paradise today; everything
> Leads us to and prostrates us upon the earth.
> It takes too much faith to overcome
> The high barrier of sadness. Instead
> It will be easy tomorrow, in the trail
> Of a season of decay,
> To recall the end of all flesh.)

Although liturgical in origin, the poems of this section fuse a personal, tender emotion with the cosmic mystery of life and death. While November is sym-

bolic of death, December brings one back to life and hope through the birth of Christ, as stated in poem 3: "E questa / La fine, non Dicembre coi suoi cieli / Di cristallo, la stella dell'Oriente / E gli uomini in ginocchio ad adorare / Il Fanciullo" (This is / The end, not December with crystal / Skies, the Star of East / And men kneeling to adore / The Child). In poem 6 mothers are seen to experience a special trepidation when they give birth to children and see the mystery of life unfold.

Guidacci's subsequent book of verse, *Paglia e polvere* (Straw and Dust, 1961), cannot be considered a poetic continuation, for it mainly includes poems written earlier that had remained unpublished; only a very few had appeared in anthologies and periodicals. The first group, "La conchiglia e altri versi" (The Shell and Other Poems), was composed in 1945 and 1946. The second group, "Consigli a un giovane poeta" (Advice to a Young Poet); the third, "Polvere" (Dust); and the fourth, "In Irlanda" (In Ireland), were written in 1947; the fifth group, "Chiaroscuro," from 1948 to 1951; the sixth group, "Un paniere di avanzi" (A Basket Full of Leftovers), from 1952 to 1953; the seventh group, "Esterni" (Outside), in 1954; and the tenth and last group, "Prime" (First Poems), from 1934 to 1940. Only part of the eighth group, "Varie" (Various) — written from 1955 to 1960 — and the five poems of the ninth group, "Le Ceneri, L'eclisse" (Ash Wednesday, The Eclipse), written in 1961, can be considered new compositions. However, all the poems, including the early ones, contain a nucleus of the themes that Guidacci developed in her mature work.

The decade from 1957 to 1967, though not rich creatively, was an intense period for her work on translations, some of which reflect her personal preferences. Guidacci translated from English, under the title *Desiderio di pace* (Desire for Peace, 1957), compositions of the great Chinese eighth-century poet Tu Fu, who laments the terrible consequences of war that mercilessly crushed his people, though he does not lose all hope of a future palingenesis. Her translations of Anglo-American literary works include four poems by Archibald MacLeish (*Quattro poesie*, 1958) and Dickinson's poems and letters (*Poesie e lettere*, 1961).

A new creative intensity for Guidacci was marked by a bilingual (Italian and French) edition of eleven poems, *Un cammino incerto* (An Uncertain Path, 1970). Prevailing existential tensions range from fervor to disappointment and from uncertainty to dismay, only to be focused in a genuine religious anxiety in search of purity, truth, and the absolute. Guidacci's lyric style is down to the very essential, so that the soul becomes almost transparent, and the images are projected in negative form: "Sopra quanti miracoli / getta luce / quello che non avviene!" (On how many miracles / throws light / that which does not occur!). Symbolic objects abound: "Alla pietra / si addice la durezza ... / Ma ogni volo trafitto / fa trasalire l'anima" (Hardness / is characteristic of rocks ... / But each pierced flight / makes the soul startle).

Between September 1958 and June 1969 Guidacci had worked on a series of poems she published under the title *Neurosuite* (1970). The compositions, partially autobiographical, are exceptional not only as testimony to the anxiety experienced by the mentally ill but also for the effective depiction of their state of being. She creates a kind of grandiose, impressive X ray of the human psyche, in its conscious and unconscious moments. Alienation and complete distortion are the norm in a technologi-

cally advanced world that gives only an illusionary and material well-being, behind which traumas consistently lurk. The book's dedication, "a quanti conobbero le acque oscure / agli scampati ai sommersi" (to all those who experienced the dark waters / to those who made it or went under), gives the impression of a universe consisting of chaos but striving toward clarity. The opening poem, "Nero con movimento" (Black with Movement), captures the darkness and horror that oppress the mentally ill. Just what is a mental clinic — the last house of the living or the first of the dead? It is a place where thoughts are scattered, visions are confused, and people do not feel safe. Even the doctors assume the aspect of Minos, Dante's infernal judge, as they assign the patients to their rooms, where they will suffer hellish tortures. The evening injection brings temporary peace, but the demons come back at dawn. There is no communication with the doctors, for they do not fully grasp the visions of the mentally ill who are alienated by their clinical jargon; the ill are torn between the desire to have visitors and see them depart, unable to speak to them yet wanting to call them back as soon as the door closes. Soul and body no longer seem to belong to the individual who keeps asking where and who she is. While tests are done, the patients rebel, not wanting to give up parts of their souls. But the torments go on. Those who return home have the feeling that they are no longer wanted. Yet all the problems are based on fear, a fear that comes from within and cannot be overcome, for there is nothing physical to which one can cling. This collection of poems is perhaps Guidacci's most original and modern work. She refuses to give up part of her inner soul and become just like the others, as declared in the poem "Non voglio" (I Do Not Want):

> Sono un poeta: una farfalla, un essere
> delicato, con ali.
> Se le strappate, mi torcerò sulla terra,
> ma non per questo potrò diventare
> una lieta e disciplinata formica.
>
> (I am a poet: a butterfly, a being
> delicate, with wings.
> If you tear them out, I'll roll on the ground,
> but I won't be able to turn
> into a happy and disciplined ant.)

Terra senza orologi (Land Without Clocks, 1973) includes fourteen new poems and a longer composition titled "Dopo il terremoto" (After the Earthquake). Guidacci's style continues to be dramatic and rapid, almost epigraphic but always powerful. She focuses on the impossibility of coexistence between ethics and beauty, contemplated explicitly through the image of three white bellflowers she observed in a 1920 painting by Paul Klee.

Taccuino slavo (Slavic Notebook, 1976) consists of twenty poems written as a result of two visits to Croatia, in 1972 and 1973, and it is dedicated to Guidacci's friends in Zagreb. The compositions are grouped under five headings: "Tre immagini dai Laghi di Plitvice" (Three Images from the Plitvice Lakes), "Pittori croati" (Croatian Painters), "In margine a un convegno" (In Margins at a Convention), "Canto dei quattro elementi" (Song of the Four Elements), and "Congedo" (Leave-taking). In the first section she does not describe the actual beauty of the sixteen terraced lakes (one of the natural wonders of Croatia), which are connected by cascades, but rather the silence of these lakes that is reminiscent of death, in contrast to their feeding river, the Korana, which runs through populated valleys and towns, symbolic of life. Similarly the painters chosen are those who depict silence and sadness in their works, frequently reflecting their own tragic lives. The rest of the poems are of a lighter tone, but the concluding poem is a glorification of an inner liberty that knows no bounds:

gli uccelli gridano la mia libertà:
i loro voli deridono la frontiera
esattamente come fa il mio cuore.

(birds shriek my liberty:
their flights deride frontiers
just as my heart does.)

Il vuoto e le forme (Emptiness and Shapes, 1977) comprises thirty-eight poems grouped under the headings "Il vuoto e le forme," "Il muro e il grido" (The Wall and the Cry), "La vecchiaia e dintorni" (Old Age and Surroundings), "Morte senza morte" (Death Without Death), "Tre poesie della fine" (Three Poems at Year's End), and "Resta la pace" (Peace Remains). The sources of inspiration are diverse. In a poem dedicated to the English composer Reginald Smith Brindle, who himself was inspired by her verses, Guidacci muses on the transformation of words into music and music into words. Two other poems are based on two sculptures by Henry Moore. The four poems of "Il muro e il grido" reflect the senseless violence in Chile at the downfall of Salvador Allende Gossens. One composition from the last part is written in English and evokes the accidental death in 1973 of two young mountain climbers, an Englishman and an Irishman, in the Bolivian Andes.

Guidacci's collections from the mid to late 1970s include references to artworks, historical events, heroic actions, and personal travel experiences, which enriched her poetic horizon but did not significantly intensify her expressive force, but the volume *L'altare di Isenheim* (The Isenheim Altar, 1980) is her best work after *Neurosuite*. The first part of the collection, from which the title is derived, is a series of meditations on the triptych of that name painted by the German Renaissance master Matthias Grünewald. In the first panel, death is reflected in the oversize figure of the crucified Christ surrounded by the lamenting Mary, Saint John the Evangelist, and Mary Magdalene on the left side, and by Saint John the Baptist with a symbolic lamb on the right side. Powerful and overwhelming with an atmosphere of gloom achieved through the use of dark colors and twisted bodies, it is in striking contrast to the second panel – a luminous, joyous depiction of the Annunciation, the Nativity, and the Resurrection. The third panel depicts the temptation of Saint Anthony and his visit to Saint Paul the Hermit. Grünewald and his contrasting depiction of temporal versus eternal life, which had previously inspired composer Paul Hindemith, gave Guidacci an example in the figurative arts that perfectly corresponded to her own concept of life, its beginning and its end, its perpetual cycle. The crucified Christ becomes the Cartesian axis of life and death, while in the figures surrounding him is expressed all human suffering, but salvation is near, indicated through the symbolic Lamb of God.

The second and final part of the volume, "Un addio" (A Farewell), comprises poems written after the death of her husband, whose absence creates a void still felt in their house. He was called to a mysterious place, she says in the poems, and left in such a hurry that he did not even have time to say goodbye. The conclusion to the collection is appropriately a poem on birth, which renews the cycle of life.

Guidacci's next book, *Brevi e lunghe poesie* (Short and Long Poems, 1980), presents a selection of thirty poems, all taken from previously published collections. The compositions all have a religious content, encompass a thirty-year period of poetic creation (1945–1975), and illustrate her consistent return to the theme that in life's cycle there is evidence of God's mystery.

The twelve poems of the collection *L'orologio di Bologna* (The Clock of Bologna, 1981) are dedicated to the memory of the victims of the terrorist bomb that exploded in the Bolognese railroad station on the morning of 2 August 1980. Three months later

Guidacci was in Bologna. As she writes in the introductory note, she woke on 3 November puzzled by a strange silence. It was snowing. Gazing from the window, she thought of the concluding words of James Joyce's story "The Dead" (in *Dubliners,* 1914), where he writes that snow was falling "upon all the living and the dead," which made her decide to write a requiem for those who had perished in the horrible blast at the station. Her model was the liturgy of the Holy Week, but the result is her own original interpretation of holy texts and contemporary reality. Time has stopped on the clock, and the travelers have departed for another destination. Death was brought upon innocent people through violence that has continued to be perpetrated ever since Cain raised his hand over Abel, bringing about the first death on earth. The disfigured bodies of the passengers cannot be comprehended by the living, who clamor for justice but can only intone a lamentation, because evil people strike openly and with impunity. But to lose consciousness of evil is another evil. The poems of this collection are a lament not only for the victims at Bologna but for all the victims of violence.

Guidacci excuses herself in a note for having entitled her next collection *Inno alla gioia* (Hymn to Joy, 1983), which so obviously recalls the compositions by Friedrich Schiller and Ludwig van Beethoven, but it seemed to her the only appropriate name for her poems that glorify the joy of life. The introductory poem on love was written in 1945 and serves as a prelude, while all others are new compositions in which the speaker exalts with nature — each growing leaf or blade of grass, seeking the sun, represents life. The universe is populated by stars, birds, insects, shells, and waters of the seas and rivers. Just as she had previously depicted the shell narrating its own story, Guidacci in the poem "Supernova" has a star describe its glowing splendor that will come to an end, but its glorious existence is part of a predestined universe in which love is eternal joy. Even a sole moment of happiness can fulfill a whole life. The speaker steps out of night with its darkness and anguish to partake of the newly discovered sun through a renewed affection, a perfect communion of souls.

In *La via crucis dell'umanità* (The Stations of the Cross of Humanity, 1984) Guidacci again turned to the figurative arts for inspiration, with poems based on the bas-reliefs of Leonardo Rosito. *Incontro con*

Margherita Guidacci (Encounter with Margherita Guidacci, 1986) is made up of her personal selections from her previous books of poetry.

The collection *Poesie per poeti* (Poems for Poets, 1987) contains compositions written in homage not only to contemporaries such as Carlo Betocchi, Febo Delfi, and Jorge Guillén but also to poets of the past, such as William Blake and Ugo Foscolo. The most interesting is the last poem, dedicated to Foscolo and subtitled "Meditazione in Santa Croce" (Meditation in Santa Croce), where Guidacci contemplates Foscolo's tomb and thinks of his ode *I sepolcri* (On Sepulchres, 1807), only to pass on to Hamlet's comments on poor Yorick. But as she looks up to the light pouring down into the church through the stained glass windows, she perceives a parallel between the various small pieces of glass, which contribute to make a harmonious whole, and individual human beings who vibrate with all others in a fraternal concert in a place assigned to them by a superior craftsman.

This approach is also evident in *Il buio e lo splendore* (Darkness and Splendor, 1989), which was published a year after *Una breve misura* (A Brief Measure), poems in the haiku style of short, classical Japanese compositions. The first of the three parts of *Il buio e lo splendore,* titled "Sibyllae," was translated into English by Ruth Feldman as *A Book of Sibyls* (1989). The other two parts are "Rileggendo Ovidio" (Rereading Ovid) and "Il porgitore di Stelle" (The Star Pointer), based on an Etruscan legend. The meditations on ancient myths, especially the ones about the ten sibyls — guardians of enigmas associated with a primitive cult of the earth and its vital force — are rendered into harmonious verse, full of intense, luminous images. The sibyls do not provide answers; they only "read" what is already written in nature:

> Ma quella che tu chiedi, e che tu chiami
> la mia risposta, non è mia, e neppure
> è una risposta. E la vita che parla
> in ogni cosa viva, mentre passa
> verso la morte.
>
> (But what you ask — and what you call
> my answer — is not mine, and is not even
> an answer. It is life that speaks
> in every living thing, while it proceeds
> toward death.)
>   — translation by Ruth Feldman

The poems of *Il buio e lo splendore,* intellectually challenging, tie not only the poet but also the reader to the timeless classical tradition, the base of Western civilization that helped Guidacci contemplate life and death with great serenity.

Guidacci's poetry rests on a solid cultural background. She frequently indicated in notes the literary or artistic source of her inspirations, from classical authors to modern times, from Italian to Anglo-American writers, and from the Bible to Chinese literature. Margherita Guidacci remained faithful to her literary ideal, even if it did not correspond to the general tendencies of her contemporaries. Conscious of the fact that poetry is no longer often considered the best way of communicating with others, she nevertheless neither compromised nor tried to become popular by catering to fashionable trends.

Interviews:

"La pietra e l'acqua: Magici emblemi della poesia di Margherita Guidacci," *Uomini e Libri,* 59 (1976): 33–34;

"La poesia non ha pace finché non ha trovato l'espressione unica e insostituibile," *Uomini e Libri,* 79 (1980): 45.

References:

Elio Filippo Accrocca, *Ritratti su misura di scrittori italiani* (Venice: Sodalizio del Libro, 1966), pp. 225–226;

Luigi Baldacci, "Parole sull'acqua: Preghiere in versi di una moderna Ofelia," *Corriere della Sera,* 20 June 1992;

Renzo Barsacchi, "Omaggio a Margherita Guidacci," *Città di Vita,* 45, no. 4 (1990): 311–318;

Donna Beckage, "Sea Imagery in Margherita Guidacci's Poetry," *Modern Poetry Studies,* 5 (1974): 145–156;

Gianpaolo Biasin, "Diario di una poetessa inquieta," Forum Italicum, 5, no. 3 (1971): 456–458;

Jean Grasso Fitzpatrick, "Margherita Guidacci's 'Feroce Tesoro,' " *Forum Italicum,* 12, no. 3 (1978): 307–323;

Margherita Harwell, "La poesia di Margherita Guidacci: Origine e sviluppo," *Annali d'Italianistica,* 7 (1989): 354–381.

Giuseppe Jovine
(20 November 1922 –   )

Luigi Bonaffini
Brooklyn College, City University of New York

BOOKS: *La poesia di Albino Pierro* (Rome: Nuovo Cracas, 1965);

Lu pavone (Bari: Adriatrica, 1970; revised and enlarged edition, Campobasso: Enne, 1983);

La luna e la montagna (Bari: Adriatrica, 1972);

Tra il Biferno e la Moscova (Rome: Cartia, 1975);

Benedetti Molisani (Campobasso: Enne, 1979);

La sdrenga (Campobasso: Enne, 1990);

Cento proverbi di Castelluccio Acquaborrana (Campobasso: Enne, 1991);

Chi sa se passa u' Patraterne (Rome: Ventaglio, 1992).

OTHER: "L'oboe prigioniero," *Il Paese* (12 November 1954);

Marcello Scarano e la sua pittura, edited by Jovine and Alberindo Grimani (Campobasso: Scarano, 1986).

Giuseppe Jovine, poet, short-story writer, journalist, politician, and literary and social critic, has emerged, after his older cousin Francesco Jovine and the poet Eugenio Cirese, as one of the leading writers and intellectuals of the region of Molise. As with his two predecessors, at the heart of his work is an abiding concern for the social, economic, and political problems confronting his relatively less-developed native region in a world dominated by mass communication and extremely rapid changes at all levels of the social spectrum. Even more pronounced is his political commitment, both in his literary production and in his intense activity as a journalist and lecturer, on the side of social reform and outspokenly against a political class that in his view is subservient to a widespread patronage system and insensitive to real economic and social needs. Therefore his use of dialect in his book of poetry *Lu pavone* (The Peacock, 1970) and in subsequent works of fiction is indicative of a precise literary stand within the context of regional and national literature, and it is grounded on a clear ideological substratum, a profound awareness of the potential for subversion and the complex symbiotic relationship of poetry with Italian language and society. As in Cirese's poems, dialect, with its deep-rooted and rich world of experiences, represents the inalienable, fundamental core of most of Jovine's writings.

Jovine was born on 20 November 1922 in Castelmauro, a small town in Molise, in an old ducal palace bought by his ancestors from the dukes of Canzano. His mother, Adele Gallina Jovine, came from Montecilfone, a descendant of the Albanian colonists who settled in Italy in the sixteenth century. A woman with a fifth-grade education, she was intelligent and sensitive, and remained dynamic and exuberant until her death (at the age of ninety) in 1974. Jovine's father, Carlo, was from Castelmauro and was a versatile man whose special interests were music and Florentine history, which he studied assiduously. He could play several instruments, but his favorite was an oboe, which he always kept locked in its case, never allowing his son to touch it. Jovine reminisces about this in "L'oboe prigioniero" (The Captive Oboe), an article in *Il Paese* (12 November 1954), in which he sees the instrument as a symbol for his father, who remained a prisoner within the walls of his house while dreaming of a different life. Jovine's father was also active in local politics, and once, when both he, a Christian Democrat, and his son, a Communist, were scheduled to give speeches on the same evening, he withdrew to avoid the possibility of a conflict. He died of cancer in 1954.

At age eleven Giuseppe Jovine was sent to study in the Salesian Institute in Macerata, where he stayed for five years. There, at the age of sixteen, he wrote his first article, which was published in a student review. The article, on Gabriele D'Annunzio's *Contemplazione della morte* (Contemplation of Death, 1912), marked the beginning of a lifelong interest in the poet from Abruzzi. In 1938 Jovine went to Chieti to continue his studies in the Liceo Classico. During this time he decided to run away with a friend to join a battalion bound for Albania,

Giuseppe Jovine, with the actress Giuliana Lojodice, presenting a copy of his Tra il Biferno e la Moscova *to the Croce Library in Rome, 1975 (photograph by Mollica)*

but he was stopped by a colonel who noticed that the boys' military disguise did not include regulation trousers. Jovine then attended the University of Florence; in his third year he joined the army with the university battalions and was stationed in the Brennero area and then in Tuscany until the fall of Benito Mussolini in 1945. During Jovine's university years he began to write his first poems, which he published in student periodicals, and critical essays, which appeared in *Gioventù*, a student publication at the University of Naples. At the University of Florence, Jovine studied with Giorgio Pasquali, the Greek scholar and author of *Pagine Stravaganti* (Extravagant Pages, 1933), and with Giuseppe De Robertis, whose teachings and formalist critical approach left a lasting mark on Jovine's process of analysis, tending toward a very close reading of the text but rejecting a strictly formalist procedure. Jovine is often critical of modern methodologies such as structuralism and deconstructionism, which in his view can come dan-

gerously close to a belated positivism; the critic must go beyond the purely linguistic phenomenon and, in the Marxist tradition, consider the text in its complex, dynamic interplay with the social context that generated it.

Toward the end of World War II, with Castelmauro under Nazi occupation, the twenty-two-year-old Jovine was named commissario prefettizio, which after the fall of Mussolini was the equivalent of the office of mayor. Since in Molise there was no real war of resistance, Jovine helped to organize one of the liberation corps, formed in every town during the partisan struggle. Jovine's group made possible the escape of several English prisoners, and he gave instructions to clear the mines the Germans had placed under the bridge leading out of town. The attempt failed, however, as the man in charge of the operation was spotted by the Germans and forced to flee. (This episode appears in one of the stories of *La luna e la montagna* [The Moon and the Mountain, 1972]). In 1948 Jovine passed a qualifying examination for a teaching position as a secondary-school teacher and moved to Rome, where he began teaching philosophy, Italian, and Latin in various secondary schools. In 1953 he married Franca Forlivesi; they have two children – Carlo and Lucia. Jovine taught from 1948 to 1973, when he decided to stop teaching because the constraints of a rigid humanistic education, which at the time still did not go beyond nineteenth-century ideas, prevented him from teaching modern poetry and contemporary literature and from carrying out a program he felt could be of real interest to his students. He became instead a secondary-school principal.

Jovine's conciliatory stance between Christian and communist thought, and between idealism and Marxism, pointing to a necessary convergence of historical and literary phenomena, is evident in his first book, *La poesia di Albino Pierro* (The Poetry of Albino Pierro, 1965). Jovine balances a penetrating textual analysis of Pierro's poetry with an effort to place it within a historical and literary framework, from its archaic and natural Christianity to Pierro's longing for the fabulous baronial world of the Mezzogiorno. In Pierro, Jovine discovered a contrast between objectivity and a personal religious introversion, which reflects on an individual level the psychological conflict of the people of southern Italy: "la storia culturale di Pierro è un po' la storia culturale di tutta la borghesia italiana di formazione cattolico-idealistica" (Pierro's cultural history is in a way the cultural history of the whole Italian middle class with a Catholic-idealist background), while his complex spiritual drama is rooted in the convergence of a nineteenth-century romantic-philological heritage and twentieth-century ideological motivations. While recognizing Pierro's faithfulness to his own poetic universe – in which his painful condition as a spiritual exile led to a near obsession with his childhood and his native region, and his compassion for others was nourished by his secret vocation for sorrow and human redemption – Jovine is critical of Pierro's occasionally excessive artistic detachment.

The multiplicity of Jovine's personal, literary, and ideological concerns converge and come sharply into focus in *Lu pavone*, the product of his long meditation on the integration and interrelationship between dominant and subordinate cultures, reflected in the most immediate and perceptible way in the complex question of language and its social implications, already touched on in his book on Pierro. Pierro, who for a while was a colleague of Jovine, is one of the foremost dialect poets in Italy,

and his poetry has been a catalyzing agent for several southern poets. The contact with Pierro's poetry was for Jovine a decisive turning point in his reflections on dialect and its wide and profound ramifications. Jovine argues that all contemporary dialect poetry is characterized by the attempt to modernize the dialect and to recover its existential roots at the psychological as well as emotional level. Without the dialectic relationship between hegemonic culture and subordinate peasant culture, much modern poetry would be unexplainable because the question of the "popular" as an emblem of linguistic subordination has a more complex articulation than is suspected. The popular is not only the realm of pathetic improvisation, superstition, and romantic irrationality but also the place of an autonomous cultural reelaboration; on the level of apparent diversionary and escapist folklore, one finds the authenticity of the so-called peasant culture, which everyone, whether dominant or subordinate, carries within oneself and in all forms of behavior, including artistic forms. For this reason Lucania and Molise, for example, cannot be confined in an area but are alive in everyone. The literary production in dialect, just as the production in standard Italian, is always an operation of cultural montage, which must aim at the preservation of the dialectal core of the poetic material but also at the assimilation, detectable in all great dialect poets, of "cultured" linguistic forms, which must, however, be readable in a dialectal key, without intellectual excesses or arbitrary literary ornateness. This Gramscian view of peasant culture as an all-encompassing moral universe, existing regardless of national or ethnic origin, is at the heart of Jovine's literary and ideological life, and it clearly precludes any reductive, paternalistic approach, literary or otherwise, to that culture or its language.

Writing dialect poetry is a critical, far-reaching process of cultural mediation, requiring constant vigilance and control, at the service of a strategy of self-limitation, adopted with success by Jovine's immediate literary predecessor Cirese and by Jovine himself in *Lu pavone*, in which the poetic persona rises from within a precisely defined cultural and linguistic universe without ever going beyond it. Yet within this well-defined world Jovine's language moves, as Tullio De Mauro points out in his preface to the book, in the most diverse directions, from satirical representation and vivid realism, to irony, to lyrical dream, to hope. The image of the peacock in the title poem, for example, is emblematic of the power of poetic transfiguration, through which the experience of the war unfolds as a dream:

> E passata la guerra,
> 'nu sunne 'ntruvedate
> che nun sacce areccuntà:
> ghianche e nire, virde e gialle,
> Marucchine e Merecane
> prutestante e mussurmane! . . .
> Ieva guerra o carnevale?
> Ieva guerra, Miserè!
> Mò tu m'a sapèddice, Miserè,
> pecchè de tutte quille terramote
> quille pavune sule m'arecorde
> ncopp'a cchella costa assulagnata,
> c'alluccava e faceia la rota
> com a 'nu ventaglie arrecamate
> mmane a 'na bella femmena affatata
> o 'na signora de lu tiempe antiche . . .

> (The war is over,
> a murky dream
> I do not know how to tell:
> white and black, green and yellow,
> Moroccans and Americans
> Protestants and Moslems! . . .
> Was it a war or a carnival?
> It was war, Miserè!
> But now you have to tell me why, Miserè,
> from all that turmoil
> I only remember that peacock
> on that sun-swept hillside,
> crying out and spreading its tail
> like an embroidered fan
> in the hand of a beautiful enchantress
> or a lady from days gone by . . .)[.]

The realism of the peacock's cry, an image of sorrow, is not always redeemed by a healing, cathartic process. In "Sò le tre nu palazze" (It Is Three O'Clock in the Building) every word becomes a cry of pain: "e nu viche ogne parola / è nu taluorne de malate / o nu llucche ammizz'a la nevefra") (and in the alley every word / is the moan of someone sick / or a cry in the middle of a snowstorm). This recurrent theme of suffering, with its all-pervasive death imagery, is often embodied by the most beautiful or fragile creatures, like the peacock, or the sparrow in "La tagliola" (The Trap):

> 'Mbaccia a lu fuche dormene le gatte;
> scrocchiene ciocche e ceppe allegre allegre.
> 'Ncopp'a la neve senza 'na pedata
> nu passarielle stritte 'na tagliola
> a vocca aperta sbatte e scennecheia.

> (The cats are all asleep before the fire;
> the log and firewood crackle cheerily.
> On the snow without footprints
> a sparrow gripped in a trap
> thrashes and flaps his wings with his mouth gaping.)

The representation of all suffering through a similar split image reaches its greatest lyric intensity in one of the best poems of the book, "Quanta volte 'ei lassate mamma sola!" (How Many Times I Left My Mother All Alone!):

> Pù partive!
> E mamma,
> nu cellucce 'mpazzute tra le mure
> ca n'artrova la via pe lu ciele,
> sbatteia le scenne a la ventura
> e zitta zitta z'abbiava
> pe chille stanze spicce
> ca parevane cisterne.

> (Then I would leave!
> And my mother,
> a bird gone mad inside the walls
> who cannot find the way to the sky,
> would beat her wings every which way
> and very silently set out
> through those empty rooms
> that looked like cisterns.)

In Jovine's memorial recovery of a slowly disintegrating world, death itself is a constant but variously modulated presence. It can become almost a playful game, even in a concentration camp, as in the poem "La morte è na pazziella de quatrare" (Death Is a Children's Game). The frequent funerals, the faces of long-forgotten friends suddenly surfacing, the wind, the snowstorms, the many memorable townspeople, a father's ties, the fairs, the sound of a boy's "cirche de fierre" (iron hoop) bouncing and singing like a bell, the moon leaving a white pearl of snow on the dresser, the sky like "'Na cuncarella spiccia, 'na chitarra! / Cuscè te fischiene le recchie" (An empty seashell, a guitar! / To make your ears whistle) — all are the objects of a redemptive memory celebrating the boundless renewability of life in the face of death.

What sets Jovine apart from other dialect poets from Molise, Cirese in particular, is the richness and versatility of his poetic language, which is capable of delicate nuances and subtle effects, yet which frequently breaks into a grating, bristling realism, guaranteeing a strict adherence to a determined linguistic (and ethical) universe. This jarring phonic density, uncommon among dialect poets but occasionally present in the work of Pierro, is probably the most distinctive feature of Jovine's dialect poetry and, as the critic Francesco D'Episcopo proposes, can be considered the anthropological result

Jovine at a 1980 writers' meeting in Rome (photograph by Mollica)

of a continuous representation of thought and feeling, of a physical sense of being. From detailed descriptions to the remake of ancient folk poems, to the humorously shocking, expressionistic dinner of a hungry old marquise, to the havoc wreaked by the wind in "Aria roscia" (Red Air): "atturcina la munnezza, / scorcia le capre, arechieca lu firre, / sdellazza porte e gente gna nu sbirre" (it tangles garbage, / flays goats, twists iron / batters doors and people like a cop), Jovine's poetic dialect sparkles and crackles with ever-renewed intensity and inventiveness.

In 1972 Jovine published his collection of short stories *La luna e la montagna*, most of which were written in the years 1948, 1949, and 1950. Four of the stories had appeared in *Paese Sera* in 1950 and 1951. All the stories are set in Molise and are teeming with a multitude of characters in a primitive, instinctive, ancestral world, which he explores in all its seething, occasionally explosive, humanity. Jovine follows the lives of his characters with a natural, profound understanding of the forces that motivate and shape them, but his participation in their joys and sorrows and his privileged insider's perspective on a world he knows so well

are counterbalanced by a pervasive narrative subtlety and guarded irony, which dispel any possibility of nostalgic musings or veiled sentimentality. Jovine's manipulation of surrealist imagery, unexpectedly arising from the commonplace and the ordinary — as in the case of the hanged dogs in "Il vento degli impiccati" (The Hanging Wind) or the horse torn to pieces by a famished crowd in "La guerra" (The War) — attest to his determination to reinterpret a native realist tradition in a personally distinctive way. Always present, whether the theme of the story is war, passion, fratricide, homosexuality, or superstition, are the historical and social forces against which the characters try to assert themselves. "L'alluvione" (The Flood), with its nightmarish description of mass destruction and death, is a rather overt political allegory, a violent invective against modern society and its corrupt ruling class; a contained undercurrent of social criticism is perceptible in the moving, complex portrayal of Signora Impedove, the main character in one of the best stories in the book. Yet the light irony running through all the stories is a self-corrective strategy that usually prevents the implied polemical stance from assuming a denunciatory tone.

In all these stories one senses a controlled narrative skill, a natural instinct for storytelling, and above all a deep understanding of human nature.

In 1975 Jovine published *Tra il Biferno e la Moscova* (Between the Biferno and the Moscow River), a collection of poems in standard Italian, written for the most part between 1950 and 1960, though a few of them had appeared as early as 1942 in *Gioventù*. While Jovine rejects any affiliation with the various literary currents and poetic schools and is openly adverse to all types of hermetic or neohermetic movements, he readily acknowledges that his first book of poetry in standard Italian betrays a diffuse cultural conditioning, especially in the constant echoing of themes and patterns made popular by D'Annunzio, whom Jovine has always considered one of the great innovators of Italian poetry, heralding the recent widespread effort to restore a more balanced critical view of D'Annunzio's poetry. His presence is felt, for example, in the frequent recurrence of anaphoric reiterations and long lists of images, as in "Il canto dell'emigrante" (The Emigrant's Song):

e ci tornavano in sogno le notti
il canto dei pollai,
le stanze odorose di strame,
le stanze odorose di grano,
la luna d'agosto sull'aia,
il fermento del mosto nei tini,
l'erba fresca e la lingua degli agnelli,
l'acqua riccia dei ruscelli . . .

(and in our dreams came the nights again,
the song of the henhouses,
the rooms fragrant with straw,
the rooms fragrant with wheat,
the August moonlight on the threshing floor,
the must fermenting in the vats,
the fresh grass and the lambs' tongue,
the swirling water of the streams . . .)[.]

The counterpoint to this sustained, unrelenting verse is the surfacing of a more subdued tone and subtle, self-deprecating irony, strongly reminiscent of *crepuscolarismo* (twilight poetry), as for instance in the affectionate, tongue-in-cheek treatment of a nun in "Suora Bianca" (Sister Bianca):

Io busso ogni mattina ad una porta
di fronte al tuo convento, in una via . . .
in Via, ahimè, delle Botteghe Oscure.
Per voi, per voi, sorelle castigate
quella porta è la porta dell'inferno!

(Every morning I knock at a door
across from your convent, in a street . . .
alas, in Via delle Botteghe Oscure.
For you, for you, chaste sisters
that door is the door to hell!)

The reference to the Communist party headquarters in Via delle Botteghe Oscure (Rome) as the door to hell in the eyes of the chaste nuns underscores Jovine's political theme, which runs through the whole book. The later amiable exhortation "Suor Bianca, orsù, prendiamoci per mano" (Come now, Sister Bianca, let us walk hand in hand) has wider implications, which point to a possible reconciliation of Christian and Marxist ideologies.

This commitment to bring to light the moral and political grounding of reality is emphasized by Massimo Grillandi in his preface to the book: "Jovine è riuscito a creare una sua personale dimensione poetica, centrata fortemente sul reale. Non poesia realistica, intendiamoci; ma semmai un realismo filtrato attraverso una ferma concezione morale, diciamo un moral-realismo, che può essere appunto una nuova dimensione della nostra poesia, dopo gli abbandoni ermetici e neorealisti" (Jovine has succeeded in creating a personal poetic dimension, sharply focused on reality. Not realistic poetry, let us be clear about this; but rather a realism filtered through a moral conception of reality, let us call it moral-realism, which could indeed be a new dimension of our poetry, after hermetic and neorealist self-indulgence). Jovine's dedication to social justice, equality, and civic duty generates a severe underlying moral tension, which is not always expressed with the ironic detachment of "Suor Bianca" and often erupts in open invective. Such is the case in "In morte of Saverio Trincia" (On the Death of Saverio Trincia), where the sadness for the death of a beloved teacher suddenly gives way to literary derision and biting sarcasm: "C'è persino un poeta fonematico, / una metasemantica poetessa / ansimanti . . . cultura" (There is even a phonemic poet / a metasemantic poetess / panting . . . culture). The polemical tone becomes even more violent and explosive and the political fervor more impassioned when Jovine deals with topical issues. "Mosca" (Moscow) is a fierce attack on the injustices and corruption of the West, while "Brescia" is a blistering excoriation of Italy's ruling class:

Vampiri d'Italia
se avete sete
andate a bere il sangue ai petrolieri
che comprano i Ministri a peso d'oro,
ma non bevete il sangue proletario.

(Vampires of Italy
if you are thirsty
go drink the blood of the oilmen
who buy off the Ministers with gold,
but do not drink proletarian blood.)

Jovine's indignation is not the inevitable by-product of a rigid ideological posture; it is born instead from his deep love for his people and for his region, which he feels is being ravished by greed and indifference. He envisions the land with its vineyards, wheat fields, olive trees, and poplars but also with its harshness and starkness:

La mia terra ha il silenzio
che dissecca i fiumi,
sbianca i boschi e l'erba dei prati,
sfianca e spolpa le montagne
come branchi di vecchie elefantesse.

(My land has the silence
that dries up the rivers,
that bleaches the woods and the meadow grass,
wears down and strips bare the mountains
like herds of old elephants.)

This description of an austere landscape in "Che venga il tuo regno Signore" (May Your Kingdom Come Lord) leads to a meditation on the difficult life of the emigrant, another key figure in Jovine's work, and finally to a sense of outrage over those "non ancora stanchi / di giocarsi le vesti logore di Cristo" (not yet tired / of gambling away Christ's tattered clothes). As critic Gianni Barrella writes, the book is "un unico, ininterrotto discorso d'amore" (a single, uninterrupted declaration of love), moving from the people and the landscapes of Molise to a more intimate, personal space that history cannot reach, and the poems dedicated to his wife are among the best in the volume.

Benedetti Molisani (Blessed Molisani, 1979) is a collection of essays on the cultural history of Molise. In his prefatory remarks Jovine warns that his way of speaking is "matta e sghemba" (crazy and crooked) and that the book is a kaleidoscope of images whose unity of design, while perhaps not immediately discernible, the reader can discover in the intricate interweaving of impressions and ideas: "Ci si può collocare dinnanzi al libro come dinnanzi a un'anamorfosi,' una deformazione prospettica, voglio dire, che consente una visione esatta solo a chi guarda dal punto giusto" (We can place ourselves before the book as before an "anamorphosis," I mean a perspective deformation that allows an exact view only to those looking from the right angle). The humorous reference to the book's inter-

nal contradictions is an acknowledgment of its thematic and structural sketchiness, no doubt due to the fact that the various pieces were written at different times and for different purposes. Yet this apparent lack of a clearly recognizable organizational pattern does not preclude an underlying thematic cohesiveness. What guarantees coherence despite the patchwork heterogeneity is an uncompromising determination to reconstruct and reposition the cultural heritage and historical significance of Molise within the wider national framework. This region, one of the smallest and poorest of Italy, "un Mezzogiorno nel Mezzogiorno" (a South within the South), as Jovine calls it, is examined from a variety of different angles, from a sociopolitical and historical analysis to aesthetic and personal judgments, all intimately connected and made relevant by his encompassing memory and critical acumen. His overview of the literature, art, and architecture of Molise, while an open-ended exhortation to further study, succeeds in restoring the full cultural and artistic significance of the region by elevating it to national levels. Reviewer Sabino D'Acunto (*Molise Oggi*, 22 February 1981) says that not everyone has understood the importance of the book for the cultural history of Molise. While some have underscored marginal elements, very few have seen it as the record of an epoch.

Three of the first four chapters of the book, "Benedetti Molisani," "I molisani e la politica" (The People of Molise and Politics), and "La luna e la provincia" (The Moon and the Province), are the most controversial and uneven, as they take up the thorny question of moral, social, and political responsibility. The picture Jovine draws of the people of Molise is generally far from flattering, and while he takes great pains to uncover their numerous faults and weaknesses, this moral portrayal lacks the distinguishing traits that would define the regional character and differentiate it from the more traditional perception of the failings of the south. The tone is even more acerbic when Jovine turns to the historical and political causes behind the eternal backwardness of his region: the greed and selfishness of the landowners and the conniving and insensitive clergy; the *trasformismo*, or quick-change artistry, of the ruling class whose power base is built on a widespread and deeply rooted patronage system; the careerism of a paternalist middle class; and the conservatism of the dominant political party with its lack of political will to address the real economic and social problems of the region.

In the subsequent chapters, which deal with literature and art, Jovine the polemicist yields to

Jovine the critic. He surveys the narrative tradition of his region in the works of writers such as Francesco Jovine, Lina Pietravalle, Sabino D'Acunto, Vincenzo Rossi, Franco Ciampitti, Felice Del Vecchio, and Giosè Rimanelli in search of a native voice, the irreducible core of a shared heritage that the multiplicity of results and experiences cannot obliterate. Jovine offers some penetrating insights on the substantial gap that can exist between technological progress and psychological adaptation, and which the novelist must always take into consideration. A modification of the process of production does not imply an immediate modification of behavior or social relationships. Even language itself can be misleading: "Può accadere che un borghese parli il linguaggio del moderno proletariato industriale e sia ancora affettivamente, sentimentalmente legato a una realtà storico-sociale conservatrice. Lo scrittore in questo caso deve guardare al comportamento del borghese, non al linguaggio" (It can happen that someone from the middle class speaks the language of the modern industrial working class and is still bound by feelings and emotions to a conservative socio-historical reality. The writer in this case must look at the behavior of the person from the middle class, not the language).

Just as insightful are Jovine's observations on the possible emergence of a new southern fiction from a new social, political, and religious consciousness within the folds of a middle-class psychology, where aestheticism, Marxism, realism, Catholicism, and anarchism are commingled, a very fertile ground for novelists. Jovine's discussion of the dialect poetry of Molise in the next chapter is the thoughtful culmination of a lifelong interest in dialect poetry that began with his study on Pierro and found its fullest expression in *Lu pavone*. After a brief review of the early poetry in the dialect of Molise (the first poems having been written toward the end of the nineteenth century), Jovine examines at some length the work of the most important poet of Molise, Cirese, who brought the dignity of the highest literary standards to a language almost devoid of literary precedents, and subsequent poets including Nina Guerrizio, Giovanni Cerri, and Giovanni Barrea. At the heart of Jovine's analysis is the necessity to keep within the expressive possibili-

ties of dialect; nothing is more pernicious to a dialect poet than borrowing linguistic structures from the Italian language that are alien to the dialect in which he is writing.

The chapter titled "Pittori Molisani" (Painters of Molise) is a perceptive introduction to the painters Gilda Pansiotti, Domenico Fratianni, and Marcello Scarano, whose works Jovine brought to national attention in numerous articles and in his later coediting of a 1986 book on Scarano. *Benedetti Molisani* closes with a series of *medaglioni* (medallions), brief sketches of notable Molisani, among which stands out the portrait of Rimanelli, who lives in the United States.

Giuseppe Jovine's political activity, which began when he was a young man, led him in the 1950s to run (unsuccessfully) for regional office and then in 1979 to try for a seat as a member of parliament, and to lecture widely both in Italy and abroad. His work as a journalist included the writing of more than two hundred articles on a remarkable variety of subjects: farmers' rights, emigration, art and architecture, the *mezzogiorno* (southern) question, dialects and dialect poetry, literary theory, pedagogy, political parties, and travel, to name a few. He wrote mainly for *Paese Sera* and *Critica Letteraria*. Between 1970 and 1973 he was coeditor with Tommaso Fiore of the *Risveglio del Mezzogiorno*. Thus his poetry has been only one facet of his expressive talent and deep commitment.

References:

Gianni Barrella, "Il Molise emblematico di Giuseppe Jovine," *Giornale d'Italia* (16 March 1976);

Tullio De Mauro, Preface to Jovine's *Lu pavone* (Bari: Adriatrica, 1970), pp. 7–9;

Francesco D'Episcopo, "Il racconto poetico di Giuseppe Jovine," *Nuovo Mezzogiorno*, 3 (March 1985): 37;

Massimo Grillandi, "La poesia di Giuseppe Jovine," *Risveglio del Mezzogiorno* (May–June 1971): 36–37;

Grillandi, Preface to Jovine's *Tra il Biferno e la Moscova* (Rome: Cartia, 1975), pp. 2–4;

Orazio Tanelli, "Poesie in dialetto molisano di Giuseppe Jovine," *Nuova Dimensione* (October 1986): 3–4.

Mario Luzi

(20 October 1914 –   )

Laura Baffoni-Licata
Tufts University

BOOKS: *La barca* (Modena: Guanda, 1935; revised and enlarged edition, Florence: Parenti, 1942);

L'opium chrétien (Modena: Guanda, 1938);

Avvento notturno (Florence: Vallecchi, 1940);

Un'illusione platonica e altri saggi (Florence: Rivoluzione, 1941; enlarged edition, Bologna: Boni, 1972);

Biografia a Ebe (Florence: Vallecchi, 1942);

Un brindisi (Florence: Sansoni, 1946);

Quaderno gotico (Florence: Vallecchi, 1947);

L'inferno e il limbo (Florence: Marzocco, 1949; enlarged edition, Milan: Saggiatore, 1964);

Studio su Mallarmé (Florence: Sansoni, 1952);

Primizie del deserto (Milan: Schwartz, 1952);

Aspetti della generazione napoleonica (Parma: Guanda, 1956);

Onore del vero (Venice: Neri Pozza, 1957);

Il giusto della vita (Milan: Garzanti, 1960);

Lo stile di Constant (Milan: Saggiatore, 1962);

Nel magma (Milan: All'Insegna del Pesce d'Oro, 1963; enlarged edition, Milan: Garzanti, 1966);

Trame (Lecce: Critone, 1963; enlarged edition, Milan: Rizzoli, 1982);

Dal fondo delle campagne (Turin: Einaudi, 1965);

Tutto in questione (Florence: Vallecchi, 1965);

Su fondamenti invisibili (Milan: Rizzoli, 1971);

Ipazia (Milan: All'Insegna del Pesce d'Oro, 1972);

Poesia e romanzo, by Luzi and Carlo Cassola (Milan: Rizzoli, 1973);

Poesie (Milan: Garzanti, 1974);

Vicissitudine e forma (Milan: Rizzoli, 1974);

Al fuoco della controversia (Milan: Garzanti, 1978);

Libro di Ipazia (Milan: Rizzoli, 1978);

Tutte le poesie (1934–1978), 2 volumes (Milan: Garzanti, 1979; enlarged, 1 volume, 1988);

Semiserie (Salerno: Galleria "Il Catalogo," 1979);

Discorso naturale (Siena: Messapo, 1980; enlarged edition, Milan: Garzanti, 1984);

Ritorno a Siena (Siena: Taccuini di Barbablú, 1981);

Rosales (Milan: Rizzoli, 1983);

Il silenzio, la voce (Florence: Sansoni, 1984);

Reportage: Un poemetto seguito dal taccuino di viaggio in Cina (Milan: All'Insegna del Pesce d'Oro, 1984);

Per il battesimo dei nostri frammenti (Milan: Garzanti, 1985);

Hystrio (Milan: Rizzoli, 1987);

Scritti (Venice: Arsenale, 1989);

Corale della città di Palermo per Santa Rosalia (Genoa: San Marco Giustiniani, 1989);

L'alta, la cupa fiamma: Poesie, 1935–1985 (Milan: Rizzoli, 1990);

Frasi e incisi di un canto salutare (Milan: Garzanti, 1990);

Il purgatorio, la notte lava la mente (Genoa: Costa & Nolan, 1990);

De quibus (Montichiari: Zanetto, 1991);

Le parole agoniche della poesia (Macerata: Alfabetica, 1991).

Edition in English: *In the Dark Body of Metamorphosis & Other Poems,* edited and translated by Isidore Lawrence Salomon (New York: Norton, 1975).

OTHER: Dino Campana and Sibilla Aleramo, *Lettere,* edited by Niccoló Gallo, preface by Luzi (Florence: Vallecchi, 1958), pp. 7–11;

Stephane Mallarmé, *Opere,* preface by Luzi (Milan: Lerici, 1963), pp. 9–32;

Giacinto Spagnoletti, ed., *Poesia italiana contemporanea (1900–1959),* includes poems and a statement by Luzi (Parma: Guanda, 1964), pp. 529–550;

"Pascoli," in *Storia della letteratura italiana,* volume 8, edited by Emilio Cecchi and Natalino Sapegno (Milan: Garzanti, 1968), pp. 733–811.

TRANSLATIONS: Charles du Bos, *Vita e letteratura,* edited and translated, with a preface, by Luzi (Padua: Cedam, 1943);

Samuel Taylor Coleridge, *Poesie e prose* (Milan: Cederna, 1949);

Mario Luzi circa 1975

Anthologie de la poésie lyrique française, edited and translated by Luzi and Tommaso Landolfi (Florence: Sansoni, 1950);

Charles Montesquieu, *Il tempio di Cnido,* in *Romanzi francesci dei secoli XVII e XVIII* (Milan: Bompiani, 1951);

L'idea simbolista, edited and translated, with an introduction, by Luzi (Milan: Garzanti, 1959);

Jean Racine, *Andromaca,* in *Teatro francese del grande secolo* (Rome: ERI, 1960);

Paul Valéry, *Cantico delle colonne* (Milan: Scheiwiller, 1960);

Jorge Guillén, *La fonte* (Milan: Scheiwiller, 1961);

William Shakespeare, *Riccardo II* (Turin: Einaudi, 1966);

Coleridge, *La ballata del vecchio marinaio* (Milan: Rizzoli, 1973);

Francamente (Florence: Vallecchi, 1980);

La Cordigliera delle Ande (Turin: Einaudi, 1983);

Tirso De Molina, Dannato per disperazione (Milan: Garzanti, 1991).

SELECTED PERIODICAL PUBLICATIONS –
UNCOLLECTED: "Il pensiero fluttuante della felicitá," *Paragone,* 210 (June 1967): 733–811;

"Pascoli psicanalizzato," *Opera Aperta,* 2 (September 1967): 129–135;

"L'azione poetica in Rebora," *Approdo Letterario,* 14 (October–December 1968);

"Nel corpo oscuro della metamorfosi," *Approdo Letterario,* 15 (April–June 1969): 19–32;

"Graffito dell'eterna zarina," *Almanacco dello Specchio,* 4 (October 1975).

Mario Luzi, one of the most important Italian poets and scholars, was born in Castello, near Florence, on 20 October 1914. His parents, Ciro and Margherita Papini Luzi, were originally from the region of Alta Maremma; his father was the station-master at Castello. Educated at schools in Florence and Siena, in 1935 Mario Luzi made his book-publishing debut with the poetry volume *La barca* (The Boat). In 1936 he graduated with a degree from the University of Florence, having majored in French literature. His thesis on François Mauriac was published two years later with the title *L'opium chrétien* (Christian Opium), which illustrates his philosophical inclinations of those early years. Luigi Foscolo Benedetto was the professor in the Florentine athenaeum who introduced him to the study of French literature. Other literary masters, as he would recall years later (in Sergio Pautasso's *Mario Luzi*, 1981), helped him define his future as a poet rather than as a philosopher: "La lettura di alcuni testi, caduta in quel tempo, fu decisiva: [Marcel] Proust, alcuni racconti di Thomas Mann e soprattutto il *Dedalus* [Portrait of the Artist as a Young Man, 1916] di [James] Joyce mi colpirono in pieno e mi dettero, oltre al resto, la convinzione che quelli erano i veri filosofi della nostra epoca" (The reading of some texts, at that time, was decisive: Proust, some short stories by Thomas Mann, and above all, *Dedalus* by Joyce impressed me greatly and gave me, among other things, the conviction that those were the true philosophers of our times).

Poetry was for Luzi a choice of life-style. In his early years it meant having to choose a difficult and arduous path that led to the awareness of the moral void left behind by the presumed vitalistic fulfillment of the Fascist era. His intense years of formation were filled with a great variety of interests and with emotional, religious, and intellectual changes that profoundly influenced his future existential and poetic dimensions. His Catholicism evolved during this time from a form linked to his mother's intense faith to a fundamental dimension of human thought and perspective, based on the reading of works by the African Saint Augustine, Blaise Pascal, and vibrant contemporary French writers such as Mauriac, Jacques Maritain, and Gabriel Marcel. Having become actively involved in the literary trends of his times, Luzi collaborated on several journals — *Letteratura, Campo di Marte, Botteghe Oscure, Poesia,* and *Frontespizio* — to which writers such as Eugenio Montale, Piero Bigongiari, Alfonso Gatto, Vasco Pratolini, and Carlo Bo, among others, had been actively contributing. In the rich literary humus of Florence in those early years, where, in the name of literature, friendships were established that would last a lifetime, Luzi's poetic experience matured. Prior to his collection of essays *Un'illusione platonica* (A Platonic Illusion, 1941) he published his second volume of poetry, *Avvento notturno* (Noctur-

nal Advent, 1940), in which a whole generation of young poets could recognize itself. On 20 June 1942 Luzi married Elena Monaci, a teacher; they have a son, Gianni.

After World War II, while keeping close ties to the intense Florentine cultural life, Luzi devoted himself to a career in education. Between 1945 and 1955 he taught in San Miniato and Parma, where he became friendly with other young poets such as Attilio Bertolucci and Enzo Paci; he also worked in Rome at Sovrintendenza Bibliografica. Luzi then returned to Florence, where he taught French literature, first at the Liceo Scientifico, then in the Department of Political Science at the University of Florence. From 1962 to 1981 he was a professor of comparative literature at the University of Urbino.

Since his early years Luzi has enjoyed traveling to faraway places as a form of cultural enrichment and as a way of coming to grasp with different aspects of the evolution of human history. In 1966 he visited Russia; in 1968, drawn by his fascination with Oriental mysticism, he went to India. Several times he was in the United States, an invited guest of various American universities; in 1980 he traveled to China. Many of his most meaningful travel experiences emerge transfigured in his verse.

Luzi's literary beginnings (1935–1940) are deeply entrenched in the hermetic movement. His poetic discourse, however, reveals immediately a new personal and lyrical voice that offers a subtle perspective, open to a judgment free of critical apriorisms. Although emerging in the mainstream of the poetic trends between the two wars, his poetry can neither be viewed as conditioned by these trends nor as a consequence of them; rather he seems to stand by himself as a promoter of a new poetic climate. As with one of his contemporaries, Vittorio Sereni, his ties to the hermetic movement are more a matter of generational solidarity and participation.

In *La barca* — described by him in *L'inferno e il limbo* (Hell and Limbo, 1949) as "la sorgente di tutto il lavoro posteriore" (the source of all my later work) — Luzi introduces the quest of a poet who slowly abandons his self-oriented search to attempt to join the flow of the world. The metaphors of the boat and of flowing, present throughout the collection, are particularly evident in the poem "Alla vita" (To Life):

Amici dalla barca si vede il mondo
e in lui una verità che procede
intrepida, un sospiro profondo
dalle foci alle sorgenti . . .
(Friends from the boat one can see the world

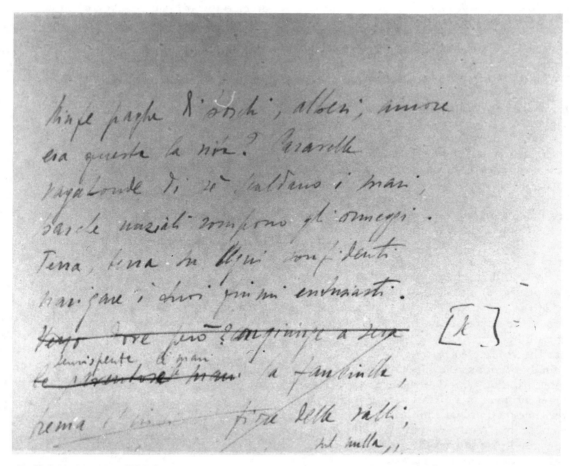

Draft for the beginning of "Ninfe pagne di boschi . . . ," a poem collected in Avvento notturno *(by permission of Mario Luzi)*

and within it a truth that proceeds
intrepid, a deep breath
from the ends to the beginnings . . .)[.]

Projecting himself toward a concrete reality, although mediated through symbolist associations, Luzi wishes to avoid any kind of pathetic or abstract viewpoint. Youthful overtones can inevitably be found in this first volume — such as a kind of bet on life played against death — but are very often redeemed by an intense feeling of Christian *pietas* (piety), as in "Canto notturno per le ragazze fiorentine" (Nocturnal Song for the Florentine Girls):

e noi andiamo con la volontà di Dio dentro al cuore
per le strade nel lieve afrore
delle vostre stanze socchiuse
nell'ombra che sommerge le vostre pupille deluse.

(and we go with God's will in our hearts
along the streets in the light pungent mist
of your rooms left ajar
in the shadow that submerges your deluded pupils.)

In *Avvento notturno* the *fisica perfetta* (perfect physics) of the first collection seems to have been replaced by a form of imperfect metaphysics. The book was greeted by many representatives of the hermetic movement as an exemplary image of their poetics. The choral utterances of the previous volumes are superseded by an intense inner dialogue of the speaker with himself, with his own soul. The poetry becomes more involved with symbols, metaphors, allusions, and analogies, as the poem "Esitavano a Eleusi i bei cipressi" (The Beautiful Cypresses at Eleusi Hesitated) illustrates:

Lungo i fiumi silenti e nella brina
il delirio è morto; sbanda un carro
di fieno sull'azzurra serpentina,
un treno subitaneo al puro marmo

dei tuoi monti s'avvinghia. Ma già assente
sul vetro della sera un viso spazia
di donna . . .

(Along the silent rivers and in the frost
the delirium is dead; a cart of hay

swerves in the azure serpentine,
a sudden train to the pure marble

of your mountains entwines itself. But already absent
on the glass of the evening a face wanders
of woman . . .) [.]

The vital, creative inspiration from which *La barca* originated has been transformed, mostly through an analogic process, into mental abstraction. The abstraction, however, does not resolve itself in pure rarefaction of images; it evolves in a metaphoric obsession that recuperates, through an orphic and symbolic process, the inner meaning of reality. There is a fundamental difference between Luzi's concept of poetry and that of the hermetics. Unlike the latter, Luzi never considered poetry an escape or evasion from reality but rather a deep and intense search. In his verse there is no perfection or isolation, but mostly the suffering of the world and, at the same time, the awareness of the impossibility of redeeming such suffering with his art.

With the volume *Un brindisi* (A Toast, 1946) Luzi gradually abandons the condition of limbo, of utmost interiorization typical of *Avvento notturno*. An obscure presentiment of a historical time no longer exclusively personal prevails in the early poems of the 1946 collection. With vast, powerful, and often-allusive images, Luzi portrays the universal tragedy of horror and death that humankind assists impotently and silently, as the poem "Un brindisi" illustrates:

Dolori informi, grida, preghiere inoggettive!
Dimenticata splende nella polvere
degli angoli la madre inaridita,
la sua voce cattolica prodiga di speranze . . .

(Inform sorrows, cries, unobjective prayers!
Forgotten the withered mother
shines in the dust of the corners,
her catholic voice prodigal of hopes . . .)[.]

The moment of crisis, however, in Luzi's poetry does not lead to negativeness and irretrievable silence but often becomes inspirational to future poetic creativity. Loneliness, tragedy, and death, woven into other realities, lead to messages of redemption and denunciation.

The Italy of the postwar years, the period of neorealism, was undoubtedly hostile to Luzi's poetry. For many who nevertheless admired his work, Luzi's path seemed noble but impractical. For him these were years of profound meditation, studying, and reading. His literary interests were significantly directed toward Anglo-Saxon culture. T. S. Eliot's poetry, mainly *Four Quartets* (1943), had a profound influence at this time in the development of Luzi's poetic discourse, as seen in the collection *Quaderno gotico* (Gothic Notebook, 1947) and above all in *Nel magma* (In the Magma, 1963).

The will to explore new literary and cognitive horizons is intertwined with his need to settle accounts with the past, in an attempt to objectify it. Along this line in 1952 he published *Studio su Mallarmé,* preceded in 1949 by *L'inferno e il limbo,* a collection of essays that is a powerful expression of his extended research on these new ideas. The book was awarded the Saint Vincent Prize for criticism for 1949. In Luzi's literary endeavors poetry and criticism proceed in parallel. The creativity of his poetic process unmistakably finds some form of verification in the reflexive stage of his work as a critic. In *L'inferno e il limbo* he warns of the risk of *petrarchismo* (Petrarchanism), which should be overcome by each poet in order to subdue "l'orgoglio delle sue qualitá e ritrovare quella modestia che lascia la sua parte al naturale, senza invaderlo . . . " (the pride of his qualities and find again that humility that leaves its part to the natural, without invading it . . .). Moreover, he identifies a great part of Italian poetry, including the hermetic school, as *petrarchesca:* "una poesia che si sviluppa su se stessa come si conviene ad uno spirito così conchiuso e concentrico, isolato appunto nel suo limbo. Una poesia . . . privata dell'orgoglio della scoperta, dei contatti più freschi e magari più bruschi dell'anima con le circostanze episodiche della vita, e volendo anche estendere il termine, con l'inferno" (a poetry that grows on itself as it is proper of a spirit so closed in and concentric, precisely isolated in its limbo. A poetry . . . deprived of the pride of the discovery, of the soul's most refreshing and even blunt contacts with life's episodic circumstances, and wishing to extend the term, with hell). As the future developments of his poetry show, Luzi chose a path that led him out of his youthful aesthetic and hedonistic "limbo" and caused him to descend, with a more concrete approach to reality, into that "hell" of Dantesque resonance. Besides *L'inferno e il limbo* he has published several collections of essays on literary criticism. Luzi's work as a translator has also been well established. He has translated works by Samuel Taylor Coleridge, Jean Racine, Paul Valéry, Jorge Guillén, and William Shakespeare, among others.

Quaderno gotico is a collection of Luzi's love lyrics, articulated through a tense and dynamic dialogue with a female in a Gothic setting. The symbols become the emblems of a potential epiphany, as in the poem "I":

L'alta, la cupa fiamma ricade su di te,
figura non ancora conosciuta,
ah di giá tanto a lungo sospirata
dietro a quel velo d'anni e di stagioni
che un dio forse s'accinge a lacerare.

(The high, dark flame falls back on you,
figure not yet known,
ah for so long sighed for
beyond that veil of years and seasons
a god is maybe about to lacerate.)

In Luzi's poetic development *Quaderno gotico,* with its diaristic nuances, acts as a connecting link between a symbolic, allegorical concept of poetry and a stance more inclined to a direct approach to reality.

Vanished are the illusions of the years immediately following the war. The speaker sees himself as surrounded by moral desolation. In *Primizie del deserto* (The Desert's First Fruits, 1952) Luzi becomes the interpreter of an existential condition in which man appears as the prey of his own spiritual desolation. The poetic persona becomes an exemplary conscience, as seen in "Né tregua" (Neither Truce):

Vuoi darmi un nome, chiamami l'angoscia,
chiamami la pazienza ed il dolore
o l'abbandono o il tedio o l'afflizione
o altrimenti se esprimono parole
la certezza di quel che so.

(You want to give me a name, call me anxiety,
call me patience and sorrow
or abandonment or boredom or affliction
or otherwise if words can express
the certainty of what I know.)

In "Gemma" (Gem), however, one of the last poems of the collection, an undisputable, although obscure, trace of existence is revealed as a counterpoint to those verses that seem to exclude any presence of life within the "desert": corre voce / di una vita che ricomincia e oscura / geme negli animali insonni, s'agita / nel mare . . . " (one hears / of a life that begins again and obscure / wails in the sleepless animals, flounders / in the sea . . .).

For the volume *Onore del vero* (Honor of Truth), published in 1957, Luzi was awarded the Marzotto Prize. The poetic journey documented by these poems leads to an external reality, to "others." These are mostly humble, picaresque characters, not at all of epic stature, whom the speaker meets in

scenic areas such as that of the poem "Lungo il fiume" (Along the River):

Se t'incontro non è opera mia,
seguo il corso di questo fiume rapido
dove s'insinua tra baracche e tumuli.
Son luoghi ove il girovago, flautista
o lanciatore di coltelli avviva
il fuoco, tende per un pó le mani,
prende sonno . . .

(If I meet you it is not my doing,
I follow the course of this rapid river
where it insinuates itself between shacks and piles.
They are places where the peddler, flautist
or knife thrower kindles
the fire, stretches his hands out for a while,
falls asleep . . .)[.]

In the lyrics of this collection a profound, almost sacred feeling, a kind of humility, emerges. It is confirmed by an almost prosaic style that seems to recall the inner drama of some medieval mystics. The poetic discourse frequently tends to transform physical data into metaphysical elements. Luzi seems obsessively intent on reaching the inner core of things in order to recuperate that hidden quality of authenticity found in humankind and nature that still resists social compromise and unnatural and insincere behavior. His new desire to capture reality beyond what is visible stems from an intense need for knowledge: "penetrare il mondo / opaco lungo vie chiare . . ." (to penetrate the opaque / world along bright ways . . .); and the deep-rooted yearning to be with others, to be part of their history: "Si ha come l'impressione di un ripopolamento del 'deserto': dove l'uomo riappare con la sua fitta trama di gesti e segni" (One has the impression of a recrowding of the 'desert': where man reappears with his intense scheme of gestures and signs). With *Onore del vero* Luzi seems to have concluded the phase of inner exploration and begun a new journey. However, *Dal fondo delle campagne* (From the Depth of the Fields, 1965) is considered by many to be still tied in many ways to the inner search of *Onore del vero.* It often reveals a dramatic tension caused by Luzi's will to measure himself against existential themes of life, death, human suffering, and bewilderment.

In 1960 *Il giusto della vita* (The Right of Life), with all his poems from 1935 to 1957, was published in Milan. *Nel magma,* initially published in 1963, was awarded the 1964 Etna-Taormina Prize. The volume was enlarged in 1966. It is regarded as a turning point in the development of Luzi's poetic discourse. The reflexive and meditative character of his poetry flows into extended dialogues. Different voices make their decisive appearance in a purgatorial and iconological atmosphere that recalls works by Dante and T. S. Eliot. A direct confrontation with history, frequently alluded to in his previous poetry, beginning with *Un brindisi,* powerfully emerges. Luzi presents a meaningful representation of the difficulty of contemporary existence, as the poem "Presso il Bisenzio" (Near the Bisenzio River):

> "O Mario" dice e mi si mette al fianco
> per quella strada che non é una strada
> ma una traccia tortuosa che si perde nel fango
> "guardati, guardati attorno . . .
> volgiti e guarda il mondo come è divenuto,
> poni mente a che cosa questo tempo ti richiede,
> non la profonditá, né l'ardimento,
> ma la ripetizione di parole,
> la mimesi senza perché né come
> dei gesti in cui si sfrena la nostra moltitudine
> morsa dalla tarantola della vita, e basta."

> ("Oh Mario" says he and comes by my side
> along that road that is not a road
> but a tortuous trail that disappears into the mud
> "look, look around yourself . . .
> turn around and look at the world how it has become,
> pay attention to what this time asks of you,
> not the depth, nor the courage,
> but the repetition of words,
> the mimesis without why nor how
> of the gestures with which our multitude gives way to
>   rage
> bit by the tarantula of life, and that is it.")

For the volume *Su fondamenti invisibili* (On Invisible Foundations, 1971) Luzi was awarded the Fiuggi Prize for Poetry. This collection is his most compact and systematic book, and the dialogues are even more dramatized. He is the *scriba* (writer) who transcribes in order to understand and record the metaphoric dynamics within creation, to perceive, mainly by intuition, the unstoppable process of metamorphosis, which is, for Luzi, the foundation of reality itself. The volume comprises three opening lyrics, followed by three long narrative poems: "Il pensiero fluttuante della felicitá (The Fluctuating Thought of Happiness), "Nel corpo oscuro della metamorfosi" (In the Dark Body of Metamorphosis), and "Il gorgo di salute e malattia" (The Vortex of Health and Disease). In these verses some of the most significant themes of modern times are poignantly examined – from the decline of Western civilization to the disappointment for "la rivoluzione mancata" (the missed revolution); from the condition of isolation of the church, as an institu-

tion, to the rare experiences that seem to redeem it; from the irretrievable disassociation of thought and reality to the incendiary violence of the technologic era. The theme of metamorphosis, described by Luzi in *Il silenzio, la voce* (The Silence, the Voice, 1984) as "il tema dei temi della mia poesia" (the theme of themes in my poetry), includes the dynamics of life and death, rebirth and extinction, and wisdom and obscurity.

In 1972 Luzi published *Ipazia,* a drama in verse. Within the context of his use of dialogue and a more extended and prosaic approach to poetry, theater seemed to offer the perfect setting for further poetic endeavors. With *Ipazia* he intended to emphasize the social crises of the 1960s, particularly the fanaticism of resurgent faiths.

After the publication of *Al fuoco della controversia* (At the Fire of Controversy, 1978) Luzi was awarded the Viareggio Prize. The complexity of the linguistic, stylistic, and thematic issues that characterize the new phase of his poetic discourse, begun with *Nel magma,* are brought forward in further magnitude and depth in *Al fuoco della controversia*. His poetic vision expands and deepens to the point of becoming prophecy. One of the first, most powerful themes in the book is that of *controversia*: controversy is conceived in the dialectic terms of a never-ending confrontation, Luzi's critical stand toward myths and their protagonists, as illustrated in "Brani di un mortale duetto" (Pieces from a Mortal Duet):

> qui nell'aria sospetta
> dove gli imperi si afflosciano
> nel loro orgoglio spremuto
> nella loro economìa a patrasso . . .

> (here in the suspicious air
> where the empires collapse
> in their squeezed pride
> in their twisted economy. . .);

and again in "Graffito dell'eterna zarina" (Graffito of the Eternal Czarina):

> Volano i grandi provveditori della pace
> con la loro coda di esperti,
> gravi, conoscitori a fondo della controversia,
> equi nel soppesare
> i diritti delle parti . . .

> (The great providers of peace fly
> with their tail of experts,
> serious, thorough connoisseurs of controversy,
> just in balancing
> the rights of the parts . . .)[.]

Luzi's poetic discourse progresses in meditation and deep reflection, enriched by memory. Places, encounters, and people are transformed through a poetic metamorphosis and become elements of a metaphorical vision of the world, with the poet at its center, ready to emphasize the existential doubt that stems from unresolved controversy. The poetic techniques mastered in *Nel magma* and *Su fondamenti invisibili* allow for more penetrating insights.

Per il battesimo dei nostri frammenti (For the Christening of Our Fragments) was published in 1985. A profound belief in the perennial fire of creation, which burns beyond the catastrophic, tragic images of daily life, emerges throughout the volume. Tormented and, at the same time, compelled by his inner sense of inquiry, search, and self-questioning, Luzi descends once more into the maze of existential and historical magma and explores the labyrinths where people, as he evinces in one of the poems from the section "Maceria e fonte" (Ruins and Source), "si strappano l'immagine dell'uomo / dalle loro opposte facce vicendevolmente" (tear their image of man off / from their opposite faces mutually). Cruel and compassionate acts, traces of crimes, defeat, abdication, and inexplicable human behavior are told of by a voice that is colloquially gentle and, at times, powerfully tragic, as in "Il mai perfetto" (The Never Perfect):

Il mai perfetto,
        il mai giunto alla fine
del suo vero compimento,
creato ancora creante —

"O, nascita di tutte le nascite!
qualcosa di me era presente"
sì, e dopo improvvisa e indefinibile
generata forse dalla distanza
da se stessa esce una moltitudine,
moltitudine da moltitudine. . . .
ma esita, non sa quello che essere
se ciò che fu sempre
nei luoghi in ombra
del mondo o altro che risplenda
di luce propria, sole nel sole —

"Per questo scesi,
per questo misi la mia vita
nella vostra morte."

(The never perfect,
        the never attained the end
of its true fulfillment,
created and still creating —

"Oh, birth of all births!
something of myself was present"

yes, and later sudden and inexplicable
maybe generated from the distance
a multitude emerges out of itself,
multitude out of multitude . . .
but it hesitates, it does not know what to be
whether what it was always
in the darker places
of the world or other that would shine
of its own light, sun within the sun —

"For this I descended,
for this I placed my life
within your death.")

Frasi e incisi di un canto salutare (Phrases and Digressions of a Salutary Song) was published in April 1990. In this volume of verse the value of Luzi's poetry is further clarified by the poet himself as "un canto di salute e di saluto" (a song of salvation and salutation).

Mario Luzi has written a substantial body of both verse and criticism, which is impressive for the originality of his thought and creativity. Having emerged from the solipsistic trends of the hermetic movement, he has succeeded in creating a deeper individual line of poetry, which, more and more often, has drawn its inspirational themes from within the mutating reality of history and the world. The tone of his poetic discourse emerges as both meditative and discursive, with a creative interplay between what is contingent and what is timeless, what can be experienced within reality and what goes beyond any experience. His poetic temperament is manifested through a particular form of symbolism that has its cultural roots more in Dante and Eliot than in Petrarch and the French symbolists, as the latest, more mature volumes of his poetry show. Through the years Luzi has managed to express the plight of modern humankind. Thus he asserts himself as one of the most creative, morally charged voices in the contemporary Italian poetic scene.

Interviews:
Carlo Bo, "Incontro con Luzi a un caffè della sua Firenze," *Europeo* (9 October 1960): 75–76;

Ferdinando Camon, "Mario Luzi," in his *Il mestiere di poeta* (Milan: Garzanti, 1982), pp. 111–120;

Luciano Lisi, "Un viaggio nella memoria: A colloquio con Mario Luzi," in *Mario Luzi: Una vita per la cultura,* by Stefano Verdino (Frosinone: Ente Fiuggi, 1983), pp. 75–95;

Rosita Copioli, "Intervista a Mario Luzi," *Anello che non Tiene: Journal of Modern Italian Literature,* 1 (Fall 1988): 55–69.

Biographies:

Giuseppe Zagarrio, *Luzi* (Florence: Nuova Italia, 1968);

Claudio Scarpati, *Mario Luzi* (Milan: Mursia, 1970);

Elio Giunta, *Mario Luzi, poeta del fluire* (Palermo: Pitré, 1977);

Luciano Luisi and Christina Becatelli, *Mario Luzi: Una vita per la cultura* (Cassino: Poligrafici, 1983).

References:

Giorgio Bàrberi Squarotti, "Luzi," in his *Poesia e narrativa del secondo Novecento* (Milan: Mursia, 1967), pp. 75–85;

Vanni Bramanti, "Note sulla poesia di Mario Luzi," *Approdo Letterario,* 61 (1973): 87–90;

Elio Chinol, "Chi chiamò i barbari?," *Espresso* (17 December 1978): 22–24;

Claudio Ferrucci, "Pasolini e Luzi: La polemica e il confronto," *Sigma,* 2–3 (May–December 1981): 157–165;

Marco Forti, "Parabola di Mario Luzi," in his *Le proposte della poesia e nuove proposte* (Milan: Mursia, 1971), pp. 234–247;

Franco Fortini, "La poesia di Mario Luzi," *Communità,* 7 (1954): 49–55;

Giovanni Giudici, "Vede il mondo da una barca," *Espresso* (5 September 1971): 16–18;

Alfredo Luzi, " 'L'enigma' e lo 'scriba' nella poesia dell'ultimo Luzi," *Anello che non Tiene: Journal of Modern Italian Literature,* 1 (Fall 1988): 17–30;

Luzi, *La vicissitudine sospesa* (Florence: Vallecchi, 1968);

Oreste Macrí, "Le origini di Luzi," in his *Realtá del simbolo* (Florence: Vallecchi, 1968), pp. 149–176;

Gaetano Mariani, *Il lungo viaggio verso la luce* (Padua: Liviana, 1982);

Barbara Nugnes, "T. S. Eliot e Mario Luzi: Un caso di Affinità," *Rivista di Letterature Moderne e Comparate,* 33 (June 1980): 129–155;

Sergio Pautasso, *Mario Luzi: Storia di una poesia* (Milan: Rizzoli, 1981);

Pensiero e poesia nell'opera di Mario Luzi (Florence: Vallecchi, 1989);

Giancarlo Quiriconi, *Il fuoco e la metamorfosi: La scommessa totale di Mario Luzi* (Bologna: Cappelli, 1980);

Giovanni Raboni, "Luzi e la storia," in his *Poesia degli anni sessanta* (Rome: Riuniti, 1976), pp. 29–39;

Silvio Ramat, "Luzi e il poema aperto," in his *La pianta della poesia* (Florence: Vallecchi, 1972), pp. 365–375;

Sergio Salvi, *Il metro di Luzi* (Bologna: Leonardi, 1967);

Achille Serrao, ed., *Atti del Convegno di Studi* (Rome: Ateneo, 1983).

Biagio Marin

(29 June 1891 – 24 December 1985)

Eliana Ricci
Rutgers University

BOOKS: *Fiuri de tapo* (Gorizia: Sociale, 1912);
Per le nozze di Mercedes: Cantico nuziale (Gorizia: Seitz/Musig, 1913);
La girlanda de gno suore (Gorizia: Paternolli, 1922);
L'ufficiale educatore (Gorizia: Divisione Fanteria, 1922);
Cansone picole (Udine: Panarie, 1927);
La corona di Graziella (Udine: Panarie, 1931);
L'isola d'oro (Udine: Panarie, 1934; enlarged edition, Grado: Comune di Grado, 1955);
Una vita (Udine: Bosetti, 1935);
La teraferma gera a tramontana (Trieste: Smolars, 1936);
Gorizia (Venice: Tre Venezie, 1940); republished as *Gorizia: La città mutilata* (Gorizia: Comune di Gorizia, 1956);
Le litànie de la Madona (Trieste: Veritas, 1949);
Lamento per Emilio Furlani deportato da gli slavi (Trieste: Giuliana, 1949);
I canti de l'isola (Udine: Del Bianco, 1951; revised and enlarged edition, Trieste: Cassa di Risparmio di Trieste, 1970; revised and enlarged again, Trieste: Lint, 1981);
Sénere colde (Rome: Belli, 1953);
Umanità e poesia di Virgilio Giotti (Trieste: Umana, 1957);
Celebrazione di Scipio Slataper (Trieste: Circolo della Cultura e delle Arti, 1957);
Poesie: Tristessa de la sera (Verona: Riva, 1957);
Per le nosse de Didi De Grassi e Mario Smareglia (Trieste: Smolars, 1957);
Tre poesie graisane a recordo de le nosse de Mauro Marocco co' Alba Marchettot (Trieste: Giuliana, 1957);
A ricordo di Donatella Slataper (Trieste: Giuliana, 1958);
L'estadela de San Martin (Rome & Caltanissetta: Sciascia, 1958);
Quattro Slataper sempre vivi: Scipio, Giuliano, Scipio Secondo, Donatella (Trieste: Fuori Commercio, 1958);
Celebrazione di Virgilio Giotti (Trieste: Circolo della Cultura e delle Arti, 1959);

Biagio Marin circa 1969

Pisino e la sua scuola (Trieste: Famiglia Pisinota, 1959);
El fogo del ponente, 1958–1959 (Venice: Neri Pozza, 1959);
In memoria de Checco Raugna (Trieste: Giuliana, 1960);
Canto d'adio a Matilde Degrassi maestra esselente (Trieste: Smolars, 1960);
Liriche di Biagio Marin (Trieste: Umana, 1960);
Umanità di Scipio Slataper (Trieste: Arti Grafiche Smolars, 1961);

Solitàe, edited by Pier Paolo Pasolini (Milan: All'Insegna del Pesce d'Oro, 1961);

I mesi dell'anno (Trieste: ALUT, 1961);

12 poesie, edited by G. B. Pighi (Milan: All'Insegna del Pesce d'Oro, 1962);

Elegie istriane (Milan: All'Insegna del Pesce d'Oro, 1963);

Il non tempo del mare, 1912–1962 (Milan: Mondadori, 1964);

Elogio delle conchiglie (Milan: Scheiwiller, 1965);

I delfini di Scipio Slapater (Milan: Scheiwiller, 1965);

Dopo la longa istàe (Milan: All'Insegna del Pesce d'Oro, 1965);

La poesia è un dono (Milan: All'Insegna del Pesce d'Oro, 1966);

El mar de l'eterno (Milan: All'Insegna del Pesce d'Oro, 1967);

Strade e rive di Trieste (Milan: All'Insegna del Pesce d'Oro, 1967);

Variazioni gradesi (Gorizia: Iniziativa Isontina, 1967);

In memoria de Genovefa Laùto nel I anniversario de la so morte (a so figia Antonieta) (Trieste, 1967);

Tra sera e note (Milan: All'Insegna del Pesce d'Oro, 1968);

Quanto più moro (Milan: Osservatore, 1969);

La vose de le scusse (Milan: Scheiwiller, 1969);

El picolo nìo (Udine: Stretta, 1969);

In memoria di Lucia Degrassi nel trigesimo de la so morte 29 magio 1970 dedica Biagio Marin (Un sigo solo: Moro) (Grado: Artigiana Gradese, 1970);

La vita xe fiama, 1963–1969, edited by Claudio Magris (Turin: Einaudi, 1970); enlarged as *La vita xe fiama e altri versi* (Turin: Einaudi, 1982);

Canto per un amico (Gorizia: Iniziativa Isontina, 1971);

Friuli-Venezia-Giulia (Milan: Touring Club Italiano, 1971);

Qualche appunto sulla storia e sull'anima di Trieste (Genoa: Italsider, 1971);

Poesie (Capua: Airone, 1972); enlarged edition, edited by Magris and Edda Serra (Milan: Garzanti, 1981);

Dialetti e lingua nazionale in Italia (Udine: Arc, 1972);

Nell'80° anniversario dell'Azienda di cura e soggiorno di Grado (Grado: Artigiana Gradese, 1972);

Acquamarina (Padua: Rebellato, 1973);

El vento de l'eterno se fa teso, edited by Serra and Elvio Guagnini (Milan: Scheiwiller, 1973);

A sol calào (Milan: Rusconi, 1974);

Tinpi passài (Fiume: Batana, 1974);

Ultime refolàe: 24 liriche (Udine: Arti Grafiche Friulane, 1975);

El critolèo del corpo fracassào: Litànie a la memoria de Pier Paolo Pasolini (Milan: All'Insegna del Pesce d'Oro, 1976);

Pan de pura farina (Genoa: San Marco dei Giustiniani, 1976);

Carne lisiere (Trieste: Cartesius, 1977);

Stele cagiùe, edited by Geda Jacolutti (Milan: Rusconi, 1977);

E tu virdisi (Padua: Rebellato, 1977);

In memoria di Guido di Serena (Milan: All'Insegna del Pesce d'Oro, 1978);

Nel silenzio più teso, edited by Serra (Milan: Rizzoli, 1980);

El fior de la morte (Udine: Panarie, 1981);

E anche el vento tase (Genoa: San Marco dei Giustiniani, 1982);

L'isola; The Island, bilingual edition, edited by Serra, translated by Gerald Parks (Udine: Del Bianco, 1982);

La grande aventura, edited by Serra (Padua: Panda, 1983);

La luse sconta (Milan: All'Insegna del Pesce d'Oro, 1983);

La vose de la sera (Milan: Garzanti, 1985).

TRANSLATION: Eduard Fueter, *Storia del sistema degli Stati europei dal 1492 al 1559* (Florence: Nuova Italia, 1932).

Biagio Marin was born on 29 June 1891 in Grado, a small island in the Lagoon of Venice, then part of the Habsburg Empire. The son of an innkeeper, he was raised by his grandmother because his mother died when he was still young. At nine he was sent to Gorizia, Italy, to attend a German-language secondary school. Later he attended the Royal High Schools at Pisino. In 1911 he moved to Florence, enrolled in the Institute of Higher Education, and actively participated in the leftist literary and political movement promoted by the literary review the *Voce.* In 1912 he went to the University of Vienna, where, for two years, he studied humanities. In 1915 he married Giuseppina Marini, with whom he had four children. He was drafted into the Austrian army during World War I and sent to Sarajevo, Yugoslavia. Marin succeeded in deserting to Italy, and after the Caporetto defeat he volunteered and fought on the Italian side. At the end of the war he received a degree in philosophy at the University of Rome. He dedicated himself to teaching for several years, with an interruption from 1923 to 1937, when he directed a Grado tourist agency. From 1938 to 1941 he was employed as a teacher of literature, history, and philosophy at a high school in Trieste. From 1941 to 1956 he worked as a librarian for the General Insurance

Company (Assicurazioni Generali) of Trieste. In 1943 the Marins lost their only son, Falco, who was killed in the war. This event profoundly affected Biagio Marin's life and verse. In 1968 he returned with his family to live in Grado, remaining there until his death on 24 December 1985.

Marin's first collection of poetry, *Fiuri de tapo* (Flowers of Cork), was published in 1912, and as Carlo Bo pointed out in his preface to Marin's *A sol calào* (To the Setting Sun, 1974), "In un certo senso c'è già tutto Marin o per lo meno ci sono già tutti i suoi temi: il vento; il mare; la luna e quelle occasioni di vita che in un paese segnano il passare del tempo e il ripetersi del destino" (In a way there is already all Marin or at least there are already all his themes: the wind; the sea; the moon and those occasions of life that in a village indicate the passage of time and the repetition of destiny). His poetry was born when the reaction to the nineteenth-century verse was in progress. Always attracted to life, free from every intellectual complication, and having absolute faith in poetry, Marin was not involved in the problematic debates of his contemporaries.

In the poetry of the *crepuscolari* (twilight poets) the use of a language that bordered on prose expressed a new reality in opposition to the high style of romantic poetry. The *crepuscolari* vision was gray, lacked vitality, and lamented the inauthenticity of human relations. Marin's dialect poetry serves instead to elevate the simple things he celebrates. Even hermeticism, which influenced the poetry of almost all the greatest poets of the twentieth century, had no effect on Marin. His language remains clear and syntactically simple. The objects are humble; the sentiments are not evoked through obscure analogies. The immediacy of the vision and the dazzling verse that, according to the hermeticists, should have been reached through a more elaborate use of analogy are reached by Marin with great simplicity. The apparently excessive simplification does not diminish the importance of what he celebrates. He knows he is part of a mystery that is impossible to explain, and he humbly accepts it, as in this untitled poem from *Poesie* (1981):

El giro de la vita
xe un gaudioso mistero:
me vivo imerso duto intiero
ne la corente sita.

(The course of life
is a joyful mystery:
I live immersed totally
in the silent current.)

He was not involved in the experimentalism of Italian poetry in his last decades. This experimentalism was testimony to a crisis not only of the individual but also of the language, which could no longer seem to represent, with traditional methods, the reality of modern life. One does not find a trace of this crisis in the poetry of Marin. There is instead always a deep adherence to the simple things that he celebrates, and his faith in poetry is never seen to diminish. For Marin there was only one thing superior to written poetry: the ability to feel and look at life with a poetic soul. Marin himself transcribed in his diary this sentence of Daniel-Rops: "Il y a seulment trois choses valables au monde: lire poésie, écrire poésie et, au dessus de tout, vivre en poésie" (There are only three things of value in the world: reading poetry, writing poetry and, above all, living in poetry).

Close to Marin's poetry are the ideals pursued by those people associated with the *Voce*. As the critic Luciana Borsetto wrote, "Del movimento della *Voce* prezzoliniana condivide la polemica contro la retorica intellettuale, il fervore disordinato, ma anche seriamente impegnato a portare alla luce . . . tutta la sensibilità necessaria a rinnovare la cultura, a promuovere una scrittura aderente alla realtà, in una ideale continuità tra arte-letteratura e vita (With the movement of [Giuseppe] Prezzolini's *Voce* he [Marin] shares the polemics against intellectual rhetoric, the untidy fervor, but is also seriously engaged in bringing to light . . . all the necessary sensitivity to renew the culture, to promote a writing that adheres to reality, in an ideal continuity between art-literature and life).

In Marin's use of dialect there is a striking absence of any intellectualism or polemics. Nor is there an intentional opposition to nondialect poetry. The reasons Marin chose to write in dialect were explained by him (to Bo) in 1974: "Perché ho scritto in gradese? Perché ero io la coscienza, la prima coscienza della piccola comunità dell'isola. E all'isola ero attaccato, e quel suo linguaggio era l'unica eredità dei padri che la mia *pietas* voleva salvare" (Why have I written in Gradese? Because I was the consciousness, the first consciousness of the small community of the island. And I was attached to the island, and that language of hers was the only inheritance of the fathers that my *compassion* wanted to save). Feeling almost a moral obligation to make Grado immortal with his poetry, Marin was, however, conscious of the limits that the choice of dialect, as his poetic language, brought with it. But dialect was the only vehicle with which he could completely express his world.

Marin circa 1982

Most critics stress the extremely personal use of dialect by Marin that makes it almost a new language. According to Fernando Bandini, "E evidente l'intenzione dell'autore di isolare il proprio dialetto dalle parlate venete attuali: ma è anche evidente la ricerca della irripetibilità della propria lingua poetica" (It is evidently the author's intention to isolate his dialect from actual Venetian dialects: but also evident is the search for the uniqueness of his poetic language). Marin did not consider the dialect an inferior language from an artistic viewpoint. His simplicity and humility of language, however, go with a very high concept of poetry and an unshakable faith in it and in his own work. For Marin, poetry was a connection between humankind and God. It is from God that poetry is directly derived, as Marin emphasizes in "Me creo in tu" (I Believe in You) in *I canti de l'ísola* (The Songs of the Island, 1951):

Me crèo in Tu, no' crèo in me, Paron:
me sento cana svoda a la to boca,
e se tu sufi, el svodo manda son,
fa musica la cana mia tarloca.

(I believe in You, I do not believe in me, Master:
I feel like an empty reed in your mouth,

and if you blow, the emptiness will make a sound,
my reed makes worthless music.)

And if poetry derives from God, with an inverse movement it leads back to him, as Marin says in "Dono de Dio" (Gift from God) in *Dopo la longa istàe* (After the Long Summer, 1965):

Me canto dolse da tanto;
me scolta i vinti che passa,
le picole onde che lassa
in pianto

la spiasa bassa del lìo;
un omo mai no' me scolta:
se leva 'l canto a la volta
de Dio.

(I have been singing sweetly for a long time;
the winds that pass listen to me,
the little waves that leave
crying

the low beach of the shore;
no one ever listens to me:
the poem rises itself
toward God.)

Marin's is a poetry he perceived in life. In the whole of life, not in its transfer to the page, he recognized the highest form of poetry. His poetry can be monotonous or sad at times, but it always flows from the heart, he says, to emphasize the nonliterary nature of his inspiration, as in this untitled poem from *El vento de l'eterno se fa teso* (The Wind of the Eternal It Is Strained, 1973):

Dal cuor sgorga perene
un filo cristalin de canto,
garghe volta xe un pianto
che intùrbida le vene.

La xe una storia sola
tre note, senpre quele:
'na vose de mandòla
in note sensa stele.

(From the heart perpetually flows
a crystalline thread of poem,
sometimes it is a cry
that muddies the veins.

It is only one story
three notes, always the same:
a voice of a mandolin
in night without stars.)

Marin's love poems always flow from a profound love of life. The natural light, the great sunniness present in his first collections (that continues to return with insistence in the poetry of his old age), testifies to the beauty that he saw in the life that surrounded him, the passion and the love that always moved him, as shown in "Me so nato dal sol" (I Am Born of the Sun) in *Dopo la longa istàe:*

> Me son nato dal sol,
> son figio d'elo e de la luse
> e amigo el vento fresco me conduse,
> me fa cantâ d'amor.
>
> (I am born of the sun,
> I am the son of him and of the light
> and as a friend the fresh wind leads me,
> it makes me sing of love.)

Love, in Marin's poetry, is always directed toward the objects and the people in his life. It expands to involve the whole universe, without, however, becoming a simple abstraction or a literary formula. Everything that he saw communicated to him a sentiment of love or admiration: for one of his *mamolusse* (little girls), for example, whose luminosity illuminates even the gray and flat landscape; or for the *colma* (high tide) and the *lìo* (shore).

Even the thought of death gave him a vital impulse, which was also an impulse of love, as in "Quanto più moro" (The More I Die), the title poem of *Quanto più moro* (1969):

> Quanto più moro
> – presensa al mondo intermitente
> e luse che se spenze, de ponente –
> tanto più de la vita m'inamoro.
>
> (The more I die
> – presence in the world intermittent
> and light that diminishes, in the west –
> the more I fall in love with life.)

Love and religion are intimately intertwined in Marin's poetry. His is like Saint Francis of Assisi's love, in which one praises and loves God by loving and praising all of his creatures. In Marin's microcosm the objects of praise are his beach, his sea, the trees near the river bank, the boats, the wind, the youngsters – all that he encountered. God was never seen or felt as a faraway abstraction. A concrete image always evoked a religious sentiment in Marin, and the spirituality is found in the most immediate concreteness of things in his poems. This metaphysical certainty allowed him to resist the pain and cruelties of life.

Grado – with its landscape, inhabitants, houses, and sea – is the constant setting for Marin's poetry. Grado is characterized by starkness; existence is simplicity itself. But everything appears illuminated by the light of the sun. *Maravegia* (marvelous) is a word that appears often in Marin's work to emphasize the constant fascination that the sights of life continue to offer. There are also moments of pain, melancholy, and desire to liberate himself from the confines of the flesh; uncertainty, doubt, and pain are accepted as a part of destiny. Yet existence is never seen as tragic. Marin always submitted to the mysteries of the universe.

Pier Paolo Pasolini saw Marin's selectivity of objects and the resulting thematic monotony as his desire to "fare di Grado il cosmo" (make of Grado the universe) by expanding "il microcosmo gradese a macrocosmo che imiti, ma *per essenzialità,* il macrocosmo religioso. Da ciò la contraddizione in termini: dilatazione attraverso riduzione" (the Gradese microcosm to a macrocosm that imitates, in *its essentials,* the religious macrocosm. Thus arises the contradiction in terms: expansion through reduction). The repetition and linguistic selectivity operate in that sense, and the language of Marin "allarga in campo semantico ciò che restringe in campo lessicale" (widens in the semantic field that which it narrows in the lexical field). In this way Marin does not reduce his island to folklore, nor his poetry to simple rustic illustration, but he confers on Grado the characteristics of universality.

Despite thematic monotony, however, the poetry of Marin is not static. In the early collections the elements celebrated are felt in their most immediate physicality, but with the passage of time his poetry became more subtle, and memory, nostalgia, and dreams appear. Also, from the formal point of view, a progressive condensation of the verse is present. He gradually progresses from longer lyrics with simple melodic movements (almost canzonets), and from extremely concrete physical presences, to a musicality and a figuration, as critic Giulio Cattaneo says, "sui confini col silenzio e l'invisibile" (on the confines of the silence and the invisible). To see this movement toward musicality and subtlety, one has only to compare some poems in which the objects celebrated are clouds, which Marin uses to express his desire to escape human limitations. In this poem of 1951, "Oh, la tristessa" (Oh, Sadness), from *I canti de l'isola,* the clouds, as well as the sky and the sea, maintain their concreteness, and the rustic description is vivid and precise:

> Che vol, che vol 'sto cuor infermo,
> che via per l'aria incòra 'l va baucando?

Una nuvola d'oro zoveneta
da vêghe navegâ pel sielo fondo,
e andâ co' ela, in svolo sora 'l mondo,
portài dal vento fin a note queta.

(What does it want, what does this ill heart want,
that through the air goes fantasizing?

A young golden cloud
seen navigating in the deep sky,
and to go with her, in flight above the world,
carried by the wind to a tranquil night.)

In "Me son el specio terso" (I Am the Clear Mirror),
from *L'estadela de San Martin* (The Summer of Saint
Martin, 1958), the precise rustic description seems
less important than what Marin wants to symbolize:

Me son el specio terso d'un fondào
do palmo d'acqua e, soto, sabia e fango:
ma 'l sielo se riflete trasognào
co' nuòli in svolo o moto d'ale stanco.

(I am the clear mirror of a shoal
two palms of water and, underneath, sand and mud:
but the sky is reflected dreaming
with clouds in flight or tired movement of wings.)

Ultimately in this untitled poem from "Versi ultimi
(1978–1980)" (The Last Verses), in the 1981 *Poesie,*
the clouds that previously were used to symbolize a
definite feeling of the speaker become a symbol of
human life in general and become presences that are
almost unreal, difficult to separate from the inner
life of the speaker:

Xe nuvole vaganti
nel sielo, site,
le nostre vite,
. . . .

Le stele fisse
tra i nuvoli sparisse
e basta el vento
pel perdimento.

(Our lives are
wandering clouds,
in heaven, silent,
. . . .

The fixed stars
disappear among the clouds
and the wind is enough
for the loss of awareness.)

Marin arrives therefore at the overcoming of
reality, not through a removal from it but through
an increasingly profound adherence to the world he
celebrates. In his later collections the thought of approaching death, the regret for his lost youth, and
the introspection absent in the first collections combine to permit moments of great vital impetus, of
wonder for the sights that the world offers him. The
profound passion he has always felt for life is integral, and the summer, which Marin identifies with
the total availability of life, even if almost finished,
continues to live in him, as seen in "Credème a me"
(Believe Me) in *Dopo la longa istàe*:

Credème a me: l'istàe
no' la finisse mai
se la portè nel sangue
co' duti i siel stelài.

(Believe me: the summer
never ends
we carry it in our blood
with all the starred heavens.)

In Marin's poetry one finds an echo of tradition. Among the poets Marin recognized as masters
were Johann Wolfgang von Goethe and other great
German Romantics. This affinity is recognizable in
Marin's attributing the value of universality to the
particular – to his own experience and to his own
world – in the same way in which, in German Romantic poetry, the voice of the individual becomes
an expression of the universal. The role that Marin
attributes to the poet, as the transmitter of a truth
that comes to him directly from God, is similar to
the role that the German Romantics attributed to
the poet.

Among Italians Marin recognized as masters
were Dante, Ugo Foscolo, Giacomo Leopardi, and
Giovanni Pascoli. Marin is similar to Dante in his
profound faith in God and in his recognition of love
as the great inspiration of his poetry. He shares with
Foscolo the desire to find and confer immortality
through poetry. With Leopardi he shares at times a
dismay when confronting life, but he is also like
Leopardi in affirming that the voice of nature unites
the poet with the voice of the eternal. A similar psychological disposition joins Pascoli and Marin: the
sense of mystery in which all things are enveloped,
and the attitude of looking at the world with the
soul of a child. But a major difference between
Pascoli and Marin is that Pascoli experimented with
the dissolution of language and syntax, whereas
Marin did not.

Finally a certain affinity can also be found
with oriental thought. The love that Marin always
nourished for all creatures of God and his seeing in
them a manifestation of God are close to the panthe-

ism of the religions of the East. Marin always had a lively interest in the works of Rabindranath Tagore and other Eastern poets and philosophers, in particular the Chinese Li Tao Po. Ironically all these myriad influences contributed to the recognizable individuality of Marin and his work. Further setting him apart is his masterful use of dialect and his attention to small things that become large in meaning.

Interview:

Fulvio Panzeri, "Marin racconta se stesso," in Marin's *Le litànie de la Madona,* third edition (Venice: Locusta, 1981), pp. 43–50.

Letters:

Un dialogo: Scelta di lettere, 1967–1981. Biagio Marin, Giorgio Voghera, edited by Elvio Guagnini (Trieste: Provincia, 1982).

Bibliography:

Elvio Guagnini, Bibliography, in Marin's *El vento de l'eterno se fa teso,* edited by Edda Serra and Guagnini (Milan: Scheiwiller, 1973), pp. 541–549.

References:

Carlo Bo, "Conoscete Biagio Marin?," *Corriere della Sera,* 10 September 1967;

Bo, "Il mar grando di Biagio Marin," preface to Marin's *A sol calào* (Milan: Rusconi, 1974), pp. 5–34;

Bo, ed., *Omaggio al poeta Biagio Marin* (Trieste: Circolo della Cultura e delle Arti, 1962);

Luciana Borsetto, "La poetica di Biagio Marin," *Rassegna della Letteratura Italiana,* 7 (September–December 1974): 456–466;

Marcello Camilucci, "Biagio Marin: Un alto canto della vita," *Osservatore Romano,* 3 August 1970;

Giulio Cattaneo, "I Canti de l'isola di Biagio Marin," *Paragone,* no. 248 (October 1970): 143–148;

Claudio Magris, "Io sono un golfo," preface to Marin's *Nel silenzio più teso,* edited by Edda Serra (Milan: Rizzoli, 1980), pp. 5–24;

Eugenio Montale, "La musa dialettale," *Corriere della Sera,* 15 January 1953;

Pier Paolo Pasolini, "Appunti per un saggio su Biagio Marin," preface to Marin's *La vita xe fiama, 1963–1969,* edited by Claudio Magris (Turin: Einaudi, 1970), pp. v–x;

Gian Paolo Resentera, *Il divino nella poesia di Biagio Marin* (Schio: Ascledum, 1976);

Andrea Zanzotto, "Poesia che ascolta l'onde," *Corriere della Sera,* 5 June 1977.

Elio Pagliarani

(25 May 1927 –   )

Fausto Pauluzzi

BOOKS: *Cronache ed altre poesie* (Milan: Schwarz, 1954);

Inventario privato (Milan: Veronelli, 1959);

Le sue ragioni, by Pagliarani and Angelo Paccagnini (Milan: Rusconi & Paolazzi, 1960);

Piero Manzoni (Milan: Scheiwiller, 1961);

La ragazza Carla e altre poesie (Milan: Mondadori, 1962); enlarged as *La ragazza Carla e nuove poesie,* edited by Alberto Asor Rosa (Milan: Mondadori, 1978);

Lezione di fisica (Milan: All'Insegna del Pesce d'Oro, 1964); enlarged as *Lezione di fisica e fecaloro* (Milan: Feltrinelli, 1968);

Pelle d'asino, by Pagliarani and Alfredo Giuliani (Milan: Scheiwiller, 1964);

Il fiato dello spettatore (Padua: Marsilio, 1972);

Rosso corpo lingua oro pope-papa scienza (Rome: Cooperativa Scrittori, 1977);

Poesie da recita, edited by Alessandra Briganti (Rome: Bulzoni, 1985);

Esercizi platonici (Palermo: Acquario, 1985);

Epigrammi ferraresi (Lecce: Manni, 1987);

La bella addormentata nel bosco (Milan: Corpo 10, 1987).

OTHER: *I maestri del racconto italiano,* edited by Pagliarani and Walter Pedullà (Milan: Rizzoli, 1964);

"Intervento," in *Gruppo '63: Il romanzo sperimentale* (Milan: Feltrinelli, 1966);

Manuale di poesia sperimentale, edited by Pagliarani and Guido Guglielmi (Milan: Mondadori, 1966);

Charles Olson, *Le lontananze,* translated by Pagliarani and William McCormick (Milan: Rizzoli, 1967);

Vittoria Bradshaw, ed. and trans., *From Pure Silence to Impure Dialogue: A Survey of Post War Italian Poetry, 1945–1965,* includes poems by Pagliarani (New York: Las Américas, 1971), pp. 677–706;

"Per una definizone dell'avanguardia," in *Gruppo '63: Critica e teoria,* edited by Nanni Balestrini (Milan: Feltrinelli, 1976);

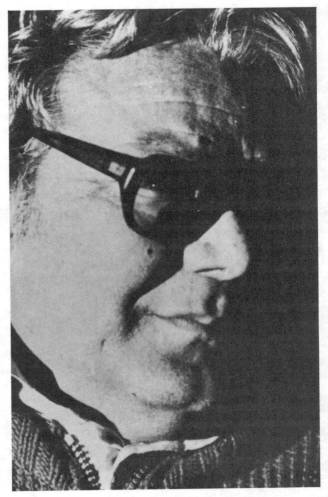

Elio Pagliarani circa 1980 (photograph by Gabriella Maleti)

Erminia Artese, ed., *Dario Fo parla di Dario Fo,* preface by Pagliarani (Cosenza: Lerici, 1977);

Ruth Feldman and Brian Swann, eds., *Italian Poetry Today: Currents and Trends,* includes poems by Pagliarani (Saint Paul: New Rivers, 1979), pp. 150–153;

Lawrence R. Smith, ed. and trans., *The New Italian Poetry: 1945 to the Present. A Bilingual Anthology,* includes poems by Pagliarani (Berkeley & Los

Angeles: University of California Press, 1981), pp. 177–195.

SELECTED PERIODICAL PUBLICATIONS –
UNCOLLECTED: "Invito al chiarimento della poesia contemporanea," *Fiera Letteraria,* 3 (July 1960): 4;
"Poesia ideologica e passione oggettiva," *Nuova Corrente,* 31 (1963): 37–40;
"Dibattito (per un bilancio dell'esperienza neo-avanguardista)," *Quaderni di Critica,* 1 (1973): 8–29;
"Poesie tra avanguardia e restaurazione," *Periodo Ipotetico,* 10–11 (1977): 3–6.

Elio Pagliarani's vigorous and exacting experimentation with language accounts for his poetic importance. By his constant and documented ideological debate with the literary establishment, especially as a member of "Gruppo '63," Pagliarani has protected artistic freedom from the encroaching, declining aesthetics of neorealism and hermeticism, and from the debilitating compromises sought by postindustrial authoritarians. In three broad periods of activity, he has chronicled the harsh stories of common people, exposed the exasperating quality of the language available to poets, and recycled traditional reflective texts to promote a calm inner debate. The poet lives in Rome with his wife, the former Cetta Petrollo; they have two children.

Born in Viserba on 25 May 1927, Pagliarani developed strong sensitivities to mathematical thinking, poetic expression, social justice, and the tenuousness of existence. He studied at the Liceo Scientifico, where he aspired to become a mathematics professor. His father, a courageous socialist persecuted since World War I, worked as a coachman for hire, especially to rich families that summered on the Rimini coast. The young poet had contact with those families, making some friendships with their children. The sum total of his experience, however, told him that he hated the ways of the rich. One friendship was with the young Giovanna Bemporad, whose publishing family Pagliarani held in high esteem. She recited poetry to him, and he began to write his own. Although as a teenager he strove to be original, he recalls a slight influence from Gabriele D'Annunzio at first, and from Giovanni Pascoli later. Childhood was marked for Pagliarani by the loss of an eye. During World War II he was arrested by the Germans and was deeply affected by the sight of a grievously wounded youth who nearly died in his presence.

In 1945 Pagliarani moved to Milan, an industrial and commercial melting pot of contradictions. It held simple people but also tyrants. Pagliarani worked for an import-export firm, where his concern with morality and fairness typed him as an undesirable. As time went on, he tried other kinds of office work. For a while he returned to Viserba, to work for a bank where the supervisor tried forcing thoughtless conformity on him. In the meantime he had enrolled at the University of Padua, where he became familiar with the language of economics and law. Graduation, in 1951, qualified him for employment in Milan's evening professional schools, where he was exposed to fresh examples of human injustice. In 1956 he joined the editorial staff of *Avanti!,* the Socialist-party daily.

In the early postwar period Pagliarani and other poets had felt the need to use a language that was prosaic, accessible to everyone, and capable of concretely conveying experiences. In Pagliarani's case this may have been because early on he had been sensitized to the honest use of speech, and because his experience in the Milan business world had taught him to dislike hype. In those days the publishing establishment was financially committed to hermetic and neorealist poetry. Pagliarani could not relate to neorealist "partisan poetry" because it spoke of flowers and stars, not of machine guns – objects considered not idyllic enough for poetry. Neither could he relate to neorealism itself, which, while concerned with humble people and their events, did not attempt a critical assessment of conditions, limiting itself to mimetic descriptions. Pagliarani perceived the estrangement of the humble, living in an increasingly technical, scientific, and mass-marketing world: he felt it was imperative to depict not merely the voice of their discomfort but also those social forces that were determining their lives. Showing causality, indicating responsibility for social conditions while telling a story, was his methodology. Pagliarani found unsuitable the type of poetry that talked about tears but did not produce them, which tried to mediate between the social wasteland and personal unhappiness. He objected to the self-enclosed lyricism of the hermetics, for example, noting that their self-involved style could not concretely show the new social conditions. In the early 1950s Pagliarani sympathized with the political Left, which, ironically, was backing "uncritical" neorealism. He had been unwilling to join the Communist party because of an aversion to Joseph Stalin and Palmiro Togliatti.

Pagliarani's involvement with magazines seeking the renewal of Italian culture – *Rendiconti, Nuovi*

Argomenti, Il Verri, and *Menabò* — began in the mid 1950s. An appreciation of Cesare Pavese's moral and truthful prose fortified him then, as likely did the goodwill of Pier Paolo Pasolini's group at *Officina.* Pagliarani's most important literary encounters, though, were with T. S. Eliot and Ezra Pound. On reading *The Waste Land* (1922), Pagliarani was struck by the style of language, which objectively referred to pimply clerks, lovemaking on a sofa, and abortion. This kind of diction, he perceived, could well serve to depict the epic but anonymous struggles of common Milanese citizens. As Italian poetry then did not have an objective language for describing daily survival in an alienating environment, Pagliarani gambled on inventing one. This style was Dantean, he has said, and opposed to Petrarchan or Francophile prosody, which historically has tended to mire Italian poets in the role of either aesthete or priest. Pagliarani learned and valued Pound's lessons on free verse, non-Western poetic traditions, the Middle Ages, and the crucial importance of being sincere with technique, rather than using it for self-adornment. Pound's civic commitment, furthermore, though not shared, was admired by Pagliarani, as were those moments of *The Pisan Cantos* (1948) in which Pound reflected on his own Medieval-like confinement.

Pagliarani's "critical" realism was a strategy with a twofold aim: to discover the proper set of guidelines for each instance of poetic creation (given the unsuitability of traditional aesthetics), and to produce a dialectic about personal values (since new social values were needed). Pagliarani's experimentation was rooted in the belief that art must promulgate new methods of thinking in order to reveal the true nature of events. A "critical" poet, therefore, would not effect mimetic playbacks of life through his own voice but rather would construct mosaic segments of it, which openly showed the reason for their union. Such segments were believable because the alienated style in which they were presented kept the reader from bonding emotionally with the story, and of distance created a sensation that allowed reflection to occur. Consequently the reader would be able to integrate poetry into his own existence. Pagliarani's new style was promoting reform.

Conscious of resistance from established literary circles to poetry with an estranged style and with language that was prosaic and pluralistic, Pagliarani explained his poetic concepts and drew distinctions. In essays such as "Intervento" (1959; collected in *Gruppo '63: Il romanzo sperimentale,* 1966), he ably demonstrated that *lirica* (lyric) was not identical with *poesia* (poetry) but was a poetic category. Furthermore *poesia* was not an essence of guaranteed, privileged existence. Most important of all, though, he explained that only a poetic language replete with everyday terms, concerned with the forces present in daily life, and held together by a nonlinear syntax could truthfully transmit the contemporary social state of affairs.

The period from 1947 to 1960 was, for Pagliarani, a stage of poetic development concerned with the contradictions of modern industrial society, the traditional poet's roles as "sensitive recluse" and "man of the people," and the need to invent a new style that could expose the reader to reality by making him face a linguistic landscape just as alienated and alienating as the socioeconomic one. During this period Pagliarani found friendship and support among younger Italian poets who were also opposing establishment literature. Works by four of these — Antonio Porta, Nanni Balestrini, Edoardo Sanguineti, and Alfredo Giuliani — appeared with poems by Pagliarani in a 1961 anthology, *I Novissimi: Poesie per gli anni sessanta* (The Very New Ones: Poems for the Sixties), edited by Giuliani and prefaced by a theoretical essay that showed their common poetic views. The anthology gave unified expression to previously independent concepts of experimentation and served as a stimulus for more mature thinking on the subject.

The twelve poems of *Cronache ed altre poesie* (Chronicles and Other Poems, 1954), written between 1947 and 1952, average twenty-two lines each. They feature prose, free atonal verses, sparse rhyming, common diction, unadorned imagery, and conversational narrative logic. At times the sense of a poem is developed by intuitive leaps rather than deliberation. The speaker is engaged in reflection, reconstructing the behavior of the world, and imagining what he would do or has done in reaction to it. Secondary voices come from city life, to inject the sense of the street into the poetry, or to expose the hopes and dreams of the humble. Irony is always reserved for those who seek safety within the establishment. A thematic concern is the effect of postwar industrial life on everyday people. Pagliarani treats topics such as the waste implicit in closing a factory, students who attend parties rather than study, soporific hopes and brutal life-styles within the faceless crowd, the confusion of eroticism with love, and the struggle to keep poetic awareness alive. The bleak details of individual life are rendered through the same language forms with which that life effects its survival: "Dopo la pioggia con i rospi in mezzo alle strade / ho fede che mi potrai trovare" (After the rain with the frogs scattered on the road / I know you will be able to find me).

Inventario privato (Private Inventory, 1959) chronicles a 1957 failed love relationship. There are Sunday strolls in the park, flowers never sent, and an inconclusive final walk near the former lover's house. The protagonist lives in a world of H-bomb testing, office-work drudgery, and working-class restaurants. He accepts the illusion that a secretary who is irritable, egotistical, and sullen can bring life to his death-pervaded consciousness. Different mentalities and values doom the illusion, and the protagonist accepts a friend's insight that his emotions were not genuine from the start. The courtly, lyrical language, present among everyday expressions, combines with an atonal, prosaic versification to portray the unresolved psychological contrast between an idealization of love and the earthy need of it. When the protagonist tries to tailor his emotions to his desires, irony is turned against him. Fundamental in this process are analogies between the personal love situation and the socioeconomic state of other people: "Ti ho perduta per troppo amore / come per fame l'affamato / che rovescia la ciotola col tremito" (I lost you because of too much love / as the hungry man who in hunger / drops the bowl by his own trembling). Through these analogies, Pagliarani combines the themes of personal love and contemporary Milanese life, and he avoids the sentimental effusions of conventional love poetry. Rather than prolonging his tale with hermetic symbolism and memories, he confronts it as it unfolds. Psychological insights are the reward. The twenty-one short poems constitute a reform of the thematic treatment and linguistic expression of love in poetry.

The poem "La Ragazza Carla" (A Girl Named Carla), written from 1954 to 1957, was a public success for Pagliarani. It was published piecemeal in *Nuova Corrente* and *Il Verri*, then whole in the *Menabò* (1960); in the anthology *I Novissimi*; and, together with his two preceding poetry collections, in *La ragazza Carla e altre poesie* (1962). The events described are those of jumbled Milanese life in 1948: political tensions spilling out; the commercial world keeping its guard; and ordinary people who have hard work, laughter, tears, fun, and preoccupations. Carla is seventeen, is from a lower-class family, and has little self-knowledge, petit bourgeois values, and idyllic aspirations. Physically repulsed by the working environment and devoid of the resources for self-actualization, she develops a sense of worth only as a sex object. This outlook prefigures the eventual betrayal of her aspirations by the system

that repulses her. A joke from the times, adapted by Pagliarani for use in the poem, lends a measure of insight to the difficulties faced by people such as Carla in their work environment: "Telefonano a un circo. / Pronto: batto a macchina e parlo francese, non basta? / So andare in bicicletta e dire il credo, non basta / per il circo? Non sentite che nitrisco, che volete di più / da un povero cavallo?" (Somebody calls a circus. / Hello: I can type and speak French, isn't that enough? / I know how to ride a bike and recite the creed, isn't that enough / for a circus? Can't you hear me neighing, what else do you want / from a wretched horse?).

"La Ragazza Carla" is a short narrative poem in three parts. To tell his story, Pagliarani brings together metric forms and print styles that project dissonance and discord, and prose excerpts – from the commercial, technical, and political worlds – that heighten the feeling of estrangement. A pervasive lack of punctuation, together with syntactic deformations, makes the flow of images tumultuous. The "noble" verses of the Italian poetic tradition are made to carry banalities and not music; they are mostly atonal and prosaic. When there is music, it either serves as a contrast to the degrading quality of office life, or it appears in the guise of nursery rhymes, presenting gentle thoughts and desires that common people are not often able to express. Pieces of the work have a choral function that confers on it an epic dimension. The creative technique of "La Ragazza Carla" was new for Pagliarani; it was motivated by the belief that an artist, in order to create works of objective use to others, must keep his personal whims from entering the action, and that reality should be presented through its material forms. Pagliarani has likened the style of this poem to the musical compositions of Arnold Schönberg. It is a style that he continued to use in his works that followed.

Le sue ragioni (The Summing Up, 1960), a musical whose script Pagliarani coauthored, is the story of a man on his deathbed, who recovers in time to confront the venality of his wife and daughter, their lack of spiritual commitment to the family. The language is commonplace and full of banalities; unlike Pagliarani's previous works, it is devoid of vernacular color. To quell his own subjective reactions to the facts and to promote reflection in the audience, he chose as conduits the stereotyped masks of the commedia dell'arte. These aptly represent the theme of alienation because they have no psychological complexity. The information they reveal enables the audience to judge, at will, the morality of any human action.

In 1961 Pagliarani moved to Rome, where he continued working full-time for *Avanti!* and part-time for Milanese publishers for one year. The Italian economic recovery was about to reach its zenith, and the publishing establishment was eager to flood the market with new materials. Pagliarani joined a group of writers, musicians, and other artists who met at the Caffè Rosati to discuss their own work and the new ideas of others. The writers focused on studies of the nature of language, seeking to learn how a transcendental poetic awareness could be induced by manipulating language itself. As they created new works, the surprising theoretical implications of linguistic structures revealed themselves. In 1963 the musicians who met at the Caffè Rosati invited their friends to read and discuss poetry at a musical congress in Palermo. Media coverage resulted in continuing notoriety for the poets, and the labels "Neoavanguardia" and "Gruppo '63" were applied to them. The individuals most often mentioned were the five who, in 1961, had been called "I Novissimi."

The 1960s and 1970s were the most fertile period of Pagliarani's career in poetry. He often engaged in public debate, rigorous intellectual experimentation with language, and theoretical publications that sought to define his innovative poetics. He participated in the Gruppo '63 congresses of 1964, 1965, and 1966; topics of discussion were the relationship of the new poetry to the other arts (especially visual poetry), the criteria for reforming the novel, and the danger of potential dogmatic stances. Pagliarani's important contribution was the idea that literature could have a social function and be art at the same time, if the artist, regardless of his ideological view, made it his duty to keep language fit and vibrant; Pagliarani believed in "una funzione sociale della letteratura . . . che non esaurisce . . . la letteratura, ma che è verificabile oggettivamente, a prescindere da ogni intenzionalità. La funzione è quella di mantenere in efficienza per tutti il linguaggio" (a social function of literature . . . that does not exhaust . . . literature, and whose influence on a work is objectively demonstrable, regardless of an artist's personal intent. Its function is to ensure that language is fit for everyone's effective use), as he says in "Per una definizione dell'avanguardia" (*Gruppo '63: Critica e teoria*, 1976). This idea implies the destruction of conventional speech and its restructuring into new semantic chains that allow the reader to perceive fresh meanings in place of previous trite ones. With this accomplished, a poet could safely give vent to his private revolutionary ferment – against bourgeois structures and institutions –

without the fear of conditioning the reader to value judgments identical to his own. Pagliarani's need to deemphasize his subjective impulses, in order to ensure autonomy for the reader, forced a break with Pier Paolo Pasolini and his group, whose poetry required the writer to isolate himself and be subjective. The belief that poetry had the social function of keeping language fit for effective use was forcing Pagliarani to oppose all sophisms that offered transcendent rationales for choosing a style. He cautioned against informality, action poetry, and pop poetry. In 1964 he declined to continue working with the avant-garde review *Grammatica* because, though open-minded and relevant, it held the position that poetic language and structures have no obligation to communicate.

The social climate of Italy in the late 1960s showed the influence of the protest movement in politics, in television, and in communications in general. Pagliarani found it increasingly important to reflect and comment on national and international political questions and on social customs. He became a contributor to *Quindici* and *Rinascita,* while in his poetic works he treated topics of sociopolitical relevance with the most broad-minded experimental techniques. As he sensed that the book, as the preferred object of social communication, was being replaced by kinetic media, he abandoned his visually stimulating style of poetry for one whose vocal qualities and accompanying gestures could shake the sensory systems of his audience. Appealing to the senses would guarantee that the new poetic style was interactive. In proposing this variation of style, which was suitable to public recitals and featured long verses whose delivery could be varied to produce any desired effect, Pagliarani relied on his theater experience (he was the theater critic for *Paese Sera*) and on Charles Olson's psychological discoveries about poetry. The 1970s, during which Pagliarani became editor in chief of *Periodo Ipotetico* and cofounder of the first writers' cooperative publishing enterprise in Italy, the Cooperativa Scrittori, saw the affirmation of Pagliarani as an oral poet and a conveyor of social truths.

In 1964 Pagliarani had published *Lezione di fisica* (Physics Lesson), comprising six letters in verse (1961–1964) and a long poem from 1956. Topics include scientific progress, southern Italy, and gold production. These are treated in a manner that reveals the clashing of nostalgic visions of preindustrial, precapitalist life with a stimulating, yet horrible, present. Extensive use is made of excerpts from physics, philosophy, psychology, economics, and politics to bring the real world and its values into the poems. Dry, learned speculations on survivability in a nuclear holocaust contrast with humanistic language not contaminated by the unfeeling diction of statistics, technology, and atomic-energy production. Strange and dissonant semantic effects are produced as a result. These are intensified by the narrative line, which is structured as if the speaker's mind were falling apart, spilling out items that only a mass culture could have put there: "siamo in un ottocento d'appendice, non si può cavarne una storia / nemmeno da mettere in versi: ci sono esperienze / che non servono a niente che si inscrivono / come puro passivo" (we are in a nineteenth-century serial novel, there is not a story you can get out of it / not even for use in a poem: you experience things / that have no use that are entered / as pure losses). The alienating effect of the style fosters the perception of a contradictory truth: even high cultural achievements, such as science and technology, can be vehicles of human estrangement. As a result, irony is displayed toward all aspects of culture (poets included) that seek to exist as ends in themselves, outside of a dialectical relationship with society.

In 1968 *Lezione di fisica* was augmented with two poems and the previously unpublished "Fecaloro" (Fecalgold). The book's shape resembles that of a folded newspaper in a jacket pocket. The verses run generously lengthwise, allowing a lively scansion; each composition, as a result, is a dramatic recitativo, delivering aggregates of sound from singular spots on the page, through speaking voices that are part of the same context. The thematic linkages of "Fecaloro" are obvious in its two parts – the first focusing on the theory of goods and its association of feces with gold and money; and the second being the personal story of a love that did not develop an honest reciprocity. Varied excerpts create contradictions, broken threads, and rhythmic distortions, as if a catastrophe in communications were taking place. These disturbances are meant to suggest that clear and simple solutions to the problems presented can only be found outside of the din, in a staging area of thought where new values can be acquired and used.

The long poem *Rosso corpo lingua oro pope-papa scienza* (Red Body Tongue Gold Pope-Father Science), published in 1977, is an original form of poetry. In the first part, Pagliarani presents, as successive blocks, two contending camps of concepts: red, body, and tongue – associated with an "us"; and gold, pope-father, and science – associated with a "them." By reshaping the narrative order of the first part, so that opposing concepts from each camp al-

ternate one-to-one in part 2 and come together within the same verse in part 3, Pagliarani renders a complete confrontation between these symbolic concepts. His style of presentation features an obsessive reiteration of key sounds, an exasperating rhythmic pattern, and a radical crescendo of speech that exclude any sequential logic. Internal rhymes, assonances, and repetitions bounce from one verse to another, creating a closed-circuit homophonic environment and an enduring echo, thus promoting an understanding of the basic truth that excess, egotism, and obsession – regardless of the camp they serve – should be avoided: "sembra più bello / ma c'è sempre il tranello / continuando a lustrare il coltello" (it seems really nice / but there's a hidden price / when you keep on shining the knife).

Pagliarani's poetic importance was confirmed by the popularity and critical reception of *La ragazza Carla e nuove poesie* (A Girl Named Carla and New Poems, 1978), made up of the complete 1962 edition of *La ragazza Carla e altre poesie,* half of *Lezione di fisica e fecaloro,* and the first part of *Rosso corpo lingua oro pope-papa scienza.* In 1985 *Poesie da recita* (Poems for Recital) was published, comprising the 1960 *Menabò* version of "La Ragazza Carla"; *Lezione di fisica e fecaloro*; and fragments from a work in progress since 1961, "La Ballata di Rudi" (Rudy's Ballad). The importance of this ballad lies in the evidence it gives of Pagliarani's continuous stylistic involvement with popular, oral culture, the dramatic power of language, and poetry's ability to shake the senses and have social impact. The lively vocal qualities of the ballad's verses and the intense bodily involvement they require for proper recitation mark them as innovative, especially in contrast with the melodic style of recitation used by symbolists and hermetics, who impressed their audiences with rhythms that were prophetic, suggestive, and hypnotic. "La Ballata di Rudi" reflects the development of a postwar society into an affluent one and makes use of many chronicled events from Pagliarani's own life. Though the ballad's topics are at times covered in such a bizarre way as to give the work the structure of a "happening," their theme is ever common: industrialized versus humane values; Milan versus Viserba; a gypsy cab driver versus an honest fisherman, and so on. Light irony highlights human excesses.

Along with many of his colleagues, Pagliarani broke with the Gruppo '63 in the late 1960s or early 1970s. His withdrawal was partly due to the increasingly technical preoccupations pervading their congresses and partly to the waves of social protest that required artists to be citizens first. In the mid 1970s, as some social protest became terrorism, as the energy crisis brought to the fore the precarious material dependency of Western cultures on cheap oil, and as the dream of unending progress stalled, the reformist concerns of Pagliarani and the *neoavanguardia* became all but ignored. Some of the poets, unable to find a new form of expression and finding the style they had developed empty and outmoded, ceased writing.

In *Esercizi platonici* (Platonic Exercises, 1985) Pagliarani attempts to infuse a modern meaning into Plato's ideas, making them more viable. For example, Pagliarani adapts Plato's words to say: "tutto ciò che diciamo essere / consta d'uno e di molti, e in sè contiene / un elemento determinante e una / indeterminazione" (everything we say exists / is comprised of one and many, and in itself contains / a substance that defines it and its own / indefiniteness).

Epigrammi ferraresi (Ferrara Epigrams, 1987) presents twenty-five short texts, poetic treatments of excerpts from Girolamo Savonarola's sermons. Coming from a genre whose objective is to foster adherence to an ethic, the poems exhibit rhetorical manipulation, the will to persuade, and an identifiable ideology. Their oral nature, however, locates them within the field of informal communications, where the senses are not easily fooled by talk. The texts are not conceived as isolated entities but are integrally related. Recurrent terms, such as *I, them,* and *Rome,* tie the texts together and stand as centers of a psychological contrast between, on the one hand, Heaven, the ire of God, and the courage of commitment, and, on the other, Hell, the abused concept of transcendence, and the libidinousness of the State. The conclusion suggested is that corruption is immanent. The estrangement created by this view, and by the use of Latin and archaic Italian words, underscores the seriousness of the alarm Pagliarani is giving, concerning those who "non credono e non possono credere" (do not and cannot believe) and who want others to share their complacency. Such an alarm reminds one of Pagliarani's constant commitment to the common good – as he prods into the open a postmodern enemy who has no convictions, who takes from the good only to create material excess. For *Epigrammi ferraresi* Pagliarani received the 1987 Mondello Prize for Poetry. He continues to live and write in Rome.

Interview:
Eugenio Battisti, "Intervista a Elio Pagliarani," *Marcatrè,* 11–13 (1965): 48–50.

Bibliographies:
Alberto Asor Rosa, "Antologia critica," in Pagliarani's *La ragazza Carla e nuove poesie,* edited by Rosa (Milan: Mondadori, 1978), pp. 30–63;

Rosa, "Bibliografia," in *La ragazza Carla e nuove poesie,* pp. 63–67;

Alessandra Briganti, "Bibliografia," in Pagliarani's *Poesie da recita,* edited by Briganti (Rome: Bulzoni, 1985), pp. 18–20;

Briganti, "Antologia della critica," in *Poesie da recita,* pp. 20–56.

References:
Luigi Ballerini, "Elio Pagliarani: Poesia come respiro (e come continuo saltare)," *New Directions,* 24 (1972);

Mario Boselli, "Procedimento metonimico e fonostilismi in *Lezione di fisica,*" *Nuova Corrente,* 42–43 (1967): 155–177;

Gianfranco Ciabatti, "La sperimentazione di Elio Pagliarani tra malizia formale e coraggio lirico," *Città,* 8 (1967);

David Demby, "Pagliarani: La rapsodia dell'import-export," *Punto,* 10 (October 1964);

Costanzo Di Girolamo, "Ritratti critici di contemporanei," *Belfagor,* 2 (1974): 187–203;

Gabriella Di Paola, *La Ragazza Carla: Linguaggio e figure* (Rome: Bulzoni, 1984);

Gian Carlo Ferretti, "Poesia di Pagliarani," *Rinascita* (12 July 1968): 25–26;

Guido Guglielmi, "Recupero della dimensione epica," *Paragone,* no. 160 (1963): 122–124;

Sergio Pautasso, "L'*Inventario* di Pagliarani," *Nuova Corrente,* 14 (1959): 59–61;

Walter Siti, "La signorina Carla," *Nuovi Argomenti,* 29–30 (1972).

Alessandro Parronchi

(26 December 1914 –   )

Romana Capek-Habekovic
University of Michigan

BOOKS: *I giorni sensibili* (Florence: Vallecchi, 1941);

Ottone Rosai (Milan: Hoepli, 1941);

Ugo Capocchini (Florence: Parenti, 1941);

Mario Marcucci (Florence: Vallecchi, 1942);

I visi (Florence: Rivoluzione, 1943);

Nomi della pittura italiana contemporanea (Florence: Arnaud, 1944);

Van Gogh (Rome: Del Turco, 1948; revised edition, Milan: Garzanti, 1954);

Rosai (Rome: Del Turco, 1948; revised as *Rosai òggi* (Florence: Pananti, 1982);

Un'attesa (Modena: Guanda, 1949; enlarged edition, Urbino: Istituto Statale d'Arte, 1962);

Lorenzo Viani (Florence: Strozzina, 1949);

L'opera di Alberto Magri (Florence: Strozzina, 1951);

L'incertezza amorosa (Milan: Schwarz, 1952);

Per strade di bosco e città (Florence: Vallecchi, 1954);

Edgar-Hilaire-Germain Degas (Milan: Garzanti / New York & Amsterdam: Abrams, 1954);

Coraggio di vivere (Milan: All'Insegna del Pesce d'Oro, 1956; enlarged edition, Milan: Garzanti, 1961);

Arrigo del Rigo (Prato: Associazione Turistica Pratese, 1956);

La noia della natura (Lecce: Pajano, 1958);

Artisti toscani del primo Novecento (Florence: Sansoni, 1958);

L'opera di Giovanni Mazzuoli (Florence: Associazione Turistica Pratese, 1959);

Studi sulla dolce prospettiva (Milan: Martello, 1964);

Pregiudizi e libertà dell'arte moderna (Florence: Le Monnier, 1964);

15 Fattori (Milan: All'Insegna del Pesce d'Oro, 1964);

L'apparenza non inganna (Milan: All'Insegna del Pesce d'Oro, 1966);

Masaccio (Florence: Sadea-Sansoni, 1966);

Opere giovanili di Michelangelo, 3 volumes (Florence: Olschki, 1968, 1975, 1981);

Michelangelo scultore (Florence: Sadea-Sansoni, 1969); translated by Pearl Sanders and Caroline Beamish as *Michelangelo: Sculpture* (New York: Grosset & Dunlap, 1968); translated by John Hale-White (London: Thames & Hudson, 1969);

Pietà dell'atmosfera (Milan: Garzanti, 1970);

Paolo Uccello (Bologna: Boni, 1974);

Il Cupido dormente di Michelangelo (Florence: Conti, 1974);

Le due cupole, by Parronchi and Eugenio Casalini (Florence: Convento SS. Annunziata, 1977);

Umori (Florence: Pananti, 1978);

Replay; L'estate a pezzi (Milan: Garzanti, 1980);

Donatello e il potere (Bologna: Cappelli, 1980);

Prime e ultime (Padua: Pandolfo, 1981);

Trattato di architettura militare (Florence: Gonnelli, 1982);

Ombra mai fu (Florence: Pananti, 1982);

Intime (Urbino: Bidiellepi, 1983);

Luna chiantigiana (Salerno: Catalogo, 1984);

Botticelli fra Dante e Petrarca (Florence: Nardini, 1985);

"Expertise" per Vittorio (Milan: Scheiwiller, 1986);

La Chiesa fiorentina presenta (Florence: Becocci, 1986);

Giorgione e Raffaello (Bologna: Boni, 1989);

Climax (Milan: Garzanti, 1990).

TRANSLATIONS: Humilis, *Poesie* (Florence: Fiorentina, 1944);

Stéphane Mallarmé, *L'Apres-Midi d'un Faune* (Florence: Fiore, 1945);

Gérard de Nerval, *Le Chimere* (Florence: Fussi, 1948);

Arthur Rimbaud, *Una stagione all'inferno* (Florence: Fussi, 1948);

Alessandro Parronchi circa 1960

Mallarmé, *Il Monologo, l'Improvviso e il Pomeriggio d'un Fauno* (Florence: Fussi, 1951);

Maurice de Guérin, *Il Centauro e altri poemi* (Florence: Fussi, 1951);

Jean Racine, *Britannico,* in *Teatro francese del grande secolo* (Turin: ERI, 1960).

SELECTED PERIODICAL PUBLICATION – UNCOLLECTED: "Alone," *Ca'balà,* 1 (July 1950).

The beginnings of Alessandro Parronchi's literary and critical endeavors occurred in Florence in the 1930s. At first, with his contemporaries Mario Luzi and Piero Bigongiari, he followed in the footsteps of the hermetic poets from the early years of the twentieth century. His early verses show how he assimilated and elaborated the hermetic style, adding his personal tone. Parronchi's images spring from the traditional poetic vocabulary, modified by new meanings, the way the hermetic poets approach the language. He adopted their use of the word as a symbol of the deepest, often ambiguous, emotions; their freely structured verses; their lyricism; and, most of all, their sensitivity. His early poetry traces the hermetic technique of translating reality into a highly subjective poetic language of obscure images that creates a rarefied, metaphysical atmosphere. What he also shares with the early works of hermetic poets (especially Giuseppe Ungaretti, Salvatore Quasimodo, and Eugenio Montale) is a refusal of any political involvement. In his later poems Parronchi's interest is directed more toward human and social reality. The presence of his family and friends replaces the hermetic exclusiveness of expression and images. His language, with the repeated use of certain themes and concepts, concentrates often on a single theme and expresses his own experience. In his later works Parronchi acknowledges that he is involved, willingly or not, in the social, political, and cultural changes Italy had been undergoing, and his escape to the past is often justified by his negative comments regarding the present.

Critics often speak about the multitude of influences on Parronchi's poetry, such as Petrarchism, neoclassicism, romanticism, and especially the poetry of French symbolists (Charles Baudelaire, Stéphane Mallarmé, Paul Valéry, and Arthur Rimbaud) – the work of some of whom he translated, and of whose influence on hermeticism he was aware. Parronchi recognizes in the surrealism of Paul Eluard and André Breton the strong influence of French symbolism and decadentism. His poetry did undergo a variety of influences, mainly in the realm of poetic language and traditional imagery, but his human experiences make it alive and personalized. The object has to exist first and, when assimilated, becomes a part of Parronchi's lyrical imagery. Carlo Bo – discussing Parronchi's *I giorni sensibili* (The Sensitive Days, 1941) – in *Nuovi Studi* (New Studies, 1946) mentions "la necessità di una vita prima conosciuta, che discussa" (the necessity of knowing life before discussing it). The strength of Parronchi's poetry originates in the interweaving of dreams and reality; in the sophisticated network of abstract, symbolic imagery of his early works; and in the return to the familiar, in search of his inner self and his past, in the later works.

Alessandro Parronchi was born on 26 December 1914 in Florence, on via Puccinotti, but his family moved a few months later to via Passavanti, which is in the quarter of Cure, where he remained almost all his life. His father, Augusto, and paternal grandfather, Enrico, were originally from Siena and were notaries. His mother, Annunziata Paoletti Parronchi, with whom he had a close relationship that endured into his adulthood, knew French and played piano, contributing in this way to a cultural atmosphere at home and setting a solid, intellectual base for the future studies of her only son. She always comforted him in difficult times. In Greve, in the region of Chianti, she owned an estate with a country house called "Terreno," which Parronchi fondly remembers as a magic place of his early childhood.

His first attempt to write poetry occurred in the summer of 1929, when Parronchi found himself emotionally distressed after the sudden death of his father. He eased his pain when he fell in love for the first time with one of the seven daughters of a nearby family; to her he dedicated his poem, written in octaves and following the classical Ariosto-Tassian tradition with which he was familiar.

Having attended Le Querce, a prestigious parochial school in Florence, Parronchi graduated in 1933 and then enrolled at the University of Florence, where he became part of a circle that included Piero Santi, Franco Fortini, and Carlo Cassola, to mention some of his best-known fellow students. The group used to gather in the Piazza dell'Olio or in Santi's house, where they would read their works. But Parronchi's ties with the group were not close, as he told interviewer Gino Gerola: "c'era, da parte mia . . . la poca o nessuna sopportazione per tutte le confraternite o conventicole quali si fossero, che mi ha sempre tenuto fin nel profondo, la curiosità di vedere quel che si facesse nella stanza accanto" (On my part, there was . . . little or no tolerance for all the fraternities or groups, whatever they might be; I always held, deep down, a curiosity to see what was happening in the next room). Parronchi graduated with a bachelor's degree in art history in 1938, with a thesis under the direction of Mario Solmi. Realizing the limitations to becoming a painter himself, he continued to express his passion for art through art criticism; Parronchi's first publication was an art critique in *Rivista d'Arte* in 1937.

Guided by curiosity, Parronchi became a member of the hermetic group, to which Luzi also belonged. He had met Luzi in 1936 in the café Giubbe Rosse, which was frequented by the Florentine literary circle. During the late 1930s Parronchi collaborated on several reviews, such as *Letteratura* and *Campo di Marte,* and was the art critic for the newspaper the *Nazione.* In addition he was an avid translator of French poetry. In 1937 he started working on the Florentine magazine *Frontespizio,* joining his friends Luzi and Carlo Betocchi. Parronchi was also in close contact with Bo, who was at the *Frontespizio* as well, and he associated with Alfonso Gatto, Vasco Pratolini, and Montale.

Parronchi's travels included a trip to Germany in the summer of 1936 and a trip to Cortina, where he went in 1940 with Luzi. Parronchi always enjoyed the countryside with its colors, openness, and freshness because it reminded him of his childhood. Often going with his friends to Greve on Sundays fulfilled an emotional need to return to the place that held many happy memories for him. The attraction of the atmosphere and picturesque landscape of Greve is visible in much of his poetry.

In 1938 Betocchi published the first poem of *I giorni sensibili,* "Eclisse" (Eclipse), in the *Frontespizio,* much to Parronchi's surprise. In 1939 he met the painter Mario Marcucci, who became his close friend and a loyal supporter of his writing. Parronchi was inspired by the paintings of Marcucci, and he found the intellectual discussions with him stimulating. That same year he began to teach at the Istituto d'Arte in Florence, but World War II interrupted his teaching career.

Parronchi's first two collections, *I giorni sensibili,* comprising verses written between 1937 and 1940, and *I visi* (The Faces, 1943), with poems dating from 1937 to 1942, are the best examples of his hermetic writings. Through images of nature — the Tuscan landscapes, the changing of the seasons, the wind that goes through the plane trees and cypresses, the noise of fountains, and the sight of shadows that pass by — Parronchi reveals his emotions of solitude. He turns inward into a world detached from objective reality, into a private cosmos that rejects the boundaries of time. Parronchi carefully chooses words that bring feelings to the surface. One of the examples of Parronchi's hermetic style is a poem in hendecasyllables — "Paesaggio primaverile" (Spring Landscape), from *I visi:*

Ricca si fa di sentieri l'ombra, la polvere
s'alza e traspaiono come da un velo le case,
le nubi, le gemme che i rami mettono intorno.
Si sono perduti i canti, ora, ferme nell'aria
le palme, un attonito bianco dai muri ci guarda,
la strada percorsa, il passato, svanito nell'ombra.

(Rich with feeling is the shadow, the dust
rises and the houses, the clouds,
the budding branches reappear as through a veil.
The songs are lost, now, the palms still in the air,
an astonished whiteness of the walls watches us,
the street traveled, the past, vanished in the shadow.)

Parronchi spent the war years traveling between Florence and Greve; the trips were tiresome and strenuous, consequently taking their toll on his health. With the normalization of life, however, his health became as good as before. He resumed his teaching career at the Istituto d'Arte in 1949, but only for a year.

In 1949 Parronchi published his collection *Un'attesa* (An Expectation), which includes verses written from 1943 to 1948. This collection was followed by "Alone" (Halo), published in the journal *Ca'balá* in 1950, but its poems actually were written earlier, in the period from 1939 to 1942. Both collections differ from his first two in several ways. In "Alone," composed of brief poems, Parronchi remains faithful to lyrical emotions, but they are no longer contemplative and ambiguous; they are felt deeply and passionately. The verses recapture the moments in which a loved woman appears. These poems are fine examples of twentieth-century love poetry in Italy. Parronchi is more in touch with reality, probably because he can no longer suppress the historical momentum of the turbulent times. The inner turmoils, anxieties, sense of tragedy, pain of separation and abandonment, longing for love and suffering for its loss, and salvation through love are the emotions that dominate the collection. Images of nature accompany the emotions, free from obscurity and abstraction, and, through the more concrete and clear language structure, express the fullness and the intensity of Parronchi's feelings:

Salvami, la dolcezza mi riprende,
questo vedere solo in te la fine
d'ogni mio desiderio: ecco ti perdo
nella notte di prima.

(Save me, sweetness seizes me,
seeing only in you the end
of my every desire: look I lose you
the night before.)

Un'attesa is divided chronologically into five sections: "Un'attesa," "Sono delle stagioni" (They Are Seasons), "Addii" (Farewells), "In ascolto" (Listening), and "Occhi sul presente" (Eyes on the Present). This collection resembles "Alone" in the willingness to face the fragility of reality, to surrender to uncertainty and doubt. The poetic language as an expression of the internal becomes more complex, finding new ways of expression. *Un'attesa* shows a more ambitious and broader intent by Parronchi to expose the hostile world of icy winters, farewells, and death. In the poem "Addio" he encompasses some of the main themes of his poetry: a love that is lost; life and youth left behind; people becoming ghosts; suffering; pain; and delusion:

Addio! Restano gli anni
del tumulto inconsueto della vita
luminosa che a vampe ci s'apriva....
Ma ora, se credi – io spettro, anche tu spettro –
troppo triste in questi occhi rivedersi
piú dolce cancellare il nostro viso
soffiare le nostre orme sulla polvere.

(Farewell! The years remain
of the strange confusion of a brilliant life
that flamed before us....

But now, if you believe — I am a ghost, you are also a
    ghost —
it is too sad to see ourselves in each other's eyes
it is sweeter to erase our faces
to blow away our traces in the dust.)

In *L'incertezza amorosa* (Love's Uncertainty),
published in 1952, Parronchi tries to find one stable point and attach himself to it, perfectly aware
that such an attempt is an illusion. Life starts in
the present; there is no future, no security.
Dreams and illusions keep people moving and existing. The awareness of changed times, where love
escapes and is as mobile as the rest of the world,
where opposites coexist and strive in a mutual
clash, sets the tone for this collection.

In 1954, to the surprise of his friends, Parronchi married a former student at the Istituto
d'Arte, Nara Somigli, by whom he had two daughters: Rosa and Agnese. Becoming a father was an
extraordinary, enriching experience, and he expresses his emotions in several poems, one of them
"Alla figlia" (To My Daughter), from the 1956 collection *Coraggio di vivere* (Courage to Live):

Il mondo a cui da poco hai aperto gli occhi
non è, piccina mia, quale vorrei
che fosse. . . . E tu, non guardarlo così,
come se — troppo presto! — lo capissi.

(The world to which a little while ago you opened your
    eyes
is not, my little one, the way I would like
it to be. . . . And you, do not look at it so,
as if — too soon! — you understand it.)

Per strade di bosco e città (Through Streets of
the Forest and the City, 1954) comprises three
small collections: "Giorno di nozze" (The Wedding Day); "Nel bosco" (In the Forest); and
"Città" (City), the last of which was republished
with some alterations in the collection *L'apparenza
non inganna* (Appearances Do Not Deceive) in
1966. "Giorno di nozze," as indicated by Parronchi, was written on Christmas Eve, 1946. Although this lyrical recital piece was written for a
wedding, the inspiration had been previously occasioned by Parronchi's admiration for Claudio
Monteverdi's opera *Orfeo* (1607) and Ottavio
Rinuccini's verses for his melodrama *Dafne*
(1597). "Nel bosco" was written after Parronchi
had seen Akira Kurosawa's movie *Rashomon* in
1951; he later read the original Japanese story by
Ryunosuke Akutagawa, and both impressed him
with their expressions of the human condition.
The result was a story Parronchi composed in

verse, in which the drama and the tragedy of the
events narrated achieve intensity through the poetic
expression. The diversity of the rhythm comes from
the cadence of the verses, which follow the uneven
climaxes of the events. The same Japanese movie inspired Parronchi to write "Città," in which he tried
to imitate the technique of the movie camera, capturing a particular situation (a failed romance) in its
"realistic-extemporary" motion. In the note that
accompanies the collection, Parronchi describes
his intentions: " 'Città' . . . tagliata fuori da
un'azione vera e propria, ruota attorno a una
situazione reale, di tempo, di luogo e di
sentimenti" ("City" . . . cut from an actual event,
turns about a situation that is real in time, place
and emotion).

By the 1950s Parronchi's career as a poet, art
critic, and translator was fairly fruitful, which could
not be said for his academic career. He had com-
peted three times for a chair in the Accademia. He
was first sent to Palermo for a year and after that to
Carrara and Bologna. In 1959 Bo put him in charge
of the Storia dell'Arte at the Università di Urbino.
He struggled for years to be present at the officially
assigned meetings throughout Italy, at the same
time preparing his lectures for the university. In
1956 Parronchi, with great regrets, had sold the
country house in Greve.

Coraggio di vivere was written from 1953 to
1956. *La noia della natura* (The Boredom of Nature) was composed in 1952 but was published
much later, in 1958, followed by "Il paesaggio
dipinto" (The Painted Landscape), with poems
from 1955 to 1960, which was included in the
enlarged edition of *Coraggio di vivere* (1961).
These collections present a departure from pure
lyric and metaphysics to the poetry of content
and topics, which vary from eternal contrasts
such as life/death, presence/absence, and
joy/pain to technological themes, including the
conquest of space, as in the poem "Sputnik"
from "Il paesaggio dipinto." Parronchi's uncertainty seems to be magnified, but the return to
his own self, to the fateful, unchanged heart, offers him comfort. By fleeing to the past, to memories and well-known faces, he negates modern
civilization, in spite of being intrigued by it. He
points to the era of technology that killed God,
and he questions it and investigates it in the
poem "Alle stelle" (To the Stars) from *La noia
della natura*: "L'etá della tecnica ha ucciso / il
pensiero di Dio" (The era of technology has
killed / the thought of God). Parronchi's words
are more forceful and concrete, negating verbs

of uncertainty are present, and the verses often conclude with a question. There is a tone of contemporaneity to them, achieved by the free structure of the verses, composed about everyday impressions and events, the modernity that Parronchi finds so difficult to accept.

L'apparenza non inganna was published again in 1970 as a part of a larger collection, *Pietà dell'atmosfera* (Mercy of the Atmosphere), with the omission of "Città." *Pietà dell'atmosfera* includes poems written between 1960 and 1970 that display Parronchi's involvement in topics stemming from the changed times. His poetic language moves toward the colloquial, as an everyday tool of expression, with anglicisms introduced in several poems; it becomes a means of conversation, rather than having mostly an emotional function. Parronchi seems to have abandoned his original hermetic style for an open address to the world, to a real or imagined listener to whom he wants to present his views on a variety of contemporary topics, among which is his new interest in the United States. Although he dislikes much of the present social climate, it supplies him with fresh inspirations and gives his poetry an invigorating pulse. The circle of his friends, his involvement in art criticism, and his family inspire him to reveal his inner soul in the clear, simple syntax of a prose-verse style. In "Autoritratto alla figlia per quando avrà ventun anni (1978)" (Self-Portrait for My Daughter When She Will Be Twenty-One Years Old [1978]), he admits he is still tilting at windmills; the Don Quixote in him never dies. He recognizes the changed world, but the past is what he appreciates. The nostalgia for the happiness of times past, for the youth that is leaving him, and for a perfect love that can save him makes readers aware that, deep inside, part of Parronchi is still in self-imposed slavery to subjectivity. However, he considers *Pietà dell'atmosfera* his best poetic work.

In 1979, after the fifth attempt, he finally was appointed to chair the Department of Art History at the Magistero in Florence. He still teaches there on occasion.

Parronchi's collection *Replay* was published in 1980 and includes poems written from 1970 to 1977, in addition to those written as a diary in two months in the summer of 1979 and titled *L'estate a pezzi* (Summer in Pieces). Here he seems to return to the lyrical style. There is a tone of resignation in these verses, a preoccupation with death and the hope that a kind of immortality may be gained

through his work. Time is an illusion, reality is relative, nature is a memory, and man has yet to find himself. These are Parronchi's conclusions. He continues searching for images that will express what poetry is, primal instincts and the deepest emotions. The heart is where everything originates. The poem "Replay" presents the everlasting human fear of mortality and finiteness, which Parronchi understands as only a component of human nature. History repeats itself, and one is only an instant in a circle that turns indefinitely. That life repeats itself is the ultimate conclusion of Parronchi's understanding of it:

> C'è una paura che le cose muoiano
> che nel tempo che è detta la parola s'estingua
> che l'urlo rimanga senza eco....
> . . . .
> Eppure c'è chi séguita
> a sentire il bisogno insopprimibile
> che tutto si ripeta,
> tutti i grani di sabbia
> tutte le onde del mare si ritrovino
> nella stessa danza d'una volta
> e i colori delle nuvole nel loro variare.

> (There is a fear that things die
> that the word dies out when it is spoken
> that the shout is without an echo....
> . . . .
> And yet there are those who persist
> in feeling the insuppressible need
> for everything to repeat itself,
> for all the grains of sand
> all the waves of the sea to join again
> in their same old dance
> and the colors of the clouds in their variations.)

The narrative and didactic style of this poem does not overshadow its lyricism, which makes one realize that Parronchi remains faithful to emotion and that through the years he has gained the wisdom of accepting life and the world as a part of perpetually repeated history.

Parronchi has been, based on his early poetry, placed by critics in the realm of hermetic poetry of the 1930s. This holds true only in part; critics have yet to evaluate fully his latest work, which occupies a special place in postwar and contemporary Italian poetry. The period when Parronchi started his literary journey was described by him to interviewer Giorgio Tabanelli, and the statement is also basically true for the other poets of his generation:

> Isolati come eravamo da una situazione politica che ci teneva all'oscuro della realtà, fu per noi naturale imparare a meditare sulle cose. Fu così che della letteratura scartammo l'aspetto superficiale.... Il desiderio di

approfondire portò con sé un uso più responsabile del linguaggio, e quindi un bisogno di scavo, punti di vista nuovi. Il nostro modo di esprimersi, forse a volte improprio, sembrò oscuro – di qui l'accusa di oscurità – e forse lo era. . . . In me particolarmente è rimasto intatto, di quell'epoca, il gusto dell'inedito, l'ansia della scoperta.

(Isolated as we were by a political situation that kept us in the dark about reality, it was natural for us to learn to meditate on things. This was why we rejected the superficial aspect of literature. . . . The desire to go deeper brought with it a more responsible use of the language, and a need to discover new points of view. Our way of expressing ourselves, maybe improper at times, seemed obscure – and thus the accusation of obscurity – and maybe it was. . . . In me remained particularly intact, from that period, the taste for the unpublished, the strong desire for discovery.)

Surrounded by friends and family, Alessandro Parronchi currently lives and writes in Florence.

Interviews:
Gino Gerola, "Una vita tra arte e poesia," *Toscana Qui,* 6 (January 1986): 76–82;

Giorgio Tabanelli, *Carlo Bo: Il tempo dell'ermetismo* (Milan: Garzanti, 1986), pp. 119–132.

References:
Sergio Antonielli, "Parronchi," *Paragone,* no. 38 (February 1953): 82–84;

Carlo Bo, *Nuovi studi* (Florence: Vallecchi, 1946), pp. 230–232;

Giuseppe De Robertis, *Altro Novecento* (Florence: Le Monnier, 1962), pp. 508–517;

Francesco Leonetti, "Riconoscimento di Parronchi," *Paragone,* no. 138 (June 1961): 74–77;

Oreste Macrì, *Caratteri e figure della poesia italiana contemporanea* (Florence: Vallecchi, 1956), pp. 171–195;

Pier Paolo Pasolini, *Passione e ideologia* (Milan: Garzanti, 1960), pp. 458–460;

Silvio Ramat, *L'ermetismo* (Florence: Nuova Italia, 1969), pp. 52–54, 101–104, 229–234.

Pier Paolo Pasolini

(5 March 1922 – 2 November 1975)

Thomas E. Peterson
University of Georgia

BOOKS: *Poesie a Casarsa* (Bologna: Landi, 1942);

Poesie (San Vito al Tagliamento: Primon, 1945; enlarged edition, Milan: Garzanti, 1970);

I diarii (Casarsa: Academiuta di Lenga Furlana, 1945);

I pianti (Casarsa: Academiuta di Lenga Furlana, 1946);

Dov'è la mia patria (Casarsa: Academiuta di Lenga Furlana, 1949);

Poesia dialettale del Novecento, by Pasolini and Mario dell'Arco (Parma: Guanda, 1952);

Tal cour di un frut (Tricesimo: Lingua Furlana, 1953);

La meglio gioventù (Florence: Sansoni, 1954);

Il canto popolare (Milan: Meridiana, 1954);

Dal diario (1945–47) (Caltanissetta: Sciascia, 1954);

Ragazzi di vita (Milan: Garzanti, 1955); translated by Emile Capouya as *The Ragazzi* (New York: Grove, 1968; Manchester, U.K. & New York: Carcanet, 1986);

Le ceneri di Gramsci (Milan: Garzanti, 1957); translated by David Wallace as *The Ashes of Gramsci* (Peterborough, U.K.: Spectacular Diseases, 1982);

L'usignolo della Chiesa Cattolica (Milan: Longanesi, 1958);

Una vita violenta (Milan: Garzanti, 1959); translated by William Weaver as *A Violent Life* (London: Cape, 1968; New York: Garland, 1978);

Passione e ideologia (1948–1958) (Milan: Garzanti, 1960);

Roma 1950: Diario (Milan: All'Insegna del Pesce d'Oro, 1960);

Sonetto primaverile (Milan: All'Insegna del Pesce d'Oro, 1960);

La religione del mio tempo (Milan: Garzanti, 1961);

Accattone (Rome: FM, 1961);

Il sogno di una cosa (Milan: Garzanti, 1962); translated by Stuart Hood as *A Dream of Something* (London & New York: Quartet, 1988);

L'odore dell'India (Milan: Longanesi, 1962); translated by David Price as *The Scent of India* (London: Olive, 1984);

Mamma Roma (Milan: Rizzoli, 1962);

Il Vangelo secondo Matteo, edited by Giacomo Gambetti (Milan: Garzanti, 1964);

Poesia in forma di rosa (Milan: Garzanti, 1964; revised, 1964);

Poesie dimenticate (Udine: Società Filologica Friulana, 1965);

Alì dagli occhi azzurri (Milan: Garzanti, 1965); selections translated by John Shepley as *Roman Nights and Other Stories* (Marlboro, Vt.: Marlboro, 1986);

Uccellacci e uccellini (Milan: Garzanti, 1966);

Edipo Re: Un film, edited by Gambetti (Milan: Garzanti, 1967); translated by John Mathews as *Oedipus Rex: A Film* (London: Lorrimer, 1971; New York: Simon & Schuster, 1971);

Teorema (Milan: Garzanti, 1968);

Medea: Un film (Milan: Garzanti, 1970);

Trasumanar e organizzar (Milan: Garzanti, 1971);

Empirismo eretico (Milan: Garzanti, 1972); translated by Ben Lawton and Louise K. Barnett as *Heretical Empiricism* (Bloomington & Indianapolis: Indiana University Press, 1988);

Calderón (Milan: Garzanti, 1973);

La nuova gioventù (Turin: Einaudi, 1975);

Trilogia della vita (Il Decameron, I racconti di Canterbury, Il fiore delle Mille e una notte) (Bologna: Cappelli, 1975);

La divina mimesis (Turin: Einaudi, 1975); translated by Thomas E. Peterson as *The Divine Mimesis* (Berkeley: Double Dance, 1980);

Il padre selvaggio (Turin: Einaudi, 1975);

Scritti corsari (Milan: Garzanti, 1975);

Le poesie (Milan: Garzanti, 1975);

Lettere luterane (Turin: Einaudi, 1976); translated by Hood as *Lutheran Letters* (Manchester, U.K.: Carcanet / Dublin: Raven Arts, 1983);

Warhol (Milan: Anselmino, 1976);

Pier Paolo Pasolini

Pasolini in Friuli, 1943–1949, by Pasolini and others (Udine: Arti Grafiche Friulane, 1976);

I Turcs tal Friúl, edited by Luigi Ciceri (Udine: Forum Julii, 1976);

Pier Paolo Pasolini e "Il Setaccio" (1942–1943), edited by Mario Ricci (Bologna: Cappelli, 1977);

Le belle bandiere: Dialoghi 1960–65, edited by Gian Carlo Ferretti (Rome: Riuniti, 1977);

San Paolo (Turin: Einaudi, 1977);

Con Pier Paolo Pasolini, edited by Enrico Magrelli (Rome: Bulzoni, 1977);

Affabulazione; Pilade (Milan: Garzanti, 1977);

I disegni, 1941–1975, edited by Giuseppe Zigaina (Milan: Scheiwiller, 1978);

Il caos (Rome: Riuniti, 1979);

Descrizioni di descrizioni, edited by Graziella Chiarossi (Turin: Einaudi, 1979);

Porcile; Orgia; Bestia da stile (Milan: Garzanti, 1979);

Poesie e pagine ritrovate, edited by Andrea Zanzotto and Nico Naldini (Rome: Lato Side, 1980);

Amado mio, preceduto da Atti impuri (Milan: Garzanti, 1982);

Sette poesie e due lettere (Vicenza: Locusta, 1985);

Ciant da li ciampanis (New York: Kaldewey, 1988);

Il portico della morte, edited by Cesare Segre (Rome: Associazione Fondo Pier Paolo Pasolini, 1988).

Editions: *Poems,* bilingual edition, translated by Norman MacAfee and Luciano Martinengo (New York: Random House/Vintage, 1982);

Selected Poems, bilingual edition, translated by MacAfee and Martinengo (London: Calder, 1984);

Roman Poems, bilingual edition, translated by Lawrence Ferlinghetti and Francesca Valente (San Francisco: City Lights, 1986).

OTHER: *Canzoniere italiano: Antologia della poesia popolare,* coedited by Pasolini (Parma: Guanda, 1955);

La poesia popolare italiana, edited by Pasolini (Milan: Garzanti, 1960);

Scrittori della realtà dall'VIII al XIX secolo, edited by Pasolini and Attilio Bertolucci (Milan: Garzanti, 1961);

Lawrence R. Smith, ed. and trans., *The New Italian Poetry,* includes poems by Pasolini (Berkeley:

University of California Press, 1981), pp. 65–111;

Herman W. Haller, ed. and trans., *The Hidden Italy*, includes poems by Pasolini (Detroit: Wayne State University Press, 1986), pp. 258–275.

TRANSLATIONS: Aeschylus, *Orestiade* (Turin: Einaudi, 1960);

Plautus, *Il Vantone* (Milan: Garzanti, 1963).

SELECTED PERIODICAL PUBLICATIONS – UNCOLLECTED: "Marxisants," *Officina* (May–June 1959): 69–73;

"Manifesto per un nuovo teatro," *Nuovi Argomenti,* 9 (January–March 1968);

"Una poesia sconosciuta di Pier Paolo Pasolini," edited by Amedeo Giacomini, *Strumenti Critici,* 10 (June 1976): 257–261.

The writing career of Pier Paolo Pasolini coincided with events of immense literary and social importance in Italy. Like many of his generation – being born at the inception of Fascism, coming of age during its defeat, and maturing in the prosperity of the 1950s and 1960s – Pasolini was a witness to a national debacle and was an artist committed to social change. In addition to poetry, he wrote novels, essays, plays, and scripts. In the 1960s he became one of the most celebrated Italian filmmakers.

Pasolini was born on 5 March 1922 in Bologna to Carlo Alberto (an army officer) and Susanna Colussi Pasolini. The family lived in the Friuli area (in the towns of Belluno, Sacile, Conegliano, and Casarsa), the Emilia region (in Cremona and Scandiano), and Bologna because of frequent moves with the military. Having begun writing poetry when he was seven, Pasolini attended high school and university in Bologna, earning a degree and establishing important friendships with Silvana Mauri, Franco Farolfi, Giovanna Bemporad, Luciano Serra, and, later, Roberto Roversi, Francesco Leonetti, and others. He participated briefly in the Fascist youth organization (G.I.L.) and coedited its magazine, the *Setaccio,* contributing writings and drawings. These early documents show an accomplished, if aestheticist and derivative, style, which evokes the peasant songs and perennial themes of bucolic life: love, camaraderie, anguish, nature, and the passing of time. His father was ordered to East Africa in 1941, captured by the English, and made a prisoner of war. Pier Paolo was called to military duty in September 1943 but escaped from his regiment after only a week; he returned to Casarsa, covering much of the distance on foot and losing the beginnings of a thesis on Italian painting. In Friuli he enjoyed close allegiances with his cousin the poet Nico Naldini as well as the painter Giuseppe Zigaina. Pasolini remained in Casarsa but traveled frequently to Bologna. He taught in a local school while engaging in frenetic intellectual and artistic activity, and he wrote and published poetry in Friulian dialect. Such literary and pedagogical pursuits became his forms of resistance to Nazism and Fascism. Pasolini's brother, Guido, who had taken up arms, died in February 1945, at the hands of a rival partisan faction. In that same month the grieving Pasolini – who had also lost his best friend, Paria (on the Russian front) – founded the Academiuta di Lenga Furlana, an institution intended to revitalize the Friulian language and tradition, politically and in terms of a romantic literary tradition dating back to the fourteenth century. After World War II he continued to teach and to organize cultural activities in Casarsa. He was then a militant communist. In autumn 1945 he defended his thesis on the poetry of Giovanni Pascoli. Pasolini's homosexuality remained largely a secret until he was accused of approaching a male student. The subsequent scandal prompted him to move with his mother to Rome in 1949. His mother was undeniably the most important person in his life. His father, increasingly disturbed after the war, was a paranoiac and an alcoholic, and the move to Rome was made without his knowledge. Three years passed before he rejoined the family. However, when Pasolini's father died in December 1958, Pasolini was at his side.

When Pasolini arrived in Rome he was in no sense a "provincial" or a stranger to that city; he made new friends and associates, among them the novelists Moravia and Elsa Morante. Rome became his element, though its presence in his psyche was never unproblematic. The periphery of Rome and its ancient center, both restructured by Fascism, are topoi in Pasolini's poetry of audacious scale, Foscolian rhythms, and Dantean narrativity.

In the 1960s, in parallel with his film career, Pasolini became a celebrity, increasingly a notorious one. His films traverse a constantly changing range of styles and contents. His handling of the medium was at times coarse and graphic. He used nonprofessional actors and avoided many standards of the industry; instead he chose subject matter from classical legends, tragedies, political diatribes, and religious gnosis. The willingness to experiment rarely diluted his efforts or resulted in anything less than a rigorous artistic product.

questo grigio patetico e ———— le
in cui la Grecia sfuma in Inghilterra,
nel maggio, *non* perso in un vento autunnale.

III

Uno straccetto rosso, ~~pari a~~ quello
che ~~xxxxxxxx~~ al collo ai partigiani,
~~xxxxxxxxx~~ e'arma, sul terreno cereo
e, ~~sull'xxx xxxx terre xxxxxxxx~~ dell'avello,

differente
~~d'un xxxxxx rosso, due gerani:
qui tu stai, "Gramsci's xxxxxx" dtxx~~

d'un differente rosso, due gerani:
qui tu stai, bandito e con dura eleganza
non cattolica, ricordato tra estranei

Tu
morti: Gramsci's xxxxxxx. Speranza
~~o scetticismo,~~ xxxx capitato
per caso in questo verde parco, innanzi

alla tua tomba, al tuo spirito restato
~~xxxxxxix xxxxxx xxxxxxix (xxxxx~~ o
quaggiù, con questi liberi. Qualcosa
forse di diverso, di più   ato

e, insieme, più umile; l'armoniosa
xxxxxxxxx della vita con la morte;
~~xxxxxxxxxxxxxxxxxxxxxxx~~ qui
e, ~~la~~ questa Italia xxxxxxxx fu

~~xxxxxxxx~~
la tua parola, sento quanto torto
e quanta ragione tu avessi insieme
nel giudicare la e le future sorte:
e che diversi frutti dia il tuo seme.

*Page from a draft for "Le ceneri di Gramsci," one of Pasolini's best-known poems
(by permission of the Estate of Pier Paolo Pasolini)*

A great deal has been written about Pasolini's dialect poetry. One of the most illustrious commentators has been the romance philologist Gianfranco Contini, who has found in the work a continuation of the spirit of Provence. Pasolini's Friulian poems excel because of their formal perfection and thematic simplicity; they also represented an open challenge to the linguistic politics of the Fascist regime. A pastoral landscape is the backdrop for the melancholy self-portrait of a youth, which expands into areas of frankness and sincerity unknown in the troubadour tradition.

With *L'usignolo della Chiesa Cattolica* (The Nightingale of the Catholic Church, 1958), this ambience and artificiality include a new conception of demonistic religiosity and sociological difference. Pasolini's customary projections, of concupiscent self-pity and of the choral religion of the peasantry, are less conventional and naive. One detects a balance between their abstract ideation and his physical presence. The balance between psyche and soma is new and remains constant in his later poetry, as does a persistent experimentalism and a profoundly oppositional, or contradictory, thematic. A key poem in the progression is "La scoperta di Marx" (The Discovery of Marx), the last one of *L'usignolo* to be written. The first stanzas constitute a gnomic devotion to the mother figure, or *genetrix*:

Può nascere da un'ombra
con viso di fanciulla
e pudore di viola

un corpo che m'ingombra
o, da un grembo azzurro
una coscienza – sola

dentro il mondo abitato?
Fuori dal tempo è nato
il figlio, e dentro muore.

(Can there be born from a shade
with a girl's face and the
modesty of a violet a body

which is a burden to me
or may a conscience
be born – alone in the inhabited
world from a blue womb?
The child is born outside
time, and inside he dies.)

Despite his atheism and commitment to the ideals of the Resistance, in his poetry a cultural catholicism endures, centered on Christ as a man who died and not a static icon. The tension between contradictory values renders the stages of Pasolini's work increasingly passionate.

In *I diarii* (The Diaries, 1945) and *Dal diario* (From the Diary, 1954) one sees the beginning of the narrativity typical of the long poems of Pasolini's maturity. In December 1945 he wrote to a friend: "sono forse l'unico in Italia . . . tra coloro che scrivono versi, che non imiti [Eugenio] Montale, né [Umberto] Saba, né altri minori ([Carlo] Betocchi, [Sandro] Penna, ecc. ecc.), né i simbolisti francesi, né infine i migliori Romantici . . ." (I am perhaps the only one in Italy . . . among those writing verse, who is not imitating Montale, or Saba, or other minor poets [Betocchi, Penna, etc. etc.], or the French symbolists, or finally the greatest Romantics . . .). Pasolini cultivated a correspondence with Contini and emulated the latter's writing, which is meticulously philological, but Pasolini was also eager to assign values and social coefficients to matters of literary technique.

Pasolini's two early novellas, *Atti impuri* (Impure Acts) and *Amado mio* (My Beloved) – eventually published together in 1982 – were suppressed by him because of their homosexuality (never as explicit in the poetry). They combine dialogue, description, figurality, and gesture with a sensibility to the various inflections and dialects of spoken Italian, resulting in a diaristic realism continuous with that of the poems.

In the late 1940s, due to the supposed amorous incident with the student, Pasolini lost his teaching job and membership in the Italian Communist party. After he moved to Rome with his mother, he again worked as a teacher while he composed the landmark essays in *Passione e ideologia* (Passion and Ideology, 1960), which extended his literary expertise into areas of philology, stylistic criticism, and political ideology. A model for such an approach was the work of Antonio Gramsci, the political organizer and founder of the Italian Communist party and a brilliant literary critic, who died in Rome in 1937 as a victim of the Fascists. Gramsci had opposed the traditional literary language as condescending, and he had proposed a national-popular literature, the reawakening of which would require reinterpretation of existing popular literature and reappraisal of the supposed simplicity and ingenuousness of previously anonymous authors. Pasolini carried forward such research with great vigor. He distilled his work on Pascoli into an essay, recognizing that poet as a major influence on twentieth-century Italian poetry. The emotional density, linguistic expressionism, and phonic variety of Pascoli's work was an experimentalist precedent for Pasolini and a way out of the strictures of a poetic canon entrenched in a monolinguistic practice (which included the work of Gabriele D'Annunzio).

Pasolini's poems of the late 1940s and those written after his arrival in Rome are characterized by a hypnotic, lyrical "wandering" through the self – an existential questioning. They are imbued with the rhythms and tones of those poets in literary Italian whom he had known and cherished, but his poems are stripped of the conceits and artifice common to the dominant, Petrarchan, tradition. He coedited the important anthology of folk verse *Canzoniere italiano* (1955) and authored the studies "La poesia dialettale del Novecento" (Dialect Poetry of the Twentieth Century), "La poesia popolare italiana" (Italian Popular Poetry), and several essays on Italian authors of the twentieth century (all in *Passione e ideologia*). He learned Roman dialect and street language – very different from the isolated Friulian he had compared to Rumanian, Catalonian, and Provençal. An intensified political awareness led Pasolini to formulate a "civic poetry" in *Le ceneri di Gramsci* (1957; translated as *The Ashes of Gramsci*, 1982). The ancient separation between written and spoken languages and literate and illiterate classes remained a dominant concern for Pasolini. The assimilation of "lesser" classes and dialects by the dominant culture was viewed through his resistance and personal subjection. The tone of his *poemetti* (long poems) is at once lyric and elegiac, the irregular hendecasyllables are usually in partially rhymed tercets, and the style is a kind of figurative realism. The themes are at once personal and civic. There is, as in Dante's poetry, an expressionistic reciprocity between the events recounted and the patterns of literary devices and between perceptions of reality and the poetic use of language (which is not allowed to become an end in itself, as in the works of the neo-avant-garde).

Some aspects of *Le ceneri di Gramsci* are contradictory: Pasolini declaims the corrupt state of a poetic tradition detached from ideological discourse, even as he identifies with the people, who are impervious to such discourse. This contradiction is extremely fertile in its intellectual and artistic polyvalence. Pasolini presents a Dantean cultural attack and a rejection of mystical or moralistic solutions to materialistic and secular problems, and he relies on a mingling of styles rather than the classic separation of styles. As elegy his poetry evokes the Italian terrain and people, using the Dantean tercet (which had resurfaced with the Romantics and then Pascoli) to create narrative continuity; as lyric his po-

etry offers traditional tropes, exclamations, striking imagery, and musicality.

One of the poems in the collection, "Récit," centers on a walk Pasolini took after learning from Attilio Bertolucci of the indictment for obscenity by a Roman magistrate because of Pasolini's novel *Ragazzi di vita* (1955; translated as *The Ragazzi*, 1968). The sixty-four rhymed couplets contain allusions to Charles Baudelaire, Dante, Guido Gozzano, and Pascoli. Neither gratuitous nor overbearing, the poem promotes a lyric sensation amid extreme duress; at the same time, one sees a pitiless view of the industrial landscape of the Roman periphery in the context of an absent religion and a hypocritical state morality. In the poem "Picasso," Pasolini criticizes the great painter for not having been involved in the major revolutionary movements of his time, and Pasolini addresses the broad question of commitment, saying that self-criticism, if authentic, is not incompatible with the "committed" work of art but represents its most intrinsic form of expression.

The title poem, "Le ceneri di Gramsci," is, like "Récit," centered on a walk. Pasolini participates in the tradition of sepulchral poetry only as a pretext that he explodes on the stage of contemporary Italy. The tendentious monologue to Gramsci and Pasolini's declared scandal of self-contradiction should be interpreted within the cultural milieu of the 1950s, in which the subaltern roles of people and poet alike seemed to point to a destiny of pure oppositions rather than a rational Hegelian dialectic. The poem's generic pretexts and copious allusions present radically diverse planes of reference united by symbols (unlike those of symbolism or hermeticism) of a relentless realism and localism; such a depiction allows the poem to emerge as a hymn to eternal objects and a testament to a historical and ethical crisis.

In Rome, Pasolini befriended Giuseppe Ungaretti, Giorgio Caproni, Sandro Penna, Attilio and Bernardo Bertolucci, and others. He corresponded with Vittorio Sereni and a host of lesser figures in the literary world. He continued to woo Contini, and in 1955 he began to write to Franco Fortini. In many respects his relationship with Fortini, conducted energetically by both men in poems, letters, and criticism, yields a portrait of the epoch. As signaled by Pasolini's essays, a strong literary debt was owed by him to Ungaretti and Montale, poets who had authenticized an internal voice suffused with lyricism while confronting the existential situation of humankind – the "evil of being." But Pasolini shifted the dramatic site of the poem away from the individualistic psyche: his psychoanalytic subject was multiple, and solitude was social. He attempted to correct Montale's skepticism and Ungaretti's vaguely heroic metaphysics. The latter is the subject of the essay "Un poeta e dio" (A Poet and God), in *Passione e ideologia,* and the essay won the Premio Le Quattro Arti in 1952.

Fortini, who had coedited the journal *Politecnico* and later worked for the newspaper *Avanti!,* joined Pasolini and his Bolognese friends Francesco Leonetti and Roberto Roversi in the publication of the review *Officina.* The attempt to forge a literary and ideological journal was intriguing and reflected the high standards of the group. There was dissension, however, and they found it hard to agree on a consistent editorial policy. Though it did not survive into the 1960s, the lessons of *Officina* were far-reaching. Fortini withdrew and refused to join Pasolini, Moravia, and Enzo Siciliano in the new *Nuovi Argomenti,* which became a primary forum for Pasolini. Fortini's reservations about Pasolini's work were shared first with the poet himself. When Pasolini's father died, Pasolini's first letter was to Fortini. In comparison to Fortini, an austere and militant Marxist, Pasolini seemed an expressionist, intent on drawing attention to his own case, impure yet exemplary, as he engaged in a personal and heretical reading of events. His Marxism features an identification with the *Lumpenproletariat,* or underclass, which Marx had scorned as being of only utilitarian importance.

In late 1959 Pasolini and his mother moved into the apartment building shared by the Bertolucci family. Shortly thereafter Pasolini began his film career, preparing and writing scripts and dialogue for other filmmakers. He conceived of cinema as a transnational language with great possibilities for political effectiveness. Asked the difference between cinema and reality, he replied, "practically none" (in an interview with Oswald Stack in *Pasolini on Pasolini,* 1969).

In 1961 Pasolini coedited with Attilio Bertolucci an important anthology of popular literature and art, *Scrittori della realtà dall'VIII al XIX secolo* (Writers of Reality from 800 to 1900). He began to see the historical, social-empirical basis of his own reality as being attached to the 1950s and to the hopes for national reconstruction that soon disappeared, banalized by industrialization and consumerism. He saw the construction of the Autostrada del Sole as a decisive moment in the passage away from agriculture and toward urbanization (despite continued underdevelopment of the south), a factor threatening to cultural diversity.

In the title poem of *La religione del mio tempo* (The Religion of My Time, 1961) Pasolini confronts the religious predicaments of contemporary Italy, indicting what he saw as the insipid and ineffectual Catholic church and pope. In the poem "La Ricchezza" (Wealth) Pasolini seeks Italy's true wealth, which is intellectual and spiritual. Throughout this understated volume his Whitmanesque speaker is a party to and an observer of the class struggle, viewed against the background of Italy's cultural patrimony. The epigrams of "Umiliato e offeso" (Humiliated and Offended) and "Nuovi epigrammi" (New Epigrams) show that Pasolini's personal desperation has become extreme. The masterful final section, "Poesie incivili" (Uncivil Poems), adds to the previous ones the bittersweet sense of departure. The tonalities are controlled, free of the implacable polemics and structural deformations of his later books, though "La reazione stilistica" (The Stylistic Reason) serves as a definitive rejection of the ambient *unilinguismo,* which aimed to homologize souls and level passions and dialects, trading the obscurity of language and clarity of reason for the purity of language and a muddied reason. Pasolini seems to emphasize that entropy (or lack of stress) decisive to perception and the creative process, an entropy "figured" in the underclass (no longer "the humble laborer") and the bourgeoisie, equally "humiliated" by power and the myth of power. The fusion of civic and lyric poetry has reached a breaking point.

A radical change was under way. *L'odore dell'India* (1962; translated as *The Scent of India,* 1984) is a document of Pasolini's penetration into a cultural "other"; the book is a combination of poetic reflections and accurate reports on the physical and spiritual identity of India. In *Poesia in forma di rosa* (Poetry in the Shape of a Rose, 1964) he abandons the sphere of the intimate or exquisite and the devices of analogism, association, and mixed metaphor. Form and tautology (literary complexity and versification) yield to process and description, the flatness of prose. Epistemological concerns slip away for the sake of a typological reconnaissance: Pasolini seems to view his poetry sociologically and ironically. The book focuses on the intellectual's role in society and is characterized by mobility and explosiveness, including references to empirical research in the sciences and in non-European cultures. It employs Dante's "candid rose" of the *Paradiso* as a graphic prop with which to "situate" the intellectuals of Pasolini's time. Though Pasolini consistently protects his poetry from intellectualism, there is a growing tendentiousness in the simplifica-

Pasolini in the role of a cleric in his 1972 film of The Canterbury Tales

tion of historical arguments to suit polemical purposes. Ostensibly this prevents the reductionism he sees as a dominant sin among those he refers to as reasoners (on the left and right) as presented in his abbreviated adaptation of the *Inferno, La divina mimesis* (1975; translated as *The Divine Mimesis,* 1980), which is initially outlined in "Progetto di opere future" (Plan of Future Works), in *Poesia in forma di rosa.*

Aiming at a public catharsis, Pasolini had turned his writing to extra-Italian themes in which the diachronic and synchronic were manifest as the *santissima dualità* (sacred duality) of social language and literary language, both of which were threatened by the new spoken language. *La divina mimesis* was described by him, in a note to the book, as "l'ultima opera scritta nell'italiano non-nazionale, l'italiano che serba viventi e allineate in una reale contemporaneità tutte le stratificazioni diacroniche della sua storia" (the last written work in non-national Italian, the Italian that keeps alive and aligned in a real contemporaneity all the diachronic stratifications of its history). This non-national "lingua dell'Odio" (language of hate) recalls Dante's

linguistic ascriptions and is made up of all possible linguistic combinations: literary, dialect, koine, Latin (classical and medieval), technological, and physiological.

While he inveighs against the destroyers of authentic wealth, Pasolini also writes of personal pain, a stance he inherited from the *vociani* (poets of the journal *Voce*) and Giacomo Leopardi, who used humble and aulic registers while rejecting paternalistic or patrician systems. Pasolini's musicality and freedom of versification – natural objects being suffused with emotions – are traits of Pascoli's work.

As a playwright and screenwriter Pasolini sought to identify static forms in society so as to induce such stress as would lead the audience to a process of self-examination. This process is enacted in the plays *Calderón* (1973), *Pilade,* and *Affabulazione* (Fabulation) – the latter two being published together in 1977 – in the films *Edipo Re* (published in 1967; translated as *Oedipus Rex,* 1971) and *Teorema* (Theorem, published in 1968), and in the script *San Paolo* (Saint Paul, 1977). Such a cultural rite seeks to disclose an alternative paradigm to that of authoritarian and consumeristic society, whose most insistent image in Pasolini's works is that of the Nazi death camps. For Pasolini the linguistic modes had grown impoverished due to a void in popular and literary culture. The marriage of corporate capital and mass media, along with the self-interested myopia of a regressive bourgeoisie, was connected perversely with a proletariat detached from the land and linguistically aphasic in the cities. The bourgeoisie was seen to rely on speculative reason at the expense of argumentative or practical reason. Pasolini stressed the unity of the oppressed class – which is the victim of violence – and the individual's participation in his particular class.

In *Trasumanar e organizzar* (Transhumanize and Organize, 1971) the corrupt social estates – the church, the rulers, the proletariat, and the press – are interpreted as mirrors of public consciousness. The book focuses on the need for an ethical reorganization in Italian culture, verifiable in the person. Pasolini elides the distinction between public and private sectors, exploiting a style that is by turns phenomenic, dialogical, and journalistic. The simplicity of the images corresponds to his sense of anonymity: "Perciò parlerò, in nome mio no, perché io son poeta dell'aria" (So I will talk, not in my own name, because I am a poet of the air). The book is an aggregate of semantic collisions and cascading syntax.

The humanistic goal is consonant with Pasolini's contemporaneous essays, many of which dwell on pedagogical issues or express unexpected opinions (for example, opposition to abortion), but the altruism seems at times masochistic. Political affirmation (and support of the Italian Communist party) is colored by the effective desanctification of any faith, including that placed in poetry or politics.

Placing in jeopardy his own seriousness, Pasolini deliberately confuses logical types, legitimizing his "impoeticità" (unpoeticness) by way of excessive descriptive material, part of the attempt to demystify and universalize personal and political figures: "solo ciò che è realistico è mitico, e viceversa" (only what is realistic is mythic, and vice versa). In "La man che trema" (The Trembling Hand) he notes the inevitable existence of reactionary motives in the revolutionary. A unifying factor in this collection is the use of dialogues and projected voices, such as that of Pope Pius XII, excoriated for his lack of Christian charity. Interlocutors include Maria Callas, the Italian Left (which Pasolini hoped to restore), a schoolchild, the national press agency, and so on. Often the voices accompany the peripatetic figure of the poet through the landscape, more cinematic than literary, its closure being a part of the Italian political chronicle.

Pasolini's conservatism – "Io sono una forza del passato" (I am a force of the past) – has been analyzed in terms of heresy, narcissism, vitalism, or regressiveness. But in his various manifestos (understood in the broadest sense) one perceives the acts and precepts of a genuine radicalism in action against a consumer-driven society. From 1959 to 1975 Pasolini endured an average of four trials a year on charges such as obscenity and defamation. Yet Pasolini was not truly pessimistic until his last year, 1975.

Significant overlaps exist among his theater, poetry, and nonfiction of the late 1960s and early 1970s, in which Pasolini's perceived "difference" acquires a universal moral sense. He rejects the aprioristic assumptions of those whose intellectual and religious practices maintain the mind-body split evident in the segregation of stylistics and philosophy, linguistics and demographics, and political theory and ethnographic studies. Increased travel outside Italy and readings in ethnography, cybernetics, and philosophy (Ludwig Wittgenstein and Zen) allowed his avid mind to temper itself and stabilize his arguments. In *Descrizioni di descrizioni* (Descriptions of Descriptions, 1979), *Scritti corsari* (Pirate Writings, 1975), and *Lettere luterane* (1976; translated as *Lutheran Letters,* 1983) Pasolini emerges as a kind of intellectual gadfly with strong pedagogical intentions.

The indictment that is implicit and explicit in Pasolini's later works extends beyond the estates to the universities, the psychoanalysts, and the political parties. Many began to speak of a Pasolinian "death wish" (especially after his death), a notion refuted by his friends and associates, who affirm his athletic zest for life, to the end. Pasolini was murdered on a beach at Ostia in November 1975 by a seventeen-year-old boy, who drove Pasolini's car over him. When he died he had been conducting a relentless critique of societal and institutional hypocrisy, and he had even called for a public trial of those who for thirty years had governed Italy: the hierarchy of the Christian Democratic party. In a 1987 book the Friulian painter Giuseppe Zigaina discusses the oracular value of his late friend's poetic work, indicating the importance of its figurative and mythic facets. Such a perspective aids in understanding the visionary nature of Pasolini's poetic practice, which is peripatetic (rather than regressive, narcissistic, or vitalistic), and the extensive meaning of its structural and formal novelty within Italian culture. His anguished attempt to recover a personal and public equilibrium, though foreshortened against a background of corrupt institutions and linguistic banalization and distorted by a persistent mannerism, is legible as that of a genuine Italian classic.

Letters:

Lettere agli amici (1941–1945), edited by Luciano Serra (Milan: Guanda, 1976);

Lettere, 1940–1954, edited by Nico Naldini (Turin: Einaudi, 1986);

Lettere, 1955–1975, edited by Naldini (Turin: Einaudi, 1988).

Interviews:

Oswald Stack, *Pasolini on Pasolini* (London: Thames & Hudson/British Film Institute, 1969; Bloomington: Indiana University Press, 1969);

Ferdinando Camon, "Pier Paolo Pasolini," in his *Il mestiere di poeta* (Milan: Garzanti, 1982), pp. 94–122;

Il sogno del centauro, edited by Jean Duflot (Rome: Riuniti, 1983).

Bibliographies:

Gian Carlo Ferretti, "Pier Paolo Pasolini," in his *Letteratura e ideologia* (Rome: Riuniti, 1964), pp. 375–386;

Pier Paolo Pasolini and others, *Pasolini in Friuli, 1943–1949* (Udine: Arti Grafiche Friulane, 1976), pp. 133–138;

Luigi Martellini, ed., *Il dialogo, il potere, la morte — Pasolini e la critica* (Bologna: Cappelli, 1979), pp. 291–352;

Franco Brevini, ed., *Per conoscere Pasolini* (Milan: Mondadori, 1981), pp. 13–17;

Keala Jane Jewell, "Bibliography," in *Pier Paolo Pasolini*, edited by Beverly Allen (Saratoga, Cal.: Anma Libri, 1982), pp. 134–137;

Carmine Amoroso, ed., "Per una bibliografia pasoliniana," *Galleria*, special issue on Pasolini, 35 (January–August 1985): 203–218.

Biographies:

Enzo Siciliano, *Vita di Pasolini* (Milan: Rizzoli, 1979); translated by John Shepley as *Pasolini* (New York: Random House, 1982);

Barth David Schwartz, *Pasolini Requiem* (New York: Pantheon, 1992).

References:

Stefano Agosti, "La parola fuori di sé," in his *Cinque analisi* (Milan: Feltrinelli, 1982), pp. 127–154;

Tommaso Anzoino, *Pasolini* (Florence: Nuova Italia, 1971);

Alberto Asor Rosa, "Pasolini," in his *Scrittori e popolo — Il populismo nella letteratura italiana contemporanea* (Rome: Samonà & Savelli, 1963), pp. 349–449;

Giorgio Bàrberi Squarotti, "Pasolini," *Paragone* (1957): 76–83;

Bàrberi Squarotti, "L'ultimo trentennio," in *Dante nella letteratura italiana del Novecento*, edited by Silvio Zennaro (Rome: Bonacci, 1979), pp. 245–277;

Leo Bersani and Ulysse Dutoit, "Merde Alors," *October*, 13 (Summer 1980): 23–35;

Laura Betti, ed., *Pasolini: Cronaca giudiziaria, persecuzione, morte* (Milan: Garzanti, 1977);

Franco Brevini, "Pier Paolo Pasolini," *Belfagor*, 37 (31 July 1982): 407–438;

Brevini, ed., *Per conoscere Pasolini* (Milan: Mondadori, 1981);

Massimo Cacciari, "Pasolini 'Provenzal'?," *Substance*, 53 (1987): 67–73;

Gianfranco Contini, "Testimonianza per Pier Paolo Pasolini," *Ponte*, 36 (30 April 1980): 336–345;

Dedicato a Pier Paolo Pasolini (Milan: Gammalibri, 1976);

Adelio Ferrero, *Il cinema di Pier Paolo Pasolini* (Venice: Marsilio, 1977);

Gian Carlo Ferretti, "La contrastata rivolta di Pasolini," in his *Letteratura e ideologia* (Rome: Riuniti, 1964), pp. 163–356;

Ferretti, *"Officina": Cultura, letteratura e politica negli anni cinquanta* (Turin: Einaudi, 1975);

Ferretti, *Pasolini: L'universo orrendo* (Rome: Riuniti, 1976);

Franco Fortini, "Esistenza e manierismo in Pier Paolo Pasolini," in his *I poeti del Novecento* (Rome: Laterza, 1977), pp. 179–189;

Fortini, "Pasolini o il rifiuto della maturità," in his *Nuovi saggi italiani* (Milan: Garzanti, 1987), pp. 208–216;

Fortini, "Le poesie italiane di questi anni," in his *Saggi italiani* (Bari: De Donato, 1974), pp. 122–133;

Pia Friedrich, *Pier Paolo Pasolini* (Boston: Twayne, 1982);

John Gatt-Rutter, "Pier Paolo Pasolini," in *Writers and Society in Contemporary Italy*, edited by Michael Caesar and Peter Hainsworth (Leamington Spa, U.K.: Berg, 1984), pp. 143–165;

Enzo Golino, *Pasolini: Il sogno di una cosa. Pedagogia, eros, letteratura dal mito del popolo alla società di massa* (Bologna: Mulino, 1985);

Ernesto Groppali, *L'ossessione e il fantasma: Il teatro di Pasolini e Moravia* (Venice: Marsilio, 1979);

Italian Quarterly Review, special issue on Pasolini (1980–1981);

The Italianist: Pier Paolo Pasolini, special issue, 5 (1985);

Keala Jane Jewell, "Deconstructing the Palimpsest: Pasolini's Roman Poems," *Substance,* 53 (1987): 55–66;

Pietro e Carla Lazagna, *Pasolini di fronte al problema religioso* (Bologna: Dehoniane, 1970);

Vincenzo Mannino, *Invito alla lettura di Pasolini* (Milan: Mursia, 1974);

Luigi Martellini, ed., *Il dialogo, il potere, la morte: Pasolini e la critica* (Bologna: Cappelli, 1979);

Nico Naldini, *Nei campi del Friuli (La giovinezza di Pasolini)* (Milan: Scheiwiller, 1984);

"Omaggio a Pasolini," *Nuovi Argomenti,* special issue, 49 (January–March 1976);

Thomas Erling Peterson, *The Paraphrase of an Imaginary Dialogue* (New York: Lang, 1993);

"Pier Paolo Pasolini," *Sigma,* special issue, 2–3 (May–December 1981);

Rinaldo Rinaldi, *Pier Paolo Pasolini* (Milan: Mursia, 1982);

Guido Santato, *Pier Paolo Pasolini: L'opera* (Vicenza: Neri Pozza, 1980);

Walter Siti, "La 'seconda vittoria' di Pasolini," *Quaderni Piacentini,* new series 5 (1982): 87–100;

Steno Vazzano, "Il dantismo di Pasolini," in *Dante nella letteratura italiana del Novecento,* pp. 279–288;

Antonio Vitti, *Il primo Pasolini e la sua narrativa* (New York: Lang, 1987);

Paul Willemen, ed., *Pier Paolo Pasolini* (London: British Film Institute, 1977);

Giuseppe Zigaina, *Pasolini e la morte: Mito alchimia e semantica del "nulla lucente"* (Venice: Marsilio, 1987).

Papers:
The two major Pasolini archives are in Rome and are held by the Associazione Fondo Pier Paolo Pasolini and the Fondo Pasolini, which is at the Biblioteca Nazionale.

Cesare Pavese

(9 September 1908 – 27 August 1950)

Gregory L. Lucente
University of Michigan

BOOKS: *Lavorare stanca* (Florence: Solaria, 1936; enlarged edition, Turin: Einaudi, 1943); translated by William Arrowsmith as *Hard Labor* (New York: Grossman, 1976);

Paesi tuoi (Turin: Einaudi, 1941); translated by A. E. Murch as *The Harvesters* (London: Owen, 1954);

La spiaggia (Rome: Tiberino, 1942);

Feria d'agosto (Turin: Einaudi, 1946); translated by Murch as *Summer Storm, and Other Stories* (London: Owen, 1966);

La terra e la morte (Padua: Tre Venezie, 1947);

Dialoghi con Leucò (Turin: Einaudi, 1947); translated by Arrowsmith and D. S. Carne-Ross as *Dialogues with Leucò* (Ann Arbor: University of Michigan Press, 1965; London: Owen, 1965);

Il compagno (Turin: Einaudi, 1947); translated by W. J. Strachan as *The Comrade* (London: Owen, 1959);

Prima che il gallo canti (Turin: Einaudi, 1949) — comprises *Il carcere* and *La casa in collina*; *La casa in collina* translated by Strachan as *The House on the Hill* (London: Owen, 1956; New York: Walker, 1961);

La bella estate: Tre romanzi (Turin: Einaudi, 1949) — comprises *La bella estate, Il diavolo sulle colline,* and *Tra donne sole*; *Tra donne sole* translated by D. D. Paige as *Among Women Only* (London: Owen, 1953; New York: Noonday, 1959); *Il diavolo sulle colline* translated by Paige as *The Devil in the Hills* (London: Owen, 1954; New York: Noonday, 1959);

La luna e i falò (Turin: Einaudi, 1950); translated by Louise Sinclair as *The Moon and the Bonfire* (London: Owen, 1952); translated by Marianne Ceconi as *The Moon and the Bonfires* (New York: Farrar, Straus & Young, 1953);

La letteratura americana e altri saggi (Turin: Einaudi, 1951); republished as *Saggi letterari* (Turin: Einaudi, 1968); translated by Edwin Fussell as *American Literature: Essays and Opinions* (Berkeley: University of California Press, 1970);

Verrà la morte e avrà i tuoi occhi (Turin: Einaudi, 1951);

Il mestiere di vivere (Diario 1935–1950) (Turin: Einaudi, 1952); translated by Murch and Jeanne Molli as *The Burning Brand: Diaries 1935–1950* (New York: Walker, 1961); also published as *This Business of Living: Diary, 1935–1950* (London: Owen, 1961);

Notte di festa (Turin: Einaudi, 1953); translated by Murch as *Festival Night, and Other Stories* (London: Owen, 1964);

Fuoco grande, by Pavese and Bianca Garufi (Turin: Einaudi, 1959);

Racconti (Turin: Einaudi, 1960); translated by Murch as *Told in Confidence, and Other Stories* (London: Owen, 1971);

Poesie edite e inedite, edited by Italo Calvino (Turin: Einaudi, 1962);

8 poesie inedite e quattro lettere a un'amica, 1928–1929 (Milan: All'Insegna del Pesce d'Oro, 1964);

Ciau Masino (Turin: Einaudi, 1969);

Poesie del disamore e altre poesie disperse (Turin: Einaudi, 1973);

Vita attraverso le lettere, bilingual edition, edited by Lorenzo Mondo (Turin: Einaudi, 1973);

La Teogonia di Esiodo e tre inni omerici (Turin: Einaudi, 1981).

Collection: *Opere,* 16 volumes (Turin: Einaudi, 1947–1968); selections translated by R. W. Flint as *Selected Works* (New York: Farrar, Straus & Giroux, 1968).

Editions in English: *The Political Prisoner,* translated by W. J. Strachan (London: Owen, 1955); republished as *The Beautiful Summer* (London: Brown, Watson, 1960) — comprises translations of *Il carcere* and *La bella estate*;

The Beach, and A Great Fire, translated by Strachan (London: Owen, 1963);

A Mania for Solitude: Selected Poems, 1930–1950, translated by Margaret Crosland (London: Owen, 1969); republished as *Selected Poems*

Cesare Pavese shortly after World War II at Langhe in the Italian Piedmont

(Harmondsworth, U.K. & Baltimore: Penguin, 1971);

The Leather Jacket: Stories, translated by Alma Murch (London & New York: Quartet, 1980).

TRANSLATIONS: Sinclair Lewis, *Il nostro signor Wrenn* (Florence: Bemporad, 1931);

Herman Melville, *Moby Dick* (Turin: Frassinelli, 1932);

Sherwood Anderson, *Riso nero* (Turin: Frassinelli, 1932);

James Joyce, *Dedalus* (Turin: Frassinelli, 1934);

John Dos Passos, *Il 42° parallelo* (Milan: Mondadori, 1935);

Dos Passos, *Un mucchio di quattrini* (Milan: Mondadori, 1937);

Gertrude Stein, *Autobiografia di Alice B. Toklas* (Turin: Einaudi, 1938);

Daniel Defoe, *Moll Flanders* (Turin: Einaudi, 1938);

John Steinbeck, *Uomini e topi* (Milan: Bompiani, 1938);

Charles Dickens, *David Copperfield* (Turin: Einaudi, 1939);

Stein, *Tre esistenze* (Turin: Einaudi, 1940);

Melville, *Benito Cereno* (Turin: Einaudi, 1940);

G. M. Trevelyan, *La rivoluzione inglese del 1688–89* (Turin: Einaudi, 1941);

Christopher Morley, *Il cavallo di Troia* (Milan: Bompiani, 1941);

William Faulkner, *Il borgo* (Milan: Mondadori, 1942);

Robert Henrique, *Capitano Smith* (Turin: Einaudi, 1947).

Cesare Pavese's life and works demonstrate a recurrent and finally unresolved contradiction. Although in many ways Pavese was the literary figure most central to the cultural life of his times and was thus the literary spokesman, along with Elio Vittorini, for his generation in Italy, Pavese never felt at ease in his social or cultural environs. He regularly held himself apart from these surroundings, always remaining on the margins of life, whether in forced or voluntary exclusion. This factor is apparent in the events of his life as well as in his novels and poems, in which it is present in the themes of solitude and alienation. The discomfort and deep-seated personal doubt that infuse Pavese's life and works do not, of course, detract from his importance as a writer. Indeed they actively contribute to the fascination that his literary corpus continues to hold for contemporary readers drawn to his works both because of the interest of the subject matter itself (regional life in Italy during the years of Fascism, World War II and the Italian Resistance, and the early postwar period) and because of the vital existential tension at the heart of his poetry and narratives.

Pavese's writing gives evidence of his desire to re-create in literary form the world of his era and, at the same time, to go against the tide. His first major publication, the poetry collection *Lavorare stanca* (1936; translated as *Hard Labor,* 1976), stands as a poetic tribute to Pavese's memories of Piedmont, the land of his birth and the region where he spent most of his adult life. This northern Italian province, bordering on the mountains and the sea, encompasses both Turin – in his time Italy's most sophisticated and "Northern European" city – and the rustic hills of the Langhe, with an ingrown rural culture steeped in the traditions of superstition, exhausting day-to-day labor, and the never-ending cycles of nature. Pavese's first volume of poetry also served to break with the dominant Italian poetics of the prewar decades (in which, due partly to Fascist censorship, the strongest poetic trend was that of opaque indirection and hermeticism) and to introduce a fresh new voice tending toward equal measures of linguistic and narrative realism, in a literary style that seemed objective and transparent.

Pavese's later major poems are collected in the volume *Poesie del disamore e altre poesie disperse* (Poems of Estranged Love and Other Scattered Poetry, 1973), which includes *La terra e la morte* (Earth and Death, 1947) and *Verrà la morte e avrà i tuoi occhi* (Death Will Come and It Will Have Your Eyes, 1951). These poems show marked changes from Pavese's early work, especially in their engaging lyrical impulse and their highly personalized subjective tone. Along with these collections of verse, in the years between 1935 and 1950 Pavese published many novels and short stories, the most important of which demonstrate an astute blend of the logically contradictory but aesthetically pleasing elements of realism and myth. Pavese also worked as an es-

sayist and translator, and he held various editorial posts, first for literary journals and then for the Einaudi publishing house in Turin, the most distinguished postwar publisher in Italy. Pavese's diary, which he almost certainly intended for publication, was published posthumously as *Il mestiere di vivere* (1952; translated as *The Burning Brand* and *This Business of Living,* 1961). This richly textured and at times disconcerting document provides ample evidence of the intensity and breadth of Pavese's cultural interests, which helped make him one of the main figures of twentieth-century Italian culture.

Although his family resided in Turin, where his father, Eugenio, was a functionary in the law courts, Pavese was born (on 9 September 1908) in Santo Stefano Belbo, a village in the Langhe, which was also where Pavese's father had been born and where the family regularly went for summer vacations. In 1914, while Pavese was still a young boy, his father died from a brain tumor. Following this loss, Pavese grew up as the sole male (with his sister, Maria, and his mother, Consolina) in a distinctly female-dominated household. His mother was a quiet and severe woman of Piedmontese origins, and she seems to have been either unwilling or unable to provide the maternal affection necessary to alleviate Pavese's overriding sense of solitude after his father's death. Only the regular returns to his birthplace in the countryside seemed to provide Pavese with pleasure and solace. These trips, and in particular the impressively resourceful people he came to know in the Langhe, form the basis for much of his mature poetry and narrative; the two best examples of such people are the worldly wise cousin of the opening poem in *Lavorare stanca,* "I mari del Sud" ("South Seas"), and Nuto, the remarkable mentor of the orphaned boy in Pavese's last novel, *La luna e i falò* (1950; translated as *The Moon and the Bonfire,* 1952).

Pavese eventually commented on the region's continuing influence on his imagination in a letter written from Santo Stefano Belbo to a close friend, Fernanda Pivano, on 25 June 1942: "la strada che gira intorno alle mie vecchie vigne . . . scompare, alla svolta, con un salto nel vuoto . . . ma presentivo di là dal salto, a grande distanza, dopo la valle che si espande come un mare, una barriera remota (piccina, tanto è remota), di colline assolate e fiorite, esotiche. Quello era il mio 'Paradiso,' i miei 'Mari del Sud' " (the road that runs along my old vineyards . . . disappears around the bend with a leap into empty space . . . but I had a presentiment, beyond

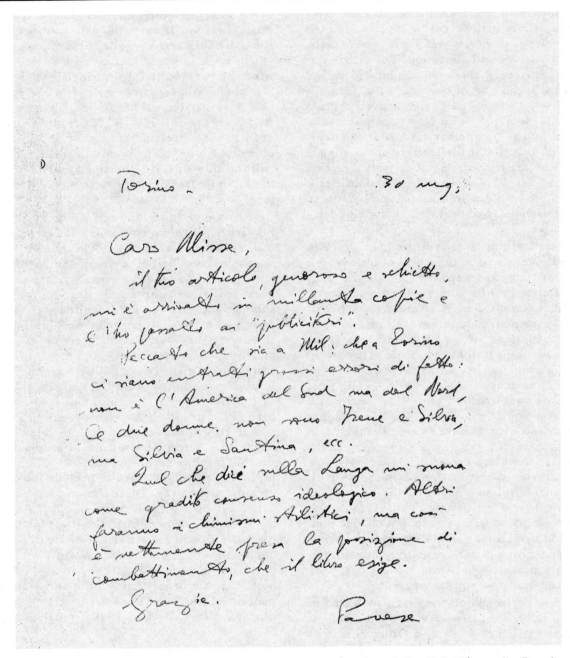

*Letter of 30 May 1950 from Pavese to his friend and fellow writer Ulisse (pseudonym for Davide Lajolo), regarding Pavese's
1950 novel,* La luna e i falò *(Collection of Davide Lajolo)*

that leap, far in the distance, after the valley that expands out like the sea, like a remote barrier [looking small, so remote it is], an image of hills drenched in sunlight, flowering, exotic. That was my "Paradise," my "South Seas").

It was nonetheless in the environs of the city rather than the countryside that Pavese found his first intellectual mentor, the anti-Fascist humanist Augusto Monti, one of Pavese's high-school instructors at the Lyceum Massimo D'Azeglio in Turin. Pavese studied the humanities with Monti from 1923 to 1926. It was in this same period that Pavese began to write poetry. In 1930, as a student at the University of Turin, Pavese earned his degree with a thesis on the work of Walt Whitman. The literary pursuits with which Pavese had been occupied during his school years continued and expanded after his graduation from the university, and until 1935 he worked on translations and collaborated on journals with some of Turin's best-known writers, editors, and critics, including friends from his youth such as Leone Ginzburg and Giulio Einaudi. However, this activity was broken off by one of the worst events of Pavese's early adult life, his trial and conviction for anti-Fascist sympathies, which led to his confinement in Brancaleone Calabro, a small town near the remote southern tip of the Calabrian coast.

Such sentences of confinement were regularly imposed on opponents of the Fascist regime as a sort of house arrest, involving displacement to remote areas. Pavese subsequently wrote a book concerning his confinement, the short novel *Il carcere* (included in *Prima che il gallo canti* [Before the Cock Crows], 1949; translated in *The Political Prisoner*, 1955). The enforced solitude and physical inactivity had the effect of intensifying Pavese's sense of himself as a northern Italian Piedmontese by way of contrast with the southern environment of Calabria. Of perhaps even greater moment in Pavese's life than the actual confinement was the event that followed, which involved, as did several of the more significant events in Pavese's life, failure with a woman. In Turin before his arrest Pavese had remained primarily on the fringes of groups with anti-Fascist sympathies, but a friend of his, Tina Pizzardo, with whom he was in love, was closely associated with the clandestine Communist party. To avoid danger, she had asked Pavese to receive letters for her at his Turin address from Altiero Spinelli, an anti-Fascist prisoner then in jail in Rome. These letters furnished the evidence that led to Pavese's ultimate sentencing to three years of confinement (which was later reduced to eight months). During Pavese's loneliness in Calabria, he seemed certain that the woman he had left in Turin (and who figured in his poetry, according to Pavese's biographer, Davide Lajolo, as "la donna dalla voce rauca," or "the woman with the hoarse voice") would be awaiting him at his return. The shocking discovery that Pizzardo had abandoned him for another man deeply affected Pavese's relationships with his art and with women.

The American actress Constance Dowling, whom Pavese met in 1949, dominates his last poems, collected in *Verrà la morte e avrà i tuoi occhi*. Pavese's final poem (written in English), "Last blues, to be read some day," has to do at least in part with his love for Dowling, and it shows the depth of his disillusionment at the failure of the relationship. Pavese refers directly to this poem in

a letter to Dowling dated 17 April 1950, in which he also states his suffering at the thought that this failure meant, for him, not merely the end of another relationship but more significantly the impossibility of finding happiness in marriage. The collapse of this love entailed exclusion from the entire social order that marriage implied. The pain of this final enforced solitude turned out to be more than Pavese could bear. Although he won the prestigious Strega Prize in June 1950 — for *La bella estate: Tre romanzi* (The Beautiful Summer: Three Novels, 1949) — he could not overcome his feelings of personal inadequacy and misery, as the final entries in his diary show. In the late summer of 1950, in a hotel room in Turin, Pavese came to terms with what he considered his life's failings by committing suicide, the one act of existential self-exclusion over which, despite everything, he still retained control. Sometime in the early hours of 27 August 1950 Pavese died of a massive overdose of sleeping pills.

Throughout his lifetime Pavese's work as a writer and translator progressed at a more or less constant pace, but there was one area of his literary activities that was of particular import in the 1940s, especially after the revival of the Einaudi publishing group following the fall of Fascism and the end of World War II. This area was that of editing. In his editorial capacity with Einaudi, Pavese was able to suggest, promote, and oversee Italian publication of some important works of the nineteenth- and twentieth-century European intellectual tradition. The works that attracted Pavese the most, from the great nineteenth-century schools of anthropology and mythology to the more current investigations into social psychology and psychoanalysis (from James George Frazer, Emile Durkheim, Bronislaw Malinowski, and Károly Kerényi to Sigmund Freud and Carl Jung), began to intermingle with Pavese's earlier experiences as a translator and essayist in helping him formulate his developing poetics.

This poetics was constituted in its various stages by fusing the fundamental elements of realism with those of myth. While grafting his understanding of psychology and mythology onto his formative reading of the work of Giambattista Vico — the Neapolitan author of *La scienza nuova* (The New Science, 1744) and the signal proponent of the equation of poetic perception with mythic perception — Pavese developed a poetics based on his own conception of the "immagine-racconto," or the poetic image containing its own story, mentioned in his diary as early as 1935 and at various points thereafter. Pavese's readings in the dynamics of the folktale, specifically his acquaintance with the formalist work of Vladimir Propp, undoubtedly assisted him in putting these theories into practice in his narrative; and his earlier work on English-language masters of realist prose with mythic underpinnings, such as Herman Melville, William Faulkner, Charles Dickens, and the young James Joyce, had pointed Pavese in this same direction. But Pavese did not restrict this sort of practice to his prose; he also relied on it in his poetry, including the early, predominantly realist poems of *Lavorare stanca,* as discussed by Pavese in a general way in the essay "Il mestiere di poeta" (The Poet's Craft, 1935), published in an appendix to later editions, such as that of 1943.

One of the most concise explanations of these concerns, dating from the mid 1940s, is the essay "Del mito, del simbolo e d'altro" ("Of Myth, Symbol, and Other Things" — collected in *La letteratura americana e altri saggi* [1951; translated as *American Literature: Essays and Opinions,* 1970]); it explains Pavese's mythic/realistic poetics in a manner that includes both narrative and poetry. In this and a group of related essays dating from 1943 to 1950 (in the section of *La letteratura* titled "Il mito," or "Myth") Pavese treats the ways in which the crucial, semimystical memories of childhood and the repetitive rhythms of events create the powerful, mythic aura of symbols — as opposed to static allegory — in poems as well as in stories and novels. This symbolic combination becomes more noteworthy in Pavese's later narratives (in particular in *La luna e i falò*), and the mythic elements become most obvious in one of his last works, the series of openly mythic "dialogues" published in 1947 as *Dialoghi con Leucò* (translated as *Dialogues with Leucò,* 1965). However, the combination is undeniably at work in Pavese's poetry as well, with the most striking results in the poems he composed in the last years of his life.

The thematic concerns of Pavese's poetry, central to the poems of *Lavorare stanca* and recurrent thereafter in his verse and his prose, can be listed in cursory fashion: the relations between men and women, with special emphasis on the isolation and integrity, or lack of it, of the individual male; the nature of human violence — including sexual violence and death — both in its bestial, destructive aspects and as a potentially positive force for ritual regeneration and renewal; the distinction between two key oppositions, on the one hand the country as opposed to the city and, on the other, the north as opposed to the south; the

relationship between individual and social action, on occasion encompassing the arena of politics and almost always including the painful, seemingly inevitable solitude of the socially alienated individual; the contest between patriarchy and matriarchy, in the early poems providing expression for Pavese's well-known misogyny; and finally the notion of the eternal return, almost always dealing with the attempt, however successful or unsuccessful, to recapture the timeless mythic truth of the memories of childhood experience in a changing world.

In the exposition of these thematic concerns, Pavese's usual practice is to begin with consideration of the individual and then to move past the individual into the larger sphere of society. This scheme is also, generally speaking, the characteristic movement of the "immagine-racconto," which begins with what seems the single instance of image or character only to broaden through rhythmic repetition into ever larger realms. However, Pavese's work does not leave the individual behind. Indeed the typical development of his work involves the return to the realm of the single character, but only as that realm is itself poeticized to include greater truth, through symbolic relations, than any individual phenomenon, as such, could encompass or suggest. This procedure was described by Pavese in a radio interview (given in the third person) broadcast in 1950 and included in *La letteratura:* "Pavese non si cura di 'creare dei personaggi.' I personaggi sono per lui un mezzo, non un fine. I personaggi gli servono semplicemente a costruire delle favole intellettuali il cui tema è il ritmo di ciò che accade.... I personaggi ... sono nomi e tipi, non altro ..." (Pavese does not worry about "creating characters." For him characters represent a means, not an end. Characters serve simply to help him construct intellectual fables the theme of which is the rhythm of what happens.... Characters ... are names and types, nothing else...). This dual movement, through individual history both into collective society and into the poetic aura of the symbol, gives form to a great deal of Pavese's work in poetry as well as prose (in the radio interview he names *Lavorare stanca* as crucial in this regard); and his stance accounts, at least in part, for his championing of novelists and poets who evince similar techniques and interests, such as Whitman, Melville, and (in a 1947 review reprinted in *La letteratura*) a gifted young Italian writer just then appearing on the scene, Italo Calvino.

The themes of Pavese's work remain fairly constant through his writing (albeit evincing a growing obsession with love and death), but the style of

Cesare Pavese

his poetry demonstrated a marked shift between the early verse of the 1930s and the poems of the later collections. When the poetry of *Lavorare stanca* first appeared in 1936, it constituted a stylistic revolution in Italian poetry. Its patently nonelegant, mundane diction echoed — but in strictly literary fashion — the simple, laconic speech patterns of the verse's "objectively" portrayed realistic subjects, who were for the most part the country people and the urban working class of Pavese's Piedmontese regions. His interest in slang (an interest that was helped along by his correspondence with a friend in America, Tony Chiuminatto) and his attentive study of the various uses of popular speech in literary discourse show up time and again in these poems. There is also a notable narrative slant to Pavese's early poetry, formed in part by a skillfully handled paratactic style that is surely Pavese's own discovery in terms of poetry but that he may have noticed in the stories of Sherwood Anderson or Ernest Hemingway, to mention only two among many possible parallels. The long and heterodox thirteen-syllable line — which, as Doug Thompson has noted in his 1982 book on Pavese, often breaks down at the caesura into two half lines of more traditional cast, septenarii and senarii — facilitates the slow pace of many of the poems.

In the late poetry of *La terra e la morte* and *Verrà la morte e avrà i tuoi occhi,* after several significant transitional poems of the late 1930s (also in *Poesie del disamore*), Pavese's style has changed considerably. Some of these changes are discussed by him in an essay titled "A proposito di certe poesie non ancora scritte" (1940; translated as "Notes on Certain Unwritten Poems"), appended to *Lavorare stanca* in 1943. In the later poems, the short lines and compact, allusive phrasing leave standard narrative concerns behind as they heighten the epiphanic effect of the lyrical moment. The overall orientation of these poems is also different, since many open by directly addressing the individual "tu" of the poem's subject, and several include the rapid metaphorization of the poem's addressee, as in the lines "Sei la terra e la morte" (You are the earth and you are death) and "Sei la vita e la morte" (You are life and you are death). Moreover, these same techniques and effects are apparent in the later poems that Pavese wrote in English (found at his death among the group written for Dowling).

The publication history of Pavese's poetry, thanks in large part to the editorial work of

Calvino, is on the whole straightforward. The first edition of *Lavorare stanca* was published by the Florence firm Solaria in 1936. This edition, from which four poems were excluded by Fascist censorship, contained slightly more than half the poems included by Pavese in the revised and augmented edition that he published with Einaudi in 1943. The standard edition of the poems in *Lavorare stanca* appeared posthumously in 1962, in *Poesie edite e inedite* (Published and Unpublished Poems), edited for Einaudi by Calvino. Extracts from the collection appear in separate volumes in Einaudi's sixteen-part series of Pavese's works, *Opere* (1947–1968; translated in part as *Selected Works*, 1968).

Perhaps the best example of both the style and the themes of Pavese's early poetry is the opening poem of *Lavorare stanca*, "I mari del Sud," dedicated to Augusto Monti. The poem begins with an often discussed and distinctively Pavesian octet:

> Camminiamo una sera sul fianco di un colle,
> in silenzio. Nell'ombra del tardo crepuscolo
> mio cugino è un gigante vestito di bianco,
> che si muove pacato, abbronzato nel volto,
> taciturno. Tacere è la nostra virtú.
> Qualche nostro antenato dev'essere stato ben solo
> – un grand'uomo tra idioti o un povero folle –
> per insegnare ai suoi tanto silenzio.

> (One evening we walk along the flank of a hill
> in silence. In the shadows of early evening,
> my cousin, a giant dressed in white,
> moving calmly along, his face browned by the sun,
> not speaking. Silence is our virtue.
> Some ancestor of ours must have been quite a solitary
>   man
>   – a great man surrounded by half-wits, or a poor crazy
>   fool –
> to teach his descendants such silence.)

This opening is characteristically direct and seemingly simple, in accord with the representational, realistically slanted style of *Lavorare stanca*. The long, slow lines suggest Pavese's intent to tell a leisurely story in poetic form, while the lexical register, echoing that of popular speech, evokes the everyday realm of common experience, which is the subject of much of Pavese's early verse. The thematic concerns are also typically Pavesian: the mingling of humans and nature; the heroic cast of silent, masculine virtue; and the openly stated fascination with roots and origins. The importance of the speaker's experience in the region of the Langhe, an importance that shows itself not only in sentiment but also in speech, in the phrases and rhythms of the local dialect, is

stressed more clearly as the poem continues as a dialogue between the speaker and his older, much admired cousin.

As the poem proceeds, the process of traveling away and returning home in spatial terms finds a parallel in temporal ones, in the speaker's memories of the formative years of his own childhood:

> Oh da quando ho giocato ai pirati malesi,
> quanto tempo è trascorso. . . . Altri giorni, altri giochi,
> altri squassi del sangue dinanzi a rivali
> più elusivi: i pensieri ed i sogni.

> (God, how long it has been since those childhood days
> when we played at Malay pirates. . . . Other days,
>   other games,
> another kind of blood, the shocks and wounds that
>   come from facing other
> more elusive rivals: thoughts and dreams.)

Then, in the present rather than the past, the speaker dwells on the force that his cousin's experience has provided as an example for him. But at the poem's end, another note creeps in, that of difference rather than similarity or simple emulation. In response to the speaker's imaginings of his cousin's marvelous south-sea adventures (reminiscent of scenes in Melville's *Moby-Dick*, 1851), the cousin replies in a manner that underscores the exotic nature of his life away from his family and his native region:

> Ma quando gli dico
> ch'egli è tra i fortunati che han visto l'aurora
> sulle isole più belle della terra,
> al ricordo sorride e risponde che il sole
> si levava che il giorno era vecchio per loro.

> (But when I tell him
> how lucky he is, one of the few people who have seen
> dawn breaking over the loveliest islands in the world,
> he smiles at the memory, saying that when the sun
>   rose,
> the day was no longer young. They had been up for hours.)

Other poems of the collection continue in this mixture of poetic statement and reminiscence, with occasionally jarring notes. "Antenati" ("Ancestors"), the next poem in the section (which bears the same subtitle), is a case in point:

> Ho trovato una terra trovando i compagni,
> una terra cattiva, dov'è un privilegio
> non far nulla, pensando al futuro.
> Perché il solo lavoro non basta a me e ai miei;
> noi sappiamo schiantarci, ma il sogno più grande
> dei miei padri fu sempre un far nulla da bravi.
> Siamo nati per girovagare su quelle colline,

senza donne, e le mani tenercele dietro la schiena.
(When I found my friends, I found my own land,
land so worthless, a man's got a perfect right
to do absolutely nothing, just dream about the future.
Work is not good enough not for my people and me;
Oh we can break our backs all right, but the dream
my fathers always had was being genuinely good at
    doing nothing.
We were born to wander and ramble these hills,
with no women, our hands folded behind our backs.)

This ancestral dream, of working past work to arrive at a state of rhythmic, pensive wandering, runs through much of *Lavorare stanca*, as it does through Pavese's narratives. But the remaining poems in the collection treat more of his favorite topics, among them sex and violence in humankind and nature, in "Il dio-caprone" ("The Goat God"); the domestic possibilities of male-female relationships, in "Lavorare stanca" and "Piaceri notturni" ("Night Pleasures"); the contrasts between the painful urban experience of the city and the pleasures of the country, throughout the section "Legna verde" ("Green Wood"); the positive, enduring, and at times ineffable aspects of feminine nature, in "Maternità" ("Motherhood"); and the ambiguity of human solitude and boredom in "Lo steddazzu" ("The Morning Star"), the poem that bears the stamp of Pavese's period of confinement in its title, which is given in Calabrian dialect.

Though the slant of Pavese's poetics is predominantly representational in his first collection, this is not the case in the later poems collected in *Poesie del disamore*. A few of these poems are of interest solely for their value in historical/biographical terms as opposed to aesthetic ones, which is especially true for "To C. from C.," an unsuccessful attempt in English to express the poetic essence of Pavese's relation with Dowling. Such aesthetic failures notwithstanding, a group of these late poems, in their blending of lyrical suggestiveness with lyrical force, stand out as Pavese's poetic masterpieces. This mastery shows up in his final complete poem, "Last blues, to be read some day," dated 11 April 1950, just a few months before his death. But his poetic capacities in this final period of his work are especially evident in two poems written slightly earlier in the spring of 1950, both of which demonstrate the rapid metaphorization of Pavese's poetic images, his use of brief lyrical lines, and the technique of direct, highly personal address. The title of the first of these is in English, "In the morning you always come back":

La città abbrividisce,
odorano le pietre —

sei la vita, il risveglio.
Stella sperduta
nella luce dell'alba
cigolío della brezza,
tepore, respiro —
è finita la notte.

Sei la luce e il mattino.

(The city shudders,
the stones give off their scent —
you are life, the reawakening itself.

Star lost
in the light of dawn,
creaking of the breeze,
warmth, breath —
the night is over.

You are the light and the early morning.)

The second of these two poems, "Verrà la morte e avrà i tuoi occhi," adds in somewhat more discursive fashion the thematics of love and death, and it gives evidence, at this point in Pavese's life, of his obsession with the ultimate suicidal gesture of willful self-exclusion, the "vizio assurdo" (absurd vice) also referred to with disconcerting repetition throughout Pavese's diaries:

Per tutti la morte ha uno sguardo.
Verrà la morte e avrà i tuoi occhi.
Sarà come smettere un vizio,
come vedere nello specchio
riemergere un viso morto,
come ascoltare un labbro chiuso.
Scenderemo nel gorgo muti.

(For everyone death has a gaze.
Death will come and it will have your eyes.
It will be as though quitting a vice,
as though seeing reemerge
in the mirror a death mask,
as though listening to lips already closed.
We will descend into the whirlpool speechlessly.)

In the decades since Pavese's death, there have been several discernible strands of critical approaches to his work. The most significant of these, all of which are discussed in Mauro Ponzi's *La critica e Pavese* (The Critic and Pavese, 1977), can be grouped into the following concerns: the psychological/biographical elements of Pavese's works; his American interests; his use of the poetics of myth; his manner of poetic style and poetic form; and the question of decadence, as opposed to political commitment, as expressed in his writings. No matter which of these approaches is adopted, however, there is no room for doubt that Pavese's work, when taken in its entirety, is among the most important artistic achievements in Italy, and indeed all of Europe, in the turbulent years between the 1930s and the 1950s.

Letters:

Lettere, 2 volumes: volume 1, edited by Lorenzo Mondo; volume 2, edited by Italo Calvino (Turin: Einaudi, 1966); selections translated by A. E. Murch as *Selected Letters, 1924–1950* (London: Owen, 1969).

Biography:

Davide Lajolo, *Il vizio assurdo: Storia di Cesare Pavese* (Milan: Saggiatore, 1960); translated by Mario and Mark Pietralunga as *An Absurd Vice: A Biography of Cesare Pavese* (New York: New Directions, 1983).

References:

William Arrowsmith, Introduction to Pavese's *Hard Labor,* translated by Arrowsmith, second edition (Baltimore: Johns Hopkins University Press, 1979), pp. ix–xxxvi;

Gian-Paolo Biasin, *The Smile of the Gods: A Thematic Study of Cesare Pavese's Works,* translated by Yvonne Freccero (Ithaca, N.Y.: Cornell University Press, 1968);

Dominique Fernandez, *L'échec de Pavese* (Paris: Grasset, 1967);

David William Foster, "The Poetic Vision of 'le colline': An Introduction to Pavese's *Lavorare stanca,*" *Italica,* 42 (1965): 380–390;

John Freccero, "Mythos and Logos: The Moon and the Bonfire," *Italian Quarterly,* 4 (1961): 3–16;

Armanda Guiducci, *Il mito Pavese* (Florence: Vallecchi, 1967);

Louis Kibler, "Patterns of Time in Pavese's *La luna e i falò,*" *Forum Italicum,* 12 (1978): 339–349;

Gregory L. Lucente, *The Narrative of Realism and Myth: Verga, Lawrence, Faulkner, Pavese* (Baltimore: Johns Hopkins University Press, 1981);

Bruce Merry, "Artifice and Structure in *La luna e i falò,*" *Forum Italicum,* 5 (1971): 351–358;

Peter M. Norton, "Cesare Pavese and the American Nightmare," *Modern Language Notes,* 77 (1962): 24–36;

Mauro Ponzi, *La critica e Pavese* (Bologna: Cappelli, 1977);

Leonard G. Sbrocchi, *Stilistica nella narrativa pavesiana* (Florence: Veroli, 1967);

Louis Tenenbaum, "Character Treatment in Pavese's Fiction," *Symposium,* 15 (1961): 131–138;

Doug Thompson, *Cesare Pavese: A Study of the Major Novels and Poems* (Cambridge: Cambridge University Press, 1982);

Tibor Wlassics, *Pavese falso e vero: Vita, poetica, narrativa* (Turin: Centro Studi Piemontesi, 1985).

Albino Pierro

(19 November 1916 –   )

Gustavo Costa
University of California, Berkeley

BOOKS: *Liriche* (Rome: Palatina, 1946);
Nuove liriche (Rome: Danesi, 1949);
Mia madre passava (Rome: Palombi, 1955);
Il paese sincero (Rome: Porfiri, 1956);
Il transito del vento (Rome: Dell'Arco, 1957);
Poesie (Rome: Dell'Arco, 1958);
Il mio villaggio (Bologna: Cappelli, 1959);
Agavi e sassi (Rome: Dell'Arco, 1960);
A terra d'u ricorde (La terra del ricordo) (Rome: Nuovo Belli, 1960);
Metaponto (Rome: Nuovo Cracas, 1963; enlarged edition, Bari: Laterza, 1966; revised edition, Milan: Garzanti, 1982);
I 'nnammurète (Rome: Nuovo Cracas, 1963);
Appuntamento (1946–1967) (Bari: Laterza, 1967);
Nd'u piccicarelle di Tursi (Nel precipizio di Tursi) (Bari: Laterza, 1967);
Eccó 'a morte? (Bari: Laterza, 1969);
Famme dorme (Milan: All'Insegna del Pesce d'Oro, 1971);
Curtelle a lu sóue (Bari: Laterza, 1973);
Nu belle fatte / Una bella storia / A Beautiful Story, translated by Edith Farnsworth (Milan: All'Insegna del Pesce d'Oro, 1976);
Quattordici poesie e nove disegni (Milan: Edizioni 32, 1977);
Sti mascre (Rome: L'Arco, 1980);
Dieci poesie inedite in dialetto tursitano (Lucca: Pacini Fazzi, 1981);
Ci uéra turnè; Vorrei ritornare (Ravenna: Girasole, 1982);
Si pó' nu jurne (Turin: Forma, 1983);
Poesie tursitane, edited by Nicola Merola (Venice: Leone, 1985);
Tante ca pàrete notte (Galatina: Manni, 1986);
Un pianto nascosto: Antologia poetica 1946–1983, edited by Francesco Zambon (Turin: Einaudi, 1986);
Com'agghi' 'a f è? / Come debbo fare? / Comment dois-je faire?, translated by Madeleine Santschi (Milan: All'Insegna del Pesce d'Oro, 1986);
Nun c'è pizze di munne (Non c'è angolo della terra), (Milan: Mondadori, 1992).

OTHER: "Nu belle fatte (Una bella storia), venti poesie," *Almanacco dello Specchio,* 4 (1975): 147–161;
"The Lovers (I 'nnammurète)," translated by Edith Farnsworth, *Forum Italicum,* 13 (Summer 1979): 225–227;
"Poesie inedite," in *Omaggio a Pierro,* edited by Antonio Motta (Manduria: Lacaita, 1982), pp. 33–39;
"Ricordi a Tursi: Feste e calamità: Poesie inedite di Albino Pierro," *Poliorama,* 1 (1982): 294–305;
"Telling Love (from *Nu belle fatte* by Albino Pierro)," translated by Anthony L. Johnson, in his *Marigolds, Stilts, Solitudes: Selected Poems, 1956–1984* (Salzburg: Institut für Anglistik und Amerikanistik, 1984), pp. 20–30;
Hermann W. Haller, *The Hidden Italy: A Bilingual Edition of Italian Dialect Poetry,* includes poems by Pierro (Detroit: Wayne State University Press, 1986), pp. 421–441.

The work of Albino Pierro is a typical example of the bilingualism that still pervades Italian society. He started writing poetry in Italian but later changed to the dialect of his birthplace, Tursi, in the Basilicata region. While the quality of his poetry in Italian is debatable, the excellence of his dialectal compositions is well recognized. Eminent critics agree that Pierro's use of the language spoken in his native town is neither a purely exterior and colorful addition to the substance of his poetry nor merely a device to embellish his verse with the enticements of the intriguing folklore of southern Italy. On the contrary, it is a strategy that enables Pierro to find and explore his own existential and cultural roots. As critic Gianfranco Folena has remarked, Pierro's dialect is an *idioletto,* a personal language bearing the imprint of his human and artistic originality. Since he was the first to use his native language in literary form, Pierro was not confronted by an accepted tradition but rather invented one. By exploring the poetic potential of the dialect of Tursi, Pierro identi-

Portrait of Albino Pierro by Carlo Levi (from Omaggio a Pierro, *edited by Antonio Motta, 1982)*

fied his poetic vision with the immemorial essence of southern civilization, untouched by consumerism and deeply aware of transience. Pierro's Orphic inspiration shows an affinity with magic; the superior quality of his best poems coincides with theurgic speech, which gives birth to a world where the living and the dead coexist in everyday life. His is not a realistic representation of southern beliefs and customs but a highly personal vision of an archetypical reality. Pierro is both a primitivist, constantly interested in the prehistoric aspects of Basilicata, and a modern writer, fully aware of the existential crisis of European culture. His style reveals a formal classicism, based on traditional comparison, and a modern sensibility, resorting to analogy and synesthesia. On a lexical level Pierro's poetry reveals a tension between existence and essence. Taken together, Pierro's poems offer a highly sophisticated blend of lyricism and irony, as well as a source of study for anthropologists and linguists.

Albino Pierro was born on 19 November 1916 to Salvatore and Margherita Ottomano Piero. Albino's mother died a few months after his birth, and he was brought up by his paternal aunts. After finishing grammar school, he continued his studies at Taranto, Salerno, Policoro, and Sulmona. He also resided in Friuli and Piedmont and finally established his residence in Rome, where he enrolled at the School of Education of the University of Rome. In 1944 he received his final degree on the basis of a thesis on Saint Augustine's political thought. At this point Pierro began his lifelong career as a poet and a high-school teacher of history and philosophy.

His first collection of poems, *Liriche* (Lyrics), was published in 1946. In this work, composed in Italian, Pierro expressed both his sensibility for the picturesque aspects of southern nature and his tragic vision of human destiny. Giovanni Pascoli's influence is evident in these traditional poems. Although they are rather diffuse and sentimental, his lyrics reveal a real poetic talent. The same characteristics are to be found in Pierro's second book, *Nuove liriche* (New Lyrics, 1949). After these first attempts Pierro rose to a much higher level with his third book, *Mia madre passava* (My Mother Went By, 1955). Despite his indulgence in eloquent flourishes, Pierro attains, especially in the title poem, an intense poetic atmosphere, founded on an amalgamation of the wild landscape of Basilicata and the theme of the dead, both of which became constant features of his art. The apparition of Pierro's deceased mother blends with the rough, mountainous terrain, which acquires dreamy connotations as it passes through the nostalgia of creative memory:

Vi passava incorporea, e ripassava,
nuvola bianca rimasta prigioniera dei monti,
ed era più lontana e misteriosa
della voce dei grilli e della luna . . .

(She went to and fro, incorporeal,
a white cloud imprisoned among the mountains,
more remote and mysterious
than the voice of crickets or the moon itself . . .)[.]

In *Mia madre passava* Pierro shows the influence of Ernesto de Martino's important studies on the attitude of southern Italians toward death. The perfect convergence of de Martino's ethnological research and Pierro's poetic inspiration is to be found also in the subsequent collections of his Italian poems, from *Il paese sincero* (The Genuine Country, 1956) to *Il mio villaggio* (My Village, 1959). One of the most penetrating assessments of Pierro's Italian poetry was written by de Martino (in *Omaggio a Pierro*, edited by Antonio Motta, 1982), who stressed the mythic dimension of Pierro's descent into the archaic, primitive world of his lost childhood. Another important contribution to the critical comprehension of Pierro's production in Italian was offered by Giorgio Petrocchi (also in *Omaggio*), who pointed out the progressive refinement of Pierro's

style, which appeared, in his later books, to be free of superfluous ornamentation and more suited for a thematic that was akin to Pascoli's in the emphasis on country and family but also open to the religious inspiration of such contemporaries as Davide Maria Turoldo and Margherita Guidacci.

In 1960 Pierro published *Agavi e sassi* (Agaves and Stones), a valuable addition to his production in Italian, and *A terra d'u ricorde* (The Land of Memory), which marked the beginning of his rediscovery of the dialect of Tursi. Pierro is fully aware of the liberating effect that dialect has on his imagination. According to Tullio De Mauro's interview, dialect was strictly forbidden in Pierro's home. When he was a child, he always used Italian in his conversations with his relatives. But Pierro liked to visit the peasants who spoke only dialect. By adopting dialect as a literary language, Pierro renewed his intimate links with the primitive society of Basilicata. However, he continued to write in Italian as well as in dialect.

Petrocchi was instrumental in promoting the publication of *A terra d'u ricorde,* which he considered a watershed in Pierro's artistic development. Petrocchi's interest was twofold, being founded both on the stylistic cogency Pierro achieved through the skillful use of dialect and the linguistic relevance of the language of Tursi, previously unknown to scholars because of the absence of written documents. Pierro's linguistic choice was justly compared to the revival of Provençal in France, and he was acclaimed as the first author of Basilicata to give a voice to the dejected peasants. However, the merit of *A terra d'u ricorde* is essentially artistic. Pierro achieves a fusion of memorial and realistic representation, as in " 'A Ravatène" (The Rabatana):

Quann'u tempe è sincire,
nturne nturne 'a terra d'i jaramme
ci 'ampìjete a lu sóue com'u specchie,
e quanne si fè notte c'è nu frusce
di vente ca s'ammùccete nd'i fosse
e rivìgghiete u cùcche e ci fè nasce
nu mère d'èrve.

(On a limpid day,
the earth of the gorges in the sun
sparkles all around like a mirror,
and when night comes
the rustling wind hides in the ditches
and awakes the cuckoo and gives birth
to a sea of grass.)

Pierro's fresh, country language is his answer to the challenge posed to modern writers by the depreciation of Tuscan as a poetic language. In the language of Tursi, Pierro indulges in childhood memories without feeling constrained by preexisting models. He experiences the happiness and suffering of his primordial world, constantly visited by the dead. The Golden Age is over, but it is still alive in memory. This state of mind is mirrored by the demonic nature represented in " 'A jaramme" (The Ravines), where the poet evokes his infancy spent among the ravines of his native land, "cchiù zinne di na frunne / mmenz'all'acqua d'u mère, / cchiù sùue di nu grille / mmenz' 'a vocia d'u munne" (smaller than a leaf / among the waters of the sea / more alone than a cricket / among the noise of the world).

In 1963 (Pierro's most memorable year) two great books of his were published: *I 'nnammurète* (The Lovers) and *Metaponto*. *I 'nnammurète* opens with the title poem. In this masterpiece Pierro depicts a young couple linked by an ecstatic love, the emblem of poetry. The words expressing this overwhelming experience may also be considered an allusion to Pierro's newly found language of Tursi:

> E t'ècchete na vòte, come ll'èrve
> ca tròvese ncastrète nda nu mure,
> nascìvite 'a paróua,
> pó' n'ate, pó' cchiù assèie:
> schitte ca tutt'i vòte
> assimmigghiàite 'a voce
> a na cosa sunnète
> ca le sintìse 'a notte e ca pó' tòrnete
> cchiù dèbbue nd' 'a jurnète.

> (And here you are once, like the grass
> that is stuck in the wall,
> a word was born,
> then another, then many more:
> only that each time
> your voice resembled
> something dreamed of
> that you heard at night that comes back
> more weakly during the day.)

The enchanted atmosphere surrounding the lovers finds its poetic equivalent in the metaphor of the soap bubble, foreboding of death: "i'èrene une cchi ll'ate / 'a mbulla di sapone culurète" (they were each for the other / a colored soap bubble). This crescendo of ominous signs climaxes in the final lines: "Nun mbogghi'a Die / ca si fècere zanghe mmenz' 'a vie" (God forbid that they turned / into mud in the streets). Another famous composition from the same collection is "T'aspette" (I Am Waiting for You), which Gianfranco Contini included in his highly selective anthology *Letteratura dell'Italia unita,*

1861–1968 (1968), where Pierro is considered one of the most significant representatives of contemporary dialectal poetry, on a par with Virgilio Giotti and Tonino Guerra.

Metaponto contains some of Pierro's best poems, such as "A maiestra" (The Teacher), "A pacciarèlle" (The Mad Girl), and "U trappite" (The Oil Press). In "A maiestra" Pierro juxtaposes present and past in his blissful remembrance of a grammar-school teacher, a charming young lady who probably excited his unconscious erotic desire. The speaker confesses that he has never met a more beautiful woman, stressing at the same time the spiritual and mystic character of her charm, as in the following comparison of the teacher's countenance to a holy wafer:

> Pó' le virìj' nda ll'arie,
> tèle e quèle,
> 'a faccicèlla rusète
> come ll'ostie nd' 'a chièsie quanne u sóue
> ci tràsete 'a matine
> cch'i vitre d'i finestre culurète . . .

> (Then I saw it again in the air,
> just as it was,
> the rosy little face
> like the holy wafer in church when the sun
> enters through the stained glass windows
> in the morning . . .)[.]

The teacher's image shows a striking similarity with the "pòura uagnone / ca i'èrete cchiù belle d'u sóue" (the poor girl / who was more beautiful than the sun), depicted in "A pacciarèlle" in the same mystic terms:

> come si ncantète lle sunnàssete
> i sante d'u paravise
> ca l'avìn' 'a chiamè.

> (as if she were dreaming spellbound
> of the blessed in Paradise
> who must have called her.)

In "U trappite" the speaker contemplates an old oil press being superseded by technological progress and feels the presence of its former owner, his dead father, who must be tired of sustaining the mound of earth under which he is buried. The abandoned room where the oil press is kept is similar to a cemetery.

Pierro's literary reputation was firmly established after the publication of *I 'nnammurète* and *Metaponto*. Yet he did not renounce his ambition to write poetry in Italian, as is evident in *Appuntamento* (Appointment, 1967), a selection of his previous

Italian compositions together with new ones, written between 1960 and 1967. *Nd'u piccicarelle di Tursi* (In Tursi's Precipice, also 1967) attests to his unabated love for dialect. Critic Antonio Piromalli has pointed out Pierro's deep concern for the anthropological changes Italian society was undergoing in the 1960s. Yet the prevailing impression one gets from *Nd'u piccicarelle* is that of an archaic agricultural society, untouched by modern values and completely isolated in the elementary cycle of life and death. The poem "U mort" (The Funeral) is a powerful representation of southern last rites. In addition to the influence of medieval dirges, this poem bears the stamp of modern anthropology and is dedicated to de Martino. Pierro's constant meditation on death reached one of its high points in *Ecc ó 'a morte?* (Why Death?, 1969). Its epigraph sets the tone of the whole book:

> Ié nun lle sacce eccó
> ci penze tante vote
> apprime di fè na cose;
>
> mbàreche àt' 'a i'èsse accussì:
> nun le uéra fè nasce mèi,
> cc'amore c'àt' 'a murì.
>
> (I do not know why
> I always think so much
> before I do anything;
>
> maybe I don't want:
> to give birth to life,
> and love something that must die.)

In the 1970s and 1980s Pierro continued to produce important books of poetry in the dialect of Tursi, such as *Curtelle a lu sóue* (Knives in the Sun, 1973), *Nu belle fatte / Una bella storia / A Beautiful Story* (1976), and *Tante ca pàrete notte* (So Much That It Seems Night, 1986). These works demonstrate Pierro's skill in enriching with new poetic nuances the established pattern of his lyrics, in which words corresponding to *heart, pain, death,* and *fear* acquire a new artistic validity in dialect. Critical acclaim has continued to accompany Pierro's literary activity, which has revealed affinities with the works of various modern writers and artists, such as Edgar Lee Masters, Thornton Wilder, Chaim Soutine, and Ingmar Bergman. Pierro has received various prizes, including the Carducci, Mediterraneo, and Brutium. In October 1982 a conference on his poetry was held at Tursi with the participation of illustrious critics such as Ettore Bonora, Alberto Frattini, Emerico Giachery, Mario Marti, and Gennaro Savarese. In 1985 a concordance of Pierro's

poetry in dialect was published. He was awarded an honorary degree by the University of Basilicata in 1992. Pierro's work has also been noted outside Italy. He is one of the Italian poets who have seen their poems widely translated into major Western languages.

Interviews:

Giorgio Varanini, "Intervista con Albino Pierro," *Italianistica*, 10 (1981): 402–407;

Tullio De Mauro, "La colazione di Donn'Albino, Conversando con Albino Pierro," in Pierro's *Si pó' nu jurne* (Turin: Forma, 1983), pp. 7–15.

Biography:

Cesare Vico Lodovici, *Albino Pierro* (Rome: Dell'Arco, 1958).

References:

Giuseppe Appella, ed., *Un poeta come Pierro* (Rome: Cometa, 1992);

Carlo Betocchi, *Incontro a Tursi, Lettere di Betocchi a Pierro, poesie, testi critici vari* (Bari: Laterza, 1973);

Luigi Blasucci, "Osservazioni sul lessico di Albino Pierro (scorrendo le concordanze delle sue poesie tursitane)," *Italianistica,* 15 (May–December 1986): 361–366;

Nino Borsellino, "Pierro e la poesia delle origini," *Poliorama,* 1 (1982): 318–321;

Borsellino and Pasquale Stoppelli, "Per Albino Pierro," in *Poesia oggi,* edited by M. Mancini, M. Marchi, and D. Marinari (Milan: Angeli, 1986), pp. 199–228;

Giovanni Pugliese Carratelli, Luigi Blasucci, Gennaro Savarese, and Pasquale Villani, *Incontro con Albino Piero* (Naples: Bibliopolis, 1992);

Giulio Cattaneo, "Poesie in dialetto lucano di Albino Pierro," *Paragone,* 20 (October 1969): 118–123;

Gianfranco Contini, "Pierro al suo paese," in his *Ultimi esercizi ed elzeviri (1968–1987)* (Turin: Einaudi, 1988), pp. 179–185;

Enzo Esposito, "Albino Pierro tra lingua e dialetto," *Osservatore Politico-Letterario,* 16 (September 1970): 54–58;

Dora Ferola Di Sabato, "L'universo magico di Albino Pierro," *Studi e Problemi di Critica Testuale,* 33 (October 1986): 159–183;

Gianfranco Folena, "Un canzoniere d'amore di Albino Pierro," *Almanacco dello Specchio,* 4 (1975): 135–145; reprinted, with English translation by J. E. Everson, in Pierro's *Nu belle fatte /*

Una bella storia / A Beautiful Story (Milan: All'Insegna del Pesce d'Oro, 1976), pp. 5–39;

Luciano Formisano, "Il linguaggio poetico di Albino Pierro: A proposito di *Com'agghi' 'a fè?*," *Albero*, 31, nos. 63–64 (1980): 181–214;

Emerico Giachery, *L'interprete al poeta, Lettere ad Albino Pierro* (Venosa: Osanna, 1987);

Giuseppe Jovine, *La poesia di Albino Pierro* (Rome: Nuovo Cracas, 1965);

Romano Luperini, "Allegoria e rielaborazione del lutto in Albino Pierro," *Autografo*, 3 (February 1986): 3–13;

Mario Marti, "La poesia di Albino Pierro tra evasione e denuncia," in his *Nuovi contributi dal certo al vero: Studi di filologia e di storia* (Ravenna: Longo, 1980), pp. 275–300;

Marti, ed., *Pierro al suo paese, Atti del Convegno su "La poesia di Albino Pierro," Tursi 30–31 ottobre 1982* (Galatina: Congedo, 1985);

Eugenio Montale, "Albino Pierro," in *Sulla poesia*, edited by Giorgio Zampa (Milan: Mondadori, 1976), pp. 341–342;

Kalikst Morawski, "La poesia di Albino Pierro," *Studia Romanica Posnaniensia*, 6 (1980): 103–120;

Antonio Motta, ed., *Omaggio a Pierro* (Manduria: Lacaita, 1982);

Antonio Piromalli, *Albino Pierro: Dialetto e poesia* (Cassino: Garigliano, 1979);

Aldo Rossi, "Albino Pierro," *Belfagor*, 32 (31 July 1978): 419–434;

"Scritti di Nino Borsellino, Mario Sansone e Antonio Piromalli," in Pierro's *Ci uéra turnè; Vorrei ritornare* (Ravenna: Girasole, 1982), pp. 41–87;

Alfredo Stussi, "Grammatica della poesia: Appunti sui versi tursitani di Pierro," *Lingua e Stile*, 22 (June 1987): 295–305;

Vincenzo Tisano, *Concordanze lemmatizzate delle poesie in dialetto tursitano di Albino Pierro* (Pisa: S.E.U.P., 1985);

Tisano, "Varianti grafiche e problemi di interpretazione fonetica nei testi dialettali di Albino Pierro," in *Il dialetto dall'oralità alla scrittura, Atti del XIII Convegno per gli studi dialettali italiani (Catania-Nicosia, 28 Settembre 1981),* volume 1 (Pisa: Pacini, 1984), pp. 279–296;

Mario Zangara, *Pierro e la Lucania* (Rome: Nuovo Cracas, 1965);

Zangara, *La poesia in dialetto di Albino Pierro* (Rome: Nuovo Cracas, 1966).

Lamberto Pignotti
(1926 –   )

Corrado Federici
Brock University

BOOKS: *Odissea* (Florence, 1954);
Significare (Bologna: Leonardi, 1957);
Elegia (Florence: Quartiere, 1958);
Come stanno le cose (Galatina: Pajano, 1959);
L'uomo di qualità (Turin: Einaudi, 1961);
Nozione di uomo (Milan: Mondadori, 1964);
Storia antica (Urbino: Istituto Statale d'Arte, 1964);
Le nudità provocanti (Bologna: Sampietro, 1965);
I postdiluviani (Milan: D'Ars, 1967);
Una forma di lotta (Milan: Mondadori, 1967);
Istruzioni per l'uso degli ultimi modelli di poesia (Rome: Lerici, 1968);
Fra parola e immagine (Padua: Marsilio, 1972);
Ma parliamo d'altro (Milan: Nuova Corrente, 1972);
Nuovi segni (Padua: Marsilio, 1973);
Pubbli-città (Florence: CLUSF, 1974);
Il supernulla (Florence: Guaraldi, 1974);
Lamberto Pignotti, bilingual edition (Rome: Carucci, 1975);
Eterografia (Pollenza: Nuova Foglio, 1976);
Parola per parola, diversamente (Padua: Marsilio, 1976);
Biografia: Verso una comunicazione verbo-visiva (Florence: Ediprint, 1978);
Marchio e femmina: La donna inventata dalla pubblicità, by Pignotti and Egidio Mucci (Florence: Vallecchi, 1978);
Il discorso confezionato (Florence: Vallecchi, 1979);
La scrittura verbo-visiva, by Pignotti and Stefania Stefanelli (Rome: Espresso, 1980);
Vedute (Rome: Florida, 1981);
Gran varietà (Cosenza: Babbalù, 1982);
Questa storia o un'altra (Naples: Guida, 1984);
Figure d'assalto (Roveto: Museo Storico Italiano di Roveto, 1985);
In principio (Cosenza: UH, 1986);
Figure e scritture (Udine: Campanotto, 1987);
Tutte le direzioni (Rome: Emporia, 1988);
Albo d'oro, edited by S. M. Martini (Rome: Morra, 1988);
Le lettrisme, by Pignotti and Aldo Bertozzi (Ravenna: Essegi, 1989);

Lamberto Pignotti circa 1980 (photograph by Gabriella Maleti)

Giro del mondo (Naples: Medusa, 1990);
Sine aesthetica, sinestetica (Rome: Emporia, 1990).

OTHER: *Antologia della poesia visiva,* edited by Pignotti (Bologna: Sampietro, 1965);
Lamberto Pignotti: Scrive versi immortali [video tape] (Taranto: Punto Zero, 1974);

Lawrence R. Smith, ed. and trans., *The New Italian Poetry: 1945 to the Present. A Bilingual Anthology,* includes poems by Pignotti (Berkeley: University of California Press, 1981), pp. 342–349;

Adriano Spatola and Paul Vangelisti, eds., *Italian Poetry, 1960–1980: From Neo to Post Avant-garde,* includes poems by Pignotti (San Francisco: Red Hill, 1982), pp. 84–85;

Il "nuovo" in poesia, edited by Pignotti and Carlo Marcello Conti (Udine: Campanotto "Zeta," 1986).

SELECTED PERIODICAL PUBLICATIONS –
UNCOLLECTED: "Le avanguardie espropriate: Dopo una memorabile colazione sull'erba," *D'Ars,* 83 (1977): 32–43;

"Le avanguardie espropriate: Baffi della Gioconda e simili," *D'Ars,* 84 (1977): 32–45;

"Le avanguardie espropriate: La dimensione onirica e l'esprit de géométrie," *D'Ars,* 85 (1977): 62–75.

Lamberto Pignotti, born in Florence in 1926, was a member of the radical "Gruppo '63" and subsequently formed the "Gruppo '70," whose membership included, among others, Luciano Ori and Lucia Mariucci. Pignotti has published poetry extensively and has experimented with a variety of poetic forms, from performance and audio to technological and visual. He has also written an impressive array of essays on poetic theory and communication modalities in the mass media. His so-called visual poems (combining words and pictures) have been widely anthologized in both Italian and English, and Pignotti has exhibited some of these poems at prestigious international showings. He was cofounder of the journals *Quartiere, Protocolli,* and *Dopotutto,* and he has been an insightful contributor to the columns of newspapers and journals such as *Paese Sera, Nazione, Unità,* and *Rinascita,* as well as several magazines within and outside Italy. His poetry was awarded the City of Florence Prize in 1958 and the Cino del Duca Prize in 1961. Currently he resides in Rome and teaches literature at the University of Bologna, where he has taught since 1971.

Pignotti's importance derives primarily from his visual poems; nevertheless he has created an almost equally significant achievement in what might be called "conventional" poetry (if one expands the parameters to accommodate the linguistic adventurism of the neo-avant-garde poets of the early 1960s). In his essays Pignotti has been especially interested in the interaction among different expressive modes of contemporary art and poetry. These areas of research and creativity are strongly interdependent in Pignotti's work because his conventional and his visual poetry are parts of a relentless quest for an appropriate vehicle for his theoretical speculations, while virtually all his prose writings deal with the topic of language and often assume the form of poetic discourse themselves. Further, Pignotti's conventional verses (limited to the use of the written word only) suggest the existence of an internal pressure to transgress the boundaries of the typographical experience in order to tap the potential of visual denotation and connotation. His visual poems, in turn, reflect the jarring discontinuities and disorienting departures from habitual pagination that are the trademarks of his standard poetry. His essays form a sturdy theoretical basis of explanation, elucidation, and rationalization for all his poetry.

Pignotti's conventional-style poetry can be discussed within the general framework of the overtly self-reflexive linguistic structures produced by the Gruppo '63, in whose debates Pignotti participated along with Edoardo Sanguineti, Antonio Porta, and Elio Pagliarani. However, Pignotti's poetry is deeply influenced by his personal views on contemporary culture and its impact on poetic language. Pignotti's visual poetry, on the other hand, links up with the montage techniques employed by the futurists, with the photomontage of the dadaists, and with other verbal/visual modes of artistic expression practiced in Italy and other countries during the first sixty years of the twentieth century. His visual poetry appeared alongside similar forms adopted by international artists, including the work produced by the exponents of mail art, narrative art, and pop art. In Italy his work complements the experimentations of Adriano Spatola, Ketty LaRocca, Michele Perfetti, and other members of the Gruppo '70.

Considering first Pignotti's conventional verses, one notices an element of consistency from the earliest collection, *Odissea* (Odyssey, 1954), to his most recent ones. However, within this continuum a distinct change or accretion of technique occurred in 1964 with the publication of *Nozione di uomo* (Concept of Man). The consistency is found in his persistent experimentation with language, which is symptomatic of the postmodernists' preeminent concern with the process of literary activity, as opposed to the product. Underlying Pignotti's casts of the linguistic dice are an acute awareness of the restrictions inherent in the capacity of words to denote empirical reality and a comparable sensitivity to the painterly or purely visual aspects of linguistic composition. Additionally Pignotti's work tenaciously comes to grips with the problem of living in the industrial epoch with the explosion of commercialism. In *Nozione di uomo* the focus is on an area of optimal interest to Pignotti: capitalist society with its deluge of information that induces alienation in humankind and in language.

Looking at the initial phase of Pignotti's conventional poetry, one discovers in *Odissea* (a series of untitled compositions) traits that bring these verses into line with those of Pignotti's neo-avant-garde contemporaries who systematically sabotaged the sense-producing mechanisms adopted in traditional poetic discourse, for the purpose of demonstrating the modernist notion that stalking a schizophrenic age cannot be adequately articulated by means of well-structured metaphors and thoughtfully crafted analogies. In *Odissea* there is a parallel tendency to arrange fragments of sentences in illogical sequences, replicating the asyntactical structures of Sanguineti or Nanni Balestrini but without necessarily evoking an identical impression of manic frenzy. Adjectival and noun phrases are customarily set side by side on the page, but the guiding, structuring presence of connectives is missing, as this sample illustrates: "figure a pezzi grossi la pianura e la punta dell'ago / e la battaglia di sangue lontano nel colore" (large segments of figures the plain and the point of a needle / and the bloody battle far into the color). Objects of the physical and psychological world seem to be presented independently of the perceiver, who, in traditional discourse, imposes his subjective rationality or interpretative constructs on the phenomena he perceives. Much in the manner of Porta, Pignotti assembles, or attempts to reproduce, the lack of objectively verified relationships among the objects and events of reality. These, then, emerge as a priori phenomena before the impassive eyes of the speaker.

The dominant motifs of *Odissea* are two: absence of inherent meaning or orderliness in the arrangements of objects and events appearing chaotically before the narrator; and the sense of void that underlies the seemingly cluttered montage. Without referring explicitly to himself, the poetic voice of the poems, at various times, rhetorically asks, "Dov'è lo scopo?" (Where is the purpose?). Illustrative of a penchant for playing with the ambiguity of terms such as *emptiness* and *fullness* is the following excerpt: "il vuoto lasciato dall'anfora vuota il silenzio fortissimo" (the void left by the amphora empties the deafening silence). There is no scarcity of tangible objects within the perceptual field of the observer, yet a sense of the impossibility of participating in their reality through visual contact or verbal invocation imbues the poems with a somber desperation, perhaps reminiscent of that which filters through the subjectless scenarios of Porta and the subjective lamentations of Eugenio Montale. A distinctive trait of *Odissea* is the painterly perspective that is frequently utilized. The compositions show an overriding concern with a design approach to the representation of objects, and Pignotti's language inescapably incorporates terms that refer to angles of vision, the presence or absence of geometric symmetry, the prominence of color schemes, and the significance of contours or lines of demarcation, such as the horizon or the spatialization of time and human experience.

This same obsession with extracting significance from the phenomenological world continues to exert its grip on Pignotti's imagination in *Significare* (Signification, 1957). Commenting on the subject of this publication, Pignotti writes, in the introduction, "La nostra è un'epoca inquieta, di transizione . . . la poesia, assuefatta alla mancanza come all'eccedenza di dogmi e non avendo la possibilità di cristallizzarsi . . . ha assunto le caratteristiche di una poesia di ricerca" (Ours is a restless, transitional age . . . our poetry, sated with the lack or the excess of dogmas, has not had the opportunity to crystallize . . . it has, therefore, assumed the characteristics of a search). This element of instability is appropriately brought into relief in the section of the book called "Ricerca" (Search). The narrator seeks to find a system for decoding the signs of reality as well as a system for encoding his perceptions so that they might be transmitted to the reader. As was the case in *Odissea*, that reality assumes the form of a haphazard accumulation of entities – conceptual as well as material – that can only be enumerated and not interpreted. The term Pignotti applies to poeticizing that does not distort empirical reality is the same term that constitutes the title of another section of *Significare*: "Inventario" (Inventory). By positioning himself neutrally in front of the phenomena of experience, the narrator becomes aware of the fictive nature of his representational schemes – hence his many intrusions with self-reflective statements, such as the suggestion to insert a parenthesis in a scene being described. Pignotti's words strain both to represent and to burst through what he calls the "monotonia di sorprese" (the monotony of surprises).

His quest for understanding the process of signification in experiential reality and for the poetic

Poesia visiva, *a collage by Pignotti (from the 1978 edition of* Verso la poesia totale, *by Adriano Spatola; by permission of Lamberto Pignotti)*

diction contrived to convey that significance is fully present in the central (title) part of the collection, "Significare." Pignotti deliberately attempts to construct meaning by elevating objects to the rank of protagonists; like many of his neo-avant-garde contemporaries, Pignotti hopes to elicit meaning by removing it from the subject and assigning it to things. In theory the language that evokes the referents permits meaning to be formed in the mind of the addressee. This mechanism would replace the customary transmission of a preconstituted or tailored meaning that the reader is asked to accept or reject.

The struggle between subject and object or between object and language rages on in Pignotti's *L'uomo di qualità* (The Man of Quality, 1961). The title is an ironic gloss on the absence of genuine quality in a modern environment characterized by the passive reception of sensorial stimuli that negates the possibility of careful discrimination. The title also alludes to humankind as a product of the neocapitalist marketplace, where images are packaged as though they were substances. In this sequence of poems the technique of accumulating fragments of sentences in an effort to reproduce an

ontological montage acquires a specifically modernist connotative power by virtue of the fact that the objects selected pertain to the metropolis, to sprawling housing developments, and to the incessant torrent of messages emanating from the electronic media, where "la religione della tecnologia" (the religion of technology) is all consuming. A central conscience battles to come to terms with the apparent lack of coherence and spiritual content in the various inventories.

This explicit concern for the debilitating effect of technology on sensibility and on the meaning-bearing capacity of language marks the transition from the first to the second phase of Pignotti's conventional poetry. Starting with certain segments of *Nozione di uomo* and extending through all the subsequent volumes of poetry up to and including *Tutte le direzioni* (In Every Direction, 1988), he adopts as his normal mode of operation the collage technique that identifies his visual poetry of the same period. In the section of *Nozione di uomo* titled "L'industria poetica" (The Poetry Industry), Pignotti abandons the neo-avant-garde's asyntactical, predominantly nominal style of composition and employs a technique of literal intertextuality, reproducing exactly excerpts of existing texts, removing them from their habitual context and defamiliarizing them (in the formalist sense) by juxtaposing these partial quotes in strange arrangements. The procedure produces a new and unpredictable reading of words already written. In a sense, the product is completely unoriginal, since it is merely a patchwork of disconnected citations; yet it is completely original for the unusual associations and the disorientation that the technique generates in the reader. In the article "Poesia sulle scatole di fiammiferi" (Poetry on Match-Book Covers), collected in *Istruzioni* (Instructions, 1968), Pignotti writes: "I poeti si stanno accorgendo che ci si può esprimere oltre che con un linguaggio privilegiato e letterario, anche col linguaggio effettivamente usato dalla comunità in cui si vive" (Poets are realizing that they can express themselves with the language used by the community in which they live as well as with a literary and privileged language). Through the adoption of this criterion, he carries on in the tradition of avant-garde experimentation with linguistic non sequiturs. At the same time, he exemplifies the postmodernist fascination with artistic fictive reality, reflects the heterogeneous glut of data spewed out by the media, and constructs a paradigm that critiques paradoxically the reality it purports to mirror, as in these lines: "La Poesia ve lo dice prima. / La Poesia ve lo dice meglio" (Poetry brings it to you first. / Poetry brings it to you better). Here the typical commercial message is lifted in its entirety from its expected context, and Pignotti substitutes "La Poesia" for the name of a newspaper. In another case he places the term in a slightly different commercial context: "La nostra poesia è resistente agli urti" (Our poetry is shock-resistant).

The process attains more powerful form in Pignotti's *Una forma di lotta* (A Kind of Struggle, 1967), in which he takes segments from the language of the media — newspapers, magazines, comic books, best-selling novels, bureaucratic pronouncements, and television broadcasts — and assembles them in quizzical montages. By juxtaposing fragments of statements that are common currency in contemporary society, Pignotti epitomizes, then satirizes, the homogenization of information: cosmetics ads, newspaper accounts of violent events, statistical reports, weather predictions, and the hackneyed dialogue of television programs are all accorded equal importance by the communications media and, therefore, become equally unimportant because they are all broadcast with identical marketing strategies. Pignotti appears to be struggling against the annihilation of thought and spontaneous self-expression, but he also seems to be trying to invent a poetic vehicle that will reinject signification and motivation into a language that has become fossilized through overuse and abuse.

In *Parola per parola, diversamente* (Word for Word, Differently, 1976), as the title plainly states, he copies texts words for word, yet he generates meaning not available in the original. He uses texts written in French, English, and Russian in separate sections of the book. The content of each segment is taken directly from the popular culture expressed in each of these languages. As before, Pignotti juxtaposes passages that seem incoherent together because they are taken from a variety of sources. In another chapter of *Parola per parola,* Pignotti cites, in completely desultory fashion, from Carlo Collodi's *Pinocchio* (1882). The result is a fable that reads like a surreal narrative, with expressions such as "il nulla" (nothingness), "il padrone" (the boss), and "il paese dei balocchi" (wonderland) acquiring connotations that Collodi could never have anticipated.

In *Questa storia o un'altra* (This Story or Another, 1984) the collage format continues to hold sway with the essential innovation being the prominence given to the motif of the seemingly lost potential of language for intimate communication. Typical of the dialogues that catch Pignotti's attention is the following: " 'Buongiorno, come stai?' / 'Non te lo dirò mai.' / Abbiamo camminato molto, è qui che sorrise, / il tempo è bello. Non ho scherzato affatto" ("Good day, how are you?" / "I'll never tell you." / We have walked a long way, and here is where he smiled, / the weather is lovely. I haven't kidded at all). Pignotti attempts to represent reality from a nonspecific or nonlocalized viewpoint, as in the poem "Il confine del linguaggio" (The Limit of Language): "ma non crede, / però nel buio della, / distolto lo sguardo da, / lo rivolge verso, / come se qui nulla, / e nero, / nella profonda oscurità" (but he does not believe, / however in the darkness of the, / his glance removed from the, / he directs it toward, / as if there were nothing here, / and blackness, / in the deep darkness).

Pignotti persistently pursues this line of linguistic inquiry in his *Vedute* (Vistas, 1981), *Gran varietà* (Great Variety, 1982), *In principio* (In the Beginning, 1986), and *Tutte le direzioni.* Untiringly he draws from the vocabulary of the modern media to weave a tapestry of the contemporary epistemological labyrinth — escape from which, Pignotti advises, may be attainable only by making a new beginning. The starting point might have to be, in his opinion, the admission that conventional language has lost the innocent capacity for figurative expression that it had in the primordial stages of its development. Pignotti tries to restore this lost quality by having his narrator confess bewilderment at the incomprehensible story that language and events are narrating to him.

The theoretical underpinnings for Pignotti's conventional poetry as well as for his visual poems are contained in his essays written between 1957 and 1987 and published in periodicals such as *Nuova Corrente, Quartiere, Protocolli, Paese Sera,* and *Dopotutto.* The most significant of the essays are collected in the following volumes: *Istruzioni, Nuovi segni* (New Signs, 1973), *Fra parola e immagine* (Between the Word and the Image, 1972), *Il supernulla* (The Supervoid, 1974), *La scrittura verbo-visiva (Verbal-Visual Writing,* 1980), and *Figure e scritture* (Figures and Writings, 1987). The primary thrust of Pignotti's essays constitutes an exploration of intermedia or multimedia artistic expression in the context of modern culture. He constantly reflects on the nature of traditional poetic language as well as on contemporary poetic discourse within a technological environment. From these reflections emerge Pignotti's personal theories, shaped to a great extent by his intelligent dialogue with various proponents of theories of information, semiotics, and cultural anthropology. Pignotti reveals, throughout his prose writings, an impressive cognizance of the views of thinkers such as Desmond Morris, Umberto Eco, Marshall McLuhan, Roland Barthes, Michel Foucault, Jacques Derrida, and Claude Levi-Strauss.

Pignotti's views on modern poetry in general and on visual poetry in particular rest on several basic presuppositions. Perhaps the most vital of these is the premise that the traditional poet is irrelevant in this technological age. Pignotti arrives at this sobering conclusion because he sees the emerging incompatibility between literature, which is often perceived as elitist and self-referential (relating as it does to predetermined aesthetic criteria), and a reader who either is incapable of comprehending the complex, extended discourse of traditional literary texts or is not interested in a product that appears to have scant relevance to the industrialized, overcommercialized, and broadly superficial world in which he lives. In light of such an evaluation of the modern nonresponsiveness to the messages uttered by the traditional poetic voice, Pignotti posits the need to render poetry accessible to the masses. Poetry must undergo a radical change, adopting the expressive jargon or techniques that are comprehen-

sible and effective to the contemporary sedated mind.

Pignotti also recommends that the poet adopt a new lexicon to convey his thoughts. He calls this auxiliary vocabulary the "neo-volgare" (new vernacular), which comprises the language currently in circulation: the language of newspapers, magazines, photo novels, comic strips, television ads, store-display signs, road signs, billboards, posters, pamphlets, and slogans. Pignotti's decision to name this plentiful linguistic resource the new vernacular stems from his argument that Dante opted in favor of the Italian language over the stately Latin tongue in order to communicate to a larger, poorly schooled public. Pignotti draws a parallel between Dante and the poet of modern times, suggesting that standard literature today has the same status that Latin had in Dante's time. Although Pignotti's theoretical writings deal with language and society, his focus remains the relationship that has always existed between the spoken or written word and visual images, a relationship that has acquired unparalleled amplitude in the technological age.

Pignotti's opinions on visual poetry per se are based on his perception that in the modern age there is an irreversible trend toward deverbalization. Communications networks are so dense and so visually oriented that the civilization of the spoken or written work is being replaced by the "civiltà dell'immagine" (culture of the image). What Pignotti proposes is the tailoring of visual information to suit the expectations of "il padrone," who personifies the corporations or institutions that control the advertising process. In the hands of dominant media monopolists, the sentence undergoes a drastic reduction.

Pignotti set out to exploit the same interdependence of word and image that the media exploit. His purpose, however, was to effect a "dirottamento del messaggio" (hijacking of the message) and its "rinvio al mittente" (return to the sender). This desired subversion could be realized by two methods. One is the stated intention of representing contemporary reality and communicating a sense of its devalued language and ideals. The second method is purely aesthetic: Pignotti's experimentation with the denotative and connotative interaction of word and image continued the tradition of intellectual inquiry into the representational properties of language and the poetic content of the visual arts. Specifically his concern was with the notion of going beyond the expressive edges of the written word by fusing the linguistic with the iconic. In this activity he joined a group of poet/artists that included LaRocca, Mariucci, Ori, and Perfetti, who were implicitly dissatisfied with the achievements of concrete poetry — which tends to explore the optical characteristics of the word itself — and were consequently curious about the possibilities of word-image collages as a new and powerful art form.

Pignotti's visual poetry has been exhibited and anthologized from the 1960s to the 1990s. In his first phase (1960–1968) Pignotti restricted himself to producing collages of visual material already available, his creativity consisting of clipping images, fragments of images, newspaper headlines, magazine headlines, slogans, and movie titles, and assembling them on a canvas that was then photographed for the purpose of publication. The juxtapositions, contrasts, and nuances of meaning prompted by this method are the result of a complex interaction among the semiotic signs. In this respect Pignotti effectively persisted in the deployment of techniques he introduced in his conventional poems. However, he expanded the borrowing practice to incorporate pictures.

After 1968 he discontinued the collage format, as such, in order to embrace a form that calls for the reproduction and enlargement of photographs from daily newspapers and magazines. Pignotti was not content to juxtapose partial images; instead, he selected entire images upon which he intruded by superimposing handwritten messages in the form of words, or merely his autograph. Often he forged the autographs of well-known artists such as Michelangelo, Raphael, and Leonardo da Vinci or of poets such as Giacomo Leopardi. In the latter part of the 1970s he incorporated handwritten original poetic utterances.

The most provocative and, indeed, poetic phase of Pignotti's work consists of the post-1968 visual poems, culminating in the lyrical compositions of *Eterografia* (Heterography, 1976). In these works Pignotti's predilection for the self-reflexive poetic utterance and for speculation on the nature of the relationship of art to subject matter come to the fore. Some photographs depict patrons in an art gallery, with statements such as "questo è un discorso sull'arte" (this is a talk on art) superimposed on them. Such coy handwritten remarks show Pignotti's fascination with modern culture as a semiotic labyrinth. Most of the photographs in *Eterografia* depict people involved in the activities of their lives, which include not only outings at the beach, peaceful demonstrations, and picnics but also brutal murders and catastrophes. All scenes are treated as forms of fiction, which Pignotti makes apparent by inscribing rhetorical or stylistic instructions on images of real life. People fleeing from an exploding building constitute an "esempio di sinestesia" (example of synesthesia); a traffic jam may be labeled "elementi di ridondanza" (elements of redundancy); masses of people in an Italian square suggest "la nascita e la caduta di parole" (the birth and death of words).

The aesthetic premise on which *Eterografia* rests is that everything in the physical world is a semiotic sign and, as such, communicates information. However, what exactly that decoded information is, or ought to be, remains debatable. Many of his handwritten messages alert readers to the semiotic nature of objects in the industrialized world: "il discorso delle scene e degli eventi" (speech of scenes and events); "ambiguità dei segni" (ambiguity of signs); "una prospettiva semiotica" (a semiotic perspective). As post-Saussurian linguists invariably do, Pignotti stresses the arbitrary nature of the link between referent and signifier and between referent and signified — hence the many suggestions of the ambiguity of signs and the obsession with signification and the production of meaning: "segni di che cosa?" (signs of what?); "segni di chi?" (whose signs?); "trova il referente di questo complesso di significati" (find the referent for this group of signifieds). It appears that Pignotti has come full circle; he began with conventional poetry to explore signification and eventually returned to that interest by including images and semiotic theories.

Despite its radical or avant-garde traits, Pignotti's verbal and verbal/visual poetry engages in the ongoing modern inquiry into the real substance of poetry. On the one hand, there is the "poesia pura" (pure poetry) stance of the hermetics and neohermetics; on the other hand, there is the "poesia impegnata" (social poetry) of the neorealists, the neo-experimentalists, and the neo-avant-garde. The first group postulates the purity of the poetic act — its autonomy with respect to variable sociohistorical contexts. The adherents of this poetics promote the poetic text as an instrument for the articulation of moral paradigms that are impervious to the fluctuations of social circumstance. The second group, in a variety of ways, envisions the poem as a versatile instrument of social change, deriving efficacy from a continuous symbiosis with, or a responsiveness to, the language and issues of a given historical moment.

Pignotti's work can be placed comfortably within the second framework, although neither aesthetic perspective necessarily invalidates the other. In a sense, both interpretations are legitimate, yet both are only partial definitions of the poetic text. In fact, each in a way incorporates the other, an interaction that can be clearly seen in the writings of Lamberto Pignotti. His technological poetry adheres to the vernacular and content of the computer age; yet, beneath the stylistic topicality, readers uncover the same search for unattainable answers to the question of human alienation, incommunicability, and oppression. By experimenting with visual poetry, Pignotti has exhibited the tendency common to most modern art: to borrow from other sources in an effort to express that which each individual art form expresses only partially or approximately.

Interview:

Ferdinando Camon, *Il mestiere di poeta* (Milan: Garzanti, 1982), pp. 207–217.

References:

Alberto Frattini, *Poesia nuova in Italia tra ermetismo e neoavanguardia* (Milan: Istituto di Propaganda Libraria, 1967), pp. 98–102;

Oreste Macrì, *Realtà del simbolo* (Florence: Vallecchi, 1968), pp. 248–251;

Franco Manescalchi and Lucia Marcucci, eds., *La poesia in Toscana dagli anni quaranta agli anni sessanta* (Messina & Florence: D'Anna, 1981), pp. 100–103, 141–150;

John Picchione, "La metamorfosi della poesia: Gli esperimenti visivi del 'Gruppo 70,' " *Canadian Journal of Italian Studies,* 3 (Fall 1979): 41–47;

Luigi Rosiello, "Pignotti tra parola e immagine," *Rinascita,* 35 (8 September 1972): 25–26;

Stefania Stefanelli, "Per una storia del Gruppo 70," *Es,* 6 (January–April 1977): 103–110;

Verri, special issue on Pignotti, 1 (1976);

Giuseppe Zagarrio, *Febbre, furore e fiele* (Milan: Mursia, 1983), pp. 250–253.

Antonio Porta
(6 November 1935 – 12 April 1989)

John Picchione
York University

BOOKS: *La palpebra rovesciata* (Milan: Azimuth, 1960);

Zero: Poesie visive (Milan, 1963);

Aprire (Milan: All'Insegna del Pesce d'Oro, 1964);

I rapporti (Milan: Feltrinelli, 1966);

Partita (Milan: Feltrinelli, 1967);

Cara (Milan: Feltrinelli, 1969);

Metropolis (Milan: Feltrinelli, 1971);

Week-end (Rome: Cooperativa Scrittori, 1974);

La presa di potere di Ivan lo sciocco (Turin: Einaudi, 1974);

Quanto ho da dirvi (Milan: Feltrinelli, 1977);

Il re del magazzino (Milan: Mondadori, 1978); translated by Lawrence R. Smith as *The King of the Storeroom* (Hanover, Mass.: University Press of New England, 1992);

Passi passaggi (Milan: Mondadori, 1980); translated by Pasquale Verdicchio as *Passenger* (Montreal: Guernica, 1986);

Se fosse tutto un tradimento (Milan: Guanda, 1981);

L'aria della fine; Brevi lettere (Catania: Lunarionuovo, 1982); selections translated by Anthony Molino as *Kisses from Another Dream* (San Francisco: City Lights, 1987);

Invasioni (Milan: Mondadori, 1984); translated by Paul Vangelisti and others in *Invasions and Other Poems* (San Francisco: Red Hill, 1986);

Nel fare poesia (Florence: Sansoni, 1985);

La festa del cavallo (Milan: Corpo 10, 1986);

Melusina: Una ballata e un diario (Milan: Crocetti, 1987); translated by Molino as *Melusine* (Montreal: Guernica, 1992);

Il giardiniere contro il becchino (Milan: Mondadori, 1988);

Partorire in chiesa, edited by Rosemary Ann Liedl (Milan: Scheiwiller, 1990).

Edition in English: *As If It Were a Rhythm,* edited and translated by Paul Vangelisti (San Francisco: Red Hill, 1978).

OTHER: "Poesia e poetica," in *I Novissimi: Poesie per gli anni '60,* edited by Alfredo Giuliani, also in-

Antonio Porta circa 1980 (photograph by Gabriella Maleti)

cludes poems by Porta (Milan: Rusconi & Paolazzi, 1961; revised edition, Turin: Einaudi, 1965), pp. 163–195;

"Interventi," in *Gruppo '63: Il romanzo sperimentale,* edited by Nanni Balestrini (Milan: Feltrinelli, 1966);

Stark [play], *Grammatica,* 2 (1967): 15-22;

Ghan Singh, ed. and trans., *Contemporary Italian Verses,* includes poems by Porta (London: London Magazine, 1968), pp. 188–189;

Poeti ispanoamericani contemporanei, edited by Porta and Marcello Ravoni (Milan: Feltrinelli, 1970);

Vittoria Bradshaw, ed. and trans., *From Pure Silence to Impure Dialogue: A Survey of Post-War Italian Poetry 1945–1965,* includes poems by Porta (New York: Las Américas, 1971), pp. 707–721;

Pin Pidìn: Poeti d'oggi per i bambini, edited by Porta and Giovanni Raboni (Milan: Feltrinelli, 1978);

Poesia degli anni settanta, edited, with an introduction and notes, by Porta (Milan: Feltrinelli, 1979);

Lawrence R. Smith, ed. and trans., *The New Italian Poetry: 1945 to the Present. A Bilingual Anthology,* includes poems by Porta (Berkeley: University of California Press, 1981), pp. 428–463.

TRANSLATIONS: André Pieyre de Mandiargues, *Il margine* (Milan: Feltrinelli, 1968);

Pierre Reverdy, *Il ladro di talento* (Turin: Einaudi, 1972);

Jude Stefan, *A Malherbe più che uomo,* translated by Porta and Sergio Solmi, *Almanacco dello Specchio,* 1 (1972): 185–207;

George Trakl, *Poesie 1914,* translated by Porta and Anna Maria Fornararo, *Almanacco dello Specchio,* 3 (1974): 15–37;

Jacques Roubaud, *Due serie di poesie, Almanacco dello Specchio,* 4 (1975): 241–271;

Titus Maccius Plautus, *La stangata persiana* (Milan: Corpo 10, 1985).

A nomadic and transgressive mode of writing, including the refusal of definitive pauses, constitutes the distinctive trait of Antonio Porta's poetic production. Restless, in constant pursuit of new beginnings and new directions, Porta writes poetry that is, first of all, an assiduous effort to explore the infinite potentialities of language by abandoning the known and determinedly demolishing the hackneyed models of tradition. This experimentation is charged with strong existential tensions. Porta's language inevitably performs a twofold function: in its reflexivity it becomes subject and object of its own operation; but through this self-investigation it moves both inward and outward, penetrating reality and attempting to perceive fragments of authentic knowledge. A dialectic between centripetal direction and centrifugal tension renders Porta's poetry one of the most dynamic and intense poetic expressions of postwar Italy.

Porta's first poems, with those of Alfredo Giuliani, Nanni Balestrini, Edoardo Sanguineti, and Elio Pagliarani, were included in 1961 in *I Novissimi* (The Very New Ones), a provocative and revolutionary anthology (edited by Giuliani) that opened the way for the formation of the "Gruppo '63," a movement soon defined as the Italian neo-avant-garde. Porta shared with the movement a conception of poetry as a negation of the "normal" linguistic code, which was refused because of its reification, commercialization, and the conservative ideological implications it conveyed. The alternative language was to be that of disorder, ambiguity, and estrangement. The deliberate construction of a language in crisis was considered the sole possibility for engendering a crisis in the normal representation of reality while, at the same time, forcing the reader to establish a more dynamic and active rapport with the text.

Porta's literary and cultural involvement, however, was not limited to the Novissimi or the Gruppo '63. Born in Vicenza on 6 November 1935, Porta (pseudonym for Leo Paolazzi) studied literature and graduated from college in Milan in 1960 with a thesis on Gabriele D'Annunzio and twentieth-century poetics. For years he worked in the publishing industry (for the Bompiani and Feltrinelli firms in particular) while involved as a member of the editorial board of the journals *Verri* (founded and directed by Luciano Anceschi, one of Porta's most important mentors, particularly in the late 1950s and early 1960s) and *Malebolge.* In 1967 he was one of the founders of *Quindici,* a monthly newspaper that soon became the artistic and political alternative voice of Italian intellectuals. In later years, as a literary critic, he contributed to the newspapers *Corriere della Sera, Giorno,* and *Tuttolibri.* More recently his activity as a militant critic was with one of the most innovative monthly newspapers in Italy, *Alfabeta.* In the 1960s Porta also experimented with visual poetry (a mixture of words and pictures), participating in various exhibits in Italy and abroad. Porta was married twice, first to Lietta Porta, whom he divorced, then to Rosemary Porta. He had two children from his first marriage and three from his second.

Although poetry was Porta's creative focus, he also published two novels – *Partita* (Game, 1967) and *Il re del magazzino* (1978; translated as *The King of the Storeroom,* 1992) – and a collection of short stories, *Se fosse tutto un tradimento* (If It Were All a Betrayal, 1981). He also wrote plays, including *La presa di potere di Ivan lo sciocco* (The Conquest of Power by Ivan the Fool, 1974) and *La festa del cavallo* (The Party of the Horse, 1986), and translated various works by others. He coedited *Pin Pidìn* (1978), a poetry anthology for children, and edited Poesia degli anni settanta (Poetry of the Seventies, 1979), an anthology tracing the development of Italian poetry from 1968 to the late 1970s. In 1985 he edited a large collection of his own poetry, Nel fare poesia (Making Poetry), a selection written over a period of about thirty years.

In Porta's initial experiments, collected in I rapporti (The Relations, 1966), comprising poems written between 1958 and 1964, readers witness his adherence to external events, assembled and presented as enigmas to be deciphered. This procedure entails a constant reduction of the "I" and is interpretable, on the one hand, as a denunciation of the traditional lyricism that had characterized twentieth-century Italian poetry and, on the other, as a realization of the poetics of the object, advocated by Anceschi in his theoretical works. The fragmented semantic structure, accompanied by metric and syntactic derangements, reaches, in some cases, a state of aphasia and nonsignification. Readers are faced with a montage of traumatic everyday occurrences: killings, brutality, anatomical horrors, and lacerated matter in a state of decay — as in "Europa cavalca un toro nero" (Europa Rides a Black Bull):

Cani azzannano i passanti, uomini
raccomandabili guidano l'assassino,
fuori, presto, scivoli.
. . . .
Gli occhi crepano come uova.
Afferra la doppietta e spara
nella casa della madre. Gli occhi
sono funghi presi a pedate.
Mani affumicate e testa
grattugiata corre alla polveriera,
inciampa, nel cielo lentamente
s'innalza l'esplosione e i vetri
bruciano infranti d'un fuoco
giallo; abitanti immobili
il capo basso, contano le formiche.

(Dogs seize passersby, men
of integrity direct the assassin,
outside, quickly, you slip.
. . . .
Her eyes crack like eggs.
He grabs the double-barreled shotgun
and shoots into his mother's house.
The eyes are mushrooms which have been kicked
to bits. Smoked hands and grated
head run to the powder magazine,
he stumbles, the explosion rises
slowly into the sky and the shattered
windows burn with a yellow
fire; immobile citizen
heads lowered, count the ants.)

— translation by Lawrence R. Smith (in *The New Italian Poetry*, 1981.)

Within this collapsing reality there is the presence of hallucinating, schizoid characters, capable only of establishing a sadomasochistic rapport with themselves and others — reminiscent of expressionist or Beckettian representations. For Porta these characters are the only possible realistic portrayals. Faced with a reality within which all possibilities of signification often break down, Porta, in dealing with the relationship of the individual with himself, with others, or with nature, is obsessed with the presence of an evil that inevitably emerges in every human manifestation and to which nature also succumbs. The poems "Vegetali e animali" (Plants and Animals) and "La pelliccia del castoro" (Beaver Skin) convey this tragic aspect of his poetry.

In this first stage, Porta's creativity was guided by the urgency to combine autonomous and heteronomous concepts of art. He believed that poetry is not a metaphor of the world but a world in itself, thus advocating a poetry not written in preconceived language. At the same time, he insisted that, in the search for truth, poetry is a cognitive medium capable not only of performing a mimetic function by representing history and reality but also of projecting hypothetical or utopian models of existence. The poetics of objects and the aversion to the "I" convey the existential need to understand reality by adopting poetry as a form of knowledge. In his essay "Poesia e poetica" (in *I Novissimi*,) Porta writes: "Direttamente alla *poetica* degli oggetti si riallaccia il problema del *vero* e della *verità*" (The *poetics* of the objects is directly tied to the problem of the *true* and of the *truth*).

However, the truth concealed behind both human and natural events speaks constantly of a tragic dimension of existence. Porta felt that the sense of the tragic was at the base of all his poetry. He was influenced by phenomenological and existential worldviews, particularly in the philosophy of Karl Jaspers. Amid social and historical catastrophes and the evils embedded in the act of living, the following is one of Porta's rare explicit admonitions (from "Europa cavalca un toro nero"):

Attento, abitante del pianeta,
guardati! dalle parole dei Grandi
frana di menzogne, lassú
balbettano, insegnano il vuoto.
La privata, unica, voce

metti in salvo: domani sottratta
ti sarà, come a molti, oramai,
e lamento risuona il giuoco dei bicchieri.

(Look out, inhabitants of earth,
beware! from the words of the Great Ones
comes a landslide of lies, they babble
up there, instructing the void.
Put the private, individual voice
in a safe place: tomorrow it will be
taken away, as with many already,
and lament echoes the clinking of glasses.)
    – translation by Smith

Although events are narrated by adopting a visual, objective mode of writing, often made up of scraps of common, everyday language carefully recycled, they constantly reveal a state of anguish, an emotional agitation.

In one of the most radical moments of this first stage of his career, Porta arrived at the conception of poetry as a form of discourse reduced to zero: the reduction of language to zero in rapport with the negation of the world. A case in point is his experiment in concrete poetry titled *Zero* (1963; reprinted in *I rapporti*) in which the verbal signs, freed from syntactic constraints and rhythmic recurrences, bring to life a montage of disconnected perceptions, forming a discourse that destroys the pseudorational order of daily communication and forces the reader to experience a signification that constantly annihilates itself. However, Porta was always far from advocating absolutist solutions.

Events without order or perspective, syntagmas clashing in antithetical or conflicting constructions, mutilated and solitary signs – these are the recurring elements that create the disquieting and crumbling reality of *Zero*. The result is a poetic world that opposes all forms of communication, as expressed by bourgeois culture, and experiences a semantic collapse that exposes a reified and alienating language and creates a tension awaiting new and liberating conditions of existence:

tante agita la sua coda, gli occhi fissi nell'ipnosi,
    roteando le gambe
tato, dilatati e richiusi, franato con un muro di mattoni,
    sotto le finestre di
per salire gli scalini, riprese a scavare sotto la torre, le
    ossa ripulite gli av
schizzò nella pianura, con una coda di scintille, annottando,
    gola palpi

(many he wags his tail, eyes in a hypnotic stare, swinging the legs
tied, dilated and closed up, collapsed with a brick wall,
    under the windows of

in order to walk up the stairs, he started to dig under
    the tower again, the cleaned up bones, the ad
he sketched on the plain, with a tail of sparks, growing
    dark, you touch throat)[.]
    – translation by Smith

In his 1969 collection, *Cara* (Dear), Porta drastically changes his stylistic register and accentuates a poetics of provocation and terrorism. Ironically titled, *Cara* is constructed in rhythmic-syntactic modulations, in antithesis to a catalogue of occurrences devoid of any narrative articulation. The overall structure seems to lead to the idea that language represents only the material presence of itself. Poetry is its inner structure, the rhythmic space in which it moves. Even though the signifiers refer to repetitive and absurd acts of daily experience, to gestures and behaviors observed with a vision of estrangement and inauthenticity, they underline primarily the poetic devices that regulate and organize them. These features make *Cara* an innovative experiment in metapoetry, as seen in the initial lines of the poem "Come se fosse un ritmo" (As If It Were a Rhythm):

si servono di uncini	si alzano dalle sedie
chiedono dei fagioli	azzannano i bambini
amano la musica	si tolgono le scarpe
ballano in cerchio	seguono lo spartito
escono dalle finestre	vanno a fare il bagno
aprono la botola	rientrano dalla finestra
cambiano posizione	si chinano sul water
controllano l'orario	escono di chiesa
pieni di medicine	cadono dalle sedie
si appendono al soffitto	colano con lentezza
si servono di forbici	li prendono a pedate
calcano sul coperchio	ci affondano le dita
scendono dall'alto	si perdono nella foresta

(they use hooks	they rise from the chairs
they order beans	they sink their teeth into the children
they love music	they take off their shoes
they dance in a circle	they follow the score
they leave through the windows	they go take a bath
they open the trapdoor	they come back through the window
they change position	they bend over the toilet
they change the schedule	they leave the church
full of medicine	they fall out of chairs
they hang from the ceiling	they pour slowly
they use scissors	they kick others around
they stamp on the lid	they sink their fingers in
they descend from above	they get lost in the forest)[.]

    – translation by Paul Vangelisti (in *Invasions and Other Poems*, 1986)

Perhaps owing to the profound sociopolitical changes that affected Italian society beginning in

Porta with Daniel Scanlon of Columbia University at a 1979 symposium held at New York University
(photograph by Elsa Ruiz)

1968, Porta's poetry also went in a decisive new direction: poetic interventions in the linguistic code are emphasized even more. The first confirmation of this tendency is *Metropolis* (1971), which contains poems written in 1969 and 1970. *Metropolis* presents two complementary operations: a contentious and demystifying inquiry into the reified linguistic repertory of contemporary culture, juxtaposed with proposals for therapeutic language models. In the first half of this collection, Porta denounces a closed, anticritical, and antidialectical language always ready to manufacture its messages in a rigid, banal, and flatly dogmatic fashion for rapid and mechanical consumption by passive consumers. In "Quello che tutti pensano" (What Everybody Thinks) catalogues of commonplaces, linguistic stereotypes, and defining topoi that range from politics to religion, from sex to psychology, and from sociology to art are compiled in a seemingly casual montage. These conflicting combinations cancel meanings, demystify them, and reveal semantic falsehoods. This destructive process demonstrates the degradation of language to an object of consumerism, to an authoritarian and alienating instrument that adopts prevaricating definitions as a form of manipulation.

Conversely, and yet complementary to this destructive tension, the second half of *Metropolis* presents defalsifying language models as a hypothesis for a recovery of communication. Phrases that present a regression to infantile linguistic procedures are aimed at regaining an elementary and primordial expressiveness, and they allow creative intervention by the reader, who is encouraged to rewrite or reelaborate them. "Modello per autoritratti" (Models for Self-Portraits), with its repetitive and fluid rhythm similar to that of nursery rhymes, offers an effective model for a therapeutic interpretation:

io non sono non c'è non chi è
non abito non credo non ho
cinquantanni ventuno dodici che c'è
quando bevo nell'acqua nuotare non so
con la penna che danza la polvere che avanza
non credo non vedo se esco né tocco
mangiare se fame digerire non do
prima corpo poi mente poi dico poi niente
è un'altra chissà se alla fine cadrà
né una vita né due né un pianeta né un altro
le lingue non capisco le grida annichilisco

(I am not there is not who is
I do not live do not believe do not have
fifty years twenty twelve what is it
when I drink in the water swimming I cannot
with the pen dancing the leftover dust

I do not believe do not see if I go out or touch
food if hunger digest I do not give
first body then mind then say then nothing
it is another if in the end it will fall
not one life not two not a planet no another
I do not understand languages and annihilate
  screams)[.]
  – translation by Pasquale Verdicchio (in *Invasions and Other
  Poems*)

Porta's shift toward a more direct investigation of sociohistorical realities, observed in *Metropolis,* reaches a transparent ideological position in *Week-end* (1974), in which the capitalist structure of society, with its debasement of life, is examined in relation to the possible function that the poet can perform. This ideological clarification is accompanied, as an immediate expressive correlative, by the recovery of a narrative style far from the semantic and syntactic fragmentation of previous experiments.

The master/slave dichotomy found in the various strata of society is presented as the underlying structure of the contemporary historical condition. The master, immobile in his role, knows only destruction and distributes only death; whereas the slave, condemned to death by servile work, aspires to life and expressions of freedom. This poetry denounces the condition of the slave in a technological, capitalist society: the depersonalizing effects of automation, the anonymity of the individual, and the atrophy and suffocation brought on by organized and alienating work. The immobility of this social structure is opposed by the self-consciousness of the slave, interpreted as a liberating possibility and as a utopian vision of other possible ways of existence.

In the poem "Utopia del nomade" the nomad's life, with constant movement, primordial simplicity, and work performed only as a necessity for survival – although presented as a precarious utopian dream – becomes a metaphor for liberation and transformation:

si muove nella stagione lo consente
ogni luogo ha regole dettate dal clima
nella stagione inclemente dispone le sue difese
si sposta per sopravvivere o vivere

(he moves as the season permits
every place has laws dictated by the climate
in inclement weather he sets up his defenses
he moves from place to place to survive or live)[.]
                              – translation by Smith

Critical awareness of the squalid conditions of the industrial, capitalist reality – a "terra predata" (plundered land) populated by "uomini disossati" (boneless men), wandering through the "Ricca . . . Cattedrale Chimica" (Rich . . . Chemical Cathedral) – generates, as an antithetical yearning, the vision of a utopian city that would not subsist as a fossilized and immobile structure but as a flexible "punto di protezione" (point of protection) in which people possessing a purified linguistic code, "il pensiero linguaggio che va preso alla lettera" (the thought language which is to be taken literally), would meet and leave according only to their own desire. The motif of the journey, interpretable as a metaphor of knowledge and liberation, is tied to that of labor restored to a nonalienating condition, strictly connected to the autonomous survival of the nomad, in a world where "non esiste proprietà del suolo" (land ownership does not exist).

The last half of *Week-end* returns to a poetry of self-exploration. Various poems under the title "Rimario" (Rhyming Dictionary) resemble experiments of minimalist art: isolated words, associated exclusively by the device of rhyme, establish rapports of semantic contiguity, and through a series of combinations and permutations they restore the polysemous nature of the verbal sign. Moreover, this process allows unconscious elements to emerge, and it forces the reader to create the text, to relive it according to his own associations.

The constant metamorphosis of Porta's poetry indicates his obstinate commitment to explore language. The poet-nomad with his project of transforming the world is continuously anxious to set out on new itineraries, on the endless journeys of language. A clear indication of a new poetic direction for him comes in "Brevi lettere" (Brief Letters), a series of poems that opens the collection *Passi passaggi* (Paces Passages, 1980; translated as *Passenger,* 1986) and which was republished in *L'aria della fine; Brevi lettere* (The Sense of an Ending; Brief Letters, 1982; selections translated as *Kisses from Another Dream,* 1987). The epistolary style of these short poems reveals the need for communication, the necessity of opening a more direct dialogue with the reader. Porta sends out messages that often stem from news reports, personal occurrences, or simply from the many elusive manifestations of daily events, transfigured in signals emitting hidden pulsations of existence.

Examined from an ideological perspective, *Passi passaggi* is rooted in the realization that poetry must regain its voice, must undergo a shift toward messages aimed at transforming the world and eliminating its horrors. However, Porta's communicative project does not regress to an easy, rigid signification. The adherence to a poetics in progress has its correlation in a signification in progress. Poetry speaks by interrogating. It is not a simple representation of reality but a thrust toward an everlasting, future-oriented transformation. It does not have any claim to transcendental truths. For Porta, poetry is a "ponte oscillante tra un punto indefinito verso un altro punto indefinibile, distante e mutevole" (bridge oscillating between an indefinite point and another point, undefinable, distant, and mutable). Such is the case in the section titled "La scelta della voce" (The Choice of Voice), comprised of texts originally written for the theater.

Metamorphic manifestations of the body, cannibalistic acts, sexual desire, birth, rebirth, and love are the emblems of regeneration and transformation. Porta, however, carefully avoids any form of seductive and reassuring lyricism: the mythical and fabulous dimension of his poetry is frequently undercut by the presence of a familiar, everyday language and by continuous outbursts of self-irony. The literary references, the problematic affirmations about writing "la scrittura / scrivendosi vuole cancellarsi" (writing / while writing itself wants to erase itself), together with the tension between silence and voice, display a poetic space far from sentimental effusions and definitive achievements. One of the closing sections of *Passi passaggi* contains a series of poems in bilingual versions (Italian and English) written during Porta's first trip to New York, in 1979.

The communicative form of the last stages of Porta's poetry results from a less traumatic rapport with reality. In other words, the recovery of a simpler, more linear formal organization interacts with a new perception of the world. The dimension of the tragic, the recurrent trait of his earlier collections, is replaced in *Invasioni* (1984; translated in *Invasions and Other Poems*) by the luminosity and transparency produced by the lightness of the images. With *Invasioni* Porta's language tends to transfigure reality in an adventure of surreal, dreamlike perceptions. He sheds new light on reality. Poetry as a "vaso rotondo, liscio e bianco, chiuso / galleggia sul fiume tumultuoso" (round vase, smooth and white, closed / floats on the tumultuous river), but the poet with his "martello pesante" (heavy hammer) smashes it to pieces and "in quell'istante e per sempre / sprigiona tutta la sua luce" (in that instant and forever / it releases all its light). Poetry's new light, however, does not lead to claims of absolute truths. Porta's desire is not to discover any improbable es-

sence but to reveal the enchantment and epiphanies of everyday events. In "Balene, Delfini, Bambini" (Whales, Dolphins, Children), Porta reminds the reader that "la mia poesia . . . / è un fare non è un essere, o l'essere, / se proprio lo volete è un fare . . . " (my poetry . . . / is a doing not a being, or the being, / if you really want, it is for me a doing . . .). Porta entrusts poetry with the task of refusing death and the emptiness of silence, demonstrating once again a transgressive will, a necessity to resist the growing contemporary metaphysics of the void, the celebration of the end of all meaning.

Porta's rapport with language and reality never arrives at a reassuring solution. Always aware of deceptions (the recurrent motif of the mirror is one example), Porta does not erase the possibilities of new discoveries: "Andate, mie parole, / calcate le tracce / dei linguaggi infiniti" (Go, my words, / follow the traces / of the infinite languages), he exclaims. *Invasioni* primarily follows a lyrical path, which leads to a form of poetry made of pictorial images and sudden revelations. The title section, a series of brief segments, constantly radiates an intense linguistic energy that, with metaphors and analogies, illuminates the world of nature:

> rinchiuso nell'armadio
> l'aquilone
> vola nella mia mente
>
> pruni fioriti a cespuglio
> la collina bruciata dai geli
> ciuffi di capelli candidi
> segnali di primavera
>
> (locked away in the cupboard
> the kite
> flies in my mind
>
> bushily flowering brambles
> a frost-burned hill
> tufts of white hair
> signs of spring)[.]
> – translation by Anthony Baldry (in *Invasions and Other Poems*)

For *Invasioni* Porta was awarded the Premio Viareggio in 1984.

Porta's recovery of the communicative force of language, together with its possibilities for penetrating reality, is born of complexity; it is the outcome of a long, tense relationship with language. In a 1987 interview with Lawrence R. Smith, Porta declared that the art that "takes refuge in non-communication serves nothing and nobody. Only an art which communicates can serve, an art which communicates critically according to a precise project for the renewal of art and society. We don't need a project for the destruction of art." Porta's constructive project represents a form of opposition and resistance to any theory that claims language is a fictive, illusory medium and affirms the collapse of all cognitive possibilities. Porta did not accept the apocalyptic claims of the absence of reality in language. For him reality did not vanish behind the displacing movement of language. Poetic language, he maintains in the introduction to his *Nel fare poesia,* is within "la lingua, come la storia degli uomini ce la consegna, non fissata per sempre ma in continua trasformazione perché la lingua a sua volta 'sta dentro' l'oceano prelinguistico, l'esperienza immediata, il sentimento che ne scaturisce, e perfino l'estasi dell'esserci" (the language, as man's history hands it to us, not fixed forever but in a continuous transformation because the language in turn is "within" the prelinguistic ocean, the immediate experience, the sentiment that derives from it, and even the ecstasy of being).

Porta's constructive project, with its linguistic and political ramifications, is also at the base of his collection *Il giardiniere contro il becchino* (The Gardener Against the Gravedigger, 1988). The opening section heralds a triumph of life over death and presents a narrative with a mythical dimension that constantly communicates the necessity of struggling, of planting, as a gardener, the seed of life:

> Che cosa fai, giardiniere?
> Hai gettato le armi?
> Sei impaurito dalla neve, dal gelo?
> Prendi una delle vanghe da trincea,
> lo sai che scavando un poco
> sotto la neve non va sottozero,
> tu conosci l'invisibile materiale
> l'utero di ogni seme.

> (What are you doing, gardener?
> Have you surrendered your arms?
> Are you frightened by the snow, by the frost?
> Take one of the hoes used for trenches,
> you know that digging a little
> beneath the snow it does not reach below zero,
> you know the invisible material
> the uterus of every seed.)

The poem "Fuochi incrociati" (Crossfires), despite the accusations, disappointments, despair, and failure (both personal and social) transpiring in the arguments of a modern couple, presents in dialogic form an attempt at communicating, at overcoming the labyrinth from which there seems to be no escape. The closing poems, in the section "Airone"

(Heron), convey a sense of liberation, of regained vitality. Poetry can reestablish its role of mediation with reality. Words are no longer estranging and reified entities but revealing media between the "I" and the world. In "Airone" words are liberating flights – essential, vital messages:

> nella mente degli uomini,
> la semplice vita,
> il nascere e morire,
> rinascere e volare via,
> aprirsi, amare,
> quello che è vivo, amore,
> sotto la semina dell'odio

> (in the mind of men,
> the simple life,
> birth and death,
> being born again and flying away,
> opening up, loving,
> that which is alive, love,
> under the sowing of hate)[.]

In Porta's poetry, language can suddenly explode and venture onto new, unexpected itineraries. The constant verbal tension and the continuous revision of the cognitive canons of reality confer on his poems a rare and fertile quality. His poetry represents one of the highest literary achievements of postwar Italy. Antonio Porta died on 12 April 1989 in Rome after a massive heart attack.

Interviews:

Renato Minore, "Devo finire un sogno," *Messaggero* (6 March 1984): 2–3;

Daryl Jung, "Bolstering Poetic Language," *Now* (8–14 May 1986): 11;

John Picchione, "A colloquio con Antonio Porta," *Quaderni d'Italianistica,* 2 (Fall 1986): 247–254;

Luisa Del Giudice, "Antonio Porta est consequentia rei," *Testuale,* 7 (1987): 117–126;

Lawrence R. Smith, "The Return to the Modernist Project: An Interview with Antonio Porta," *Caliban,* 3 (1987): 88–95.

Biographies:

Luigi Sasso, *Antonio Porta* (Florence: Nuova Italia, 1980);

Mario Moroni, *Essere e fare* (Rimini: Luisè, 1991).

References:

Stefano Agosti, "Due sistemi in relazione," *Giorno,* 28 May 1975, p. 11;

Renato Barilli, "Poesia forte," *Alfabeta,* 18 (October 1980): 16–17;

Peter Carravetta, "Limine Postmoderno," *Nuova Corrente,* no. 33 (1986): 321–333;

Giorgio Celli, "Antonio Porta e la 'coscienza cattiva,' " in *Gruppo '63: Critica e teoria,* edited by Barilli and Angelo Guglielmi (Milan: Feltrinelli, 1976), pp. 117–123;

Maria Corti, Introduction to Porta's *Week-end* (Rome: Cooperativa Scrittori, 1974), pp. 9–15;

Fausto Curi, "Poetica del nuovo terror," *Verri,* 32 (March 1970): 104–113;

Curi, "Il sogno, la crudeltà, il gioco," *Verri,* 29 (December 1968): 18–30;

Biancamaria Frabotta, "Lettere in busta chiusa," *Manifesto* (25 February 1983): 6;

Alfredo Giuliani, Preface and introduction to *I Novissimi: Poesie per gli anni '60,* revised edition, edited by Giuliani (Turin: Einaudi, 1965), pp. 3–32;

Giuliano Gramigna, "Quando la rima non serve a rimare," *Fiera Letteraria,* 48 (1 December 1974): 24;

Niva Lorenzini, "Quanto ha da darci Antonio Porta," in her *Il laboratorio della poesia* (Rome: Bulzoni, 1978), pp. 81–111;

Francesco Muzzioli, "La poesia di Antonio Porta e l'ideologia dell'avanguardia," *Argine,* 2–3 (September 1972): 868–878;

Marco Papa, "Paragrafi su 'Passi passaggi' di Antonio Porta," *Rassegna della Letteratura Italiana,* 3 (September–December 1981): 540–548;

John Picchione, "Antonio Porta e le varianti dell'azzeramento," *Verri,* 13–16 (1979): 306–316;

Picchione, "Linguaggio come terapia nell'ultimo Porta," *Strumenti Critici,* 39–40 (October 1979): 349–362;

Picchione, "Il nomadismo poetico di Antonio Porta," *Esperienze Letterarie,* 1 (1987): 37–46;

Picchione, "Poesia come provocazione: Itinerari espressivi di Antonio Porta," *Quaderni d'Italianistica,* 2 (Fall 1983): 167–182;

Picchione, "Il ruolo del lettore di fronte all'aspro stil novo dei Novissimi," *Studi Novecenteschi,* 27 (June 1984): 103–117;

Giuseppe Pontiggia, Preface to Porta's *Quanto ho da dirvi* (Milan: Feltrinelli, 1977), pp. 7–13;

Edoardo Sanguineti, "Il trattamento del materiale verbale nei testi della nuova avanguardia," in his *Ideologia e linguaggio* (Milan: Feltrinelli, 1965), pp. 123–131;

Gianni Scalia, "La nuova avanguardia (o della 'miseria' della poesia)," in *Avanguardia e Neoavanguardia* (Milan: Sugar, 1966), pp. 22–84;

Walter Siti, "Metropolis," in his *Realismo dell'avanguardia* (Turin: Einaudi, 1975), pp. 47–62;

Enrico Testa, "Il linguaggio della poesia di Antonio Porta," *Nuova Corrente,* no. 98 (1986): 267–285;

Stefano Verdino, "Caratteri di una poesia," *Nuova Corrente,* no. 98 (1986): 247–266;

Giuseppe Zagarrio, "Porta, la libertà e la coscienza del non," in his *Febbre, furore e fiele* (Milan: Mursia, 1983), pp. 223–227.

Giovanni Raboni

(22 January 1932 –   )

David Ward
Wellesley College

BOOKS: *Il catalogo è questo* (Milan: Lampugnani Nigri, 1961);

L'insalubrità dell'aria (Milan: All'Insegna del Pesce d'Oro, 1963);

Le case della Vetra (Milan: Mondadori, 1966);

Gesta romanorum (Milan: Lampugnani Nigri, 1967);

Economia della paura (Milan: All'Insegna del Pesce d'Oro, 1970);

Cadenza d'inganno (Milan: Mondadori, 1975);

Almanacco degli almanacchi (Milan: Bompiani, 1976);

Poesia degli anni sessanta (Rome: Riuniti, 1976);

Il più freddo anno di grazia (Genoa: San Marco dei Giustiniani, 1977); translated by Stuart Friebert and Vinio Rossi as *The Coldest Year of Grace* (Middletown, Conn.: Wesleyan University Press, 1985);

La fossa di Cherubino (Milan: Guanda, 1980);

Quaderno in prosa (Milan: Lampugnani Nigri, 1981);

Poesia italiana contemporanea (Florence: Sansoni, 1981);

Nel grave sogno (Milan: Mondadori, 1982);

Operai di sogni (Catania: Comune di Randazzo, 1985);

Canzonette mortali (Milan: Crocetti, 1986);

A tanto caro sangue (Milan: Mondadori, 1988);

I bei tempi dei libri brutti (Milan: Lampugnani Nigri, 1988);

Versi guerrieri e amorosi (Turin: Einaudi, 1990).

OTHER: Vittoria Bradshaw, ed. and trans., *From Pure Silence to Impure Dialogue: A Survey of Post-War Italian Poetry,* includes poems by Raboni (New York: Las Américas, 1971), pp. 584–601;

Nelo Risi, *Poesie scelte (1943–1975),* edited by Raboni (Milan: Mondadori, 1977);

Bartolo Cattafi, *Poesie scelte (1946–1973),* edited by Raboni (Milan: Mondadori, 1978);

Ruth Feldman and Brian Swann, eds. and trans., *Italian Poetry Today: Currents and Trends,* includes poems by Raboni (Saint Paul: New Rivers, 1979);

Giorgio Caproni, *L'ultimo borgo: Poesie, 1932–1978,* edited by Raboni (Milan: Rizzoli, 1980);

Arnaldo Ederle, *Il fiore d'Ofelia e altre tenerezze,* introductory note by Raboni (Milan: Societa' di Poesia / Verona: Bertani, 1984);

Marco Ceriani, *Fergana: 1978–1986,* introduction by Raboni (Maser: Amadeus, 1986);

Francesco Riviera, *L'orefice,* introduction by Raboni (Milan: Crocetti, 1986);

Enrico Gabrielli Scalini, *Erotogheia,* introduction by Raboni (Milan: Crocetti, 1987);

"Dopoguerra e secondo novecento," in *Storia della letteratura italiana: Il Novecento,* edited by Natalino Sapegno (Milan: Garzanti, 1987), pp. 209–248;

Enzo Siciliano, *Rosa pazza e disperata,* introduction by Raboni (Milan: Mondadori, 1987);

Alda Merini, *Testamento,* edited by Raboni (Milan: Crocetti, 1988).

TRANSLATIONS: Gustave Flaubert, *L'educazione sentimentale* (Milan: Garzanti, 1966);

Louis Aragon, *Bianca o l'oblio* (Milan: Mondadori, 1969);

Francis Simons, *Discorso sull'infallibilità* (Milan: Mondadori, 1969);

François Mauriac, *Un adolescente d'altri tempi* (Milan: Mondadori, 1971);

Charles Baudelaire, *Poesie e prose* (Milan: Mondadori, 1973);

Guillaume Apollinaire, *Bestiario* (Milan: Guanda, 1977);

Baudelaire (Turin: Einaudi, 1987).

A regular and highly visible presence in the frenetic world of Italian culture, Giovanni Raboni is one of the leading exponents of the Italian school of poetry loosely known as the *Linea lombarda* (Lom-

Giovanni Raboni circa 1980 (photograph by Gabriella Maleti)

bard Line), which emerged in the early 1950s as part of the explosive resurgence in postliberation cultural activity that Raboni has referred to as "una chiamata alla poesia" (a call to poetry). Drawing on a rich tradition of Lombardian enlightenment and progressive thinking, stretching back at least as far as Alessandro Manzoni, Giuseppe Parini, and Cesare Beccaria, the poets of the Linea Lombarda – Nelo Risi, Luciano Erba, Giorgio Orelli, Bartolo Cattafi, Elio Pagliarani, and Giancarlo Majorino – were among the first to challenge the primacy of the role hermeticism had played in Italian poetry and culture of the pre– and immediate post–World War II years. Hermeticism and, to a lesser extent, the poetry wing of neorealism, dismissed by Raboni as in-

consequential in the panorama of postwar Italian poetry, became the poles against which the Lombardian poets defined themselves. In his 1987 essay "Dopoguerra e secondo novecento" (Postwar and Second [Half of the] Twentieth Century) Raboni defines the poetics of the *Linea lombarda*: "una lombardità in poesia fatta da un lato di attenzione alle cose, al paesaggio, a una quotidianità dimessa e pungente, e di una vocazione morale (di matrice cattolica in alcuni, laica e progressista in altri) . . . dall'altro lato, di una pronuncia in sottile e sempre affabile equilibrio fra tenerezza elegiaca e ironia, fra precisione e understatement" (a Lombardness in poetry consisted on the one hand of attention to things, to the landscape, to an unassuming and sharp everydayness, and to a moral calling [of catholic origins in some, of a lay and progressive origin in others] . . . on the other, it consisted of a subtle and affable balance between elegiac tenderness and irony, accuracy and understatement).

Hermeticism was attacked and ultimately rejected for its refusal to address social and political issues, as well as for its tendency toward a self-referential, self-enclosed poetic mode. The Lombardian school extended its critique of the direction postwar Italian culture had taken to include the neorealistic tendency that had emerged forcefully in film and narrative (but less so in poetry), as a viable alternative to hermeticism, and that had come to take pride of place in the period of radical optimism that followed the Italian liberation from both domestic and Nazi Fascism. However, neorealism was criticized for its insistence on the absolute primacy of the social fact to the exclusion and detriment of any more transcendent or metaphysical claims.

The term *Linea lombarda* is something of a misnomer. Actual residence in Milan or Lombardy was never a prerequisite for membership, and many of the poets, if they chose the Lombardy region at all, chose it only as their adopted home. This, however, is not the case with Raboni. Born on 22 January 1932 in Milan, he was raised there and still lives there with his wife and children; the epicenter of Raboni's entire life has been the city of Milan and its environs, a fact that emerges forcefully from his poems, many of which mention the mists and fogs of the long Milan and Lombardy winters. After initially embarking on a career in law, Raboni took up what was to become the major activity of his life: his work in publishing. He has worked for many of Italy's leading publishing houses, including Mondadori, where he is presently an editor. As his notoriety as a critic and poet grew, he took on other commitments. For example, he is the theater critic for *Corriere della Sera,* the Milan-based daily newspaper; he is a member of the editorial board of the journal *Paragone;* and he is vice-president of the *Fondo "Associazione Pier Paolo Pasolini."*

In marked contrast to the frequency of his activity as critic, reviewer, editor, screenwriter, and translator, Raboni's work as a poet has been marked by its extreme intermittence. In nearly thirty years of writing poetry, Raboni has published few collections comprised of only new poems. In 1966 two earlier broadsheets – *Il catalogo è questo* (This Is the Catalogue, 1961) and *L'insalubrità dell'aria* (The Unwholesomeness of the Air, 1963) –

became the basis for his first book-length collection, *Le case della Vetra* (The Houses of the Vetra), consisting of poems mostly set in the working-class quarters in the Naviglio area of Milan. His second collection, *Cadenza d'inganno* (Cadence of Deceit), was published in 1975, and *Nel grave sogno* (In the Deep Dream) in 1982; both are made up of previously uncollected works, none of which was separately published. Poems from all three of these collections were included in a compendium, *A tanto caro sangue* (To Such Dear Blood, 1988). Dictated by the practical need to reissue volumes that had gone out of print, but undoubtedly also spurred on by Raboni's near-fatal heart attack, *A tanto caro sangue* is more than a simple volume of collected works. The driving force behind the venture was an attempt to draw together the strands of Raboni's thirty-year career as a poet. *A tanto caro sangue,* then, is something other than a republication of poems that had already appeared in earlier volumes. Indeed many of the poems were rewritten, while some were jettisoned, and new, previously unpublished poems were added. The order in which the poems appear in the compendium volume does not respect the original chronology of their publication, nor are the poems themselves identified by date or provenance. In his 1989 interview with Paolo Ruffilli, Raboni spoke of *A tanto caro sangue* as "non più un'antologia, né tantomeno, l'opera completa. La chiamerei una raccolta ragionata" (no longer an anthology, not even a collected work. I'd call it a reasoned collection). He called the volume his testament, the book of his life: "anche se a distanza di mesi dal lavoro finito, continuo a sentirlo come il libro della mia vita. Potrebbero esserci dei codicilli, ma è un testamento già scritto" (even months after the work has been finished, I still feel that this is the book of my life. There could be one or two codicils, but the testament has already been written).

Raboni's niche within the *Linea lombarda* is characterized by the strong influence that French and Anglo-American poets have had on his work, and he has made a name for himself as a successful translator. In a more domestic context the Italian influence that is most distinct in Raboni's poetry is that of Eugenio Montale. In addition to many stylistic resonances, Raboni also seems to share the same essentially humble view of poetry's function in the world as that held by Montale. As Raboni made clear in his interview with Ruffilli, he has no pretensions of shaking the foundations of the world or reshaping the sphere of postwar Italian poetry.

Raboni's view of the relationship between poetry and knowledge of the world puts the accent on poetry's slow and gradual conquest of small areas of lucidity, pockets of knowledge, oases in a desert of incomprehension, but he makes no claim to completion or plenitude in his poetry. The possibility of knowledge that poetry opens up is, then, not a sudden and striking moment of epiphany or enlightenment but a long-term, forward-moving process of gradual and ever-increasing elucidation. For Raboni the role of the poet and poetry is to forge, in the work-manlike manner that befits the active and practicing poet, a coherent space where, however provisionally, some degree of certitude may be formed. Raboni's own reworking and rewriting of his previous texts, which is the characteristic mark of *A tanto caro sangue,* is an illustration of the revisionary and provisional roles he assigns to poetry and to the achievements of poets.

Although often based on mundane topics – such as soccer, birthdays, bookies, the stock market, tax returns, and overcrowded cemeteries – Raboni's poems present a motif also present in Montale's, that of the fragility of an order whose deeper meanings elude the grasp of the narrator. "Portale" (Doorway), from *L'insalubrità dell'aria,* is the poem that opens *A tanto caro sangue,* and it poses questions to which there are no coherent answers:

Difficile dire
quante spade, quante lance, quanti elmi di cuoio
su profili romani,
quanti fabbri e pescatori col cappelluccio a cono
e le orecchie puntute,
quante facce di porco o di drago, quanti piedi
con cinque dita

e ruote e focacce sbilenche e proiezioni
di tavole imbandite

nella ressa, nel fuoco, nella gioia
della neve che approssima, del vino
bevuto in gioventù,
della folla irta e viva, di un'intera nazione
che pesca caccia ecc. e prepara
l'acre festa sul legno.

(It is hard to say
how many swords, how many lances, how many
    leather helmets
on Roman profiles,
how many smiths and fishermen with their coned
    hoods
and pointed ears,
how many pig or dragonlike faces, how many feet
with five toes

and wheels and misshapen cakes and projections
of groaning tables

in the crush, in the fire, in the joy
of the snow that is on its way, of the wine
drunk in youth,
of the bristling and lively crowd, of an entire nation
that fishes hunts etc. and prepares
the acrid feast on wood.)

The opening words of the poem (and, perhaps more significantly, of the whole collection) – "Difficile dire" – suggest that no single, unequivocal, or easy sense can be extracted from the plethora of information with which the observer is faced. In a similar way, "I fatti del diavolo" (The Devil's Facts) nears its conclusion with a complaint that "resta / sempre fuori qualcosa" (there is / always something that is left out), followed by a list including "il memoriale dell'impiccato, le smorfie dell'amore / sulle pareti degli orinatoi" (the memorial of the hanged man, the grimaces of love / on the walls of the urinals).

Whereas "Portale" deals with the uncertainty inherent in past events, "Il giocatore" (The Player) transfers that uncertainty into future time. Contrasting the familiar and reassuring present of his gambling vice with an as-yet-unknown and differently named possible future vice, the narrator confesses, "Ma ecco, quasi / ho paura a pensarci: che sarà / qualche vizio più squallido, o segreto, / o cupo – da non riderne, da avere / un altro nome, altri nomi in certe bocche" (But here, I am / almost afraid to think about it: it could be / a more squalid or secret vice, / or darker – nothing to laugh about, with / another name, or other names in certain mouths).

But it is in "Dopo" (After) and in "Dilazione seconda" (Second Respite) that Raboni's concern with the insubstantial and ever-changing nature of things finds two of its most eloquent images. In "Dopo" the world appears as if drawn in chalk on the pavement and slowly rubbed out: "Disegnato col gesso come era / sul marciapiede il mondo si cancella" (Drawn in chalk as it was / on the pavement the world erases itself). In "Dilazione seconda" the narrator speaks of invisible links – missing in poems such as "Portale" and "I fatti del diavolo" – that would join together and give a unified sense to the objects: "la traccia che dovresti seguire / per scoprire invisibili legami di oggetti lontani fermi o in movimento" (the trace that you should follow / to discover the invisible links of objects distant motionless or moving).

On other occasions, however, Raboni's sense of puzzlement at the events of the present is translated into a sense of nostalgia for the familiarity and reassurance of his own formative years. "Risanamento" (Restoration), for example, contrasts the changed state of the Naviglio area of Milan, where Raboni grew up, with his memories of what it used to be like: "Ma quello / che hanno fatto, distruggere le case, / distruggere quartieri, qui e altrove, / a cosa serve?" (But what / have they done, destroy houses, / destroy neighborhoods, here and elsewhere, / what for?).

However, this apparent valorization of a past to which one can confidently turn in time of crisis is undercut by "Gli addii" (Goodbyes), a poem in which turning back to the familiarity of past events is accompanied not by a sense of regained synthesis but by fear. The passing of time enacts disturbing changes on the former assumed stability of the past: "Strano gioco, / ho paura, è assai poco redditizio. / Tanto tempo è passato!" (Strange game, / I am afraid, and it is hardly rewarding. / So much time has passed!).

Accompanying and bolstering this generalized sense of uncertainty – what Ruffilli has called "una poetica dell'incertezza e della precarietà esistenziale" (a poetics of uncertainty and of existential precariousness) – is the presence at the heart of Raboni's poetry of a self-questioning, unstable, decentered subjectivity. Often in his poems a gap or distance exists between the narrating voice and the narrated events. Pinpointing the exact provenance of the voice or giving it a well-defined identity is a problem. At other times, the interrogative mode with which the voice addresses the reader, as in "Portale," raises doubts about the status of the voice as the stable origin and authoritative central presence of the poem. This tendency is accentuated by the often down-to-earth and colloquial register in which Raboni writes. Not only is the provenance of the voice often hard to locate but so is the addressee of the poems. In "Il cotto e il vivo" (The Cooked and the Raw), which deals with overcrowded cemeteries, although the third character present in the poem can safely be assumed to be the narrator's dead father, and the first person to be Raboni himself, the identity of the second person, to whom the voice addresses itself – "Non vorrai lasciarlo" (You will not want to leave him); "Ma lascia stare" (Do not worry yourself) – remains ambiguous and unspecified.

As the opening words of *A tanto caro sangue* suggest, Raboni's attempts to come to terms poetically with an uncertain world is also a struggle with and against language. It is not, however, a struggle lost at the outset. Even though the opening poem dramatizes the difficulties inherent in the task faced by the poet, its very existence as a poem also signals the ultimate viability of the poetic enterprise. Poems are written, Raboni feels, through and against language. To give in to any supposed impossibility of language is not to investigate fully the resonances and expressive/communicative possibilities it may hold. Despite its inherent difficulties, the resilient power of language and the word is underlined by a poem such as "Congedo" (Farewell):

Le parole scambiate col barbiere
sapendole aride e vane, credendole fraintese
e sepolte per sempre in un orecchio peloso
ritornano. Più fioche, più crudeli . . .

(The words exchanged with the barber
knowing them to be arid and vain, believing them to
  have been misunderstood
and buried forever in a hairy ear
come back. Weaker, more cruel . . .).

Words may be buried and misunderstood in banal conversations with a barber, they may be inadequate signs, but they also come back; they reverberate, even perhaps as nightmares or elements of turbulence. Words once uttered remain and return, as events they cannot be erased, and as such they have a status as signs in and of the world. Herein lies the potential of language. Indeed the continued belief in the inherent possibility of the linguistic enterprise to break new ground and make a difference is given political legitimization in "Rammarico del Viceré" (The Complaint of the Viceroy). Words, if listened to or used carefully, can make a difference in a world ever more dominated by the tyrannical forces of sameness and standardization where "Tutto, ormai, / filerebbe secondo le istruzioni" (Everything by now would go as per the instructions).

It is tempting to read Raboni's defense of the possibilities inherent in language, and the hint of the political repercussions that follow, in the same light as his own critical comments on the poet Antonio Porta. In Raboni's essay "Dopoguerra e secondo novecento" the terms of his appreciation of Porta's work could well be applied to Raboni himself and understood as a kind of manifesto or declaration of his own ethical and political stake in poetry. In a world of chaos and catastrophe, the poet must not give in to silence and sameness but must always be on the front lines ready and prepared for a meaningful engagement with reality, no matter how overwhelming it may be.

The notion that the practice of poetry has become a necessary rearguard action to be carried out against a hostile world, to which one must not surrender, has an analogue in Raboni's attitude toward death. If death is akin to the catastrophe against which Porta (and also Raboni) write and practice poetry, then it is an equal act of cowardice to submit oneself meekly to it, no matter how ineluctable its coming. In the Ruffilli interview Raboni speaks of how "In fondo, i conti con la morte li ho sempre un po' fatti" (Essentially, I have always come to terms with death). Of his work on *A tanto caro sangue*, published soon after his heart attack, he says, "ho lavorato in questa nuova prospettiva: di chi avrebbe potuto morire. Così, il libro si è fatto libro di bilancio, spingendosi naturalmente ad inglobare le poesie più recenti ed ultimissime. Tuttavia, questa prospettiva della morte non mi ha dato affatto angoscia, anzi, una sorte di euforia. Mi sono accorto che quello che dovevo fare, l'avevo fatto; e che quello che dovevo scrivere, l'avevo scritto" (I worked from this new point of view: as one who could have died. In this way, the book became a balance sheet, which went on to take in the most recent and very recent poems. Still, the standpoint of death I adopted did not trouble me at all; rather, it gave me a sense of euphoria. I realized that I had done what I had to do, that I had written what I had to write).

Interview:
Paolo Ruffilli, "Intervista a Giovanni Raboni a cura di Paolo Ruffilli," *Anello che non Tiene,* 1 (Spring 1989): 53–57.

References:
Piergiorgio Bellocchio, "Intervento di P. Bellocchio: L'itinerario poetico di Raboni," *Quaderni Piacentini,* 14 (November 1975): 147–153;

Maurizio Cucchi, "Giovanni Raboni," *Belfagor,* 32 (September 1977): 523–542;

Gilberto Finzi, "Raboni e Cesarano," in his *Poesia in Italia: Montale, novissimi, postnovissimi, 1959–1978* (Milan: Mursia, 1979), pp. 59–60;

Marco Forti, "Raboni: Le *Canzonette mortali,*" *Paragone,* 38 (April 1987): 77–81;

Forti, "Testimonianza per Raboni," *Nuovi argomenti,* new series 59–60 (1978): 243–251;

Cesare Garboli, "L'impero dei sensi," *Paragone,* 38 (April 1987): 82–90;

Stefano Pastore, "Fra pubblico e privato: *Cadenza d'inganno,*" *Paragone,* 38 (April 1987): 91–99;

Silvio Ramat, *L'intelligenza dei contemporanei* (Padua: Rebellato, 1968), pp. 247–250;

Walter Siti, "Cadenza d'inganno," *Nuovi Argomenti,* new series 47–48 (September–December 1975): 288–291.

Silvio Ramat

(2 October 1939 –   )

Gaetana Marrone
Princeton University

BOOKS: *Le feste di una città* (Florence: Quartiere, 1959);

Lo specchio dell'afa (Bologna: Leonardi, 1961);

La rissa dei salici (Urbino: Argalia, 1963);

Gli sproni ardenti (Milan: Mondadori, 1964);

Montale (Florence: Vallecchi, 1965);

L'intelligenza dei contemporanei: Saggi, note, interventi sulla poesia italiana del Novecento (Padua: Rebellato, 1968);

L'ermetismo (Florence: Nuova Italia, 1969);

Psicologia della forma leopardiana (Florence: Nuova Italia, 1970);

La pianta della poesia (Florence: Vallecchi, 1972);

Corpo e cosmo (1964–1972) (Milan: All'Insegna del Pesce d'Oro, 1973);

Fisica dell'immagine (Manduria: Lacaita, 1973);

Crisi di lettura: Anticronache dal vero (1969–1973) (Naples: Guida, 1974);

Storia della poesia italiana del Novecento (Milan: Mursia, 1976);

In parola (Milan: Guanda, 1977);

Protonovecento (Milan: Saggiatore, 1978);

Invito alla lettura di Piero Bigongiari (Milan: Mursia, 1979);

L'inverno delle teorie (Milan: Mondadori, 1980);

L'arte del primo sonno: Quintetti 1979–1980 (Genoa: San Marco dei Giustiniani, 1984);

L'acacia ferita e altri saggi su Montale (Venice: Marsilio, 1986);

Orto e nido (Milan: Garzanti, 1987);

In piena prosa, 1980–1981 (Montebelluna: Amedeus, 1987);

I sogni di Costantino (Milan: Mursia, 1988);

Una fonte (Milan: Crocetti, 1988);

Serials (Treviso: Cominiana, 1988);

Firenze vuol dire (Lugano, Switzerland: Laghi di Plitvice, 1989);

Ventagli (Montebelluna: Amadeus, 1991).

OTHER: Dino Campana, *Canti orfici e altri scritti,* includes notes by Ramat (Florence: Vallecchi, 1966);

Omaggio a Montale, edited by Ramat (Milan: Mondadori, 1966);

Edoardo Calandra, *A guerra aperta; La signora di Riondino (1690); La marchesa Falconis (1705–1706),* edited by Ramat (Florence: Vallecchi, 1971);

Vittorio Alfieri, *Polinice,* edited by Ramat (Milan: Mursia, 1971);

Piero Bigongiari, *Poesie,* edited by Ramat (Milan: Mondadori, 1982);

Bino Rebellato, *L'oza leggera, 1938–1989,* includes an essay by Ramat (Milan: All'Insegna del Pesce d'Oro, 1989).

In the historical context of contemporary poetic modes, Silvio Ramat's work represents the most significant continuation of the Florentine hermetic school. Ascribed by Giovanni Raboni to the so-called generation of 1956 and chronologically belonging more to the avant-garde of the 1960s, Ramat has a motive power that lies in an innate, pressing urge to renovate poetic language and to reconcile previous thematic and formalistic treatments with an openness to emotional impressions of autobiographical integrity and sensitivity. He enriches the poetic systems promulgated by Mario Luzi and Vittorio Sereni with realistic and social stimuli. His poetry evokes all the canonical criteria of the hermetic tradition: preference for the synthetic blend of expression, composition, and inflection; widespread reference to a spiritual condition that is ambiguous and undefinable; an interest in the sonority of the word and the associative function of language; a lyric tonality that oscillates between mental perception and narrative *occasione* (occurrence); and a symbolism that embodies the dramatic interaction of the artistic subject and the external world. This poetic discourse eventually leads to a distinct obscurity and to an allusive, analogical component. Ramat's linguistic and thematic purism is not, however, cerebral, programmatic artifice. He is a great poet of analogy, of suggestive reflection, who feels imprisoned by the human inadequacy to find definite truths. Ultimately he exalts the journey of the self to a profound inner state: the enticing depth of dreams; the alluring realm of the waking state of mind; and the divine fight of memory and fantasy against time and death.

The son of Raffaello Ramat, the eminent critic, and Wanda Pieroni Ramat, Silvio was born in Florence on 2 October 1939; he pursued classical studies at the local university and graduated in 1962, with a thesis on Eugenio Montale. On 3 August 1964 Ramat married Luisella Bernardini; they later had a daughter, Silvia, and a son, Giuliano. In 1967 Ramat began teaching the history of criticism at the Facoltà di Magistero in Florence, and since 1976 he has been a professor of modern and contemporary Italian literature at the University of Padua. Ramat is a prolific poet and literary critic. His most significant theoretical contributions are in the field of twentieth-century Italian poetry. A regular contributor to journals and newspapers, such as *Paragone, Letteratura, Approdo, Corriere della Sera,* and *Tempo,* he is also an associate editor of *Forum Italicum.* Ramat has received numerous poetry prizes, including the Cittadella Opera Prima in 1960, the Carducci two years later, the Cervia in 1969, and the Ceppo in 1973. In 1984 he was awarded the Premio Montale and in 1987 the Tagliacozzo and Traiano prizes.

Ramat's work presents a noticeable absence of speculation. His poetics can be traced in the poems themselves and in the sphere of his critical thought. He believes, for example, that apathy toward theories is a distinct feature of the post-Montalian, posthermetic generation. Paradigmatic of Ramat's poetic praxis is what he calls in *La pianta della poesia* (The Plant of Poetry, 1972), "la fatica del mio inventare" (the hardship of having to invent), which is often counterbalanced by an "affaticato lettore di professione" (a tired professional reader). His style has a clear tendency to identify the word with its hidden meaning. He says that "il linguaggio non è solo lo strumento, ma il centro e il fine della poesia. Appare altrettanto logico il valore sperimentale del linguaggio, nella poesia e altrove: ché anzi l'àmbito del suo sperimentare è prettamente linguistico, non essendo il linguaggio in nessun caso un *dato* (nemmeno quello di una presunta tradizione) ma un impulso e al contempo la finalità obbiettiva di quell'impulso" (language is not only the instrument, but the very center and purpose of poetry. The experimental value of language appears to be equally logical, in poetry and elsewhere: the sphere of its experimentation is purely linguistic, since in no case language can be considered a *datum* [not even that of a

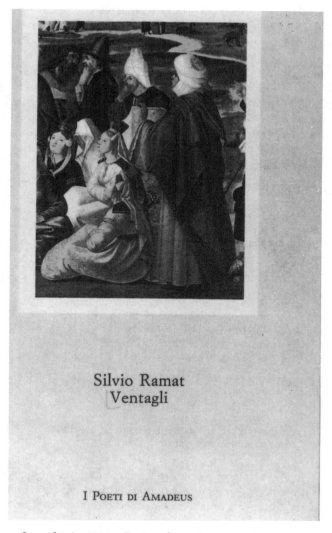

Silvio Ramat
Ventagli

I POETI DI AMADEUS

Cover for the 1991 collection of verse by a poet whose work is considered an important continuation of the Florentine hermetic school

presumed tradition] but an impulse and at the same time the objective aim of such an impulse).

Ramat's first collections of poems, *Le feste di una città* (The Feasts of a City, 1959) and *Lo specchio dell'afa* (The Mirror of Sultriness, 1961) – both republished in *La rissa dei salici* (The Brawl of the Willow Trees, 1963) and, with additions, in *Fisica dell'immagine* (Physics of the Image, 1973) – show technical maturity and an extensive imagination. At twenty he received flattering critical reviews and was acclaimed as the most distinguished disciple of the Florentine hermetic movement. Ramat's highly structured poetry is rich with complex allusiveness, but it is evident, from these early lyrics, that he was not to be influenced by the technical experimental trends of the 1960s. His future poetic growth, denoted by a constant desire to master a skillful formalism, would establish the *occasione* as the nucleus that best condenses a descriptive and moral rapport with the phenomenal world. For Ramat teleological design sustains the reality of all things; an insistence upon details transforms objects into emerging visions and memories. His poetry is a *reductio* of the external world to sound units, which are apprehended and classified in organic patterns. Giuseppe Zagarrio named this apparatus "cellularismo" (cellular structure), the representation of small, vital worlds refracted in a maze of mirrors. For Ramat the *occasione* expresses the story and portrays his poetic projection onto the undefinable, his way of "interrogating" universal anxieties. His stylistic elaboration formalizes a subjective zone of consciousness, which often relies on memory. In "Le ore di punta" (Rush Hours), from *Fisica dell'immagine,* he writes:

La memoria, che terreno consumato, indurito
anno per anno, da racimolarvi ben poco
se non in giorni rari, di fortuna,
che l'immagine cresce da sé e di colpo
ho il privilegio di guardarmi vivere.

(Memory, what a worn-out territory, hardened
year after year, so that little can be gathered in it
except on rare, lucky days,
when the image grows by itself and suddenly
I have the privilege of watching myself live.)

The awareness of a temporal fragmentation – "fatico a raccordare / tempo con tempo" (I can hardly connect / time with time) – is extended into a conception of the individual world: "ma quattro pareti sono una pellicola tenera" (but four walls are a tender film). Within this confining physical space, a human being can strengthen dramatically the degree of his sensory perceptions. Every external presence can be transformed into an occasion of inexhaustible life. The poet invests the object with an emblematic essence so that it becomes the locus of introspection and reflexive action – a function normally designated to the narrative self. In the textual structure of the poems, the object belongs to the realm of the consciousness of the perceiving subject: both self and object are protagonists, while any neoromantic, heroic nature of the self is abrogated. This organic dynamism of objects and *occasione,* observed in its potentiality, represents one of Ramat's major poetic traits.

A three-year interval separated his first poems from *Gli sproni ardenti* (The Burning Spurs, 1964). The volume confirms Ramat as a leading figure in contemporary Italian poetry. His literary, semantic structures pertain to the lyrical traditions of Petrarch and baroque mannerism. Piero Bigongiari appropriately compares Ramat's hermetic, intransitive word with the unlimiting transitiveness of the stylized Petrarchan code. *Gli sproni ardenti* is full of surrealist associations; it is a work of renovation within traditional articulations. Ramat does not, however, repropose classical and modern lyrical modes; he reinvents them by means of exquisite decadent effects. His style is characterized by an intense use of consonance, enjambment, assonance, antithesis, and a pounding, paratactic, iterative tonality. There is a perilous balance between verbal richness and hypnotic apparitions. His poetry begins in the conscious mind, with a cadence of recurrent sound patterns, and then shifts from the elaborateness of conventional forms to an inner dimension. As for many of the Florentine poets, his tendency to formal assimilation turns into a nocturnal celebration of sounds and images. *Gli sproni ardenti* attests a conception of poetry as lyrical experience. By returning to Petrarch, Ramat acknowledges a need for stylistic discipline. His lyricism is controlled and pellucid, and his "bravura barocca" (as Luigi Baldacci calls it) displays an ambitious mix of syntactic units. Furthermore he does not indulge in the negativity of tormented interrogation but stresses the exaltation of momentary freedom.

Fundamental to Ramat's poetry is "il ricorso frequente all'ambiguo tema del viaggio" (the frequent return of the ambiguous theme of the journey), by which the first-person narrator re-creates the past and conquers an absolute condition of totality, as Ramat explains in his notes to *Corpo e cosmo* (Body and Space, 1973). He assigns the regressive journey of the self to a latent Orphic vein and associates it with recurrent motifs: "l'impulso a una concentrazione, la più razionale possibile, dell'eccentrica rosa dei sensi; la spola fra metafisica e politica, indice dei complessi di colpa del poeta" (the impulse to concentrate, most rationally, on the eccentric rose of the senses; the shuttle between metaphysics and politics, an index of the poet's guilt complexes). The poetic "confession" is neo-Platonic in its conception: memory, dream, sleep, and enchantment lead to an eternal idea. The search for authenticity can only be found at a primordial, preconscious state of existence, which implies a release from marginality. Time and love unfold toward a final goal where limits are transcended.

Corpo e cosmo is divided into three sections: "Terza persona," "Gli uomini trasparenti," and "Un grafico ricostruito a senso" (Third Person, Transparent Men, and A Graph Freely Reconstructed); and the book is prefaced by an epigraph from Austrian poet Hugo von Hofmannsthal: "La gente cerca volentieri dietro una poesia ciò che essa chiama il 'vero senso.' Come le scimmie, che così cacciano le mani dietro uno specchio, quasi *là* ci fosse un corpo da afferrare" (People willingly search behind a poem for its 'true meaning.' Like monkeys, who put their hands behind a mirror, as if *there* were a body to grab onto). This theoretical statement recognizes an organic unity focused on the musical rhythm of words – as Ramat had already made clear in *Gli sproni ardenti* and was later going to develop fully in *In parola* (In Word, 1977). His commitment to enhance the melodious power of words, which represent, shape, and interrogate the world, is evident in "Tempo e Luogo" (Time and Place):

Anche a metà della vita
c'è una notte in cui l'incubo nidifica
secondo forme chiuse nell'infanzia.
E il precipizio, è la caduta a piombo
da una cima di ponte o da un decimo piano
con i piedi pesanti fino a terra
e a terra il corpo non esplode – solo
ti risveglia il colpo dell'aria smossa.

Ma intanto, per la durata del volo,
chi ha conosciuto l'aria, l'elemento
di questa via larvale ricomparsa
inaspettata in un sogno di adulto?

(Also in the middle of life
there is a night when the nightmare nests
according to shapes enclosed within childhood.
It is the precipice, it is the perpendicular fall
from the top of a bridge or from a tenth floor
with heavy feet down to the ground
and on the ground the body does not explode – only
the gust of the shifted air wakes you.

Meanwhile, for the duration of the flight,
who has experienced the air, the element
of this latent path reappeared
unexpected in an adult's dream?)

Corpo e cosmo is a diaristic record of love, death, defeat, God, time, and destiny; it expresses a melancholic dimension of life and the consciousness of an unnamed personal crisis.

Ramat and his wife were divorced in 1980, and for him the following decade was a time for a systematic rethinking of his views on life and poetry. In the previous fifteen years his literary activity had become predominantly critical: several volumes of criticism by him were published between 1965 and 1980. His lyrics had been inspired by loneliness, death, and nightmares. From *L'inverno delle teorie* (The Winter of Theories, 1980) to *Ventagli* (Fans, 1991) Ramat perfected the sublime art of the verse and

achieved, through suffering, an intense level of self-awareness. His later poetic form is based on anaphoric repetitive patterns; repetition became the chief organizational unit of his poetic discourse.

In *L'inverno delle teorie* the poet's journey is structured on the topos of the dream and sleep (not as an existential condition of passivity but as a dialectic opponent of insomnia). The prison metaphor mythicizes the condition of one who, by accepting self-enclosure, finds an unforeseen type of freedom. Ramat's latest poems represent the dialectic of the visual and the emotional as a form of inspiration, and the image is transformed into a newly conquered space.

Silvio Ramat's poetry is representative of the essential thematic structures of his generation. However, it stands out as a personal statement. Ramat aims at reestablishing the subjective autonomy of the word over reality. This is the voice of the artist who goes beyond the temporal alienation of marginality by engaging in the power of fantasy, which can transform limitations into freedom.

References:

Luigi Baldacci, "Le poesie di Ramat tra l'ermetismo e la bravura barocca," *Epoca* (1 November 1964): 130, 132;

Enza Biagini, "Continuo e discontinuo nella poesia di Ramat," *Italianistica*, 7, no. 2 (1978): 428–436;

Piero Bigongiari, "Introduzione alla poesia di Ramat," *Forum Italicum*, 3, no. 1 (1969): 105–108;

Neria De Giovanni, "Il 'Poema intempestivo' ovvero l'insonne viaggiatore di Silvio Ramat," in her *Da Sebastiano Satta a Eugenio Montale: Studi sulla poesia italiana del Novecento* (Pisa: Giardini, 1984), pp. 83–120;

Elio Giunta, "La coscienza del limite," in his *Antideologia e linguaggio: Discorso sui testi di Ramat e di Cattafi* (Palermo: Vittorietti, 1978), pp. 14–29;

Ruggero Jacobbi, "Il 'Poema intempestivo' di Silvio Ramat," *Nuova Rivista Europea,* 4 (1980): 189–190;

Oreste Macrì, "Due poeti dell'avanguardia fiorentina," in his *Realtà del simbolo: Poeti e critici del Novecento italiano* (Florence: Vallecchi, 1968), pp. 252–258;

Mirella Billi Mancioli, "Sulla poesia di Silvio Ramat," *Forum Italicum*, 9, no. 2 (1975): 74–89;

Mario Richter, "Un poeta, una città su una poesia 'padovana' di Silvio Ramat," *Padova e il Suo Territorio,* 13 (1988): 28–29;

Giuseppe Zagarrio, *Struttura e impegno: La poesia* (Florence: Quartiere, 1966), pp. 41–50.

Mario Ramous

(18 May 1924 –   )

Giovanni Sinicropi
University of Connecticut

BOOKS: *La memoria, il messaggio* (Bologna: Cappelli, 1951);

Il presente, l'affetto (Rocca San Casciano: Libreria Antiquaria Palmaverde, 1954);

Nuove poesie (Bologna: Cappelli, 1956);

109/26965 (Urbino: Svolta, 1965);

Programma n. (Bologna: Immagine, 1968);

Interventi (Bologna & Turin: Geiger, 1968);

Quantità e qualità (Bologna & Turin: Geiger, 1968);

1962–1969 (Bologna: Immagine, 1970);

Registro 1971 (Bologna: Cappelli, 1971);

Battage per Valeria (Bologna: Cappelli, 1973);

Macchina naturale (Milan: Feltrinelli, 1975);

A discarico (Turin: Geiger, 1976);

Dopo la critica (Milan: Società di Poesia, 1984);

La metrica (Milan: Garzanti, 1984);

Interferenze (Milan: Garzanti, 1988).

OTHER: *Giorgio Morandi: I disegni,* edited, with an essay, by Ramous (Bologna: Cappelli, 1949);

Marino Marini: Disegni, includes an essay by Ramous (Bologna: Cappelli, 1951);

Marino Marini: Litografie e Disegni, includes an essay by Ramous (Bologna: Cappelli, 1951);

Selections from *Macchina naturale,* translated by Giovanni Sinicropi, *International Poetry Review,* 2 (Fall 1976).

TRANSLATIONS: *Esopo: Le favole del lupo, le favole del leone, le favole dell'asino, le favole della volpe* (Bologna: Cappelli, 1952);

Il libro delle Odi: Versioni da Orazio (Bologna: Cappelli, 1954; enlarged edition, 1963);

Dal libro di Catullo (Bologna: Immagine, 1966);

Catullo, Virgilio, Orazio: Traduzioni (Bologna: Cappelli, 1971);

Catullo: Le poesie (Milan: Garzanti, 1975);

Orazio: Satire (Milan: Garzanti, 1976);

Virgilio: Georgiche (Milan: Garzanti, 1982);

Orazio: Epistole (Milan: Garzanti, 1985);

Orazio: Odi, Epodi (Milan: Garzanti, 1986).

One of the most original personalities in the development of experimental poetry in the 1960s and 1970s, Mario Ramous was born on 18 May 1924 in Milan and lives in Bologna. He started his career as an art and literature critic for various periodicals, including the *Progresso d'Italia* and *Emilia,* and the Italian national radio (RAI). For several years he was editorial director for a publishing house. He now teaches at the University of Urbino. He was an active member of the Italian Communist party until the crushing of the Hungarian uprising in 1956 led him, along with many other Italian intellectuals, to believe that the trust they had placed in the justice of "realized socialism" was illusory. His break with that political organization, however, did not diminish his adherence to the ideal of social justice that had attracted him to it in the first place. His allegiance to the ideal was pursued in his daily work and writing. In his poetry Ramous refuses the role of observer, considering it his duty to intervene in the events of the world.

His apprenticeship is documented by his first essays, collected in his first three books, where Ramous proves to be a good critic and promoter of a poetic language and rhetorical system that three or four decades of aging had brought to a limpidness of intonation rarely attained in Italian poetry since the work of Giacomo Leopardi. Salvatore Quasimodo, for example, is a poet with whom Ramous feels a great deal of affinity, probably due to their sharing a neoclassic style of treating the precariousness of the present instant by writing it into the well-sculpted classical line, and also because of their ideological concurrence in the repugnance they felt for an adulterated reality. In Ramous's first poems the hendecasyllable, bridled by the solemnity of a Quasimodian prosody, gives him the sense of security that derives from the awareness of moving on an ancient and well-traveled path.

Ramous's apprenticeship in poetic language was also done directly with the classics, especially the works of Roman poets, whose study he sedulously pursued throughout his career. The list of authors he studied and translated with greatest interest is significant: Horace, Virgil, and Catullus — authors in whose poems the practice of poetic language was exercised in unison with that of life in the present. Poetry was not a mirror of life, but poetry and life were integral parts of one existential practice. Few poets and translators have understood this unity as well as Ramous. Perhaps for this reason his renderings of the classics are — rather than word-perfect translations or mockingbird imitations — echoes in a different key, representations from without: living re-creations of what was once lived, actualizations of the original authenticity.

Among the new experimental poets, Ramous is the one who remains most faithful to the lesson imparted by the classics, as seen in the Catullian intonation or Horatian pace of some of his lines, and especially in the rhythmic structure of the line, the prosodic components of which can be retraced to classical molds. He not only remains faithful to the hendecasyllable, his basic measure, but to some of the most classical metric forms: frequently the sonnet — as especially seen in *Macchina naturale* (Natural Machine, 1975), in which one section consists entirely of twenty-two sonnets — but also the canzone and the sestina.

Even though Ramous never properly belonged to the avant-garde movement, he walked the same road in search of personal solutions to what for him was a fundamental question going beyond that concerning the function of poetry and its expressive means in present society; Ramous's question concerned rather the social and cultural position of the poet. An intelligent positing of the question required a thorough analysis of present society not in its appearance but in its reality, in the actual structures that make it possible. Ramous's poetics developed during the 1960s under the direct influence of the sociopolitical tensions that culminated in the unrest of 1968.

To him once a capitalistic organization became, by the necessity inherent in its own logic, pandemic and totalitarian, it transformed itself into a power machine exercising control over every aspect of reality. Far from representing an aberrant moment of history, this machine becomes history. By passing itself off as the only producer and regulator of "sense," this machine constantly endeavors to eliminate dissent while constraining freedom. The machine produces self-regulating rationality: its calculations are, therefore, never erring. One finds in this position several of the fundamental critical concepts elaborated by the so-called Frankfurt School, and especially those linked to Herbert Marcuse. The only hope one can have to escape the power machine is to induce or discover an error in its calculations or destroy its rationality and credibility. Hence, insofar as the poet is concerned, the operation must be carried out first and foremost on the structure of language in order to free meaning, not from the accretions of time but from the rhetorical and logical preemptive coercions placed on meaning by the power machine. The preempting of meaning exercised by the power machine on the totality of phenomenological reality leaves no other choice than to seek freedom beyond the statutory relations between word and object. The *inventio* (finding) of the "other" word does not postulate a mystical or mythical search for the nonexistential, nor for a "probable" point in an infinite series; it does not concern the relation between *vox* (word) and *res* (object). It rather concerns the conceptual mechanism of semantic relations in an attempt to free it from the regulatory monopoly exerted by the power machine. In a poem in *Interferenze* (1988) he writes:

è da considerare
come articolare elementi
isolati da ogni contesto
per una teoria reale
di significati, nel senso
non più di quello che si dice
ma di che si potrebbe dire

il prevedibile
      già consumato
non ti consente attendibilità

      (to be considered
is how to articulate elements
isolated from any context
towards a real theory
of significations, no longer
in the sense of what is said
but of what might be said

the predictable
      worn out by use
does not yield dependability)[.]

Ramous, however, carefully avoids rushing into the blind alley of dogmatic negativism in which many a rash follower of the avant-garde movement became trapped. His deconstruction of institutionalized poetic discourse aims at restructuring the components in order to yield a renovated possibility of meaning. However, Ramous's poetry is not without hesitation; his reasoning includes doubt. Among the poets of his generation he is perhaps the one most aware of the paradox threatening all iconoclastic experimentalism. As with all his metric forms, developed in relation to institutionalized metrics, the negative dialectics pursued by the neo-avant-garde can remain alive only by presupposing a positive ideological structure as a referential pole. In his more recent works Ramous seems to have progressively abandoned or overcome most of his experimental positions, due probably to the strictures of his theoretical doubts. The result is the crystal-clear poetic expression of refreshing simplicity, based on feelings bred by what he calls the "sana abitudine di vivere" (healthy habit of living) — as seen in these lines from *Interferenze*:

viene il tempo in cui la speranza sciocca
puoi affidarla solo a quel futuro
che ti consentono gli affetti, tu,
amore mio, chi è nato da noi,
e voi amici

(the time comes when foolish hope
you can only entrust to the future
your feelings allow for, you,

my love, who is born of us,
and your friends)[.]

Interviews:

Gina Lagorio, "Incontro con Mario Ramous," *Corriere Mercantile* (16 October 1971);

Fiora Vincenti, "Poesia contemporanea: Orientamenti degli anni '70," *Uomini e Libri,* 40 (September–October 1972).

References:

Gina Lagorio, "Poesia di Ramous," *Uomini e Idee,* 11 (December 1969): 80–85;

Antonio La Penna, "Mario Ramous traduttore di classici latini," *Maia,* 25 (April–June 1973): 137–140;

Claudio Marabini, "I ricorsi stilistici di Mario Ramous," *Resto del Carlino* (7 May 1969);

Gianni Scalia, "La poesia di Mario Ramous," *Letteratura Moderne,* 8 (March–April 1958): 205–207;

Adriano Spatola, "Situazione della poesia italiana d'avanguardia," *Battana,* 5 (October 1968).

Amelia Rosselli

(1930 –)

Pietro Frassica
Princeton University

BOOKS: *24 poesie* (Turin: Einaudi, 1963);
Variazioni belliche (Milan: Garzanti, 1964);
Serie ospedaliera (Milan: Saggiatore, 1969);
Documento, 1966–1973 (Milan: Garzanti, 1976);
Primi scritti, 1952–1963 (Milan: Guanda, 1980);
Impromptu (Genoa: San Marco dei Giustiniani, 1981);
Appunti sparsi e persi (Reggio Emilia: Aelia Laelia, 1983);
La Libellula (Genoa: SE, 1985);
Antologia poetica, edited by Giacinto Spagnoletti (Milan: Garzanti, 1987).

OTHER: Carlo and Nello Rosselli, *Epistolario familiare,* edited by Amelia Rosselli (Milan: Sugarco, 1979);
Lawrence Smith, ed. and trans., *The New Italian Poetry: 1945 to the Present. A Bilingual Anthology,* includes poems by Rosselli (Berkeley: University of California Press, 1981), pp. 351–369;
Beverly Allen, Muriel Kittel, and Keala Jane Jewell, eds. and trans., *The Defiant Muse: Italian Feminist Poems from the Middle Ages to the Present. A Bilingual Anthology,* includes poems by Rosselli (New York: Feminist Press, 1986), pp. 75–79.

The poetry of Amelia Rosselli presents an extremely disconcerting linguistic environment: traditional logical and expressive syntax is replaced by bold verbal combinations. Each poem seems the result of an improvisation, which, at the same time, is the fruit of great deliberation, of ideals and feelings of love nurtured for years, all of which find expression within her verse as a means of touching the heart of things. Pier Paolo Pasolini, in 1963, introduced some poems by Rosselli to the readers of the journal *Menabò*. He emphasized the importance of the linguistic and grammatical *lapsus* (error), not an involuntary infraction but a conscious creation. Language expands and becomes malleable in her poems. Nevertheless, the decidedly spare linguistic expression and the formal technicalities do not hide the human values of the works.

Her language expresses the anguish of a psyche that was shaken but not overcome, her strength being nourished by the concurrent presence in her mind of her three native languages – English, French, and Italian – aiding her communicative abilities. The daughter of an Italian father and an English mother, Rosselli was born in Paris in 1930 and spent her childhood in France, Switzerland, England, and the United States, finally settling in Italy. The future poet thus experienced different places and languages. The fact that she was not limited to a single linguistic identity contributed to complicating her already-difficult poetics. Moreover one must also take into consideration the fact that music plays a fundamental role in the poetry of Rosselli, because she is also a composer of musicals and film scores. In the brief essay "Spazi metrici" (Metrical Spaces), in the appendix of the collection of poems *Variazioni belliche* (War Variations, 1964), she expounds on her thoughts in this regard: "Una problematica della forma poetica è stata per me sempre connessa a quella sempre più strettamente musicale, e non ho mai in realtà scisso le due discipline, considerando la sillaba non solo come nesso ortografico ma anche come suono, e il periodo non solo come un costrutto grammaticale ma anche un sistema" (For me there has always been a connection between the problems involving poetic form and those specifically related to musical form, for I have never differentiated the two disciplines, considering the syllable not only as a written sign but also as sound, and the phrase not only as a grammatical construction but also as a system).

Verbal distortions, in which logical and traditional linguistic connections are undermined by unexpected associations, provide drama within the fabric of her writing, in which she expresses the truths of an existence tormented by the circumstances of her childhood. Amelia Rosselli is the daughter of the anti-Fascist martyr Carlo Rosselli

Quaderni della Fenice
65

Amelia Rosselli
Primi Scritti 1952-1963

Guanda

Cover for the 1980 book that collects some of Amelia Rosselli's early poetry and prose

and Marion Cave. Amelia's life was suddenly and profoundly marked by the killing of her father, who was brutally murdered (by order of Benito Mussolini and Galeazzo Ciano) at Bagnole-de-l'Orne, Normandy, along with his brother Nello, by members of Cagoule, a secret right-wing French organization funded by Italian Fascists. It was 1937, and Amelia was barely seven years old. In 1940, after the Nazi invasion of France, Amelia, her grandmother Amelia, the widows of Carlo and Nello, and their children began their long peregrination to various countries. They returned to Italy in 1946.

As Rosselli stated in her 1987 interview with Cetti Addamo, the memory of her socialist-activist father greatly influenced her intellectual development: "La sua morte ha creato in me uno scompenso affettivo proprio.... Per questo ho voluto interessarmi alla sua scrittura. Da giovane giravo per le piccole città toscane alla ricerca dei suoi libri, prevalentemente di contenuto tecnico-scientifico. Una piccola scoperta la feci quando, a distanza di anni, ripresi a leggere *Fuga in quattro tempi,* l'unico libro non volontariamente letterario di mio padre. Si trattava di un racconto sulla sua fuga da Lipari. Con enorme sorpresa, quasi con spavento, io vi ho ritrovato in parte la mia scrittura" (His death left in me an emotional void. . . . For this reason I became interested in his writing. As a child I used to wander through small Tuscan cities in search of his books, which were predominantly technical-scientific in nature. I made a small discovery when, years later, I reread *Fuga in quattro tempi* [Escape in Four Movements], the only of my father's books that turned out literary despite his intentions. It was the story of his escape from [exile in] Lipari. With great surprise, almost shock, I recognized in a way my own style of writing).

After a brief stay in Florence, Rosselli moved to England, where she began to study music, violin, piano, and composition. The following year, when she was eighteen years old, while she was at her grandmother's house in Florence, the news of her mother's death reached her. Left alone, she found a job as a translator at the publishing house of Comunità in Rome, and she moved there. Memories of those first few years in Rome emerged in her 1987 interview with Francesco Mannoni: "Qui continuai le letture sia filosofiche che quelle più tecniche e mi imbattei in Alberto Moravia, cugino di mio padre (vero nome di Moravia è Alberto Pincherle: suo padre era fratello di mia nonna Amelia Rosselli), il quale mi indirizzò ad altre letture di autori italiani benché allora studiassi composizione musicale" (Here I continued with my readings, the philosophical as well as the more technical, and I met Alberto Moravia, my father's cousin [Moravia's real name is Alberto Pincherle: his father was the brother of my grandmother Amelia Rosselli], who directed me toward other Italian authors although in reality I was then studying musical composition).

Of great importance was Rosselli's meeting in those years with the poet Rocco Scotellaro, a great interpreter of the passion and social vindications of the southern peasants; he played an important role in her writing. They met in 1950 at a meeting of former resistance partisans. The memory of that encounter and of the close friendship that bound them together for three years, until Scotellaro's death in 1953, was relived by her in an interview with Giacinto Spagnoletti, published at the end of Rosselli's *Antologia poetica* (1987): "Diventammo amici, ma proprio amici come fratello e sorella. . . .

Era un uomo assai maturo, e senza che me ne accorgessi, mi formava. Non esagero dicendo che era un essere eccezionale. Io avevo proprio in quel tempo cominciato a scrivere. E si parlava naturalmente anche di poesia. . . . E con lui c'era abbastanza spesso Carlo Levi, che era stato molto amico di mio padre" (We became friends, just like brother and sister. . . . He was a very mature man, and without my being aware of it, he molded me. I am not exaggerating when I say that he was an exceptional human being. I had begun to write at exactly that moment, and naturally we used to discuss poetry as well. . . . Carlo Levi, who had been a good friend of my father, was frequently in his company).

While Rosselli was working as a translator for Comunità, her interest in literature was growing. She was convinced that she should become a writer. Attracted more and more by poetry, she read works by Giuseppe Ungaretti, Cesare Pavese, Sandro Penna, and Eugenio Montale. Toward the end of the 1950s, poetry became the primary interest in her life; she felt assured that she had "forza e sistema metrico fra le mani" (strength and meter in hand).

In 1958 she wrote the poem "Libellula" (Dragonfly), collected in *Serie ospedaliera* (Hospital Series, 1969). The pursuit of a universal expression in which the most varied sounds harmonize is evident. Vowels and consonants are at the same time sounds and thoughts, which allow the reader to single out the characteristics of a diction that is both difficult and refined, indicating influences from the poetry of Dino Campana, as Rosselli herself has emphasized.

Variazioni belliche shows variations whose prosaic, narrative tendencies point to Franz Kafka as an implicit source of inspiration. But it is in the poems of *Serie ospedaliera* that Rosselli attains her greatest achievements. Although the products of years of pain resulting from a serious illness, these poems chronicle the rediscovery of a certain kind of hope that nature at times is able to grant. But she is not sentimental about such hope, as evidenced in these lines:

Di sera il cielo spazia, povera
cosa è dalla finestra il suo bigio
(ma era verde) ondulare. Oppure

colori che mai speravo riconquistare
abbaiavano tetri al davanzale.

(In the evening the sky expands, a poor
thing is its gray billowing
[but it was green] from the window. Or

colors I had never hoped to regain
were barking gloomy at the windowsill.)

Rosselli's third major collection of poetry, *Documento, 1966–1973,* published in 1976, bears witness in varying ways to her poetic vision and talent, as seen in this poem:

io non ho nella mia mano alcuna erba
medicamentosa, non ho alcuna speranza
di potere un giorno cangiarti a vista
mentre sperimentando con il mio corpo
tu ti accingi a visitarmi, insapiente
mentre neghi ogni altra ricetta alla
tua vanagloria di saperne di più degli
alberi, e più dei fiumi che scorrono
borbottando tra le vigne.

(I do not have in hand any medicinal
herbs, I have no hope
of being able to change you suddenly
one day while, experimenting with my body,
you are preparing to visit me, unknowing
while denying every other prescription
for your self-conceit in claiming to know
more than the trees, and more than the rivers
that flow murmuring amid the vineyards.)

After the completion of *Documento* Rosselli took a long hiatus from poetry. In 1980 she published a small volume, *Primi scritti* (Early Writings), which brings together works written between 1952 and 1963. There one can find many points of interest that not only contribute to a deeper understanding of Rosselli's preceding books but also of the growth of her innovative prosodic methods.

The long poem *Impromptu,* published in 1981, was born of Rosselli's personal desires and her study of Dante's sound patterns:

se
la misericordia era con me
quando vincevo, e invero

se la tarda notte non fosse
ora ora di mattino, io non
scriverei più codeste belle
note! – Davvero mi torturi?
e davvero mi insegni a non
torturare la mente in agonia

d'altri senza agonia, ma mancanti
al sole di tutti i splendidi

soldi che hai riconosciuto
nella Capitale del vizio

che era Roma?

(if
mercy was with me
when I was winning, and if

late night were not on
the brink of morning, I would
no longer write these beautiful
notes! – Are you really torturing me?
Are you really teaching me how
not to torture everyone else's

agonized mind without agony, those who lack
in the light of all the shining money

that you recognized
in the Capital of vice

that was Rome?)

Following the publication of *Impromptu* Rosselli was awarded the 1981 Pasolini Prize for poetry.

In *Appunti sparsi e persi* (Scattered and Lost Notes, 1983) the mysterious and mediumistic mood found in the preceding collections (and which seems to reach its climax in *Documento*) is lightened by a simpler style composed of more everyday elements. The result is a more gentle, tamed irony, inasmuch as it is the product of a different type of creative effort. In a brief, incisive preface, Rosselli narrates the story of her book and observes how public readings accustomed her to offering more accessible texts: "siccome l'autore corre dietro l'impossibile e non sempre il pubblico corre svelto, un po' di ovvio o di medio pensai non guastasse anche in pubblicazione" (since the writer pursues the impossible and the public is not always quick to catch on, I think that a bit of the obvious and familiar is not a bad thing in print). Her style occasionally becomes epigrammatic as she reexamines and modifies certain themes found in her previous books:

Non vi è luce
senza gloria, e non vi è inferno
senza diffamazione.

(There is no light
without glory, and there is no hell
without calumny.)

From this concept she gets such verses as the following:

I forchettoni della gloria. Enfaticamente
traduci in prosa il tuo viaggio all'inferno
addomesticato come si usa bene e infine anche
    valorizzato.

(The gluttons of glory. Emphatically
you translate into prose your trip to hell
domesticated as it should be and in the end even validated.)

Pier Vincenzo Mengaldo, in his *Poeti italiani del Novecento* (Italian Poets of the Twentieth Century, 1978), summarizes Rosselli's typical creative patterns: "Si potrebbe parlare di identificazione tendenzialmente assoluta della lingua poetica col registro del privato, del vissuto quotidiano personale: equazione realizzata per la prima volta e coi risultati finora poeticamente più efficaci, io credo, dalla Rosselli" (One could say that Rosselli's poetic language tends toward an almost absolute identification with her everyday speech, with her daily personal existence: a correspondence realized for the first time and achieved with the most poetically effective results to date, I believe, by Rosselli).

An existence wrought with hardships, a life of peregrination, a lack of national or regional identity, a talent for trilingualism, the study of music and philosophy, and the burden of a fatherless childhood are keys to understanding the poetry of Amelia Rosselli. This unspoken tension leads Rosselli toward a conscious, lucid, and rigorous study of language in order to develop it to the utmost possibilities. Hers is a poetry of psychic inquiry, where the writing transmits ambiguity, hallucinations, and an obsession with the subconscious. For these reasons Rosselli may be of interest to those in the fields of psychoanalysis, politics, women's studies, linguistics, and literature. A woman with many facets, she has always had to struggle in an unfriendly environment. Her poetry is a part of that struggle.

Interviews:

Francesco Mannoni, "Intervista ad Amelia Rosselli," *Giornale di Bergamo,* 3 December 1987;

Cetti Addamo, "La persecuzione del nome Rosselli," *Sicilia,* 21 December 1987;

Giacinto Spagnoletti, "Intervista ad Amelia Rosselli," in Rosselli's *Antologia poetica,* edited by Spagnoletti (Milan: Garzanti, 1987), pp. 149–163.

References:

Giovanni Giudici, Preface to Rosselli's *Impromptu* (Genoa: San Marco dei Giustiniani, 1981);

Marco Papa, "Gli *Appunti* di Amelia Rosselli," *Lettore di Provincia,* 16, nos. 61–62 (1985): 46–48;

Pier Paolo Pasolini, "Notizia," *Menabò,* 6 (1963): 66–69.

Roberto Roversi

(28 January 1923 –   )

Antonio Vitti
Wake Forest University

BOOKS: *Poesie* (Bologna: Landi, 1942);
Umano (Bologna: Landi, 1943);
Rime (Bologna: Landi, 1943);
Ai tempi di re Gioacchino (Bologna: Palmaverde, 1952);
Poesie per l'amatore di stampe (Caltanissetta: Sciascia, 1954);
Caccia all'uomo (Milan: Mondadori, 1959);
Dopo Campoformio (Milan: Feltrinelli, 1962; revised edition, Turin: Einaudi, 1965);
Cinque descrizioni in atto per la cartella di Guerreschi (Padua: Prandstraller, 1963);
Registrazione di eventi (Milan: Rizzoli, 1964);
Unterdenlinden (Milan: Rizzoli, 1965);
Le descrizioni in atto (Bologna: Privately printed, 1969);
Tempo viene chi sale e chi discende (Bologna: Incontri, 1975);
I diecimila cavalli (Rome: Riuniti, 1976);
L'Italia sepolta sotto la neve (Valverde: Girasole, 1989).

PLAY PRODUCTION: *Il crak* Milan, Piccolo Teatro, 1969.

RECORDINGS: *Il giorno aveva cinque teste,* by Roversi and Lucio Dalla, Milan, RCA, DPSL 10583, 1973;
Anidride solforosa, by Roversi and Dalla, Milan, RCA, 1975;
Il futuro dell'automobile, by Roversi and Dalla, Milan, RCA, 1976;
La canzone di Orlando, Milan, RCA, 1979.

OTHER: Giuseppe Addamo, *I segni topografici,* preface by Roversi (Padua: Rebellato, 1967);
Vittoria Bradshaw, ed. and trans., *From Pure Silence to Impure Dialogue,* includes poems by Roversi (New York: Las Américas, 1971), pp. 418-443;
Tonino Guerra, *I bù: Poesie romagnole,* translated by Roversi (Milan: Rizzoli, 1972);
Rolando Certa, *Lettera a Leonida Breznev: Roberto Roversi and Others Take Part in the Debate* (Mazara del Vallo: Impegno 70, 1976), pp. 51-54;
Pietro Aretino, *I ragionamenti,* preface by Roversi (Rome: Savelli, 1979);
Ruth Feldman and Brian Swann, eds. and trans., *Italian Poetry Today: Currents and Trends,* includes poems by Roversi (Saint Paul: New Rivers, 1979), pp. 185-188;
Lawrence R. Smith, ed. and trans., *The New Italian Poetry: 1945 to the Present. A Bilingual Anthology,* includes poems by Roversi (Berkeley: University of California Press, 1981), pp. 271-293;
Alberto Cadioli, ed., *Dialogo con Pasolini: Scritti, 1957-1984,* includes an essay by Roversi (Rome: Unità, 1985), pp. 207-290.

SELECTED PERIODICAL PUBLICATIONS – UNCOLLECTED: "Il margine bianco della città," *Officina,* 1 (May 1955): 9-16;
"Momenti," *Officina,* 2 (July 1955): 77-78;
"Il mulino," *Officina,* 3 (September 1955): 111-113;
"Digressione per 'I Gettoni,' " by Roversi and Francesco Leonetti, *Officina,* 4 (December 1955): 158-164;
"Il tedesco imperatore – Periferia," *Officina,* 6 (April 1956): 228-237;
"Periferia," *Officina,* 12 (April 1958): 498-503;
"Lo scrittore in questa società," *Officina,* new series 1 (March-April 1959): 16-19;
"Il linguaggio della destra," *Officina,* new series 2 (May-June 1959): 57-62;

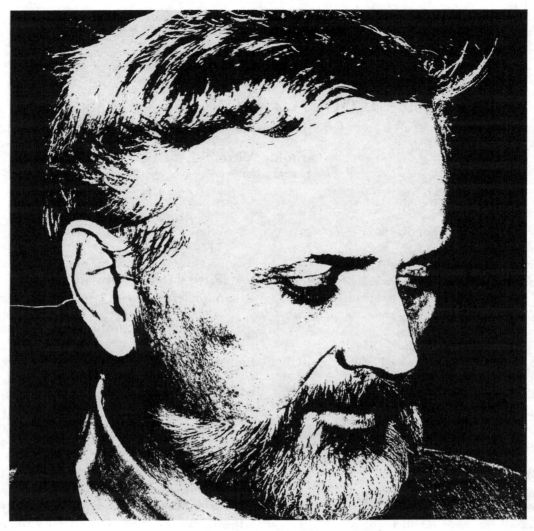

Roberto Roversi (photograph by Massimo Listri)

"Realtà e tradizione formale nella poesia del dopoguerra," *Nuova Corrente*, 16 (1959): 104–106;

"Risposta a 7 domande sulla poesia," *Nuovi Argomenti*, 55–56 (March–June 1962): 77–88;

"La settima zavorra," *Rendiconti*, 4–6 (November 1962): 5–17;

"Gli edipi grammaticali," *Rendiconti*, 8 (October 1963): 12–28;

"10 Domande su Neocapitalismo e Letteratura," *Nuovi Argomenti*, 67–68 (March–June 1964): 109–116;

"Piero Jahier," *Paragone*, no. 188 (October 1965): 103–107;

"La lucida organizzazione del presente," *Nuovi Argomenti*, new series (January–March 1966): 174–186;

"Una nota su Rebora," *Paragone*, no. 194 (April 1966): 90–93;

"Vittorio Sereni," *Paragone*, no. 204 (February 1967): 98–101;

"Il crak" [sketches for a play], *Sipario*, no. 275 (March 1969): 49–64;

"La macchina da guerra più formidabile," *Quaderni del Cut-Bari*, 9 (February 1971), 5–81;

"Esecuzione di un piano," *Quasi*, 1 (May–August 1971): 10–13;

"Il codice operativo autunno 1966," *Giovane Critica*, 31–32 (Fall 1972): 35–41;

"Scrivere o non scrivere i volantini" and "Un circo, e quattro gladiatori," *Rendiconti*, 26–27 (January 1974): 169–171; 172–176;

"Enzo Re," *Quaderni del Cut-Bari*, 20 (December 1978): 5–74.

Roberto Roversi's poetry is characterized by experimentalism – semantic research applied to the current usage of poetic language. However, in his later poetry he rejects the unrestricted technical experimentation of the neo-avant-garde and the neofuturists, searching instead for a new kind of poetic expression. *Le descrizioni in atto* (Descriptions in Progress, 1969) is the culmination of all his previous work. These poems are not easily read: they use the techniques of collage and of fragmentary reporting. With that collection Roversi can be acclaimed as the chronicler of the contradictions and tensions of modern historical events, described in a tone showing his anger against cultural and political degradation. Atypical of Italian intellectuals, though, Roversi considers himself neither a poet nor a professional writer but simply a lover of letters. Unlike most Italian writers, he avoids publicity and shuns the release of overt personal opinions on any public, political, or cultural event.

Roversi was born in Bologna on 28 January 1923 to a middle-class family. During World War II, after the Italian surrender in 1943, he was imprisoned by the Germans in a concentration camp from which he escaped to join the liberation movement in Piedmont. At the end of the war he went back to school and earned a degree in philosophy from the University of Bologna. Subsequently he worked for a while for a manufacturer before opening a bookstore specializing in antique and rare books. In 1955, in collaboration with some of the most notable young Italian writers of the time (Pier Paolo Pasolini, Francesco Leonetti, Gianni Scalia, Angelo Romano, and Franco Fortini), Roversi became cofounder and coeditor of *Officina,* a bimonthly magazine dealing mainly with Italian culture and poetry. This early editing experience led Roversi to the founding of Palmaverde Printing Company. As chief editor he allowed young, unknown writers and poets to publish their works, and then in 1961 he started a new bimonthly magazine of literature and science, *Rendiconti,* to replace the defunct *Officina.*

During the 1950s Roversi became directly involved with the debate surrounding the form and role of modern literature. His ideological position on the role of the intellectual in culture and history underwent a profound development. On one hand, *Officina* reexamined and condemned the hermetic poetic tradition and the sociopolitical role played by its supporters. On the other hand, it rejected the neorealistic approach, characterized by the schematic rigidity of populism, as a lasting alternative to

the past tradition. Roversi became aware that the problems being confronted were not only historical and cultural but related to language as well. From these basic formulations Roversi started his semantic, linguistic, and methodological research, using details from all periods of Italian history for his poetic experimentations. This choice was ideological and at the same time stylistic, because it allowed Roversi to use the richness of topical and historical events from both the present and the past for poetic imagery.

His first two collections of poems, *Poesie* (Poems, 1942), and *Rime* (Rhymes, 1943), show the strong influence of Petrarch and a vigorous moralism similar to that of Guido Cavalcanti. Although this classical tone disappears from his later work, Roversi always maintains a predilection for classical poise and romantic tension. Perhaps the most striking aspect of his early poems is Roversi's natural disposition to create tragicomic figures who are so forcefully imprinted in the reader's mind that they acquire a sculptural stature. A third collection of poems, *Poesie per l'amatore di stampe* (Poems for the Lover of Prints, 1954), which includes a section titled "Libretto d'appunti" (Small Notebook), presents the best of his early poetry. In "Libretto d'appunti" Roversi reveals a preference for everyday description narrated in simple language. His poems appear antirhetorical and antihermetic to the point of rendering the title "Libretto d'appunti" more suggestive and fitting for the entire collection. Like most of his later work, the poems are pessimistic, revealing a high sense of morality and strength of mind. The general tone of *Poesie per l'amatore di stampe,* written mainly between 1947 and 1948, is pervaded by an idyllic vision accompanied by a taste for descriptive and scenic images. The collection marks the beginning of a new phase in Roversi's development, culminating with the first edition of *Dopo Campoformio* (After Campoformio) in 1962. These later poems mark a definitive break from the solipsism of his early transitional period.

In the new style of *Dopo Campoformio* Roversi tries to accelerate the flow and rhythm of the verses by eliminating many articles and prepositions. The subject pronoun *I* is almost completely absent, along with diminutives and descriptive adjectives. The best examples of these changes are found in the different versions of the poem "Ritratto del vecchio Celso" (Portrait of Old Celso). The first poem of *Poesie per l'amatore di stampe,* it reappears in the 1962 edition of *Dopo Campoformio,* but it is omitted from the 1965 edition. The rewriting and reordering of Roversi's poems were influenced by his collaboration with the other editors of *Officina*. Roversi realized that he had to experiment with new modes of expression in order to redefine the concept of poetry in the changing historical situation of Italy. The underlying concept behind the terms *prose* and *poetry* had a different meaning in a society faced by industrialization and neocapitalism. The stylistic changes made in his continuous rewriting of many of the same poems and short stories show a dissatisfaction with the language of traditional literature. In 1959 he published his first novel, *Caccia all'uomo* (Manhunt), which combines a rewriting of his first collection of short stories, *Ai tempi di re Gioacchino* (At the Time of King Joachim, 1952), with a transformation into prose of some of his short poems originally written in 1952.

By 1960 Roversi felt that the great political hopes of the postwar period had been replaced by the hegemony of the Christian Democrats, who had put a stop to the cultural renovation of Italy. The new economic growth had positioned Italy in a new cultural phase. The neorealistic idea that literature could create a new culture had ended in the mid 1950s. Neocapitalism was affecting literature and language. For Roversi the dilemma faced by all the Italian intellectuals of the time became an intense search for a new and meaningful opposition to the system. As a reaction to this historical period Roversi formulated his own conception of patience, which he defined as a strategy to be used against the power and the supremacy of the political establishment. Patience allowed an astute search for truth. This notion should not be confused or associated with traditional submission or resignation and blind acceptance of events. Pasolinian desperation about the future of Western culture assumes a tone of pessimistic moralism and resistance in Roversi's work. His earlier direct political commitment has been replaced by a social one, as revealed in the tone of the forty-six poems of the group titled "La raccolta del fieno" (The Hay Harvest), in the revised (1965) edition of *Dopo Campoformio*. The cultural regression of the 1960s is viewed as another sign of the many compromises made by the Italian political class and as another missed opportunity for authentic changes. Roversi deplores the conformism of many intellectuals in a society ruled by a false sense of liberalism and neopositivism.

The second edition of *Dopo Campoformio* includes, for the most part, Roversi's best poems written up to 1962. Written in unrhymed free verse, the poems are full of images presented in a style rich with passion and tension. The themes are numerous and reflect the degradation of life under neocapitalism, memories from the Resistance, and the pusillanimity typical of the times. Campoformio becomes another Waterloo, or stands as a parallel to the failed risorgimento and the unkept promises of the liberation, all of which were dwarfed by their respective restorations. The former Jacobin confined in a small city of the Papal States can be compared to the postwar partisan forced to give up his hopes and dreams. The transformation and destruction of the peasant culture can be compared to the cultural degradation of Italy. In the poem "La bomba di Hiroshima" (The Hiroshima Bomb) Roversi switches the action from the remains of the devastated city in Japan to Italy:

> Nel Giappone una città nuova
> cresce adesso funebre violenta
> sopra uomini esanimi che al sole
> si scuoiano nei fossi.
> E qua è l'Italia, non intende, tace,
> si compiace di marmi, di pace
> avventurosa, di orazioni ufficiali,
> di preghiere che esorcizzano i mali. . . .
> Tutti i morti oramai dimenticati.
> Il ventre della speranza è schiacciato
> nella polvere da una spada antica;
> anni interminabili, senza amore,
> inchiodano col fuoco alla fatica.

> (In Japan a new city
> now grows funereal violent
> over lifeless men skinned
> in ditches in the sun.
> And here is Italy, it does not understand, it keeps
>   quiet,
> it delights in marble, in adventurous
> peace, in public orations,
> in prayers that exorcise the evils. . . .
> All the dead by now are forgotten.
> The womb of hope is crushed
> in the dust by an ancient sword;
> without love, endless years,
> nail labor with fire.)

The sense of reality and self-awareness in Italy is lost and replaced by rhetoric and empty phrases. All the poems of *Dopo Campoformio,* with the exception of the last, which is a montage, are placed in a specific historical context with which the reader is forced to reckon. The tone is imbued with pain even when it assumes a malicious irony. Roversi struggles with a dismal cultural situation in order to keep alive a dialectical debate in a time dominated by passive intellectual resignation and a lack of conclusive ideas.

It was clear to Roversi that the poet, in order to escape futility, had to find a way to place the literary event in a social context. In order to join poetry and prose for the purpose of psychological, linguistic, and sociological research, he needed to end the intellectual's traditional estrangement from the world. Roversi's search for the proper expression must not be associated or confused with the experiments of the new avant-garde. The poets of this group rejected the political ideology of the Resistance, favoring a language stripped of its sociopolitical connotations. The language became an autonomous system with no necessary references to or dependence on external social reality. Roversi's disagreement with the movement became more evident with the polemic aroused after the publication in 1964 of his second novel, *Registrazioni di eventi* (Postings of Events). Even though it is a novel, it contains many poems — a fact that exasperated the critics. The avant-garde accused him of being unable to write prose without lyricism and of resorting to outdated language even in his poetry. Roversi defended his position by reaffirming his cultural formation and rejecting the neo-avant-garde, neofuturism, and the nostalgia of the reemerging hermetic school. He believed in a complete restructuring by means of new ideas, not by a mere revival of a past mode of expression. Roversi further explored these ideas in a short play, *Il crak* (The Crack), first performed at Piccolo Teatro in Milan in 1969.

Perhaps his best collection of poems, *Le descrizioni in atto* was an underground publication never placed on the market. Roversi had it printed on a cyclostyle at his own cost, and three thousand copies were sent free of charge to interested readers upon request. *Le descrizioni in atto* is a collection of poems dating from 1963 to 1969 in which Roversi deals with the widespread neocapitalistic culture without resorting to his previous lyricism. The book comprises forty-six poems, but if one takes into consideration that thirteen of them consist only of a few lines, which could be read as prefaces to other poems, one is left with thirty-three descriptions of events. These descriptions are polemical attacks sparked by newspaper articles, headlines, letters, essays, and philosophical treatises. Theoretically the collection is the culmination and fusion of Roversi's main topics: anger and reason, which he had been

using and redeveloping since 1962. As in the majority of his poetry, the Resistance is seen as a landmark for a cultural change that did not take place. It is not remembered with nostalgic tenderness but as a past event that caused the deaths of many people without bringing about a revolution. The poetry is generated by the Roversian idea that modern society has a false sense of consciousness. Contemporary poetry must break with this blindness by assuming a role of furious protest against conformity. This form of political anger must be accompanied by reason, whose role is to point out passive complicity. Therefore, reason and anger are dialectically united in a poetry of action used to describe events. Since reason alone can never change the course of historical events, it will always further necessitate the role of anger, which becomes a catalyst for the annotation of recurring events.

In order to voice clearly his protest and denunciation, in the 1970s Roversi started a collaboration with the popular Italian singer and composer Lucio Dalla. In 1973 Roversi wrote ten poems for Dalla, which were recorded on an RCA album, *Il giorno aveva cinque teste* (The Day Had Five Heads). The same collaboration produced other recordings, including *Il futuro dell'automobile* (The Future of the Automobile, 1976). Roversi wanted to reach as many listeners as possible to put a stop to what he defined as ideological contamination, which he believed to be as harmful and deadly as aquatic and atmospheric pollution.

As a poet and writer Roversi has always maintained an open cultural debate with the establishment. He has always refuted the practice of publishers assigning awards and prizes to literary works. This characteristic distinguishes him in the chaotic literary world, giving him an air of moral integrity. Repeatedly he has reasserted his underlying desire to unmask cowardice and conformism.

Roberto Roversi's literary works of the 1950s and early 1960s are a significant testimony to the hopes felt and expressed by many Italian intellectuals after the liberation of Italy from the Nazi occupation. After the Christian Democrats' victory in 1948 his work reflects the pain and anger over the virtual disenfranchisement of many leftist intellectuals. His active participation in the journals *Officina* and *Rendiconti,* his involvement in polemics, and his obsession with the language as a means of poetic expression must be evaluated within the context of postwar discussions and as a continuation of the poetic experimentations before World War II. During the contradictory and confusing period of recent Italian literary and cultural issues, Roversi disagreed with the neofuturists, the neohermetics, the neorealists, and even with the Pasolinian definition that labeled him a neoexperimentalist. Roversi's poetry demonstrates a strong conviction that art is a reflection of how reality is perceived, rather than a mere retreat from the outside world.

Interviews:

Ferdinando Camon, *Il mestiere di scrittore* (Milan: Garzanti, 1973), pp. 162–180;

Gian Carlo Ferretti, in Roversi's *I diecimila cavalli* (Rome: Riuniti, 1976), pp. ix–xxi;

Silvia Batisti and Mariella Bettarini, *Chi è il Poeta?* (Milan: Gammalibri, 1980), pp. 62–63;

Stefano Mecatti, *La Poesia in mostra: Quarantacinque autoritratti a voce alta* (Florence: Lettere, 1982), pp. 153–160;

Tiziano Merlin, *La Piassa* (Verona: Bertani, 1984), pp. 9–18.

References:

Ferdinando Camon, *La moglie del tiranno* (Rome: Lerici, 1969), pp. 174–177;

Luciano Caruso and Martini Stelio, *Roberto Roversi* (Florence: Nuova Italia, 1978);

Gian Carlo Ferretti, *La letteratura del rifiuto* (Milan: Mursia, 1968), pp. 211–227;

Marco Forti, *Le proposte della poesia e altre proposte* (Milan: Mursia, 1971), pp. 403–409;

Franco Fortini, "Le poesie italiane di questi anni," *Menabò*, 2 (1960): 103–142;

Pietro Mainoldi, *Vocabolario del dialetto bolognese* (Bologna: Forni, 1967), pp. 8–9;

Giuliano Manacorda, *Vent'anni di pazienza* (Florence: Nuova Italia, 1972), pp. 407–411;

Eugenio Miccini, "Ideologia, avanguardia e altro in Leonetti e Roversi," *Nuova Corrente,* 34 (Fall 1964): 132–153;

Walter Pedullà, *La letteratura del benessere* (Rome: Bulzoni, 1973), pp. 481–485;

Elio Vittorini, "Notizia su Roberto Roversi," *Menabò*, 2 (1960): 100–102;

Giuseppe Zagarrio, *Febbre, furore e fiele* (Milan: Mursia, 1983), pp. 387–402.

Edoardo Sanguineti
(9 December 1930 –   )

John Picchione
York University

BOOKS: *Laborintus* (Varese: Magenta, 1956);
Erotopaegnia (Milan: Rusconi & Paolazzi, 1961);
Opus metricum (Milan: Rusconi & Paolazzi, 1961);
Interpretazioni di Malebolge (Florence: Olschki, 1961);
Tra liberty e crepuscolarismo (Milan: Mursia, 1961);
Tre studi danteschi (Florence: Le Monnier, 1961);
Alberto Moravia (Milan: Mursia, 1962);
K. e altre cose (Milan: All'Insegna del Pesce d'Oro, 1962);
Capriccio italiano (Milan: Feltrinelli, 1963);
Triperuno (Milan: Feltrinelli, 1964);
Ideologia e linguaggio (Milan: Feltrinelli, 1965; enlarged, 1970);
Guido Gozzano: Indagini e letture (Turin: Einaudi, 1966);
Il realismo di Dante (Florence: Sansoni, 1966);
Poeti e poetiche del primo Novecento (Turin: Giappichelli, 1966);
Il giuoco dell'oca (Milan: Feltrinelli, 1967);
T.A.T. (Verona: Sommaruga, 1968);
Teatro (Milan: Feltrinelli, 1969);
Orlando furioso (Rome: Bulzoni, 1970);
Il giuoco del Satyricon (Turin: Einaudi, 1970);
Storie naturali (Milan: Feltrinelli, 1971);
Wirrwarr (Milan: Feltrinelli, 1972);
Catamerone: 1951–1971 (Milan: Feltrinelli, 1974);
Giornalino (Turin: Einaudi, 1976);
Liguria (Florence: Alinari, 1978);
Postkarten: 1972–1977 (Milan: Feltrinelli, 1978);
Giornalino secondo (Turin: Einaudi, 1979);
Stracciafoglio (Milan: Feltrinelli, 1980);
Segnalibro: Poesie 1951–1981 (Milan: Feltrinelli, 1982);
Faust: Un travestimento (Genoa: Costa & Nolan, 1985);
La Valle d'Aosta (Florence: Alinari, 1985);
Scribilli (Milan: Feltrinelli, 1985);
Smorfie (Rome: Etrusculudens, 1986);
Novissimum testamentum (Lecce: Manni, 1986);
La missione del critico (Genoa: Marinetti, 1987);
Bisbidis (Milan: Feltrinelli, 1987);
Ghirigori (Genoa: Marinetti, 1988);

Commedia dell'Inferno (Genoa: Nolan, 1989);
Senzatitolo (Milan: Feltrinelli, 1992).

OTHER: *Il sonetto,* edited by Sanguineti and Giovanni Getto (Milan: Mursia, 1957);
Alfredo Giuliani, ed., *I Novissimi: Poesie per gli anni '60,* includes poems and essays by Sanguineti (Milan: Rusconi & Paolazzi, 1961; revised edition, Turin: Einaudi, 1965);
"Poetica e poesia di Gozzano," in *Novecento: I contemporanei,* volume 1, edited by Gianni Grana (Milan: Marzorati, 1963), pp. 897–913;
"Tommaso Landolfi," in *Novecento: I contemporanei,* volume 2, edited by Grana (Milan: Marzorati, 1963);
Giuliani and Nanni Balestrini, eds., *Gruppo '63: La nuova letteratura,* includes comments by Sanguineti (Milan: Feltrinelli, 1964);
Dante, *La vita nuova,* preface by Sanguineti (Milan: Lerici, 1965);
Sonetti della scuola siciliana, preface by Sanguineti (Turin: Einaudi, 1965);
Elio Vittorini, *Conversazione in Sicilia,* preface by Sanguineti (Turin: Einaudi, 1966);
Balestrini, ed., *Gruppo '63: Il romanzo sperimentale,* includes comments by Sanguineti (Milan: Feltrinelli, 1966);
Philippe Sollers, *Il parco,* preface by Sanguineti (Milan: Bompiani, 1967);
Carlo Vallini, *Un giorno e altre poesie,* preface by Sanguineti (Turin: Einaudi, 1967);
Roberto Di Marco, *Telemachia,* preface by Sanguineti (Turin: Einaudi, 1968);
Poesia italiana del Novecento, 2 volumes, edited by Sanguineti (Turin: Einaudi, 1970);
Ludovico Ariosto, *Orlando Furioso,* adapted and abridged by Sanguineti (Rome: Bulzoni, 1970);
Giovanni Pascoli, *Poemetti,* edited, with a preface, by Sanguineti (Turin: Einaudi, 1971);

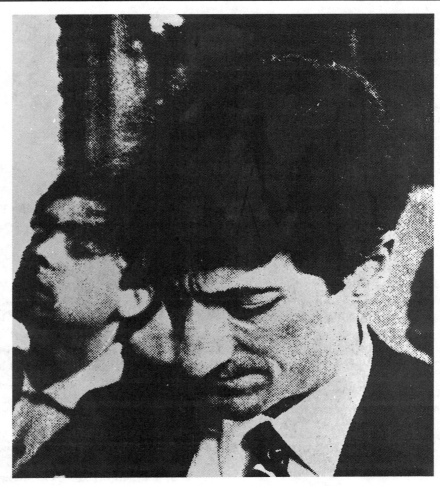

Edoardo Sanguineti circa 1987

L'opera di Pechino, edited by Sanguineti and Balestrini (Milan: Feltrinelli, 1971);

Vittoria Bradshaw, ed. and trans., *From Pure Silence to Impure Dialogue: A Survey of Post-War Italian Poetry, 1945–1965,* includes poems by Sanguineti (New York: Las Américas, 1971), pp. 722–752;

Guido Gozzano, *Poesie,* preface by Sanguineti (Turin: Einaudi, 1973);

Gian Pietro Lucini, *Revolverate e Nuove revolverate,* edited by Sanguineti (Turin: Einaudi, 1975);

Renato Barilli and Angelo Guglielmi, eds., *Gruppo '63: Critica e teoria,* includes essays by Sanguineti (Milan: Feltrinelli, 1976);

Ruth Feldman and Brian Swann, eds. and trans., *Italian Poetry Today: Currents and Trends,* includes poems by Sanguineti (Saint Paul: New Rivers, 1979), 198–202;

Lawrence R. Smith, ed. and trans., *The New Italian Poetry: 1945 to the Present. A Bilingual Anthology,* includes poems by Sanguineti (Berkeley: University of California Press, 1981), pp. 372–391;

Guido D. Guinizelli, *Poesie,* edited by Sanguineti (Milan: Mondadori, 1986).

TRANSLATIONS: James Joyce, *Poesie,* translated by Sanguineti, Alfredo Giuliani, Antonio Rossi, and R. J. Wilkcock (Milan: Mondadori, 1962);

Euripides, *Le baccanti,* translated by Sanguineti (Genoa: Teatro Stabile, 1968);

Seneca, *Fedra,* translated by Sanguineti (Turin: Einaudi, 1969);

Sophocles, *Edipo tiranno,* translated by Sanguineti (Bologna: Cappelli, 1980).

Edoardo Sanguineti is one of the most influential theorists and writers of the Italian neo-avant-garde. First as a member of the rebellious, anti-traditional group known as the *novissimi* (newest ones) and later as a leading figure of the iconoclastic "Gruppo '63," he has contributed profoundly to the innovation and deprovincialization of Italian literature. A precocious writer with a strong intellectual background in European art and aesthetics, Sanguineti, especially in his poetry, represents a decisive turning point for postwar Italian literature.

Edoardo Sanguineti was born in Genoa on 9 December 1930 to Giovanni and Giuseppina Cocchi Sanguineti; he spent his formative years in Turin, where, in 1956, he graduated from the local university. His thesis was on Dante. Remaining at the University of Turin, he began his teaching career as a lecturer in Italian literature, later (in 1968) moving to the University of Salerno, where he taught until 1974. He then returned to his native city to hold the chair in Italian literature at the University of Genoa. On 30 September 1954 he married Luciana Garabello; they have three sons and one daughter.

Sanguineti's intense intellectual activity has taken many directions: his long list of publications includes – in addition to his poetry and literary criticism – novels, plays, and translations. He also wrote the script for Luca Ronconi's successful 1970 theater adaptation of Ludovico Ariosto's *Orlando Furioso,* and Sanguineti has collaborated with the musicians Luciano Berio and Globokar Vinko in producing opera librettos. Concurrently he has engaged in a great deal of journalistic activity. His articles dealing with a wide range of subjects have appeared in newspapers, particularly the *Paese Sera* and *Giorno,* and in magazines such as the *Espresso.* In 1979 he was elected a member of the Italian parliament. Sanguineti has often claimed that his biography clearly emerges in his works and that the fundamental events of his life are his marriage and the birth of the couple's four children. He told biographer Gabriella Sica that "Il resto non è che psicologia" (The rest is nothing but psychology).

At the base of Sanguineti's theory of literature, which he particularly developed during the debates of the Gruppo '63 (1963–1967), lies the postulate that literature is in essence a metalinguistic production of ideologies. Convinced that a writer's form of language is his ideology, Sanguineti declares that "l'esperienza delle parole condiziona (precede) quella delle cose" (the experience of words forms [precedes] that of things). Transformation of reality (things) can occur solely through a transformation of ideology, which in turn can be transformed only through the demolition of conventional language. Literature in Sanguineti's poetics is not a simple epi-

phenomenon but an activity that has a practical function and is ultimately political action. Literature becomes a revolutionary act by contesting and destroying the ordered system of traditional language and by throwing into question the accepted vision of reality and opposing the dominant ideology. By experimenting with language in a critical fashion, neo-avant-garde literature – the literature of cruelty, as Sanguineti defines it – "non è al servizio della rivoluzione, ma *è* la rivoluzione sopra il terreno delle parole" (is not working for the revolution, but *is* the revolution at the level of words).

The verbal revolution, in its contraposition to the linguistic code, attendant ideologies, and dominant literary models, represents a negative aesthetics capable of providing a radical new perspective on the world in a struggle against the deceptive normality of contemporary reality. The new destructive form translates itself into a new content: the project of formal disorder denounces the false harmonies and reconciling modes of bourgeois writing, the function of which is to conceal alienation and social contradictions. Formal dissonance carries within itself a message of dialectical antithesis, the negation of the present system and the desire for a new one.

In his analysis of the relationship between the economic system and literature, Sanguineti comes to the conclusion that neocapitalism inevitably reduces all aesthetic works to commodities. According to his theory the revolt of the avant-garde artist follows three structurally interconnected stages. The "heroic" aspiration of escaping the market by producing uncontaminated works is followed by the "pathetic" moment in which art is absorbed by the market and reduced to an exchange value. Last is the "cynical" attitude: the artist with daring innovations outmaneuvers competing products by aiming for either immediate or future markets. Consequently Sanguineti concludes that any avant-garde product is eventually absorbed and neutralized by museums or libraries: market and museum are in essence two sides of the same coin. The only possible way out is to "ideologize" the avant-garde by exposing the contradictions of the mercantile heteronomy and by adopting a language of disorder capable of transforming itself into a dialectical antithesis to the prevailing bourgeois ideologies. Such a linguistic disorder, which manifests itself in Sanguineti's poetry as a pathological, schizophrenic language with a shattered and lacerated syntax, is not to be interpreted as a transcription of a personal nervous breakdown but as an objective representation of historical and social alienation relived from the inside, on the page. For Sanguineti such a strategy stems from the urgency to plunge into the "Palus putredinis," the historical, collective chaos of irrationality and alienation, with the hope of coming out of it "con le mani sporche, ma con il fango anche lasciato davvero alle spalle" (with dirty hands, but with the mud definitively left behind).

Sanguineti's first collection, *Laborintus* (Labyrinth, 1956), should be read within this context. Written between 1951 and 1954, when Sanguineti was in his twenties, *Laborintus* represents one of the most radical breaks from the tradition of hermetic and neorealistic literary models. *Laborintus* opened the road to the poetic experimentation of the 1960s and beyond. The title, taken from a thirteenth-century treatise on rhetoric written by Everardus Alemannus, suggests, through the symbol of the labyrinth, the difficulty if not the impossibility of escape, and a condition of psychological distress and labor. *Laborintus* portrays the descent into a historical hell, the swamp of capitalist alienation in which the conscience is lost in the falsity and contradictions of bourgeois ideologies.

Through this Dantean journey into the psychological and social chaos of contemporary reality, Sanguineti transcribes a delirious *naufragio mentale* (mental collapse) with the intent of resolving the *complicatio* into a liberating, therapeutic process. What makes *Laborintus* a modern epic of the alienated and neurotic state of mind is the fact that such a condition is represented by the form itself, an abnormal, quasi-aphasic use of language. *Laborintus* is constructed as a plurilinguistic text in which fragments of sentences, quotations from foreign languages (English, French, Greek, and Latin), neologisms, scientific terms, and scraps of banal conversations are assembled in an anarchic montage that indiscriminately combines the language of erudition with that of the colloquial:

> ma distratto da futilità ma immerso in qualche cosa
> and CREATURES gli amori OF THE MIND di spiacevole realmente
> très-intéressant mi è accaduto dans le pathétique un incidente
> che dans le comique mi autorizza très-agréable
> a soffrire!
> e qui convien ricordarsi che Aristotile
> sí c'è la tristezza mi dice c'è anche questo ma non questo
> soltanto, io ho capito and REPRESENTATIONS non si vale mai
> OF THE THINGS delle parole passioni o patetico per significar
> le perturbazioni and SEMINAL PRINCIPLES dell'animo . . .

> (but distracted by futilities but immersed in something
> and CREATURES loves OF THE MIND disagreeable indeed
> très intéressant an accident dans le pathétique happened to me
> which dans le comique authorizes me très-agréable to suffer!
> and here it's worth remembering that Aristotle
> yes there is sadness he tells me there is also this but not only this,
> I understand and REPRESENTATIONS he never benefits
> OF THE THINGS of the words passions or pathetic to signify
> the perturbations and SEMINAL PRINCIPLES of the soul . . .)[.]

It seems as if Sanguineti, with *Laborintus,* was attempting to uproot the lyrical tradition of Italian poetry by assimilating styles that were developing outside the field of literature. One of Sanguineti's goals was that of bridging the gap between the traditional, exhausted language of Italian poetry and innovative means of expression from other art forms. The atonality of *Laborintus* — together with the semantic dissonances, agitated rhythms, and the disappearance of hierarchical coordinations of discourse — is the poetic equivalent of the conflicting and disharmonizing elements present in dodecaphonic music or in abstract expressionism. To these influences the works of Ezra Pound and T. S. Eliot can be added. However, all these artistic models that converge in *Laborintus* are integrated by the phenomenological approach (the suspension of the "I") and by neo-Marxist aesthetics. Sanguineti has been particularly influenced by the theories of Theodor W. Adorno and Walter Benjamin.

The main recurrent themes of *Laborintus* are tied to the archetypal symbols of Jungian psychology: the process of individuation; the search for the totality of one's self; the unity of the private and collective; and the integration of conscious and unconscious. However, *Laborintus* represents the *bolgia* (hell) of historical contradictions with no hope of redemption or salvation. Through constant irony, parody, and demystification, Sanguineti is relentlessly set on demolishing any myth that aims at providing a resolution. The only possible strategy is to subvert the system by practicing "anarchia come complicazione radicale" (anarchy as radical complication), a reflection of a "coscienza eteroclita" (anomalous conscience) that has explored all the negativity of "permanente alienazione" (permanent alienation).

The transgressive language of *Laborintus* is retained in many ways in Sanguineti's second volume of verse, *Erotopaegnia* (Erotic Games, 1961), a collection of erotic poems. The apocalyptic vision, however, finds a liberating outlet in the verbal excitement of *Erotopaegnia*. The playful, comic, bizarre, and grotesque eroticism of love games is mirrored by linguistic, philological wordplay. Although, as in *Laborintus*, the linguistic playing cannot be detached from a tragic perception of reality, the corporality and sexuality of *Erotopaegnia* promote something of an orgiastic catharsis, the first indication of a possible constructive contact with reality. The predominantly oneiric narration has a rhetorical and ideological energy that indicates Sanguineti is beginning to move away from the collapse of all myths toward the proposal of a counter ideology as an alternative to bourgeois values and models. For instance, the dream images acquire the function of revealing a possible truth, a state of authenticity concealed behind an alienated bourgeois existence.

In fact "Purgatorio de l'Inferno" (Purgatory of Hell), comprising poems written between 1960 and 1963 and published together with the two previous volumes in the 1964 trilogy *Triperuno* (a title reminiscent of Teofilo Folengo's *Chaos del Triperuno*, 1527), presents on a linguistic level the recovery of a more linear discourse and on a thematic level a more articulated and rational criticism of dominant ideologies. This new perspective displays, if not the certainty of a social and political paradise, at least a hope, a utopian dream expressed from a recovering condition. As the poems addressed to his son Alessandro demonstrate, Sanguineti's shifting toward a poetry of content often takes on the form of a direct attack on the negative values of bourgeois society:

> piangi piangi, che ti compero una lunga spada blu di
> plastica, un frigorifero
> Bosch in miniatura, un salvadanaio di terra cotta, un
> quaderno
> con tredici righe, un'azione della Montecatini:
>   piangi piangi, che ti compero
> una piccola maschera antigas, un flacone di sciroppo
> ricostituente,
> un robot, un catechismo con illustrazioni a colori, una
> carta geografica
> con bandierine vittoriose . . .

> (cry cry, I will buy you a long blue plastic sword, a
> miniature
> Bosch refrigerator, a clay piggy bank, a notebook
> with thirteen lines, a Montecatini share:
>   cry cry, I will buy you
> a little gas mask, a bottle of revitalizing syrup,

> a robot, a catechism book with color illustrations, a
> map
> with victorious little flags . . .)[.]

From 1963 to the beginning of the 1970s Sanguineti focused his attention on writing critical and theoretical studies, such as *Ideologia e linguaggio* (1965), and prose narratives. Between 1963 and 1970 Sanguineti wrote and published three of the most important novels to come out of the Italian Neoavanguardia movement — *Capriccio italiano* (Italian Whimsy, 1963), *Il giuoco dell'oca* (The Game of the Goose, 1967), and *Il giuoco del Satyricon* (The Game of the Satyricon, 1970). In 1972 a new collection of his poetry was published: *Wirrwarr* (a German term meaning disorder). It is divided in two distinct, antithetical sections, "T.A.T." (published separately in 1968) and "Reisebilder" (Travel Pictures), and only the first part reflects the chaos alluded to by the title of the book. With "T.A.T.," which stands for "Testo di Appercezione Tematica" (Thematic Apperception Test), Sanguineti appears to abandon drastically the communicative project initiated with "Purgatorio de l'Inferno" and reverts to linguistic derangement, which in many aspects is even more drastic than that in *Laborintus*. In "T.A.T." the linguistic sign often undergoes the process of a total desemantization, effecting an irreconcilable split between signifier and signified. The dismemberment of normal language is carried out not only on a syntagmatic level but also within words, which are often shredded into phonemes or assembled on the page in a cluster of solitary fragments:

> e sopra: nel caso che LUI fosse (e: nel caso che LUI); e
> sotto: nel
> caso (e: nel; e: ne; e: n);
>   e: in tormento; (e per incutere
> terrore: (disgusto, forse); nelle ragazze, anche);
>   e il 24
> febbraio scrisse: je ne pense plus . . .

> (and over: in case HE were (and: in case HE); and
> under: in
> case (and: in; and: i; and: n);
>   and: in torment; (and to arouse
> terror: (disgust, perhaps); in the young ladies, also);
>   and the 24th of
> February he wrote: je ne pense plus . . .)[.]

This reduction of language, to a signification that constantly annihilates itself, not only represents the insurmountable division between word and reality but declares the impotence of poetry and of all literature to make sense of the intricate manifestations of history and conscience. Tragically nihilistic, "T.A.T.," with its aphasic gibberish, communicates the impossibility of communication and denies literature any redeeming function.

At the opposite pole is the second part of the volume, "Reisebilder," which, like Heinrich Heine's homonymous works, is structured as a medley of travel notes recounting a 1971 trip Sanguineti took to Belgium, Holland, and Germany. The most pronounced feature of this section is the recovery of a linguistic normality that repeatedly aims at approximating colloquial language. The poems reveal a narrative breadth absent in all his preceding poetry and the emergence of a subjectivism that seems to enwrap the "I" in a totally private dimension. These elements should not be interpreted as a simple return to bourgeois forms of poetry or as the fatal collapse of a political engagement resulting from disillusionment with post-1968 social realities. On the contrary, with "Reisebilder" the political dimension of literature is shifted toward the personal and private, with the intent to interpret them in Marxist terms. Marxism becomes, in Sanguineti's words, "un'antropologia generale: che spiega tutta la vita" (a general anthropology: which explains all of life).

This is not to say, however, that "Reisebilder" does not present a sense of disappointment or an existential and intellectual crisis. Closed within the bourgeois limits, life in its everyday manifestations cannot but exude, according to Sanguineti, "una mortale malattia morale" (a mortal moral malady), which degrades and deforms all experiences. These poems, reminiscent of the lowbrow, antilyrical language of the crepuscular poets and laced with the heavy doses of irony typical of the works of Guido Gozzano, a poet important to Sanguineti, offer disenchanted self-portraits. Nonetheless, these portraits do not represent so much a self-victimizing, defeatist attitude as a demystifying view of the poet's role in a capitalist society. Having dissolved the traditional aura that surrounded poetry, bourgeois society has also transformed the poet into a "dipendente salariato" (wage earner). In "Reisebilder," utopia gives way to the uneventful actions of everyday reality and, to such a perception of existence corresponds, as a necessary reflection, a similar use of poetic language. "Reisebilder," with its diaristic monologues, self-irony, and parodistic use of poetic language, marks another stage of Sanguineti's writing, a stage that continues and is expanded in other collections, such as *Postkarten* (Postcards, 1978) and *Stracciafoglio* (Torn Sheet, 1980).

Postkarten, as the German title suggests, is a series of notes written on postcards. The collection continues the trend set by "Reisebilder" in the use of a colloquial, domestic lexicon and in the epistolary, epigrammatic style centered on irony and parody. The dejected tone of "Reisebilder" is still present in *Postkarten*, enveloping more and more not only the poet but also poetry and literature as a whole: "vi lascio cinque parole, e addio: / non ho creduto in niente" (I leave you five words, and goodbye: / I never believed in anything). All possible styles are refused — "oggi il mio stile è non avere stile" (today my style is not to have a style) — and poetry sinks to such a level of domesticity as to be equated with a banal cooking recipe: "per preparare una poesia, si prende 'un piccolo fatto vero ... ' " (to prepare a poem, take "a small true fact ...").

With the exception of "Fuori Catalogo" ("Unclassified") which groups together a series of heterogeneous poems written between 1957 and 1979, including a diatribe against Pier Paolo Pasolini — "Una polemica in prosa" (A Polemic in Prose) — *Stracciafoglio* continues, together with political themes, the intimate diary of a poet who, in the guise of an antihero wandering among the ruins of ideological utopias, can offer only one heroic act: the courage of self-parody. Poetry becomes a medium of derision and self-derision, a language of destruction and self-destruction. Sanguineti is inevitably confronted with an unsurmountable paradox: as a bourgeois superstructure, poetry (and literature as a whole) must be sabotaged: but the task of sabotage is assigned to literature itself. Examined from this metalinguistic perspective, this stage of Sanguineti's poetry cannot be interpreted as a simple return to earlier traditions of Italian twentieth-century poetry (though many critics have indicated the resemblances not only to crepuscularism but also to the work of Giovanni Pascoli or Eugenio Montale); it is a renewed transgression of literary models.

In his collections of the 1980s Sanguineti pursues two opposite directions. At one extreme, poetry is presented as a medium stylistically impoverished, as an "emorragia di parole" (hemorrhage of words), which often seems to reflect a mental aphasia or the decaying and enfeebling process of the body. (The motifs of the body incarnated in the text and of the body as a text are recurrent.) This direction — summarized by a line from *Bisbidis* (Whispering, 1987), "sapere bene come scrivere male" (to know well how to write badly) — expresses Sanguineti's attack on literature and the urgency to demystify such a bourgeois institution. Literature must question itself and its ways of ordering the world; such is Sanguineti's parodoxical struggle. At the other extreme Sanguineti presents a linguistic vigor and a poetic erudition extraordinarily rich; these transform his writing into pleasure and eroticism. Poems such as "Alfabeto apocalittico" (Apocalyptic Alphabet), in *Bisbidis,* exploit linguistic nuances and, with capricious combinations, reveal the ideological urgency to free poetic discourse from any form of inhibition, thus showing poetry to be a manifestation of the libido. At the same time, such poems indicate that Sanguineti is a materialist poet in that he works with the materiality of language. He works with the conviction that tinkering with the signifiers can eventually effect changes in the signifieds.

Tragic and comic, grotesque and oneiric, parodistic and clownish, Sanguineti's pastiches are not evasive, formal exercises born of an ultrarefined literary culture. Literature is never conceived by Sanguineti as a metahistorical system; writing is always a mirror of an ideology and, as such, is the locus in which the poet carries out his social and intellectual struggles. Sanguineti's poetry, with its innovative and provocative language, constantly places the reader in a state of conflict, not only with literary models but with reality itself.

Interviews:

Ferdinando Camon, "Edoardo Sanguineti," in his *Il mestiere di poeta* (Milan: Lerici, 1965), pp. 215–242;

Adriana Casalegno, "Il pensiero nasce sulla bocca: Intervista con Edoardo Sanguineti," *Ponte,* 40 (May–June 1984): 94–105.

Biography:

Gabriella Sica, *Sanguineti* (Florence: Nuova Italia, 1974).

References:

Renato Barilli, "La normalità 'autre' di Sanguineti," in his *La barriera del naturalismo* (Milan: Mursia, 1964), pp. 290–308;

Filippo Bettini, "La scrittura materialistica di Sanguineti," *L'Ombra d'Argo,* 1–2 (1983), 107–117;

Maria Corti, "Neoavanguardia," in her *Il viaggio testuale: Le ideologie e le strutture semiotiche* (Turin: Einaudi, 1978), pp. 111–130;

Fausto Curi, "Il sogno, la crudeltà, il giuoco," in his *Metodo Storia Strutture* (Turin: Paravia, 1971), pp. 167–180;

Luciano De Maria, "Ricognizione sui testi," in *Avanguardia e Neo-avanguardia* (Milan: Sugar, 1966), pp. 137–163;

Umberto Eco, "The Death of the Gruppo '63," *Twentieth Century Studies,* 5 (1971): 60–71;

Alfredo Giuliani, Introduction to *I Novissimi: Poesie per gli anni '60,* edited by Giuliani (Turin: Einaudi, 1965), pp. 15–32;

Gianni Grana, "I ripercorsi storici della neo-avanguardia," in his *Le avanguardie letterarie,* volume 3 (Milan: Marzorati, 1986), pp. 744–892;

Niva Lorenzini, "L'effettuale ragione pratica della poesia nel *Catamerone* di Sanguineti," in her *Il laboratorio della poesia* (Rome: Bulzoni, 1978), pp. 17–44;

John Picchione, "Il ruolo del lettore di fronte all'aspro stil novo dei Novissimi," *Studi Novecenteschie,* 27 (1984): 103–117;

Jacqueline Risset, "Edoardo Sanguineti, ou: Ce lapsus qui nous habite," *Critique,* nos. 447–448 (1984): 617–627;

Walter Siti, "Purgatorio de l'Inferno," in his *Il realismo dell'avanguardia* (Turin: Einaudi, 1975), pp. 77–93;

Lucio Vetri, "Riduzione, dispersione, disseminazione dell'io," *Verri,* 20–21 (1971): 36–65.

Rocco Scotellaro

(19 April 1923 – 15 December 1953)

Giovanni Sinicropi
University of Connecticut

BOOKS: *E fatto giorno* (Milan: Mondadori, 1954; revised and enlarged by Franco Vitelli, 1982); translated by Paul Vangelisti as *The Sky with Its Mouth Wide Open* (Los Angeles: Red Hill, 1976);

Contadini del sud (Bari: Laterza, 1954); republished in *L'uva puttanella; Contadini del Sud* (Bari: Laterza, 1964);

L'uva puttanella (Bari: Laterza, 1955); republished in *L'uva puttanella; Contadini del Sud;*

La poesia di Scotellaro, edited by Franco Fortini (Rome & Matera: Basilicata, 1974);

Uno si distrae al bivio (Rome & Matera: Basilicata, 1974);

Margherite e rosolacci, edited by Vitelli (Milan: Mondadori, 1978);

Giovani soli, edited by Rosaria Toneatto (Rome & Matera: Basilicata, 1984);

Un poeta come Scotellaro (Rome: Cometa, 1984).

Edition in English: *The Dawn Is Always New,* translated by Ruth Feldman and Brian Swann (Princeton, N. J.: Princeton University Press, 1980).

OTHER: Vittoria Bradshaw, ed. and trans., *From Pure Silence to Impure Dialogue: A Survey of Post-War Italian Poetry 1945–1965,* includes poems by Scotellaro (New York: Las Américas, 1971), pp. 91–109;

Levi Robert Lind, ed., *Twentieth-Century Italian Poetry,* includes poems by Scotellaro (Indianapolis & New York: Bobbs-Merrill, 1974);

Lawrence R. Smith, ed. and trans., *The New Italian Poetry,* includes poems by Scotellaro (Berkeley: University of California Press, 1981), pp. 114–125.

Drawing of Rocco Scotellaro (from Omaggio a Scotellaro, *edited by Leonardo Mancino, 1974)*

Perhaps no other poet in twentieth-century Italy has aroused such passionate discussions of his works as Rocco Scotellaro, known as "the little mayor of Tricarico." Hailed by some as a Lucanian Claude-Joseph Rouget de Lisle – providing a new Marseillaise to the oppressed farmworkers of the Italian south – scorned by others as the last epigone of the *crepuscolari* (twilight poets); saluted as a new Francis of Assisi with class consciousness, or damned as a sentimental imitator of the *ermetici* (hermetic poets); and believing in the redemption of the masses through poetry and good intentions, Scotellaro became a legend when, compelled by harrowing circumstances, he began to practice his irresistible vocation for poetry with a sincere dedication to political action.

Scotellaro was born on 19 April 1923 into a poor family in the little town of Tricarico, in the Basilicata area of Lucania. His father was a shoemaker and tradesman, his mother the town midwife. Rocco's precocious talents induced his parents moderna senza peraltro raggiunge

Eccovi *Villa d'Este.*

Entra che ti sfiora
un fresco di vesti di edere
e un ventagliare di fronde.
Che incantano i viali
eccedano i fiori;
scivola l'uccello pei rami;
ondeggiano calme
le vette dei pini
e glicini scendono scendono
con lo scroscio de l'acque.
Da ovunque sui podi
dormono statue,
china la pietra del capo
su ruscelletti cascanti.
Vela il muschio sottile

Page from a fair copy of a poem by Scotellaro (from Omaggio a Scotellaro; *by permission of the Estate of Rocco Scotellaro)*

to sustain, through great sacrifices, his education, at first in a convent as a novice (for two and a half years), then in Matera, Potenza, Trento (where his married sister lived), and Bari; he rarely spent two consecutive years at the same school. He learned well and quickly, cultivating at the same time his secret passion for poetry and writing. Having completed his *liceo classico* (degree in classics), he went on to study law in Rome, working at the same time in Tivoli as a tutor in a private school. In 1942, when his father died from a thrombosis and while the war was still raging, he transferred from the University of Rome to that of Naples, living in Tricarico and going to the university only to take his exams. With the rapid worsening of the situation in Italy and, especially, in his own family, he had to abandon temporarily any hope of finishing his studies. Consequently he never earned his degree in law.

In the heated political climate following the end of the war, he became interested in politics, and by 1944 he was a militant member of the Socialist party, involving himself in feverish activity as a political and union organizer. An effective and galvanizing orator, when the first elections of the postwar period were held in Italy in 1946, he was elected mayor of Tricarico by the people whose needs and aspirations he knew well. He administered public affairs more with his heart and imagination than by political strategies.

Scotellaro brought to civic administration those virtues always hoped for and rarely found in public administrators: compassion, profound honesty, a genuine love of freedom, and an authentic sense of democracy. His activity was intense. He mobilized various sectors of the population, including the local bishop, and, a year after Scotellaro was elected, Tricarico had its first hospital. Under his administration the town soon had a new aqueduct, improved roads, and social services, including a program to fight illiteracy. At this time, all over Basilicata, farm laborers were being organized in cooperatives, and a bitter struggle for the occupation of uncultivated land was beginning.

Scotellaro identified with the aspirations of the farmworkers of the Basento Valley, and the workers identified with him, in whose poetry they heard the expression of their ancestral griefs and hopes. The epic quality found in Scotellaro's "social" poems stems from such identification. Whether his apprenticeship was carried on under the sign of the *ermetici* (including Salvatore Quasimodo, Alfonso Gatto, and, especially, Leonardo Sinisgalli) or under that of the neorealists (including Elio Vittorini, Cesare Pavese, and Carlo Levi) is, from this viewpoint, a relatively unimportant question that concerns his cultural formation, or, at most, the literary validity of his poetry measured in the cold reading of the page. The important fact is that, with Scotellaro, poetry came down once again among the masses and was once again conceived among the real suffering people who recognized it as their own voice and were moved by it.

The mayor and poet had earned the devoted loyalty of most of his people, but not of all. An accusation of embezzlement, which had been lurking around for some years, took definite shape in 1950: he was charged with trying to sell clothes distributed by the United Nations Relief and Rehabilitation Administration (UNRRA). He was jailed from 8 February to 25 March, awaiting trial. Scotellaro, acquitted of all charges, was saddened by the whole situation. He resigned from the local administration and left town.

By this time he had become widely known in Italy, both for his political action and for his poems, which, from 1947 on, were being published in several local and national periodicals, such as the *Strada, Basilicata, Botteghe Oscure, Comunità, Ponte, Fiera Letteraria,* and *Pattuglia.* He had also won some prizes, including the Premio dell'*Unità* (1947) and the Premio Roma (1950); in 1952 he won the Premio Monticchio. He met and corresponded with poets and writers, first of all Levi, who developed a profound, paternal affection for him.

Scotellaro never had a steady source of income; the office of mayor carried no stipend. What little money he had came from his family. For 1948 and 1949 he had received a fellowship from the Center for Social Studies and Researches of *Comunità* in Ivrea. In 1949 he had gone to Turin in an attempt to establish contacts with powerful intellectuals gravitating around the Einaudi publishing house; he was coldly ignored. Following the 1950 trial he was offered a research fellowship at the agricultural school in Portici (a suburb of Naples), directed by another of his supporters, Manlio Rossi-Doria, whom he knew through Levi. Scotellaro worked on a long research project: "Illiteracy in Basilicata." While in Portici he was commissioned by the Laterza publishing house to write a series of biographical "case studies" illustrating, in a direct way, the situation of farmworkers in the south. Scotellaro traveled through various regions looking for appropriate subjects. At the time of his death he had somewhat completed only four of these studies, which were later published in *Contadini del sud* (Farmworkers in the South, 1954). In the meantime he had started to work on an autobiographical novel, *L'uva puttanella* (Strumpet Grapes, 1955), in five or six parts, which was interrupted after part 4 due to his death.

Being away from his town did not help him politically. In 1952 he returned to Tricarico to run as a representative in the provincial election and was defeated. In the following year he was forced to resign as president of the hospital he had founded. He died in Portici on 15 December 1953 from an undiagnosed circulatory ailment from which, unaware, he had been suffering for years. With the exception of a few poems printed in periodicals during his lifetime, all his works were published posthumously. *E fatto giorno* (The Day Breaks, 1954; translated as *The Sky with Its Mouth Wide Open,* 1976) won the Pellegrino Prize and the prestigious Viareggio Prize.

Scotellaro's vocation for poetry started very early, probably in childhood. The first extant poem by him is dated 1940, when he was seventeen. Titled "Lucania," it includes this stanza:

M'accompagna lo zirlío dei grilli
e il suono del campano al collo

d'un'inquieta capretta.
Il vento mi fascia
di sottilissimi nastri d'argento
e là, nell'ombra delle nubi sperduto,
giace in frantumi un paesetto lucano.

(Along my path the crickets' screech
and the dinging of the bell on the neck
of a restless goat.
Wind binds me
in tenuous silvery ribbons,
a little Lucanian town lies in fragments
lost up there in the shadows of clouds.)

The poem is important because it shows the two basic constants in Scotellaro's poetic discourse: an incessant return to the land from which he had been dragged away too many times and an epiphany of details suspended in memory, which become charged with meaning, as in "Vespero" (Vespers), from *E fatto giorno:*

Verranno le campane dei conventi
a tuonare vicino al mio capo.
E sono leggere e mute
hanno i volti delle statue
le femmine ai lumi.

(The convent bells will come
thundering over my head.
And light and silent are
women with faces of
statues by the lamplights.)

Through these details suspended in memory, the myth of the land to which one must return and from which one must leave is shaped, and the sense of longing can be placated. In "Stazione" (Railroad Station) Scotellaro writes:

Ho cacciato lo sguardo
infino alla mia terra lontana
attraverso i binari.
Hanno suonato tardi
i campanelli dei muli alla fontana

(I threw a glance
as far as my faraway land
through the rail tracks.
Late have rung
the bells of mules at the fountain)[.]

The magic of memory offers the only way in which the time and things of childhood can still be salvaged.

Scotellaro's nostalgic poetry was nourished as an intimate, interiorized answer to circumstantial reality and developed alongside his political and social songs in which he expresses his presence in history. But Scotellaro brought to his interiorized poetry the same passionate voice of the downtrodden, just as he brought to his social songs the yearning for what was and what should never have been lost.

Bibliographies:

Franco Vitelli, *Bibliografia critica su Scotellaro* (Rome & Matera: Basilicata, 1977);

Pompeo Giannantonio, *Rocco Scotellaro* (Milan: Mursia, 1986), pp. 247–280.

Biography:

Anna Angrisani, *Rocco Scotellaro* (Naples: Napoletana, 1982).

References:

Anna Angrisani, *L'alba è nuova* (Casalvelino: Galzerano, 1980);

Ennio Bonea, A. Marrasco, and C. A. Augieri, *Trittico su Scotellaro* (Galatina: Congedo, 1985);

Giovanni Caserta, *La poesia di Rocco Scotellaro* (Matera: BMG, 1966);

Michele Dell'Aquila, *Giannone, De Sanctis, Scotellaro* (Naples: Napoletana, 1981);

Franco Fortini, Introduction to *La poesia di Scotellaro,* edited by Fortini (Rome & Matera: Basilicata, 1974);

Pompeo Giannantonio, *Rocco Scotellaro* (Milan: Mursia, 1986);

Pino Iorio, *Limiti e lezioni di Scotellaro* (Naples: Hyria, 1980);

Leonardo Mancino, ed., *Omaggio a Scotellaro* (Manduria: Lacaita, 1974);

Riccardo Monaco, *Rocco Scotellaro* (Abano Terme: Piovan, 1981);

Rosalma Salina Borello, *A giorno fatto: Linguaggio e ideologia in Rocco Scotellaro* (Matera: Basilicata, 1977).

Vittorio Sereni

(27 July 1913 – 10 February 1983)

Laura Baffoni-Licata
Tufts University

BOOKS: *Frontiera* (Milan: Corrente, 1941);

Poesie (Florence: Vallecchi, 1942);

Diario d'Algeria (Florence: Vallecchi, 1947);

Una polvere d'anni di Milano (Milan: Maestri, 1954);

Non sanno d'essere morti (San Rafael: Brigadas Liricas, 1955);

Frammenti di una sconfitta: Diario bolognese (Milan: Scheiwiller, 1957);

Gli immediati dintorni (Milan: Saggiatore, 1962; enlarged, 1983);

Appuntamento a ora insolita (Milan: Allegretti di Campi, 1964);

L'opzione (Milan: Scheiwiller, 1964);

Gli strumenti umani (Turin: Einaudi, 1965);

Dodici poesie (Verona: Sommaruga, 1966);

Lavori in corso (Luxembourg: "Origine," 1969);

La guerra girata altrove (Verona: Dominicae, 1970);

Ventisei (Rome: Aldina, 1970);

Addio Lugano bella (Florence: Upupa, 1971);

Da tanto mare (Milan: Galleria l'Incontro, 1971);

Sei poesie e sei disegni, by Sereni and Franco Francese (Milan: Trentadue, 1972);

Poesie scelte (1935–1965), edited by Lanfranco Caretti (Milan: Mondadori, 1973);

Letture preliminari (Padua: Liviana, 1973);

Toronto sabato sera (Milan: Galleria Rizzardi, 1973);

Un posto di vacanza (Milan: All'Insegna del Pesce d'Oro, 1973);

A Venezia con Biasion (Urbino: Ca' Spinello, 1975);

Franco Francese: La bestia addosso (Milan: Scheiwiller, 1976);

Tre poesie per Niccolò Gallo (Florence: Galleria Pananti, 1977);

Nell'estate padana (Milan: Spirale, 1978);

Rapsodia breve (Brescia: Farfengo, 1979);

Il sabato tedesco (Milan: Saggiatore, 1980);

Stella variabile (Milan: Garzanti, 1981);

Senza l'onore delle armi (Milan: All'Insegna del Pesce d'Oro, 1986);

Tutte le poesie (Milan: Mondadori, 1986);

Il grande amico: Poesie 1935–1981 (Milan: Rizzoli, 1990).

Editions in English: *Sixteen Poems of Vittorio Sereni,* translated by Paul Vangelisti (Fairfax, Cal.: Red Hill, 1971);

The Disease of the Elm and Other Poems, translated by Marcus Perryman and Peter Robinson (London: Many, 1983).

OTHER: Sergio Solmi, *Levania e altre poesie,* introduction by Sereni (Milan: Mantovani, 1956), pp. 7–25;

Claudio Sartori, ed., *Giacomo Puccini,* includes an essay by Sereni (Milan: Ricordi, 1959), pp. 27–32;

Giacinto Spagnoletti, *Poesia italiana contemporanea 1909–1959,* includes a statement and poems by Sereni (Parma: Guanda, 1964), pp. 575–592;

Luciano Anceschi, ed., *Lirici nuovi,* includes the essay "Posizione verso Montale" and poems by Sereni (Milan: Mursia, 1964), pp. 491–508;

"La cattura," in *Racconti italiani* (Milan: Reader's Digest, 1967);

Tommaso di Salvo and Giuseppe Zagarrio, eds., *Lombardia,* introduction by Sereni (Florence: Nuova Italia, 1970);

Vittoria Bradshaw, trans. and ed., *From Pure Silence to Impure Dialogue,* includes poems by Sereni (New York: Las Américas, 1971), pp. 16–21;

Giorgio Seferis, *Poesia prosa,* translated by F. M. Pontani, introduction by Sereni (Milan: Club Degli, 1971), pp. 58–75;

"A Vacation Place," translated by Ruth Feldman and Brian Swann, *New Direction,* 27 (1973): 61–71;

La traversata di Milano, in *Poesia Uno* (Milan: Guanda, 1980).

TRANSLATIONS: Julien Green, *Leviatan* (Milan: Mondadori, 1947);

Paul Valéry, *Eupalinos; L'anima e la danza; Dialogo dell'albero* (Milan: Mondadori, 1947);

Vittorio Sereni circa 1965

William Carlos Williams, *Poesie* (Milan: Triangolo, 1957);

René Char, *Fogli d'Ipnos* (Turin: Einaudi, 1968);

Char, *Ritorno sopramonte* (Milan: Mondadori, 1974);

Guillaume Apollinaire, "Otto poesie," *Almanacco dello Specchio,* 8 (1979);

Pierre Corneille, *L'illusione teatrale* (Milan: Guanda, 1979);

Apollinaire, *Eravamo da poco intanto nati* (Milan: Scheiwiller, 1980);

Il musicante di Saint-Merry (Turin: Einaudi, 1981).

SELECTED PERIODICAL PUBLICATIONS –
UNCOLLECTED: "Una proposta di lettura," *Aut-Aut,* 61–62 (January–March 1961): 110–118;

"A proposito di letteratura e industria," *Nuova Corrente,* 25 (January–March 1962): 8–10;

"25 aprile a Casablanca," *Unità* (11 April 1965);

"Ognuno conosce i suoi," *Letteratura,* 79–81 (1966): 306–307;

"Giorgio Seferis," *Verri,* 38 (1971–1972): 6–21.

Emerging in the 1930s from the then-prevalent hermetic school, Vittorio Sereni soon abandoned its solipsistic tendencies for a more personal and realistic approach to writing poetry. As he told interviewer Leone Piccioni: "Non si può fare a meno di tenere conto di un certo grado di dipendenza, inevitabile per la mia generazione, dai cosidetti maestri del nostro inquieto tirocinio, nell'ambito di quella fase che fu detta ermetismo e dalla quale anch'io provengo" (One cannot help taking into account a certain degree of dependence, inevitable for my generation, from the so-called masters of our restless apprenticeship, within that phase that was called hermeticism where I too come from). Several examples of such *dipendenza* can be found in Sereni's early verse, from the frequent, allusive, and vague use of adjectives to the extenuated rhythm, rich with enjambments. Pursuing the orientation of the *Linea lombarda* (Lombard Line), the literary-geographic grouping introduced by Carlo Bo, Sereni found himself leaning toward the concept of a poetry "in re" – as Luciano Anceschi defines it – a poetry that "can be touched." Consequently Sereni dismissed the solipsistic orientations of his Florentine contemporaries who, while searching for the "absolute" and essential word, rejected most contacts with reality. Sereni maintained neither the metaphysical conceits of the Florentine hermetics nor their aristocratic extremism, and the reason for his stance was principally his Lombardian origin and upbringing, which favored the idea of literature accepting life in its totality.

Sereni was born in the town of Luino, near Varese, Lombardy, on 27 July 1913. His mother, Maria Colombi Sereni, was Lombardian; his father, Enrico, a customs officer, was from the south. Sereni's youthful years spent in Luino had a significant importance in the development of his poetic sensibility: many of the sites on the shores of Lago Maggiore reappeared in his early verse, though transformed and enriched. In 1933 he settled in Milan, where he studied Italian literature at the local university. After graduating in 1936, with a thesis on Guido Gozzano, he devoted himself to a high-school teaching career. In Milan he also became actively involved in the philosophical and literary trends of the times, collaborating on several journals, such as *Corrente, Campo di Marte*, and *Letteratura*. In 1937 he published two poems, his first poetic attempts, in the Florentine journal *Frontespizio*, in an issue edited by Carlo Betocchi. In those early years Sereni established long-lasting friendships with Anceschi, Alfonso Gatto, and Salvatore Quasimodo, to name a few.

During World War II Sereni fought as an infantry officer in Greece and in Sicily, where, at Trapani, he was taken prisoner and eventually held in an Algerian prison camp. After the liberation Sereni returned to Milan, where he briefly resumed his teaching career, leaving it later for the world of industry; he became chief news director and press officer at the Pirelli tire factory and then literary editor in chief at the Mondadori publishing house. The latter job was closer to his own interests and allowed him to establish meaningful contacts with well-known figures in the cultural world. Sereni also worked as a newspaper editor for the *Rassegna d'Italia*, and from 1950 to 1951 he was the literary critic for *Milano-Sera*.

Sereni received several literary prizes: in 1956 he won the Libera Stampa Prize; in 1965 the Montefeltro Prize was conferred upon him in Urbino; and in 1972 he received the Feltrinelli "Accademia dei Lincei" Prize for poetry. For his collection of translations *Il musicante di Saint-Merry* (The Musicians of Saint Merry, 1981) he won the Bagutta Prize, and also in 1981 he received the Viareggio Prize for poetry for his volume *Stella variabile* (Variable Star, 1981). Although he retired in the mid 1970s from active employment at Mondadori, Sereni continued to work untiringly in many areas of interest on the Italian cultural scene until his death on 10 February 1983. His body was buried in the family tomb in Luino.

The development of Sereni's poetic discourse can be traced through his four major collections: *Frontiera* (Frontier, 1941); *Diario d'Algeria* (Algerian Diary, 1947); *Gli strumenti umani* (Human Instruments, 1965); and *Stella variabile*. The poems in *Frontiera*, set on the idyllic Lombardian lakeside, reveal his youthful hesitations and anxieties. One notices Sereni's ability to transform concrete places into idealized symbols. Time becomes a mythical present, according to editor and critic Lanfranco Caretti: "i suoi luoghi deputati sono certe strade e sobborghi di Milano, Luino, Creva e soprattutto la vagheggiata Europa, al di là della frontiera" (its appointed places are certain roads and suburbs of Milan, Luino, Creva and above all the cherished Europe, beyond the frontier). The "sentimento della frontiera" (sentiment of the frontier) was defined by Sereni in his interview with Ferdinando Camon: "prendeva significato proprio tra la chiusura antidillica della vita italiana di quegli anni e la tensione verso quello che stava al di là, verso un mondo più grande . . . " (it actually acquired meaning as a result of the antidyllic diminution of the Italian lifestyle in those years and the tension toward what was beyond, toward a bigger world . . .). That "mondo più grande" was Europe, idealized by Sereni as a "terra promessa" (promised land), which he intended to set against the rude and noisy myths of the Fascists.

Gozzano and Eugenio Montale are the poets who, to a great degree, influenced Sereni's work. To Gozzano, Sereni dedicated his doctoral dissertation; to Montale, one of his first articles. Both writers are very important in understanding the genesis of Sereni's poetry. From Montale he derived the idea of a poetry yielding to objects, to the physical world as a normal basis for poetry, and he also derived a deeply felt attitude that he was a "minor" poet without ambitions to create eternal poetry. The themes of irony and melancholy, typical of Gozzano and the *crepuscolari* (twilight poets), were adopted by Sereni not only because they were consistent with his own perplexed nature but also as measures to eliminate the "d'annunzianesimo" (imitation of Gabriele D'Annunzio's style and mannerisms) that plagued Italian society between the two world wars. After D'Annunzio fell from literary grace, much of his negative influence still afflicted the social and cultural life of the country during the apprenticeship years of Sereni. Consequently a tone of nonviolence emerges in Sereni's early poetry along with what is considered his most recurrent theme: the negative myths – the presence of death seen as disintegration and a sign of absolute nothingness, as the poem "Strada di Zenna" (Road to Zenna) illustrates:

Ma ora
nell'estate impaziente
s'allontana la morte.
...con labile passo
c'incamminiamo su cinerei prati
per strade che rasentano l'Eliso....
Vedi sulla spiaggia abbandonata
turbinare la rena,
ci travolge la cenere dei giorni....
Voi morti non ci date mai quiete...

(But now
in the impatient summer
death swerves away.
...with unsteady pace
we are walking on ash-colored meadows
through roads that border upon Elysium....
On the abandoned shore
you see the sand twirl,
we are swept away by the ashes of the days....
You dead never leave us in peace...)[.]

The presence of death is undoubtedly there, as well as a sense of inevitable existential defeat; untiringly, however, the speaker searches for glimmers of hope through which to attempt the impossible escape. Sereni writes in "Inverno a Luino" (Winter in Luino), "Fuggirò quando il vento / investirà le tue rive" (I will flee when the wind / invests your shores); in "Strada di Zenna" (Zenna Road), "Ci desteremo sul lago a un'infinita / navigazione" (We will awaken on the lake to a boundless / sailing); and in "Soldati a Urbino" (Soldiers in Urbino), "poi parli di una stella / che ancora un giorno / sulla tua strada forse spunterà" (then you speak of a star / that still one day / on your path will perhaps rise). The instrument of escape, in these cases, is the verb in the future tense, through which he projects a

hopeful alternative to the reality of death, disintegration, and uncertainty.

The psychological state of perennial suspension, inherent in Sereni's nature, is amply illustrated in his early verse by the persuasive frequency of adjectives such as "stupito" (amazed) and "irrequieto" (restless), which emphasize a recurrent leitmotiv of uncertainty. With this mood of perplexity Sereni's verse conforms to a primary condition of Italian poetry in the 1940s. One of the poems in *Frontiera* that illustrates this point is "Terrazza" (Terrace), with its expansion of a particular event into "un mito che tende all'infinito" (a myth that tends to the infinite), and its atmosphere, dense with ambiguous meanings validated even more by the warning signs of imminent drama:

Siamo tutti sospesi
a un tacito evento questa sera
entro quel raggio di torpediniera
che ci scruta poi gira se ne va.

(We are all suspended
from a silent event this evening
within that ray of a torpedo boat
that probes us then turns and leaves.)

Sereni recounts, in *Diario d'Algeria,* the reality of war, destruction, and defeat. The first part of the book portrays a flight from the frail myths centered in the Lombardian countryside; an idea of coerced motion seems to be the recurrent theme. The second part reflects his experience of imprisonment in North Africa (from 1943 to 1945); it is characterized by a sense of inactivity, forced rest, and anxiety. In these poems readers find a dramatic fracture, "due epoche morte dentro di noi" (two epochs dead within us), causing "un improvviso vuoto del cuore" (a sudden void in the heart). Indeed in the sands of the Algerian desert Sereni's poetry acquired the vitality and strength that allowed it to stand as an autonomous, ideological structure, able to denounce the insanity of war and the downfall of ideals and to place him in a position of constructive criticism within history.

With constant and persuasive recurrence two of the most meaningful aspects of Sereni's poetry emerge in *Diario d'Algeria:* the theme of isolation and the dialectics of estrangement and involvement. The events of World War II kept him in a state of forced "absence," but an underlying involvement with the common drama of humankind can be felt in almost every poem of the collection. The theme of isolation finds its symbolic representation in the condition of the prisoner: the world falls apart all around; the soldier suffers the abasement of the conquered; and some presences are ghosts who mysteriously touch a neighbor's shoulder or emerge, for an instant, against faraway hills and then vanish. The only music is the one of tents banging against the poles; the only truth is the one of concrete sight:

> Ora ogni fronda è muta
> compatto il guscio d'oblio
> perfetto il cerchio.

> (Now every branch is silent
> compact the shell of oblivion
> perfect the circle.)

The speaker seems to have reached the "zero" hour: an absolute stasis reigns; the spirit is mute, apathetic, indifferent, and completely immersed inside a "compatto guscio d'oblio." The world and the poetic persona are annulled. The circle of isolation, absenteeism, and estrangement has closed around the speaker, immersing him in a compact and atonic atmosphere of oblivion. The circle offers no opening or escape. In the circle metaphor probably the most meaningful aspect of Sereni's poetic discourse, as he himself acknowledged, can be found: the sense of uncertainty, perplexity, and absenteeism leads to the consciousness of an irretrievably missed participation in human existence. The experiences in *Diario d'Algeria* therefore emerge at the epicenter of an existential dialectic, and the book describes, according to critic and poet Franco Fortini, "l'incontro fra una predestinazione psicologica ed una realizzazione storica" (the encounter between a psychological predestination and a historical realization).

The poems in *Gli strumenti umani* address the difficult postwar period from 1945 to 1965. Sereni comments on his encounters with a changed society, which he yearns to understand fully and responsibly, and also comments on the realization of his inability, in his role as a poet, to change things. Those who count, the writer says, are those who fight, suffer, and die for an idea — the heroes of the resistance and, in the 1960s, the workers in the factories, as he points out in the poem "Una visita in fabbrica" (A Visit to the Factory):

> Dove piú dice i suoi anni la fabbrica,
> di vite trascorse qui la brezza
> è loquace per te?
>   Quello che precipitò
> nel pozzo d'infortunio e di oblio:
> quella che tra scali e depositi in sé e
> accolse crebbe il germe d'amore

> e tra scali e depositi lo sperse:
> l'altro che prematuro dileguò
> nel fuoco dell'oppressore.
> Lavorarono qui, qui penarono.
> (E oggi il tuo pianto sulla fossa comune).

> (Where the factory speaks more of its years,
> of lives spent here is the breeze
> talkative for you?
>   The man who plunged
> into the well of misfortune and oblivion:
> the woman who among wharves and warehouses received into herself
> and in herself grew the seed of love
> and among wharves and warehouses scattered it:
> the other who prematurely disappeared
> into the fire of the oppressor.
> They worked here, here they suffered.
> [And today your mourning on their common grave].)

The poet, capable only of offering words, is left with no other choice but to denounce the inadequacy of his art — its creative, communicative, and cathartic function, as the poem "I versi" (The Verses) illustrates: "non c'è mai / alcun verso che basti / se domani tu stesso te ne scordi" (no poem / is ever enough / if tomorrow you yourself forget it).

From a social and historical standpoint Sereni stresses the inability of poetry to express the feeling of estrangement, contempt, and basic dislike for his own time. Finally, from an existential perspective, the poem expresses the inability of poetry to fulfill its cathartic function of deliverance from life's burdens. This denunciation of the inadequacy of poetry is especially manifested in the last poems of *Gli strumenti umani*. Through the persistent use of the iterative process, the poetic word seems to empty itself of its thematic content while openly denouncing its own inadequacy to communicate. However, having reached this point that could be defined as "zero," the poetic persona gradually regains new strength: psychological, gnomic, and aesthetic. Through the iterative form Sereni, while recognizing the failure of his act, struggles for a more authentic use of the word; it is a search for a communicative means that somehow connects him to others. Moreover he is able to acquire some certainties, usually lacking in his natural predisposition to perplexity, on which to base his cognitive processes, directed not as much toward an external reality as toward his inner world.

Stella variabile presents variations on basic themes in Sereni's poetic discourse. Prevailing is the theme of death. Words such as *vuoto* (emptiness), *notte* (night), and *silenzio* (silence) confirm the daily meditation on death and are accompanied by perturbed visions of threatened reality: small swastikas in New York, old Indian motifs, and so on. Alongside these signs of disorientation and premonition – in an oscillatory movement of light and darkness – inventive outbursts emerge, revealing proof of the vitalistic energy and great transfiguring power of Sereni's poetry. Sereni's poetic inspiration in the book is an existential metaphor founded on contrasts: the perspective of an enlightening and enlightened life that borders – through a myriad of intermediary phases – on its contrary, darkness, the nonexistent, and death. Consequently Sereni does not describe the "being" but describes the "becoming" of the infinite *io* (self) – adapting his poems to particular moments. The sea, a presence that frequently emerges in this last collection, becomes "una metafora della vita cangiante" (a metaphor of ever-changing life), as in "Un posto di vacanza" (translated in 1973 as "A Vacation Place"): "il mare incanutito in un'ora / ritrova in un'ora la sua gioventù" (the sea turned white in an hour / recovers in an hour its youth). Frightened and perplexed, the speaker realizes that only with the guidance of a "variable star" – that is, poetry – can he cross the fluctuating and unsettled sea of existence.

Of the five sections of *Stella variabile,* the third, which includes only three poems – "Un posto di vacanza," "Niccolò," and "Fissità" (Stillness) – is the most compact and plays a central role. Some of the most significant themes in Sereni's poetry are there, such as the theme of friendship tied to that of a colloquium with the dead. Another theme is the persistent memory of the war. Finally – begun in *Gli immediati dintorni* (The Immediate Vicinities, 1962), his diary in prose, which runs parallel, often as an explanatory text, to his poetry, and carried on in *Gli strumenti umani* – are his reflections on poetry, in "Fissità," one of the most intense poems of the collection:

Quell'uomo.
Rammenda reti, ritinteggia uno scafo.
Cose che io non so fare. Nominarle appena.
Da me a lui nient'altro: una fissità.
Ogni eccedenza andata altrove. O spenta.

(That man.
He mends nets, he repaints a hull.
Things I cannot do. I can hardly name them.
From me to him nothing else: a stillness.
Any excess gone elsewhere. Or extinguished.)

In this poem, writing poetry is regarded as an act of existence, comparable to mending nets. The poet's task is to name things, and naming them is what he must do: it is what others expect of him, and it is also the act that connects him, in a broader existential vision, to other people. Anything else is "fissità": a lack of movement and life, a dead excess.

One of the most significant aspects of Sereni's literary achievements is his work as translator. Critics have frequently emphasized the undisputed lyrical qualities of his translations. His volume *Il musicante di Saint-Merry* is a collection of his most important translations, including works by Albert Camus, Guillaume Apollinaire, René Char, Ezra Pound, and William Carlos Williams. While working on someone else's text, the writer is able to infuse it with his own creativity, and the translations can often be read as separate creations.

Sereni's total poetic contribution is one of the most significant of the second half of the twentieth century. The importance of his presence can be attributed not only to his gradual refusal of the hermetic tradition and its solipsistic mode but also to his ability and determination in finding a more personal and realistic mode of expression, which cannot be easily linked to any particular school but only to the inspiration of his inner world. The development of his poetic discourse, spanning four decades, shows Sereni's extraordinary loyalty to his private vision, poetic message, and expressive mode, and, at the same time, to the controversial events of history. This sense of dual, yet inseparable, coexistence runs through his collections of verse. Sereni disseminated a message of hope and unyielding faith in the demiurgic power of the poetic word.

Interviews:

Elio Filippo Accrocca, *Ritratti su misura* (Venice: Sodalizio del Libro, 1960), pp. 383–384;

Pier Annibale Danovi, *Scrittori su nastro* (Milan: Scheiwiller, 1961), pp. 181–198;

"Risposta a sette domande sulla poesia," *Nuovi Argomenti,* 55–56 (March–June 1962): 232–237;

Leone Piccioni, "Intervista a Sereni," in his *Maestri e amici* (Milan: Rizzoli, 1969), pp. 68–70;

Sandra Petrignani, "Che ognuno vi cerchi il suo senso," *Messaggero,* 3 February 1982;

Ferdinando Camon, "Vittorio Sereni," in his *Il mestiere di poeta* (Milan: Garzanti, 1982), pp. 121–128;

Laura Baffoni-Licata, "Intervista a Vittoria Sereni – Milano, 22 luglio 1982," in her *La poesia di Vittorio Sereni: Alienazione e impegno* (Ravenna: Longo, 1986), pp. 109, 176.

Biographies:

Massimo Grillandi, *Vittorio Sereni* (Florence: Nuova Italia, 1972);

Francesco Paolo Memmo, *Vittorio Sereni* (Milan: Mursia, 1973).

References:

Luciano Anceschi, "Di una possibile poetica lombarda," in his *Del Barocco e altre prove* (Florence: Vallecchi, 1953), pp. 199–221;

Laura Baffoni-Licata, *La poesia di Vittorio Sereni: Alienazione e impegno* (Ravenna: Longo, 1986);

Carlo Bo, "Parlando di Sereni," *Letteratura,* 82–83 (July–October 1966): 3–16;

Lanfranco Caretti, "Il perpetuo 'presente' di Sereni," introduction to Sereni's *Poesie scelte (1935–1965),* edited by Caretti (Milan: Mondadori, 1973), pp. ix–xxi;

Giansiro Ferrata, "Il libro 'unico' di Sereni," in his *Presentazioni e sentimenti critici (1942–1965)* (Cremona: Mangiarotti, 1965), pp. 246–256;

Giancarlo Ferretti, "L'ultima spiaggia di Sereni," in his *La letteratura del rifiuto* (Milan: Mursia, 1968), pp. 179–193;

Marco Forti, "I tre 'tempi' di Vittorio Sereni," in his *Le proposte della poesia* (Milan: Mursia, 1963), pp. 253–283;

Franco Fortini, "Le poesie italiane di questi anni," *Menabó,* 2 (April–June 1960): 124–126;

Pier Vincenzo Mengaldo, "Iterazione e specularitá in Sereni," afterword to Sereni's *Gli strumenti umani* (Turin: Einaudi, 1980), pp. 107–115;

Remo Pagnanelli, *La ripetizione dell'esistere: Lettura dell'opera poetica di Vittorio Sereni* (Milan: All'Insegna del Pesce d'Oro, 1980);

La poesia di Vittorio Sereni: Atti del Convegno su Vittorio Sereni (Milan: Librex, 1985);

Giovanni Raboni, "Sereni e l'inclusivitá dello spazio poetico," *Aut-Aut,* 61–62 (January–March 1961): 87–93;

Rudolf Schuerch, *Vittorio Sereni e i messaggi sentimentali* (Florence: Vallecchi, 1985);

Natale Tedesco, "Frustrazione esistenziale e rivalsa etica nel nuovo 'parlato' di Vittorio Sereni," in his *La condizione crepuscolare* (Florence: Nuova Italia, 1970), pp. 237–271.

Adriano Spatola

(4 May 1941 – 23 November 1988)

Elena Urgnani
Rutgers University

BOOKS: *Le pietre e gli dei* (Bologna: Tamari, 1961);
L'oblò (Milan: Feltrinelli, 1964);
Poesia da montare (Bologna: Sampietro, 1965);
Zeroglifico (Bologna: Sampietro, 1966); translated by
   Giulia Niccolai and Paul Vangelisti as *Zeroglyphics* (Los Angeles: Red Hill, 1977);
L'ebreo negro (Milan: All'Insegna del Pesce d'Oro, 1966);
Algoritmo (Turin: Geiger, 1968);
Verso la poesia totale (Salerno: Rumma, 1969);
Majakovskiiiiiij (Turin: Geiger, 1971); translated by
   Vangelisti (Los Angeles: Red Hill, 1975);
Quadri, miraggi, ritratti di Francesco Guerrieri (Turin: Geiger, 1972);
Diversi accorgimenti (Turin: Geiger, 1975); translated
   by Vangelisti as *Various Devices* (Los Angeles: Red Hill, 1978);
La composizione del testo (Rome: Cooperativa Scrittori, 1978);
Cacciatore di mosche (Modena: Telai del Bernini, 1980);
La piegatura del foglio (Naples: Guida, 1983);
Impaginazioni (San Paolo d'Enza: Tam Tam, 1984);
Recenti Zeroglifici (San Paolo d'Enza: Tam Tam, 1985);
Il futurismo (Milan: Elle Emme, 1986);
La definizione del prezzo (Sant'Ilario d'Enza: Tam Tam, 1991).

OTHER: Lamberto Pignotti, ed., *Poesie visive,* includes poems by Spatola (Bologna: Sampietro, 1965);
"Dodici schede e musica," in *Teatro italiano,* edited by Massimo Dursi (Bologna: Sampietro, 1966), pp. 437–444;
Parole sui muri, edited by Spatola and Claudio Parmiggiani (Turin: Geiger, 1968);
Ezio Gribaudo: Il peso del concreto, edited by Spatola (Turin: Arte Fratelli Pozzo, 1968);
Miroglio: Qualcosa di metafisico, edited by Spatola (Turin: Geiger, 1970);
Giuliano Della Casa, *Alfabeto,* introduction by Spatola (Modena, 1971);

Adriano Spatola circa 1980 (photograph by Gabriella Maleti)

Ruth Feldman and Brian Swann, eds. and trans., *Italian Poetry Today: Currents and Trends,* includes poems by Spatola (Saint Paul: New Rivers, 1979), pp. 204–211;
Paul Vangelisti, ed., *Another You,* includes poems by Spatola (Los Angeles: Red Hill, 1980);
Lawrence R. Smith, ed. and trans., *The New Italian Poetry: 1945 to the Present. A Bilingual Anthology,*

includes poems by Spatola (Berkeley: University of California Press, 1981), pp. 466–483;

Italian Poetry, 1960–1980: From Neo to Post Avant-Garde, edited by Spatola and Vangelisti (San Francisco: Red Hill, 1982);

"Gli assassini innamorati," *Anello che non Tiene,* 1 (Spring 1989): 65–66.

TRANSLATIONS: Anne Vilmont, *Le Carnivore* (Turin: Dellavalle, 1969);

Violette Leduc, *Teresa e Isabella e la donna col renard,* translated by Spatola and Ginetta Vittorini (Milan: Feltrinelli, 1969);

Michael Edwards, *Nell'India Antica,* translated by Spatola and Giulia Niccolai (Milan: LM, 1975);

Ellen MacNamara, *Gli Etruschi,* translated by Spatola and Niccolai (Milan: LM, 1975);

Marjorie Rowling, *Nel Medioevo,* translated by Spatola and Niccolai (Milan: LM, 1975);

John Cage, "Aria per John Cage," in *John Cage: Dopo di me il silenzio* (Milan: Emme, 1978), p. 93.

Adriano Spatola's first appearance in the literary world was associated with the neo-avant-garde, a literary movement active in Italy between the end of the 1950s and the beginning of the following decade; the group was initially associated with the magazine *Verri.* One of its important accomplishments was the publication of the anthology of poetry *I Novissimi* (The Very New Ones, 1961), which includes texts and poetic declarations by Elio Pagliarani, Alfredo Giuliani, Edoardo Sanguineti, Nanni Balestrini, and Antonio Porta. This literary group was also open to other intellectuals (Spatola among them) and had been officially founded in Palermo in 1963 under the name "Gruppo '63". Its essential goals were a drastic renewal and an opening of contemporary literature, a sharp rupture with the preceding movements (from neorealism to the circle supporting the magazine *Officina*) and with every form of ideology, and a recovery of the historic avant-garde movements, including futurism. The neo-avant-garde was also linked to analogous European movements, such as that surrounding the French magazine *Tel Quel* and that of the *nouveau roman* (new novel) writers. In concrete terms the neo-avant-garde favored a deeper attention to the particular problems of poetic language and a complex opening to different forms of expression, even highly experimental ones (visual poetry and poetic experiments with electronic calculators, collages, and performances), in the attempt to give a greater vitality to the poetic experience. Spatola regularly contributed poetry criticism to the *Verri,* published poems in *Nuova Corrente,* and also directed the magazine *Quindici,* thus meeting the poetess Giulia Niccolai, who became his collaborator on various translations and other projects.

Spatola was born Bruno Spatola in Sapjane, Yugoslavia, on 4 May 1941; he later adopted Adriano as his first name because his family had called him that since he was a child. During his youth his family lived in Imola, Italy, but in 1958, at the end of his high-school education, he moved to Bologna to enroll in law school. At this time he began to edit and publish the magazine *Babilu.* There were only two issues, but it had some valuable contributors, such as Gianni Celati, for example, who contributed two poems.

In 1961, after listening to one of Luciano Anceschi's lectures on poetry, Spatola decided to quit law school and get a degree in Italian literature. Spatola was not academically oriented enough to take his studies seriously, yet he never dropped out of school. He finally received his degree from the University of Bologna at the beginning of the 1980s.

Anceschi was not only Spatola's mentor but also the link between him and the neo-avant-garde. Anceschi introduced the young poet to the board of *Verri* and commissioned him to write an essay on realism, which was published. Shocked by his unexpected success, also having had poems published, Spatola was ready to change his profession, but for a long time he was able to make ends meet only through his job as a proofreader for the Mulino publishing house.

Spatola's first marriage was to Anna Fausta Neri, on 12 June 1965. In May 1966 they had a son, Riccardo.

In 1964 Spatola had participated in the circle associated with the journal *Malebolge,* formed in Reggio Emilia. It was a small parasurrealist circle, which also included G. Celli, Corrado Costa, and, marginally, Porta. Celli was studying the entomological aspects of surrealism and oneirism, Costa took care of political issues, and Spatola created posters. *Malebolge* was trying to coagulate Italian surrealist ferments, and its polemic targets were writers such as Alberto Moravia and Pier Paolo Pasolini. The group was also characterized by a sort of anarchism. For Spatola *Malebolge* had been an inventive inspiration. *Quindici* was to give him a theoretical and political impetus beginning in the mid 1960s.

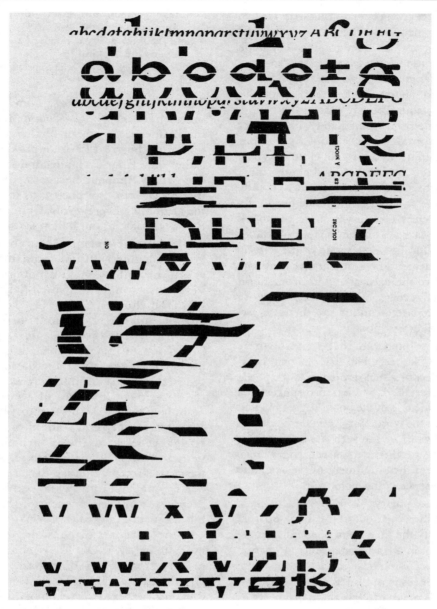

One of Spatola's zeroglifici *("zeroglyphics"), combining poetry and graphic design (from his* Verso la poesia totale, *1969; by permission of the Estate of Adriano Spatola)*

Quindici had its headquarters in Rome, where Spatola soon began living with Niccolai, having separated from his wife. He lived with Niccolai until 1979, divorce being illegal in Italy at the time. (Spatola was finally able to obtain a divorce in spring 1984.) On the board of editors of *Quindici* there were not only poets but also sociologists, critics, and political activists. Renato Barilli was contributing criticism, and Umberto Eco was in charge of semiotics. The group at *Quindici* came to a crosspoint at the end of the 1960s. Balestrini insisted on further opening the magazine to currently hot political issues. When he succeeded, the magazine was popular at the University of Rome and

was often sold out. But the editorial board was split, and as a group it came to an end.

Spatola's first published volume was the collection of poems *Le pietre e gli dei* (The Stones and the Gods, 1961), which is now almost impossible to find. He later published a novel, *L'oblò* (The Porthole, 1964), which won the Ferro di Cavallo Prize. *L'oblò* is written in a difficult, lyrical, surrealist, convoluted prose. Spatola's other novel, "Achille," is still unpublished.

In 1965 Adriano Spatola published the puzzle poem *Poesia da montare* (Poetry to be Assembled), and in 1966 the book *Zeroglifico* (translated as *Zeroglyphics,*

1977), a package of "concrete" poems on cards. He had already taken part in many exhibitions of experimental poetry — visual, concrete, and ideographic. The book is headed by a quotation from Max Bense: "to write means to construct language, not to explain it." Barilli, in his introduction to the translated edition, points out that, though Spatola courageously crosses the boundaries of the literal, he stops immediately, like a diver who does not confront depths but stops right under the surface. The graphic layout is still close to typography, whereas Spatola could have used handwriting, private and somewhat distant from public and codified forms. For these first experiments he purposely chose printed characters as anonymous as possible — very large and bold-faced, as in newspaper headlines or advertisements. But the breaking up of the writing is rather clear and elementary. It maintains a rational appearance, similar to the vertical and horizontal grid on which the normal typecase is based. His purpose was to correct the apparent candor and the false pretenses in linear or "literary" poetry.

Niccolai has pointed out that some of these poems have a layout that resembles that of a piano keyboard, adding an effect of visual resonance to the poetic sounds that are represented. She has also suggested a brief explanation of the title of the book, suggesting that *zeroglyphic* stems from the word *hieroglyphic,* derived from the Greek *hieroglyphicos* (from the verb *glyphein,* meaning to incise, to sculpt), pertinent to sacred engravings. Thus the title conveys the annulment of the semantic message and the presence of the iconic one.

The collection of poetry *L'ebreo negro* (The Black Jew) was also published in 1966. In this book Spatola seems to recover fully the fluency of poetic discourse, though certainly not in a traditional sense. Punctuation, for example, is completely omitted, so that the stream of consciousness is not interrupted. The first letter of each verse is never capitalized, in order not to break the fluidity. The book contains seven poems, each presenting a series of narrative sequences, generally descriptive in their development. In the first, "Catalogopoema" (Cataloguepoem), the proposed images are those of everyday violence, as in metropolitan suburbs: "tram batte nella notte occhiuta lingua trappola che scatta" (bus rattles in the night sharp tongue trap that snaps). Occasionally the insistence upon a bloodcurdling detail is so intense as to become almost ironic toward the literary canon:

>   la maionese con l'insalata e le olive e il feto sul bordo
>   del piatto
>   il sugo denso compatto e la saliva salata macchia sul
>   tovagliolo

>   (the mayonnaise with salad and the olives and the fetus
>   on the edge of the dish
>   and the thick gravy condensed and the salty saliva
>   stains the napkin)[.]
>   — all translations by Paul Vangelisti

The dead fetus is a recurrent image in the poetry of nineteenth-century *scapigliatura* (libertine art) and in the Baudelairean stream that crossed Italian literature after the great Parisian poet's death. However, rather than Charles Baudelaire, Spatola preferred to cite Arthur Rimbaud because Spatola was conscious that his devotion to poetry, as much as his passion for alcoholic beverages, was building him a reputation as the last of the Italian *maudit* (damned) poets.

The title poem, "L'ebreo negro," shows a more accented rhythmic scansion than some others in the collection. It is composed of forty-two verses, the longest of which has thirty-nine syllables, the shortest eight. The semantic turns are abrupt, and the reader must provide creative cooperation. The poem is descriptive only in a broad sense; images generate other images as if by parthenogenesis. Punctuation is absent, and the first verse is all in lowercase letters. It tells of the imaginary invasion of a city by an army of zombies; they are the memories of a holocaust Western society had wanted to erase: "inutile distruggere le carte, inutile bruciare i documenti / vengono fuori in processione, cauti e pazienti, nascosti dietro cenciose divise" (unnecessary to destroy papers, unnecessary to burn documents / they come out in a procession, wary and patient, hiding inside ragged uniforms). Later throughout a refined process of phonological derivation the morpheme *orfeo* (Orpheus) changes to *ebreo* (Hebrew): "orfeo! gli dice uno, erfeo! gridando, efreo! battendogli la / faccia con i piedi, ebreo! gli dice allora: 'canta'" (orpheus! one of them says, erpheus! yelling ephreus! stamping / on his face, hebrew! he then says: "sing"). During World War II some Jews were forced by the Nazis to entertain their tormentors.

In another poem Spatola posits a boomerang as a double-edged weapon with which a degraded society hits itself. The poem "Boomerang" includes one of Spatola's most ironic self-portraits:

>   frutto maturo l'ascensore appeso e come il verme nella
>   mela
>   dentro eccomi assiso a battere spondei
>   . . . .
>   mi guadagno la paga stando in bagno due ore,
>   scrivendo
>   versi galanti per le vecchie signore

(ripe fruit the elevator hanging and like the worm in
the
apple here I sit beating out spondees
. . . .
I earn my pay staying two hours in the bath writing
gallant verse for the old gentle ladies)[.]

The most frequently repeated terms in the book concern nature: *stone, incrustation, rock, sand, mud, fish, water, frog, oil, hands, feet, nails, abdomen,* and so on. Clearly the goal is a superabundant suggestive effect rather than the development of a linear discourse. It is a poetry where the semantic accumulation goes so far as to replace grammatical order, aiming at a more direct and almost synesthetic communication.

Among the many happenings and exhibitions in which Spatola took part, worth mentioning is one that took place in Fiumalbo, a small village between Florence and Modena, from 6 to 18 August 1967. The events are described in *Parole sui muri* (Words on the Walls, 1968). Fiumalbo was a conservative and religious village whose mayor was a patron of poets and artists. Desiring to make his experience as a mayor fruitful, he decided with friends to organize a meeting of the neo-avant-garde movement, which would certainly shock the people. On 6 and 7 August about one hundred artists arrived and started to exhibit their works: posters of all kinds; concrete poetry; and op, pop, and kinetic art. From the balcony of the town hall a loudspeaker blasted phonetic poetry and electronic sounds, in a village where people usually only heard the bells of the church. Spatola's younger brother, Tiziano, walked around with a sandwich-board sign; written on both sides were the words "I am a poem." Another artist put a chair in a circle drawn on the street and was issuing a certificate to anybody ready to sit for a moment in that circle. The document said that the passerby had become a permanent work of art. A tree of the village was painted red, and cement and electrical poles were disguised as trees. The villagers became restless and angry when an artist hung a poster near the church; the sign read, "Don't call me a Catholic please." At this point many of the locals refused to allow any more posters on their houses, and the mayor had to keep some of the posters in his office (particularly those that were too strongly against religion or morality) in order to prevent intervention by the provincial police, whose cars were nearby and ready.

There was a hiatus of about five years between the publication of *L'ebreo negro* and *Majakovskiiiiiij* (1971; translated, 1975). The title is supposed to sound like a dying scream. Spatola real-

ized at the end of the 1960s that not only the decade but also an entire epoch was ending, and Vladimir Majakovskij, with his poetic experimentalism and his personal and political contradictions, had been an appreciated and recognized emblem of this epoch. The book was published by Geiger, a publishing house Spatola founded and directed.

During this time Spatola made a major life change: in 1970, after the experience of *Quindici* was definitely over, he left Rome, where he was living with Niccolai, to retire with her in a farmhouse in the country near Mulino di Bazzano (in the province of Parma). The house was the property of his friend Costa and was a solid sixteenth-century peasant house, with no heating or telephone. There the couple edited the poetry magazine *Tam Tam: Rivista di Poesia, Apoesia, e Poesia Totale.* Spatola also recorded the series of cassettes he called an "audiomagazine" – *Baobab.* Niccolai left him in 1979, and he later met Bianca Maria Bonazzi, who moved in with him in October 1980.

The title poem of Spatola's 1971 book, "Majakovskiiiiiij," is divided into six sections, each of them bearing a title that identifies the topic and contents in rhetorical terms: "exordium," "narratio," "partitio," "probatio," "repetitio," and "peroratio." However, this is merely a frame effect whose only goal is to stress the contrast with the nonnarrative flow of the poetic text itself:

questa estrema dissoluzione sistematicamente portata ai
limiti della violenza e fino alle terre del fuoco fino
all'eccitazione stagnante nel rendimento del ritmo alle
catastrofi degli organismi in circolazione casuali
nelle città fagocitate nei corpi incrostati di sale
sotto la luna ecchimotica che rotola sopra il biliardo

(this extreme dissolution systematically carried
to the limits of violence and up to the land of fire
up to the static agitation in the rending of rhythm
to the catastrophes of organisms in casual circumstances
inside the cities sewn together with bodies incrusted
with salt
under a moon bruised that rolls across a pool table)[.]

"Majakovskiiiiiij" is the first sign of a discourse Spatola expands in the rest of the poems: the use of poetry as a metapoetic discourse itself, which finds its first full development in the poem "La composizione del testo" (The Composition of the Text), which later became the title poem of his 1978 collection. "La composizione del testo" tends to communicate to the reader the exact sensation of the circumstances in which the writer works, by placing both of them — reader and writer — on the same perceptive level:

> un aggettivo la respirazione la finestra aperta
> l'esatta dimensione dell'innesto nel fruscio della pagina
> oppure guarda come il testo si serve del corpo
> guarda come l'opera è cosmica e biologica e logica
> nelle voci notturne nelle aurorali esplosioni
> nel gracidare graffiare piallare od accendere
> qui sotto il cielo pastoso che impiastra le dita
> parole che parlano
>
> (an adjective breathing the window open
> the exact dimension of the incision in the rustling of
>   pages
> or see maybe how the text uses the body
> see how the work is cosmic and biologic and logic
> in nocturnal voices in auroral explosions
> in the croaking scratching scraping setting fire
> here under the soft sky sticking all over the fingers
> words that speak)[.]

Tactile circumstances, nouns, and verbs are connected to concrete actions, creating an atmosphere of a blacksmith forge, chemical laboratory, or carpenter shop. And the appeal to the reader is constant, heartily direct, with the insistent repetition of the imperative *guarda* (see): "guarda ma guarda come la negazione modifica il testo / con parole possibili con parole impossibili / ma il testo è un oggetto vivente fornito di chiavi" (see this how negation modifies the text / with words possible with words impossible / but the text is an object living furnished with keys). Sometimes the text is seen as an object to be shaped: "è questo il momento che aspetti comincia a tagliare" (this is the moment you wait for start cutting). Some other times it is seen as a severely sick person whose sickness appears to be very difficult to diagnose and treat. More often, though, it is an object that becomes more and more foreign, more subject to conventional rules, while its composition proceeds toward the end:

> nel testo tutto si accumula tutto si scioglie in vapore
> ricordati è tardi ricordati è ora di andare di salutare
> con poche precise innocue parole. . . .
> fra poco nel testo avrà inizio la parte finale
> catalogo di manierismi e di stupri canzone e narcosi
> sul calendario segnare con la matita la data della consegna
>
> (in the text everything accumulates everything melts in
>   vapor
> remember it's too late remember time to go to say
>   goodbye
> with a few careful innocuous words. . . .
> before long in the text the final part will have begun

> catalog of mannerisms and raped songs and narcotic
> on the calendar marking with a pencil the date of the appointment)[.]

Through this writing procedure, the reader perceives the text almost physically; he is forced to visualize it, not with his own eyes but from the writer's point of view, thus losing his own perspective.

Poetic writing, then, was for Spatola the possibility of re-creating an elementary and total linguistic system; poetic language could not only express the world but also could become critical reflection, as in *Diversi accorgimenti* (1975; translated as *Various Devices*, 1978). In the poem "L'abolizione della realtà" (The Abolition of Reality) the language claims the privilege of art criticism, commenting on artworks such as *Pomeriggio domenicale all'isola della Grande Jatte* (Sunday Afternoon on the Island of the Grande Jatte) by Georges Seurat. *Various Devices* is a book of refined experiments. A remarkable poem in this collection is "L'esistenza della descrizione" (The Existence of Description), which starts as a reflection on genres and becomes a detailed description of a well-known poem by Aldo Palazzeschi, "La fontana malata" (The Sick Fountain), of which Spatola writes:

> La fontana il suo impegno alla tortura
> alla fragile docile soavemente ingegnosa
> macchina che mastica inghiottisce digerisce
> il cavallo sbandato dall'urto della grida
> tra le palme gli ulivi le logiche trascritte
> il peso è puro stagno mercurio escremento
> elementi proclivi all'ansia del desiderio
> al segmento spezzato irrorato dall'acqua
>
> (The fountain its commitment to torture
> to the fragile docile sweet ingenious
> machine that masticates swallows digests
> the astonished horse by the impact of screams
> among the palms the olives the transcribed logics
> the weight is pure tin mercury excrement
> elements tending to anxiety and desire
> to the fragment fractured sprayed by water)[.]

There is another lucid, surrealist, and metapoetic reflection in "Considerazioni sulla poesia nera" (Considerations on Black Poetry), in *La composizione del testo*. This poem is preceded by a quotation from Alfred Hitchcock: "Ho un amico che ha il cuore di un bambino / lo tiene sulla scrivania in un vaso pieno d'alcool" (I have a friend who has a child's heart / he keeps it on his desk in a bottle of alcohol). In one stanza, Spatola writes:

Queste perorazioni formalmente locutorie
in qualche gioco degne di se stesse determinate
proprietà e simmetrie una funzione dell'onda
biliardiche suzioni un'oasi matematica
l'avviso al caratterista il ferro varie leghe
poniamo che tra questi risultati manchi l'odio.

(These perorations formally locutions
in some sort of game worthy of themselves determined
property and symmetrics a function of the wave
billiard-like suctions a mathematical oasis
a call for a character actor the iron various settings
suppose that among these results hate is missing.)

A thematic reading of Spatola's works would also highlight the political, in spite of his apolitical declarations in *Tam Tam.* The first poem indicative of his political point of view is in *Majakovskiiiiiij:* "Il poema Stalin" (The Poem Stalin), which indicates how Spatola became the lucid critical conscience of the Italian leftist movement, for which Stalin had been a mythic figure. Blunt and rhymeless, the poem communicates a sensation of solemnity in spite of everything:

un poema Stalin dovrebbe essere scritto senza aggettivi
senza virgole né decimali senza opportune parentesi
l'esclamazione un veleno l'interrogazione una stanca
    orditura
ma niente di meno accettabile dell'ingiuria del punto
    fermo
1879–1953

(a poem Stalin ought to be written without adjectives
without commas or decimals without convenient pa-
    renthesis
the exclamation a poison the question mark a tired plot
but nothing less acceptable than the insult of a period
1879–1953)[.]

Spatola is equally critical of the detractors as well as the unconditional admirers of a historical character who was troublesome in every sense, even to his party comrades, although they often tried to justify his actions in terms of historical necessity.

The poem "Che giorno è oggi" (What Day Is It Today), in *Diversi accorgimenti,* has a topic that is equally political. The poem is a circumvolution around the word *democrazia* (democracy), and the insistence is almost surprising. One of the polemic targets of the Gruppo '63 had been the ideologized poetry of the group at *Officina.* However, there is no overt trace of ideology in Spatola's discourse in the poem, which flows fluidly and surrealistically, as he is conscious of the contradictions that language itself elicits:

Democrazia una parola
agevolmente lingua corruttibile
        plausibilmente negabile
e rinnegabile la causa della giustizia
        la sottrazione
rinnovabile al ritmo è la distanza
sussidiaria mestizia
o teofania.

(Democracy a word
easily a corruptible tongue
        plausibly negatable
and deniable the cause of justice
        the subtraction
renewable to the rhythm is the distance
subsidiary sadness
or theophany.)

A few years earlier, in *Verso la poesia totale* (Toward Total Poetry, 1969), Spatola had written: "La speranza di un'arte proletaria-collettivistica del futurismo russo si dissolve nella industrializzazione planetaria, nello spazio-tempo delle leggi di mercato, nella pseudodemocratizzazione attuata dalla televisione, dall'analfabetismo, dalla pubblicità, dalla catena di montaggio, dalla produzione in serie . . ." (The hope for a proletarian-collectivistic art that belonged to Russian futurism dissolves into planetary industrialization, into the time-space of market laws, into pseudodemocratization carried out by television, by analphabetism, by publicity, by the assembly line, by serial production . . .)[.] Spatola's position demonstrates a consciousness of the limits of preceding historic movements. Thus the revaluation of futurism, which derives from his participation in the ideas of Gruppo '63, is accompanied by an open adhesion to surrealist poetics, from which he derives answers to distressing questions: "il surrealismo ha cercato di portare alle estreme conseguenze quelli che erano e sono i dati di una situazione tragica e grottesca di impasse, di un'alternativa apparentemente senza sbocco tra 'la carriera letteraria (borghese) e quella rivoluzionaria (marxista),' come ha scritto André Breton" (surrealism has tried to bring to its extreme consequences those which were and are the data of a tragic and grotesque situation of impasse, of an alternative apparently without solution between the "[bourgeois] literary career and the [Marxist] revolutionary one" as André Breton put it).

The problem of *impegno* (engagement) should not be denied, but neither can it be reconnected to that tradition of discursive and pathetic poetry that overuses nineteenth-century, outdated, petit bourgeois formulas. Such a poetry does not question any worldview, and it develops with the trend of current opinion, inviting the reader to resignation. Spatola prefers to substitute for the ambiguity of *engagement* the word *participation,* a concept used by Brazilian writers of concrete poetry. In *Verso la poesia totale* Spatola furnished one of the first and most exhaustive theoretical/historical treatments of modern and experimental avant-garde poetry. He places himself inside rather than outside the cultural movements he writes about, making his testimony more reliable.

One of Spatola's last collections of poetry is *La piegatura del foglio* (The Folding of the Sheet), published in 1983, and at times one can perceive a softening of the hard, avant-garde language, perhaps even justifying the label of "neohermetism." Nevertheless his entire oeuvre is deeply antihermetic because it is antielegiac, focused on a diverging, fractioned, discordant, pluritonal phraseology, exactly the opposite of what the hermetics were pursuing. As Guido Guglielmi points out in his introduction to *La piegatura del foglio,* Spatola had too much of a taste for tautology, for paradoxes, and for phonic dilatation to be labeled hermetic. He exploits disparities between words and looks for resemblances and strident relationships. Guglielmi defines Spatola's writing as oriented toward a mixture of abstract and notional language, both high and low, and of objectifying language, with a preference for hard and strongly polysyllabic words and thus for phonic expressionism.

For example, the poem "Cacciatore di mosche" (Hunter of Flies) cannot be called neohermetic because it is impregnated with antilyricism:

Immonde sarebbero le concezioni del mondo
le macchie arrugginite sulla pelle maculata
le stasi della mano posata sul vecchio pacco
abbandonato da tempo sull'angolo del quadrato
in prospettiva aristotelica non molto distante
dal concetto perfetto di geometria o impertinenza
dell'occhio delle mosche in volo nella stanza
fosforescente intorno alla pista d'atterraggio
immondo è ucciderle senza averne il coraggio

(filthy would be the world conceptions
the rusty spots on the speckled skin
the stasis of the hand placed on the old package
abandoned a long time since on the edge of the square
in Aristotelian perspective not very far
from the perfect concept of geometry or impertinence
of the flies' eye flying in the room
phosphorescent around the landing runway
filthy is to kill them without having the courage to)[.]

Notice Spatola's usual use of concrete words among which, almost abruptly, abstract ideas emerge: "in

Aristotelian perspective not very far / from the perfect concept of geometry or impertinence." There is also the recurrence of assonance and a certain taste for surrealist humor.

One finds scalding irony, self-irony, and metaliterary notations in "Una poesia d'amore" (A Love Poem), where there is boredom and a consciousness of literary commonplaces:

Scrivere una poesia d'amore
è già una poesia d'amore
ma invertebrata ma viva
gettata nell'acqua bollente
asciugamani un po' malmenati
saponetta a forma di cuore

(To write a love poem
is already a love poem
but invertebrated but alive
tossed into the hot water
bathtowel a little mistreated
barsoap in a heart shape)[.]

Nevertheless, a symbolist, even lyric, background without a shadow of irony appears in "Fasi della luna e altrove" (Phases of the Moon and Somewhere Else):

Luminosa argilla appannata
apparsa sul greto del torrente
nel profilo dell'acqua viziata
da un appassionato temporale
ormai addensato nella memoria
di un terriccio ipernutrito
ai bordi di una marcita
per un uomo che calza stivali
in un'aria umida e calda
fradicia e suppurata
gonfia di cicuta e detriti
tra foglie appena cadute
da alberi incanutiti
da una luttuosa radiazione
sparsa sui campi incantati

(Luminous clay tarnished
appeared on the dry gravel bed of the torrent
in the profile of the water polluted
by a passionate thunderstorm
by now thickened in the memory
of an hypernourished top soil
at the border of a water-meadow
for a man wearing boots
in a humid and warm air
rotten and suppurated
swollen with hemlock and debris
among the leaves recently fallen
of gray-headed trees
from a doleful radiation
spread over the enchanted fields)[.]

A sublime appearance is imparted to images of the natural world.

Spatola's *La definizione del prezzo* (The Definition of Prize, 1991) completes what he called his linear trilogy: *La composizione del testo, La piegatura del foglio,* and *La definizione del prezzo.* The shape and thrust of the poetry are similar in all three books.

During the 1980s Spatola lived with Bonazzi and edited *Tam Tam* while continuing to write poems. He was often invited to lecture and read abroad, and such activities included a poetry reading in Sydney, Australia, on 29 August 1978, as well as a visit to Harvard in 1981 and a poetry performance inside a mine in Belgium in fall 1986. He married Bonazzi a few months before dying on 23 November 1988.

Adriano Spatola was a poet with expressive strength and social sensibility; he engaged in changing the surrounding world in both aesthetic and political terms. He was an organizer of culture, a theoretician, and at the same time a historian of those movements in which he took part.

References:

"Adriano Spatola," *MILANOPOESIA '89* (Milan: Ansaldo, 1989), pp. 71–75;

Renato Barilli, "A Word from Renato Barilli," in Spatola's *Zeroglyphics,* translated by Giulia Niccolai and Paul Vangelisti (Los Angeles: Red Hill, 1977), p. 5;

Peter Carravetta, "A Reading of Spatola's *Majakovskiiiiiij,*" in *Altro Polo* (Sydney, Australia: University of Sydney, Fredrick May Foundation for Italian Studies, 1980), pp. 89–110;

Pier Luigi Ferro, ed., *Adriano Spatola, Poeta totale: Materiali critici e documenti* (Genoa: Costa & Nolan, 1992);

Luigi Fontanella, "Corrispondenza a Mulino di Bazzano," *Produzione e Cultura,* 3 (January–June 1988): 11–12;

Milli Graffi, ed., "Omaggio a Spatola," *Verri,* special issue, 4 (1991);

Guido Guglielmi, Introduction to Spatola's *La piegatura del foglio* (Naples: Guida, 1983), p. 5;

Giulia Niccolai, "A Possible Way of Interpreting Some Zeroglyphics," in Spatola's *Zeroglyphics,* p. 7;

Antonio Porta, "Adriano Spatola," *Alfabeta* (December 1989): 114;

Testuale, special issue on Spatola and Antonio Porta (December 1991);

Paolo Valesio, "In memoriam Adriani Spatulae," *Polytext,* 5 (Spring 1989): 12–25.

Maria Luisa Spaziani

(7 December 1924 –   )

Rebecca West
University of Chicago

BOOKS: *Primavera a Parigi* (Milan: Scheiwiller, 1954);

Le acque del Sabato (Milan: Mondadori, 1954);

Luna lombarda (Venice: Neri Pozza, 1959);

Il gong (Milan: Mondadori, 1962);

Utilità della memoria (Milan: Mondadori, 1966);

L'occhio del ciclone (Milan: Mondadori, 1970);

La Pléiade (Messina: Genal, 1972);

Ronsard fra gli astri della Pléiade (Turin: ERI, 1972);

Il teatro francese del Settecento (Rome: Faro/Nuova Biblioteca Universitaria, 1974);

Il teatro francese dell'Ottocento (Rome: Faro/Nuova Biblioteca Universitaria, 1975);

Il teatro francese del Novecento (Messina: EDAS, 1976);

Ultrasuoni (Samedan: Munt, 1976);

Storia dell'Alessandrino (Messina: EDAS, 1977);

Transito con catene (Milan: Mondadori, 1977);

Alessandrino e altri versi fra Ottocento e Novecento (Messina: EDAS, 1978);

Poesie, edited by Luigi Baldacci (Milan: Mondadori, 1979);

Geometria del disordine (Milan: Mondadori, 1981);

La stella del libero arbitrio (Milan: Mondadori, 1986);

Giovanna d'Arco (Milan: Mondadori, 1990);

Donne in poesia (Venice: Marsilio, 1992).

OTHER: Elio Filippo Accrocca, ed., *Ritratti su misura,* includes an autobiographical sketch by Spaziani (Venice: Sodalizio del Libro, 1960), pp. 398–399;

Biancamaria Frabotta, ed., *Donne in poesie: Antologia della poesia femminile in Italia dal dopoguerra ad oggi,* includes poems and an essay by Spaziani (Rome: Savelli, 1976), pp. 51–53, 143–145;

Ruth Feldman and Brian Swann, eds. and trans., *Italian Poetry Today: Currents and Trends,* includes poems by Spaziani (Saint Paul: New Rivers, 1979), pp. 212–214;

Beverly Allen, Muriel Kittel, and Keala Jane Jewell, eds., *The Defiant Muse: Italian Feminist Poems from the Middle Ages to the Present: A Bi-*

Maria Luisa Spaziani circa 1980 (photograph by Gabriella Maleti)

lingual Anthology, includes poems by Spaziani (New York: Feminist Press, 1986), pp. 68–71.

TRANSLATIONS: Winston Clewes, *Amicizie violente* (Milan: Mondadori, 1951);

E. H. Gombrich, *Il mondo dell'arte* (Milan: Mondadori, 1952);

Jacques Audiberti, *Il padrone di Milano* (Milan: Bompiani, 1956);

Desmarets de Saint-Sorlin, *I visionari* and Philippe Quinault, *Commedia senza commedia,* in *Teatro francese del gran secolo,* edited by Giovanni Macchia (Turin: ERI, 1960);

Marguerite Yourcenar, *Il colpo di grazia; Alexis* (Milan: Feltrinelli, 1962); *Alexis,* published separately (Milan: Feltrinelli, 1983);

Langston Moffet, *Il diavolo e la sua coda* (Milan: Club degli Editori, 1962);

George Sand, *Francesco il trovatello* (Turin: ERI, 1963);

Sully Prudhomme, *Poesie* (Milan: Fratelli Fabbri, 1965);

Conte di Gobineau, *Sull'ineguaglianza delle razze* (Milan: Longanesi, 1965);

Paul-Jean Toulet, *Poesie* (Turin: Einaudi, 1966);

Saul Bellow, *La vittima* (Milan: Feltrinelli, 1968);

Charles d'Orléans (Rome: Faro/Nuova Biblioteca Universitaria, 1970);

Marceline Desbordes-Valmore (Rome: Faro/Nuova Biblioteca Universitaria, 1971);

Jean Racine, *Bajazet* (Rome: Faro/Nuova Biblioteca Universitaria, 1973);

Johann Wolfgang von Goethe, *Götz von Berlichingen,* in *Teatro* (Turin: Einaudi, 1973);

Michel Tournier, *Le Meteore* (Milan: Mondadori, 1979);

André Gide, *Oscar Wilde* (Florence: Giusti, 1979).

The question of Maria Luisa Spaziani's feminine identity is of pertinence to any consideration of her poetry. Critics have tended to identify her work as "feminine," although this is a category to which Spaziani does not ascribe. Answering a series of questions concerning the place of feminism and feminine experience (both personal and literary) in her poetry in *Donne in poesie: Antologia della poesia femminile in Italia dal dopoguerra ad oggi* (Women in Poetry: Anthology of Feminine Poetry in Italy from the Postwar Period to Today, 1976), Spaziani asserted that "la singola voce di un poeta-donna valeva e vale di per sé, per una unicità sensibile e morale, la stessa che differenzia i libri importanti scritti da uomini" (the individual voice of a woman poet was and is valuable in and of itself, for its emotional and moral uniqueness, the same singularity that differentiates important books written by men). She does not in any sense oppose feminism, the acceptance of which she sees as "una delle superstiti tappe da varcare nella trasformazione dell'uomo tolemaico in uomo copernicano" (one of the remaining stages to be passed through in the transforma-

tion of Ptolemaic man into Copernican man), but she insists that even though she can see a connection between her "presunta femminilità" (presumed femininity) and her "concreto operare" (real-life activities), "in poesia è diverso" (in poetry it is different). For Spaziani, poetry is poetry, whether written by men or women, and she does not, therefore, consciously privilege or foreground the feminine elements in her verse.

Spaziani was born in Turin "in un giorno freddissimo . . . di dicembre" (on a very cold . . . December day), according to her. She further wrote in her autobiographical sketch in *Ritratti su misura* (Custom-Made Portraits, 1960) that this fact perhaps determined her "violenta, quasi esclusiva simpatia per i paesaggi rigidi e nordici" (violent, almost exclusive liking for harsh Nordic landscapes). However, she spent much of her youth traveling to sun-drenched places such as Rome and parts of southern Italy, and it was only when she visited Paris, Chartres, Cologne, and Ostend that she found a physical climate compatible with her inner sense of an ideal poetic landscape. Her future poetry was to be dominated by the wintry, more austere ambience of this ideal north, which conditions her verse both psychologically and rhetorically. *Austerity* is perhaps too severe a term, however, because Spaziani's poetry is in no sense coldly Parnassian. Her adherence to certain principles of control, her formal elegance, and her domination of effusive and intimistic confession results in a clarity of expression and a subdued intensity that are emotionally resonant. Literature and life are held in constant tension, as Spaziani seeks to transform mere autobiography into more mythically and universally resonant themes and images.

She began her literary activities at an early age. As a high-school student she founded the journal *Il Dado* (The Die), published in 1942 and 1943, to which she contributed translations from the French, English, and German, as well as original pieces. She had a particular interest in issues pertaining to style, and tradition rather than innovation or radical experimentation attracted and inspired her. In 1953, with the support of a scholarship, she went to Paris, a trip she describes as "fatidico" (fateful). The northern landscape of her imagination, supported by the real ambience of Paris and the surrounding countryside, inspired her first collections of poetry, both published in 1954: *Primavera a Parigi* (Springtime in Paris); and *Le acque del Sabato* (The Sabbath's Waters), into which was incorporated the earlier small volume. Her debt to the hermetics, especially Eugenio Montale, and to earlier models, such as the crepuscular poets and Giovanni Pascoli, is obvious in these early collections, but already Spaziani goes beyond imitation toward the creation of an unmistakably original voice that is private and autobiographical and yet tends toward a classically depersonalized and universally elegiac tone. There is a constant interplay between specific details – such as place, time, and season – and mythically timeless intimations of the hidden meanings beneath quotidian detail. Spaziani inserts her images into traditional hendecasyllabic verse, rarely departing from this classically determined musicality.

The moon is a recurrent presence in many of these early poems, casting a tender, elegiac, crepuscular light over the scenes and evoking a Leopardian pensive longing. In addition to Montale, whose importance as a model is sometimes too explicit, Giacomo Leopardi's presence is dominant, and not just thematically. Her recourse to certain ancient lyric traditions, such as high musicality and formal elegance, came at a time when many poets of her generation were seeking to liberate themselves from the preceding generation's dominant hermeticism through a diaristic, journalistic, and quotidian "lower" tonality. Spaziani's love of and respect for the sublime beauty of which poetry is capable, as well as her firm belief in inspiration, placed her work, from the very beginning, squarely within the tradition of high lyricism, both ancient and modern, rather than the experimental, novelty-oriented spirit of self-conscious contemporaneity. This dedication to tradition continued throughout her subsequent work, although she soon moved farther away from the heavy reliance on certain formal and thematic models evident in the first collection.

Le acque del Sabato, awarded the Premio Internazionale Byron, was received positively by critics such as Emilio Cecchi, Domenico Porzio, and Luigi Baldacci, as well as by other poets. Montale wrote – in a 1954 letter to Albert Camus quoted in Spaziani's *Poesie* (1979) – that she was "l'unique femme écrivain d'Italie ... qui ait le droit de se dire un poète" (the only woman writer in Italy who has the right to call herself a poet). Montale and Spaziani were of tremendous mutual importance to each other's poetry during the late 1940s and early 1950s.

As Spaziani continued to develop as a poet, she also began an academic career. She had written a thesis on Marcel Proust (as part of earning her degree at the University of Turin in 1948), and eventually, in 1964, after having taught in a boys' high school, she took a position as professor of French at the University of Messina. That career has resulted in various scholarly publications and translations from French, American, and German literature, and it still continues. Although she has traveled widely in England, the Soviet Union, Belgium, and Greece, and spent sustained periods in France and the United States, Spaziani has for many years lived and worked primarily in Rome. She is currently the president of the Centro Internazionale Eugenio Montale, a Roman foundation for the dissemination and study of poetry, which awards an annual prize for translations and publications of Italian verse. A frequent contributor to the newspaper the *Stampa,* Spaziani has also appeared often on Italian and Swiss television.

The scholarly and professional activities to which Spaziani has dedicated a great portion of her time have not stifled her poetic inspiration. In 1959 she published another collection of verse, *Luna lombarda* (Lombard Moon), followed by *Il gong* (The Gong) in 1962, the latter of which won the Premio Firenze. These two volumes were incorporated into the 1966 collection *Utilità della memoria* (Utility of Memory), which won the Premio Carducci. In 1970 a new volume titled *L'occhio del ciclone* (The Eye of the Cyclone) was published and recognized with the award of two prizes, the Cittadella and the Trieste. In 1976 Spaziani published *Ultrasuoni* (Ultrasounds), later incorporated into *Transito con catene* (Passage with Chains, 1977), the winner of the Premio Vallombrosa. The 1980s saw the publication of *Geometria del disordine* (Geometry of Disorder, 1981), which won the Premio Viareggio, and *La stella del libero arbitrio* (The Star of Free Will, 1986). The narrative poem *Giovanna d'Arco* was published in 1990. Her body of work is generally recognized as one of sustained seriousness and excellence, and it has earned her an eminent position within modern Italian letters.

The titles of all Spaziani's collections are indicative of an underlying poetics informing the individual poems. She has explicitly stated that the titles are all metaphors for poetry itself. In a note in *Le acque del Sabato,* for example, she writes that the title is an "Antichissima e perfetta immagine ebraica per 'poesia,' intesa come contemplazione, da un punto di vista di immobilità o serena distensione o catarsi (il sacro riposo del Sabato) di ogni cosa terrena soggetta al fluire del tempo, di cui normalmente, per distrazione o eccessiva vicinanza o fatica, la visione è offuscata" (Ancient and perfect Hebrew image for "poetry," understood as contemplation, from the point of view of immobility or serene relaxation or catharsis [the sacred rest of the Sabbath] of every earthly thing subject to the flow of time, the vision of which is normally obfuscated, due to distraction or excessive closeness or exertion). That Spaziani's poetry is as much about poetry as it is about lived experience is thus made clear: poetry as contemplation; as a ritualistic, yet natural function; as a connection between life and dreams. Throughout her works the importance of memory — collective and personal — is constant, just as the deep sonorities (the "heartbeat" of poetry) and the transpersonal truths of expression are always given priority.

The autobiographical element evident in her first collection in the form of both elegiac and vitalistic responses to places, people, and events is still present, although tempered, in *Luna lombarda* and *Il gong*. Regarding the former, Spaziani states in a note that the collection is "una rievocazione . . . del 1956–57, quando insegnavo al liceo scientifico del collegio maschile 'Facchetti' di Treviglio" (a reevocation . . . of 1956–57, when I taught at the technical high school for boys, the "Facchetti" in Treviglio). However, the symbolic dominates the narrative dimension. She also simultaneously projects herself into an imagined future, when her own intensely lived story will be a part of history, inscribed along with so many other personal stories into the cycle of time: "Ritornerà con le nuvole, con le stagioni, / tremando ebbrezze seppellite: / ottenebrato, inutile, senza respiro" (It will come back with the clouds, with the seasons, / stirring up buried rapture: / faded, useless, without breath). An epic, mythic quality begins to emerge in *Il gong*. Spaziani creates a poetry of more breadth and sweep through the construction of suites that maintain tonal and thematic unity. One of the most successful is "Il fuoco dipinto" (Painted Fire), a series of rhymed tercets in hendecasyllables, the technical concision and formal control of which contrast with the intensity of the emotions being portrayed — love, anger, longing, and desolation.

The title poem of *Utilità della memoria* (which includes the two previous volumes) provides a hint of that collection's focus: "io ricordo tutto, grazie al Cielo, / la memoria l'ho giovane e forte" (I remember everything, thank Heaven, / memory I have young and strong). The inescapability of memory, as well as its positive and negative functions, are effectively captured in this poem. As Spaziani makes clear, memory reminds one of what one no longer has while providing treasures that help one to go on. It is useful, therefore, but also painful and ruthlessly indifferent to the ironies it serves to highlight. The self-ironic stance is a new element in this collection; no longer submerged by waves of nostal-

Spaziani circa 1960

gia or rendered ecstatic by epiphanic flashes, Spaziani is psychologically and rhetorically more distanced from her own experience and the expression of it.

L'occhio del ciclone is made up of two long sections, "Il Mare" (The Sea) and "La Terra" (The Earth), divided by an "Intermezzo" of six prose poems. Readers see the influence of Montale once more, both in the salient role of the sea (reminiscent of his early "Mediterraneo" suite in the 1925 collection *Ossi di seppia* (Cuttlefish Bones) and the mixture of poetry and prose pieces such as in his 1956 book *La bufera e altro* (The Storm and Other Things). Yet the influence is more diffuse and less determinant of the tonalities and emphases of structure and lexicon than in Spaziani's earlier verse. Her poetry in *L'occhio del ciclone* is still more neoclassical than experimental, but it often resembles the rhythms of spoken speech. The autobiographical and memorialistic elements are still dominant, however, especially in "La Terra," where Spaziani situates several poems in Rome and includes several others that speak to a lost love.

The poem mentioned in a note by Spaziani as a clarification of the title of the collection is itself untitled and included in "Il Mare":

> Dicono i marinai, quegli ormai vecchi
> lupi di mare che sugli usci fumano
> pipe portoricane, che fra tutti
> i ricordi tremendi dei tifoni
> e l'ululo di morte dei naufragi,
> nulla atterrisce più di quella calma
> che per ore si crea al centro stesso
> della tregenda: l'occhio del ciclone.

> (Sailors say, those old
> salts who sit in doorways smoking
> Puerto Rican pipes, that among all
> the terrible memories of typhoons
> and the death's howl of shipwrecks,
> nothing strikes more fear than that calm
> that for hours is created in the very center
> of the uproar: the eye of the cyclone.)

As in Spaziani's explanation of the title of *Le acque del Sabato,* here again poetry is connected to stasis, to *calma,* but now it is the fearful eye of the cyclone rather than the ideal repose of the Sabbath. In the poem above, Spaziani goes on to call this calm "una gabbia" (a cage) and "un trabocchetto" (a snare), where "la morte è in agguato" (death lies in wait). People are likened to "ragni fra i mozzi delle ruote" (spiders in the hubs of wheels), poised in a deceptively firm and fixed center while events whirl like "l'uragano più nero" (the blackest storm) around the eye. This emphasis on blindness and on the inability of poetry to capture the storm of life even from its ostensibly privileged center continues throughout this and subsequent collections. More and more the cruel ironies of experience are the subjects of Spaziani's verse, and the limits and dangers of poetic re-creation that relies on rationality and control are emphasized.

The ironic, mysterious, and fateful aspects of living are highlighted in the prose pieces included in "Intermezzo." For example, in "Gli uccelli" (The Birds) Spaziani writes of being trapped in her fate of living far from her beloved northern climes, just as certain prey are trapped in the jaws of fish by means of "meccanismi ancora misteriosi" (still mysterious mechanisms). In "La mano" (The Hand) she relates how the strongest image of a past love affair came to her in the Sistine Chapel when she looked at the hand of Adam reaching out for the Creator's hand. Similarly she and her lover had once touched hands by chance across the space between their beds in a train compartment, and she realizes that her hand "chiedeva senza ancor saperlo, con la grazia della mano di Adamo, di venire eletta alla creazione, di approdare alla vita" (asked without yet knowing it, with the grace of Adam's hand, to be chosen for creation, to reach life as a destination). Such hypotheses, analogies, and connections are part of an avid search for the expression of truths that might explain the fateful elements that make up the calm eye and the whirling winds of the storm of life.

Both *Transito con catene* and *Geometria del disordine* reveal in their titles Spaziani's continued interest in the contradictory and ultimately unknowable aspects of experience. In an epigraph to the former volume she indicates her stance:

> Follia non è sapere che di tutti
> quei trentamila giorni che viviamo
> ne resteranno forse dieci o venti
> ben vivi alla memoria. . . .

> (Madness is not knowing that of all
> those thirty thousand days that we live
> perhaps only ten or twenty will remain
> strongly alive in our memory. . . .)

Spaziani's writing remains faithful to her early clarity and control, revealing her urgency to capture those authentic days. There are included in these two collections poems that, as usual, rely on remembered places and people, including a beautiful suite dedicated to Spaziani's mother – "Stella polare" (Polar Star) in *Transito con catene.*

The 1986 collection *La stella del libero arbitrio* includes examples of Spaziani's most radically changed voice to date. As stated in the cover blurb, it has "il timbro di una sprezzatura fra colloquiale e diaristica, un piglio che del suo più illustre parnaso sa essere il perfetto rovescio e persino l'ironica o sommessa 'prosa' " (the timbre of a nonchalance between the colloquial and the diaristic, a style that knows how to be the perfect reverse and even the ironic and subdued "prose" of her most illustrious Parnassian style). Again Montale's influence shows, for he, too, had presented the "reverse" of his earlier high lyrics in his last diaristic collections. There is much the same aphoristic, epigrammatic quality to both poets' more prosaic, quotidian poetry, just as in both there was a desire to sum up certain final insights concerning both experience and art. In her group of poems "La poesia" (Poetry) Spaziani includes three poems directly inspired by Montale, one written on the day of his death. Alluding to his *Ossi di seppia,* she writes: "Il meglio della seppia è l'osso. / Il resto è per i cuochi" (The best of the cuttlefish is the bone. / The rest is for cooks).

The ironic and satiric bent that underlies the quotidian verses in *La stella del libero arbitrio* is commented on in Spaziani's explanatory note regarding the title of the collection. She writes that free will no longer seems to be a practical option, given the scholarly findings regarding such subjects as economics and DNA. She has, therefore, ironically conjoined the words *libero arbitrio* (free will) with the word *stella* (star), a term that for her represents the negation of free choice. She further specifies that *stella* is used in its "significato bonario e degradato, ormai borghesemente o proletariamente secolarizzato e prosciugato all'osso" (kindly and degraded sense, by now secularized and made bone dry by bourgeois or proletarian use). In her poetry, Spaziani both accepts and plays against this "degradation." In the section "Domenica zodiacale" (Zodiacal Sunday), for example, there are several poems in which she trivializes the concept of fate by referring to the astrological profiles printed in newspapers, yet her belief in the mysterious junctures and odd occurrences of life is still evident:

Il Sagittario promette gran viaggi
(ma il mio problema è di viaggiare meno).
Dice che ispiro furenti passioni
ma che in breve ogni furia si spegne.
Il Sagittario è un fascio di saette,
segno di fuoco promette miracoli.
Resta a vedere se quelle saette
le scocco o le ricevo.

(Sagittarius promises great trips
[but my problem is to travel less].
It says that I inspire furious passions
but that in a brief time all fury is spent.
Sagittarius is a bundle of arrows,
the fire sign promises miracles.
It remains to be seen if those arrows
I shoot or I receive.)

There is strong self-irony in many of these poems. As if kidding herself for her well-known attachment to the hendecasyllable, Spaziani includes as an epigraph to the final section of the collection, "Crisi" (Crisis), what she labels as an "endecasillabo spontaneo, da una bolletta della Società Romana Gas" (a spontaneous hendecasyllable, from a bill from the Rome Gas Company): "Se c'è una fuga non cercar con fiamma" (If there's a leak, do not look for it with a match). As she confronts her aging self, she writes in "Vecchia fotografia" (Old Photo-

graph) that many times in the past she had strange intimations of her possible Etruscan parentage, but she now feels an equal sense of mystery in looking at a photograph of herself taken many years ago: "Ma un eguale mistero mi collega stasera / a quegli occhi, a quei ciuffi, a quel vento dimenticato" (But an equal mystery connects me tonight / to those eyes, those tufts of hair, that forgotten wind). More explicitly, in "Le fasi" (The Phases), she expresses her sense of disjuncture from her own aging body: "Ferma! Fatemi scendere! Per sbaglio / mi hanno rinchiusa in un corpo che invecchia" (Stop! Let me off! By mistake / they have shut me up in a body that is getting old). The tone of her poetry has been radically lowered, and it is much closer to the spoken word than to the music of high lyric by which her earlier work is most typically characterized.

Maria Luisa Spaziani took a certain direction early in her career as poet, and she has deviated little from it. It has proven to be a positive direction, not only in the individual development of her "poetry of voice" but also in the collective history of modern Italian verse of the postwar period. Spaziani was and continues to be an alternative to the various other paths followed by poets of her and later generations; neither slavishly imitative of the hermeticism of earlier twentieth-century Italian verse nor radically innovative as much of the neo-avant-garde and postmodernist poetry of the last twenty-five years has been, Spaziani's poetry reveals the richness to be found in a modern and thoroughly personalized use of tradition combined with the highest form of autobiography, in which one's own life takes on resonances that echo meaningfully beyond individual chronology. Her body of work achieves that emotional and moral singularity wherein, according to Spaziani herself, lies the value of important books whether written by men or women, and her poetry stands as an important contribution to the achievements of the modern Italian lyric.

References:

Glauco Cambon, "La voce di Maria Luisa Spaziani," *Italica,* 41 (June 1964): 158–161;

Marco Forti, "Due situazioni poetiche," in his *Le proposte della poesia e nuove proposte* (Milan: Mursia, 1971), pp. 410–414;

Giovanna Wedel De Stasio, "La memoria divinatoria di Maria Luisa Spaziani," *Italian Quarterly* (Fall 1986): 45–49.

Giovanni Testori

(12 May 1923 – 16 March 1993)

Elena Urgnani
Rutgers University

BOOKS: *La morte; Un quadro* (Forlì: Pattuglia, 1943);

Il dio di Roserio (Turin: Einaudi, 1954);

I segreti di Milano: I, Il ponte della Ghisolfa (Milan: Feltrinelli, 1958);

I segreti di Milano: II, La Gilda del Mac Mahon (Milan: Feltrinelli, 1959);

I segreti di Milano: III, La Maria Brasca (Milan: Feltrinelli, 1960);

I segreti di Milano: IV, L'Arialda (Milan: Feltrinelli, 1960);

I segreti di Milano: V, Il fabbricone (Milan: Feltrinelli, 1961); translated by Sidney Alexander as *The House in Milan* (New York: Harcourt, Brace & World, 1962; London: Collins, 1963);

Il Brianza e altri racconti (Milan: Feltrinelli, 1962);

Giovanni Paganin: Scultore dal 1952 al 1963 (Milan: Milione, 1964);

Palinsesto valsesiano (Milan: All'Insegna del Pesce d'Oro, 1964);

Il gran teatro montano: Saggi su Gaudenzio Ferrari (Milan: Feltrinelli, 1965);

I trionfi (Milan: Feltrinelli, 1965);

Crocifissione (Milan: All'Insegna del Pesce d'Oro, 1966);

In trigesimo (Milan: All'Insegna del Pesce d'Oro, 1966);

Manieristi piemontesi e lombardi del '600 (Milan: Pizzi, 1967);

La monaca di Monza (Milan: Feltrinelli, 1967);

L'amore (Milan: Feltrinelli, 1968);

Erodiade (Milan: Feltrinelli, 1969);

Fra Galgario (Turin: ERI, 1969);

Per sempre (Milan: Feltrinelli, 1970);

Thorn Prikker (Milan: All'Insegna del Pesce d'Oro, 1970);

"Nature morte" di Ernesto Ornati (Milan: All'Insegna del Pesce d'Oro, 1970);

Grunewald (Milan: Rizzoli, 1972);

L'Ambleto (Milan: Rizzoli, 1972);

Alain (Milan: Sciardelli, 1973);

Nel tuo sangue (Milan: Rizzoli, 1973);

Macbetto (Milan: Rizzoli, 1974);

La cattedrale (Milan: Rizzoli, 1974);

Passio Laetitiae et Felicitatis (Milan: Rizzoli, 1975);

Edipus (Milan: Rizzoli, 1977);

Conversazione con la morte (Milan: Rizzoli, 1978);

Interrogatorio a Maria (Milan: Rizzoli, 1980);

Il senso della nascita: Colloquio con Don Luigi Giussani (Milan: Rizzoli, 1980);

Factum est (Milan: Rizzoli, 1981);

La maestà della vita (Milan: Rizzoli, 1982);

Post-Hamlet (Milan: Rizzoli, 1983);

Bacon a Brera (Milan: Multhipla, 1983);

Ossa mea (Milan: Mondadori, 1983);

I promessi sposi alla prova (Milan: Mondadori, 1984);

Azione teatrale in due giornate (Milan: Mondadori, 1984);

Confiteor (Milan: Mondadori, 1985);

Kei Mitsuuchi (Milan: Mazzotta, 1985);

Diadèmata (Milan: Garzanti, 1986);

In Exitu (Milan: Garzanti, 1988);

– et nihil (Florence: Arnaud, 1989);

Sfaust (Milan: Longanesi, 1990);

Sdisorè (Milan: Longanesi, 1991).

Collection: *I libri di Giovanni Testori* (Milan: Mondadori, 1984).

OTHER: "Coro della sera," *Politecnico*, 6 (3 November 1945): 7;

"Guardati intorno e impara," in *Racconti* (Milan: Nuova Accademia, 1964), pp. 175–192;

Carlo Borromeo, *Memoriale ai Milanesi*, introduction by Testori (Milan: Giordano, 1965), pp. 1–28;

"Stanze per la flagellazione di San Domenico Maggiore," *Paragone*, no. 226 (December 1968): 3–5;

"Bestemmie e preghiere," in *Almanacco internazionale dei poeti 1973*, edited by Giancarlo Vigorelli (Milan: Borletti, 1973), p. 194;

"Un uomo in una donna, anzi un Dio," preface to Michelangelo Buonarroti's *Rime* (Milan: Rizzoli, 1975), pp. i–xviii;

Giovanni Testori circa 1983

"Dodici poesie da a te," *Almanacco dello Specchio,* 8 (1979): 175–180;

Luca Doninelli, *Intorno a una lettera di Santa Caterina,* introduction by Testori (Milan: Rizzoli, 1981), pp. 5–14;

Traduzione della I Lettera ai Corinti, translated by Testori (Milan: Longanesi, 1991).

Giovanni Testori first presented himself to the public during World War II with two one-act plays, *La morte* (Death) and *Un quadro* (A Painting), published together in 1943, but his major work consists of prose, in the form of essays, novels, and short stories. His first attempt at narrative, *Il dio di Roserio* (The God of Roserio, 1954), started a cycle of novels and plays with the overall title *I Segreti di Milano* (Secrets of Milan), 1958–1961) — obviously inspired by the *Mysteries of Paris* (1842–1843) by Eugène Sue. Testori's style led critics to label him a verist or a naturalist. The setting of his novels is geographically limited to the Milanese hinterland, where the petite bourgeoisie and lumpenproletarians try to survive and improve their status through sport competitions but find themselves in a vicious cycle of prostitution, pornography, and underworld homosexuality. The usage of Milanese dialect becomes more and more rare in the books, while stress is placed on the tangle between the persecuted and the persecutors.

Born on 12 May 1923 in Novate Milanese, a suburb of Milan, Testori came from a family of textile industrialists. His parents were Edoardo and Lina Testori. He received a Catholic education, attending the lyceum at the Collegio Arcivescovile San Carlo and the Catholic University of Milan, where he graduated with a degree in philosophy in 1947. Later he dedicated himself to literature, literary criticism, and art history.

The production of Testori as a poet began in 1965 with the book *I trionfi* (The Triumphs), whose title recalls Petrarch. It is a long autobiographical poem, a collection of cultural and intellectual experiences and of religious and intellectual anxieties. The result of Testori's exasperated and sometimes artificial effort of introversion is a poetry of screams and convulsive cries that derives colorism and violence from the literary influences of Paul Verlaine, Arthur Rimbaud, and Gabriele D'Annunzio. Testori accumulates linguistic and stylistic materials in an attempt to dilute into poetry the dense autobiographical mixture of contradictions, such as morbidly erotic homosexual and heterosexual obsessions, which do not meld with the restrictiveness of a dark, counterreformist religiosity. Writing becomes a form of self-damnation and, at the same time, a form of spiritual safety. Testori's poetic narration breaks abruptly into questions, excited cries, and violent, desperate confessions. Moments of such confession are mingled with the inclination toward a scenographic and allegorical grandiosity. Any love refrain is immediately counterbalanced by a death refrain. Death is invoked and awaited as a liberation from sensual, material passion, incarnated deep within the body. This poem is the diary of an "irregular" love between the older poet and his younger male lover, referred to as the blond "agile cervo" (agile deer), descended from the north. Tender, melancholy, and exciting moments are inserted into the allegorical scheme of a long, hymnographic poem.

Separation and regret come to signify the triumph of life, through love, over the fragility of substance and thus over death, the triumph of existence and understanding over nothing and nonsense, and the triumph of unity over separation: "Non è indifferenza; / forse è passione / che la demenza porta, / di scatto in scatto / e di groviglio in strame, / dall'immane crosta / verso lo strazio di sentire, / verso la difficile luce / di capire" (It is not indifference; / it could be passion / that craziness brings, / from click to click / and from tangle to litter, / from the giant crust / toward the pain of feeling, / toward the difficult light / of understanding). This scheme, however, is not sustained by a certitude of faith. It is rather a continuous oscillation that leads to blasphemy. The triumph of positive values is often only apparent and illusory; it is the everlasting self-repetition of the "sussulto infinito della creta" (the infinite convulsion of clay), while the only triumph that seems to be permanent is that of separation and death.

One year after *I trionfi,* Testori published another book of poetry, *Crocifissione* (Crucifix-

ion, 1966), which is a long poem in several untitled sections and which follows the same thematic path of theological doubts accompanied by sexual obsessions. In *Crocifissione* there is a thematic and stylistic continuity with the "Intermezzi" of *I trionfi.* The composition has the tonality of a more extreme exasperation and verbal violence, and it more vividly recalls the invective style of Jacopone da Todi.

The foreground consists of the image of Christ ascending Calvary. What was a background in *I trionfi* now becomes the foreground. Time, space, and the image of Christ's face are transformed: they become all the possible faces of living creatures, through a process of condensation that evokes an oneiric vision, a nightmare, or a surrealistic picture. Such an effect is the result of a lexical mixture motivated by the blending of places and people in a common condition:

> Nella landa ingrigita,
> tra scheletri di schisti,
> pietre, brina,
> arranca la palpebra tremante,
> la veste mortuaria,
> calcinata,
> stanca.
> Fetono le arterie;
> il gasolio
> stipa le cloache.
> Ombre sfatte
> cadono dai cieli,
> gemini,
> pianeti.

> (In the gray land,
> among skeletal schists,
> stones, rime,
> the trembling eyelid waddles,
> the mortuary garments,
> calcined,
> tired.
> The arteries stench;
> the gas oil
> fills the cloaca.
> Shapeless shadows
> fall down from the skies,
> gemini,
> planets.)

Theological doubt later becomes more and more radical, almost blasphemous. The man who hobbles, carrying death over his shoulders, is "the son of man," the atavistic carcass of a tired humanity, in a landscape where the modern crust holds together the layers underneath, the residual of the past centuries, and covers the universal emptiness. The bleeding image that imprints the linen offered by Veronica's piety to the suffering man is "senza

Testori (far left) and friends celebrate publication of the one-hundredth issue of Paragone, *a Florentine journal for which Testori was art critic*

senso" (meaningless). At the moment of the last agony, of the final defeat, we feel the failure of the vanquished god/man.

The stylistic indications that emerge from *I trionfi* and from *Crocifissione* ripen in the 1968 collection *L'amore* (Love). Testori abandons the ambitious idea of a long poem or hymn in favor of a more intimate mood. Thematically readers find the suffering of homosexuals and the distress caused by having a socially different nature. Obsession with sin draws a shadow over the sensual and mystical relationship with a son/brother/lover. The form of the composition shifts from the chant to the fragmentation of the lyrical poem, mitigated and concentrated on the image of Alain (the lover), who works as a catalyst for images, metaphors, and obsessions. The type of love Testori writes about is strongly sensualized and is a pretext for metaphors that constitute an elegant, but still obsessive, description of sex acts.

In Testori's search for a significance, there is another recurrent theme, already outlined in *I trionfi* — the father-son relationship — inside the emblematic relationship between him and Alain: "O figlio amato / mai avuto che in te / di cui accolgo nel bacio / lo

spasimo dei sensi" (Oh my beloved son / son that I never had other than in you / in whose kiss I receive / the spasm of the senses). At other times the roles are reversed: "Da grande che sono / divento tuo bambino, / tu il mio pastore" (Adult though I am / I become your child / you are my shepherd). Sensuality deepens into a dimension in which the significance of life is questioned. Religious experience becomes a metaphor for sexual experience or verges on blasphemy:

Il Cristo,
la corona di lagrime
e di spine
che frammenti fiorisce
di cervice,
sostanze eterne
incorpore
nel grembo vergine aspettato;
il Cristo che urla,
maledice,
latra,
non scacciarlo da me.

(Christ,
the crown of tears
and thorns

that flowers fragments
of nape,
eternal substances
incorporated
in the awaited virgin womb;
the howling Christ,
cursing,
barking,
do not drive him away from me.)

The poetry of *L'amore,* like that of *I Trionfi,* speaks through associations, sometimes hallucinations, and is marked by the recurrence of terms and images. The verse has an irregular measure — from two to fifteen or sixteen syllables — and does not seem restricted to any formal criterion. Punctuation is abundant, almost always at the end of the lines, but there are numerous cases of enjambment. Testori's strongly expressionistic style makes use of punctuation to emphasize certain focal points.

The passage from *I trionfi* to *L'amore* represented a substantially new and different mood in Testori's poetry. The form of his composition became more restrained, more dense. This change is carried further in *Per sempre* (Forever, 1970), which confirms the appearance of a second stylistic manner that will continue to exist beside the early fluid, complex style. In *Per sempre* the sentence becomes more incisive, the poems are as short as fragments, and their first requisite is their simplicity. The semantic expressionism is utilized as a shock factor, and rhymes are more frequent and precise.

The central theme is again love, and the poems constitute a further testimonial to a mystical kind of eroticism, not only because the area of metaphorization is often extrapolated from religious terminology, and more specifically from Christian terminology, but also because the experience of love itself becomes total, an experience of an absolute. Testori explores the ways through which love, a temporal reality that usually perishes after a while, may reach a total dimension and last forever: "Baciami ancora, / baciami con più gioia, / baciami finito ed infinito, / baciami infinitamente. / — e che si baci il mondo / nella pace dei martiri e dei santi . . ." (Kiss me again, / kiss me more joyfully, / kiss me as I am finite and infinite, / kiss me infinitely. / — and let the world kiss / in the peace of martyrs and saints . . .).

Another central theme is the fluency of time, which the title emphasizes. The theme of paternity is also prevalent:

Ecco la sposa:
l'ha amato,
t'ha creato.

Benedetta la rosa
che il ventre ha lacerato.
Dall'ombra la ringrazio
per averci un angelo donato
in questo tempo grigio
e sconsacrato.

(Here is the bride:
she loved him,
she created you.

Blessed be the rose
which the groin lacerated.
From the shadows I thank her
for having given us an angel
in this time gray
and desecrated.)

For Testori "la rosa" is a common metaphor for the male organ, and the image of the mother remains in the background. Often the lover is perceived as a son, as in *L'amore.*

Remaining active as a playwright, in 1971 Testori founded the theater group Cooperative Franco Parenti, with Parenti and André Ruth Shammah. The goal was to revitalize the Theater Pier Lombardo. Testori took the opportunity to show his plays to a larger audience, and he started to write his well-known *triologia: L'Ambleto* (1972), *Macbetto* (1974), and *Edipus* (1977). *Nel tuo sangue* (With Your Blood, 1973) is the first collection Testori published after the radical religious questioning that he engaged in subsequent to his mother's death in 1970. In this collection Testori seems to go back to the theological doubts seen in his first two books. *Nel tuo sangue* has a preface that informs readers of the kind of blasphemous prayer, or sacred blasphemy, that these poems constitute. They can be very disturbing. From the formal point of view, these compositions have brevity as an essential characteristic, and often the rhymes have a provocative and desecrating effect:

Tu sei il Dio marcio
il Dio incarnato.
Sei il Dio Cristo,
il Dio sangue,
il Dio *peccato.*

(You are the putrid God
the incarnated God.
You are the Christ God,
the blood God,
the *sin* God.)

The book is divided into four sections, each without a title. The first concentrates on the personal relationship between Testori and God:

T'ho amato con pietà
con furia T'ho adorato.
T'ho violato, sconciato, bestemmiato.

Tutto puoi dire di me
tranne che T'ho evitato.

(I loved You with piety
with fury I adored You.
I raped You, I spoiled You, I cursed You.

You can say anything about me
except that I avoided You.)

The second section is dedicated to San Giovanni, the disciple most loved by Christ. The irreligious reading key is once again homosexuality:

L'hai amato più degli altri.
Sul desco della Cena
appoggiava la sua guancia
al Tuo volto.

Non era solo predilezione,
era un'atroce, carnale
peccatrice dedizione.

(You loved him more than the others.
On the Last Supper table
he was leaning his cheek
on your face.

It was not only predilection,
it was an atrocious, carnal
sinful devotion.)

The third part is completely dedicated to Mary, and a biological dimension is added to the eucharistic mystery:

Hai lasciato anche Tu
sulla neve di quel lontano Natale
una rosa di sangue,
un liquido sconcio e fetale.

(You too left
on the snow of that long gone Christmas
a bloody rose,
an obscene and fetal liquid.)

Sometimes a tender familial scheme is inserted to represent Christ's infancy:

Quando Tua madre
Ti stendeva sul grigio giaciglio
baciava suo figlio
o un mostro atroce e divino,
una carne di pane e di vino?

(When Your mother
laid You down
on the gray straw bed
was she kissing her child
or a dreadful and divine monster,
a flesh of bread and wine?)

The divine mystery is given a human dimension.

In 1975 Testori wrote a short preface to a new edition of Michelangelo's *Rime*. The title Testori chose for his text is "Un uomo in una donna, anzi un Dio" (A Man Within a Woman, Rather a God), which is the incipit of a well-known madrigal Michelangelo wrote for Vittoria Colonna. It is a significant choice because Testori is the first critic to recognize fully, explicitly, and sympathetically Michelangelo's homosexuality. Testori also emphasizes Michelangelo's fifty epitaphs for Cecchino Bracci and the ambiguity of Michelangelo's relationship with Colonna. This act of criticism acquires its fullest and most meaningful form because of the complete adherence of Testori to the feelings expressed by Michelangelo.

The year 1977 was rather crucial in Testori's life; it was the year of his final conversion to Catholicism, a conversion that had been accelerated by his mother's death. The late 1970s were also years in which Italian public opinion was divided because of the referendum on abortion; Testori was resolutely opposed to abortion. This intense political participation led to a time of meditation and renewed theatrical ardor that overcame Testori's activity as a poet — until the publication of the book *Ossa mea* (My Bones, 1983), which is centered on the concept of the *poète maudit* (damned poet) and presents macabre images that are projections of the insistent sense of guilt toward a God that makes himself more and more unattainable.

These are images that the poet draws directly from the Lombardian tradition of *scapigliatura* (unconventionality), borrowing them from poets such as Cletto Arrighi or Igino Ugo Tarchetti. Testori also shares with them the same disgust toward any form of the so-called progress that the *scapigliati* feel. To him there is no progress in human history, only a monotonous repetition of the same primordial and apocalyptic horror. The city is perceived as chaos and emptiness, as a horrible lump of degenerated humanity. But the most powerful images, peculiar to Testori, are those that spring out of Catholicism, and they accompany social criticism:

Società
tradita soglia;

società
mentita spoglia,
senza seni.
Eva sei,
senza utero
né denti.
Non ti penti?
. . . .
Come feti
qui profeti,
Toro a corna,
fisse d'Aquila pupille,
ruggì d'Africa il Leone,
venne l'Angelo scrivano.

(Society
betrayed threshold;
society
belied garments,
breastless.
You are Eve,
wombless
teethless.
Don't you repent?
. . . .
like fetuses
here prophets,
horned Bull,
fixed Eagle's pupils,
the African lion roared,
the scrivener Angel came.)

The images of the four evangelists are symbolized according to the allegories canonized by the scholastic tradition, while the attitude of the four beasts forecasts the imminent apocalypse.

The love talk prevailing in *L'amore* and *Per sempre* is over, and what prevails is the screaming, blasphemy, and invective, which is on three levels: theological, social, and private. Generally speaking, the verse is free, whereas the syntax is hammering and paratactic. In his poetry Testori keeps refusing the lesson of the *avanguardia,* from which he also distances himself because of his political position. Testori seems an anomalous Christian Democrat.

In the collection *Diadèmata* (1986) the mysticism of Testori's eroticism is overcome. He descends to the chronicling of facts, in a series of episodes that might have been taken from a police accident report. Sex is a stimulus, but it is not looked at as a sin. What is emphasized is the violence of man against man, the abuse of and the wish for the annihilation of the "other." Dialogue is frequent, but it is more realistic and bleak than that in *L'amore* and *Per sempre.*

Late in his life Giovanni Testori collaborated with various periodicals, including the *Sabato,* a Catholic militant weekly newspaper, linked to the integralist Catholic movement Comunione e Liberazione. He died of cancer on 16 March 1993 after being hospitalized in Milan for three years.

References:

Ignazio Baldelli, *Varianti di prosatori contemporanei* (Florence: Le Monnier, 1965), pp. 76–91;

Giovanni Cappello, *Giovanni Testori* (Rome: Nuova Italia, 1983);

Annamaria Cascetta, *Invito alla lettura di Testori* (Milan: Mursia, 1983);

Angelo Guglielmi, *Vero e falso* (Milan: Feltrinelli, 1968), pp. 123–127;

Leone Piccioni, *Maestri veri e maestri del nulla* (Turin: SEI, 1979);

Rinaldo Rinaldi, *Romanzo come deformazione* (Milan: Mursia, 1985), pp. 63–177.

Patrizia Valduga

(20 May 1953 –)

Guido Mascagni
Rutgers University

BOOKS: *Medicamenta* (Milan: Guanda, 1982);
La tentazione (Milan: Crocetti, 1985).

OTHER: "Quattordici sonetti," *Almanacco dello Specchio,* 10 (1981): 321–331.

The form of Patrizia Valduga's poetry – its most striking component – attracts the attention of critics and readers. Her rich, ponderous, minutely examined language has been full of philological refinements and neologisms since the publication of her first fourteen sonnets in the *Almanacco dello Specchio* (1981). In composing her poetry, she borrows from contemporary and classical Italian poetry, and various sources in between. After she won the Premio Viareggio in 1982, Valduga's work began to be examined for more intrinsic values and meanings. She is now regarded in a more complex and profound light, as more than just a stylist and the author of a collection of erotic lyrics – *Medicamenta* (Medicine, 1982).

Patrizia Valduga was born on 20 May 1953 in Castelfranco Veneto, a small town in the northern Italian region of Treviso, not far from Venice. Soon she moved with her large family to Belluno, a nearby city. In the mid 1970s Valduga attended medical school at the University of Padua, concentrating on psychology. In 1978 she transferred to the Department of Modern Languages and Literatures at the University of Venice, where she graduated in French literature with a thesis on Louis-Ferdinand Céline under the direction of professor Francesco Orlando. She was married at that time but then separated and began a relationship with the poet and literary critic Giovanni Raboni. In the late 1970s Valduga moved to Milan, where she started working as an editor for the Guanda publishing house.

Valduga is a woman of definite cultural views. Her love for poetry began when she was only seven. She prefers Dante – with his "plurilinguism" – to Petrarch, and Torquato Tasso to Ludovico Ariosto.

Patrizia Valduga circa 1985

She prizes the doubt that constantly permeates Tasso's work and his transitional position between the Renaissance and early baroque mannerism. She admires Giambattista Marini for his excellent technical skill: his musicality, difficult and rare rhymes, and alliteration. Among her contemporaries, she admires Raboni, Maurizio Cucchi, and Cesare Viviani. Her true passion, though, is for a contemporary playwright, Tadeusz Kantor, for being "uno stemma – il colore che racchiude in sé l'inferno dell'umiliazione umana e il cielo di ogni possibile redenzione" (an emblem – the color containing in itself the hell of human humiliation and the heaven of all possible redemption), as Franco Cordelli states in his introduction to her *La tentazione* (Temptation, 1985). Her musical taste runs to baroque music and the works of Richard Wagner. She prefers the poetry and prose of the seventeenth and eighteenth centuries over twentieth-century fiction, which – except for that of Guido Ceronetti and Céline – she finds boring and flat.

She received the Premio Viareggio for her first work, *Medicamenta,* a book she disavowed immediately after its publication, while her second collection, *La tentazione,* was in progress. At present Valduga lives and works in Milan, where she directed for some months *Poesie,* a monthly journal. She is one of the most prominent and characteristic personalities of the new generation of Italian poets.

The formal peculiarity of Valduga's poetry partly concerns her reversion to poetical forms no longer common. She uses the sonnet, for instance, in most of *Medicamenta,* in which ottava rima appears throughout a whole section. She also uses the triplet. *La tentazione* comprises ten cantos of thirty-three triplets and one hendecasyllable each, a scheme that unmistakably recalls Dante's poetry.

Why this interest in classical form with the choice of traditional rhymes? Why this rejection of the "freedom" of the free verse? In her 1985 interview with Antonio D'Orrico, Valduga admits that the use of rhymes helps one not only to read but to create poetry. The rhymes lend more musicality to her poetry and, at the same time, offer a way back to the classical material from which she has borrowed so heavily. This material, which has a unity of sound rather than concepts, has its roots in the musicality of language itself. At the end of *La tentazione* she quotes Giacomo Lubrano, the eighteenth-century Jesuit preacher and poet who praises memory as the heritage of imagery, and she sadly recognizes the difficulty of memorizing the rhymeless poetry of the twentieth century.

The technical result of Valduga's poetry is remarkable, although wavering here and there. At some points it is hard to reckon with the syllables, rhymes, and assonances. Occasionally the equilibrium is jeopardized by a compelling and constraining lexical choice, which appears like a patch on a torn cloth. Occasionally readers see hypometric lines or obscure semideveloped concepts that require long explanations. These lines – with their stylistic incoherence – sometimes break the overall equilibrium unpleasantly, probably the most evident proof of her effort to go back to patterns in disuse for about a century and her incomplete mastery of them.

In regard to the elements borrowed from tradition, it is not hard to recognize in Valduga's poetry the echoes of Dante, Petrarch, Tasso, and Marini, as well as the *stilnovo* (new style) and the poetesses of the sixteenth century. Sometimes echoes emerge from lines taken as they are or from rearrangements of the lines. At other times certain techniques are employed, among which the typical baroque metaphor stands out. The beginning of *La tentazione,* for instance, is obviously Dantesque:

> In questa maledetta notte oscura
> con una tentazione fui assalita
> che ancora in cuore la vergogna dura.
>
> (In this cursed dark night
> I was assaulted with a temptation
> so that the shame still lasts inside.)

Baroque conceits and metaphors are also evident in these lines from *Medicamenta:*

> O marea d'amore
> sul ramo di mare del cuore . . .
> ma invera o invanisce il cuore?
>
> (O tide of love
> on the arm of the sea of the heart . . .
> does the heart become true or idle?)

Valduga's vocabulary is rich, too – the fruit of diligent linguistic studies and research, even in antiquarian dictionaries – and it includes neologisms. The product is always the result of long reflection and intense, constant work and research.

The content and themes of *Medicamenta* deserve attention. The book is divided into three sections and opens with the quotation of a triplet from Dante's *Inferno* (canto 25):

> Coi piè di mezzo gli avvinse la pancia,
> e con gli anterior le braccia prese,
> poi gli addentò l'una e l'altra guancia.
>
> (Its middle feet sank in the sweat and grime
> of the wretch's paunch, its forefeet damped his arms,
> its teeth bit through both cheeks).
> – translation by John Ciardi

In a circle of thieves a damned soul is being attacked by a reptile, and following the assault the sinner turns into a serpent while the reptile turns into the sinner. The emphasis is on mutation, an exchange of two natures that in Valduga's work appears to touch on the double nature of humankind and the dualism "idealized life versus real life." Dante's image is also highly carnal and erotic, as well as one of physical possession, the first of many such images in *Medicamenta* and *La tentazione.*

The first poem of *Medicamenta* is an anticipation of a later one that begins the same way:

> Sa sedurre la carne la parola,
> prepara il gesto, produce destini. . . .

> (The word knows how to seduce the flesh,
> prepares the gesture, produces fates. . . .)

Later the thought continues:

> E martirio è il verso,
> è emergenza di sangue che cola
> e s'aggruma ai confini
> del suo inverso sessuato, controverso.

> (And the verse is distress,
> an emergency of bleeding
> and clotting blood at the boundaries
> of its sexuated, controversial reverse.)

Poetry is proclaimed to be an "other life," a sublimated, parallel world opposed to daily life; at the same time it is distress, martyrdom, suffering, and the pain of creation. Yet to lack the word or the skill to use it means not to be able to understand and act, and to fall into despair and frustration. The meaning of the Latin title of this collection becomes clear: *medicamenta* can mean medicine, remedy, poison, or filter.

Taken one by one, the images could appear merely as different aspects of the same thing – sex; but taken together they provide a grid of meaning that includes Valduga's perception of life, her own personal reality. Most of the erotic images are expressed in terms of violence, almost rape, and not simply of passion:

> Legami annegami e infine annientami.
> Addormentami e ancora entra . . . riprovami.
> Incoronami. Eternami. Inargentami.

> (Tie me drown me and then destroy me.
> Dull me and come in again . . . retry me.
> Crown me. Immortalize me. Silver me.)

At other times the sensuality is a weird eroticism – frantic, made up of alliterations and neologisms:

> E nottetempo la gente si arrappa,
> s'ingrifa, al serra serra si disgroppa.
> Ah . . . eh . . . ah . . . bada ansimare . . . di tappa
> in tappa svelta s'accoppia, s'aggroppa.

> (And overnight the people get horny,
> snout off, at the clench jump on each other.
> Ah . . . eh . . . ah . . . watch their panting . . .
> from stage to stage quickly they couple, they rump off.)

Eroticism is later tied to the trouble of living, to an incompatibility that has to be worked out at any cost.

The main theme in *Medicamenta* and *La tentazione* is the sense of loss involved in purely physical sex, which leads to a "non-life," the death of the soul. In fact, death appears throughout *Medicamenta*. Sometimes it is invoked as a relief, as when death poses as shelter against fear.

La tentazione, like most of *Medicamenta,* is a "nocturnal" book including the frustrating erotic activities and recollections of the speaker. The night therefore assumes the connotations of the Dantesque forest of the first canto of the *Inferno,* with all its dismay and loss of the self. The night is an enemy caging the thought; whereas in *Medicamenta* night is the container of the anguishes of a life perceived as wasted and unlived. In *La tentazione* the night means pleasure and death, indissolubly tied together. The night is like poetry, which creates and solves situations at the same time, which gives them meaning, and which explains the questions about life in new ways through its expressive unpredictability.

In *La tentazione* sex is mostly described with disgust. When the theme of sex develops, it takes on an even stronger sense of repulsion. The lover – the most animal part of the self or the id – constantly asks for sex but is constantly rejected. The consequence is having to reckon with the impossibility of an escape from that id: "Non c'è scampo dall'uomo, non c'è scampo" (There's no escape from being human, no escape).

The final invocation is eloquently addressed to the night, the most propitious time for poetic creation. It is a prayer of liberation from obsessive carnality in order to be able to express all the potential of a fully lived life, to understand, and, like Saint Augustine exhorting Petrarch in Petrarch's *Secretum,* to take advantage of that understanding by a constant will aiming at personal improvement: "Confusamente l'anima comprende / e non volere più infine vuole" (Confusedly the soul understands / and wants not to want anymore). *La tentazione,* therefore, as does Dante's *Commedia,* has a cathartic aspect of personal purification, although it is not an actual Christian redemption. There is no God in Valduga's work; instead there is a void in which she is groping. There is a hope for something that is hard to know but which can save, which seems to be very close to the awareness created by poetry:

> O notte, notte, invano tu nascondi
> nei tuoi capelli il mio vile nemico,
> invano vuoi che in quel vomito affondi:

io non ti supplico, io ti maledico.
Apri, ti prego, fa' che veda il cielo,
contro il tuo buio invano mi affatico.

(O night, night, in vain you hide
in your hair my vile foe,
in vain you want me to sink in that vomit:

I am not imploring, I am cursing you.
Open, I pray you, let me see the sky,
I tire myself against your darkness.)

Salvation, the light in the darkness of night, is a poetic experience. The speaker is looking for an opening by following Dante's method, a way out of the forest of existential confusion by pursuing in verse what one cannot understand or say any other way. Night becomes a darkness producing poetical light.

Without poetry, according to Valduga, life is nothing but a blind transit through meaningless banalities, an absurd routine, unintelligible daily repetitions, and above all a renunciation of the present for a futile illusion of a fully true life in the future: "Aspettando la vita che vivrai? / o duri sonni o altra cosa più dura" (What can you live waiting for life? / Either hard sleeps or something else harder). Such hints at the pain of living are frequent and coherent in Valduga's work. In order to survive, one has to construct one's own pseudolife from mere matter, a fake efficiency hiding an existential nothingness.

La tentazione is not new in recognizing loveless eroticism as a mishap that can occur in a fully lived life. However, one's awareness can lead to an existential solution through psychological and poetic action. Sex and shame, desire and guilt, and temptation and redemption are perceived in a Christian way as polar oppositions. Obviously the dualism "love-death" is nothing new, but in *La tentazione* one can hear those echoes of traditional religious literature in a modern way. Flesh is life and the grave, and poetry is one key to understanding this dualism.

Interview:
Antonio D'Orrico, "Il mio poema è un furto," *Unità,* 11 November 1985.

References:
Franco Cordelli, Introduction to Valduga's *La tentazione* (Milan: Crocetti, 1985);
Antonio Porta, "Scrivere un sonetto con le parole di oggi," *Corriere della Sera,* 26 September 1982, p. 3;
Giovanni Raboni, "Introduzione a Quattordici sonetti," *Almanacco dello Specchio,* 10 (1981): 318–321.

Diego Valeri

(25 January 1887 – 28 November 1976)

Thomas E. Peterson
University of Georgia

BOOKS: *Monodia d'Amore* (Padua: Società Co-operativa Tipografica, 1908);

Le gaie tristezze (Milan, Palermo & Naples: Sandron, 1913);

Umana (Ferrara: Taddei, 1916);

Crisalide (Ferrara: Taddei, 1919);

Il canto di Farinata (Ravenna: Ravegnana, 1922);

Ariele (Milan: Mondadori, 1924);

Poeti francesi del nostro tempo (Piacenza: Porta, 1924):

Montaigne (Rome: Formiggini, 1925);

Il campanellino (Turin: SEI, 1928);

Poesie vecchie e nuove (Milan: Mondadori, 1930);

I colli Euganei (Florence: Nemi, 1932);

Guerrino il Meschino (Turin: UTET, 1932);

Fantasie veneziane (Milan: Mondadori, 1934);

Scherzo e finale (Milan: Mondadori, 1937);

Scrittori francesi (Milan: Mondadori, 1937);

Saggi e note di letteratura francese moderna (Florence: Sansoni, 1941);

Tempo che muore (Milan: Mondadori, 1942);

Guida sentimentale di Venezia (Padua: Tre Venezie, 1942); translated by Cecil C. Palmer as *A Sentimental Guide to Venice* (Florence: Sansoni, 1955);

Città materna (Padua: Tre Venezie, 1944);

Giuseppe Cesetti (Rovereto: Arte Delfino, 1944);

Cinque secoli di pittura veneta (Padua: Tre Venezie, 1945);

Taccuino svizzero (Milan: Hoepli, 1947);

Il fraticello re (Turin: SEI, 1948);

Il teatro comico veneziano (Venice: GEV, 1949);

Terzo tempo (Milan: Mondadori, 1950);

Sand e Musset (Turin: Radio Italiana, 1950);

Giacomo Favretto (Venice: Ferrari, 1950);

Nature morte di Tosi (Milan: All'Insegna del Pesce d'Oro, 1952);

Il simbolismo francese da Nerval a Régnier (Padua: Liviana, 1954);

Fiorenzo Tomea (Milan: Centro Culturale San Fedele, 1954);

Jeux de mots (Paris: Divan, 1956);

Diego Valeri circa 1963

Da Racine a Picasso: Nuovi studi francesi (Florence: Sansoni, 1956);

Metamorfosi dell'angelo, edited by Giovanni Scheiwiller (Milan: All'Insegna del Pesce d'Oro, 1957);

Venise (Paris: Hachette, 1957);

Il flauto a due canne (Milan: Mondadori, 1958);

Un poemetto inedito del satirico veneziano Pietro Buratti (Florence: Sansoni antiquariato, 1958);

Padova duemila anni dopo, edited by Luigi Gaudenzio (Padua: Rebellato, 1959);

La poesia di Clemente Rebora (Milan: All'Insegna del Pesce d'Oro, 1961);

I nuovi giorni, edited by Scheiwiller (Milan: All'Insegna del Pesce d'Oro, 1962);

Poesie (Milan: Mondadori, 1962; enlarged, 1967);

La sera (Milan: All'Insegna del Pesce d'Oro, 1963);

Tempo e poesia (Milan: Mondadori, 1964);

Poesie piccole (Milan: All'Insegna del Pesce d'Oro, 1965);

I "soli" di Saetti, by Valeri and Bruno Saetti (Milan: All'Insegna del Pesce d'Oro, 1966);

Soregina: Fiaba in due atti (Milan: All'Insegna del Pesce d'Oro, 1967);

Amico dei pittori (Milan: All'Insegna del Pesce d'Oro, 1967);

Conversazioni italiane (Florence: Olschki, 1968);

Verità di uno (Milan: Mondadori, 1970);

Petit testament (Verona: Dominicae, 1970);

Trentatrè poesie (Milan: M'arte, 1973);

Giardinetto (Milan: Mondadori, 1974);

Calle del vento (Milan: Mondadori, 1975), translated by Michael Palma as *My Name on the Wind* (Princeton, N.J.: Princeton University Press, 1989);

Poesie scelte, 1910–1975, edited by Carlo della Corte (Milan: Mondadori, 1977);

Invito al Veneto (Bologna: Boni, 1977);

Poesie inedite o come (Genoa: San Marco dei Giustiniani, 1978);

La domenica col poeta (Venice: Marsilio, 1979).

OTHER: *Credere e operare: Antologia italiana per le scuole medie superiori,* edited by Valeri and F. Cologero (Turin, 1933);

"Il sentimento della natura in D'Annunzio," in *Gabriele D'Annunzio,* edited by Jolanda de Blasio (Florence: Sansoni, 1939), pp. 11–26;

"Caratteri e valori del teatro comico," in *La civiltà veneziana del Rinascimento,* edited by Valeri and others (Florence: Sansoni, 1958), pp. 1–25;

Fiabe teatrali, edited by Valeri (Turin: ERI, 1958);

"Il centenario delle 'Fleurs du Mal'" in *Studi sulla letteratura dell'ottocento,* edited by Giovanni Macchia and Glauco Natoli (Naples: ESI, 1959), pp. 316–326;

"L'arte del Rinascimento," in *Conosci l'Italia,* volume 6 (Milan: Touring Club Italiano, 1962);

Dante, *Divina Commedia,* preface by Valeri (Milan: Motta, 1966);

Padova, i secoli, le ore, edited by Valeri (Bologna: Alfa, 1967):

"Diego Valeri" [self-introduction], in *Antologia popolare di poeti del Novecento,* edited by V. Masselli and G. A. Cibotto, includes poems by Valeri (Florence: Vallecchi, 1973), pp. 97–111.

TRANSLATIONS: Frédéric Mistral, *Da "Lis isclo d'or" e dal "Calendau"* (Castiglione delle Stiviere: Pignotti, 1912);

Mistral, *Piccola antologia* (Milan: Istituto Editoriale Italiano, 1916);

Mistral, *Mirella* (Turin: UTET, 1930);

Le leggende del Graal (Turin: UTET, 1934);

Il romanzo di Candullino (Turin: UTET, 1936);

Gustave Flaubert, *La Signora Bovary* (Milan: Mondadori, 1936);

Il romanzo di Sigfrido (Turin: UTET, 1942);

Romanzi e racconti d'amore del Medio Evo francese (Milan: Garzanti, 1942);

Liriche tedesche (Milan: All'Insegna del Pesce d'Oro, 1942);

Maupassant (Milan: Garzanti, 1942);

Stendhal, *Il rosso e il nero* (Turin: Einaudi, 1946);

Jean La Fontaine, *Quaranta favole* (Florence: Sansoni, 1952);

Johann Wolfgang von Goethe, *Cinquanta poesie* (Florence: Sansoni, 1954);

Goethe, *Ifigenia in Tauride* (Venice: Neri Pozza, 1954);

Antichi poeti provenzali (Milan: All'Insegna del Pesce d'Oro, 1954);

I lirici tedeschi (Milan: All'Insegna del Pesce d'Oro, 1955);

Da "Lyrisches Intermezzo" di Heinrich Heine (Padua: Centro d'Arte degli Studenti, 1956);

I lirici francesi (Milan: Mondadori, 1960);

Molière, *Il signor di Pourceaugnac* (Turin: Einaudi, 1967);

Quaderno francese del secolo (Turin: Einaudi, 1967);

Goethe, *Settanta liriche* (Milan: Rusconi, 1970).

Diego Valeri represents a twentieth-century continuation of the classical lyric tradition in its purest form. Peripheral to contemporary ideological crises, his voice is imbued with the music and Arcadian imagery of Anacreon, Petrarch, Angelo Politian, and Giacomo Leopardi. Valeri's subject matter is nature and humankind, in love, melancholy, anguish, and struggle. He did not believe in tendentious poetry, yet, beneath the pristine and consistently metrical surface of Valeri's poems, one finds a stylistic complexity rich in moral intonations, qualifying Valeri as a poet of rectitude as well as melody and harmony.

Diego Valeri was born on 25 January 1887 in Piove di Sacco, between Padua and Venice. Among his important early readings was Petrarch's sonnet

"Levommi il mio pensier in part ov'era." In 1909, after receiving a *laurea* (doctorate) in letters at the University of Padua, Valeri won a scholarship to the Sorbonne; he later returned to Italy to teach Italian and Latin in the classical lyceums, and subsequently French literature at the University of Padua. He became an active cultural presence there, while Venice remained at the heart of his poetic imagination. Some of his early poems melodically represent Venice as a pure environment of the sentiments, a place where the senses are lulled and fooled. Valeri examined both cities in various articles, essays, and books. After World War II he briefly assumed the editorship of the Venetian newspaper *Gazzettino*, aiding in its post-Fascist rehabilitation. But his role was not primarily that of journalist, and his occasional writings only pointed the way to his achievements in literary criticism, translation, and poetry. By all indications his personal life was quiet and uneventful, providing a sense of solace that is a constant in his writing,

Valeri's first book of poetry, *Monodia d'Amore* (Monody of Love), was published in 1908 after he left the money and manuscript with an associate and traveled to Paris. In 1913, after the sudden death of his brother, Ugo, Valeri published *Le gaie tristezze* (The Joyful Sadness), a book he later suppressed. The influence of the *crepuscolari* (twilight poets) is apparent in the narratives, refrains, and exclamations and in the dark, pathetic, psychological dimension. The eulogies for a lost family member recall those of Giovanni Pascoli and Giosuè Carducci, who, with Gabriele D'Annunzio, were the major literary influences on Valeri's generation. His early poems are saturated with these and other literary sources. Yet already Valeri's own voice stands out, with an aulic message phrased in common speech:

No, non m'illudo: l'opera fornita
per alacre fatica senza tregua
al desiderio mio non mai s'adegua
di fonder la parola con la vita.

(No, I'm not deceived: the work
produced by eager unceasing toil
will never equal my desire
to fuse the word with life.)

The melic simplicity and rhyme retain a freshness throughout Valeri's work; the occasion prevails over the writing; the word is greater than the work.

Once past the self-indulgence and imitations in his earliest verse, Valeri is closer to the essence of

the Italian lyrical canon. His early collections *Umana* (Human, 1916), *Ariele* (Ariel, 1924), and *Crisalide* (Chrysalis, 1919) contain several poems later included in *Poesie* (Poems, 1962), stripped of refrains, vignettes, and exclamations. In his revisions Valeri turns frequently to an austere and meditative verse focused on the themes of self-discovery and love, a process he describes in his *Conversazioni italiane* (Italian Conversations, 1968): "venivo imparando . . . che la realtà non ha altra sostanza né funzione se non di motivo alla creazione individuale di una soprarealtà, in cui splenda almeno un raggio del sole dell'anima; che all'infuori di ciò, la vita non è che disordine e essenza: vanità" (I was learning . . . that reality has no substance or function outside the motive for individual creation of a superreality, in which at least there shines a ray of the soul's light; since beyond that, life is only disorder and essence: vanity). An example of this stylistic purification may be seen in the 1962 revision of "Sera suburbana" (Suburban Evening). The opening lines that appear in *Crisalide* contain a typical "twilight" pathos: "Sol morente e prima luna / polverio di croco ardente e azzurro gelo. / Su la terra che s'imbruna / piovon lacrime dolcissime di cielo. / Tutto il cielo scende in pianto" (Dying sun and first moon / dusting of burning crocus and blue frost. / Over the darkening earth / rain the sky's tenderest tears. / The whole sky descends in weeping). In the revision, Valeri writes:

Veli madidi di pianto
su la muta sconfinata prateria
dove stanno per incanto
quattro case, grandi e nude, in simmetria.

(Veils wet with tears
over the limitless silent meadows,
where four houses stand by enchantment
large and naked, in symmetry.)

The first volume of Valeri's mature production, *Poesie vecchie e nuove* (Poems Old and New, 1930) has Venice as its obvious protagonist — not the romanticized and abstract city of dreams but the concrete environs of a wise and rugged people, a universal city of love and aspirations. Readers encounter a wistful evocation of its elegiac past, its bittersweet and quietly momentous sense of place, as in "Primavera di Venezia" (Spring in Venice): "io non so cosa piú soave e bella / di te, che fai tua festa d'un riflesso / blando d'acque e di cieli" (I know nothing sweeter or lovelier / than you, who create and celebrate a mild / reflection of waters and skies). In Valeri's world the only authority a poet may seek has its origin in per-

Drawing of Valeri by Eugenio Montale (from Ritratti su misura, *edited by Elio Filippo Accrocca, 1960; by permission of the Estate of Eugenio Montale)*

sonal experience. The persistence of the theme of locale links a representation of nature with a generic figuring of human sensibility; natural and divine orders are superimposed. In "Romanza" (Romance) the city frames sin, despair, and romance:

> E così mi son fermato
> ai piedi del ponte.
> E così ti sei fermata anche tu
> un gradino più su.
> Non sapevo ch'era un addio.
> L'ho saputo un attimo dopo
> sentendo le tue labbra sfiorare le mie.
> Era la prima, era l'ultima volta.
> Così.

> (And so I stopped
> at the foot of the bridge.
> The same way you stopped
> one step higher.
> I did not know it was a good-bye.

> I knew it a moment later
> feeling your lips brush against mine.
> It was the first, it was the last time.
> Just like that.)

The critic Giuseppe Raimondi has linked Valeri's impressionism to the brief format of a poem "painted" onto a page, and Raimondi postulates "Woman" as a kind of arch metaphor for Valeri's poetry: "Le donne non sono solo senso. Sono capriccio, e sofisma; sono dispetto, e insolubile scontentezza" (Women are not simply sense. They are caprice, and sophism; they are scorn, and unresolvable unhappiness). Yet women are also presented as redeemers and comforters, as in "Sister Gesuina." Woman as redeemer appears through such amorous/religious figures as Venus, Rebecca, and Ophelia. The underlying erotic component in the poetry is compatible with its projected sense of well-being.

Metrically, the hendecasyllable and septenary dominate, as does the quatrain with the rhymes *abba*. The poetry's monotone also recalls nineteenth-century French works and the language of the Gospels. The repetition of images, rather than exhausting them, tends to universalize them, much as in poems by Petrarch. In place of dialogue one finds the supplications and ruminations of the poet. However, there is none of the intellectual turbulence of Eugenio Montale, with his personal legend endowed with contradictory and tangled sentiments. Valeri's internalized images accrue as in nature, quietly and almost motionlessly.

Scherzo e finale (1937) and *Tempo che muore* (Time that Dies, 1942), which are edited and combined in *Terzo tempo* (Third Time, 1950), show a more troubled voice and a more violent and descriptive view of nature. The season is winter, also perhaps an allusion to the war years. In the muted chromaticism, colors shine forth in isolated, synesthetic wonder.

In the poems after 1950 one notes even more attention given to the theme of time and its harbinger the rose, an image that appears in at least twenty-six post-1950 poems by Valeri. The rose defies specific meaning, summoning up feelings of indeterminacy, agreeable sensations of sonority and visual harmony, and the sense of habitual pleasures. The rose is a chalice and a plant, a metaphor for woman, and a gift to her. It is not a sterile convention but, like other recurrent nouns, a means to suffuse the text with generality. For example, in "Sole lontano" (Distant Sun), from *Poesie*, the sun emerges after a rain:

Dopo la pioggia brilla un sole
d'improvviso staccato dalle cose,
salito in cima al cielo,
di là dal cielo, com'esule: assente
dalla terra che ancora è verde e calda.
Vive la terra; ma spogliata
di peso, dentro i suoi fermi contorni
d'alberi e case; e sono i suoi colori
splendidi senza raggio. Laggiù un grido
rosso di salvie, stranamente muto.

(Suddenly after the rain a sun
is shining detached from things,
risen high in the sky,
beyond the sky, as if in exile: absent
from earth that is still green and warm.
The earth is living; but stripped
of weight, within the sharp outlines
of trees and houses; and its colors are
splendid but not bright. Down there a red
cry, strangely hushed, of sage.)

The collected poems in *Poesie* possess the unity of a Petrarchan *canzoniere* (songbook): the ephemeral sense of the self, the monolinguistic containment of literary borrowings, and the apparently cyclical nature of time. The accountability of the volume as a unified autobiographical statement rests more on the absence of Valeri's persona than on his presence; the oeuvre does not circumscribe the life. Poems such as "Fiorita" (Bloomed), "Le violette" (Violets), "Canzonetta" (Little Song), "L'oro d'autunno" (The Gold in Autumn), "Passaggio" (Passage), "Altro vento" (Other Wind), "Risveglio" (Awakening), and "Aspettazione" (Expectation) are characteristically inconclusive, ending in questions or oppositions. The cyclical sense of time is not the same as an arbitrary ordering of events. In fact *Poesie* represents a sophisticated model of the poetic event, which is both synchronic and diachronic, reflecting Valeri's life as a man and his historical vision. Due to the gentleness and volubility of his artistry, it is important to emphasize its underlying mystery and power, as in "Campo di esilio" (Field of Exile):

Il giorno è nero di corvi e ricordi,
di tonfi sordi, di passi di morti.
La notte ha il viso dell'amore vicino.
La notte è un volo di bianche colombe.

(Day is dark with crows and memories,
deaf thuds, footsteps of the dead.
Night has the face of one's love close by.
Night is a flight of white doves.)

According to critic Piero Nardi, in Vittorio Zambon's *La poesia di Diego Valeri* (1968), Valeri's thought is "una forma di vitalismo, il quale ha poco da vedere, in verità, con il crepuscolarismo, sì piuttosto si apparenta con la tendenza, nella tradizione più nostra, classica, a simpatia con le cose, pur nella coscienza . . . della loro vanità" (a form of vitalism, having very little to do with crepuscularism, but related to the tendency, in that classical tradition closest to us, toward a sympathy with things, even in the consciousness . . . of their vanity). In terms of the Leopardian distinction between poets of the "heart" (the ancients) and poets of the "imagination" (the romantics), Valeri belongs to the former; his uniform phrasing and compact rhythms, his direct "imitation" of nature, make him a poet of sentiment and sensation, of grace and suffering. If he breathes the spirit of vitalism, it is without impetuosity or verbal conceit. When sentiments emerge they are behind the forms of the phenomenal world, as if to recognize the utter differences.

The 1967 edition of *Poesie* includes thirteen additional poems and deletes four of the earliest poems that were in the 1962 edition. Valeri had begun to publish poems in French in 1956, and one might suspect literary borrowing from those poets translated and studied in such detail. But that is not the case.

In Valeri's compositions in French there remain the principles of harmony and parsimony, the same melic tonal values, and a concentration on form and colors that are chromatic and tonal; rhythm prevails over concept. As Valeri states in the preface to his *Jeux de mots* (Joy of Words, 1956): "Il a pensé, ce vieux poète, qu'en écrivant en français il lui serait possible, peut-être, d'éviter l'automatisme (de parole, de phrase, de vers) qui lui parait menacer la substance meme de sa poésie" (This old poet thought that by writing in French it would be possible perhaps to avoid the automatism [of speech, phrase, and verse] that seemed to threaten the very substance of his poetry). His French poetry does show an obvious debt to Charles Baudelaire and Stéphane Mallarmé.

In Valeri's later works the familiar Venetian landscape is more distinctly human, rendered in bold conflations of human and natural imagery. Venice is a living paradigm for what fellow poet Carlo Betocchi calls Valeri's sense of free isolation: "una condizione di singolarità unica al mondo" (a condition of singularity unique to the world). Names of seasons and months proliferate (autumn in the later poems). As Valeri says in *Tempo e poesia* (Time and Poetry, 1964), "Tutta fuori del tempo la grande poesia. E nondimeno soltanto il grande poeta può darci una compiuta immagine del *nunc* in cui gli è toccato di vivere in mezzo a milioni di uomini come lui" (Great poetry is entirely outside time. And yet only the great poet can give us a complete image of the *present* in which he happens to live amid millions of men like himself). Such a transcendent appreciation of the temporal is evident in Valeri's lexicon, in which the repeated spatiotemporal indicators establish a mood of suddenness and stillness.

Valeri's last book published before his death was *Calle del vento* (1975; translated as *My Name on the Wind,* 1989). In his remembrance of the war, Valeri recalls his role as an anti-Fascist who resisted the temptation to be an "engaged" or "committed" writer:

Io vidi già sotto un cielo d'inferno
rotto avvampato dai fuochi di guerra
schiudersi la corolla di una rosa
bianca, amorosa.

(I just saw under a hellish sky
burnt and broken by the flames of war
a white, amorous rose
open its corolla.)

Valeri's rose wants nothing to do with specificity and singularity, preferring instead the indeterminate, those agreeable sensations of sonority and visual harmony one often finds without seeking them.

In documenting the uncertainty of the affective moment, Valeri resisted the fragmentist and expressionist tendencies of his contemporaries. As a modernist he engaged in the willful confusion of syntax and semantics that was the heritage of symbolism, but he found there a realm of perfect Platonic forms, the source of his landscapes and the end of his solitude. In confronting symbolism, Valeri reversed the tone of predecessors and contemporaries, in pursuit of those Italian ideals of harmony and balance that had only been parroted by Fascism and which were ignored by the literature of engagement. He avoided the "literary" symbols of D'Annunzio and Pascoli, whom he describes as an orthodox symbolist in *Conversazioni italiane*: "con la sua inquieta e ombrosa sensibilità, col suo naturismo misticheggiante, col suo gusto tra alessandrino e impressionistico, con la sua sintassi involuta e spezzata" (with his restless and gloomy sensibility, with his mystifying naturism, with his taste between Alexandrine and impressionistic, with his cut-up and involuted syntax).

Critic Luigi Baldacci has called Valeri a nontragic poet who is "sostanzialmente 'antiumanistico,' nel senso che egli naturaliza l'umano, ma si rifiuta di umanizzare la natura" (substantially "antihumanistic" in the sense that he naturalizes the human but refuses to humanize nature). Valeri's poems are a recognition of the limits of cognition and discourse, and he points to the incapacity of "economic man" to find an earthly paradise. Valeri was not politically indifferent, but wrote of the tragicality of naturalism, as found in Anacreon and the Old and New Testaments. Yet there is none of Leopardi's so-called negative theology. The pervasive negativity present in the works of Montale is transformed by Valeri into temporal and secular sorrows. Neither specifically a love poet or a religious poet, Valeri spoke to the word's narrow capacity to express supreme emotions. His remarks on Clemente Rèbora, who became a priest in 1936, are enlightening in this regard (in *Conversazioni italiane*):

la poesia religiosa di Rèbora mi pare, in qualche misura, impedita, ostacolata dall'ossequio naturale e legittimo e necessario del sacerdote verso la Verità ricevuta.... Tuttavia le pagine poeticamente più vive tra quelle d'ispirazione religiosa mi paiono le poche in cui ancora vige il contrasto tra l'umano e il sopraumano, lo sforzo della volontà a sollevare il peso morto della umanità comune, in cui l'anima ancora si dibatte tra il credere e il dubitare, ancora e sempre cerca, benché abbia trovato. Non è, del resto, proprio in ciò l'eterno lievito del cristianesimo: nell'ansia e nell'inquietudine dell'anima, che pur crede e sa?

(Rèbora's religious poetry seems to me in some degree impeded, blocked, by the natural, legitimate, and necessary deference of the priest to the Truth received.... Nevertheless the most poetically alive pages among those of religious inspiration seem to me those few in which the contrast between the human and the superhuman is vigorous: that effort of the will to lift up the dead weight of common humanity, in which the soul is still debating between believing and doubting, is still and forever searching, though it has already found. Isn't the eternal uplifting of Christianity precisely here, in the soul's anxiety and disquietude, even as it knows and believes?)

In the divergence from perfect harmony, as from the idyll, one discovers the tension inherent in classic poetry. In *Tempo e poesia* Valeri defines such a canon by alluding to Petrarch: "Valga sempre l'esempio del Petrarca, unico abitatore del proprio mondo lirico, unico parlante il misterioso linguaggio da lui stesso creato, e, ciò nonostante, poeta altamente (aristocraticamente) popolare" (May the example of Petrarch stand, the only inhabitant of his own lyrical world, the only speaker of the mysterious language he himself created, and, nevertheless, a highly [aristocratically] popular poet). Valeri's homage to Petrarch is also apparent in the limpid meditations on old age in *Poesie*:

E una distanza come di colline
posate dalla luce della sera
su l'estremo orizzonte.
Cosí nette di segno e cosí tenere,
che non osa toccarle l'amoroso
desiderio dei sensi.
Questa è la tua distanza.

(It is a distance as of hills
laid by the evening light
upon the distant horizon.
So crisply marked and so tender,
that the amorous desire of

the senses dares not touch them.
This is your distance.)

In the tradition of Leopardi and Pascoli, the *fanciullino* (child) for Valeri represented the artist within the person, capable of unadorned natural observation and wonder. Valeri's extreme verbal economy may be seen to be modeled on the child's trust for the senses, intuition, and memory, as seen in these lines from *Poesie*:

La giovinetta che davanti al mare,
splende, incantando il mare,
ha negli sguardi, nei gesti qualcosa
di esitante: è
felice e dubitosa.
Bellezza, di che temi?
Forse non d'altro
che dell'esser bella,
di portar nella carne gloriosa
un cosí gran mistero,
. . . .
Forse soltanto di vederti nuda
come un tenero fiore.

(The girl who shines before
the sea, charming the sea,
has in her glance, in her gestures, something
hesitant: she is happy and doubtful.
O beautiful one, what are you afraid of?
Perhaps of nothing more than being beautiful,
of carrying in your glorious flesh
such a great mystery,
. . . .
Perhaps only of seeing yourself naked
as a tender flower.)

Valeri has written of the prominence of the child in his work, and of the spiritual nature of his early childhood. He published several volumes of poetry for children, and in *Amico dei pittori* (The Painters' Friend, 1967), a collection of poems dedicated to fourteen contemporary Italian painters, he shows that painters, like children, have a language of their own and an immediacy of perceptions: "Bastano pochi fili al vento sparsi / per aprire infiniti il mare il cielo; / una scrittura di contorni, lieve / come il pensiero, basta a formare le forme delle cose, / semplici trasparenti impenetrabili" (A few threads scattered in the wind / are enough to open the infinite sea and sky; / a writing of outlines, light like / thought, is enough to shape the forms of things, simple transparent impenetrable).

In addition to his poetry, literary essays, and editing of anthologies, Valeri wrote books of remembrance and dedicatory prefaces for other writers and artists and did many important translations.

The monolinguistic uniformity of Valeri's formal poetic presentation and the emotional intensity surrounding images of Venice and of Woman constitute a continual rephrasing of the paean to nature. Like nature, Valeri's projected voice, or "I," does not comment on his poetry or devise a fictional persona. Throughout Valeri's opus his poetry is typified by clarity of language, understatement, song, and mystery and by direct communication, as in these lines from *Poesie inedite o come* (Poetry Unpublished or As If, 1978): "Ho in cuore una città / che nasce ogni giorno dal mare / e ogni sera nel mare si dissolve" (I have a city in my heart / that is born every day from the sea / and every night dissolves in the sea).

Interview:
Ferdinando Camon, "Diego Valeri," in his *Il mestiere di poeta* (Milan: Garzanti, 1982), pp. 53–58.

Bibliography:
Vittorio Zambon, *La poesia di Diego Valeri* (Padua: Liviana, 1968), pp. 123–136.

Biographies:
Ugo Piscopo, *Diego Valeri* (Rome: Ateneo, 1985);
Paolo Tieto, *Diego Valeri e la sua città natale* (Noventa Padovana: Panda, 1987).

References:
Luigi Baldacci, "Per un'antologietta di Diego Valeri," in his *Libretti d'opera e altri saggi* (Florence: Vallecchi, 1974), pp. 108–129;
Carlo Betocchi, "L'indimenticabile Valeri," in Valeri's *Poesie inedite o come* (Genoa: San Marco dei Giustiniani, 1978), pp. 11–17;
Giacomo Debenedetti, "Brixen-Idyll," in Valeri's *Poesie* (Milan: 1962), pp. 371–390;
Carlo della Corte, Introduction to Valeri's *Poesie scelte, 1910–1975,* edited by della Corte (Milan: Mondadori, 1977), pp. xi–xvii;
Giuseppe De Robertis, "Valeri: Fantasie veneziane," in his *Scrittori del Novecento* (Florence: Le Monnier, 1940), pp. 243–247;
Ugo Fasolo, ed., *Omaggio a Diego Valeri* (Florence: Olschki, 1974);
Franco Fortini, "Le apparizioni di Arturo Onofri e le presenze di Diego Valeri," in his *I poeti del Novecento* (Bari & Rome: Laterza, 1977), pp. 41–46;
Giuseppe Raimondi, "Premessa a *I nuovi giorni*" in Valeri's *Poesie,* pp. 391–399;
Giovanni Titta Rosa, "Diego Valeri," in his *Vita letteraria del Novecento* (Milan: Ceschina, 1972), pp. 641–645;
Vittorio Zambon, *Le poesia di Diego Valeri* (Padua: Liviana, 1968);
Andrea Zanzotto, "Il maestro universitario," *Fiera Letteraria* (3 March 1957): 3;
Zanzotto, "L'ultimo Valeri," *Comunità,* 50 (June 1957): 95.

Sebastiano Vassalli

(25 October 1941 –)

Leonard G. Sbrocchi
University of Ottawa

BOOKS: *Lui (egli)* (Florence: Rebellato, 1965);
Narcisso (Turin: Einaudi, 1968);
Disfaso (Rome: Trevi, 1969);
Tempo di màssacro (Turin: Einaudi, 1970);
La poesia oggi (Novara: Ant, 1971);
Il millennio che muore (Turin: Einaudi, 1972);
Il libro dell'utopia ceramica (Ravenna: Longo, 1974);
L'arrivo della lozione (Turin: Einaudi, 1976);
Brindisi (Bergamo: Bagatto, 1979);
Belle lettere, by Vassalli and Giovanni Bianchi (Bergamo: Bagatto, 1979);
La distanza (Bergamo: Bagatto, 1980);
Abitare il vento (Turin: Einaudi, 1980);
Mareblù (Milan: Mondadori, 1982);
Manuale di corpo (Siena: Barbablu, 1982);
Vani e servizi (Alessandria: Piombino, 1983);
Ombre e destini (Naples: Guida, 1983);
Arkadia (Bergamo: Bagatt, 1983);
Il finito (Bergamo: Bagatt, 1984);
La notte della cometa (Turin: Einaudi, 1984);
L'antica Pieve di Casalvolone in provincia di Novara (secoli XI–XII) (Bergamo: Bagatt, 1984);
Sangue e suolo (Turin: Einaudi, 1985);
L'alcova elettrica (Turin: Einaudi, 1986);
L'oro del mondo (Turin: Einaudi, 1987);
Marradi, by Vassalli and Attilio Lolini (Brescia: Obliquo, 1988);
Il neoitaliano (Bologna: Zanichelli, 1989);
La chimera (Turin: Einaudi, 1990);
Marco e Mattio (Turin: Einaudi, 1992).

OTHER: *Dino Campana: Opere; Canti Orfici; Versi e scritti sparsi pubblicati in vita; Inediti,* edited by Vassalli and Carlo Fini (Milan: TEA, 1989).

Sebastiano Vassalli circa 1980 (photograph by Gabriella Maleti)

Sebastiano Vassalli, a painter, poet, photographer, essayist, and translator, was born in Genoa on 25 October 1941. His father, Luciano, is Milanese, and his mother, Falaschi Alfreda, is Tuscan. Vassalli considers himself Tuscan, although he has spent most of his life in Piedmont and some of it in Milan. In 1966 Vassalli graduated with a degree in psychology from the University of Milan.

He began writing at the age of twenty but soon felt that he could better express himself through the plastic arts. Pop art was gaining a larger audience, and between 1960 and 1964 Vassalli created pop art, having several important showings to his credit. When, in 1964, works of American pop artists arrived at the Biennale di Venezia, Vassalli understood that pop art, as he conceived it and was expressing it, already existed. Furthermore, he also understood that he could not be a painter all of his life. After 1964 he devoted more time to writing, having joined the loose association of writers known as "Gruppo '63." For him the group represented the progressive aspect of Italian literature. There was substantial experimentation taking place, but it produced few works. It did bring about a flood of translations of works by foreign writers. From all this experimentation and modernization of art, Vassalli realized that experimentation alone was not sufficient and that poetry did not equate with crossword puzzles, simple movement, or getting together every two years to examine what had been accomplished. According to Vassalli, in this atmosphere "con un po' di cultura e di tecniche cerebrali chiunque può fare il poeta" (anyone with a bit of culture and cerebral techniques could be a poet). Toward the end of the 1960s he became more disenchanted and left the group. He later said that "l'avanguardia di per se non esiste. Esiste un'avanguardia storica perché bisogna sempre fare i conti con la tradizione" (avant-garde per se does not exist. What does exist is a historical avant-garde because one must always deal with tradition).

The period between 1968 and 1978 Vassalli considers a temporary hell. He made a living by teaching Italian and history, and he repudiates everything he wrote during that time. The only ray of hope came in 1968 when he met Luciana Ariatta, the woman who five years later became his wife and who, in 1975, gave birth to their son, Marco. However, life was not easy or simple in the ensuing years. Beginning in 1979 he wrote for several papers and magazines. In 1982 he decided to live in the country by himself while his wife and child stayed in Novara. He would see them two or three days a week. Having two houses meant giving new life to their own relationship, but, in terms of Vassalli's writing, "la parola può avere una forza solo se è filtrata attraverso il silenzio. Forse è possibile trovarlo anche in città; ma io non potrei farlo in altro modo che in campagna" (the word can have power only if it is filtered through silence. Perhaps it is possible to find it in the city; but I can do so only in the country). The turning point in Vassalli's career came about with his autobiographical novel *Abitare il vento* (To Inhabit the Wind), published in 1980. However, the real point of arrival – as he put it – was his book on Dino Campana, *La notte della cometa* (The Night of the Comet, 1984).

Also in 1984, in *Il finito* (The Finite), he expressed his views on the current state of poetry: "La

poesia o è un messaggio per chi non c'è, gesto non rapportabile a qualsivoglia presente, o è relazione sociale, sistema di convenzioni linguistiche e di rapporti personali che si creano da soli il loro *humus* di estetiche, le loro verità di giornata, forniture per uffici e per aule e per salotti dove vegetano freschi e compiaciuti di sé i parolieri del nulla, cosiddetti (da loro stessi) poeti" (Poetry is either a message for someone who is not there, a gesture not relatable to any particular present, or it is a social relation, a system of linguistic conventions and personal relationships that by themselves create their own *humus* for aesthetics, their daily truths, furniture for offices, classrooms, and drawing rooms where wordy speakers of nothing [they call themselves poets] vegetate, cool and complacent). In September of the previous year, 1983, Vassalli had published a pamphlet titled *Arkadia,* in which he analyzes the various poetic schools of the 1970s and points out the damage some of them have done, the lack of responsibility they have toward society, how their members are not poets, and how their greatness is measured in direct proportion to that of their publishers.

Vassalli's own poetry is not very substantive in terms of volume. However, it reflects the various phases of his development and changes in ideology as well as his fidelity to basic points: the use of a language that has semantic substance; the need for social denunciation; and the value of the lyric fragment.

Brindisi (Toasts, 1979), at first glance, seems to be a collection celebrating anniversaries of weddings and births, each with a different wine. In fact it is a series of reflections on life, daily toil, and the hopes of youth, culminating in the fall of "i sensi e le parole e i sogni e i regni e i segni e le illusioni . . ." (senses and words and dreams and kingdoms and signs and illusions . . .).

In *La distanza* (Distance, 1980), Vassalli points out the great distance that exists between words and deeds: "Una parola che si sente appena / e non nomina niente; / distanza è un complemento dell'assenza, / è una voce felice / del verbo distanziare" (A word one can hardly hear / and it does not signify anything; / distance is a complement of absence, / it is a felicitous form / of the verb to leave behind). Nonetheless, "Distanza è un'infinita adolescenza" (Distance is an unending adolescence) because when experiences such as anguish, love, hope, waiting, ideals, and sunsets are seen from a distance, they lose their harsh contours and acquire a patina of timelessness.

Vani e servizi (Rooms and Services, 1983) is a series of poems in which Vassalli, in a sarcastic way, presents values that have always been the subjects of serious poetical presentations. Truth is "una stanza con scrivania / sopra alla scrivania c'era il telefono" (a room with a desk / on the desk there was a telephone). Justice comes to the house twice a week to do the cleaning – "Era una Giustizia a ore" – (It was a Justice that worked by the hour). Security is at the end of the hall: "Era una corda appesa / a un gancio del soffitto, con un nodo" (It was a cord hanging by a hook in the ceiling, with a knot). Virtue is "nascosta nell'armadio dei libri. Non sapevo / che fosse la Virtù della memoria / finché un giorno per caso l'ho trovata / secca, perfettamente imbalsamata / dentro un libro di storia" (hidden in a bookcase. I did not know / it was the Virtue of memory / until one day by chance I found it dry, perfectly embalmed in a history book). Pride "stava appeso all'ingresso / o in camera da letto" (was hanging in the entrance / or in the bedroom). Hope is a boat that has tried to move in a motionless sea:

Dipinto sul soffitto c'era un mare
senza onde né vento e sempre uguale.

La barca al centro con la vela bianca
portava scritto sulla prua: SPERANZA.

La vela si gonfiava, palpitava.
Le corde si tendevano. Schiumava

l'acqua sotto la chiglia là nel mare
senza onde né vento e sempre uguale.

(Painted on the ceiling was a sea
without waves or wind and always the same.

The boat in the middle with a white sail
had written on its prow: HOPE.

The sail filled, palpitated.
The ropes tightened.

The water foamed under the keel there in the sea
without waves or wind and always the same.)

Giovanna Ioli, in her introduction to *Ombre e destini* (Shadows and Destinies, 1983), a collection with most of Vassalli's best poems up to that time, notes that Vassalli's rhythms are exercised "nell'apparente semplicità delle rime, nella scelta trasgressiva della filastrocca come parodia e satira di uno stile che non può più affermare valori e concetti sublimi, regole etiche e moraleggianti di valore assoluto, che rifiuta la vena dell'elegia" (in the apparent simplicity of the rhymes, in the transgressive

choice of the rigmarole as parody and satire of a style that can no longer affirm values and sublime concepts, ethics and moralizing rules of absolute value, [and] which refuses the form of the elegy). She concludes that "l'apparente semplicità delle definizioni diventa strumento di satira politica, etica e letteraria . . ." (the apparent simplicity of the definitions becomes the instrument of political, ethical, and literary satire . . .). There is irony and sarcasm in Vassalli's lyrics, but there is also a genuine concern for humanity, even if a person's destiny may be like that of a caterpillar, which before dying "emette impercettibili / suoni ben modulati in un lamento / cadenzato e ossessivo" (utters imperceptible / sounds well modulated / in a cadencelike and obsessive lamentation). Moreover, in language, Vassalli seeks (as he put it) "una certa corposità" (a kind of body or consistency), which perhaps may be identified in images such as these: "Gli amori son fatti di nasi. / Gli amori hanno forma di vasi . . ." (Love affairs are made of noses. / Love affairs have the shape of vases . . .) and "Le angosce hanno aspetto di bisce. / Le angosce hanno forma di cosce . . ." (Anguish has the appearance of snakes. / Anguish has the shape of thighs . . .).

Il finito is divided into three parts, what Vassalli calls the finite (translations), the infinite (fragments), and poetry (prose compositions). The nine poems in the first part are not pure translations but parodies of works by Giacomo Leopardi, Arthur Rimbaud, Jautré Rudel, Gérard de Nerval, and Catullus. In the poem "Il finito," as in Leopardi's *L'infinito* (1819), the speaker seeks solace in solitude but cannot escape his destiny. He does not flounder in the sea of infinity but identifies with the perfection of a stone: "annullo / l'ansia del tempo nella carne e il vuoto / della ragione riempio e chiudo e sono" (I annul / the anxiety of time in the flesh and I fill the void / of reason and I close and I am).

In the third part Vassalli presents a series of sketches outlining characters and situations, and he concludes with a declaration of why he writes: "Scrivo per i mutanti, per i licantropi, per i superstiti del presente e per gli analfabeti a venire. Scrivo per il fiore purpureo che s'aprirà nella notte del tempo; per il fuoco che scaturirà dalle tenebre, necessità e verità, esito e inizio. Al finito" (I write for the mutants, for the lycanthropes, for the survivors of the present and for the illiterates to come. I write for the purple flower that will bloom in the night of time; for the fire that will rise out of the darkness, necessity and truth, denouement and beginning. To the finite).

The most lyrical part of this collection is the second part. The fragment is linked to the instant in which the individual becomes totally identified with nature: "M'invento / nel vento / divento / di vento / frammento" (I invent myself / in the wind / I become / like the wind / a fragment). Vassalli reiterates his realization that one really has to be alone in order to succeed: "I soli stanno soli e fanno luce / nel pensiero . . ." (The solitary ones stand alone and create light / in thought . . .). However, like a spider in its web or a poet in a dream about doing something about the world, Vassalli realizes that he cannot change the world, and he "grida / la sua disperazione. E negli spazi / vuoti dell'universo quella voce / sembra il ronzìo nervoso di una mosca / che vuole uscire da una stanza chiusa" (shouts / his desperation. And in the empty / spaces of the universe that voice / seems the excited buzzing of a fly / wanting to get out of a closed room). His is not only a vision of desperation, though, because "Oltre la nebbia ci sarà il tuo viso / fatto ad anfora, tondo, come un vaso; / il mezzo al viso ci sarà il tuo naso / e attorno al naso ci sarà un sorriso" (Beyond the fog will be your face / in the shape of an amphora, round, like a vase; / in the middle of the face will be your nose / and around your nose there will be a smile).

In his 1988 interview with Paolo Di Stefano, Vassalli said, "ho scoperto che non lo sono [poeta] . . . di poesie ne ho scritte poche e in questa produzione spaventosa di segatura poetica italiana, io di segatura ne ho fatta pochissima e l'ho ammucchiata in un angolo. Maturando come scrittore e come uomo ho una idea della poesia che non può scendere a compromessi. La poesia è qualcosa di assurdo e di indefinibile in quanto tale, non può essere una norma. . . . La poesia e l'arte sono qualcosa di troppo grande perché se ne possa parlare in termini di quotidianità e di routine" (I have discovered that I am not a poet . . . I have written few poems . . . and in this dreadful production of Italian poetic sawdust, I have made very little of it and I have stashed it in a corner. As I matured as a writer and as a man, I conceived an idea of poetry that cannot bow to compromise. Poetry is something absurd and indefinable and because of that it cannot be a norm. . . . Poetry and art are something too great to speak about in daily or routine terms). Whether or not he will write any more poems, Vassalli has found that the word has power because it is filtered through silence.

Interview:

Paolo Di Stefano, "A colloquio con Sebastiano Vassalli: Accettare la verità," *Corriere del Ticino,* 21 May 1988.

References:

Giovanna Ioli, Introduction to Vassalli's *Ombre e destini* (Naples: Guida, 1983), pp. 5–8;
Giuseppe Zagarrio, *Febbre, furore e fiele* (Milan: Mursia, 1983), pp. 123–125.

Cesare Viviani

(22 April 1947 –   )

John P. Welle
University of Notre Dame

BOOKS: *Confidenza a parole* (Parma: Nuovi Quaderni di Poesia, 1971);

L'Ostrabismo cara (Milan: Feltrinelli, 1973);

Psicanalisi interrotta (Milan: Sugarco, 1975);

La pazzia spiegata dai bambini (Milan: Formichiere, 1976);

Piumana (Milan: Guanda, 1977);

Papà linguaggio mamma paura (Milan: Emme, 1980);

L'amore delle parti (Milan: Mondadori, 1981);

Summulae, 1966–1972 (Milan: All'Insegna del Pesce d'Oro, 1983);

La scena: Prove di poetica (Siena: Barbablù, 1985);

Merisi (Milan: Mondadori, 1986);

Folle avena (Pordenone: Studio Tesi, 1987);

Pensieri per una poetica della veste (Milan: Crocetti, 1988);

Il sogno dell'interpretazione: Una critica radicale all'ideologia psicanalitica (Genoa: Costa & Nolan, 1989);

Preghiera del nome (Milan: Mondadori, 1990).

OTHER: Alfonso Berardinelli and Franco Cordelli, eds., *Il pubblico della poesia,* includes statements by Viviani (Cosenza: Lerici, 1975), pp. 76–77;

"Poesie d'amore e altre," *Almanacco dello specchio,* 8 (1979): 369–379;

Il movimento della poesia italiana degli anni settanta, edited by Viviani and Tomaso Kemeny, includes an introduction and an essay by Viviani (Bari: Dedalo, 1979), pp. 28–35;

I percorsi della nuova poesia italiana, edited by Viviani and Kemeny, includes an introduction and an essay by Viviani (Naples: Guida, 1980), pp. 1–5;

"La percezione assoluta," *Verri,* 1 (March–June 1990): 23–27.

TRANSLATIONS: Paul Verlaine, *Feste galanti,* edited and translated, with an introduction, by Viviani (Milan: Guanda, 1979);

Verlaine, *Feste galanti; La buona canzone,* translated, with an introduction, by Viviani (Milan: Mondadori, 1988).

With one of the most original styles to appear in the 1970s and 1980s, Cesare Viviani represents the fruitful continuation of the experimentalism that characterized Italian poetry in the 1960s. After the culmination of the polemics of the *novissimi* (newest ones) – poets such as Edoardo Sanguineti, Antonio Porta, Alfredo Giuliani, Nanni Balestrini, and others who wanted to destabilize the traditional codes of Italian poetry in the interest of a new experimentalism – Viviani has been able to benefit from the ground-breaking efforts of his predecessors while finding his own distinctive voice. In Viviani's poetry the ideological scaffolding, historical issues, and critical positions of the previous decades give way to the exploration of a new subjectivity, informed by the revolutionary impact of psychoanalysis and by developments in the human sciences, most notably linguistics. In his introduction to *Il movimento della poesia italiana degli anni settanta* (The Movement of Italian Poetry in the 1970s), published in 1979, Viviani describes this new subjectivity:

Della vasta trasformazione culturale avvenuta negli ultimi due decenni, un punto su cui torno volentieri è il processo di rinnovamento del "soggetto." Lo spazio, la forza, la fisionomia, il movimento del soggetto sono cambiati. L'io vive e si percepisce in modo nuovo, e ricorda e agisce, crede e prevede in modo nuovo. Legge e scrive, realizza le sue fantasie e stabilisce rapporti in modo nuovo. . . . Così, oggi il soggetto ha un rapporto diverso anche con l'esperienza poetica. E, quindi, anche la scrittura poetica è cambiata: emergono le spinte sconosciute del desiderio e tanti altri impulsi, le realtà si moltiplicano, l'io è decentrato. . . .

(Of the vast cultural transformation that has occurred in the past two decades, a point to which I return willingly concerns the process of the renewal of the "subject." The space, the force, the physiognomy, the movement

Cesare Viviani (photograph by Uliano Lucas)

of the subject have changed. The I lives and perceives itself in a new way, remembers and acts, believes and looks ahead in a new way. It reads and writes, realizes its fantasies and establishes relationships in a new way.... Therefore today the subject has a different relationship also with poetic experience. And, therefore, poetic writing has changed: unknown forces of desire and so many other impulses are emerging, realities are multiplying, the I is decentered....)

This decentered *I* figures prominently in Viviani's poetry. A psychoanalyst by profession, Viviani has written, in addition to his poetry, four books on psychoanalysis. Not surprisingly his poetry addresses the new realities of human personality uncovered by psychoanalysis. Like the "talking cure" itself, Viviani's poetry inquires into impulses caught in the tropes and figures of language. Rather than a facile commentary on psychoanalysis, however, his poetry explores human consciousness and the world from the new poetic perspectives made possible by science. He has emerged as a poet well worthy of critical attention.

Cesare Viviani was born in Siena on 22 April 1947 to Antonio (a lawyer) and Biancamaria Vivi-

ani. After completing his high school studies, Cesare enrolled in the University of Siena and later graduated with a law degree. His first poems were published in 1970 and 1971 in the reviews *Bimestre* and *Quasi,* respectively. In 1972 he became interested in psychoanalysis and moved to Milan, where he began working as a professional psychologist in 1973. Later he earned a degree in education at the University of Florence. In 1976 he married his wife, Francesca.

In 1971 Viviani had published his first volume, *Confidenza a parole* (Confidence in Words), which he later revised substantially before its inclusion in *Summulae* (Summaries, 1983). While he has distanced himself from his early poetry, written between 1964 and 1969, this work is useful for understanding his poetic sources, the evolution of his themes, and the development of his poetic language.

Already in *Confidenza a parole,* as the critic Giuseppe Zagarrio has noted, the instincts and the primary biological-psychological condition of the person provide the bases for Viviani's poetry, as in these lines:

Tra l'essere
e il non essere
la pausa. Dell'istinto.

(Between being
and nonbeing
the pause. Of instinct.)

The epigrammatic nature of Viviani's early poetry, a few terse lines surrounded by immense white space, has caused critics to point to certain influences in his early work, among them the classical hermeticism of the 1930s and 1940s as well as the neohermeticism of the 1950s and 1960s. Michel David, for example, in his preface to *L'Ostrabismo cara* (a neologism that might be rendered as "The Ostracized-cross-eyed-ism, Dear," 1973), has emphasized the echoes of Sandro Penna, Giuseppe Ungaretti, and Eugenio Montale in Viviani's work; his spare diction and bare minimalism recall his predecessors' attempts to recharge the vitality of the poetic word. Viviani soon developed a more distinct and complex poetic style, but his early work already expresses a sense of wonder and a joyful playfulness that remain dominant characteristics.

On the surface *L'Ostrabismo cara* seems to have little in common with the poetry that preceded it. Viviani picks up the challenges presented by the most radical poetic experiments of the 1960s. A mature, difficult poetic language results from his interest in the psychoanalytic theories of Jacques Lacan, the poststructuralist direction of Saussurean linguistics, and the deconstructive tendencies of Jacques Derrida, Roland Barthes, and Michel Foucault. Viviani's poetry also continues the morphological and syntactic violence of the neo-avant-garde Italian poets of the 1960s. An avid explorer and bold creator of metalanguage, Viviani frequently relies on assonance, wordplay, substitution, lapses, and a broad lexicon to create his poetic effects. *L'Ostrabismo cara* forms part of the writerly tradition in contemporary literature — literary works that explore the nature of writing itself. At the same time, his voice distinguishes itself with a certain poetic bravado, a gift for comedy, and a sense of humor that, at times, bring to mind the futurists, as in this excerpt:

mi abbasso alla scomposta
macchia sull'abbecedario come l'insetto
lucido trascina la traccia impolverata dalla luna.

(I lower myself onto the decomposed
stain on the spelling book like a lucid
insect who drags the dusty trace from the moon.)

In 1977, with the publication of *Piumana* (another neologism, which could be rendered as "Feather/Stream"), Viviani continued his exploration of the decentered *I* and built on the accomplishments in *L'Ostrabismo cara*. In *Piumana* he investigates the mind's relationship to the body. In gathering fragments from the flux of experience, Viviani gives birth to dreamlike fantasies. As the title to this work suggests, there is a fascinating lightness to these verses. His compositions are longer, and brief narratives are extended. The pleasing musical flow of *Piumana* contributed to a greater critical awareness of the poet's work and inspired Porta, in his anthology *Poesia degli anni Settanta* (Poetry of the 1970s) – published in 1979 – to single out Viviani's poetry as one of the most interesting new developments.

L'amore delle parti (The Love of the Parts, 1981) shows Viviani delving deeper into the vein that distinguishes his poetry from some of the earlier poetic experiments. There is a greater harmony and counterpoint in *L'amore delle parti* than in his earlier books. The individual poems are organized into twelve sections, which give a greater sense of consistency, continuity, and substance to the poetry. The decentralization of the *I* yields its most fruitful results as Viviani begins to engage traditional poetic forms in an innovative, intriguing way. The opening verses, for example, recall epic poetry in a self-consciously postmodern fashion:

avvicinandosi alla lunga storia o poema
come hanno chiuso i due la giornata!
lascia che gli altri seguano la corte
cambiano posizione vai
più forte fai vedere più cose . . .

(approaching the long story or poem
how the two of them closed their day!
let the others follow the court
they are changing position go
more swiftly show more things . . .)[.]

Viviani's multiple points of view, the succession of voices, and the frequent interruption of the narrative are held together by an elusive approximation of the address to the reader in classic poetry.

The originality of Viviani's poetry becomes more apparent in *L'amore delle parti*. Psychoanalysis and the eruption of desire into poetic language continue to provide the main focus, as he seeks to name desire:

Vorrei parlare di quello che ha preso
erano le misure del corpo passavano
nella mia stanza: a dire

quello che portano i seni
e le caviglie e le vene

(I would like to talk about that which has taken
they were the sizes of the body passing
in my room: to say
that which the breasts carry
and the ankles and the veins)[.]

Seen in this context, the allusion to epic poetry or to a long story, in the volume's opening lines, makes this collection, as critic Giuliano Gramigna rightly emphasized in 1986, a romance or love story – not a love story in the traditional sense but a stuttering account of primary eroticism.

In 1983 Viviani published *Summulae,* a selection from his work prior to *L'Ostrabismo cara.* With this slim selection he intended to rectify the situation created by the premature publication of *Confidenza a parole.* As Viviani states in a note in *Summulae:*

Nel '73 sarebbe uscito *L'Ostrabismo cara.* E più cresceva la nuova fisionomia del mio linguaggio più aumentava l'imbarazzo per le prime prove. . . . Avevo deciso di non nominarlo più, quando l'ho visto rammentato da alcuni critici. Allora con la testa di oggi, ho pensato di fare una selezione del lavoro che ha preceduto *L'Ostrabismo cara,* eliminando ciò che non tiene, e trascurando il concetto prudente per il quale una simile revisione il poeta la può fare solo dopo i cinquant'anni.

(In 1973 *L'Ostrabismo cara* was to appear. And the more the new physiognomy of my language grew the greater was my embarrassment at my first attempts. . . . I had decided not to mention the [1971] book anymore when I saw it recalled by some critics. Therefore with the mind of today, I thought I would make a selection of the work that preceded *L'Ostrabismo cara,* eliminating the weaker parts, and overlooking the prudent concept by which a revision such as this can only be done by a poet after the age of fifty.)

Of the seventy-one poems in *Confidenza a parole* only seven reappear in *Summulae,* which also includes six early poems originally published in magazines and thirteen previously unpublished poems. Because they represent poems from the late 1960s and early 1970s that are revised according to Viviani's techniques of the 1980s, these texts help clarify the trajectory of his poetic practice. They also demonstrate the development of his poetics, which finds expression in his *La scena: Prove di poetica* (The Scene: Attempts at a Poetics, 1985).

In *Summulae* and more frequently in *Merisi,* published in 1986 (the title being a proper name invented by Viviani), he stages brief scenes, miniature

dramas, and lyrical spectacles with a minimalist-epic style. The following sample from *Summulae* is an example of the brief encounters that typify Viviani's poetry:

Due fratelli contadini sono al campo.
Uno lavora, l'altro
riposa e lo guarda.

(Two brothers, peasants, are in the field.
One works, the other
rests and watches him.)

The simplicity of the diction and the brevity of the narrative recall the discounted poems in *Confidenza a parole.* At the same time, a tension emerges that was lacking in the early poems. In the poem above, the action consists in the unfolding of the spectacle. The poem is "about" two brothers; the reader looks at them and at the scene. In this way, vision becomes the main theme of Viviani's poetry.

The scene, the spectacle, and the gaze form a dominant triangle in *Merisi.* Like Italo Calvino's book of short stories *Palomar* (1983), *Merisi* explores contemporary human perception. The incorporation of traditional poetic elements in a reflexive manner – a technique Viviani began in *L'amore delle parti* – produces pleasing results. The twenty-nine poems solidified his reputation and are capable of surprising the reader with their lyrical intensity:

E quest'Italia sarà cantata sui colli
ai passi di confine scenderà chiunque
non solo il capo i prati
dove una volta lui si era fissato di essere
un animale inferocito e sentiva già
la bava la pelle e ora porta
la vittoria apre con il canto la valle.

(And this Italy will be sung in the hills
whoever descends along the frontier passes
not only the chief the meadows
where he once was intent on being
an enraged animal and he already felt
the slaver the skin and now he brings
the victory he opens with his song the valley.)

This poem brings to mind the high lyricism of the Italian tradition. The epic sweep or movement is cut short, however. The Italy sung about by great poets in the past is celebrated here by a decentered, polycentric I. The poetic text is no longer rigidly controlled by an egomaniacal lyric presence that sees and knows all. Rather, the changing points of view create surprising twists and turns connected by frequent enjambments.

In 1990 Viviani published *Preghiera del nome* (The Prayer of the Name). These brief, lapidary verses continue his project of recharging the poetic word by exploring invocation and incantation as primary poetic functions. As Viviani states in a note to the volume, "La pronuncia dei nomi è sempre invocazione e preghiera. I nomi sono parole inspiegabili, resistenti ai significati. In poesia le parole acquistano l'autonomia dei nomi" (The pronunciation of names is always invocation and prayer. Names and words without explanation, resistent to meanings. In poetry words acquire the autonomy of names). Viviani's poems, according to reviewer Biancamaria Frabotta (*Espresso,* 11 March 1990), succeed in communicating the poetic charge associated with hieratic writings. Influenced by the later poetry of Porta, Viviani seeks to maintain the explosive energy of the individual lyric while constructing a narrative sequence.

A young poet of considerable talent, Cesare Viviani has already shown a marked growth and evolution. His work has evolved from its neohermetic matrix and the morphological and syntactic experiments that characterized the 1960s. Viviani has developed a distinct style that is capable of reg-istering lyric intensity while remaining intellectually challenging, and it holds great promise for the future of Italian poetry.

References:

Michel David, Preface to Viviani's *L'Ostrabismo cara* (Milan: Feltrinelli, 1973), pp. 7–13;

Marco Forti, "Viviani: Decostruzione, esperimenti e fantasmi," *Lunario Nuovo,* 42 (1987): 3–16;

Giuliano Gramigna, "Iscritto nello scritto (Viviani, Cagnone)," in his *Le forme del desiderio: Il linguaggio poetico alla prova della psicoanalisi* (Milan: Garzanti, 1986), pp. 152–167;

Gramigna, Preface to Viviani's *Summulae, 1966– 1972* (Milan: All'Insegna del Pesce d'Oro, 1983), pp. 7–12;

Manfred Hardt, "Zur italienischen Lyrik der Gegenwart: Cesare Viviani, Milo De Angelis, Valerio Magrelli," *Italienisch,* 20 (November 1988): 57–70;

Giuseppe Zagarrio, "Del nonsenso, dei lapsus e di Viviani, di una (im)probabile fine del gioco," in his *Febbre, furore e fiele* (Milan: Mursia, 1983), pp. 486–494.

Andrea Zanzotto

(10 October 1921 -   )

John P. Welle
University of Notre Dame

BOOKS: *Dietro il paesaggio* (Milan: Mondadori, 1951);

Elegia e altri versi (Milan: Meridiana, 1954);

Vocativo (Milan: Mondadori, 1957; revised, 1981);

IX Ecloghe (Milan: Mondadori, 1962);

Sull'altopiano: Racconti e prose, 1942-1954 (Venice: Neri Pozza, 1964);

La beltà (Milan: Mondadori, 1968);

Gli sguardi i fatti e senhal (Pieve di Soligo: Bernardi, 1969);

A che valse? Versi, 1938-1942 (Milan: Scheiwiller, 1970); enlarged and edited by Stefano Agosti as *Poesie, 1938-1972* (Milan: Mondadori, 1973); enlarged again and edited by Giorgio Luzzi as *Poesie, 1938-1986* (Turin: L'Arzanà, 1987);

Pasque (Milan: Mondadori, 1973);

Filò: Per il Casanova di Fellini (Venice: Ruzante, 1976); revised as *Filò e altre poesie* (Rome: Lato Side, 1981); revised again as *Filò* (Milan: Mondadori, 1988);

Il galateo in bosco (Milan: Mondadori, 1978);

Circhi e cene / Circuses and Suppers, bilingual edition, translated by Beverly Allen (Verona: Plain Wrapper, 1979);

Mistieròi Poemetto dialettale veneto (Feltre: Castaldi, 1979); revised and translated into Friulian by Amedeo Giacomini (Milan: Scheiwiller, 1984);

Fosfeni (Milan: Mondadori, 1983);

Idioma (Milan: Mondadori, 1986);

Racconti e prose (Milan: Mondadori, 1990);

Fantasie di avvicinamento (Milan: Mondadori, 1991).

Edition in English: *Selected Poetry of Andrea Zanzotto,* edited and translated by Ruth Feldman and Brian Swann (Princeton, N.J.: Princeton University Press, 1975).

OTHER: "Noventa tra i 'moderni,' " in *I metodi attuali della critica in Italia,* edited by Maria Corti and Cesare Segre (Turin: RAI, 1970), pp. 153-158;

Vittoria Bradshaw, ed. and trans., *From Pure Silence to Impure Dialogue: A Survey of Post-War Italian Poetry, 1945-1965,* includes poems by Zanzotto (New York: Las Américas, 1971), pp. 296-344;

"Petrarca fra il palazzo e la cameretta," in Francesco Petrarca's *Rime,* edited by Guido Bezzola (Milan: Rizzoli, 1976), pp. 5-16;

"Pedagogia," in *Pasolini: Cronaca giudiziaria, persecuzione, morte,* edited by Laura Betti (Milan: Garzanti, 1977);

"Fiches Leiris," *Verri,* 18 (1980): 92-101;

Franco Fortini, *Una obbedienza: 18 poesie 1969-1979,* introduction by Zanzotto (Genoa: San Marco dei Giustiniani, 1980), pp. 7-12;

"Ipotesi intorno alla *Città delle donne,*" in Federico Fellini's *La città delle donne* (Milan: Garzanti, 1980), pp. 19-31;

"Pasolini poeta," in *Pasolini: Poesie e pagine ritrovate,* edited by Zanzotto and Nico Naldini (Rome: Lato Side, 1980), pp. 203-212;

Lawrence R. Smith, ed. and trans., *The New Italian Poetry: 1945 to the Present. A Bilingual Anthology,* includes poems by Zanzotto (Berkeley: University of California Press, 1981), pp. 200-217;

"Pasolini nel nostro tempo," in *Pier Paolo Pasolini: L'opera e il suo tempo,* edited by Guido Santato (Padua: CLUEP, 1983), pp. 235-239;

"Pasolini, L'Academiuta di lenga furlana," in Naldini's *Nei campi di Friuli* (Milan: All'Insegna del Pesce d'Oro, 1984), pp. 65-74.

TRANSLATIONS: Michel Leiris, *Età d'uomo e Notti senza notte* (Milan: Mondadori, 1966);

George Bataille, *Nietzsche, il culmine e il possibile* (Milan: Rizzoli, 1970);

Bataille, *La letteratura e il male* (Milan: Rizzoli, 1973);

Honoré de Balzac, *La ricerca dell'assoluto* (Milan: Garzanti, 1975);

Balzac, *Il medico di campagna* (Milan: Garzanti, 1977).

Andrea Zanzotto circa 1960

Andrea Zanzotto is widely considered one of the most important Italian and European poets of the twentieth century. From the fall of Fascism in the 1940s to the economic boom of the late 1950s, and from the student protests and "hot autumn" of the 1960s to the advent of a mass culture in the 1970s, Zanzotto's poetry has registered the profound social and cultural changes that have transformed postwar Italy. An articulate witness and engaged interlocutor whose roots are deep within the culture of his native region (the Veneto), Zanzotto examines the events of contemporary history as well as international scientific, philosophical, and artistic developments. In a distinctive poetic style noted for its surprising changes in each new volume, Zanzotto's work represents the search for a link between tradition and experimentation. In addition to his books of poetry, he is also an accomplished translator and an important literary critic, and he has done some writing for two of Federico Fellini's films, *Casanova* (1976) and *E la nave va* (And the Ship Sails on, 1983).

Born in Pieve di Soligo on 10 October 1921, Zanzotto grew up during the Fascist years, and after earning his degree in literature from the University

of Padua in 1942, he took part in the Resistance movement. Following the war, he spent some time in France and Switzerland and later returned to his hometown, where he has been a public-school teacher and administrator for over forty years and where he currently resides. In 1959 Zanzotto married, and he and his wife, Marisa, have two sons, Giovanni and Fabio.

Zanzotto's poetry began to appear on the literary scene in the early 1950s. His first book, *Dietro il paesaggio* (Behind the Landscape, 1951), consists of forty-five poems written between 1940 and 1948; it won the Premio Saint-Vincent in 1950. The prize committee comprised Giuseppe Ungaretti, Eugenio Montale, Salvatore Quasimodo, Leonardo Sinisgalli, and Vittorio Sereni — whose critical approval of Zanzotto's early efforts has been since corroborated by other discerning critics. In discussing Zanzotto's early work, critics often underline such literary sources as Friedrich Hölderlin, Rainer Maria Rilke, Federico García Lorca, Paul Eluard, Giacomo Leopardi, Ungaretti, and Mario Luzi. While Zanzotto's poetry evolved from within the hermetic mode, his work has also been marked by experimental energy, intellectual depth, and a conscious attempt to renew the Italian poetic tradition.

Dietro il paesaggio evinces the themes and imagery that form the nucleus of Zanzotto's poetic vision. His native landscape provides a springboard for an exploration of inner space: "Qui non resta che cingersi intorno il paesaggio / qui volgere le spalle" (Here there remains only to gird oneself with the landscape / to turn one's back here). The land is a continual reference point and becomes a kind of alter ego, an "other" in relation to which Zanzotto's subjectivity defines itself. The recurring symbols of sun, moon, grass, snow, mother, and child depict the flux of the seasons and the fluidity of subjectivity.

Elegia e altri versi (Elegy and Other Verses, 1954) continues in the vein of his first collection, but Zanzotto's third book, *Vocativo* (Vocative, 1957), announces a growing disquietude with the nature of language in general and a concern for the changing Italian linguistic situation in particular. Stylistically more complex than his previous two volumes, *Vocativo* is divided into two sections, "Come una bucolica" (Like a Bucolic) and "Prima persona" (First Person), which indicate his ongoing concern with the pastoral landscape and the nature of subjectivity. Visited by specters of World War II, he seeks refuge in his native terrain. In a poem dedicated to his deceased comrades, "I compagni corsi avanti" (The Comrades Who Have Gone on Ahead), Zanzotto writes: "Oh stringiti alla terra, a terra premi / tu la tua fantasia. Strugge la mite / notte Hitler" (Oh cling fast to the earth, to the earth press / your imagination. The gentle night / dissolves Hitler). The experience of the war and the moral impulse born in the resistance to Fascism are continual presences throughout Zanzotto's work. In *Vocativo*, however, his dialogue with the land has eroded into the reverberations of a single querulous voice. In "Dove io vedo" (Where I Look), Zanzotto writes:

dove sei che davanti a te e nel tuo
sottile definirti io sto per sempre e invano
ed invano ti parlo mio solo nutrimento?

(Where are you for I am always in front of you
within your subtle self-defining though in vain
and in vain address you my only nourishment?)

The vocative voice symbolizes Zanzotto's growing mistrust of language as an authentic instrument for depicting reality.

This attitude becomes more acute in *IX Ecloghe* (Nine Eclogues, 1962) — twenty-eight poems written between February 1957 and October 1960. The dialogue with the landscape becomes an object of satire: "un diagramma dell'anima? Un paese che sempre / piumifica e vaneggia di verde e primavere?" (a diagram of the soul? A town that always preens and raves with green and springtimes?). With Zanzotto the eclogue attains a neoclassical elegance. While calling attention to the contours of rhetorical devices, he questions and affirms the validity of the lyric mode. In "Un libro di ecloghe" (A Book of Eclogues) Zanzotto addresses this classical poetic form: "forte / come il vero ed il santo, questo canto che stona / ma commemora norme s'avvince a ritmi a stimoli: / questo che ad altro modo non sa ancora fidarsi" (strong / like the true and the holy, this song that clashes / but commemorates conventions binds itself to rhythms and stimuli: / this song that still does not know how to entrust itself to another mode). In *IX Ecloghe* Zanzotto's diction expands beyond its Petrarchan and symbolist bases to include the most recent scientific and technological discourses. There is a greater exploration of metalanguage:

Significati allungano le dita,
sensi le antenne filiformi.
Sillabe labbra clausole
unisono con l'ima terra.

(Signifieds stretch out their fingers,
senses their filiform antennae.
Syllables lips clauses
in harmony with the deepest earth.)

Bristling with energy like a new comet on the literary horizon, *La beltà* (Beauty, 1968) breaks with the style of Zanzotto's earlier work. This book amplifies the iconoclastic bent of *IX Ecloghe*. Broadening his investigation of linguistic truth, the forty-one poems of *La beltà* fracture the connecting link between signifier and signified: "male s'aggancia / il fatto semantico al fatto fonematico" (poorly the semantic / fact hooks up with the phonemic fact). Zanzotto animates lexical resources in the Italian language through alliteration, wordplay, and the manipulation of morphological and syntactical elements. Zanzotto's grammatically deconstructive poetry forces the reader to abandon normal reading habits and to confront a discourse that defies the accepted perimeters of articulation:

Canzoniere epistolario d'amore
di cui tutto fosse fonemi monemi e corteo,
in ogni senso direzione varianza,
babele e antibabele.

(Songbook epistolary of love
in which everything would be phonemes monemes and

procession,
in every sense direction variation
Babel and anti-Babel.)

Zanzotto's *La beltà* mirrors the anger, frustration, and disorientation of the 1960s. A period of social transformation in Italy, this decade saw the eclipse of the peasant civilization, the formation of a new urban proletariat, and the advent of a consumer society. One of the most important literary works of the period, *La beltà* registers this changing tide and includes some of Zanzotto's most significant lyrics. For example, in "Retorica su: Lo sbandamento, il principio 'resistenza'" (Rhetoric About: The Disbanding, the "Resistance" Principle) he examines the possibility of developing critical consciousness at a time when the notion of history has dissolved into innumerable microhistories. "L'elegia in petèl" (The Elegy in Baby-Talk), on the other hand, treats the origins of language, identity, and poetry in childhood.

From *La beltà* onward the utilization of widely divergent linguistic registers becomes even more pronounced in Zanzotto's works. The rapid shift from one semantic field to another provides the dominant technique of *Gli sguardi i fatti e senhal* (Gazes Facts and Secret Names, 1969), a long poem. Modeled on the Rorschach test, *Gli sguardi i fatti e senhal* presents, on one level, the television coverage of the American moon landing as a puncturing of the mythic fabric that once surrounded the moon in popular imagination.

In *Pasque* (Easters, 1973) Zanzotto plays on the etymology of *pasqua,* a Hebrew and Latin word meaning "passage" and "pasture" respectively. Easters for Zanzotto are "Passovers" or passages from one state of being to another: from the impossible to the possible, from the past to the future, and from Calvary to Emmaus. Various reference points keep these poems from becoming overly abstract: Alice's tumble down the rabbit hole, the descent of Orpheus into the underworld, the passage of protein into the bloodstream, and the transfer of knowledge. In *Pasque* Zanzotto again conveys the sense of wonder, the interest in the sacred, and the commitment to progressive social reform that permeate his entire opus.

In 1976 Zanzotto published an important book of poems in dialect, *Filò: Per il Casanova di Fellini* (The Peasants' Wake: For Fellini's *Casanova*). The first half of the book includes dialogue written in a pseudo-Venetian koine of the eighteenth century; it is a dialect Zanzotto invented at the request of Fellini for his film *Casanova*. The second part,

consisting of one of Zanzotto's most significant poems, "Filò," is written in the vernacular of Pieve di Soligo. Zanzotto uses the ancient mother tongue of a small agricultural community to praise and to attack the cinema as the new visual language of an increasingly global society:

E ò squasi maledì
tante òlte 'sti posti de cine
che cofà bue sbusa fin fora pa' i camp,
no pi sol che in paesi e zhità:
a inpastrociarne i nostri insònii
. . . .
Ma qualche òlta 'l cine arzh brusa e fa ciaro
. . . .
e 'l cine – squasi – 'l par lu la poesia

(And I have almost cursed
many times these movie places
that like wounds leave holes in the back country,
no longer only in villages and towns:
gumming up our dreams
. . . .
but sometimes movies are on fire they burn and throw
    off light
. . . .
and movies – almost – seem themselves to be poetry)[.]

"Filò" stages an encounter between a regional peasant culture and a spreading mass culture of international proportions. A poem in dialect on the death of dialect, "Filò" participates in and reflects on the revitalization of dialect poetry in the twentieth century. The relationship between Italian dialects and the standard, written, national language has been a salient feature of Italian culture since the Renaissance. In the postwar period, however, with the advent of television and the mass media, a truly national idiom has emerged for the first time in Italian history. To a greater extent perhaps than any other Italian poet since Dante, Zanzotto examines the Italian linguistic situation, which is also indicative of changing social relations.

In an important brief essay on dialect, which serves as an afterword to "Filò," Zanzotto observes that "Oggi meno che mai si sa che cosa siano i dialetti, nelle loro capillarizzazioni infinitesimali, e le lingue, specie quelle a diffusione tendenzialmente panterrestre; né come i loro destini s'intersechino" (Today less than ever do we know what dialects are, in their infinitesimal capillary movements, or languages, especially those tending toward a panterrestrial diffusion; nor do we know how their destinies intersect).

The biological symbolism of various sign systems and the pursuit of all possible forms of communication characterize the direction of Zanzotto's poetry from the early 1950s to the late 1980s. The central concerns of his early period – the pastoral beauty masking a tragic landscape, the pain of history, the exploration of the psyche, and the Italian linguistic situation – remain constant throughout his middle period and into the new phase inaugurated by his masterpiece, the trilogy consisting of *Il galateo in bosco* (The Forest Book of Etiquette, 1978), *Fosfeni* (1983; the title referring to the small dots of light a person can see after rubbing his eyes), and *Idioma* (Idiom, 1986). This trilogy has been described by various critics as one of the most significant poetic and linguistic experiments in twentieth-century Italian literature.

Il galateo in bosco consists of fifty-two poems written between 1975 and 1978; it expands on Zanzotto's earlier treatment of language and communication. Like that of Giovanni Pascoli, whose fin de siècle poetry often imitates the language of birds, Zanzotto's poetry extends beyond the range of human life to include other living beings. Thus he casts his voice into remote and minute life forms and depicts the genetic code as an elemental form of communication. The biological exchange of information and the flow of energy between various creatures and their environments provide Zanzotto with a model for poetry, itself a form of communication and communion. His paraphrase of Dante (*Paradiso,* book 6) in the final line of the sonnet "Postilla" (Gloss) typifies Zanzotto's frequent use of literary quotations and sheds light on his analogy of poetry as food:

> Così ancora di te mi sono avvalso,
> di te sonetto, righe infami e ladre –
> mandala in cui di frusto in frusto accatto
>
> (Thus again from you I have grown strong,
> from you sonnet, infamous and thieving verse –
> mandala in which bit by bit I go begging)[.]

In this volume Zanzotto spins diverse fragments of the Italian literary tradition – from Dante to the futurists – into a seamless poetic fabric.

The key elements of Zanzotto's mature poetic practice (the use of resemanticized literary allusions, the creative violation of syntactical and morphological norms, and a boundless lexicon) reach still further heights in *Fosfeni,* which resembles *Pasque* in its themes of transcendence. Zanzotto portrays the Logos at play in the genetic code, in the silicon chip, and in every attempt at communication:

> Logos, in ogni cristallo di brina di neve glorioso
> anche se forse non sei più che un'ipotesi
>
> (Logos, in every crystal of frost of glorious snow
> even if you are nothing more than a hypothesis)[.]

Utilizing Greek letters, ideograms, and an innovative graphic design, *Fosfeni* explores the theme of the Logos, the arbitrariness of the sign, and the relationship of the grapheme to the phoneme.

With *Idioma* Zanzotto brings the trilogy to a remarkable close. Whereas *Il galateo in bosco* depicts the elemental biological life of the Montello forest and *Fosfeni* reflects the radiant snow fields of the Dolomites, *Idioma* describes the people who make up the town where Zanzotto has lived throughout his life. This volume incorporates the earlier plaquette *Mistieròi* (Mysterious Trades, 1979). Written in Zanzotto's native dialect, these poems are among his finest lyrics.

Idioma includes an elegy to the murdered Pier Paolo Pasolini; a beautiful poem occasioned by the eightieth birthday of Montale; and a remarkable "film poem" (similar to "Filò" in this respect) on the death of Charlie Chaplin. By adopting a conversational tone characteristic of dialect as a primarily oral form of communication, Zanzotto reaches a level of emotion that is sometimes missing from his poems in Italian. Paradoxically, in addressing the various interlocutors of *Idioma* in the language of his native village, Zanzotto manages to render his personal experience universal.

Zanzotto's poetry, which was awarded the Premio Viareggio in 1978 and the Premio Eugenio Montale-Librex in 1983, expresses the tensions of postwar European culture from an Italian perspective. His linguistic experience mirrors that of a large part of his generation. Furthermore, Zanzotto's interest in science, philosophy, psychoanalysis, linguistics, and semiotics enriches his poetry, making its significance stretch beyond the demarcations traced by dialects and national or international languages.

Interviews:

Ferdinando Camon, "Andrea Zanzotto," in his *Il mestiere di poeta* (Milan: Garzanti, 1965), pp. 169–181;

Wallace P. Sillanpoa, "An Interview with Andrea Zanzotto," *Yale Italian Studies,* 2 (1978): 297–307;

Giuliana Massini and Bruno Rivalta, eds., *Sulla poesia: Conversazioni nelle scuole* (Parma: Pratiche, 1981), pp. 63–107;

Beverly Allen, "Interview with Andrea Zanzotto," *Stanford Italian Review,* 4 (1984): 253–265.

Bibliography:

Armando Balduino, "Scheda bibliografica per Zanzotto critico," *Studi Novecenteschi,* 4, nos. 8–9 (1974): 341–348.

References:

Velio Abati, *L'impossibilità della parola: Per una lettura materialistica della poesia di Andrea Zanzotto* (Rome: Bagatto Libri, 1991);

Stefano Agosti, "Introduzione alla poesia di Zanzotto," in Zanzotto's *Poesie, 1938–1972,* edited by Agosti (Milan: Mondadori, 1973), pp. 7–25;

Beverly Allen, *Andrea Zanzotto: The Language of Beauty's Apprentice* (Berkeley: University of California Press, 1988);

Lucia Conti Bertini, *Andrea Zanzotto o la sacra menzogna* (Venice: Marsilio, 1984);

Piero Falchetta, *Oculus Pudens: Venti anni di poesia di Andrea Zanzotto (1957–1978)* (Padua: Francisci, 1983);

P. P. Franchi, "Clausole di una memoria infelice: Appunti sul *clavus* venetico nel *Filò* di Andrea Zanzotto," in *Lingua, dialetto e culture subalterne,* edited by Giordano De Biasio (Ravenna: Longo, 1979), pp. 73–110;

Peter R. J. Hainsworth, "The Poetry of Andrea Zanzotto," *Italian Studies,* 37 (1982): 101–121;

Thomas J. Harrison, "Andrea Zanzotto: From the Language of the World to the World of Language," *Poesis,* 5, no. 3 (1984): 68–85;

Eugenio Montale, "La poesia di Zanzotto," in *Sulla poesia,* edited by Giorgio Zampa (Milan: Mondadori, 1976), pp. 337–349;

Giuliana Nuvoli, *Andrea Zanzotto* (Florence: Nuova Italia, 1979);

Pier Paolo Pasolini, "*La beltà* (appunti)," in his *Il portico della morte,* edited by Cesare Segre (Rome: Associazione Fondo Pier Paolo Pasolini, 1988), pp. 267–270;

Studi Novecenteschi, special issue on Zanzotto, 4 (July–November 1974);

Luigi Tassoni, *Il sogno del caos: "Microfilm" di Zanzotto e la geneticità del testo* (Bergamo: Moretti & Vitali, 1990);

John P. Welle, "Dante and Poetic *Communio* in Zanzotto's Pseudo-Trilogy," *Lectura Dantis,* 10 (Spring 1992): 34–58;

Welle, *The Poetry of Andrea Zanzotto: A Critical Study of* Il galateo in bosco (Rome: Bulzoni, 1987);

Welle, "Zanzotto: Il poeta del cosmorama," *Cinema & Cinema,* 14 (June 1987): 51–55.

Checklist of Further Readings

Accrocca, Elio Filippo, and Valerio Volpini, eds. *Antologia poetica della resistenza italiana*. Florence: Landi, 1956.

Albisola, Giancarlo, Nella Audisio, and others. *Nuovi poeti italiani*. Turin: Einaudi, 1980.

Allen, Beverly, Muriel Kittel, and Keala Jane Jewell, eds. *The Defiant Muse: Italian Feminist Poems from the Middle Ages to the Present. A Bilingual Anthology*. New York: Feminist Press, 1966.

Anceschi, Luciano. *Le poetiche del Novecento in Italia*. Turin: Paravia, 1972.

Anceschi, ed. *Linea lombarda*. Varese: Magenta, 1952.

Antonielli, Sergio. *La letteratura del disagio*. Milan: Comunità, 1984.

Asor Rosa, Alberto, ed. *Dizionario della letteratura italiana del Novecento*. Turin: Einaudi, 1992.

Asor Rosa, ed. *Letteratura italiana*. Turin: Einaudi, 1989.

Balestrini, Nanni, ed. *Gruppo '63*. Milan: Feltrinelli, 1966.

Ballerini, Luigi, ed. *Scrittura visuale in Italia*. Turin: Galleria Civica d'Arte Moderna, 1973.

Ballerini, ed. *"Shearsmen of Sorts: Italian Poetry 1975–1993." Forum Italicum: Italian Poetry Supplement* (1992).

Bàrberi Squarotti, Giorgio. *Poesia e narrativa del secondo Novecento*. Milan: Mursia, 1978.

Bàrberi Squarotti, ed. *Storia della civiltà letteraria italiana*. Turin: UTET, 1992.

Bàrberi Squarotti and Anna Maria Golfieri. *Dal tramonto dell'ermetismo alla neoavanguardia*. Brescia: Scuola, 1984.

Barbuto, Antonio. *Da Narciso a Castelporziano: Poesia e pubblico negli anni Settanta*. Rome: Ateneo, 1981.

Barilli, Renato, and Angelo Guglielmi, eds. *Gruppo '63: Critica e teoria*. Milan: Feltrinelli, 1976.

Basile, Bruno. *La poesia contemporanea, 1945–1972*. Florence: Sansoni, 1973.

Batista, Silvia, and Mariella Bettarini. *Chi è il poeta*. Milan: Gammalibri, 1980.

Berardinelli, Alfonso, and Franco Cordelli, eds. *Il pubblico della poesia*. Cosenza: Lerici, 1975.

Bertacchini, Renato. *Letteratura italiana: I Contemporanei*. Milan: Marzorati, 1975.

Bigongiari, Piero. *Poesia italiana del Novecento*. Milan: Saggiatore, 1978.

Bonora, Ettore, *Montale e altro Novecento*. Caltanissetta & Rome: Sciascia, 1989.

Bonora, ed. *Dizionario della letteratura italiana*. Milan: Rizzoli, 1977.

Bordini, Carlo, and others, eds. *La poesia dei marginali.* Rome: Savelli, 1978.

Bradshaw, Vittoria, ed. and trans. *From Pure Silence to Impure Dialogue: A Survey of Post-War Italian Poetry 1945–1965.* New York: Las Américas, 1971.

Branca, Vittore, ed. *Dizionario critico della letteratura italiana.* Turin: UTET, 1986.

Brevini, Franco. *Parole perdute: Dialetti e poesia nel nostro secolo.* Turin: Einaudi, 1990.

Caesar, Michael, and Peter Hainsworth, eds. *Writers and Society in Contemporary Italy.* Leamington Spa, U.K.: Berg, 1984.

Camerino, Giuseppe Antonio. *Poesia senza frontiere e poeti italiani del Novecento.* Milan: Mursia, 1989.

Camon, Ferdinando. *Il mestiere di poeta.* Milan: Garzanti, 1982.

Cavallini, Giorgio. *Strutture, tendenze, esempi della poesia italiana del Novecento.* Rome: Bulzoni, 1988.

Cavallo, Franco, ed. *Zero: Testi e anti-testi di poesia.* Naples: Altri Termini, 1975.

Cavallo and Mario Lunetta, eds. *Poesia italiana della contraddizione.* Rome: Newton Compton, 1989.

Cecchi, Emilio, and Natalino Sapegno, eds. *Storia della letteratura italiana,* volume 2: *Il Novecento.* Milan: Garzanti, 1987.

Cherchi, Luciano, ed. *La situazione poetica: 1958–1968.* Milan: Naviglio, 1970.

Chiara, Piero, and Luciano Erba, eds. *Quarta generazione.* Varese: Magenta, 1954.

Chiesa, Mario, and Giovanni Tesio, eds. *Il dialetto da lingua della realta a lingua della poesia.* Turin: Paravia, 1978.

Coletti, Vittorio. *Momenti del linguaggio poetico novecentesco.* Genoa: Melangolo, 1978.

Contini, Gianfranco. *Schedario di scrittori italiani moderni e contemporanei.* Florence: Sansoni, 1973.

Cordelli, Franco. *Il poeta postumo.* Cosenza: Lerici, 1978.

D'Ambrosio, Matteo. *Bibliografia della poesia italiana d'avanguardia.* Rome: Bulzoni, 1977.

Debenedetti, Giacomo. *Poesia italiana del Novecento.* Milan: Garzanti, 1988.

Di Francesco, Tommaso, ed. *Veleno: Antologia della poesia satirica contemporanea italiana.* Rome: Savelli, 1980.

Di Nola, Laura, ed. *Poesia femminista italiana.* Rome: Savelli, 1978.

Dizionario biografico degli Italiani. Rome: Instituto della Enciclopedia Italiana, 1960– .

Doplicher, Fabio, and Umberto Piersanti, eds. *Il pensiero, il corpo.* Rome: Stilb, 1986.

Doplicher, ed. *Poesia della metamorfosi.* Rome: Stilb, 1984.

Doplicher, ed. *Il teatro dei poeti: Antologia catalogo.* Rome: CTM, 1987.

Esposito, Roberto. *Ideologie della neoavanguardia.* Naples: Liguori, 1976.

Falqui, Enrico, ed. *La giovane poesia.* Rome: Colombo, 1956.

Feldman, Ruth, and Brian Swann, eds. and trans. *Italian Poetry Today: Currents and Trends.* Saint Paul: New Rivers, 1979.

Fini, Carlo, ed. *La poesia italiana degli Anni Settanta*. Siena: Amministrazione Provinciale, 1980.

Finzi, Gilberto. *Poesia in Italia: Montale, novissimi, postnovissimi 1959–1978*. Milan: Mursia, 1979.

Folena, Gianfranco, and others. *Ricerche sulla lingua poetica contemporanea*. Padua: Liviana, 1966.

Forti, Marco. *Le proposte della poesia e nuove proposte*. Milan: Mursia, 1971.

Forti and Giancarlo Pontiggia, eds. *Almanacco delle Specchio*. Milan: Mondadori, 1972– .

Fortini, Franco. *I poeti del Novecento*. Bari: Laterza, 1978.

Frabotta, Biancamaria, ed. *Donne in poesia*. Rome: Savelli, 1976.

Frattini, Alberto. *Dai crepuscolari ai novissimi*. Milan: Marzorati, 1969.

Frattini. *Poesia nuova in Italia tra Ermetismo e Neoavanguardia*. Milan: IPL, 1968.

Frattini, ed. *Poesia e regione in Italia*. Milan: IPL, 1983.

Frattini and Pasquale Tuscano, eds. *Poeti a Roma*. Rome: Bonacci, 1983.

Frattini and Tuscano, eds. *Poeti italiani del XX secolo*. Brescia: Scuola, 1974.

Frattini and Marcella Uffreduzzi, eds. *Poeti a Roma*. Rome: Bonacci, 1983.

Friedrich, Hugo. *The Structure of Modern Poetry*. Evanston: Northwestern Illinois University Press, 1974.

Fusini, Nadia, and Mariella Gramaglia, eds. *La poesia femminista*. Rome: Savelli, 1977.

Gelli, Piero, and Gina Lagorio, eds. *Poesia italiana: Il Novecento*. Milan: Garzanti, 1980.

Getto, Giovanni. *Poeti del Novecento e altre cose*. Milan: Mursia, 1977.

Giannone, Antonio Lucio. *Tradizione e innovazione nella poesia italiana del Novecento*. Lecce: Milella, 1983.

Giuliani, Alfredo. *Autunno del Novecento: Cronache di letteratura*. Milan: Feltrinelli, 1984.

Giuliani, ed. *I Novissimi: Poesie per gli anni '60*. Milan: Rusconi & Paolazzi, 1961.

Giùttari, Teodoro, Adriana Nicolini and Pierpaolo Serarcangeli, eds. *I Trovieri: Antologia critica di poeti dialettali italiani*. Milan: Todariana, 1975.

Golino, Carlo, ed. and trans. *Contemporary Italian Poetry: An Anthology*. Berkeley: University of California Press, 1962.

Gramigna, Giuliano. *Le forme del desiderio: Le linguaggio poetico alla prova della psicanalisi*. Milan: Garzanti, 1988.

Grana, Gianni. *Avanguardie letterarie*. Milan: Marzorati, 1986.

Grana, ed. *Letteratura italiana. Novecento: I contemporanei*. Milan: Marzorati, 1979.

Guglielmi, Guido, and Elio Pagliarani, eds. *Manuale della poesia sperimentale*. Verona: Mondadori, 1966.

Haller, Herman W., ed. and trans. *The Hidden Italy: A Bilingual Edition of Italian Dialect Poetry*. Detroit: Wayne State University Press, 1986.

Kemeny, Tommaso, and Cesare Viviani, eds. *Il movimento della poesia italiana negli anni Settanta*. Bari: Dedalo, 1979.

Kemeny and Viviani, eds. *I percorsi della nuova poesia italiana*. Naples: Guida, 1980.

Lanuzza, Stefano. *L'apprendista sciamano: Poesia italiana degli anni settanta.* Messina & Florence: D'Anna, 1979.

Lanuzza, *Lo sparviero sul pugno: Guida ai poeti italiani degli anni ottanta.* Milan: Spirali, 1987.

Lind, Levi R., ed. *Twentieth-Century Italian Poetry.* Indianapolis & New York: Bobbs-Merill, 1974.

Livi, François. *La parola crepuscolare.* Milan: IPL, 1986.

Lorenzini, Niva. *Il laboratorio dell poesia.* Rome: Bulzoni, 1978.

Lunetta, Mario, ed. *Poesia italiana oggi.* Rome: Newton Compton, 1981.

Luti, Giorgio, ed. *Critici, movimenti e riviste del '90 letterario italiano.* Rome: Nuova Italia Scientifica, 1986.

Luti, ed., *Novecento.* Milan: Vallardi, 1990.

Luti, ed. *Poeti italiani del Novecento.* Rome: Nuova Italia Scientifica, 1985.

Luzzi, Giorgio. *Poeti della Linea lombarda (1952–1985).* Milan: Nuova Stampa, 1987.

Luzzi, ed. *Poesia italiana (1941–1988): La via Lombarda/Diciannove poeti contemporanei.* Milan: Marcos y Marcos, 1989.

Macrì, Oreste. *Caratteri e figure della poesia italiana contemporanea.* Florence: Vallecchi, 1956.

Macrì. *Realtà del simbolo.* Florence: Vallecchi, 1968.

Majorino, Giancarlo, ed. *Poesia e realtà: '45–'75.* Rome: Savelli, 1977.

Malagò, Elia, and Gianluca Prosperi, eds. *Care donne.* Forlì: Forum/Quinta Generazione, 1979.

Manacorda, Giuliano. *Letteratura italiana d'oggi: 1965–1985.* Rome: Riuniti, 1987.

Manacorda. *Storia della letteratura italiana contemporanea: 1940–1965,* third edition. Rome: Riuniti, 1967.

Mancinelli, Franco. *Poeti e frontiera.* Rome: Stilb, 1983.

Manescalchi, Franco, and Lucia Marcucci, eds. *La poesia in Toscana dagli anni Quaranta agli anni Settanta.* Messina & Florence: D'Anna, 1981.

Marabini, Claudio. *Le città dei poeti.* Turin: SEI, 1976.

Marchi, Marco. *Alcuni poeti.* Florence: Vallecchi, 1981.

Marchione, Margherita, ed. and trans. *Twentieth-Century Italian Poetry.* Rutherford, N.J.: Fairleigh Dickinson University Press, 1974.

Marianacci, Dante. *La cultura degli anni '80.* Foggia: Bastogi, 1984.

Mariani, Gaetano. *Letteratura italiana: I contemporanei.* Milan: Marzorati, 1969.

Mariani and Mario Petrucciani, eds. *Letteratura italiana contemporanea.* Rome: Lucarini, 1982.

Martelli, Mario, ed. *10 poeti italiani contemporanei.* Florence: Istituto Gramsci/Sezione Toscana, 1980.

Mazzotti, Artal. *Letteratura italiana. Orientamenti culturali: I contemporanei.* Milan: Marzorati, 1963–1969.

Mengaldo, Pier Vincenzo, ed. *Poeti italiani del Novecento.* Milan: Mondadori, 1978.

Mondello, Elisabetta. *Gli anni delle riviste.* Lecce: Milella, 1985.

Morrocchi, Giuseppe. *Scrittura visuale: Ricerche ed esperienze delle avanguardie letterarie.* Messina & Florence: D'Anna, 1978.

Noferi, Adelia. *Le poetiche critiche novecentesche.* Florence: Le Monnier, 1970.

Occhipinti, Giovanni. *Uno splendido medioevo: Poesia anni Sessanta.* Poggibonsi: Lalli, 1978.

Pansa, Francesco, and Marianna Bucchich, eds. *Poesia d'amore: l'assenza, il desiderio: Le più importanti poetesse contemporanee presentate da trentasei critici.* Rome: Newton Compton, 1986.

Paris, Renzo, ed. *L'io che brucia: La scuola romana di poesia.* Cosenza: Lerici, 1983.

Pautasso, Sergio. *Anni di letteratura.* Milan: Rizzoli, 1979.

Pecora, Elio. *Poesia italiana del Novecento.* Rome: Newton Compton, 1990.

Petrollo, Concetta, ed. *Poesia in Italia 1945–1980.* Rome: Biblioteca Nazionale Centrale, 1982.

Petrucciani, Mario. *Poesia pura e poesia esistenziale.* Turin: Loescher, 1957.

Pieri, Marzio. *Biografia della poesia: Sul paesaggio mentale della poesia italiana del Novecento.* Parma: Pilotta, 1979.

Pignotti, Lamberto, ed. *Antologia della poesia visiva.* Bologna: Sampietro, 1965.

Pontiggia, Giancarlo, and Enzo Di Mauro, eds. *La parola innamorata: I nuovi poeti 1976–1978.* Milan: Feltrinelli, 1978.

Porta, Antonio, ed. *Poesia degli anni settanta.* Milan: Feltrinelli, 1979.

Porta and Giovanni Raboni, eds. *Pin Pidin: Poeti d'oggi per i bambini.* Milan: Feltrinelli, 1978.

Quasimodo, Salvatore, ed. *Poesia italiana del dopoguerra.* Milan: Schwartz, 1958.

Quiriconi, Giancarlo, ed. *I miraggi, le tracce: Per una storia della poesia italiana contemporanea.* Milan: Jaca, 1989.

Raboni, Giovanni. *Poesia degli anni Sessanta.* Rome: Riuniti, 1976.

Ramat, Silvio. *Storia della poesia italiana del Novecento.* Milan: Mursia, 1976.

Ravegnani, Giuseppe, and Giovanni Titta Rosa. *L'antologia dei poeti italiani dell'ultimo secolo.* Milan: Aldo Martello, 1972.

Ronconi, Enzo, ed. *Dizionario generale degli autori italiani contemporanei.* Florence: Vallecchi, 1974.

Sanguineti, Edoardo, ed. *Poesia italiana del Novecento.* Turin: Einaudi, 1970.

Scalia, Gianni. *Avanguardia e Neo-avanguardia.* Milan: Sugar, 1966.

Singh, Ghan S., ed. and trans. *Contemporary Italian Verse*. London: London Magazine, 1968.

Siti, Walter. *Il realismo dell'avanguardia*. Turin: Einaudi, 1975.

Smith, Lawrence R., trans. *The New Italian Poetry: 1945 to the Present. A Bilingual Anthology*. Berkeley & Los Angeles: University of California Press, 1981.

Smith, William J., and Dana Gioia, eds., *Poems from Italy*. Saint Paul: New Rivers, 1985.

Spagnoletti, Giacinto. *La letteratura italiana del nostro secolo*. Milan: Mondadori, 1985.

Spagnoletti, ed. *Poesia italiana contemporanea, 1909–1959*. Parma: Guanda, 1959.

Spagnoletti, ed. *Poeti del Novecento*. Milan: Mondadori, 1977.

Sparta, Santino. *Sacerdoti-poeti del '900 italiano*. Roma: Spada, 1978.

Spatola, Adriano. *Verso la poesia totale*. Salerno: Rumma, 1969.

Spatola and Paul Vangelisti, eds. *Italian Poetry, 1960–1980: From Neo to Post Avant-garde*. San Francisco: Red Hill, 1982.

Tanturri, Riccardo. *I simboli del malessere: La poesia italiana 1964–1975*. Samedam, Switzerland: Mount, 1977.

Tedesco, Natale. *La condizione crepuscolare*. Florence: Nuova Italia, 1970.

Uffreduzzi, Marcella, ed. *Poeti italiani d'ispirazione cristiana del Novecento*. Genoa: Sabatelli, 1979.

Vitielli, Ciro. *Teoria e analisi del linguaggio poetico*. Naples: Guida, 1984.

Vivaldi, Cesare, ed. *Poesia satirica nell'Italia d'oggi*. Parma: Guanda, 1964.

Volpini, Valerio, ed. *Antologia della poesia religiosa italiana contemporanea*. Florence: Vallecchi, 1952.

Zagarrio, Giuseppe. *Febbre, furore e fiele*. Milan: Mursia, 1983.

Zagarrio. *Poesia fra editoria e anti*. Trapani: Caelèbes, 1971.

Contributors

Laura Baffoni-Licata ....*Tufts University*
Luigi Bonaffini ....*Brooklyn College, City University of New York*
Romana Capek-Habekovic...*University of Michigan*
Elio Costa ....*York University*
Gustavo Costa...*University of California, Berkeley*
Natalia Costa-Zalessow ....*San Francisco State University*
Giovanna Wedel De Stasio..*Rome, Italy*
Rosetta Di Pace-Jordan...*University of Oklahoma*
Corrado Federici ....*Brock University*
Pietro Frassica ....*Princeton University*
Hermann W. Haller.................................*City University of New York*
Thomas Harrison ....*University of Pennsylvania*
Claire De Cesare Huffman ....*Brooklyn College, City University of New York*
Louis Kibler...*Wayne State University*
Ernesto Livorni...*Yale University*
Maria Nina Lombardo ....*University of Chicago*
Gregory L. Lucente..*University of Michigan*
Gaetana Marrone ....*Princeton University*
Guido Mascagni...*Rutgers University*
Mario B. Mignone....................*State University of New York at Stony Brook*
Fausto Pauluzzi...*Columbia, South Carolina*
Pietro Pelosi.......................................*University of Salerno*
Joseph Perricone...*Fordham University*
Thomas E. Peterson...................................*University of Georgia*
John Picchione ....*York University*
Mark Pietralunga..*Florida State University*
Giancarlo Quiriconi ....*University of Florence*
Eliana Ricci ....*Rutgers University*
Leonard G. Sbrocchi...................................*University of Ottawa*
Achille Serrao..*Rome, Italy*
Giovanni Sinicropi ....*University of Connecticut*
Emilio Speciale...................................*University of Chicago*
Elena Urgnani..*Rutgers University*
Lawrence Venuti ....*Temple University*
Antonio Vitti ....*Wake Forest University*
David Ward..*Wellesley College*
John P. Welle ....*University of Notre Dame*
Rebecca West...*University of Chicago*

Cumulative Index

Dictionary of Literary Biography, Volumes 1-128
Dictionary of Literary Biography Yearbook, 1980-1992
Dictionary of Literary Biography Documentary Series, Volumes 1-10

Cumulative Index

DLB before number: *Dictionary of Literary Biography,* Volumes 1-128
Y before number: *Dictionary of Literary Biography Yearbook,* 1980-1992
DS before number: *Dictionary of Literary Biography Documentary Series,* Volumes 1-10

A

E

F

G

H

I

L

O

P

Q

U

W

ISBN 0-8103-5387-3

9 780810 353879

1860, edited by Catharine Savage Brosman (1992)

120 *American Poets Since World War II,* Third Series, edited by R. S. Gwynn (1992)

121 *Seventeenth-Century British Nondramatic Poets,* First Series, edited by M. Thomas Hester (1992)

122 *Chicano Writers,* Second Series, edited by Francisco A. Lomelí and Carl R. Shirley (1992)

123 *Nineteenth-Century French Fiction Writers: Naturalism and Beyond, 1860-1900,* edited by Catharine Savage Brosman (1992)

124 *Twentieth-Century German Dramatists, 1919-1992,* edited by Wolfgang D. Elfe and James Hardin (1992)

125 *Twentieth-Century Caribbean and Black African Writers,* Second Series, edited by Bernth Lindfors and Reinhard Sander (1993)

126 *Seventeenth-Century British Nondramatic Poets,* Second Series, edited by M. Thomas Hester (1993)

127 *American Newspaper Publishers, 1950-1990,* edited by Perry J. Ashley (1993)

128 *Twentieth-Century Italian Poets,* Second Series, edited by Giovanna Wedel De Stasio, Glauco Cambon, and Antonio Illiano (1993)

Documentary Series

1 *Sherwood Anderson, Willa Cather, John Dos Passos, Theodore Dreiser, F. Scott Fitzgerald, Ernest Hemingway, Sinclair Lewis,* edited by Margaret A. Van Antwerp (1982)

2 *James Gould Cozzens, James T. Farrell, William Faulkner, John O'Hara, John Steinbeck, Thomas Wolfe, Richard Wright,* edited by Margaret A. Van Antwerp (1982)

3 *Saul Bellow, Jack Kerouac, Norman Mailer, Vladimir Nabokov, John*

Updike, Kurt Vonnegut, edited by Mary Bruccoli (1983)

4 *Tennessee Williams,* edited by Margaret A. Van Antwerp and Sally Johns (1984)

5 *American Transcendentalists,* edited by Joel Myerson (1988)

6 *Hardboiled Mystery Writers: Raymond Chandler, Dashiell Hammett, Ross Macdonald,* edited by Matthew J. Bruccoli and Richard Layman (1989)

7 *Modern American Poets: James Dickey, Robert Frost, Marianne Moore,* edited by Karen L. Rood (1989)

8 *The Black Aesthetic Movement,* edited by Jeffrey Louis Decker (1991)

9 *American Writers of the Vietnam War: W. D. Ehrhart, Larry Heinemann, Tim O'Brien, Walter McDonald, John M. Del Vecchio,* edited by Ronald Baughman (1991)

10 *The Bloomsbury Group,* edited by Edward L. Bishop (1992)

Yearbooks

1980 edited by Karen L. Rood, Jean W. Ross, and Richard Ziegfeld (1981)

1981 edited by Karen L. Rood, Jean W. Ross, and Richard Ziegfeld (1982)

1982 edited by Richard Ziegfeld; associate editors: Jean W. Ross and Lynne C. Zeigler (1983)

1983 edited by Mary Bruccoli and Jean W. Ross; associate editor: Richard Ziegfeld (1984)

1984 edited by Jean W. Ross (1985)

1985 edited by Jean W. Ross (1986)

1986 edited by J. M. Brook (1987)

1987 edited by J. M. Brook (1988)

1988 edited by J. M. Brook (1989)

1989 edited by J. M. Brook (1990)

1990 edited by James W. Hipp (1991)

1991 edited by James W. Hipp (1992)

1992 edited by James W. Hipp (1993)